JOHN BENSON'S A to Z BASEBALL PLAYER GUIDE 1996

DIAMOND LIBRARY

Executive Editor:
Marc Bowman

Associate Editors:
Lary Bump and Lawr Michaels

Layout and Design:
Stephen Wade Lunsford and Brian Weaver

Copyright (c) 1995 by John Chapman Benson with licenses to Diamond Analytics Corporation

All rights reserved under International and Pan-American Copyright Conventions

Library of Congress Catalog Data: Benson, John, *Baseball Player Guide A to Z 1996*
1. Baseball -- United States -- History
2. Baseball -- United States -- Records
I. Title

ISBN 1-880876-03-5

No part of this book may be reproduced or transmitted in any form by any means, electronic or mechanical, including photocopying, recording, electronic imaging or scanning, or by any information storage and retrieval system or method, unless expressly permitted in writing by the author and the publisher.
For information contact Diamond Library Publishers.

Published by Diamond Library Publishers, a division of Diamond Analytics Corporation, with offices at 196 Danbury Road, Wilton, Connecticut, 06897. Telephone 203-834-1231.

PRINTED IN THE UNITED STATES OF AMERICA

Cover design by - Stephen Wade Lunsford
Production Manager - Brian Weaver
Editorial Consultant - Rob Curley
Editorial Associate - James Benson

Statistics are provided by STATS, Inc. 8131 Monticello Ave. Skokie, IL 60076-3300
Telephone 708-676-3322.

Rotisserie League Baseball is a registered trademark of The Rotisserie League Baseball Association, Inc. For information, contact RLBA at 370 Seventh Avenue, Suite 312, New York, NY 10001.

This book is sold for entertainment purposes only. Neither the writers, nor the editors or publishers assume any liability beyond the purchase price for any reason.

Table of Contents

Credits   4

Acknowledgments   5

Introduction   7

Position Players   10

Pitchers   164

1995 Draft Report Card   319

Scouting Resources   324

Credits:

James Benkard
James Benson
Tony Blengino
Marc Bowman
Lary Bump
Jim Callis
Rob Curley
Greg Gajus
Bill Gilbert
Peter Graves
David Luciani
Stephen Lunsford
Fred Matos
John Perrotto
Steven Rubio
Brian Weaver
Alan Woodard

Acknowledgments

It feels a little funny to tell people, "I wrote this book," because there were so many other people who did so much of the writing. Actually, what I did was to manage a project that produced this book. The writers whose names appear on the facing page are the core of a team of which I am just one guy on the field, if you know what I mean -- fairly useless without the others.

To all of the writers, I offer a hearty "thank-you" with a special appreciation for the splendid attention to timing, by everyone. In a book of this type, the pieces must fit together in the right place at exactly the right moment, or the team can't move along. Like the daylight play at second base, the run-and-hit, and the rotation play when executed perfectly, this year's teamwork was (again!) just right. Thanks and congratulations for a job well done.

While I am always reluctant to single out individual efforts in a teamwork project where everyone is indispensable, I must say a special word of appreciation, for the second consecutive year, to Marc Bowman for his work as executive editor. A project such as this one -- making the book that has most players and the most current information of anything on bookstore shelves -- could easily become frustrating if not impossible. The word "comprehensive" sounds easy and smooth, but the word implies a depth of effort that is, frankly, beyond description in the context of this book. Marc knows what I mean. Many of the writers who searched deep into the minor league levels of their selected teams also know what I mean, but you haven't been there, words attempting to describe "comprehensive" will always fall short. The point is: I salute Marc for knowing, better than any of us, what it means to be comprehensive.

Special thanks also go to John Dewan of STATS, Inc. for the many helpful and light-shedding statistics and wise counsel over the years. Whenever anyone asks (and sometimes before they ask) I recommend STATS as the best source for baseball factual information, and the fastest production of that information, and the sharpest presentation, and the most useful state-of-the-art media including their amazing on-line service.

In conclusion, I urge all readers to take a long, hard look at the "credits" list on the facing page, and understand this book as springing from the hearts and minds of those individuals. I wish I could put all their names on the cover, because they deserve it.

John

Marc Bowman's Acknowledgments

John has given me a unique opportunity to acknowledge the efforts of our writers this year. In order to provide an accurate glimpse of those efforts you should first understand what is entailed in writing for this book.

We ask each of our writers to cover specific teams and to write about any players who may appear in the major leagues in the next season or two, providing a brief description of each players' strengths and weaknesses as well as what can be expected of him in the immediate future. An easy way to think about this task is to pretend you are at a ballpark with a friend and are trying to describe an individual player as he strides to the plate or trots in from the bullpen (or saunters in, if you are describing Lee Smith). You have just a few seconds to describe the traits of the player before he actually performs. Try it some time and you'll discover how hard it really is to "say something insightful, clever, concise and comprehensive, quickly, now."

The hardest part isn't finding enough to say about each of these players, but being relatively brief while still capturing their essential qualities. Several players in this volume have had entire books devoted exclusively to their exploits. Now multiply the singular task of writing about one specific player by the over 2500 players who appear in these pages and then limit the task at hand to less than a month and you can get an appreciation of what these writers have accomplished.

Among the credited writers are many familiar names and a couple of new ones. I'm happy to say that several of these people have been involved with Benson's books for years, and many of us have developed a nationwide network of friendship through this work. These writers have a great love for the game of baseball in addition to bringing their own special talents into these books. They are good people to know:

John Perrotto, a writer for Baseball America, provided his usual highly professional examination of Pirates, Cardinals and Expos players. His work is always a joy to read. Tony Blengino covered Indians, Marlins and Phillies players in his own unique style. Additional material from Tony and from Lary Bump can be found in a soon-to-be-published volume called "Future Stars" reviewing the minor league player population in depth. Bill Gray (Mariners and Brewers) and Steven Rubio (Athletics and Giants) were able to accomplish their always superb work despite each of them dealing with personal family losses during the most critical period of work. Heartfelt thanks to two real professionals. Greg Gajus' timely and precise writing on Reds and Dodgers players is always among the best in this book. Fred Matos took on a large volume of work this year, covering the Orioles, Padres and Angels in fine detail. In addition to keeping all of us entertained with the various machinations of each side during last year's labor problem, Bill Gilbert turned out excellent work on the Astros. Peter Graves' coverage of the Rangers continues to be well-reasoned and well-written. As usual, David Luciani provided superior coverage of the Blue Jays. James Benkard is one of our newer contributors, first writing for the 1995 editions of Benson's books. His coverage of the Twins and Tigers has been especially insightful.

One of our rookie writers this year, Al Woodard, gave us excellent coverage of the Rockies, and did so on very short notice with fine results. Lary Bump manages to see hundreds of young players in the minor leagues every year and we would be lost without his annual contributions. Lary's fine work can also be found in expanded form in the aforementioned "Future Stars" book. Another rookie who provided supreme effort this year was Rob Curley, who gave us greatly detailed coverage of players from the American Association and the Texas League. He also took on a large workload yet did a quality job in a short time frame.

Brian Weaver and Stephen Lunsford took care of the many thousands of small details necessary to make this book a reality and improved the readability in so many different ways. Last, but certainly not least, John Benson did the Yankees and Mets and many individual players in his own thoughtful manner.

Marc Bowman November, 1995

INTRODUCTION

The uniquely American game of baseball, like fine art, great music, and meaningful literature, has the power to make people profoundly happy. On diverse levels, fans may be captivated by each tiny play. Over the course of a year-long competition, the tiny plays accumulate to create an ever-growing context for the next split-second outcome. Longtime fans follow with passion the rise of dynasty teams and the fruitless struggles of league doormats.

Baseball has no equal as a metaphor for life itself. Individuals stand alone and observable, in their specialized roles, unlike any other team sport. While the object of the game is unquestionably team-oriented, individual accomplishments in baseball can be noted, tabulated, scrutinized and evaluated in daily results and in annual and career totals.

In what other sport do fans sit and write down, play by play, how each athlete performs in each contest? None. The baseball scoresheet has no equivalent in basketball or football or any other team sport. Likewise the baseball box score tells a story, showing the linkage of all individual achievements to team success, unlike any daily record from any other game. And the length and magnitude of the season -- six months containing 162 games for every team -- provide a cumulative context of information like no other sport.

Inevitably, baseball attracts people who like books. Sure, there are plenty of fans who never read anything more than a daily newspaper, but there are also large numbers who delight in research, nostalgia, and strategic thinking. Any bookstore will show you, by the quantity of shelf space devoted to baseball, which sport is a clearly number one among the upper end of the literate population in America.

This particular book is made for serious fans, especially for those who like books. The *Baseball Player Guide A-Z* came into being largely through my own personal desire to have, at my fingertips, one book that identified every player instantly. As a baseball writer, especially as one who covers the entire player population in essays and books, it is necessary for me to have comprehensive reference materials.

Over the years it struck me that there was no single book that included "everyone." Finding some background on any established major leaguer is usually easy, of course. The annual *Scouting Notebook*, for example, has a good essay on 95% or more of the players who will have any major league impact in the coming season (I cover the Mets and Yankees for them myself), and there are numerous annual previews in the "fan" market covering popular players. Many of the most comprehensive books, however, focus on statistics exclusively.

Looking at just a table of statistics for any player, of course, you can't tell if he's dead or alive, much less see if the player is injured or healthy, retired or active. Sometimes when searching for a player who had simply disappeared, it might take me half an hour to find if that player had gone to Japan, missed an entire year because of injury, retired, or simply took a year off. And soon I learned that I was not alone in lacking information. My next step when I can't find a player after looking in every publication and database, is to call the front office of the team that last had him in their information guide, and ask, "What ever happened to Joe Bimbleman?" Usually the team media or minor league officer will know what happened, but often the answer at the other end was, "Gee, I don't know."

This book -- the one that you have in your hands now -- is my effort to get "everybody" in or near the major leagues into one book. My purpose is to have one volume at my fingertips all the time, so that I can quickly find ANY player and see immediately who he is, what he can do, and whether he is rising or falling in his career. Wanting that book for myself, I figured other people would want it too.

To make the "one book" idea reasonable to accomplish, and to make the end result something that would fit inside a briefcase without cramming, I decided to be (1) brief and (2) selective.

WHO'S IN THIS BOOK

Being brief is easy. There are minor problems, of course, when you try to write something clever and insightful, in 50 words or less, about any established star who has already been the subject of thousands and thousands of words in print; but being brief was not the hardest part of producing this book.

Being selective is quite a bit more difficult than being brief. I needed a method to choose slightly more than one third from the 5000 or so players now getting paid to play baseball and/or performing as college stars. My method was to include the following:

1. Players who were in the major leagues last year. In general, I left in the players who had retired, with a note about their retirement. Most of those players about whom you may be wondering, "Is he, or isn't he?" are in this book.

2. Players who have been in the major leagues and might return. In the post-expansion world that favors recycling as a quick and easy form of player development, that means just about all ex-major leaguers who choose to hang on. And I don't mean just the obvious Triple-A extension of the major league bench that can be found in every major league organization. In 1994 Tommy Gregg was hanging on in Mexico, unable to hook on with any of the 28 franchises north of the border; but we kept him in these pages with reference to his 1989 presence in the majors and the fact that he remained a good pinch hitter and backup outfielder. Maybe Dave Dombroski or Gary Hughes saw that comment; more likely they already knew about Gregg. Anyway when he became a major leaguer again in 1995, he was here in these pages for anyone who needed a quick identification: yes, that Tommy Gregg.

3. Minor leaguers who are close to a major league roster. This group includes many of those Triple-A players who probably won't be in the major leagues in 1996, or ever, but are close enough to the major league depth charts that one or two serious injuries on the major league roster could elevate them.

4. Minor leaguers who will probably reach the major leagues some day on the basis of their talent. We have tried to include every top prospect, every can't-miss phenom, every first round draft pick (two thirds of them reach the majors), and every minor leaguer who has been touted, publicized, recommended, or who won a prize, award, or batting title, etc.

Some players are both close to a major league roster, as in (3) above, and likely to reach the major leagues some day as in (4) above -- and these players are the best of the minor league population, at least for 1996.

WHO'S NOT IN THIS BOOK

Having told you who's in, now I will tell you who's not in this book. We have ruled out many players who have no hope of ever reaching the major leagues. You would be surprised how many players fit this description, if you are not in the baseball business yourself. The minor leagues are simply jammed full of players who don't have the potential to move up. Most of them got into baseball when they were young and developing, and then they stopped developing. Why would a baseball team keep them around? Many of them can perform OK at their minor league level, they are good role models, and they provide a useful service by filling out the rosters of enough teams for the true prospects to play enough games against enough other players so that their skills can be developed.

There are, of course, some players not in this book, who will nonetheless reach the major leagues some day, maybe even in 1996. Sometimes players suddenly show development after years of stagnation, or their team's needs change radically and unforeseeably. The reason they are not in is that they have not shown yet, to me or anyone who gives me information, enough evidence that they are probably bound for the majors. "Enough evidence" is of course a matter of opinion. I have tried to be generous and inclusive, but being too generous would make this book less useful.

PLAYER VALUES

Some baseball traditionalists using this book may be turned off when they find "Rotisserie" dollar values. There is one very good reason why those dollar values are in here: people buy this book to get them, and I like people to buy this book.

There is a very particular type of audience that cares about my work. Obviously, some people in the business of baseball have an interest in what I have to say. I don't know the extent to which they value my observations or trust my predictions; but I do know that a few people who make baseball personnel decisions get my annual books and my monthly updates. Some of them may even call my 900 number; it's a little eerie when an unfamiliar voice asks me about a player, and I say, well, the guy hasn't drawn a walk in his last 40 plate appearances, and his minor league roommate says he never could hit a slider, and one pitcher just told me it's easy to make a guy look bad when he's so eager to swing ... and the next day, I see on the AP wire that this player got sent down or released. Anyway, a large segment of the baseball fans who follow my work are competitors in contests to see who can pick the best players before the season starts. The so-called Rotisserie phenomenon has revolutionized the way America watches baseball, and in my opinion very much for the better. Baseball is show business, and the object of the game off-the-field is to sell tickets and video access and to maintain fan interest. Rotisserie has done more for that purpose than any development since television. And didn't the traditionalists say that television was going to ruin baseball? Rotisserie makes fans buy tickets, read more publications, learn more and enjoy more. Great!

Too often, sitting in the press box, I hear someone speaking with an air of authority talk about how those damn Rotisserie people have ruined baseball, with all their home/road, grass/turf, day/night, left/right stats that now appear everywhere. Fact is: split stats and breakdowns and all those "meaningless" numbers that weren't around 20 years ago have nothing to do with Rotisserie, or any other player selection contests. Rotisserians and most other such competitions use only the simplest, widely-accepted baseball measures, namely: batting average, home runs, runs batted in, and stolen bases for hitters; and ERA, wins, saves, and opponents' on-base percentage (baserunners per inning, or B/I) for pitchers. That stuff about what a player does at home, on grass, in night games, against lefties, comes from broadcast booths, not from Rotisserie leagues.

Another false myth about Rotisserie enthusiasts is that they don't know much about baseball. Of the million or so people who annually get into some kind of contest to see who can pick the best players, there are probably a few thousand dullards (I once saw one with the word "zero" written on his forehead). But what group of a million people, selected on any basis, doesn't have a few like that?

In my experience, the people who enjoy matching their knowledge against others, in any field, tend to have superior knowledge, or they would not enjoy the competition. The people who read my annual books and my monthly updates, and the people who call me on the phone, are a very knowledgeable group. There may not be a million people who care about my work, but there are many thousands of them, and their interest is intense.

STATS AND PROJECTIONS

This book is not a stats book. There are plenty of excellent statistical references available every year, including the books from STATS, Inc. described in the latter pages of this volume for the benefit of my readers. Stat lines from the last year or two are included for selected players where that information appears to be helpful in understanding who the player is, and what he is capable of doing.

Projections for 1996 are based on a very preliminary assessment of where the player was trending when we went to press. "Tendency" might be a better word than projection to describe this effort. Certainly I have avoided using the word "forecast" because that has a special and more definite meaning.

Just before each season starts, I publish true forecasts for every player, taking into consideration all the player moves and injuries right up until the finals days of spring training, and considering with appropriate weight exactly what managers are saying about who will play, and in what role. Much of the context and reasoning for these forecasts will appear in my Rotisserie Baseball Annual which reviews every position on every team from a depth-chart point of view.

There are various ways to stay current with my forecasts as they take shape and change continuously right up until Opening Day. The Projections in this book are just the starting point for that annual forecast process.

John Benson
November, 1995

ABAD, ANDY - OF - BL - Age 23
The leadoff batter in this book couldn't cut it in the Trenton Thunder's lineup, so he was demoted to Sarasota. He doesn't have much power, and has been a very ineffective base-stealer.

ABBOTT, JEFF - OF - BR - Age 23
The former University of Kentucky player has pounded the ball for a .357 average in his two pro seasons. He has been promoted three times, and his statistics have slipped at each step. But there's nothing wrong with his .382 on-base percentage and .431 slugging average for Double-A Birmingham. The White Sox are awaiting his arrival as patiently as they can.

ABBOTT, KURT - SS - BR - Age 26
Abbott led all NL shortstops in homers in 1995. He developed into a legitimate power threat, but continued to be deficient in most areas that define the worth of major league shortstops. His defensive range and overall reliability both rank in the bottom third of the NL population, and he is an undisciplined hitter with an unsightly 228/55 career K/BB ratio in 826 at bats. Abbott should return and be a creditable sixth or seventh hitter for the Marlins in 1996, but afterwards, phenom Edgar Renteria is a good bet to seize his job.

	AB	R	HR	RBI	SB	BA	$
1994 Florida NL	345	41	9	33	3	.249	7
1995 Florida NL	420	60	17	60	4	.255	11
1996 *Projection* >>>	462	63	16	58	5	.262	11

ABNER, SHAWN - OF - BR - Age 29
A former first pick in entire draft (1984) who never blossomed.

ABREU, BOB - OF - Age 22
Abreu was selected as the fourth best prospect in the Pacific Coast League in by Baseball America in his first year at Triple-A Tucson. A consistent .300 hitter with 10-16 stolen bases, Abreu has moved up a level each year in his five minor league seasons. Abreu projects as a solid major league player after he improves his defense, cuts down his strikeouts and refines his temperament. Abreu should take over as the Astros' leftfielder at age 23 in 1997 after another year at Triple-A.

ADRIANA, SHARNOL - 2B - BR - Age 25
With more at bats than he enjoyed his previous four professional seasons, Adriana finally got a few hits after a mediocre start to his career. He strikes out way too often to expect everyday action, especially with his lack of power. Adriana should see more playing time at the Double-A level in 1996 and might be at Triple-A by the end of the year.

ALDRETE, MIKE - 1B/OF - BL - Age 35
The Angels obtained veteran first baseman-outfielder from the A's to provide bench strength for the stretch run. He's a smooth lefty hitter with a career .266 average over nine major league seasons. Aldrete got substantial playing time with the A's when Mark McGwire was injured for long periods, but it's doubtful that he will see as much playing time with the Angels.

	AB	R	HR	RBI	SB	BA	$
1994 Oakland AL	178	23	4	18	2	.242	2
1995 California AL	149	19	4	24	0	.268	2
1996 *Projection* >>>	101	13	2	14	0	.258	0

ALEXANDER, MANNY - 2B - BR - Age 25
Alexander was primarily a shortstop in the minors, but second base was his best chance to get substantial playing time in the majors. He was learning how to play second in the majors, and although he has good physical tools and excellent range, his reaction times were a little slow at times, something that should improve with experience. He chokes up on the bat but is not considered a contact hitter as he comes up hacking including swinging at a lot of bad pitches. Alexander doesn't have any power, but he has good base-stealing speed.

	AB	R	HR	RBI	SB	BA	$
1994 Rochester AAA	426	63	6	39	30	.249	
1995 Baltimore AL	242	35	3	23	11	.236	6
1996 *Projection* >>>	163	24	2	16	7	.236	2

ALFONZO, EDGAR - SS/3B - BR - Age 28
Don't confuse Edgar, the older Oriole farm hand, with Edgardo Alfonzo the bright young Mets infield prospect. Edgar is not making very good progress toward the major leagues. Last year was his third in Double-A, and he was injured, further limiting his progress.

ALFONZO, EDGARDO - 3B/2B - BR - Age 22
When Dallas Green saw Edgardo Alfonzo playing winter ball in Venezuela a year ago, that was the end of any plan for Alfonzo to spend a year at Triple-A. His defense is already superior, and his offense will go steadily upward for the next few years as he matures in the majors.

	AB	R	HR	RBI	SB	BA	$
1995 New York NL	335	26	4	41	1	.278	6
1996 Projection >>>	510	54	12	78	5	.284	14

ALICEA, LUIS - 2B - BB - Age 30
A very slow start made Alicea's off-season acquistion by the Red Sox seem like a bust. But Boston stayed with him and he hit .295-4-27-8 in the second half while playing steady defense. He reached career highs in many categories, including games played and at-bats. It was the first time he'd really had the second base job all to himself; expect more of the same from Alicea in 1996.

	AB	R	HR	RBI	SB	BA	$
1994 St. Louis NL	205	32	5	29	4	.278	7
1995 Boston AL	419	64	6	44	13	.270	12
1996 Projection >>>	405	62	6	46	12	.273	11

ALLANSON, ANDY - C - BR - Age 34
Veteran Andy Allanson seems to get a major league job every year as there is usually a team in dire need of a veteran backup catcher. He's not much of a hitter.

	AB	R	HR	RBI	SB	BA	$
1995 California AL	82	5	3	10	0	.171	-

ALLENSWORTH, JERMAINE - OF - BR - 24
Selected by the Pirates as a supplemental first-round pick from Purdue in 1993, Allensworth jumped to Double-A in 1994, then Triple-A in 1995. However, he has struggled some at the upper levels and his trip on the fast track has slowed down. He could still become a decent major-league center fielder but probably not a star.

ALMANZAR, RICHARD - 2B - BR - Age 18
A .401 OPB won Almanzar a midyear promotion to high Class A. He's got speed.

ALOMAR, ROBERTO - 2B - BB - Age 28
Alomar hit .300 for the fourth straight year and his speed returned to where it was a couple of years ago. He is still a complete package and should be in his prime. Entering the winter, he was a free agent destined for big bucks and a long contract so he will be under increased pressure to produce. He sat out the final few games of the season with a mysterious injury that some suggested was his way of ensuring a .300 average.

	AB	R	HR	RBI	SB	BA	$
1994 Toronto AL	392	78	8	38	19	.306	23
1995 Toronto AL	517	71	13	66	30	.300	29
1996 Projection >>>	573	92	14	70	34	.303	31

ALOMAR, SANDY - C - BR - Age 29
The next time a meteorite falls out of the sky, don't be surprised if it hits Alomar. He continues to be an injury waiting to happen, missing over half of the 1995 season. He hasn't had 300 at bats in a season since 1990, but has been extremely productive when healthy during the past two seasons.

	AB	R	HR	RBI	SB	BA	$
1994 Cleveland AL	292	44	14	43	8	.288	16
1995 Cleveland AL	203	32	10	35	3	.300	8
1996 Projection >>>	281	42	13	45	4	.288	9

ALOU, MOISES - OF - BR - Age 29
After emerging as one of the National League's top young players, Alou had a tough 1995 that ended early with arthroscopic surgery on both shoulders. He appears to be stagnating a bit with the Expos and probably needs to move on if he's to become a superstar. He was stung by the Expos' fire sale last spring and doesn't always see eye-to-eye with the manager, even though it's his father Felipe.

	AB	R	HR	RBI	SB	BA	$
1994 Montreal NL	422	81	22	78	7	.339	30
1995 Montreal NL	344	48	14	58	4	.273	12
1996 *Projection* >>>	458	73	20	80	7	.300	20

ALVAREZ, CLEMENTE - C - BR - Age 27
The only remote resemblance to the other Clemente is Alvarez's arm. He's a good defensive catcher who can barely carry Mario Mendoza's bat. He'll probably be a minor league free agent every winter for as long as he can pick up his mask.

AMARAL, RICH - OF - BR - Age 34
A .282 average and twenty-one stolen bases is fine, and he can do it again if he gets enough playing time. Watch his role carefully. There are a lot of nervous veteran middle infielders on the Mariners roster looking over their shoulder at Alex Rodriguez. Somebody has to go, and it could be Amaral.

	AB	R	HR	RBI	SB	BA	$
1994 Seattle AL	228	37	4	18	5	.263	6
1995 Seattle AL	238	45	2	19	21	.282	13
1996 *Projection* >>>	208	36	2	18	13	.277	7

AMADOR, MANNY - SS - BB - Age 20
Very quietly, Amador has begun to assert himself as a viable future contender for the Phils' starting second base job. He was one of the younger starters in the Class-A Florida State League in 1995, and he made consistent contact with gaps power at the plate and, as a converted shortstop, was well above average defensively. His 6'0", 165 lbs, body is still developing, promising more power and with an addition of plate discipline, he could become a top notch offensive player. He needs two more years in the minors, but will then threaten Mickey Morandini.

AMARO, RUBEN - OF - BB - Age 31
Amaro is firmly established as a player who will routinely excel in the minors, but leave little or no mark in the majors. He is a capable defender at all three outfield positions, and possesses decent speed which translates into few stolen bases. He is a switch-hitter who has historically been a much better hitter from the right side, though that wasn't the case with the Indians in 1995. His role will never increase from his current fifth outfielder status - he is more likely to spend 1996 in Triple-A than in the majors.

	AB	R	HR	RBI	SB	BA	$
1994 Cleveland AL	23	5	2	5	2	.217	0
1995 Cleveland AL	60	5	1	7	1	.200	-
1996 *Projection* >>>	55	6	2	7	2	.215	-

ANDERSON, BRADY - OF - BL - Age 32
Anderson is an excellent outfielder and hitter, but the Orioles are disappointed that he is not a better lead-off man. For example, he is fast and could bunt more, but he doesn't. He could also work the count more to get more walks. Thus, the Orioles are looking for a good lead-off man, and when one is found, Anderson will move to second in the batting order or sixth or seventh.

	AB	R	HR	RBI	SB	BA	$
1994 Baltimore AL	453	78	12	48	31	.263	28
1995 Baltimore AL	554	108	16	64	26	.262	23
1996 *Projection* >>>	570	105	13	62	23	.261	20

ANDERSON, CHARLIE - IF - BR - Age 26
A late-round 1992 draft pick, Anderson was in a platoon situation at Double-A Arkansas in 1995, so his .283-4-29 batting line might not really represent his abilities. He's a singles hitter and an above-average fielder with a good arm. If he can put up comparable numbers in 350 at-bats during 1996, you've got to think he could turn some scouts' heads.

ANDERSON, GARRET - OF - BL - Age 23
Garrett Anderson was a solid hitter in Triple-A, so his solid rookie season with the Angels was not a surprise. His best years are still ahead of him, and it's likely that he will approach 25 homers and 100 RBI in 1996. Anderson should develop even more power as he matures, so look for 30 homers in a few years.

	AB	R	HR	RBI	SB	BA	$
1994 Vancouver AAA	505	75	12	102	3	.321	
1994 California AL	13	0	0	1	0	.385	-
1995 California AL	374	50	16	69	6	.321	18
1996 Projection >>>	508	75	24	96	8	.316	24

ANDERSON, MARLON - 2B - BL - Age 22
The Phils' 1995 second round pick dazzled in the Rookie level New York-Penn League. Defensively, he has above average range and is extremely surehanded. Offensively, he has gap power, makes consistent contact, and has above average basestealing ability. Since he is an experienced, All-America collegian, the Phils would be wise to aggressively promote him. Along with Manny Amador, Anderson will likely be a contender for the Phils' starting second base job two to three years down the road.

ANDREWS, SHANE - 3B/1B - BR - Age 24
Andrews proved the scouts right in 1995, his first full season in the major leagues with the Expos. His legs are too heavy to play third base and his bat is too slow to catch up with good major-league heat. Andrews, though, is 24 and could conceivably improve. However, it's hard to imagine him blossoming into a star.

	AB	R	HR	RBI	SB	BA	$
1994 Ottawa AAA	460	79	16	85	6	.254	
1995 Montreal AL	220	27	8	31	1	.214	2
1996 Projection >>>	210	25	7	30	1	.226	0

ANDUJAR, JUAN - SS - BR - Age 24
Andujar spent too much time at Single-A Kinston in the Indians' chain. He has developed decent power for a middle infielder. However, his lack of progress to date and free-swinging nature at the plate suggest that he won't advance much farther.

ANSLEY, WILLIE - OF - BR - Age 26
Houston's number one draft pick in January, 1989. He is excellent at getting on base and stealing bases, but he hasn't developed the power potential he showed in high school.

ANTHONY, ERIC - OF/1B - BL - Age 28
The former Astros phenom was signed by the Reds as a free agent in April and performed well on the rare occasions he was not on the DL with knee and hamstring injuries. Anthony displayed flashes of power last year and has a good chance to expand his playing time in 1996 if he can stay healthy.

	AB	R	HR	RBI	SB	BA	$
1994 Seattle AL	262	31	10	30	6	.237	8
1995 Cincinnati NL	134	19	5	23	2	.269	4
1996 Projection >>>	209	28	8	29	3	.251	3

ARIAS, ALEX - SS/3B - BR - Age 28
Very silently, Arias has developed into one of the most versatile, reliable utilitymen in the National League. In all of 677 major league at bats in four seasons, Arias has contributed a grand total of five homers and two steals. With the abundance of Grade A middle infield prospects in the Marlins' chain, Arias has no chance of garnering a fulltime major league spot in Florida - he is at best a multipositional 23rd-man who will not play much.

	AB	R	HR	RBI	SB	BA	$
1994 Florida NL	113	4	0	15	0	.239	-
1995 Florida NL	216	22	3	26	1	.269	3
1996 Projection >>>	113	10	1	14	1	.259	0

ARIAS, GEORGE - 3B - BR - Age 24
Third baseman George Arias made the Double-A All-Star team last year. He has showed some good hitting and power in the minors and could break into the Angels' starting lineup in 1996.

ARNOLD, KEN - SS - BR - Age 26
Arnold is a weak hitting shortstop in the Orioles farm system. He appears to be a career minor leaguer.

ASHLEY, BILLY - OF - BR - Age 25
Ashley's big swing was exploited by major league pitchers in 1995 as he struck out a staggering 88 times in only 215 at bats. It didn't help matters that he battled injuries and LaSorda would not leave him in the lineup with any consistency. He is Dave Kingman's little brother until proven otherwise, and the other Dodger outfield prospects may take his position before he gets a chance to win it.

	AB	R	HR	RBI	SB	BA	$
1994 Albuquerque AAA	388	93	37	105	6	.345	
1994 Los Angeles NL	6	0	0	0	0	.333	-
1995 Los Angeles NL	215	17	8	27	0	.237	3
1996 *Projection* >>>	303	30	10	36	1	.251	4

AUDE, RICH - 1B - BR - Age 24
One of the few players in the Pirates' organization with power, the big first baseman hasn't received a fair chance at the major-league level. He's reminiscent of Dick Stuart, though Pirates manager Jim Leyland doesn't seem all that interested in him.

	AB	R	HR	RBI	SB	BA	$
1994 Buffalo AAA	520	66	15	79	9	.281	
1995 Calgary AAA	195	34	9	42	3	.333	
1995 Pittsburgh NL	109	10	2	19	1	.248	1
1996 *Projection* >>>	276	25	4	47	4	.270	4

AURILIA, RICH - SS - BR - Age 24
Aurilia hit very well at Double-A, not as well for Triple-A Phoenix, then crushed the ball in half a dozen games for the Giants at the end of the season. He has OK power for a shortstop, will steal the occasional base, and may be given a chance at a regular job in 1996. However, last year was his second at Double-A, which is a sign his numbers there need to be looked at with a little skepticism. Nowhere near a sure thing, Aurilia is likely to be overrated by those who place too much importance on nineteen major-league atbats.

	AB	R	HR	RBI	SB	BA	$
1994 Tulsa AA	458	67	12	57	10	.234	
1995 Phoenix AAA	258	42	5	34	2	.279	
1995 San Francisco NL	19	4	2	4	1	.474	1

AUSMUS, BRAD - C - BR - Age 26
Ausmus is a baseball rarity...a catcher with base-stealing speed. He had stolen as many as 19 in a minor-league season, so his 16 last year were not a surprise. Neither was his good hitting last year a surprise as he was young with some major league experience and he had reached age 26 when many hitters have a good breakout year. Ausmus should continue his solid hitting in 1996.

	AB	R	HR	RBI	SB	BA	$
1994 San Diego NL	327	45	7	24	5	.251	7
1995 San Diego NL	328	44	5	34	16	.293	13
1996 *Projection* >>>	375	50	7	34	13	.273	10

AUSTIN, JAKE - OF - BL - Age 25
Austin had a poor season for the Pirates' Double-A Carolina farm club last year and is not considered a prospect.

AVEN, BRUCE - OF - BR - Age 24
Aven, the Indians' 30th round pick in 1994, emerged as a solid power/speed threat in his first full pro season at Class-A Kinston. However, he has an unlikely build for a power hitter (5'9", 180), and will likely be severely challenged at Double-A in 1996. He is also a wild swinger who has accumulated a 154/61 K/BB ratio in 699 pro at bats. A modest increase in selectivity could enable him to remain in the running for an eventual big league backup role.

AVERSA, JOE - SS/2B - BB - Age 27
A scrappy hitter in the mold of Kansas City's David Howard, Aversa is also a tremendous defensive player. His glove draws attention, so if he can hit the ball at all he might get a late-season callup.

AZUAJE, JESUS - 2B - BR - Age 23
A speedy middle infielder with a good eye and a knack for scoring runs. He could advance rapidly, as second base pickings are pretty slim in the Indians' farm system.

BAERGA, CARLOS - 2B - BB - Age 27
Hard to believe that this guy, with his 971 career hits, is only 27 years old. Baerga is a pure hitter who combines hitting for average with power unmatched among major league second basemen. However, his lack of selectivity at the plate has acted as a bottleneck in the Indians' vaunted batting order. His 1995 .355 OBP, though a career best, was below the Indians' team OBP of .361.

	AB	R	HR	RBI	SB	BA	$
1994 Cleveland AL	442	81	19	80	8	.314	27
1995 Cleveland AL	557	87	15	90	11	.314	25
1996 *Projection* >>>	582	99	20	99	12	.315	27

BAEZ, KEVIN - SS - BR - Age 29
Surfaced with the Mets as a good-field no-hit shortstop in 1990-1993. Baez spent 1995 at Triple-A Toledo, hitting .231.

BAGWELL, JEFF - 1B - BR - Age 27
Bagwell's production dropped off sharply in 1995 from his MVP year in 1994 due to a very slow start and another hand injury which caused him to miss the month of August. He should be expected to come back with a strong year in 1996 in the range of .320-30-120-15. Modest and hardworking, Bagwell should be in his prime years and should be one of the top players in the league for many years.

	AB	R	HR	RBI	SB	BA	$
1994 Houston NL	400	104	39	116	15	.368	48
1995 Houston NL	448	88	21	87	12	.290	22
1996 *Projection* >>>	524	111	30	116	11	.310	31

BAINES, HAROLD - DH - BL - Age 37
The sweet swinging Harold Baines had another solid season last year, showing no signs of slowing down. His role is almost exclusively left handed hitting DH in a platoon situation. Baines is good for 20-25 homers and 60-70 RBI in 1996.

	AB	R	HR	RBI	SB	BA	$
1994 Baltimore AL	326	44	16	54	0	.294	15
1995 Baltimore AL	385	60	24	63	0	.299	15
1996 *Projection* >>>	412	61	22	66	0	.280	12

BALL, JEFF - 1B/3B - BR - Age 26
Ball is a capable Triple-A hitter (.293-4-56 in 1995) who has had trouble finding a defensive position. Although there is a potential opening at third base in Houston, Ball will have to excel in the Arizona Fall League to be considered a candidate for the job. He could have a chance as a utility player in the majors because of his bat and experience at several positions.

BARBARA, DON - 1B - BL - Age 27
Barbara returned to his usual low-power output and his batting average dropped to a career low in 1995. He earned his release from the Red Sox' Triple-A affiliate at Pawtucket and was out of a job by mid-season. His career is teetering on the edge of oblivion.

BARBERIE, BRET - 2B - BB - Age 28
Barberie hit a combined .289 over 1993 and 1994, so his weak .241 last year was a big disappointment to the Orioles, so much so, that he was not in their plans for 1996. He can bounce back in 1996, especially in the National League. Barberie's not a Ryne Sandberg or Craig Biggio, but he can hit a productive .280.

	AB	R	HR	RBI	SB	BA	$
1994 Florida NL	372	40	5	31	2	.301	11
1995 Baltimore AL	237	32	2	25	3	.241	2
1996 *Projection* >>>	242	30	3	25	2	.270	2

BARKER, GLEN - OF - BR - Age 24
Barker added some power to his main asset -- speed (122 stolen bases in three pro years) -- but will have to make much better contact (143 strikeouts at Double-A Jacksonville) to register as a Tigers prospect.

BARKER, TIM - 2B/SS - BR - Age 27
Barker has been in three organizations, and was eligible to become a minor league free agent. He can get on base, and steal once he gets there.

BARNES, SKEETER - 1B - BR - Age 39
A long-time favorite of Sparky Anderson, Barnes bowed out after 36 games at Triple-A Toledo in 1994.

BARRON, TONY - OF - BR - Age 29
Barron is a thoroughly professional player who has labored nine years in the minors, even going back to Double-A each of the last two seasons, in his quest to play in the big leagues. He has a right field arm and some speed in the outfield, and can turn around a pitcher's mistake in a hurry. Barron may get a chance for a reserve role with Montreal.

BARRY, JEFF - OF - BB - Age 27
A long-time farmhand who had his career year at Double-A in 1994, Barry's arrival in the majors was more a symptom of post-expansion recycling than it was a tribute to his fair tools and exemplary attitude.

	AB	R	HR	RBI	SB	BA	$
1995 Binghampton AA	290	49	11	53	4	.269	
1995 Norfolk AAA	41	3	0	6	0	.220	
1995 New York NL	15	2	0	0	0	.133	-

BARTEE, KIMERA - OF - BB - Age 23
The player to be named in the Scott Erickson deal, Bartee is an outfielder with excellent speed who needs another two years in the minors. He could use more plate discipline, and he sustained an injury in the second half of '95. Bartee now looks like the next Chuck Carr, but he could still progress farther.

BASS, KEVIN - OF - BB - Age 36
Signed to be the part-time 4th outfielder, Bass wound up playing regularly as several Oriole outfielders were injured. He was productive early in the season, but tired and went into a prolonged slump going 107 at-bats after July 6 with only one RBI. Even as a part time outfielder and pinch hitter, it may be difficult for Bass to latch on somewhere in 1996.

	AB	R	HR	RBI	SB	BA	$
1994 Houston NL	203	37	6	35	2	.310	9
1995 Baltimore AL	295	32	5	32	8	.244	6
1996 Projection >>>	240	26	3	27	5	.238	2

BATES, JASON - 2B/3B/SS - BB - Age 25
This scrappy rookie grabbed the starting job at second base when Roberto Mejia struggled. When his hot bat cooled, Bates became the Rockies' designated fifth infielder. He's a far better hitter lefthanded than righthanded. Bates' determination and versatility make up for his lack of foot-speed and power.

	AB	R	HR	RBI	SB	BA	$
1994 Colorado Springs AAA	458	68	10	76	4	.286	
1995 Colorado NL	322	42	8	46	3	.267	8
1996 Projection >>>	217	28	5	31	2	.270	4

BATISTA, TONY - SS - BR - Age 22
He's a raw middle infielder with lots of flaws, but any shortstop who hits 33 homers in two seasons before he reaches 22 years of age is worth a mention. Bautista is at least two years away; his poor K/BB ratio suggests he may never succeed, but he's intriguing nonetheless.

BATISTE, KIM - 3B/SS - BR - Age 28
Batiste spent all of parts of four years in the majors with the Phillies where he hit a career .241 in 528 at-bats. He doesn't have any power or speed, and must now play in the minors waiting for an injury to a regular or other opportunity to get more major league playing time.

BATTLE, ALLEN - OF - BR - Age 27
He had a terrific 1994 with Triple-A Louisville but could not crack the Cardinals' starting outfield last season. He has good speed and decent gap power. However, at age 27, his future is limited to being a fourth or fifth outfielder.

	AB	R	HR	RBI	SB	BA	$
1995 Louisville AAA	164	28	3	18	7	.280	
1995 St. Louis NL	118	13	0	2	3	.271	1
1996 *Projection* >>>	138	20	1	14	4	.269	2

BATTLE, HOWARD - 3B - BR - Age 24
Battle finally made his major league debut last year despite a dropoff in performance at Triple-A. He has a big swing and a great throwing arm. With Ed Sprague finally performing up to expectations, Battle entered the winter blocked from cracking the Toronto lineup.

	AB	R	HR	RBI	SB	BA	$
1995 Syracuse AAA	443	43	8	48	10	.251	
1995 Toronto AL	15	3	0	0	1	.200	-

BAUTISTA, DANNY - OF - BR - Age 23
This young Dominican experienced some growing pains in '95. Bautista brings Detroit much needed speed and plays right field well, so Sparky Anderson gave him the first half of the '95 season to produce with the bat. He didn't and was benched, then demoted. Bautista eventually will be a regular player, but look for him to assume a part time role until he is fully ready, about '97 or '98.

	AB	R	HR	RBI	SB	BA	$
1994 Detroit AL	99	12	4	15	1	.232	1
1995 Detroit AL	271	28	7	27	4	.203	1
1996 *Projection* >>>	231	29	8	30	4	.242	3

BEAMON, TREY - OF - BL - Age 22
After winning the Double-A Southern League batting title for Carolina in 1994, Beamon had another solid season with the Pirates' Triple-A Calgary farm club last year. He hits for average but will need to add more power or speed to become a star player at the major-league level. Beamon could well return to Calgary for another season.

BEAN, BILLY - OF - BL - Age 31
Veteran Billy Bean has spent parts of six years in the majors with a career batting average of .228 in 478 at-bats. But he made the Triple-A All-Star team last year. He has very little power and no speed.

BEASLEY, TONY - 2B - BR - Age 29
After being released just prior to the 1994 season, Beasley returned to the Pirates as a replacement player last spring. He's never played in the majors and is not a prospect. Beasley is likely to return to his father's logging business in Virginia soon.

BECKER, RICH - OF - BB - Age 24
After stepping in for Alex Cole, Becker didn't shine on offense like fellow rookie Marty Cordova did. He still played well in center field and started to hit better late in the year. Becker is capable of producing Chad Curtis' numbers in time, and he should raise his average to .260 in '96.

	AB	R	HR	RBI	SB	BA	$
1994 Minnesota AL	98	12	1	8	6	.265	3
1995 Minnesota AL	392	45	2	33	8	.237	4
1996 *Projection* >>>	500	64	4	50	18	.261	13

BELK, TIM - OF - BR - Age 26
Belk was considered one of the Reds better prospects at the start of the season, but his year was destroyed by a serious beaning that broke several bones in his face. In the minors, Belk has been a righthanded Hal Morris type, hitting for high average, many doubles, and few home runs.

BELL, DAVID - 3B/2B - BR - Age 23
The son of Buddy Bell, David was acquired by the Cardinals from Cleveland in the Ken Hill deal last season. Though a third baseman like his father while coming up through the Indians' system, St. Louis also played him at second base

late last season. He'll start at one of the two positions this year and should eventually become a dependable player like his father.

	AB	R	HR	RBI	SB	BA	$
1995 Buffalo AAA	254	34	8	34	0	.272	
1995 Louisville AAA	76	9	1	9	4	.276	
1995 St. Louis NL	144	13	2	19	1	.250	1
1996 *Projection* >>>	306	30	4	40	3	.257	3

BELL, DEREK - OF - BR - Age 27
Bell is an aggressive player who was having an excellent season for Houston before being sidelined with a leg injury for the last five weeks. He should be back at full strength in 1996 and another big year can be expected as he moves into his prime. Bell reached career highs in batting average and stolen bases in 1995, but his home runs were down. A realistic expectation for 1996 would be more power with a lower average.

	AB	R	HR	RBI	SB	BA	$
1994 San Diego NL	434	54	14	54	24	.311	32
1995 Houston NL	452	63	8	86	27	.334	29
1996 *Projection* >>>	542	73	13	88	31	.308	29

BELL, JAY - SS - BR - Age 30
Bell got off to a bad start last season and was obviously not ready after spending his time during the strike as a member of the union's negotiating committee. Still one of the best all-around shortstops in baseball, he has five more good years ahead of him. It may not be in Pittsburgh, though; the Pirates are going with youth and would like to unload the $9.3 million he's guaranteed in salary over the next two seasons.

	AB	R	HR	RBI	SB	BA	$
1994 Pittsburgh NL	424	68	9	45	2	.276	11
1995 Pittsburgh NL	530	79	13	55	2	.262	10
1996 *Projection* >>>	596	92	13	61	4	.270	14

BELL, JUAN - 2B/SS - BR - Age 28
"Suitcase" Bell has spent all or parts of the last five seasons with five different teams. He's not really even a good Triple-A player and is only a reserve infielder during his brief major league stints. Bell is a poor hitter who can handle the glove well; he'll likely end up with some new team in 1996.

	AB	R	HR	RBI	SB	BA	$
1994 Montreal NL	97	12	2	10	4	.278	3
1995 Boston AL	26	7	1	2	0	.154	-

BELLE, ALBERT - OF - BR - Age 29
Belle posted one of the single most devastating individual seasons in baseball history in 1995. In a strike-shortened 144-game season, he did things never before done in 162-game campaigns, like reaching the half-century mark in both doubles (52) and homers (50). For a power hitter, he strikes out relatively infrequently, and has learned to work the count in his favor consistently. Though 1995 will be very difficult to top, look for Belle to continue to compete for MVP awards and homer titles in the short to intermediate term.

	AB	R	HR	RBI	SB	BA	$
1994 Cleveland AL	412	90	36	101	9	.357	41
1995 Cleveland AL	546	121	50	126	5	.317	35
1996 *Projection* >>>	588	122	49	130	9	.325	37

BELLIARD, RAFAEL - SS/2B - BR - Age 34
The weak-hitting Belliard again gave Atlanta sparkling defensive play as a substitute. He can't hit a lick, however, and is quickly losing his reserve role to Mike Mordecai.

	AB	R	HR	RBI	SB	BA	$
1994 Atlanta NL	120	9	0	9	0	.242	-
1995 Atlanta NL	180	12	0	7	2	.222	-
1996 *Projection* >>>	170	11	0	9	1	.224	-

BELLINGER, CLAY - SS - BR - Age 27
Bellinger has spent seven years in the minors without hitting over .274. He's a career minor leaguer with no bat.

BELTRE, ESTEBAN - SS - BR - Age 28
Beltre was Benji Gil's caddy in 1995, and he has no realistic chance of a larger role. Beltre is a decent-field, no-hit player who could hang around for a few more seasons as a reserve.

	AB	R	HR	RBI	SB	BA	$
1994 Texas AL	131	12	0	12	2	.282	2
1995 Texas AL	92	7	0	7	0	.217	-
1996 Projection >>>	117	10	0	10	1	.248	-

BENARD, MARVIN - OF - BL - Age 26
A late-bloomer, Benard can hit for average and steal the occasional base, and he impressed in a brief stint with the Giants at the end of the 1995 season. At age 26, Benard will never be a superstar, but like many talented but relatively old rookies, he could be a pleasant surprise in his first season if given a chance.

	AB	R	HR	RBI	SB	BA	$
1995 Phoenix AAA	378	70	6	32	10	.304	
1995 San Francisco NL	34	5	1	4	1	.382	1
1996 Projection >>>	123	16	3	14	4	.277	1

BENAVIDES, FREDDIE - SS - BR - Age 29
A solid utility man who can play any of the infield positions, Benavides' playing future is uncertain because of his age. Last year, he hit .241-4-26 for Triple-A Iowa and was a vital part of that club.

BENITEZ, YAMIL - OF - BR - Age 23
Benitez's 1995 statistics in Triple-A were so similar to his '94 numbers in Double-A that it was scary. He arrived in Montreal in September on a hot streak, and kept it going. His biggest improvement ;last year was in his base-stealing percentage. Now it's time to work on his strike-zone judgment. There's no reason to think the talented Benitez can't do it, even in the majors with Montreal.

	AB	R	HR	RBI	SB	BA	$
1995 Ottawa AAA	474	66	18	69	14	.259	
1995 Montreal NL	39	8	2	7	0	.385	1
1996 Projection >>>	126	24	4	24	0	.244	0

BENJAMIN, MIKE - 2B/SS - BR - Age 30
Benjamin had the hottest three-game streak in major league history in 1995, which is all the more amazing because Benjamin has always been a very limited hitter. He is a career .196 hitter even with the six hits in one game and is not good enough for regular play. Benjamin has succeeded in 21 of 22 stolen base attempts in the majors and he'll serve as the Phillies main reserve player at shortstop and third base in 1996.

	AB	R	HR	RBI	SB	BA	$
1994 San Francisco NL	62	9	1	9	5	.258	3
1995 San Francisco NL	186	19	3	12	11	.220	4
1996 Projection >>>	106	12	2	8	6	.224	-

BENNETT, GARY - C - BR - Age 23
Following in the footsteps of former Phillie catcher Doug Lindsey, who struck out in his only four at bats with the club (three against David Cone in a season-ending one-hitter in 1991), unlikely major leaguer Bennett struck out in his only 1995 at bat, which will likely represent the body of his major league career. A six year minor league veteran with a sub-.300 career slugging percentage and decent defensive skills, Bennett is probably one of the least impressive players with a line in Total Baseball.

BENZINGER, TODD - 1B - BB - Age 33
One of the weakest hitting first base regulars of 1994, Benzinger was released early in 1995 and never would have compared favorably with Will Clark anyway.

	AB	R	HR	RBI	SB	BA	$
1994 San Francisco NL	328	32	9	31	2	.265	8
1995 San Francisco NL	10	2	1	2	0	.200	-

BERBLINGER, JEFF - 2B - BR - Age 25
Berblinger is probably the best second-base prospect in the Cardinals' farm system. He has a good batting eye and

above average speed. A stress fracture in his right leg caused his numbers for Double-A Arkansas to drop off slightly, but he still finished at .319-5-29 with more walks than strikeouts. Next stop, Triple-A Louisville.

BERRIOS, HARRY - OF - BR - Age 24
Outfielder Harry Berrios had a monster year in 1994, mostly in Class A, and was named the Orioles Organization Player of the Year. He was promoted to Double-A in 1995, struggled mightily, and was demoted back to Single-A for awhile and then back up to Double-A where he again struggled before getting it all together for his last 100 or so at-bats. Berrios is 25, and needs to make a major upward career move very soon or else he will become a career minor leaguer able to hit only at the lower levels.

BERROA, GERONIMO - OF - BR - Age 31
Berroa has always hit; his success at the major-league level was a surprise only to all the GMs who refused to recognize the legitimacy of the Chief's production in the minors. He'll be playing when he's 40 if there is still a DH rule. He provides decent average, solid power, occasional steals and walks far more often than you'd think, given his reputation as a free swinger.

	AB	R	HR	RBI	SB	BA	$
1994 Oakland AL	340	55	13	65	7	.306	20
1995 Oakland AL	546	87	22	88	7	.278	19
1996 Projection >>>	533	85	21	90	8	.282	19

BERRY, SEAN - 3B - BR - Age 30
As always, Berry seemed on the verge of being run out of town; instead he responded with the best season of his career for the Expos in 1995. Though not the classic power-hitting third baseman, Berry is a good hitter and an OK fielder. He's a lot better than given credit for and finally seemed to win manager Felipe Alou's respect last summer.

	AB	R	HR	RBI	SB	BA	$
1994 Montreal NL	320	43	11	41	14	.278	18
1995 Montreal NL	314	38	14	55	3	.318	15
1996 Projection >>>	376	49	15	59	9	.289	14

BERRYHILL, DAMON - C - BB - Age 32
Why the Reds wanted Berryhill is a mystery, but they wasted a number one draft pick to sign him after Boston cut him loose in 1994. Only weaknesses are lack of power, low average, poor strike zone judgement, speed and defense.

	AB	R	HR	RBI	SB	BA	$
1994 Boston AL	255	30	6	34	0	.263	5
1995 Cincinnati NL	82	6	2	11	0	.183	-
1996 Projection >>>	70	7	2	9	0	.237	-

BETTS, TODD - 3B - BL - Age 22
Very quietly, Betts has developed into a strong offensive force in the Indians' low minors. A la Wade Boggs, Betts simply does not go outside the strike zone to swing at a pitch. He has accumulated an excellent 111/174 K/BB ratio in his three pro seasons, and also possesses gaps power, with 10 homer capability. The 1993 14th round pick finds a wide open field ahead of him at third base in the minors, and he could graduate to Triple-A by the end of 1996. He could eventually be a productive bench player in Cleveland, or a starting third sacker elsewhere.

BETZSOLD, JAMES - OF - BR - Age 23
The 1994 Indians' 20th round pick was a consistent power source at Class-A Kinston in 1995. However, he is a strikeout machine who has whiffed 205 times in 667 pro at bats. He has a long, looping swing that may have a hard time catching up with higher grade fastballs. He is also a little old to be just reaching Double-A - it should only take about 100 at bats at that level in 1996 to determine whether he has the requisite bat speed to eventually rate a chance at a major league bench role.

BIASUCCI, JOE - 2B/SS - BR - Age 26
Biasucci has stalled at Double-A after slow progress in the low minors. Power is his main asset, but he showed little of that while hitting .244 at Double-A Canton-Akron in 1995. He's not a good fielder, so he'll make it with the bat, or not at all; bet on the latter.

BICHETTE, DANTE - OF - BR - Age 32
Bichette turned in another All-Star year, but critics continue to give more credit to Coors Field's altitude for his bodacious offensive numbers than they do to Bichette's prowess with the bat. In addition to the prodigious power output, he also had the longest hitting streak (23 games) in the NL in 1995. Defensively, he still has one of the strongest arms in the game, but fly balls hit to Bichette's right (or behind him) sometimes turn into unexpected adventures in the art of outfielding. Bichetter signed a big dollar contract to return to Colorado in 1996.

	AB	R	HR	RBI	SB	BA	$
1994 Colorado NL	484	74	27	95	21	.304	39
1995 Colorado NL	579	102	40	128	13	.340	42
1996 *Projection* >>>	599	101	30	102	14	.305	31

BIESER, STEVE - OF - BB - Age 27
The fact that the Phils' 1989 32nd round draft pick has lasted this long is a testament to the system's weakness over the years. He doesn't hit for average or power (three homers in 1640 career plate appearances), and has middling speed. He is a versatile gamer who can catch in a pinch. The arrival of the Phils' best prospects at Triple-A in 1996 will hasten his departure from the organization.

BIGGIO, CRAIG - 2B - BR - Age 30
Biggio had an outstanding season with the Astros in 1995, solidifying his position as the best second baseman in the National League, if not the major leagues. He led the majors in runs scored and was second in the National League in on base average. Biggio is an aggressive player who excels in every phase of the game and should continue to produce at a high level for several years.

	AB	R	HR	RBI	SB	BA	$
1994 Houston NL	437	88	6	56	39	.318	38
1995 Houston NL	553	123	22	77	33	.302	33
1996 *Projection* >>>	598	126	18	79	39	.300	35

BLANKENSHIP, LANCE - OF - BR - Age 32
Blankenship has missed all of the last two years due to injury; he last played for Oakland in 1993. When he plays he hits for a low average, draws a lot of walks and has some speed. He's a versatile player who can be used at any number of infield and outfield positions. Until he's fully healthy again it's hard to predict what the future holds for Blankenship.

BLASINGAME, KENT - OF - BL - Age 26
Blasingame, the son of Phils' roving minor league instructor and former major leaguer Don Blasingame, is a scrappy battler who simply does not have the physical skills to excel in the upper reaches of the minor leagues. He is above average defensively and has decent speed, but he has no power and his bat is simply too slow to compete against higher level pitching. His pro career seems to have run its course.

BLAUSER, JEFF - SS - BR - Age 30
Blauser's season started out badly and just got worse. His season long slump left him sharing the shortstop role with Rafael Belliard. Blauser still has some power and decent strike zone judgment but isn't a good shortstop. He's an excellent candidate for a big rebound in 1996.

	AB	R	HR	RBI	SB	BA	$
1994 Atlanta NL	380	56	6	45	1	.258	7
1995 Atlanta NL	431	60	12	31	8	.211	4
1996 *Projection* >>>	490	72	12	45	7	.247	8

BLOSSER, GREG - OF - BL - Age 24
The Red Sox first-round draft choice in 1989 has seen his star tarnished. He reached Boston in 1993 and '94, but was sent down to Double-A during last season. A minor league free agent, he took his strong arm and power-hitting bat to the Baltimore organization.

BLOWERS, MIKE - 3B - BR - Age 30
He's played well before, and while last year was not entirely a fluke, that's as good as it'll get for Blowers. He's useful at third, first, leftfield and DH.

	AB	R	HR	RBI	SB	BA	$
1994 Seattle AL	270	37	9	49	2	.289	11

	AB	R	HR	RBI	SB	BA	$
1995 Seattle AL	439	59	23	96	2	.257	14
1996 Projection >>>	348	47	12	61	2	.267	8

BOGAR, TIM - SS - BR - Age 29
An overachieving role player, Bogar has been in the right place at the right time frequently in his career. That luck will run out as the Mets young infield stars emerge in 1996. And that .290 average in '95 was a fluke.

	AB	R	HR	RBI	SB	BA	$
1994 New York NL	52	5	2	5	1	.154	-
1995 New York NL	145	17	1	21	1	.290	3
1996 Projection >>>	110	12	2	15	1	.252	-

BOGGS, WADE - 3B - BL - Age 37
Although the batting titles and .360 seasons are gone, Boggs remains a solid (even improved) defensive third baseman and an underappreciated force at the plate. The Yankees aimed to keep this player who was instrumental in their last-season surge. Expect the graceful aging to continue.

	AB	R	HR	RBI	SB	BA	$
1994 New York AL	366	61	11	55	2	.342	20
1995 New York AL	460	76	5	63	1	.324	14
1996 Projection >>>	498	82	8	69	1	.326	17

BOLICK, FRANK - 1B/DH - BB - Age 29
Bolick is a nine year minor league vet who actually had a short stint as the Expos' starting third baseman in 1993. He is a stocky (5'10", 180) switch-hitter who has perennially hit for power with excellent plate discipline in the minors, but has never had an extended major league trial. It is unlikely that he will ever get that chance - especially if he remains with the Indians. To put it mildly, Bolick is no threat to Jim Thome, and he doesn't play defense well enough to be his caddy.

BONDS, BARRY - OF - BL - Age 31
His power and average dropped off a bit, but otherwise Bonds had yet another MVP-level season in 1995. As this future Hall-of-Famer gradually declines in his thirties, he may be overrated by people who remember what Bonds did in his prime, but otherwise there is nothing negative to say about the best player of his era.

	AB	R	HR	RBI	SB	BA	$
1994 San Francisco NL	391	89	37	81	29	.312	45
1995 San Francisco NL	506	109	33	104	31	.294	37
1996 Projection >>>	560	124	42	117	36	.302	43

BONIFAY, KEN - 3B - BL - Age 25
The nephew of Pirates General Manager Cam Bonifay had a big 1993 in the small ballpark at Class A Salem but struggled through an injury-plagued season at Class AA Carolina in 1994 and went back to Class A in 1995.

BONILLA, BOBBY - OF/3B - BB - Age 33
Slugger Bobby Bonilla hit .333-10-46 for the Orioles indicating that he won't have any problems adjusting to American League pitching. Look for him to approach the 30-homer mark. He will play third base or the outfield, with his position dependent on the Orioles' signing of a free-agent outfielder.

	AB	R	HR	RBI	SB	BA	$
1994 New York NL	403	60	20	67	1	.290	19
1995 Two Teams	554	96	28	99	0	.329	26
1996 Projection >>>	523	84	25	90	1	.288	18

BOONE, AARON - 3B - BR - Age 23
Yet another Boone in pro ball, this one was the Reds third round draft pick in 1994 and displays good power and speed. He briefly reached Double-A Chattanooga in 1995, where he should start 1996. By 1997 he could easily be playing alongside brother Bret in Riverfront Stadium.

BOONE, BRET - 2B - BR - Age 26
Despite a lengthy second half slump that dropped his average to .267, Boone established himself as one of the best

second basemen in the league in 1995. Boone is an unusual combination for a middle infielder, with very good power (34 doubles and 15 home runs), not much speed (five steals) and spectacular defense (only four errors all year with excellent range). Boone has reached the age/experience level where rapid improvement is likely.

	AB	R	HR	RBI	SB	BA	$
1994 Cincinnati NL	381	59	12	68	3	.320	20
1995 Cincinnati NL	513	63	15	68	5	.267	14
1996 Projection >>>	533	70	17	80	5	.295	18

BOOTY, JOSH - 3B - BR - Age 21
Major concerns are beginning to develop regarding the Marlins' 1994 first round draftee. In two years of rookie ball, Booty has been unable to make consistent contact and is batting well below .200. Booty became so despondent by the end of 1995 that he is said to be considering going to college to play football - he spurned a full ride to play quarterback at LSU to sign with the Marlins. At 6'3", 215 lbs, he's got the physical tools to advance through the ranks, but one has to question his will at this point.

BORDERS, PAT - C - BR - Age 32
Borders was acquired by Houston from Kansas City to provide a steadying influence during the stretch drive. Nearing the end of his career, Borders now hits for a low average with little power.

	AB	R	HR	RBI	SB	BA	$
1994 Toronto AL	295	24	3	26	1	.247	3
1995 Two Teams	178	15	4	13	0	.208	-
1996 Projection >>>	192	16	3	16	1	.232	-

BORDICK, MIKE - SS - BR - Age 30
Your typical good field, no hit shortstop, and will steal ten bases and hit .260 with lots of at-bats. His .300 batting average in 1992 grows dimmer every year.

	AB	R	HR	RBI	SB	BA	$
1994 Oakland AL	391	38	2	37	7	.253	8
1995 Oakland AL	428	46	8	44	11	.264	11
1996 Projection >>>	498	53	8	51	11	.259	10

BORRELLI, DEAN - C - BR - Age 29
Borelli ended last season as a reserve catcher in Triple-A. At the age of 28, the light-hitting Borelli has little chance of playing in the major leagues.

BOSTON, DARYL - OF - BL - Age 33
Boston hit .188 in 64 at-bats for Triple-A Charlotte and was released. He had over 2600 major league at-bats in eleven seasons, but is probably finished.

BOSTON, D.J. - 1B - BL - Age 24
Daryl's younger brother struggled with his batting average most of the 1995 season. His power and speed now look ordinary although he'd help himself by not trying to swing for the fences much of the time. He should be hoping for nothing more than another chance as an everyday player at Double-A.

BOURNIGAL, RAFAEL - 2B/SS - BR - Age 29
After more than eight years in the Dodgers organization, including some time as a player-coach, Bournigal arrived with the Expos' top farm team at Ottawa in time to help show its young players how to win the International League title. The minor league free agent may have another year or two as a utility player, but appears headed for a lengthy career in coaching.

BOWERS, BRENT - OF - BL - Age 24
Bowers continued to swing at everything last year and after his promotion to Triple-A, it hurt every element of his game. Even though he can run well, he doesn't take walks and therefore doesn't get many opportunities to steal. He's not quite up to the major leagues just yet.

BOWIE, JIM - 1B - BL - Age 31
After nine years in the minors, Bowie finally made it to the majors in 1994, getting fourteen at bats just before the strike. Don't be surprised if those are the only at bats Bowie gets in his major league career; there isn't much need for a 30-year-old, low power first baseman.

BOYKIN, TYRONE - DH/OF - BR - Age 27
At 27 last year, outfielder Tyrone Boykin was a little old and experienced for Double-A. It was his second year in Double-A, and the .285 is poor because it was with Midland in the hitter-friendly Texas League.

BRADY, DOUG - 2B - BB - Age 26
Brady is a good fielder and has excellent speed, but probably won't hit enough to survive in the majors. He turned a few heads with a 30-game hitting streak at Triple-A Nashville - the longest streak in professional baseball in 1995. Brady might pressure Ray Durham for platoon time in 1996, but won't be a regular.

BRADSHAW, TERRY - OF - BL - Age 27
Perhaps the greatest quarterback ... oops, wrong Terry Bradshaw. This one is a Cardinals' outfield prospect who didn't show much in his first major-league shot last year and is getting long in the tooth at age 27. Four Super Bowl, er World Series, rings don't appear to be in his future.

	AB	R	HR	RBI	SB	BA	$
1995 Louisville AAA	389	65	8	42	20	.283	
1995 St. Louis NL	44	6	0	2	1	.227	-
1996 *Projection* >>>	90	12	1	8	3	.247	-

BRAGG, DARREN - OF - BL - Age 26
Bragg was a big disappointment after winning the Mariners leftfield job in spring training, hitting .222 before his demotion. He redeemed himself with a .306 performance at Triple-A Tacoma, but had lost his job to Vince Coleman by the time he returned later in the year; he got just 28 at-bats the rest of the year. Bragg will have another chance to win the Mariners regular left field job in 1996. He's got good speed and some power, and has displayed a good batting eye in the past.

	AB	R	HR	RBI	SB	BA	$
1995 Tacoma AAA	212	24	4	31	10	.307	
1995 Seattle AL	145	20	3	12	9	.234	4
1996 *Projection* >>>	88	12	2	7	5	.230	0

BRAGGS, GLENN - OF - BR - Age 33
Braggs continues to be a power hitting hero for the Yokohama BayStars in Japan.

BRANSON, JEFF - 3B/SS - BL - Age 29
Branson is another example of Davey Johnson's extraordinary ability to get the most out his extra players. Starting the season as a reserve infielder/lefthanded pinch hitter, Johnson moved Branson moved into what turned out to be a very effective third base platoon after Willie Greene busted again. Per 600 at bats, his season translates to 22 home runs, 82 RBI, and 80 walks. Branson is not likely to expand his role, but his power and versatility make him a useful player.

	AB	R	HR	RBI	SB	BA	$
1994 Cincinnati NL	109	18	6	16	0	.284	3
1995 Cincinnati NL	331	43	12	45	2	.260	8
1996 *Projection* >>>	287	38	10	36	2	.251	4

BRANYAN, RUSSELL - 3B - BB - Age 20
Branyan teased Indians' brass with glimpses of his incredible potential at Class-A Columbus in 1995, but also grandly displayed his flaws. Branyan crushed 19 homers in only 277 at bats, but also managed to cram in 120 strikeouts, with only 27 walks. The 1994 7th round selection is a switch-hitter and has a projectable 6'3", 195 lbs, body, but he must become more selective to rate a major league chance. His upside is extremely high, but the risks are enormous. The Indians will start Branyan at Class-A Kinston in 1996 - they would like him to make it to Double-A by season's end, with safer, less spectacular prospect Todd Betts sliding up to Triple-A.

BREAM, SCOTT - 2B - BB - Age 25
Infielder Scott Bream has improved his hitting in recent years, and he can steal some bases. It's doubtful that he can

beat out the established Padres' veterans, so his best opportunity for major league playing time is as a utility man or a replacement for an injured regular.

BREAM, SID - 1B - BL - Age 35
Several injuries slowed Bream in 1994 and he was out of professional baseball in 1995. He was a good fielding first baseman and a successful pinch-hitter for the Braves in the early 1990's, but he's now finished as a ballplayer.

BREDE, BRENT - OF - BL - Age 24
Here's the story of the man named Brede. He has surprisingly little power for a guy 6-4, and surprisingly good ability to draw a walk. He's a leadoff type who can steal a base and play adequately in the outfield.

BREWER, ROD - OF/1B - BL - Age 30
After spending 1994 in Japan, the former Cardinals' journeyman returned to the states as the Marlins' Triple-A first baseman. That was not a particular challenge for Brewer, who hit for average and power in 1995. However, he has proven over time that his bat is not quick enough for a significant major league role. Expect him to settle in for the long haul as a Triple-A first sacker, with brief major league opportunities a possibility.

BRIDGES, KARY - 2B - BL - Age 24
Bridges has hit for average but not power in each of his three seasons (.301-3-43-10 at Double-A in 1995) in the Astro system. He is a contact hitter who rarely strikes out and he has some speed. Bridges is a marginal prospect who needs at least one more strong year before making a bid for a major league job.

BRIGGS, STONEY - OF - BR - Age 24
Briggs went from the Blue Jays to the Padres in the Derek Bell trade. He is a power hitting outfielder who is still learning to be a more consistent and aggressive hitter. Last year in Double-A, Briggs struck out 35 per cent of the time yet hit only eight homers.

BRILEY, GREG - OF - BL - Age 30
Diminuitive Briley continues to decline, hitting a combined .235 at two Triple-A stops in 1995. He's just barely hanging onto a professional baseball job at this point.

BRITO, BERNARDO - DH/OF - BR - Age 32
Brito got five at-bats for the Twins before going to Japan. He has legendary power as a minor leaguer; it might be interesting to see what he could actually do in the majors. Brito may be beyond that opportunity now.

BRITO, JORGE - C - BR - Age 29
Brito played an important backup role behind Girardi in the early part of 1995. A strong defensive catcher, Brito was optioned to Triple-A Colorado Springs in July to make way for newly-signed Matt Nokes, and later, the stronger hitting Jayhawk Owens. He'll be unlikely to break spring training with the parent club in 1996.

BRITO, LUIS - SS - BB - Age 25
Surprise - another SS from San Pedro de Macoris. The Phils jumped him over a level to Double-A Reading in 1994 with uninspiring offensive results. He's your basic low average, no power type with little speed and no discipline.

BRITO, TILSON - SS - BR - Age 23
His debut season at Triple-A saw his average drop to the lowest it has been in his four professional seasons. He has great speed but is only beginning to time his base stealing properly. Brito is probably going to spend most of 1996 at Triple-A again.

BROCK, TARRICK - OF - BL - Age 22
He doesn't show any power and needs to improve his hitting in order to start receiving serious attention.

BROGNA, RICO - 1B - BL - Age 25
The Mets have coached young Brogna to hit line drives wherever the ball is pitched. The Tigers had him trying to pull everything, a method that didn't work. Now he's a major power source and on the upswing in his career, ready to graduate from a platoon-plus role to full-time in 1996.

	AB	R	HR	RBI	SB	BA	$
1994 New York NL	131	16	7	20	1	.351	8
1995 New York NL	495	72	22	76	0	.289	17
1996 *Projection* >>>	526	74	24	81	1	.280	17

BROOKS, ERIC - C - BR - Age 26
He continued to look unsuited for professional baseball last year. He has no power at all, doesn't make much contact and the fact that he will take a walk isn't enough to make up for the rest. At his age and considering his struggles of the last five years, he's almost gone from pro ball.

BROOKS, JERRY - OF - BR - Age 29
Brooks got a cup of coffee with the Dodgers in 1993, but that's been his career highlight so far. He had a decent year at Triple-A Indianapolis in 1995, hitting .283 with 14 homers and 52 RBI and has a shot as a backup in the majors somewhere in 1996.

BROSIUS, SCOTT - OF - BR - Age 29
Brosius is a useful utility player with legitimate homerun power (43 HR in 1081 major-league at-bats). He took as many walks in 1995 as he had in his three previous Oakland stints combined.

	AB	R	HR	RBI	SB	BA	$
1994 Oakland AL	324	31	14	49	2	.238	9
1995 Oakland AL	388	69	17	46	4	.262	10
1996 *Projection* >>>	420	62	18	54	4	.254	10

BROWN, ADAM - C - BL - Age 29
A veteran minor league catcher who appears to have topped out at Triple-A.

BROWN, BRANT - 1B - BL - Age 24
Brown is highly regarded by the Cubs due to his raw power, which hasn't yet developed. He can't run and rarely walks. Brown wields a mean glove but needs to expand his game quickly.

BROWN, JARVIS - OF - BR - Age 28
Jarvis Brown is a speedy little outfielder formerly in the majors with the Twins, Padres, and Braves. He's not much of a hitter, and although he's fast, he doesn't steal very many bases. His best role in the majors appears to be a 4th or 5th outfielder and pinch runner.

BROWN, KEVIN - C - BR - Age 22
A 1994 first round pick, Brown made good progress in the Florida State League and was scheduled to play in the Arizona Fall League. He has a strong arm, and projects as an above-average hitter. Brown should arrive in the majors by 1998.

BROWNE, JERRY - 2B/OF - BB - Age 30
Though Browne was not nearly as valuable to the Marlins in 1995 as he was in 1994, he remained a key player because of his ability to play at least six positions. Browne is a spray hitter who will take a pitch, but his lack of speed or power makes him a liability as an everyday player.

	AB	R	HR	RBI	SB	BA	$
1994 Florida NL	329	42	3	30	3	.295	9
1995 Florida NL	184	21	1	17	1	.255	1
1996 *Projection* >>>	194	24	1	18	1	.274	1

BRUETT, J.T. - OF - BL - Age 28
A good fielding outfielder, Bruett hits for a decent average and can steal a few bases, too, although he hasn't stolen more than twelve in any season since 1992. He served as Omaha's fourth outfielder for most of 1995; he got into 73 games for the Twins in 1992 and 1993. Bruett is basically Triple-A roster filler who would only return to the majors as a defensive replacement and pinch-runner.

BRUMFIELD, JACOB - OF - BR - Age 30
Brumfield finally got the chance to play on a regular basis with the Pirates last season after being buried behind a group

of talented outfielders in Cincinnati. He finished with a flourish after a horrid start. Brumfield figures to be the Pirates' leadoff hitter and center fielder again in 1996 but he's 30, not exactly the age at which he'll suddenly blossom into a superstar.

	AB	R	HR	RBI	SB	BA	$
1994 Cincinnati NL	122	36	4	11	6	.311	7
1995 Pittsburgh NL	402	64	4	26	22	.271	13
1996 *Projection* >>>	412	70	6	28	22	.277	14

BRUMLEY, MIKE - SS - BB - Age 32
Brumley is a veteran utility player who has appeared in the major leagues with six different teams. His top minor league home run year was 12 and his peak in stolen bases was 41. If he appears again in the majors, it will likely be as a pinch hitter or pinch runner. He was sent outright to Triple-A after the season.

	AB	R	HR	RBI	SB	BA	$
1994 Oakland AL	25	0	0	2	0	.240	-
1995 Houston NL	18	1	1	2	1	.056	-

BRUNANSKY, TOM - OF - BR - Age 35
Bruno was once a feared power hitter for the Twins, but quickly faded to hit .207 over his last two seasons. He's now retired.

BRUNO, JULIO - 3B - BR - Age 23
Third baseman Julio Bruno began last year in Triple-A, but struggled and was demoted back to Double-A, not a good sign, especially since it was his second year in Triple-A. Despite the demotion, the Padres still have a very high regard for Bruno and consider him a top prospect who will develop power and consistency.

BRUNSON, MATT - 2B - BB - Age 21
The Tigers' first round pick in the '93 draft, Brunson has been a disappointment so far. He brings speed and infield defense to the team but has been unable to hit for an acceptable average. Brunson still has time to create a Joey Cora type of career, and he has earned rave reviews for his makeup.

BRYANT, PAT - OF - BR - Age 23
Bryant continued to tease the Indians with flashes of his power/speed potential in 1995. Bryant is a low-average hitter with 20/20 potential. He needs to improve upon his 1995 116/52 K/BB ratio, which is indicative of his six-year pro career. He was eligible to become a six-year minor league free agent following the 1995 season, and his array of skills and relative youth should attract interest from several clubs. A change of scenery to an organization without three superstars in their twenties in the outfield is what Bryant needs to reach the majors.

BUCCHERI, JIM - OF - BR - Age 27
Buccheri was one of the few players who benefited from last spring's strike. With Montreal's outfield prospects on the 40-man roster, new Ottawa manager Pete Mackanin was forced to play Buccheri, and liked him so much he was in the lineup almost every day in center field. The International League leader in stolen bases was a minor league free agent again during the winter.

BUCHANAN, BRIAN - OF - BR - Age 22
Buchanan, a first-round pick by the Yankees in 1994, was off to an excellent start in the Sally League before a broken ankle ended his season.

BUECHELE, STEVE - 3B - BR - Age 34
Buechele ran out of gas in 1995 and retired.

	AB	R	HR	RBI	SB	BA	$
1994 Chicago NL	339	33	14	52	1	.242	9
1995 Chicago NL	106	10	1	9	0	.189	-

BUFORD, DAMON - OF - BR - Age 25
Buford has good leadoff hitter skills (on base ability and speed) on a team that may not be looking for leadoff help in 1996. Dallas Green likes to shuffle and mix, however, so Buford will get his share of time -- especially against lefty pitching.

	AB	R	HR	RBI	SB	BA	$
1995 Rochester AAA	188	40	4	18	17	.309	
1995 New York NL	136	24	4	12	7	.235	3
1996 *Projection* >>>	180	30	3	15	8	.250	2

BUHNER, JAY - OF - BR - Age 31
His technoid persona as the rightfielder from the University of Jupiter belies the fact that he is one of the great power hitters in the game. With his Simonized noggin and ALCS exposure, Buhner is no longer a well kept secret. He'll go on cranking at this level for years.

	AB	R	HR	RBI	SB	BA	$
1994 Seattle AL	358	74	21	68	0	.279	17
1995 Seattle AL	470	86	40	121	0	.262	21
1996 *Projection* >>>	524	94	35	108	0	.265	18

BULLETT, SCOTT - OF - BL - Age 27
The Cubs think more of this guy than his performance would usually warrant. He's strictly a fifth outfielder - a pinch-hitter, pinch-runner and defensive fill-in. His playing time might increase should Luis Gonzalez depart via free agency, just don't expect him to earn a regular job.

	AB	R	HR	RBI	SB	BA	$
1994 Iowa AAA	530	75	13	69	27	.308	
1995 Chicago NL	150	19	3	22	8	.273	5
1996 *Projection* >>>	107	13	2	15	6	.269	1

BULLOCK, ERIC - OF - BL - Age 36
Bullock has bounced around the majors and minors and through several organizations, and the Padres are his fifth organization. He has played in 131 major league games hitting .205, but he has hit as high as .309 in the high minors. His best major league role is spare outfielder and pinch runner.

BURKS, ELLIS - OF - BR - Age 31
Burks' wrist surgery after the shortened 1994 campaign was not fully healed at the start of the 1995 season. This, coupled with inconsistent play both at the plate and in the field, resulted in Burks being platooned in center field with Mike Kingery during most of the 1995 season. Burks showed flashes of the superb fielding skills and quick bat of which he is capable, but was a strikeout victim in more than one-quarter of his at-bats. Still, he's penciled in as the Rockies starter in center for 1996.

	AB	R	HR	RBI	SB	BA	$
1994 Colorado NL	149	33	13	24	3	.322	11
1995 Colorado NL	278	41	14	49	7	.266	11
1996 *Projection* >>>	360	59	20	61	8	.280	15

BURNITZ, JEROMY - OF - BL - Age 26
Though the former Mets' #1 pick is no longer projected to be a star, he does possess a power/speed combination which should earn him a permanent ticket back to the majors before long. Acquired by the Indians in the Dave Mlicki/Jerry DiPoto/Paul Byrd trade, Burnitz had an excellent all-around season at Triple-A Buffalo, with his career-high .284 a major surprise. Obviously, there are not going to be any full-time outfield spots available in Cleveland anytime soon, but Burnitz will either be very attractive trade bait or a prime fourth or fifth outfielder candidate for the Tribe. He could be the next Geronimo Berroa.

	AB	R	HR	RBI	SB	BA	$
1994 New York NL	143	26	3	15	1	.238	1
1995 Buffalo AAA	443	72	19	85	13	.284	
1996 *Projection* >>>	91	19	3	10	1	.257	-

BURTON, DARREN - 2B - BB - Age 23
Burton stalled at Double-A for the Royals, then was given a second chance by the Cubs in 1995. He has speed and hit .306 for Double-A Orlando - his best average at any level. Burton is a limited player who can only hope for a fifth outfielder role in the majors.

BURTON, ESSEX - 2B - BR - Age 25
Burton has batted consistently around .260 in his five minor league seasons. He also can draw a walk to get on base, and once he does, he goes (292 career stolen bases). But the White Sox have better, younger second base prospects.

BUSCH, MIKE - 3B - BR - Age 27
Lost in all of the controversy over his promotion to majors is the fact that he is probably as good as the 38 year old Tim Wallach and the slap hitting Dave Hansen. Busch is big (6-5, 222) low average slugger in the Billy Ashley mold who is too old to be considered a serious prospect. However, he could sneak a year or two of regular play for the Dodgers at third base if Wallach ever decides to retire.

	AB	R	HR	RBI	SB	BA	$
1995 Albuquerque AAA	443	68	18	62	2	.269	
1995 Los Angeles NL	17	3	3	6	0	.235	0

BUSH, HOMER - 2B - BR - Age 23
Shortstop Homer Bush has hit very well in the minors including a league batting championship. He's a fast base stealer who could break into the Padres starting line-up in 1996 or '97.

BUTLER, BRETT - OF - BL - Age 38
The re-acquisition of Butler was the key in-season move by the Dodgers in 1995, solving their leadoff and center field problems that were created when they let Butler go at the beginning of the season. At age 37 he turned in one of his better years, setting a career high in stolen base percentage with 80% and hitting extremely well after the break. At his current rate of decline, Butler probably only has five years left.

	AB	R	HR	RBI	SB	BA	$
1994 Los Angeles NL	417	79	8	33	27	.314	29
1995 Two Teams	513	78	1	38	32	.300	22
1996 *Projection* >>>	502	81	3	38	32	.298	22

BUTLER, ROB - OF - BL - Age 25
Butler is a spray-hitting outfielder whom the Blue Jays once envisioned as the heir apparent to their left field position. The Phils' Triple-A left fielder in 1995, Butler no longer possesses the foot speed that once made him an attractive leadoff option - he also is too overzealous at the plate to be a regular at the top of the order. His ability to play above average defense at all three outfield positions gives him an edge over his organizational peers for a 1996 backup job in Philadelphia.

	AB	R	HR	RBI	SB	BA	$
1994 Toronto AL	74	13	0	5	0	.176	-
1995 Scranton WB AAA	327	46	3	35	5	.300	
1996 *Projection* >>>	156	21	1	13	1	.240	-

BUTLER, RICH - OF - BL - Age 22
Butler went back to Double-A after a sub-par year a level higher in 1994. He has no power but is getting better at taking pitches. He's young enough to overcome the odds but his stock has fallen considerably. His brother Rob played with the Blue Jays in 1992 and 1993.

BYINGTON, JOHN - 3B - BR - Age 28
Byington is a contact hitter with little speed or power. Although Texas used five third basemen in 1995, Byington never got the call. He is unlikely to have a significant role in the majors.

BYRD, ANTHONY - OF - BR - Age 25
Byrd improved in his second season with a Twins Double-A affiliate, primarily because he sliced his strikeout total from 114 to 85. But he has a long way to go, and little time to do it.

BYRNE, CLAYTON - OF - BR - Age 24
Byrne is a weak hitter without much power. He needs a great deal of improvement to make progress towards the majors.

CABRERA, FRANCISCO - 1B - BR - Age 29
Back from Japan, Cabrera hit little in a short stint for Triple-A Richmond. His major league days are long gone.

CACERES, EDGAR - 2B - BB - Age 31
Career minor leaguer Caceres got his chance with the Royals by being a replacement player and showing his versatility on the infield. His hot bat at the beginning of the season was balanced by a cold spell to end it and Caceres finished the year with a marginally useful performance for a reserve infielder. While Caceres has the versatility to play anywhere on the infield, he's not skilled enough as a hitter or fielder to play anywhere regularly. He's a utility infielder who will likely bounce between the high minors and major league bench for the next few years.

	AB	R	HR	RBI	SB	BA	$
1995 Kansas City AL	117	13	1	17	2	.239	1

CAIRO, MIGUEL - 2B - BR - Age 21
A good fielder and a consistent hitter, this speedy second baseman needs some time at Triple-A, but he's a very solid prospect.

CAIRO, SERGIO - OF - BR - Age 25
Cairo is limited defensively, and at 165 pounds is hardly a prototypical run producer. He's a long shot to advance to the majors.

CAMERON, MIKE - OF - BR - Age 23
A good defensive outfielder and good baserunner, Cameron can't hit well enough in the majors. He jumped to the majors from Double-A Birmingham in 1995 but will return to the minors in 1996. When he returns to the big leagues it will be as a pinch-runner and defensive replacement.

CAMERON, STANTON - OF - BR - Age 26
Injuries wrecked the whole year for Cameron, just as they did in 1994. In two years since his acquisition from Baltimore late in 1993, he hasn't shown the Pirates anything useful. Cameron's health and power better return soon or his career will likely be over.

CAMINITI, KEN - 3B - BB - Age 32
Getting away from the spacious Astrodome, Ken Caminiti's long drives are now home runs in the Padres' stadium. He had his career-best year last season, even stealing a career-high 12 stolen bases. Caminiti had a strong second half hitting .326-25-49, and it should carry over into 1996.

	AB	R	HR	RBI	SB	BA	$
1994 Houston NL	406	63	18	75	4	.283	19
1995 San Diego NL	526	74	26	94	12	.302	27
1996 Projection >>>	520	72	20	88	10	.280	19

CAMPANIS, JIM - C/DH - BR - Age 28
Formerly in the Mariners organization where he spent two years in class A and three years in class AA, Campanis is a career minor leaguer.

CANALE, GEORGE - 1B - BL - Age 30
Canale had a big 1995 as the Pirates' Double-A Carolina farm club won the Southern League title. But the former Milwaukee prospect was also 30 years old. His last chance at the majors would have been as a replacement player, though he refused to cross the line last spring.

CANATE, WILLIAM - OF - BR - Age 24
Canate didn't perform last year but is improving as a hitter. Even though he has limited potential as a basestealer, he has nice speed and covers the outfield well with a good throwing arm. He's well back of the pack as an immediate major league prospect but has the advantage of some major league bench-warming experience with Toronto in 1993.

CANDAELE, CASEY - OF/2B - BB - Age 35
It's been ten years now since this mighty mite (5'9", 165) made his big league debut with the Expos. He spent his eleventh consecutive season at Triple-A or above in 1995, with his third organization (Indians) in three years. Candaele is a gamer who will play any position, will run through a brick wall, etc., but he is hanging around on guts alone at this point. His chances for a big league return are nil at this point, but he is relatively certain to get a crack at a job as a coach or minor league instructor.

CANGELOSI, JOHN - OF - BB - Age 33
Cangelosi had a career year with Houston in 1995 in the ninth season that he has appeared in the major leagues. He should be able to stay in the majors as a fourth outfielder. He is especially valuable for his ability to get on base and steal bases.

	AB	R	HR	RBI	SB	BA	$
1994 New York NL	111	14	0	4	5	.252	2
1995 Houston NL	201	46	2	18	21	.318	13
1996 *Projection* >>>	142	29	1	11	12	.250	3

CANIZARO, JAY - 2B - BR - Age 22
Canizaro had a fine, four-category season at Double-A Shreveport, making Baseball America's Texas League All-Star team. His numbers look a lot like Robby Thompson's Shreveport numbers, and Thompson made a jump the next season to the majors. Canizaro is an interesting prospect, maybe a year away, but quietly impressive thus far.

CANSECO, JOSE - DH - BR - Age 31
Although he didn't hit 75 homers in Fenway Park like some people thought he might, Canseco overcame an injury early in the year to give Boston a consistent power stroke most of the year. He even played in the outfield at season's end. Canseco will again DH for the Red Sox, likely batting fifth behind Mo Vaughn, and produce 25-30 homers and 90 RBI.

	AB	R	HR	RBI	SB	BA	$
1994 Texas AL	429	88	31	90	15	.282	32
1995 Boston AL	396	64	24	81	4	.306	19
1996 *Projection* >>>	421	74	27	87	4	.288	18

CAPPUCCIO, CARMINE - OF - BL - Age 26
Cappuccio is a pull hitter with some power and a good batting eye. However, his fielding needs work and he's too old to be a real prospect; 1995 was his first season above Class A. He'll have to improve his glove work to get much farther.

CAPRA, NICK - OF - BR - Age 38
The Energizer Bunny of the minor leagues kept right on rolling in his twelfth consecutive Triple-A season in 1995. The diminutive (5'8", 165) Capra has exceeded 20 steals and recorded more walks than whiffs in all of those seasons. He has had five brief stints in the majors, but none since 1991. For good behavior, the Marlins should give one last fling to a guy who truly loves the game.

CARABALLO, GARY - 3B - BR - Age 24
He has little speed and a decent batting eye. Caraballo is an adequate defensive player who needs to improve his hitting in all phases to become a real prospect.

CARABALLO, RAMON - 2B - BB - Age 26
Once considered Atlanta's second baseman of the future, his career hasn't turned out as planned. He got a major-league shot last year with a Cardinals team desperate for second base help after Geromino Pena got hurt again; he did absolutely nothing. He was taken off the 40-man roster late in the season.

	AB	R	HR	RBI	SB	BA	$
1995 St. Louis NL	99	10	2	3	3	.202	
1996 *Projection* >>>	112	16	2	10	3	.232	-

CAREY, PAUL - 1B - BL - Age 28
Paul Carey is a big first baseman who struggled in Triple-A last year. It was his third year of Triple-A, and although he had some injuries last year, the bad year and his age indicate that time is running out on him.

CARR, CHUCK - OF - BR - Age 27
Carr's term as a Marlin regular likely ended in 1995, as the club finally realized that he would never fully learn how to parlay his speed into acceptable offensive production. Carr has absolutely no power, and though he has become more selective, his on-base percentages have been nowhere near the level desired for a leadoff man, a role now capably filled by Quilvio Veras. Carr does hit lefties well, and could live on as part of a platoon. More likely, the Marlins will spend some cash on a center fielder/leadoff hitter, with Carr moving on or becoming a fourth outfielder.

	AB	R	H	RBI	SB	BA	$
1994 Florida NL	433	61	2	30	32	.263	23
1995 Florida NL	308	54	2	20	25	.227	9
1996 *Projection* >>>	293	40	2	20	24	.247	8

CARR, JEREMY - 2B - BR - Age 25
If he can hit for a higher average, he could be a good leadoff candidate. The Royals drafted him in the 23rd round in 1993 out of Cal State-Fullerton.

CARREON, MARK - OF - BR - Age 32
Carreon had his best season last year at the age of 31, playing regularly for the first time. He has useful power when he plays, won't kill you in batting average, and has no speed. Not an overwhelming performer in comparison to others at his positions, and won't improve at his age.

	AB	R	HR	RBI	SB	BA	$
1994 San Francisco NL	100	8	3	20	0	.270	2
1995 San Francisco NL	396	53	17	65	0	.301	15
1996 *Projection* >>>	404	51	16	70	0	.290	12

CARRILLO, MATIAS - OF - BL - Age 32
Carrillo is a former Mexican League superstar whose major league play to date only serves to underscore the inferiority of the Mexican League. After averaging 32 homers in his two seasons south of the border, he's still looking for his first major league blast. With the Marlins' younger outfield prospects in the wings, Carrillo's major league career is likely near its end.

CARTER, JEFF - OF - BB - Age 32
This minor league journeyman had a new organization (Marlins) and a new position in 1995, his first year as an infielder. In his sixth straight Triple-A season, Carter again was an extremely reliable top of the order hitter, consistently drawing walks and reaching double figures in steals for the eleventh straight season. His versatility gives him a shot at a major league cameo appearance as a utilityman.

CARTER, JOE - OF - BR - Age 36
He missed knocking in 100 runs for only the second time in the last ten years and his swing slowed dramatically from what it was a year earlier. He looked like the Joe Carter we saw with San Diego back in 1990, who couldn't get around on anything. Of course, he still has good power and makes contact as often as always. He will play everyday and the odds are in his favor for a comeback year.

	AB	R	HR	RBI	SB	BA	$
1994 Toronto AL	435	70	27	103	11	.271	28
1995 Toronto AL	558	70	25	76	12	.253	18
1996 *Projection* >>>	590	82	30	102	13	.245	19

CARTER, MIKE - SS - BR - Age 26
Carter led the American Association in hitting for Triple-A Iowa in 1995. His compact swing lets him make contact while generating some power. An average outfielder, Carter can play either rightfield or centerfield. He's right on the verge of getting called up to Wrigley.

CARVAJAL, JOVINO - OF - BB - Age 27
Carvajal is a fast outfielder who steals bases. A little older for a minor-league prospect, he has nevertheless showed some talent in the past two years, rising to Triple-A at the end of last year where he hit decently. Last year, managers and coaches voted Carvajal as both the fastest and best baserunner in the Texas League.

CASANOVA, RAUL - C - BB - Age 23
Casanova is an excellent hitting catcher who could challenge for the Padres' starting job very soon. He has shown some power already, and will show even more as he matures. Casanova could develop into a 20-homer per year hitter in the majors.

CASE, MIKE - OF - BR - Age 27
Case's .276-11-80-21 season for Single-A Central Valley earned him a late season promotion to AAA Colorado

Springs, but he's too old to be considered a serious prospect. Besides, he strikes out way too much (120 strikeouts in 452 at bats).

CASEY, SEAN - 1B - BL - Age 22
Casey is a hitter - pure and simple. He signed promptly, and hit for average and gaps power in rookie ball. He is expected to substantially increase his homer output, based upon his prototype 6'3", 200, body, but he has serious defensive and footspeed deficiencies. Look for Casey at Class-A Columbus or Class-A Kinston in 1996.

CASILLAS, ADAM - OF - BL - Age 30
Good singles hitter, but little power and no speed. Your basic minor league extension of the major league bench.

CASTALDO, GREGG - 2B/SS - BR - Age 25
Castaldo is your typical weak hitting infielder. He has never hit very well in three years in the minors.

CASTELLANO, PEDRO - 3B - BR - Age 26
Castellano was a regular in the Rockies' Triple A cast which won the Pacific Coast League crown. His numbers, while solid, didn't warrant a September call-up. Youth is still on his side, but the emergence of Vinny Castilla on the parent club in 1995 dictates that Castellano will again spend most of the 1996 season in the minors.

CASTILLA, VINNY - 3B - BR - Age 28
This 1995 All-Star pick was the surprise of the year for the Rockies. At best a projected back-up or a platooner (with Jason Bates) at the start of the season, Castilla appeared in all but five games and made Rockies fans forget about the departure of Charlie Hayes. His "career-year" 1995 batting numbers may not be possible to duplicate in 1996, but it is safe to bet that he will again be strong in the field and will continue to hit for power in Coors Field.

	AB	R	HR	RBI	SB	BA	$
1994 Colorado NL	130	16	3	18	2	.331	6
1995 Colorado NL	527	82	32	90	2	.309	26
1996 *Projection* >>>	550	79	18	86	2	.303	20

CASTILLO, ALBERTO - C - BR - Age 26
Not as young as most New Yorkers have been led to believe (Todd Hundley is only nine months older) Castillo is type of catcher loved by pitchers but not much in the way of offense. Think of an inexperienced Charlie O'Brien, and you get the idea.

	AB	R	HR	RBI	SB	BA	$
1995 Norfolk AAA	217	23	4	31	2	.267	
1995 New York NL	29	2	0	0	1	.103	

CASTILLO, BRAULIO - OF - BR - Age 27
Castillo was once a hot prospect in the Dodgers' organization, showing both speed and power, but then he had a bad year in 1990, which, combined with some off-field problems, led to his arrival with the Phillies and subsequent exposure in the expansion draft.

CASTILLO, LUIS - 2B - BR - Age 20
Castillo made a major impact in his first full pro season in 1995 and became one of the finest all around second base prospects in baseball. He was recognized as the best defensive second baseman and fastest baserunner in the Class-A Midwest League by circuit managers, and was named the league's fifth best prospect at season's end by Baseball America. At 5'11", 146 lbs., he has no power and doesn't look the part of an offensive threat, but he slaps the ball on the ground to utilize his speed, and has exceptional knowledge of the strike zone for such a youngster.

CASTLEBERRY, KEVIN - 2B - BL - Age 27
Castleberry made his Triple-A debut with the Expos' top farm at Ottawa, and proved to be a particularly pesky hitter. He did not show exceptional defense. A veteran of three other organizations, he was a minor league free agent again after last season.

CASTRO, JUAN - SS - BR - Age 23
Castro made his major league debut last year even though he has neither power nor speed and didn't hit very well at Triple-A Albuquerque. Good defense? You bet.

CASTRO, RAMON - C - BR - Age 20
Castro was Houston's No. 1 draft choice in 1994. He has played two years in short season leagues and has impressed with his power (.299-9-49 in 1995). He was selected as the eighth best prospect in the New York-Pennsylvania League in 1995 by Baseball America. Castro has a lot of work ahead of him to reach the majors, but he has plenty of time.

CEDENO, ANDUJAR - SS - BR - Age 26
Cedeno's offensive production dropped considerably last year, disappointing the Padres to the point where they were ready to trade him. Cedeno's slugging percentage dropped from the .412 and .418 levels of 1993 and 1994 all the way down to .308, caused primarily by his hitting a pathetic .190 against right handed pitching, down from .252 in 1994. But Cedeno is still young, and he could bounce back to his previous levels.

	AB	R	HR	RBI	SB	BA	$
1994 Houston NL	342	38	9	49	1	.263	9
1995 San Diego NL	390	42	6	31	5	.210	1
1996 *Projection* >>>	457	51	11	55	6	.255	8

CEDENO, DOMINGO - SS/2B - BB - Age 27
Cedeno started strong given little playing time but faded down the stretch and saw his average fall under .240 at the end of the season. He's a slick fielder who is useful in that he can play either second base or shortstop comfortably. Going into the winter, Cedeno might have been crossing his fingers that Roberto Alomar signed with another team.

	AB	R	HR	RBI	SB	BA	$
1994 Toronto AL	97	14	0	10	1	.196	-
1995 Toronto AL	161	18	4	14	0	.236	0
1996 *Projection* >>>	154	19	3	14	1	.233	-

CEDENO, ROGER - OF - BB - Age 21
Extremely fast outfield prospect who was overmatched in his first major league trial, but is still well regarded due to his age. Cedeno hit .305 at Albuquerque, which is not overwhelming given the league, but he showed decent strike zone judgment and led the team in triples and steals. Cedeno is the Dodger centerfielder of the future, but when that future begins depends on how long Brett Butler sticks around.

	AB	R	HR	RBI	SB	BA	$
1995 Los Angeles NL	42	4	0	3	1	.238	-
1996 *Projection* >>>	171	21	2	20	5	.245	1

CENTENO, HENRI - 2B - BB - Age 26
Centeno is one of the many players Houston has signed out of Venezuela. Based on his performance to date (.256-2-12-6 at Double-A in 1995), he is not likely to rise above that level.

CHAMBERLAIN, WES - OF - BR - Age 29
A wide open battle for outfield jobs in Boston provided Chamberlain with a chance to show his talents. In two weeks of play he went 2-for-30 and got a ticket to Pawtucket. Although he hit much better there, Chamberlain was gone to the Royals Triple-A franchise in a late season deal. He has some power, especially against lefthanders, but he's only a fringe major leaguer at this point; he has little future with the Royals.

	AB	R	HR	RBI	SB	BA	$
1994 Two Teams	233	20	6	26	0	.262	4
1995 Boston AL	42	4	1	1	1	.009	-
1996 *Projection* >>>	155	15	4	16	1	.239	-

CHARLES, FRANK - C/1B - BR - Age 26
Charles developed a little power in 1995, but is unlikely to hit well enough to play in the majors.

CHAVEZ, RAUL - C - BR - Age 23
Chavez was signed by the Astros at the age of 16 in Venezuela. In six years he has progressed to the Triple-A level where he hit .262 in 1995. He projects as a possible backup catcher in the majors.

CHIMELIS, JOEL - 3B - BR - Age 28
Chimelis caused an uproar with the Giants and their fans when he became the first replacement player to be called up to the majors by San Francisco, then was abruptly returned to the minors without seeing action after the players

rebelled. One hundred years from now, those few abortive days with the Giants will be his only claim to fame. He has been a decent minor leaguer for years, but has no chance of ever succeeding at the major-league level.

CHOLOWSKY, DAN - 1B/OF - BR - Age 25
Cholowsky is a pretty versatile fielder who can play any of the outfield positions. A supplemental first round draft pick in 1991, Cholowsky has to cut the strikeouts without losing the power if he wants to keep moving up.

CHRISTENSEN, McKAY - OF - BL - Age 20
The Angels selected the speedy Christensen in the first round of the 1994 draft, even though he'll be on a mission for the Mormon church until 1996.

CHRISTOPHERSON, ERIC - C - BR - Age 26
This former first-round draft pick for the Giants hits even worse than Kirt Manwaring, and does it in the offense-crazed Pacific Coast League. He's absolutely not a major-league hitter; in fact, he is still having trouble hitting minor-league pitchers. He's no prospect.

CIANFROCCO, ARCHI - 1B/SS - BR - Age 29
Cianfrocco was recalled from Triple-A late last year and went on a hitting tear, hitting grandslams and driving in runs. He also played six different positions, making him a valuable all-purpose utility man. Cianfrocco is about a .250-.260 hitter, and he could hit a dozen home runs playing full time, but part time is his role.

	AB	R	HR	RBI	SB	BA	$
1994 San Diego NL	146	9	4	13	2	.219	1
1995 San Diego NL	118	22	5	31	0	.263	
1996 Projection >>>	171	22	4	31	1	.244	1

CIRILLO, JEFF - 3B/2B - BR - Age 26
Cirillo offers light offense but can steal and homer on occassion. A perfectly serviceable reserve.

	AB	R	HR	RBI	SB	BA	$
1994 Milwaukee AL	126	17	3	12	0	.238	0
1995 Milwaukee AL	328	57	9	39	7	.277	10
1996 Projection >>>	352	59	9	40	6	.269	8

CLARK, DAVE - OF - BL - Age 33
Clark had a sub-par 1995 primarily because he missed a good chunk of the season with a broken collarbone. He's still a fine role player with power, though, and the Pirates will find him at bats this season.

	AB	R	HR	RBI	SB	BA	$
1994 Pittsburgh NL	223	37	10	46	2	.296	11
1995 Pittsburgh NL	196	30	4	24	3	.281	5
1996 Projection >>>	233	37	6	37	3	.285	6

CLARK, JERALD - OF/1B - BR - Age 32
Clark returned to the major leagues after one year in Japan and proved he could still hit, as he smacked a few home runs before sustaining a knee injury. Clark could repeat some of this success in '96 if used correctly, yet he's not capable of the production needed from a regular.

	AB	R	HR	RBI	SB	BA	$
1995 Minnesota AL	109	17	3	15	3	.339	4
1996 Projection >>>	154	23	5	21	3	.262	2

CLARK, PHIL - OF - BR - Age 27
Clark is a utility infielder and outfielder who had a bad year at the plate hitting only .216. He's a better hitter than that, and is capable of hitting .260 or higher while popping an occasional home run.

	AB	R	HR	RBI	SB	BA	$
1994 San Diego NL	149	14	5	20	1	.215	1
1995 San Diego NL	97	12	2	7	0	.216	-
1996 Projection >>>	117	13	3	12	1	.251	-

CLARK, TIM - OF - BL - Age 27
Clark has always been one of the older regulars in his respective minor leagues, and though he has generally hit for a solid average, he does not possess the power necessary for a starting major league first sacker. He might inch forward to Triple-A in 1996, but he clearly does not have a substantial major league future.

CLARK, TONY - 1B - BB - Age 23
Detroit's future first baseman and cleanup hitter, Clark has made tremendous strides in the past two years and stands on the brink of a major league job. He could use another year in Triple-A; besides Cecil Fielder is not overjoyed at moving to DH full time. Clark will eventually produce numbers closer to Fielder's when he has three or four years of major league experience.

	AB	R	HR	RBI	SB	BA	$
1994 Toledo AAA	92	10	2	13	2	.261	
1995 Detroit AL	101	10	3	11	0	.238	0
1996 *Projection* >>>	367	38	11	38	0	.245	3

CLARK, WILL - 1B - BL - Age 32
Last season was fairly typical for Clark, despite being pitched around more frequently due to injuries to Juan Gonzalez and Dean Palmer and the trade of Jose Canseco to Boston. Clark has now hit over .300 in four of his last five seasons, and there is little reason to expect anything different in the near future.

	AB	R	HR	RBI	SB	BA	$
1994 Texas AL	389	73	13	80	5	.329	24
1995 Texas AL	454	85	16	92	0	.302	16
1996 *Projection* >>>	519	96	18	103	2	.308	20

CLAUDIO, PATRICIO - OF - BR - Age 23
Not many minor league outfielders have less power than this guy, but he has averaged over 30 steals in his first three seasons in the Indians' chain. A flawed talent, he must first bulk up and develop some patience at the plate before he can be labeled a prospect.

CLAYTON, ROYCE - SS - BR - Age 26
Two very disappointing seasons in a row have marked Clayton as a player unlikely to reach the heights many predicted for him. His glove gets him playing time and his steals give him some offensive value, but his inability to get on base and his frequent strikeouts are increasingly problematic. At an age when most players are reaching their peak, Clayton is going backwards at the plate. He's still capable of a few Mariano Duncan-like seasons, but no longer a potential superstar.

	AB	R	HR	RBI	SB	BA	$
1994 San Francisco NL	385	38	3	30	23	.236	15
1995 San Francisco NL	509	56	5	58	24	.244	14
1996 *Projection* >>>	560	59	5	59	27	.256	15

CLYBURN, DANNY - OF - BR - Age 21
Taken in the second round of the 1992 draft from a rural South Carolina high school, Clyburn has shown power and speed in the minors. He's still very raw but some members of the Pirates' front office feel he may be the best player in the system. Clyburn won't reach the majors for a while, though, as the Pirates must polish his rough edges.

COCHICK, EMMITT - OF - BL - Age 27
Last year was outfielder Emmitt Cochick's third with Midland in the Double-A Texas League. The bad thing is that it was his worst year. Cochick will have to turn things around quickly to get to the majors, otherwise he's a career minor leaguer.

COCKRELL, ALAN - OF - BR - Age 33
This longtime minor leaguer's least remembered highlight in 1995 may be his part in igniting a ninth-inning come-from-behind victory by the Colorado (replacement) Rockies against the New York (replacement) Yankees during the (unofficial?) grand opening series at Coors Field last spring. Cockrell played on a semi-regular basis for the Triple-A Colorado Springs Sky Sox after the "real" players returned, but his chances for a cup of coffee in the majors in 1996 are about as slim as they were in 1995, albeit for different reasons. He's savvy, but too old, too slow, and has no pop.

COLBERT, CRAIG - C - BR - Age 31
Colbert is a veteran of 10 minor league seasons, including six in Triple-A. He made it to the show in 1992 and '93, getting into 72 games and hitting .215. If he gets back to the majors, it will be as a back-up catcher.

COLBRUNN, GREG - 1B - BR - Age 26
Colbrunn developed into a credible offensive force in 1995, his first extended shot at a major league fulltime job. He did so despite a meager .215 average against lefties, whom he had ravaged in his previous major league trials. His main weakness is his overaggressiveness at the plate - he only managed 22 walks in 1995, and he got himself out on a regular basis. If he can overcome this flaw, he could eventually reach the upper echelon of NL first basemen, as he is capable of a .300 average, 25 HR, and double digits in steals.

	AB	R	HR	RBI	SB	BA	$
1994 Florida NL	155	17	6	31	1	.303	7
1995 Florida NL	528	70	23	89	11	.277	22
1996 Projection >>>	539	69	22	92	8	.280	19

COLE, ALEX - OF - BL - Age 30
Cole broke his leg in May and missed the bulk of the '95 season. He played well in '94 and started '95 in excellent shape, so he could be a pleasant surprise in '96 provided the broken leg hasn't significantly cut his speed. He has demonstrated the capacity to make adjustments in his career.

	AB	R	HR	RBI	SB	BA	$
1994 Minnesota AL	345	68	4	23	29	.296	24
1995 Minnesota AL	79	10	1	14	1	.342	2
1996 Projection >>>	203	35	2	19	12	.284	7

COLEMAN, VINCE - OF - BB - Age 34
Vince's value is from stolen bases. With the lively ball he's added a bit of power, and his average is respectable. Thought to be down the tubes after the firecracker incident, Coleman has rebounded nicely. Note that he was nabbed stealing sixteen times in fifty-eight attempts, so his age is beginning to show.

	AB	R	HR	RBI	SB	BA	$
1994 Kansas City AL	438	61	2	33	50	.240	31
1995 Two Teams	455	66	5	29	42	.288	28
1996 Projection >>>	528	77	4	36	40	.269	23

COLE, STU - IF - BR - Age 30
Cole finished his second full year as a dependable utility infielder for the Rockies' Triple-A affiliate in 1995. He's no prospect.

COLES, DARNELL - 3B/OF - BR - Age 33
Coles was released by the Cardinals last August after a fairly dreadful season. He's had more lives than a cat but it seems quite possible that his career is now over. His versatility no longer makes up for a weak bat.

	AB	R	HR	RBI	SB	BA	$
1994 Toronto AL	143	15	4	15	0	.210	0
1995 St. Louis NL	138	13	3	16	0	.225	0
1996 Projection >>>	59	6	1	7	0	.223	-

COLLIER, LOUIS - SS - BR - Age 22
Collier's arm was voted the best of any infielder in the South Atlantic League before he earned a promotion to the Carolina League. He's a threat on the bases.

COLON, CRIS - SS - BB - Age 27
Former Rangers' farmhand Colon is good with the glove and versatile enough to play any position. He struggled early on for Triple-A Iowa, then spent the rest of the year trying to catch up. Colon played briefly for Texas in 1992 and began 1995 on the Cubs' 40-man roster. His stock clearly declined after last season.

COLON, DENNIS - 1B - BB - Age 22
Colon is young but, as a first baseman who doesn't hit for power or average (.225-5-31 at Double-A in 1995), he does not appear to have a major league future.

CONINE, JEFF - 1B/OF - BR - Age 29
Conine has developed into the Marlins' most reliable, if not their best player, based on his excellent performance over the past two seasons. He hits for average and power, rarely misses a game, and has worked hard to make more consistent contact and draw more walks with each passing season. Though 1995 was likely his peak, he is more than worthy to fill the sizeable role of Gary Sheffield's protector in the batting order. Expect Conine's production to gradually moderate over the next few seasons.

	AB	R	HR	RBI	SB	BA	$
1994 Florida NL	451	60	18	82	1	.319	24
1995 Florida NL	483	72	25	105	2	.302	23
1996 Projection >>>	575	81	23	109	2	.298	22

COOKSON, BRENT - OF - BR - Age 26
Cookson escaped Barry Bonds shadow when the Royals claimed him from Triple-A Phoenix after he was removed from the Giants' 40-man roster. After hitting .401 for the Omaha Royals, Cookson got a brief look in the majors, although a minor injury prevented him from playing at full strength. He has a powerful stroke and a good batting eye; he could hit 25 homers in a full season of major league play. Easy come, easy go: after the 1995 season Cookson was claimed off of Royals' waivers by the Red Sox where he'll compete with their cast of thousands for an outfield spot in 1996.

COOLBAUGH, SCOTT - 3B - BR - Age 29
Coolbaugh has become one of the Hanshin Tigers' leading power threats in Japan. While he has some power, he fans too frequently to be much more than bench help in the USA.

COOMER, RON - 3B - BR - Age 29
Coomer came over to the Twins from Los Angeles in the Kevin Tapani trade. He has some power and can play third or first base. Coomer might have a full time job if the Twins don't bring back Scott Leius, or he could share a platoon role at first base with Scott Stahoviak, Dan Masteller, or Steve Dunn.

	AB	R	HR	RBI	SB	BA	$
1995 Albuquerque AAA	323	54	16	76	5	.322	
1995 Minnesota AL	101	15	5	19	0	.257	1
1996 Projection >>>	125	19	4	23	0	.251	0

COOPER, GARY - 3B - BR - Age 31
High noon arrived for Cooper when he got 16 at-bats for Houston in 1991. He faded gradually from a .300 hitter at Triple-A in 1991-2 to a part-time player in 1993-4, then hit .276-18-66 for Double-A Jacksonville in 1995; it was his fourth organization in as many years. Cooper is a good hitter, but his opportunity to play in the big leagues has come and gone.

COOPER, SCOTT - 3B - BL - Age 28
Sometimes the best-laid plans go awry. The Cardinals needed a third baseman going into last season and Cooper appeared to be the perfect fit when they acquired him in a trade with Boston during spring training. He had played in the previous two All-Star Game and was a hometown boy from St. Louis. However, Cooper struggled miserably and almost certainly will be leaving home before 1996 opens.

	AB	R	HR	RBI	SB	BA	$
1994 Boston AL	369	49	13	53	0	.282	12
1995 St. Louis NL	374	29	3	40	0	.230	1
1996 Projection >>>	360	37	6	44	1	.253	3

CORA, JOEY - 2B - BB - Age 30
Cora is primarily a singles hitter capable of hitting an occasional homer. He can also steal few bases. He's useful and with Seattle now a contender in the AL West, (who isn't?) his veteran play and defensive skills might serve to extend his role as a starter before the kids take over.

	AB	R	HR	RBI	SB	BA	$
1994 Chicago AL	312	55	2	30	8	.276	9
1995 Seattle AL	427	64	3	39	18	.297	17
1996 Projection >>>	316	50	2	29	10	.288	9

CORDERO, WILFREDO - SS/OF - BR - Age 24
Cordero is truly a baffling guy. He was a major disappointment to the Expos until breaking through with a fine 1994. But just when he appeared on his way to stardom, Cordero regressed in 1995 and was even moved from shortstop to leftfield. He appears to have worn out his welcome in Montreal and will have to try to become a superstar somewhere else, and considering his age and accomplishments already, he will succeed.

	AB	R	HR	RBI	SB	BA	$
1994 Montreal NL	415	65	15	63	16	.294	26
1995 Montreal NL	514	64	10	49	9	.286	15
1996 *Projection* >>>	569	76	15	69	15	.290	21

CORDOVA, MARTY - OF - BR - Age 26
Cordova enjoyed a very consistent rookie season, as he hit for power and a good average, stole a few bases, and gunned out eleven runners from left field. He also showed a better eye at the plate than he had in the minors and punished lefthanders. Only potential injuries can prevent him from becoming a reliable run producer.

	AB	R	HR	RBI	SB	BA	$
1994 Salt Lake AAA	385	69	19	66	17	.358	
1995 Minnesota AL	512	81	24	84	20	.277	26
1996 *Projection* >>>	544	86	26	90	23	.281	27

CORREIA, ROD - SS - BR - Age 28
The Angels tried Correia last year following the injury to Gary DiSarcina. Correia is a very weak singles hitter and was overmatched at the plate.

	AB	R	HR	RBI	SB	BA	$
1994 California AL	17	4	0	0	0	.235	-
1995 Vancouver AAA	264	42	1	39	8	.303	
1995 California AL	21	3	0	3	0	.238	

COSTELLO, BRIAN - OF - BR - Age 21
Costello has held his own as one of the younger starters in his league in each of the past two seasons, hitting for low average with little plate discipline, but with decent power and speed. The Phils' 1993 13th round pick will be sternly challenged at Double-A in 1996 - a breakout season at that level would entrench him firmly in the organization's future plans.

COSTO, TIM - OF - BR - Age 27
Costo was considered possibly the premier power prospect in the 1990 draft, but has never made the adjustment to the wooden bat, and is now a mere minor league journeyman. Costo has a pro body (6'5", 230), but his bat remains too slow for eventual major league success. First traded from the Indians to the Reds for then-megaprospect Reggie Jefferson, and later sent back to the Indians for then-megaprospect Mark Lewis, Costo is now typical Triple-A roster filler.

COTTO, HENRY - OF - BR - Age 35
Cotto returned from his Japanese experiment to get into a few dozen games for Triple-A Nashville in 1995. He hit just .131 with 20 strikeouts in 61 at-bats, though, and would appear to be finished.

COTTON, JOHN - 2B - BL - Age 25
After struggling at the plate for six minor-league seasons, second baseman John Cotton improved greatly last year, in a relative sense. He was a tremendous base stealer earlier in his career, once stealing 56 bases in Class-A, but he hasn't run nearly as much in recent years. Cotton should be a candidate for the Padres second base job in 1996.

COUGHLIN, KEVIN - OF - BL - Age 25
Coughlin runs decently, but doesn't walk much, has no power and won't stick out unless he hits at least .320.

COUNSELL, CRAIG - SS - BL - Age 25
Counsell was the regular shortstop for the Rocks' Triple-A Colorado Springs affiliate in 1995 after a productive season at Double-A New Haven in 1994. He is a steady if not spectacular hitter for a middle infielder, with a strong glove and

arm. He was called up to the parent club at the end of the minor league season, and was groomed for the transition to second base in the Arizona Fall League this past winter. If the Rockies tire of Eric Young's spotty fielding and Roberto Mejia's recalcitrant attitude, Counsell could see substantial time in the bigs in 1996.

COX, DARRON - C - BR - Age 28
Despite his good defensive reputation, Cox won't advance past the level of Triple-A reserve due to his weak bat.

COX, STEVE - 1B - BL - Age 21
Cox hit 30 homers for Class A Modesto, with a .298 average and 84 walks, making the California League All-Star team.

CRANFORD, JAY - 3B - BR - Age 24
Cranford suffered through an injury-marred season with the Pirates' Double-A Carolina farm club last season. He's put up some decent numbers in the past but is a borderline prospect.

CRESPO, FELIPE - 3B - BB - Age 23
He spent his first season at Triple-A and was better than he's ever been. His power keeps getting better and he's become a decent contact hitter that can get a few walks. Crespo was a second baseman earlier in his career and could make the move back if a major league situation warranted it. He is close to the big leagues.

	AB	R	HR	RBI	SB	BA	$
1995 Syracuse AAA	347	56	13	41	12	.294	

CROMER, TRIPP - SS - BR - Age 28
Cromer got an extended shot to play shortstop for the Cardinals last season when Ozzie Smith underwent shoulder surgery. However, he did little with the opportunity. He's now 28 and looking more like a utility infielder than The Wizard's heir apparent.

	AB	R	HR	RBI	SB	BA	$
1994 Louisville AAA	419	53	9	50	5	.274	
1995 St. Louis NL	345	36	5	18	0	.226	0
1996 *Projection* >>>	158	17	2	11	0	.228	-

CRON, CHRIS - 1B - BR - Age 32
This career minor leaguer has now accumulated over 4400 minor league at-bats, and only 25 in the majors. He barely hit his weight for Triple-A Charlotte in the Indians' organization, but had more extra-base hits than singles. He has virtually no hope of establishing himself as a major leaguer at this point.

CROSBY, MIKE - C - BL - Age 27
Why, exactly, is this man in this book? Well, as the Indians' primary Double-A catcher, he's only two heartbeats from the big leagues. Unfortunately, the man simply cannot hit, with a sub-.200 career average to prove it. He swings at everything, as evidenced by his amazing 181/27 career K/BB ratio in 738 career at bats. His adequate defensive skills have kept him in the pros this long, but true prospect Einar Diaz should shove Crosby out of baseball in 1996.

CRUZ, FAUSTO - SS - BR - Age 24
An interesting prospect, Cruz is still young and can hit for average, but he slipped a bit in his first full stint at Triple-A, although he made the Pacific Coast League All-Star team. He's still worth watching, but with perhaps lower expectations than one might have had a year ago.

	AB	R	HR	RBI	SB	BA	$
1994 Tacoma AAA	218	27	1	17	2	.321	
1994 Oakland AL	28	2	0	0	0	.107	-
1995 Edmonton AAA	448	72	11	67	7	.281	
1995 Oakland AL	23	0	0	5	1	.217	-

CRUZ, IVAN - 1B - BL - Age 27
Cruz found his power stroke in '95 when he returned to Double-A after spending two years trying to break through at Triple-A Toledo. He might have a future as a pinch hitter, but he won't be a factor in '96. Cruz has been passed by Tony Clark on the Tigers' first base depth chart.

CRUZ, JACOB - OF - BL - Age 23
Cruz had an impressive season for Double-A Shreveport, with good-not-great production in all four categories. He made Baseball America's Texas League All-Star team, and is worth watching.

CRUZ, JOSE - OF - BR - Age 22
Cruz was one of the top ranked amateur players of 1995 before being selected in the first round by the Mariners in the June draft. He got all the way to higher Class A Riverside where he connected for seven homers in 144 at-bats. He's an excellent power hitting prospect with decent speed, too. Cruz will soon be another "Junior" playing in the Mariners outfield.

CUMMINGS, MIDRE - OF - BL - Age 24
He has been a flop for the Pirates after being acquired from Minnesota in 1992. It has become clear that his potential was overrated. Compounding the matter is that he doesn't even seem to care. Still, he's young.

	AB	R	HR	RBI	SB	BA	$
1994 Pittsburgh NL	86	11	1	12	0	.244	0
1995 Pittsburgh NL	152	13	2	15	1	.243	1
1996 Projection >>>	302	33	6	32	2	.252	3

CURTIS, CHAD - OF - BR - Age 27
Curtis prospered in center field for Detroit after California traded him for Tony Phillips. He hit exactly his career average, tied his career high in walks, and doubled his home run average from previous seasons. Curtis is a hustling player whose excellent work habits will have a positive effect upon the young and rebuilding Tigers.

	AB	R	HR	RBI	SB	BA	$
1994 California AL	453	67	11	50	25	.256	23
1995 Detroit AL	586	96	21	67	27	.268	26
1996 Projection >>>	604	96	18	68	28	.265	24

CURTIS, RANDY - OF - BL - Age 25
Curtis began the season in Triple-A, but he slumped and was demoted to Double-A where he had a solid season. In about two years he should be a fine leadoff hitter for the Padres.

CUYLER, MILT - OF - BB - Age 27
Cuyler has shown signs of life the past two seasons at Triple-A Toledo, where he has hit .300. He needs to use his speed to start anew as a reserve outfielder. Detroit's outfield is very crowded, so Cuyler might be helped by moving to another organization.

	AB	R	HR	RBI	SB	BA	$
1994 Detroit AL	116	20	1	11	5	.241	2
1995 Detroit AL	88	15	0	5	2	.205	-
1996 Projection >>>	163	28	0	12	6	.230	1

GOT A QUESTION? CALL JOHN BENSON LIVE

Your Question - Your Roster - Your Situation

Let the top analyst in the business help you!!

1-900-773-7526

$2.49/minute

1 pm to 11 pm Eastern Time - 7 days a Week

DALESANDRO, MARK - OF - BR - Age 27
Although Catcher Mark Dalesandro has hit well in Triple-A for the past three years, he has a very wek bat. He's essentially a singles hitter without any power or speed. Dalesandro's hitting statistics are reminiscent of a young Andy Allanson.

DALTON, DEE - 3B - BR - Age 23
Dalton needs to make more frequent contact if he is to become a hot prospect in the Cardinals' chain.

DAMON, JOHNNY - OF - BL - Age 22
The gemstone of the Royals crown of youngsters, Damon tore up the Double-A Texas League and skipped Triple-A entirely to be promoted to the bigs in mid-August. He produced immediately, batting over .300 with emerging power and good speed for much of the rest of the year. He'll hit leadoff and play centerfield for the Royals in 1996, eventually moving to the third spot in the batting order once his power develops. Damon led all professional players with 198 hits in 1996; he had 145 for Wichita, then 53 for the Royals.

	AB	R	HR	RBI	SB	BA	$
1995 Wichita AA	423	83	16	54	26	.343	
1995 Kansas City AL	188	32	3	23	7	.282	6
1996 *Projection* >>>	478	83	11	60	21	.290	21

DANAPILIS, ERIC - OF/DH - BR - Age 24
Danapilis made a bit of a splash coming out of Notre Dame when he batted .341 in the New York-Penn League, then followed it up with 23 homers in the Sally League. When he moved up to Double-A last year, he found the going tougher. Danapilis has little speed, so the Tigers may have to use him at first base. He'll be at Jacksonville again, or possibly Toledo.

DASCENZO, DOUG - OF - BB - Age 31
The former Cub and Ranger felt right at home with a number of other faded journeymen on the Marlins' Triple-A Charlotte club. Dascenzo had speed once, but is now just a feisty hustler who makes pitchers throw strikes. The Marlins' best prospects are just now beginning to reach Triple-A, so Dascenzo and friends are likely to be at a new Triple-A address in 1996.

DAUGHERTY, JACK - OF - BB - Age 35
An aging pinch-hitter and reserve outfielder, Daugherty is finished. He last appeared in the majors for Cleveland in 1993 and hit just .152 in 33 at-bats before his release from Triple-A Phoenix in 1995.

DAULTON, DARREN - C - BL - Age 34
Yet another knee surgery ended Daulton's 1995 season prematurely. Though his power potential has dissipated quite rapidly, Daulton remains an offensive threat (for a catcher) because of his patience at the plate. He should be a candidate for a move to first base, but Gregg Jefferies is set there and has a no-trade contract. Daulton too has a long-term deal and is virtually untradeable. Expect his effectiveness to gradually diminish over the next two seasons, as he holds the fort for prospect Bobby Estalella, a likely 1998 arrival.

	AB	R	HR	RBI	SB	BA	$
1994 Philadelphia NL	257	43	15	56	4	.300	16
1995 Philadelphia NL	342	44	9	55	3	.249	7
1996 *Projection* >>>	390	57	15	71	3	.248	9

DAUPHIN, PHIL - OF - BL - Age 26
In six seasons in the Cubs, Reds and Expos organizations, Dauphin has shown he's a pretty good center fielder who can steal a base but not hit much. He has spent the last three years in Double-A and Triple-A, and isn't likely to get any higher.

DAVIS, ALVIN - 1B - BL - Age 35
Elderly Davis spent several years in Japan trying to find his power stroke. It was gone permanently and now so is he.

DAVIS, BUTCH - OF - BR - Age 37
Last seen with the Rangers in 1994, this retired reserve outfielder was a career .243 hitter in the big leagues.

DAVIS, CHILI - DH - BB - Age 36
Aches and pains caused Angel DH Chili Davis to miss 35 games last year. Nevertheless, he still came through with another strong year. Oddly enough, in 15 major league years, last year was the first one when his walks exceeded his strikeouts, 89 to 79. New batting coach Rod Carew must have influenced the old veteran to be more selective at the plate as his strikeout rate stayed about the same, but his percentage of walks per plate appearance increased substantially.

	AB	R	HR	RBI	SB	BA	$
1994 California AL	392	72	26	84	3	.311	26
1995 California AL	424	81	20	86	3	.318	20
1996 Projection >>>	430	75	22	82	2	.287	15

DAVIS, ERIC - OF - BR - Age 33
Formerly one of the most feared hitters in the National League, Davis faded rapidly after an injury suffered in the World Series in 1990 and protracted contract battles thereafter. Last seen with the Tigers in 1994, where he hit .184 in 37 games. Davis is one of the homesteaders who didn't make it.

DAVIS, GLENN - 1B - BR - Age 35
Davis had an outstanding year for Triple-A Omaha, but didn't get so much as a sniff from the Royals, so he left for Japan in 1995 where he became a power threat for the Hanshin Tigers.

DAVIS, RUSSELL - 3B - BR - Age 26
Davis was on the power streak of his life in '94 when a pitch broke his wrist in August. Still he reached the majors in 1995. Playing off the bench wasn't exactly what he wanted ("It's the hardest thing I've ever had to do") but at least he made the majors to stay. A move to a team that needs a third baseman, or a move of Wade Boggs over to first or out of New York, are the clearest chances for Davis to play full-time in 1996.

	AB	R	HR	RBI	SB	BA	$
1994 New York AL	14	0	0	1	0	.143	-
1995 Columbus AAA	76	12	2	15	0	.250	
1995 New York AL	98	14	2	12	0	.276	-
1996 Projection >>>	172	22	2	23	0	.265	0

DAWSON, ANDRE - DH/OF - BR - Age 41
Dawson returned home to South Florida and played much more than he or his battered knees expected, due to a barrage of injuries to Marlin regulars. At this stage, Dawson is a useful power threat against lefthanded fastball pitchers, and that's about it. Never a patient sort (career high in walks is 44), Dawson can now be relied upon to swing at nearly every pitch. It is simply painful to watch him play defense anymore. It is uncertain whether he will return in 1996 - if he does, expect his role to be significantly diminished.

	AB	R	HR	RBI	SB	BA	$
1994 Boston AL	292	34	16	48	2	.240	10
1995 Florida NL	226	30	8	37	0	.257	5
1996 Projection >>>	130	14	4	19	0	.253	1

DEAK, BRIAN - C - BR - Age 28
Deak had a great season at the plate for Triple-A Las Vegas in 1994, but was slowed by injuries in 1995 and missed the last third of the season. Although he's not a great prospect, Deak could get a callup as a backup catcher if he swings the bat well enough.

DEAK, DARREL - 2B - BB - Age 26
Deak lost his spot on the Cardinals' 40-man roster due to a slumping bat. A good switch-hitter, he isn't very handy with the glove. Deak can hit better than he did for Triple-A Louisville in 1995 (.241-7-34).

DECILLIS, DEAN - SS - BR - Age 28
Decillis spent parts of three years in Triple-A and Double-A. He is not improving so his baseball future is very limited.

DECKER, STEVE - C - BR - Age 30
Decker won the Marlins' backup catching job and was solid defensively but weak with the bat. The former top Giants'

prospect has always hit in the minors, but has fallen woefully short in his last four major league trials. 1995 was probably his last full shot at a major league role, and the Marlins cut their ties with Decker at season's end. He's likely to latch on with someone and resurface as a backup.

	AB	R	HR	RBI	SB	BA	$
1994 Edmonton AAA	259	38	11	48	0	.390	
1995 Florida NL	133	12	3	13	1	.226	0
1996 *Projection* >>>	131	16	3	18	1	.235	-

DEER, ROB - OF - BR - Age 35
Veteran free-swinging power hitter Rob Deer returned from Japan last year, but the best contract he could get was in Triple-A. Released by the Angels' Triple-A club, he latched on with the Padres's Triple-A team, hoping to get a call-up, but it never came. Deer is best remembered for all his strikeouts.

DELANUEZ, REX - OF - BR - Age 28
Younger Tigers outfielders who are better prospects passed him by in 1995. Time is ticking.

DeJARDIN, BOBBY - BB - Age 29
Dejardin is an older veteran of the minor leagues in the Orioles system last year. He was formerly in the Yankees organization, and got just 35 at-bats with Triple-A Rochester in 1995.

DELEON, ROBERTO - SS - BR - Age 25
The Padres drafted infielder Roberto DeLeon out of the University of Texas. He has hit in the .250-270 range in his last three minor league years popping an occasional home run. He could make the majors as a utility infielder.

DELGADO, ALEX - C - BR - Age 25
In his first full year above Class A, Delgado showed some power. He was inconsistent when promoted to Triple-A Pawtucket and his defensive skills were below average. Delgado could make it to the majors as a backup catcher.

DELGADO, CARLOS - 1B/OF - BL - Age 23
He had another great season at Triple-A and earned a well-deserved September callup. With tremendous power and a good eye, Delgado made the move to first base with Syracuse and looked comfortable. With his catching days behind him, he has accomplished everything required in the minor leagues. Delgado will start 1996 in the major leagues.

	AB	R	HR	RBI	SB	BA	$
1994 Toronto AL	130	17	9	24	1	.215	3
1995 Syracuse AAA	333	59	22	74	0	.318	
1995 Toronto AL	91	7	3	11	0	.165	-
1996 *Projection* >>>	274	28	14	43	0	.277	6

DELLICARRI, JOE - 3B - BR - Age 29
Formerly in the Mets organization, Dellicarri was in Triple-A for parts of 1992 and 1993, and has now moved back down to Double-A. There is nothing in his minor league career that suggests that he can make it to the majors.

DELVECCHIO, NICK - 1B - BL - Age 26
The Harvard-educated Delvecchio was off to a great start in the Florida State League before a broken wrist sidelined him.

DENSON, DREW - 1B - BB - Age 30
Once a hot prospect with the Braves (a 1984 top draft choice), Denson has gotten a mere 41 major league at-bats over twelve pro seasons. This career minor leaguer had a good season for Triple-A Indianapolis, hitting .277 with 18 homers and a team-leading 69 RBI. He'd be an extra bat off the bench should he return to the big leagues.

DESHIELDS, DELINO - 2B - BL - Age 27
In July, DeShields had missed most of the season and was talking openly of retiring. His plans, and the Dodgers plans may have been changed by his strong finish (14 RBI and 14 steals the last five weeks). His only real weakness is durability - his defense, strike zone judgment and speed are all outstanding. He was a free agent and would probably be more effective playing on astroturf.

	AB	R	HR	RBI	SB	BA	$
1994 Los Angeles NL	320	51	2	33	27	.250	18
1995 Los Angeles NL	425	66	8	37	39	.256	21
1996 *Projection* >>>	509	79	7	46	46	.270	24

DEVAREZ, CESAR - C - BR - Age 26
For the most part, catcher Cesar Devarez has struggled at the plate in the minors. If he gets any major league playing time, it will be as a back-up catcher, called up when one of the other catchers is injured.

DEVEREAUX, MIKE - OF - BR - Age 32
To the victors go the spoils. Such was the case when the pennant pretender White Sox dealt Devereaux to the Braves to improve their playoff roster. It paid off as he helped the Braves return to the World Series. Devereaux proved he can still hit with his showing in Chicago. He became a free agent again and should earn a decent contract offer, but beware of that batting average; Devereaux is not really a .300 hitter.

	AB	R	HR	RBI	SB	BA	$
1994 Baltimore AL	301	35	9	33	1	.203	2
1995 Chicago AL	333	48	10	55	6	.306	
1995 Atlanta NL	55	7	1	8	2	.255	16
1996 *Projection* >>>	241	32	7	35	3	.266	4

DIAZ, ALEX - OF - BB - Age 27
Speedy, spray type switch hitter who never produced a high batting average before 1993, hitting under .269 in all six of his minor league seasons.

	AB	R	HR	RBI	SB	BA	$
1994 Milwaukee AL	187	17	1	17	5	.251	3
1995 Seattle AL	270	44	3	27	18	.248	10
1996 *Projection* >>>	118	17	1	11	7	.243	1

DIAZ, EINAR - C - BR - Age 23
Despite his questionable size (5'10", 165 lbs.), Diaz is an excellent defensive catcher with raw offensive skills which could be refined into major league material. Diaz loves to swing the bat - he has never walked more than 20 times in his five pro seasons. However, he also makes consistent contact, as he has never struck out more than 34 times in a season, and drives the ball into the gaps. If Diaz can learn to take a pitch, he could evolve into a useful offensive player who could bat behind a speedster, take pitches to allow the rabbit to steal, and also be a reliable hit-and-run man. He's got the bat-handling ability and just needs the patience.

DIAZ, LINO - 3B - BR - Age 25
Diaz tore up the Texas League in 1995, including hitting nearly .470 in the month of August. He has shown a flair for the dramatic by continually coming through with clutch hits late in games, especially last season at double-A Wichita. With the Royals emphasizing youth, Diaz' chances of making the majors with Kansas City are good, but not great.

	AB	R	HR	RBI	SB	BA	$
1995 Wichita AA	226	40	6	43	0	.350	

DIAZ, MARIO - 2B - BR - Age 34
Diaz was Alex Arias' understudy as the Marlins' 1995 infield utilityman. The gritty Diaz has amazingly now played in nine consecutive major league seasons and accumulated a grand total of only 773 mediocre at bats, with only five homers and one steal. That streak may now be at an end, as the Marlins waived Diaz following the season and he became a free agent.

	AB	R	HR	RBI	SB	BA	$
1994 Florida NL	77	10	0	11	0	.325	1
1995 Florida NL	87	5	1	6	0	.230	-
1996 *Projection* >>>	68	6	1	7	0	.265	-

DIGGS, TONY - OF - BB - Age 28
This Cardinals' replacement player is an average hitter with little power and above-average speed, although he doesn't steal a lot of bases. Diggs is on the downside of his career as a minor leaguer.

DiSARCINA, GARY - SS - BR - Age 28
Gary DiSarcina was having his career-best year when he tore a ligament in his thumb sliding into second on August 3 missing most of the remainder of the season. He was a key element of the Angels team and their drive to the pennant, and their record went into a tailspin soon thereafter. DiSarcina's hitting improvement is a good example of the successful teaching of new Angel batting coach Rod Carew.

	AB	R	HR	RBI	SB	BA	$
1994 California AL	389	53	3	33	3	.260	6
1995 California AL	362	61	5	41	7	.307	12
1996 Projection >>>	500	76	6	51	8	.284	13

DiSARCINA, GLENN - SS - BL - Age 25
He's Gary's brother, and, like his brother, runs fairly well and hasn't hit much in his early twenties. His fielding is why he's been considered a prospect.

DISMUKE, JAMIE - 1B - BL - Age 26
Considered a solid prospect after a fine season at Chattanooga in 1993, Dismuke struggled in AAA in 1994. Dismuke hit well at Chattanooga again in 1995 but has been passed within the Reds organization by Tim Belk. Both Dismuke and Belk are good average, some power type of hitters.

	AB	R	HR	RBI	SB	BA	$
1995 Chatanooga AA	347	56	20	69	0	.285	
1995 Indianapolis AAA	36	6	0	2	0	.250	

DODSON, BO - 1B - BL - Age 25
Dodson, once an up-and-comer in the Brewers organization, now has to sit behind Scott Talanoa on their prospect train.

DONNELS, CHRIS - 3B/1B - BL - Age 29
A mid-season acquisition from Houston, Donnels gave the Red Sox an extra lefty bat off of the bench and a temporary replacement at third base when Tim Naehring was hurt briefly. He's a below average hitter in every respect and is a fringe major leaguer no matter where he ends up in 1996.

	AB	R	HR	RBI	SB	BA	$
1994 Houston NL	86	12	3	5	1	.267	1
1995 Houston NL	30	4	0	2	0	.300	
1995 Boston AL	91	13	2	11	0	.253	0
1996 Projection >>>	90	12	2	9	1	.264	-

DORSETT, BRIAN - 1B/C - BR - Age 34
Dorsett isn't great, but you would think a catcher who is considered a good handler of pitchers and has some pop (15 HR in 285 at bats last year) could find a major league job as a third catcher. The signing of Damon Berryhill and Benito Santiago ended any chance for Dorsett to make it back to the majors with the Reds.

DOSTAL, BRUCE - OF - BL - Age 31
Dostal didn't hit at Triple-A and was released. A speedy singles hitter, Dostal is probably out of chances at this point, and being a former replacement player won't help.

DOSTER, DAVID - 2B - BR - Age 25
Doster is a hustling, grinding middle infielder with surprising power - he has had 59 and 63 extra base hits, respectively, in the last two seasons. The 1993 27th round pick makes up for a lack of raw ability by positioning himself properly in the field, and never giving away an at bat.

DOTY, DERRIN - OF - BR- Age 25
Still a marginal prospect after three years in Class A, Doty has good speed. He's a product of the University of Washington.

DOWLER, DEMITRIUS - OF - BR - Age 24
A very raw player, Dowler has pretty good speed, but just not enough bat. He rose to Double-A for the first time in 1995 and should return there in 1996. But he's too old to be a real prospect.

DRINKWATER, SEAN - 3B - BR - Age 24
The Padres drafted Drinkwater out of North Carolina State. He hasn't hit much in the minors, but he has had some very hot streaks. He made the California League All-Star team in 1993 and was the MVP in the game. He could make the Padres as a spare infielder, but he won't hit in the majors.

DUCEY, ROB - OF - BL - Age 30
Ducey could never earn more than a reserve outfield role in the US, so he left for Japan in 1995 where he became a good power hitter for the Nippon Ham Fighters.

DUNCAN, ANDRES - SS - BB - Age 24
Mariano Duncan's younger brother hasn't had even Andres Thomas' success. Duncan the Younger hasn't stuck in two brief Triple-A trials, and didn't help himself with his performance for the Twins' Double-A team at New Haven last year.

DUNCAN, MARIANO - 2B/SS - BR - Age 33
In the past, Duncan has been a useful semi-regular, playing four positions and contributing good speed and extra base power, particularly against lefthanded pitching. In 1995, he lost his speed and his strike zone judgement was laughable playing for the Phillies and Reds. Any future employment depends on how cheaply he is willing work for.

	AB	R	HR	RBI	SB	BA	$
1994 Philadelphia NL	347	49	8	48	10	.268	14
1995 Cincinnati NL	265	36	6	36	1	.287	7
1996 *Projection* >>>	212	29	4	29	3	.269	3

DUNN, STEVE - 1B - BL - Age 25
Dunn spent his second consecutive year at Triple-A Salt Lake, and is in line for a shot at the first base job in Mnnesota in '96. His likely level of production in '96, a .260 average with ten home runs, is not enough to secure him the job outright. Down the road, he will be a good platoon player at first base or DH.

	AB	R	HR	RBI	SB	BA	$
1994 Minnesota AL	35	2	0	4	0	.229	-
1995 Salt Lake AAA	402	57	12	83	3	.316	

DUNN, TODD - OF - BR - Age 25
The third of Milwaukee's four first-round draft picks in '93, and the most successful to date. Drafted out of the University of North Florida, where he had transfered after first attending Georgia Tech on a football scholarship. Played center field at Helena.

DUNSTON, SHAWON - SS - BR - Age 33
Dunston has a back problem and wore down near the end of 1995 but still managed one of his most productive years ever. He's a very erratic player and was expected to go elsewhere via free agency. If healthy Dunston can be among baseball's better hitting shortstops.

	AB	R	HR	RBI	SB	BA	$
1994 Chicago NL	331	38	11	35	3	.278	11
1995 Chicago NL	477	58	14	69	10	.296	19
1996 *Projection* >>>	480	57	15	63	8	.279	14

DUNWOODY, TODD - OF - BL - Age 21
The Marlins' 1993 7th round pick evolved into a solid all around prospect in 1995, as he was named the best defensive outfielder in the Class-A Midwest League in his first full pro season. He can hit for average and power, which will improve as his 6'2", 185 lbs, body fills out. He also has excellent speed and a plus throwing arm. The Marlins expect Dunwoody to progress rapidly and might skip him over a level to Double-A in 1996 - he is the one minor league Marlin outfielder most capable of eventually starting in the majors.

DUPLESSIS, DAVE - 1B - BL - Age 25
Duplessis is a Montreal first base prospect who hits for a decent average with little power. Not exactly the offensive attributes one looks for at that position.

DURHAM, RAY - 2B - BB - Age 24
Durham turned in a good rookie year despite a September slump; he appeared to wear down at the end of the year. He has good range, but is very rough in the field, although his double play pivot is improving. Athletic Durham is a terrific baserunner who had large platoon splits in 1995 (.350 BA against righthanders, .230 against lefties). Durham will get 500 at-bats in 1996; watch him grow as one of the league's better young second basemen.

	AB	R	HR	RBI	SB	BA	$
1994 Nashville AAA	527	89	16	66	34	.296	
1995 Chicago AL	471	68	7	51	18	.257	15
1996 *Projection* >>>	500	72	8	53	14	.269	14

DURANT, MIKE - C/DH - BR - Age 26
Durant, who shared time with Tim McIntosh at Salt Lake, is not a particularly good defensive catcher. He can hit, and can run a bit.

DYE, JERMAINE - OF - BR - Age 22
Dye is part of the outfield prospect phalanx moving on Atlanta. Last year with Double-A Greenville, he didn't match his production the year before, but he was making a big jump from the Sally League. A slow start in the Arizona Fall League reduced his luster, but the youngster has plenty of prospect promise.

DYKSTRA, LENNY - OF - BL - Age 33
In 1995, a serious back injury shut him down for the season. Interestingly, in the days immediately preceding his shutdown, Dykstra played left field, with Andy Van Slyke in center field. The back injury is of major concern - it could be a career ender if he does need major surgery, and could rob him of a major asset, power, if it lingers in any form. Look for Dykstra to be an on-base threat in 1996, but without his trademark power or speed.

	AB	R	HR	RBI	SB	BA	$
1994 Philadelphia NL	315	68	5	24	15	.273	14
1995 Philadelphia NL	254	37	2	18	10	.264	6
1996 *Projection* >>>	310	54	4	24	11	.274	10

EASLEY, DAMION - 3B/2B - BR - Age 26
Easley's future looked bright after he hit an excellent combined .291 in 381 at-bats in 1992 and '93. But the past two years hitting .216 have been a disaster, and he couldn't step up when he was really needed to replace the injured Gary DiSarcina.

	AB	R	HR	RBI	SB	BA	$
1994 California AL	316	41	6	30	4	.215	3
1995 California AL	357	35	4	35	5	.216	2
1996 *Projection* >>>	397	44	5	38	6	.236	4

EASON, TOMMY - C - BR - Age 25
After missing the entire 1993 season, Eason had an excellent offensive campaign, especially after his midseason promotion to Double-A Reading, where he flirted with a .500 slugging percentage. Despite his resurgence, it's highly unlikely that he will ever be a major league starter.

ECHEVARRIA, ANGEL - OF - BR - Age 24
This Eastern League All-Star had a big year with the Rockies' Double-A New Haven affiliate. He reached career bests in homers (21) and batting average (.300), while also leading the club with 100 RBI. He'll likely spend 1996 at Triple-A Colorado Springs. The Rockies crowded outfield makes an early major league appearance unlikely for Echevarria.

EDGE, TIM - C - BR - Age 27
This good-fielding, terrible-hitting journeyman minor-league catcher in the Pirates' farm system will someday make a good coach or manager.

EDMONDS, JIM - OF - BL - Age 25
The good batting average was not unexpected, but the 30 home runs and 104 RBI were a complete surprise to everyone, and more surprisingly, most of the RBI came from Edmonds hitting in the second hole in the order. Hitting instructor Rod Crew: "If he applies himself, he can be a good hitter for a long time. He's got what it takes."

	AB	R	HR	RBI	SB	BA	$
1994 California AL	289	35	5	37	4	.273	9
1995 California AL	558	120	33	107	1	.290	23
1996 *Projection* >>>	555	102	26	97	2	.285	20

EDWARDS, JEROME - OF - BR - Age 27
A 1990 13th-round pick, Edwards got his first crack at Double-A in 1994 and failed miserably, getting shuttled back to Single-A Clearwater. He stole over 20 bases in each of his first three pro seasons, but hit a for low average with negligible power. He'll probably be released by the time you read this.

EDWARDS, MIKE - 3B - BR - Age 26
Edwards was relegated to backup duty in his second season at Double-A. He is unlikely to hit well enough to advance further.

EENHOORN, ROBERT - SS - BR - Age 28
In his native Netherlands, Eenhoorn could have been a standout soccer pro, but he chose the esoteric path toward major league baseball. Even with allowances for a delayed learning curve, it's pretty clear he won't go far beyond the bounds of unusual publicity.

	AB	R	HR	RBI	SB	BA	$
1994 New York AL	4	1	0	0	0	.500	-
1995 New York AL	14	1	0	2	0	.143	-

EHMANN, KURT - SS - BR - Age 25
Ehmann has a good arm, but he has yet to hit in the minors and is getting old for a prospect. He's very unlikely to have a major-league career of any note.

EISENREICH, JIM - OF - BL - Age 36
Eisenreich has been a revelation in his three seasons with the Phillies, lashing the ball consistently into the gaps and fielding masterfully while garnering much more playing time than anyone could have expected. The Phils hold to a fairly strict platoon due to both his inability to hit lefties (.213 in 1995) and the effects of his medication for Tourette's Syndrome. He showed signs of slowing late in 1995 and should be expected to begin a gradual career downturn in 1996.

	AB	R	HR	RBI	SB	BA	$
1994 Philadelphia NL	290	42	4	43	6	.300	12
1995 Philadelphia NL	377	46	10	55	10	.316	17
1996 *Projection* >>>	296	39	4	39	5	.292	7

ELLIS, KEVIN - 3B - BR - Age 24
Ellis showed power, but struck out a lot in 1994 and remained at Class-A in 1995. The Cubs hope he'll be a late bloomer.

ELLIS, PAUL - C - BL - Age 27
Ellis was once a big prospect who has now fizzled out. A "Crash Davis" type of player, Ellis handles pitchers extremely well and is an asset in the minor league clubhouse.

ELSTER, KEVIN - SS - BR - Age 31
How bad did things get for the Phillies in 1995? One needed only to look up and see this guy playing first base in September to effectively know the answer to that question. He used to be an effective fielder, but those days are long gone, due to 1990 shoulder surgery. Elster did provide one exclamation point in 1995, with a startling center field homer, one of the Phils' longest of the season, and most likely his longest ever. After the season, he became a free agent after refusing an outright Triple-A assignment.

	AB	R	HR	RBI	SB	BA	$
1994 New York AL	20	0	0	0	0	.000	-
1995 New York AL	17	1	0	0	0	.118	-
1995 Philadelphia NL	53	10	1	9	0	.208	-

ENCARNACION, ANGELO - C - BR - Age 22
He makes decent contact and has a rifle arm but is clearly the Pirates' second-best catcher in the organization behind 1995 Southern League MVP Jason Kendall. Encarnacion is a little guy and durability is a question behind the plate. However, he has a chance to have a long major-league career as a second-string catcher.

	AB	R	HR	RBI	SB	BA	$
1995 Pittsburgh NL	159	18	2	10	1	.226	0
1996 Projection >>>	169	19	2	11	2	.235	-

ERSTAD, DARIN - SS - BL - Age 23
Talented outfielder Darin Erstad was the first draft pick overall in 1995, taken by the Angels. He's a power hitter out of the University of Nebraska. He tore up two leagues: the Class-A California League, and the Arizona Fall League. Erstad is very talented, and he might even make the Angels coming out of spring training.

ESPINAL, JUAN - 3B - BR - Age 20
Espinal hit just .208 at Class-A in 1995. Still very young but looked more promising a year ago.

ESPINOSA, RAMON - OF - BR - Age 24
Espinosa had a decent 1995 as an outfielder with the Pirates' Double-A Carolina farm club but is not considered a prospect. In a five year minor league career he has a .306 OBP and .384 SLG.

ESPINOZA, ALVARO - 3B/SS - BR - Age 34
Alvaro Espinoza played at second base, shortstop and third base. Espinoza is a veteran leader on a young squad.

	AB	R	HR	RBI	SB	BA	$
1994 Cleveland AL	231	27	1	19	1	.238	1
1995 Cleveland AL	143	15	2	17	0	.252	0
1996 Projection >>>	198	22	2	22	1	.249	0

ESTABELLA, BOBBY - C - BR - Age 21
The Phils' 1992 23rd round draft pick made a quantum leap forward in 1995, transforming himself from a free swinging low average hitter into a patient, power hitting, durable receiver who was named the sixth best prospect in the Class-A Florida State League by Baseball America. He also held his own in a late season Double-A trial in the heat of the Eastern League pennant race. Two more years of similar development will put him squarely in line to succeed Darren Daulton in Philadelphia and possibly approach his production.

ESTRADA, JOSUE - OF - BR - Age 21
Estrada, a supplemental first-round draft choice by the Expos in 1993, swung and missed in his first full pro season.

ESTRADA, OSMANI - 3B - BR - Age 27
Estrada had a solid season as one of Double-A's older players, but lacks speed and power. He's not a prospect.

EUSEBIO, TONY - C - BR - Age 28
Eusebio was a pleasant surprise in 1995 with his consistent hitting as Houston's regular catcher. He is average defensively and will probably not have another year when he receives as much playingtime as he did in 1995.

	AB	R	HR	RBI	SB	BA	$
1994 Houston NL	159	18	5	30	0	.296	5
1995 Houston NL	368	46	6	58	0	.299	10
1996 Projection >>>	315	39	6	52	0	.285	6

EVERETT, CARL - OF - BB - Age 26
Everett developed immensely as a hitter in 1995. Observers from a distance have said that he developed more patience and discipline, but Everett claims he's simply shifted his aggressiveness to active watching for just the right pitch -- and then, bam! He's got speed, too, and a Grade A arm. Will play right as the Mets pursue an established veteran for center.

	AB	R	HR	RBI	SB	BA	$
1994 Florida NL	51	7	2	6	4	.216	1
1995 Norfolk AAA	260	52	6	35	12	.300	

	AB	R	HR	RBI	SB	BA	$
1995 New York NL	289	48	12	54	2	.260	9
1996 *Projection* >>>	505	81	20	99	9	.282	20

FABREGAS, JORGE - C - BL - Age 26
Angels catcher Jorge Fabregas is one of those rare hitters who hits better in the majors than he did in the Pacific Coast League. He hit .247 last year, and that's about the best you can expect. Fabregas may be relegated to a deep back-up role, or even the minors, when top slugging prospect Todd Greene arrives.

	AB	R	HR	RBI	SB	BA	$
1994 California AL	127	12	0	16	2	.283	2
1995 California AL	227	24	1	22	0	.247	0
1996 *Projection* >>>	207	21	1	22	1	.248	0

FANEYTE, RIKKERT - OF - BR - Age 27
After three seasons at Triple-A, Faneyte has nothing left to prove in the minors, but at this point he would appear to come up short as a major-leaguer. His production at Phoenix fell off in his third year, while his major-league average in limited play was under .200 for a third straight season. OK speed but is nothing special even there.

	AB	R	HR	RBI	SB	BA	$
1994 San Francisco NL	26	1	0	4	0	.115	-
1995 San Francisco NL	86	7	0	4	1	.198	
1996 *Projection* >>>	90	12	1	11	1	.234	-

FARIES, PAUL - 2B - BR - Age 31
He's a better player than many major leaguers, but he didn't hit in early callups and is now merely an aging minor leaguer.

FARISS, MONTY - OF - BR - Age 28
Fariss missed his chance to earn a major league job when he hit .217 in 104 games for Texas several years ago. He didn't help himself with his .182 performance for Triple-A Iowa in 1995.

FARNER, MATT - OF - BR - Age 22
Toronto's second first-round pick in the '93 draft. Has good speed, which he wasn't able to showcase in pro ball because he rarely got on base.

FARRELL, JON - OF - BR - Age 24
The Pirates' top pick in the 1991 draft, Farrell has yet to play at the Triple-A level. He doesn't hit for average, has terrible plate discipline, is a poor outfielder and is unlikely to play in the major leagues.

FARRIS, MARK - SS/3B - BL - Age 20
The Pirates made Farris their surprise first-round draft pick in 1994. A high school player from Angleton, Texas, he had a scholarship to play quarterback at Texas A&M and the football option scared away many clubs. He was a shortstop in high school but the Pirates project him as a third baseman in the Robin Ventura mold.

FASANO, SAL - C - BR - Age 24
After getting off to an incredibly slow start at Double-A Wichita in 1995, Fasano eventually showed why he was the Royals Minor League Player of the Year in 1994. His power coupled with his ability to hit for average make him an asset to the hitting-weak Royals. Fasano's weight can cause him a problem behind the plate, but it's his hitting that will get him to the big leagues.

FAULKNER, CRAIG - C/1B - BR - Age 30
Faulkner is a weak hitting reserve catcher and first baseman last seen with Triple-A Rochester in 1994.

FELDER, KENNY - OF - BL - Age 25
A big (6'3", 220 lbs.) and strong first round draft pick (1992), Felder made better contact while hitting 12 homers and driving in 55 runs after advancing to Double-A El Paso in 1995. Felder is the Brewers' best power prospect and is one full season away from a major league shot.

FELDER, MIKE - OF - BB - Age 33
Ex-major leaguer was hanging on in Independent ball in 1995, hitting .352 in 307 at bats.

FELIX, JUNIOR - OF - BB - Age 28
There have been questions about how old he really is, and he may be showing those final signs of age before being released by Triple-A Ottawa in 1995. He has rebounded before, but it's doubtful that Felix can ever win a regular role in the majors again.

FERMIN, FELIX - SS - BR - Age 32
How a player can drop 122 points in batting average and stay in the majors with somebody like Alex Rodriguez on the horizon is the question. Fermin's offense in 1995 made Raphael Belliard look like Ernie Banks.

	AB	R	HR	RBI	SB	BA	$
1994 Seattle AL	379	52	1	35	4	.317	13
1995 Seattle AL	200	21	0	15	2	.195	-
1996 *Projection* >>>	191	23	1	16	2	.261	0

FERNANDEZ, TONY - SS - BB - Age 33
Signed for another year, Fernandez offers an above-average veteran alternative to the imminent arrival of Derek Jeter at shortstop in New York. Still, Fernandez' nagging injuries (rib cage and then a knee in 1995) and declining batting average are a plus for Jeter.

	AB	R	HR	RBI	SB	BA	$
1994 Cincinnati NL	366	50	8	50	12	.279	17
1995 New York AL	384	57	5	45	6	.245	6
1996 *Projection* >>>	337	46	5	40	4	.257	5

FIELDER, CECIL - 1B/DH - BR - Age 32
Fielder turned in a respectable season in '95, as he connected for his yearly total of thirty home runs and maintained a decent on base average. His declining batting average and doubles total show the pressure he puts on himself to produce the long ball for the traditionally power oriented Tigers. As he enters the strictly DH portion of his career, Fielder remains a quality run producer, albeit one whose batting average will be low.

	AB	R	HR	RBI	SB	BA	$
1994 Detroit AL	425	67	28	90	0	.259	19
1995 Detroit AL	494	70	31	82	0	.243	13
1996 *Projection* >>>	544	79	34	100	0	.246	15

FINLEY, STEVE - OF - BL - Age 31
Finley took over the Padres' lead-off spot when Bip Roberts was injured, and came through beautifully as the new Padres' sparkplug. In one stretch, he went 48-for-129 hitting .372. Traded from Houston, he took a liking to San Diego and had his career-best year. He also got back to stealing bases aggressively. Finley should continue his excellent play in 1996.

	AB	R	HR	RBI	SB	BA	$
1994 Houston NL	373	64	11	33	13	.276	17
1995 San Diego NL	562	104	10	44	36	.297	27
1996 *Projection* >>>	586	93	10	48	30	.284	23

FINN, JOHN - 2B - BR - Age 28
A diminuitive (5'8") contact-hitter who lacks power, Finn struck out just seven times in 117 at-bats for Triple-A New Orleans in 1995. He has pretty good speed, but is not a good prospect.

FISHER, DAVID - 2B - BR - Age 26
He hits doubles, draws walks, but has the look of a minor league journeyman.

FLAHERTY, JOHN - C - BR - Age 28
Flaherty appeared to be a major find for Detroit early in the '95 season, as he hit for average and played well defensively behind the plate. A poor second half dimmed the lustre on his year, yet he heads into '96 as the favorite to play every day for the Tigers. He is capable of producing as a regular catcher for the next two to three years.

	AB	R	HR	RBI	SB	BA	$
1994 Detroit AL	40	2	0	4	0	.150	-
1995 Detroit AL	354	39	11	40	0	.243	4
1996 Projection >>>	258	27	7	29	0	.236	1

FLETCHER, DARRIN - C - BL - Age 29
Fletcher is one of the National League's better hitting catchers but his defense borders on awful. His defensive woes are such that the Expos will look to trade him and insert young Tim Laker as the starter behind the plate in 1996.

	AB	R	HR	RBI	SB	BA	$
1994 Montreal NL	285	28	10	57	0	.260	9
1995 Montreal NL	350	42	11	45	0	.286	9
1996 Projection >>>	396	43	13	60	0	.275	9

FLETCHER, SCOTT - 2B - BR - Age 37
Detroit signed Fletcher to spell Lou Whitaker against lefthanders in '95, but Fletcher didn't find a groove offensively. He will hope to land a job as a pinch-hitter and veteran leader in '96, and he can still run the bases and play defense.

	AB	R	HR	RBI	SB	BA	$
1994 Boston AL	185	31	3	11	8	.227	4
1995 Detroit AL	182	19	1	17	1	.231	0
1996 Projection >>>	181	25	1	15	4	.240	0

FLORA, KEVIN - 2B - BR - Age 26
Once upon a time, Flora was an excellent all around second base prospect in the Angels' chain. The Phils obtained him late 1995 and gave him his first extended big league trial, as an outfielder. He disappointed, hitting for a low average with little power, and scant evidence of the speed.

	AB	R	HR	RBI	SB	BA	$
1995 Vancouver AAA	124	22	3	14	7	.298	
1995 Philadelphia NL	75	12	2	7	1	.213	-
1996 Projection >>>	102	17	2	10	3	.237	-

FLORES, MIGUEL - 2B - BR - Age 25
Flores had steadily advanced through the Indians' chain from 1990-93 based on contact hitting, surehanded defense and basestealing ability. It had become clear, however, that he was no threat to Carlos Baerga, and he needed to learn other positions in order to make the bigs as a utilityman. Two years later, injuries have sapped Flores' speed, and he remains solely a second baseman. Flores has stagnated at the Triple-A level, and will remain there only until the Indians find a better alternative.

FLOYD, CLIFF - 1B - BL - Age 23
Floyd is one of the most hyped prospects of this decade; his doctors feared his career was over last May when he suffered a shattered wrist. Incredibly, he was back in action by September. Floyd will move from first base to rightfield this season. He really hasn't done much in the majors yet and the time has come for him to prove the hype has been justified.

	AB	R	HR	RBI	SB	BA	$
1994 Montreal NL	334	43	4	41	10	.281	13
1995 Montreal NL	69	6	1	8	3	.130	-
1996 Projection >>>	427	49	11	64	13	.280	14

FOLEY, TOM - 2B - BL - Age 36
After spending most of last season with Montreal's Triple-A Ottawa farm club, Foley retired to become director of minor-league operations for the expansion Tampa Bay Devil Rays. A solid utility infielder for more than a decade, he is a terrific guy and will be a first-rate manager in the big leagues some day.

	AB	R	HR	RBI	SB	BA	$
1994 Pittsburgh NL	123	13	3	15	0	.236	0
1995 Montreal NL	24	2	0	2	1	.208	-

FONVILLE, CHAD - SS - BB - Age 25
Tommy LaSorda gave Fonville much of the credit for the Dodgers success in 1995, which is interesting given that Fonville had an on-base average of .328 and slugged a robust .303. He finished the year as the Dodgers regular shortstop. Bip Roberts first season was similar (.253 BA, .293 OBA, .303 SLG) but Bip was 22 when he came up and he eventually developed some doubles power and good strike zone judgment. Fonville hits some singles, steals, and can play several positions - a nice combination for a bench player but a liability as a regular (even at shortstop) if he doesn't add some other skills.

	AB	R	HR	RBI	SB	BA	$
1995 Two Teams	320	43	0	16	20	.278	11
1996 *Projection* >>>	292	31	1	18	14	.268	6

FORBES, P. J. - 2B - BR - Age 28
Back in 1993, P.J. Forbes hit .319-15-64 in Double-A, and the "On the Fly" column in "The Sporting News" predicted that he would start for the Angels and become rookie-of-the-year. Alas, Forbes was never rookie-of-the-year, and worse yet, he has never made it past Triple-A. The Angels were desperate for infield help last year, but Forbes never got the call, and at age 28, he looks like a career minor leaguer.

FORD, CURT - OF - BL - Age 35
He's back after a lengthy absence from the A-Z book and is more mediocre than ever. Ford was one of many older journeymen on the Marlins' 1995 Triple-A roster, which included such notables as Nick Capra, age 38, Doug Dascenzo, 32, and their youngest starter, Eddie Zosky, 28. Ford is an aging lefty with little power and faded speed. He swings at everything.

FORDYCE, BROOK - C - BR - Age 25
A good defensive catcher with a fair bat, Fordyce has been unfortunate to come of age in an organization with surplus talent behind the plate. A change of scenery would help.

FOSTER, JIM - C - BR - Age 24
Hits with power, but his most dangerous weapon is his throwing arm. In the Appalachian League, where runners often steal at will, Foster gunned down four of four Johnson City base-stealers in one game. A 22nd round pick in 1993's draft, out of Providence College.

FOX, ANDY - 3B - BL - Age 25
Fox was voted both the best defensive third baseman and the infielder with the best arm in the Eastern League. He's behind Russ Davis in the Yankees organization.

FOX, ERIC - OF - BB - Age 32
Fox got another cup of coffee in 1995 with the Rangers, and at his age, it probably was his last. Fox is a decent defensive player, but offers too little offense to take up a roster spot in the majors.

	AB	R	HR	RBI	SB	BA	$
1994 Oakland AL	44	7	1	1	2	.205	-
1995 Texas AL	15	2	0	0	0	.000	-

FRANCISCO, DAVID - OF - BR - Age 24
He has a great glove, stole 30 bases at Double-A in 1995, but has no power and way too many strikeouts. He's two years away at the least and unlikely to be anything more than a fifth outfielder at the major league level.

FRANCO, JULIO - DH - BR - Age 34
The White Sox sorely missed Franco in 1995. Instead he became one of the Japanese Leagues' top hitters for the Chiba Lotte Mariners. Don't be surprised to see Franco make a triumphant return to the US in 1996. He's no longer a batting champion contender, but he can still drive in runs; he'd be well suited to a DH/RBI role.

FRANCO, MATT - 1B - BL - Age 26
As a hitter, Franco is much like Mark Grace, only less potent. He moved across the diamond to third base in 1995, his third season at Triple-A Iowa, and earned a September promotion to Chicago. For 1996 he has a chance for a reserve role in the big leagues, or a larger role should Grace leave via free agency.

	AB	R	HR	RBI	SB	BA	$
1994 Iowa AAA	437	63	11	71	3	.277	
1995 Iowa AAA	455	51	6	58	1	.281	
1995 Chicago NL	17	3	0	1	0	.294	-
1996 *Projection* >>>	90	9	1	8	1	.257	-

FRANKLIN, MICAH - OF - BB - Age 23
A switch-hitting outfielder with power, Franklin was obtained by the Pirates from the Cincinnati organization prior to last season. He looked good in spring training and had a decent year for Triple-A Calgary. However, he didn't endear himself to management by jumping the club for a week last season when his wife gave birth, again raising long-standing questions about his attitude. He was left off the 40-man winter roster.

FRAZIER, LOU - OF - BB - Age 31
After having back-to-back good seasons as a reserve outfielder, Frazier slumped in 1995 and was traded to Texas where he was briefly a starter. He has tremendous speed and is a valuable bench player if he hits. And it's hitting that will determine how much longer Frazier can stay in the big leagues because we all know the cliche about not being able to steal first base.

	AB	R	HR	RBI	SB	BA	$
1994 Montreal NL	140	25	0	14	20	.271	12
1995 Montreal NL	63	6	0	3	4	.190	-
1995 Texas AL	99	19	0	8	9	.212	4
1996 *Projection* >>>	150	24	0	12	15	.233	4

FRIAS, HANLEY - SS - BB - Age 22
After struggling at the Class A level for four seasons, Frias turned it on for Double-A Tulsa last season. He has no power, but he has good speed and can hit for average. His agility on the bases might get him an extra look from big league scouts.

FRIEDMAN, JASON - 1B - BL - Age 26
First baseman Jason Friedman was formerly in the Red Sox system where he won a batting championship in Class-A. But he struggled in Double-A last year in the Orioles organization, and his future looks limited. Friedman doesn't have a very strong bat.

FRYE, JEFF - 2B - BR - Age 29
Frye put together another solid season despite a nagging hamstring injury. Frye is a career .284 hitter with very little power, and he can't stay healthy enough to play a full season. He ended last season in Johnny Oates' doghouse by complaining about lack of playing time.

	AB	R	HR	RBI	SB	BA	$
1994 Texas AL	205	37	0	18	6	.327	9
1995 Texas AL	313	38	4	29	3	.278	6
1996 *Projection* >>>	270	37	3	25	5	.292	6

FRYMAN, TRAVIS - 3B - BR - Age 27
Fryman made some significant improvements in his game after a subpar '94 season to reestablished himself as one of the AL's young stars. He led the Tigers in hits, runs, and batting average, and paced AL third basemen in innings and double plays. Fryman also reduced his strikeouts from '94, and he will be an MVP candidate when he returns to form against lefthanders (.211 in '95).

	AB	R	HR	RBI	SB	BA	$
1994 Detroit AL	464	66	18	85	2	.263	17
1995 Detroit AL	567	79	15	81	4	.275	15
1996 *Projection* >>>	597	85	19	94	4	.281	18

FRYMAN, TROY - 1B - BL - Age 24
After tearing up the Midwest League in 1993, Travis Fryman's younger brother hit the wall the last two years with the White Sox Southern League affiliate at Birmingham. His future is cloudy at best.

FULLER, AARON - OF - BB - Age 24
Reaching Double-A in his third pro season might have been overreaching for Fuller as he hit just .196 with no homers. He has excellent speed but will need to show a lot more with the bat to get any farther.

FULLY, ED - OF - BR - Age 24
Outfielder Ed Fully has spent three years in Single-A and two in Double-A, struggling at the plate every year. Maybe it's time for Fully to think about another career.

GAETTI, GARY - 3B/1B - BR - Age 37
As the only thing standing between the Royals and offensive oblivion, Gaetti produced perhaps his finest season ever, collecting career highs in homers and several other offensive categories. A pull-hitting slugger, Gaetti has almost no speed but is still sharp on defense. A free agent over the winter, Gaetti is assured a regular role for the foreseeable future. Expect a sharp drop off over the next two seasons.

	AB	R	HR	RBI	SB	BA	$
1994 Kansas City AL	327	53	12	57	0	.287	13
1995 Kansas City AL	514	76	35	96	3	.261	19
1996 Projection >>>	477	68	24	80	2	.251	12

GAGNE, GREG - SS - BR - Age 34
The Royals infield glue, Gagne had a disappointing third season in Kansas City. His offensive totals were about what he has always produced - marginal batting average and moderate power for a middle-infielder - but he made far more errors in 1995 than in previous years. Still, Gagne remains one of the league's best gloves; he'll again find regular work in 1996 and turn out his usual steady performance.

	AB	R	HR	RBI	SB	BA	$
1994 Kansas City AL	375	39	7	51	10	.259	13
1995 Kansas City AL	430	58	6	49	3	.256	6
1996 Projection >>>	502	62	8	60	7	.260	10

GAINER, JAY - 1B - BL - Age 29
Gainer played a key role in helping the Triple-A Colorado Springs Sky Sox to the Pacific Coast League Championship in 1995, and consistently showed a steady bat and good power throughout the season. His past stints in the bigs revealed an inability to hit the breaking ball, but his biggest obstacle to a major league future with the Rockies is probably Andres Galarraga.

GALARRAGA, ANDRES - 1B - BR - Age 34
The Big Cat's batting average dropped substantially in 1995 from the previous two seasons, but the power numbers remained impressive. Galarraga joined Bichette, Castilla and Walker, a/k/a The Blake Street Bombers, as the only four members of the same team to each have at least 30 homers in a season since the 1977 Dodgers. Look for a big year for Galarraga in 1996, when he becomes a free agent at season's end, but keep a wary eye on his strikeout/at-bat ratio.

	AB	R	HR	RBI	SB	BA	$
1994 Colorado NL	417	77	31	85	8	.319	32
1995 Colorado NL	554	89	31	106	12	.280	27
1996 Projection >>>	596	100	32	111	12	.276	26

GALLAGHER, DAVE - OF - BR - Age 35
The Angels acquired veteran outfielder Dave Gallagher from the Phillies for their pennant run. His best role is pinch hitting and a backup 4th or 5th outfielder. Gallagher doesn't have any power, thus limiting his usefulness as a bench player.

	AB	R	HR	RBI	SB	BA	$
1994 Atlanta NL	152	27	2	14	0	.224	-
1995 Philadelphia NL	157	12	1	12	0	.318	2
1995 California AL	16	1	0	0	0	.188	-
1996 Projection >>>	151	18	2	13	0	.271	-

GALLEGO, MIKE - SS/2B/3B - BR - Age 35
He has a job because of his glove: all 28 of his hits last season were singles, leaving him with a slugging percentage

of .233. He might be a useful backup infielder for some teams.

	AB	R	HR	RBI	SB	BA	$
1994 New York AL	306	39	6	41	0	.239	4
1995 Oakland AL	120	11	0	8	0	.233	-
1996 *Projection* >>>	136	16	2	17	0	.244	-

GANT, RON - OF - BR - Age 31
Gant justified Jim Bowden's 1994 gamble with an MVP type year in 1995, returning to his Atlanta form in every category including stolen bases (23 for 31). One of the top power/speed combinations in the game, Gant is a free agent and is unlikely to sign again with the Reds, who refused to pay an $86,000 fine that Gant incurred for a suspension.

	AB	R	HR	RBI	SB	BA	$
1994 Atlanta-Cincinnati NL			Did Not Play				
1995 Cincinnati NL	410	79	39	88	23	.276	28
1996 *Projection* >>>	495	95	31	102	26	.273	29

GARBER, JEFF - 2B - BR - Age 29
After four years at Double-A and Triple-A, Garber has proven himself to be no more than a career minor leaguer. He's steadier than many other players of his ilk, but isn't likely to get a real shot at the majors.

GARCIA, CARLOS - 2B - BR - Age 28
Tried at various times as a No. 1, 2 or 8 hitter by the Pirates, Garcia was finally placed in the No. 6 hole by manager Jim Leyland late last season. An RBI spot should be just right for a guy who has rare power for second baseman. 1996 will be the year when he blossoms into one of the game's better players at his position.

	AB	R	HR	RBI	SB	BA	$
1994 Pittsburgh NL	412	49	6	28	18	.277	18
1995 Pittsburgh NL	367	41	6	50	8	.294	12
1996 *Projection* >>>	505	60	8	60	13	.285	16

GARCIA, FREDDY - 3B - BR - Age 23
Garcia was selected from Toronto in the Rule 5 Draft and had to spend all of last season on the Pirates' major-league roster - he was clearly overmatched. However, he has outstanding raw power and is a good defensive third baseman. Garcia needs another year or two in the minors but he has star potential.

	AB	R	HR	RBI	SB	BA	$
1995 Pittsburgh NL	57	5	0	1	0	.140	-

GARCIA, KARIM - OF - BL - Age 20
Garcia is the top prospect in the Dodgers organization and appears to be a lefthanded version of Raul Mondesi, a right fielder with a strong arm, good power, some speed, and poor strike zone judgment. He was rated as the number two prospect in the PCL by Baseball America should have a good chance of making the Dodgers in 1996. The Dodgers need a left fielder and a lefthanded hitter and Roberto Kelly and Billy Ashley are not my idea of tough competition for the job.

	AB	R	HR	RBI	SB	BA	$
1995 Albuquerque AAA	474	88	20	91	12	.319	
1995 Los Angeles NL	20	1	0	0	0	.200	-
1996 *Projection* >>>	244	28	6	30	3	.260	3

GARCIA, OMAR - 1B - BR - Age 24
In addition to having a high-average bat, Garcia is a solid defensive first baseman. He doesn't have enough power to make it big in the bigs.

GARCIAPARRA, NOMAR - SS - BR - Age 22
Garciaparra was one of three first-round draft choices from Georgia Tech in 1994. Defensively, he's already as good as any shortstop, even in the majors. After adjusting his hitting style by moving off the plate, he started stinging the ball at Double-A Trenton. With John Valentin on hand in Boston, the Red Sox don't have to rush Garciaparra. For that, Pawtucket fans are grateful.

GARDNER, JEFF - 2B - BL - Age 32
A scrappy utility infielder, Gardner has now retired to become a scout for the Padres.

GARRISON, WEBSTER - SS - BR - Age 30
Had Garrison not elected to play replacement ball, at least one writer believes he would have had an excellent chance to stick as a utility man on the Rockies' major league roster in 1995. As it was, he wasn't even called up in September after a solid Triple-A season, in part because management was concerned about possible repercussions. Garrison has a steady bat with decent pop, and is a consistent infielder with good speed and range, but at age 30, the career minor-leaguer's opportunities are dwindling.

GATES, BRENT - 2B - BB - Age 25
Perhaps the biggest victim of Tony LaRussa's odd motivational strategies, Gates saw his job taken away from him in the spring (LaRussa wanted Mike Gallego at second base). Gates was asked to learn a new position, which didn't take. As he was also coming off an injury, the early part of his 1995 season was a disaster, although he improved over the course of the year. Gates is unlikely to reach double digits in either homers or steals.

	AB	R	HR	RBI	SB	BA	$
1994 Oakland AL	233	29	2	24	3	.283	6
1995 Oakland AL	524	60	5	56	3	.254	7
1996 *Projection* >>>	505	59	5	55	4	.284	10

GEISLER, PHIL - 1B - BL - Age 26
A strong 1994 spring training made him a favorite in the Phils' organization, despite the fact that he had barely played above Single-A at age 24. Since then, his once above average power has totally disappeared, he has consistently gotten himself out by swinging at bad pitches, and he has batted below .200 in both of his Triple-A trials. Geisler's career appears to be in reverse, and the 1991 9th round draftee may need to find a new organization in which to bounce around.

GENNARO, BRAD - OF - BL - Age 24
Outfielder Brad Gennaro should be popular with the Padres fans as San Diego is his home town. He has hit solidly but not spectacularly in the minors. Gennaro showed power in the hitter-friendly minor leagues, but had a tougher time last year in the Southern League.

GIAMBI, JASON - 3B - BL - Age 25
With nothing left to prove at Triple-A, he's ready to make his mark on major league pitching. He's willing to take a walk, has a good line-drive power, still young enough to improve. Giambi should be a pleasant surprise in 1995.

	AB	R	HR	RBI	SB	BA	$
1995 Edmonton AAA	190	34	3	41	0	.342	
1995 Oakland AL	176	27	6	25	2	.256	3
1996 *Projection* >>>	198	30	5	28	2	.258	2

GIANNELLI, RAY - 3B - BL - Age 30
A free-agent acquisition from the Blue Jays, Giannelli was Triple-A Louisville's MVP in 1995. His bat earned him a late-season callup to St. Louis. Giannelli could figure in as a utility player for the 1996 Cardinals.

GIBRALTER, STEVE - OF - BR - Age 23
Gibralter was leading the American Association in home runs and RBI when torn thumb ligaments ended his season. Gibralter has no single outstanding skill (except perhaps his defense) but he features above average power, speed, and average. His only weakness is strike zone judgement (70 strikeouts in 263 at bats). Considered one of the top prospects in the American Association, Gibralter will compete for the left field job in 1996 if the Reds do not sign Ron Gant.

	AB	R	HR	RBI	SB	BA	$
1994 Chattanooga AA	460	71	14	63	10	.270	
1995 Indianapolis AAA	263	49	18	63	0	.316	
1996 *Projection* >>>	255	38	9	45	2	.270	6

GIBSON, KIRK - DH/OF - BL - Age 38
The Gamer bowed out of a fine career in mid-'95 when he was "traded to his family." His second retirement will last much longer than his first.

	AB	R	HR	RBI	SB	BA	$
1994 Detroit NL	330	71	23	72	4	.276	19
1995 Detroit AL	227	37	9	35	9	.260	9

GIL, BENJI - SS - BR - Age 23
Gil made tremendous strides defensively in 1995, but struck out more than once in every three at bats. Only Mo Vaughn had more strikeouts in the American League last season, and Mo hit a bit better than did Gil. Gil has tremendous potential and appears to be on the track toward developing it, but the hitting part of his game is about two years away. Until then, he's good for double-digit homers and a very low batting average.

	AB	R	HR	RBI	SB	BA	$
1994 Oklahoma City AAA	487	62	10	55	14	.248	
1995 Texas AL	415	36	9	46	2	.219	3
1996 *Projection* >>>	493	43	10	53	2	.238	4

GILBERT, SHAWN - SS - BR - Age 31
Gilbert now has 3937 career minor league at bats over nine seasons, without a single major league trial to show for it. He is versatile and has above average speed, but has marginal offensive skills. Despite Kevin Stocker's struggles in 1995, Phils' brass never even considered giving Gilbert a big league trial. He will seemingly linger as Triple-A roster filler material for an indefinite period.

GILES, BRIAN - OF - BL - Age 25
Giles is one of the best kept secrets in baseball. He is a career .306 hitter in seven minor league seasons, and has developed power in the past two seasons. He has significantly more walks than strikeouts in his career, and his career OBP is narrowly under .400. He wasn't intimidated in a late season major league trial, batting .556 with a homer. He can play all three defensive positions, and is above average in center field. He is ready for the majors, and should assume and upgrade the Wayne Kirby role in Cleveland.

GILKEY, BERNARD - OF - BR - Age 29
After nearly being released last spring in a cost-cutting move, Gilkey woke up and had a fine season for the Cardinals. He has the tools to be a fine player but has fluctuated between good and bad seasons. He lacks the consistency to ever become a star.

	AB	R	HR	RBI	SB	BA	$
1994 St. Louis NL	380	52	6	45	15	.253	14
1995 St. Louis NL	480	73	17	69	12	.298	21
1996 *Projection* >>>	516	78	15	69	15	.285	20

GILLIS, TIM - 3B - BR - Age 28
Marginal power is Gillis' best trait; he lacks a good batting eye, is not a good defensive player and is far too free-swinging for his power output. In his second full season at Greenville, Gillis may have reached his high water mark. He simply has too many holes in his game to advance very much farther.

GILMORE, TONY - C - BR - Age 27
Gilmore was set to start for the 1995 Houston replacement team and that appears to be as close to the major leagues as he will get. He played at Double-A Jackson in 1995 (.214-1-15).

GIOVANOLA, ED - SS - BL - Age 27
There's something about Richmond that brings out the best in marginal infield prospects. Mike Mordecai had his career year there in 1994; last year it was Giovanola's turn. He batted 40 points higher than his previous full-season high, and finished second in the International League batting race. He also has played some shortstop, so could battle Mordecai and Rafael Belliard for a utility job in Atlanta.

GIRARDI, JOE - C - BR - Age 31
Girardi's most valuable asset to the Rockies is his ability to handle a relatively young and oft-maligned pitching staff. He had some clutch hits which resulted in several Rockies victories in 1995, but his OBP and SLG figures were the lowest and second lowest among Rockies starters, respectively. In addition, his defense weakened uncharacteristically as the campaign reached its dog days.

	AB	R	HR	RBI	SB	BA	$
1994 Colorado NL	330	47	4	34	3	.276	8
1995 Colorado NL	462	63	8	55	3	.262	9
1996 *Projection* >>>	451	52	5	42	2	.248	8

GIVINS, JIM - 2B - BB - Age 28
Givens is weak hitting shortstop who can also play second base.

GLANVILLE, DOUG - OF - BR - Age 25
Glanville has good speed, so his thirteen stolen bases for Triple-A Iowa were a disappointment. He has progressed a lot slower than the Cubs had hoped. Glanville is a solid defensive player and should be back in Iowa to start 1996.

GLENN, LEON - OF/DH - BL - Age 26
Glenn is a struggling minor-league power hitting outfielder who strikes out about 30 percent of the time. It would be better if he hit lot of home runs, but he doesn't connect very often, and therefore has a limited future.

GOFF, JERRY - C - BL - Age 31
Goff is a veteran Triple-A player who was signed to a minor league contract by Houston in 1995 as protection in the event of an injury at the major league level. He received some major league playing time when Rick Wilkins was hurt but failed to hit and probably won't get another chance.

	AB	R	HR	RBI	SB	BA	$
1994 Pittsburgh NL	25	0	0	1	0	.080	-
1995 Pittsburgh NL	26	2	1	3	0	.154	-

GOMEZ, CHRIS - SS/2B - BR - Age 24
Gomez displayed good power for a middle infielder in '95, totaling 33 extra base hits, and his average suffered as a result. He must stay healthy and improve versus righthanders (.201 in '95). By '98, Gomez will be capable of having yearly .270-10-60 production.

	AB	R	HR	RBI	SB	BA	$
1994 Detroit AL	296	32	8	53	5	.257	10
1995 Detroit AL	431	49	11	50	4	.223	5
1996 *Projection* >>>	438	49	10	55	4	.244	6

GOMEZ, LEO - 3B - BR - Age 29
Gomez struggled early in the season losing the Orioles starting third base job to Jeff Manto. Manto was later injured, and Gomez regained his job, hitting decently until he fractured his ankle requiring surgery. Gomez is prone to long batting slumps, but playing full time, he is capable of hitting .260-.275 with 20 homers.

	AB	R	HR	RBI	SB	BA	$
1994 Baltimore AL	285	46	15	56	0	.274	12
1995 Baltimore AL	127	16	4	12	0	.236	0
1996 *Projection* >>>	130	19	6	19	0	.252	0

GONZALES, RENE - 3B/1B - BR - Age 34
Rene Gonzales is a veteran utility infielder who has spent all or parts of 10 years in the majors, hitting .239 in 1435 at-bats. Now he plays at Triple-A, awaiting a call from a major league team needing an experienced utility man.

	AB	R	HR	RBI	SB	BA	$
1994 Cleveland AL	23	6	1	5	2	.348	1
1995 California AL	18	1	1	3	0	.333	-

GONZALEZ, ALEX - SS - BR - Age 22
Gonzalez posted acceptable numbers for his first full season in the major leagues. He has good power for an infielder and although he makes a lot of errors (17 in 97 games last year) his range is good enough to keep him in the majors for a while.

	AB	R	HR	RBI	SB	BA	$
1994 Toronto AL	53	7	0	1	3	.151	-
1995 Toronto AL	367	51	10	42	4	.243	6
1996 *Projection* >>>	418	57	11	45	6	.254	8

GONZALEZ, JUAN - DH/OF - BR - Age 26
Gonzalez played last season with a very bad back, which restricted him to DH duty by the end of the season. Although his overall production was down significantly, Gonzalez' ratio of homers to at bats and slugging average rebounded to near 1993 levels. While back injuries in young players are always a cause for concern, a winter of rest and therapy without the excessive weight training Gonzalez has done in the past could result in a return to previous levels of productivity.

	AB	R	HR	RBI	SB	BA	$
1994 Texas AL	422	57	19	85	6	.275	21
1995 Texas AL	352	57	27	82	0	.295	17
1996 *Projection* >>>	490	76	32	108	3	.289	21

GONZALEZ, LUIS - OF - BL - Age 28
The Cubs were happy with Gonzalez's hustle in 1995 despite some adjustment problems after he was acquired by trade from the Astros. He's a good defensive outfielder and all-around contributor, a player that Manager Jim Riggleman likes a lot. The Cubs will work to bring free agent Gonzalez back to Chicago in 1996.

	AB	R	HR	RBI	SB	BA	$
1994 Houston NL	392	57	8	67	15	.273	20
1995 Chicago NL	471	69	13	69	6	.276	14
1996 *Projection* >>>	517	76	13	79	12	.284	18

GONZALEZ, PETE - C - BR - Age 26
Gonzalez is good defensively. He was passed over for a promotion to the Tigers in favor of John Flaherty.

GONZALEZ, RAUL - OF - BR - Age 22
In his fifth pro season Gonzalez reached Double-A. He can do a little of everything with the bat. Gonzalez needs a consistent year in the high minors to become a real prospect.

GOODWIN, CURTIS - OF - BL - Age 23
Goodwin hit like Ty Cobb for a month or two, but then the pitchers caught up with him, exploiting his impatience at the plate. He then slumped badly, hitting only .172 in his last 145 at-bats, a far cry from the get-on-base leadoff man the Orioles wanted. He was stubborn and uncoachable and fell into management's disfavor. Goodwin has blinding speed, but with all his problems, he may start 1996 back in Triple-A.

	AB	R	HR	RBI	SB	BA	$
1995 Baltimore AL	289	40	1	24	22	.263	13
1996 *Projection* >>>	332	46	2	27	23	.265	11

GOODWIN, TOM - OF - BL - Age 27
Another old Royals rookie, Goodwin battled Kenny Lofton for the stolen base crown into the final weekend of the season. He always had the speed, but 1995 provided the first proof that he can hit enough in the majors. Despite the outstanding season, Goodwin remained a free agent during the off-season, so his future is difficult to predict. He'll be a regular in centerfield or leftfield for a weak team, or could become a valuable bench/platoon player for a stronger franchise.

	AB	R	HR	RBI	SB	BA	$
1995 Kansas City AL	480	72	4	28	50	.288	32
1996 *Projection* >>>	422	63	4	26	39	.275	20

GORDON, KEITH - OF - BR - Age 27
The Reds second round draft pick in 1990, Gordon had a good year at Triple-A in 1995, and has trimmed down his strike zone judgement problems.

GRABLE, ROB - 3B - BR - Age 26
Journeyman Grable was a reliable, patient power/speed source for the Phils' Double-A Reading affiliate, but failed

in a Triple-A trial due to overaggressiveness at the plate. 1995 was his first foray above Double-A, not a good sign for someone of his age. Grable will kick around in the minors because of his above average offense and ability to play third base in addition to the outfield. However, his bat simply is not quick enough for him to have a major league future.

GRACE, MARK - 1B - BL - Age 31
Grace signed a one-year contract before the 1995 season, returning to the Cubs with a vengeance; his .326, 51 doubles and 16 homers were all career bests. His strong play belied his reputation as a whiner who was more focused on personal goals than team goals; he became much more of a team leader last season. Free agent Grace now wants to return to Chicago for 1996.

	AB	R	HR	RBI	SB	BA	$
1994 Chicago NL	403	55	6	44	0	.298	11
1995 Chicago NL	552	97	16	92	6	.326	25
1996 *Projection* >>>	562	88	14	84	5	.315	23

GRAFFANINO, TONY - 2B - BR - Age 23
It was a lost year for Graffanino, a 1994 Double-A all-star who couldn't do anything right for the Richmond Braves and lost his job to journeyman Ed Giovanola. Graffanino is young enough to make a comeback; this will have to be the year for it.

GREBECK, BRIAN - SS - BR - Age 28
Grebeck, Craig's brother, is an Angels minor-league shortstop who hit about .300 in the minors until he got to Triple-A last year where he found the going much tougher. Even when he hits .300, he has a weak bat and doesn't produce many runs. If he was a good prospect, he would have been called up to play in place of the injured Gary DiSarcina, but he wasn't, so his future prospects are a little cloudy.

GREBECK, CRAIG - SS - BR - Age 31
Grebeck's window of opportunity to win a regular job has probably closed, but he's still a top flight utility player. A good shortstop and not a bad second baseman, either, he can play anywhere on the infield and is a spunky hitter. A platoon with Ozzie Guillen wouldn't work because Grebeck doesn't hit lefties well at all. So, in 1996 Grebeck will continue his utility role and be one of the league's better reserves.

	AB	R	HR	RBI	SB	BA	$
1994 Chicago AL	97	17	0	5	0	.309	1
1995 Chicago AL	154	19	1	18	0	.260	0
1996 *Projection* >>>	134	18	1	12	0	.262	-

GREEN, GARY - SS - BR - Age 34
Your typical ex-prospect, Green has surfaced in the major leagues five times, with three different organizations, never getting more than 88 at bats in a season. Career .222 hitter.

GREEN, SHAWN - OF - BL - Age 23
Green showed unexpected power and was everything the Blue Jays hoped he would be in his first full major league season. His swing has been compared to John Olerud and despite defensive problems in his first year, he has a very good throwing arm. Some awkward moments in the outfield last year will not stop him from getting 400-500 at bats as the regular right fielder.

	AB	R	HR	RBI	SB	BA	$
1994 Toronto AL	33	1	0	1	1	.091	-
1995 Totonto AL	379	52	15	54	1	.288	11
1996 *Projection* >>>	444	62	18	65	5	.290	16

GREENE, TODD - C - BR - Age 24
Todd Greene is a power-hitting machine. Last year was his third season as a pro, and he continues to hit well at every minor-league level. He hits for a good average and power and his strikeouts are low. Last year, he became the first minor leaguer to hit 40 home runs since Danny Taratbull in 1985. He was Baseball Weekly's 1996 Minor League Player-of-the-Year, and he should be catching for the Angels in 1996.

	AB	R	HR	RBI	SB	BA	$
1995 Midland AA	318	59	26	57	3	.327	

	AB	R	HR	RBI	SB	BA	$
1995 Vancouver AAA	168	28	14	35	1	.250	
1996 *Projection* >>>	233	32	12	37	2	.244	4

GREENE, WILLIE - 3B - BL - Age 24

Greene has been considered a legitimate prospect for the last four years, but bad luck (and possibly a bad attitude) have delayed his arrival. In 1995, he reported over weight, and hit .105 in his first eight games with the Reds while the team was going 1-7. This earned another trip to Indianapolis where he struggled and suffered from an elbow injury. Greene is still an excellent power prospect despite being perceived as a failure at the major league level - his last three trials have totaled only 106 at bats. The Reds could use a lefthanded power hitter.

	AB	R	HR	RBI	SB	BA	$
1994 Cincinnati NL	37	5	0	3	0	.216	-
1995 Indianapolis AAA	325	57	19	45	3	.243	
1995 Cincinnati NL	19	1	0	0	0	.105	-
1996 *Projection* >>>	265	29	9	31	3	.255	4

GREENWELL, MIKE - OF - BL - Age 32

Lost among the great seasons turned in by Mo Vaughn and John Valentin, Greenwell gave the Red Sox steady play at bat and in the field, posting his most productive season of the 1990's. Overall, Greenwell has been one of most consistent hitters from year to year; as long as he's healthy, he'll hit .290 to .310, smash 15 homers and drive in 80 runs.

	AB	R	HR	RBI	SB	BA	$
1994 Boston AL	327	60	11	45	2	.269	10
1995 Boston AL	481	67	15	76	9	.297	19
1996 *Projection* >>>	516	78	16	77	7	.291	17

GREER, RUSTY - OF - BL - Age 27

Greer turned in another solid season, mostly in a platoon role. He is a line-drive hitter with occasional power and a good batting eye. Although he is likely to remain a role player, Greer should improve in average and power over his 1995 totals.

	AB	R	HR	RBI	SB	BA	$
1994 Texas AL	277	36	10	46	0	.314	12
1995 Texas AL	417	58	13	61	3	.271	11
1996 *Projection* >>>	429	58	14	65	2	.274	11

GREGG, TOMMY - OF - BL - Age 32

After taking his act to Mexico for a season, journeyman Gregg brought his lefthanded line drive bat back stateside, and performed his ritual strafing of Triple-A pitching. Gregg is a prototypical lefty bat off of the bench who has the ability to go on short power tears. He has neither the power nor the speed, however, to secure a significant big league role. Gregg was cut loose by the Marlins shortly after the end of the regular season and will likely land a Triple-A job for 1996.

	AB	R	HR	RBI	SB	BA	$
1995 Charlotte AAA	124	30	9	32	7	.387	
1995 Florida NL	156	20	6	20	3	.237	3
1996 *Projection* >>>	95	13	4	13	2	.250	0

GRESHAM, KRIS - C - BR - Age 25

Gresham is a weak hitting catcher in the Orioles farm system. He needs to greatly improve his hitting to move upward.

GRIEVE, BEN - OF - BL - Age 19

The first position player taken in the 1994 draft. Grieve struggled in his first full minor league season, but hit .262 with 75 walks, stole 13 bases, and was promoted late in the season from low to high Class A. He's still only 19 years old, with excellent potential.

GRIFFEY, KEN JR - OF - BL - Age 26

With the broken wrist sidelining him for months, his dad could have posted better numbers last year. This year we might need a seismograph to measure his performance. We really haven't seen his best yet. When Kevin Mitchell was a teammate in Seattle, he claims Griffey asked him; "Why is this game so easy?" Mitchell thinks it'll get a little tougher when the wear and tear of running into walls, and making diving catches take their toll as Griffey ages. If he plays until age 40 he could hit 800 home runs for his career.

	AB	R	HR	RBI	SB	BA	$
1994 Seattle AL	433	94	40	90	11	.323	39
1995 Seattle AL	260	52	17	42	4	.258	9
1996 *Projection* >>>	556	116	43	114	12	.311	33

GRIFFIN, TY - 2B - BB - Age 27
A Cardinals replacement player, Griffin fought injuries in 1995 but played pretty well for Double-A Arkansas. He led off four consecutive games with homers last year - thought to be a minor league record - and should start 1996 at Triple-A Louisville.

GRIFOL, PEDRO - C - BR - Age 26
There's one word for Grifol: Dee-fense. That has enabled him to play the last four years in Double-A, where he hasn't even hit his weight (205).

GRIJAK, KEVIN - 1B - BL - Age 25
When Grijak was growing up in Michigan, he had a batting cage in his yard. That explains why he's a hitter but not a very good fielder. He spent long hours in the cage with a neighbor kid named Aldo Pecorilli, who finished last season platooning with Grijak at first base for the Richmond Braves.

GRISSOM, ANTONIO - OF - BR - Age 26
It took Marquis Grissom's younger brother more than five years to get out of Class A. It doesn't appear that Antonio, who made it to Harrisburg in the Montreal organization last season, will follow in big brother's big-bucks footsteps.

GRISSOM, MARQUIS - OF - BR - Age 28
Despite his gradually improving hitting over the course of the season, Grissom has to be viewed as a big disappointment for the Braves. Expected to be the table-setter that their high-powered offense needed, he pressed too hard to succeed and sputtered through the first half of the year. With his speed and defense, Grissom can still be one of the better leadoff hitters in the league, but first he'll have to learn how to deal with life under the microscope.

	AB	R	HR	RBI	SB	BA	$
1994 Montreal NL	475	96	11	45	36	.288	34
1995 Atlanta NL	551	80	12	42	29	.258	19
1996 *Projection* >>>	580	96	14	52	37	.274	26

GROPPUSO, MIKE - 3B - BR - Age 26
Groppuso was a first round compensation pick by the Astros out of Seton Hall in 1991 who appears to be topping out at Double-A. He has never hit for a high average because of a tendency to strike out.

GROTEWOLD, JEFF - 1B - BL - Age 30
This replacement player fared pretty well in limited action with the Royals, but spent the majority of the 1995 season with Triple-A Omaha. Grotewold is a consistent hitter with good power, but is too old to make it big in the major leagues. He is, however, a handy guy to have in your organization. Once considered Philadelphia's top prospect, Grotewald had only two brief stints with the Phillies.

	AB	R	HR	RBI	SB	BA	$
1995 Kansas City AL	36	4	1	6	0	.278	-

GRUDZIELANEK, MARK - SS - BR - Age 26
The Expos would love nothing more than to trade Wil Cordero and move Grudzielanek, the MVP of the Double-A Eastern League, into the starting shortstop role. Many scouts compare Grudzielanek to Pittsburgh shortstop Jay Bell because of his steady fielding and hitting.

	AB	R	HR	RBI	SB	BA	$
1995 Montreal NL	269	27	1	20	8	.245	4
1996 *Projection* >>>	332	44	5	40	11	.268	8

GUERRERO, JUAN - IF - BR - Age 29
Guerrero lost his chance when he missed the entire 1993 season due to legal problems in the Dominican Republic.

He appears to be on the downside now and probably won't get another opportunity in the majors.

GUERRERO, PEDRO - 1B/DH - BR - Age 39
This is the same Pedro Guerrero who tore up the National League in the 1980's as a Dodger slugger.

GUREEREO, VLADIMIR - OF - BR - Age 20
Guerrero (.333 with 16 homers in A-ball) is a future star who is still developing.

GUERRERO, WILTON - SS - BR - Age 21
Guerrero led the Texas League in hitting and has shown some speed in his brief minor league career, but has exhibited no secondary offensive skills (only 19 extra base hits and 26 walks in 389 at bats). He is considered to be an excellent defensive shortstop, which may earn him a chance sooner rather than later given the Dodgers problems at that position. Maury Wills was probably the last Dodger shortstop who could actually field.

GUEVARA, GIOMAR - 2B - BR - Age 23
Guevara was the Midwest League's best defensive second baseman. For a little guy (5-8, 150), Guevara has pop.

GUIEL, AARON - 2B - BR - Age 23
Guiel showed good power and base stealing speed and he could move up quickly if he continues to hit well at higher levels. Middle infielders with the power and stolen base combination are rare, so Guiel bears watching.

GUILLEN, JOSE - OF - BR - Age 23
This young outfielder led the short-season Class A New York-Penn League with 12 home runs last season for Erie. Besides his power, he has an incredible throwing arm and draws comparisons to Raul Mondesi. What makes the story even better is that Guillen grew up with Mondesi in the Dominican Republic and considers the Los Angeles right fielder his best friend.

GUILLEN, OZZIE - SS - BL - Age 32
The heart and soul of the team, Guillen started well enough, then said some nasty things about the White Sox fans before going into an extended slump. He sulked and played listlessly for much of the year (after a personal loss). The White Sox are down on Guillen at this point and he could be platooned if he doesn't start off well in 1996.

	AB	R	HR	RBI	SB	BA	$
1994 Chicago AL	365	46	1	39	5	.288	10
1995 Chicago AL	415	50	1	41	6	.248	5
1996 Projection >>>	425	51	1	43	5	.256	5

GULAN, MIKE - OF - BR - Age 25
After beginning the season at Double-A Arkansas, Gulan became the Cardinals' minor league player of the year. He earned a late-season promotion to Triple-A Louisville and needs time there to develop. Gulan has a good glove and decent power but whiffs too much - over 100 times each of the last three seasons.

GUTIERREZ, RICKY - SS - BR - Age 25
Gutierrez was a key member of the Class-A Carolina League champions, the Kinston Indians. He contributed solid defense, plate discipline and blazing speed to the championship effort. League managers voted him as the circuit's best baserunner in a midseason survey. He is a spray-hitting 1994 28th round pick who is quite old to have never played above Class A. However, the lack of a true second baseman prospect in the organization should keep him on the upward track. At best, he has major league utilityman potential.

	AB	R	HR	RBI	SB	BA	$
1994 San Diego NL	275	27	1	28	2	.240	2
1995 Houston NL	156	22	0	12	5	.276	3
1996 Projection >>>	265	34	1	22	5	.256	2

GWYNN, CHRIS - OF - BL - Age 31
Gwynn has spent nine years in the majors as a lefty pinch-hitter, but 1995 was his worst pro season. Gwynn is not a good outfielder and has little power or speed; he's a one trick pony. Even so, he'll have to hit more than .214 to keep his major league role in 1996.

	AB	R	HR	RBI	SB	BA	$
1994 Los Angeles NL	71	9	3	13	0	.268	1
1995 Los Angeles NL	84	8	1	10	0	.214	-
1996 *Projection* >>>	50	6	1	7	0	.249	-

GWYNN, TONY - OF - BL - Age 35
Future Hall-of-Famer won another batting championship last year, and his elaborate video taping and studying of pitchers helps him to keep ahead of them. He fractured his toe on August 3 and was a little hobbled thereafter. But he hit .372 playing with the fractured toe, even better than when he was completely healthy. Amazing!

	AB	R	HR	RBI	SB	BA	$
1994 San Diego NL	419	79	12	64	5	.394	31
1995 San Diego NL	535	82	9	90	17	.368	33
1996 *Projection* >>>	551	88	10	80	14	.348	30

HACOPIAN, DEREK - OF - BR - Age 26
He has limited defensive skills, but was named as one of the "Best of the Rest" outfield prospects by USA Today Baseball Weekly. At his age, and with the Indians' stable of outfield prospects, the pressure's on him.

HAJEK, DAVE - 2B - BR - Age 28
Hajek has put together two almost identical seasons at Triple-A,(.324-7-70-12 in 1994 and .327-4-78-12 in 1995). However, in his six year career in the Houston system, he has not been considered even a marginal major league prospect until this year. He is the type of player who has to be seen every day to be appreciated. A fundamentally sound contact hitter who rarely strikes out, Hajek should be able to play in the majors if given the opportunity.

HALE, CHIP - 2B - BL - Age 31
Hale has played well for the Twins in his role as a pinch hitter/DH. He will face challenges from Brian Raabe and Mitch Simons in '96, but should keep his job for at least another year.

	AB	R	HR	RBI	SB	BA	$
1994 Minnesota AL	118	13	1	11	0	.263	0
1995 Minnesota AL	103	10	2	18	0	.262	1
1996 *Projection* >>>	130	14	2	18	0	.272	0

HALL, BILLY - 2B - BB - Age 26
Hall is a fast base-stealing second baseman who has hit as high as .356 in the lower minors. It doesn't look good that he struggled last year in the Pacific Coast League because it was his second year in the league. The Red Sox scouts saw some talent in Hall and made him a Rule V draft pick in 1993, but he couldn't cut it in spring training and was returned to the Padres. Hall needs to hit better to compete for the Padres' second base job.

HALL, JOE - OF - BR - Age 30
Recalled by Detroit for a midsummer cup of coffee, Hall is a decent fill in outfielder who is experienced and can hit .270 in a limited role.

	AB	R	HR	RBI	SB	BA	$
1994 Chicago AL	28	6	1	5	0	.393	0
1995 Toledo AAA	319	52	11	47	4	.320	
1995 Detroit AL	15	2	0	0	0	.133	-

HALL, MEL - OF - BL - Age 35
Lack of regular playing time drove Hall to Japan a few years ago. In 1995 he was a part-time player for the Chunichi Dragons, and didn't have a very good year. It's doubtful he could still play big league ball in the states.

HALTER, SHANE - SS - BR - Age 26
Halter is a great defensive shortstop with good range and an impressive arm; he just needs his bat to catch up with his fielding prowess. He has shown occasional power, but his strong suit is clearly his glove. Halter's chances of making the big leagues are nominal, but he'll have to hit a lot better to be anything more than a defensive replacement.

HAMELIN, BOB - 1B - BL - Age 28
The 1994 American League Rookie of the Year did a Joe Charboneau impression in his sophomore campaign, getting

demoted twice to Triple-A Omaha; he was a non-factor by the end of the Royals season. Hamelin will strike out a lot, but he has sufficient power to be successful as a regular DH or first baseman. However, he was struggling mightily and not seeing eye-to-eye with Royals coaches - he may need a change of scenery to get untracked. Hamelin is still a good bet for a major rebound in 1996.

	AB	R	HR	RBI	SB	BA	$
1994 Kansas City AL	312	64	24	65	4	.282	20
1995 Kansas City AL	208	20	7	25	0	.168	-
1996 *Projection* >>>	276	41	13	45	2	.223	3

HAMILTON, DARRYL - OF - BL - Age 31
The Brewers let him file for free agency without an offer. He can still run, and in another setting can be productive.

	AB	R	HR	RBI	SB	BA	$
1994 Milwaukee AL	141	23	1	13	3	.262	2
1995 Milwaukee AL	398	54	5	44	11	.271	11
1996 *Projection* >>>	398	57	5	42	12	.269	10

HAMMONDS, JEFFREY - OF - BL - Age 25
A shoulder injury caused Jeffrey Hammonds to miss most of last season. Even healthy, he is not the Rickey Henderson-type of offensive impact player the Orioles expected. He needs to improve his plate discipline as he frequently swings at the first pitch, even from wild pitchers. Hammonds also needs to learn to lay-off high fastballs, especially the very high ones.

	AB	R	HR	RBI	SB	BA	$
1994 Baltimore AL	250	45	8	31	5	.296	11
1995 Baltimore AL	178	18	4	23	4	.242	3
1996 *Projection* >>>	316	43	8	40	7	.279	9

HANEY, TODD - 2B - BR - Age 30
The Cubs really liked Haney's effort in 1995. Haney hit well for Triple-A Iowa, then was promoted in late August. He hit very well and played a lot until he got hurt. Ryne Sandberg's return will hurt his chance for regular play in 1996 but he should win a utility role.

	AB	R	HR	RBI	SB	BA	$
1994 Chicago NL	37	6	1	2	2	.162	-
1995 Chicago NL	73	11	2	6	0	.411	3
1996 *Projection* >>>	119	16	2	11	0	.270	-

HANSEN, DAVE - 3B - BL - Age 27
Hansen is a line drive hitter who excels as a pinch hitter, but keeps missing out on a chance at a regular or at least a platoon job as the Dodger third baseman. In 1994 Tim Wallach put Hansen on the bench with a great comeback season and in 1995 when Wallach was hurt, LaSorda was reluctant to give Hansen a chance at the job. If Wallach retires, Hansen may finally get a chance at the job in 1996 - he would be a .280 hitter with some (10-15 home run) power as a regular.

	AB	R	HR	RBI	SB	BA	$
1994 Los Angeles NL	44	3	0	5	0	.341	0
1995 Los Angeles NL	181	19	1	14	0	.287	2
1996 *Projection* >>>	228	23	2	23	0	.299	3

HANSEN, TERREL - 1B/OF - BR - Age 29
Hansen has always had good power but dropped to just nine homers in part-time duty at Double-A Jacksonville, while hitting only .227. The lustre has faded on this once-bright prospect. Hansen is not a good fielder, so he has to rely on his bat for a pro career; his 1995 results show he may not even be able to count on his bat, though.

HARDGE, MIKE - 2B/SS - BR - Age 24
Hardge's bat held him back in the Montreal organization. He hit better with the Red Sox top two farm teams last year. His greatest improvement was in cutting his strikeout total. He'll need to make similar gains this year to remain a prospect.

HARDTKE, JASON - 3B - BB - Age 24
The Mets acquired Hardtke from the Padres organization, and he anchored the infield for Double-A Binghamton in 1995. His batting eye makes him a top-of-the-order hitter.

HARE, SHAWN - OF - BL - Age 29
In parts of four major league seasons, Hare has never had more than 40 at bats. Don't look for him to break that barrier in 1996.

	AB	R	HR	RBI	SB	BA	$
1994 New York NL	40	7	0	2	0	.225	-
1995 Texas AL	24	2	0	2	0	.250	-

HARKRIDER, TIM - SS - BB - Age 24
The Angels drafted shortstop Tim Harkrider out of the University of Texas. He hasn't exactly set the minors on fire with his bat, which he hit .295 last year, but it was in the hitter-friendly Texas League. Harkrider is fast and has excellent fielding, skills could carry him to the majors even if he doesn't hit well.

HARLEY, QUENTIN - 2B - BB - Age 24
After a very good 1994 in Class-A, Padres infielder Quentin Harley struggled at the plate when promoted to Double-A last year, his 6th year in the minors. He needs to improve his hitting to make progress towards a Padres' major league job.

HARMES, KRIS - C - BL - Age 24
Harmes' production at the plate fell off in his Double-A debut with the Blue Jays' Knoxville farm. That's not a good sign for a player whose resume includes the words "designated hitter."

HARPER, BRIAN - C - BR - Age 36
Harper retired after going hitless in seven at bats for Oakland in 1995. He was not a good catcher, but was a good hitter for average with a little power. Harper is an example of a player who re-invented himself as a catcher after being a reserve outfielder for nine seasons with five teams.

	AB	R	HR	RBI	SB	BA	$
1994 Milwaukee AL	251	23	4	32	0	.291	6
1995 Oakland AL	7	0	0	0	0	.000	-

HARRIS, DONALD - OF - BR - Age 28
Going, going, gone. Harris never developed any plate discipline and faded out of the Rangers organization after just 40 at-bats for Triple-A Oklahoma City in 1995.

HARRIS, LENNY - 3B/2B - BL - Age 31
Once a useful role player, the veteran utility infielder did not hit in 1995 and may be at the end of the line. Harris displayed good speed, stealing 10 bases in 11 attempts but his effectiveness (along with all of the Reds reserve players) will be in question under another manager. Davey Johnson was a genius at getting the most out of his reserves

	AB	R	HR	RBI	SB	BA	$
1994 Cincinnati NL	100	13	0	14	7	.310	6
1995 Cincinnati NL	197	32	2	16	10	.208	2
1996 Projection >>>	130	15	1	12	7	.239	1

HARVEY, RAY - OF - BL - Age 27
Harvey is a marginally skilled player who has been unable to break out of Double-A in the past three seasons in the Indians' chain. He has never reached double figures in steals, his career high in homers is ten, and he's so good defensively that he winds up at DH a good percentage of the time. He has plateaued, and his days in the pros appear numbered.

HASELMAN, BILL - C - BR - Age 29
Haselman filled in well as a backup catcher, just as he has done in each of the last three years. He isn't really a very good hitter, but he can pop an occasional homer while playing once or twice a week.

	AB	R	HR	RBI	SB	BA	$
1994 Seattle AL	83	11	1	8	1	.193	-
1995 Boston AL	152	22	5	23	0	.243	1
1996 *Projection* >>>	151	22	4	20	1	.236	0

HATCHER, BILLY - OF - BR - Age 35
Hatcher's rapid descent was discussed in these pages a year ago. He can no longer run well enough to offset his otherwise below average skills. Hatcher had a chance to fill in for injured Juan Gonzalez in May, but couldn't help the Rangers. He went to Triple-A Omaha, grew bored of minor league life and retired in mid-season.

	AB	R	HR	RBI	SB	BA	$
1994 Boston AL	298	39	3	31	8	.245	7
1995 Texas AL	12	2	0	0	0	.083	-

HATCHER, CHRIS - OF - BR - Age 27
Hatcher is a power hitter who has been in the Astro system for six years. His progress has been impeded by injuries and excessive strikeouts. Hatcher was once on the 40 man roster, but was never called up. Time appears to be running out.

HATTEBERG, SCOTT - C - BL - Age 26
Already a good defensive catcher, Hatteberg had his best season for Triple-A Pawtucket, hitting .271-7-27 with more walks than strikeouts to earn his first major league cup of coffee. He'll be back for more since the Boston backup catcher job is up for grabs in 1996.

HAYES, CHARLIE - 3B - BR - Age 30
A late spring bargain signing, Hayes, an excellent fielder on turf, paid dividends in the field all season, and at the plate in the season's first half, before sharply faltering down the stretch. Hayes and the Padres' Ken Caminiti towered over the rest of the league with the glove, and Hayes was seemingly the only Phillie who didn't get injured. The Phils are posed with a dilemma for 1996 - Hayes wants a multi-year contract, but the Phils are solidly committed to starting phenom Scott Rolen in 1997.

	AB	R	HR	RBI	SB	BA	$
1994 Colorado NL	423	46	10	50	3	.288	14
1995 Philadelphia NL	529	58	11	85	5	.276	15
1996 *Projection* >>>	546	62	13	81	6	.275	14

HAZLETT, STEVE - OF - BR - Age 26
Hazlett is a young outfielder who had a good year at Triple-A (.300 batting average) and could build a career as a reserve if he could take his game a level higher.

HECHT, STEVE - BL - 2B - Age 30
Hecht is a Triple-A veteran with very little chance to play in the majors. He is a contact hitter with a little speed.

HECKER, DOUG - 1B - BR - Age 25
In his first year above A-ball, Hecker hit just .204 with below average power. He'll have to step it up quite a bit just to get noticed.

HELD, DAN - 1B - BR - Age 25
The Phils' 42nd and last draft pick in 1993, Held continued to defy the odds, as he was named the best power prospect in the Class-A Florida State League by league managers in 1995. He strikes out a ton, and needs to develop plate discipline, but when you're a 42nd round draftee, surviving this long is an accomplishment. However, any player who is 25 and has yet to reach Double-A must be viewed with some skepticism. At best, he appears to a future bat off the bench in the majors.

HELFAND, ERIC - C - BL - Age 27
Helfand posts poor offensive numbers in the hit-happy Pacific Coast League, which means his .171 career major-league average should come as no surprise.

	AB	R	HR	RBI	SB	BA	$
1994 Oakland AL	6	1	0	1	0	.167	-

	AB	R	HR	RBI	SB	BA	$
1995 Oakland AL	86	9	0	7	0	.163	
1996 Projection >>>	92	10	0	7	0	.192	-

HEMOND, SCOTT - IF/C - BR - Age 30
A reliable reserve with Oakland, Hemond had a dreadful first season with the Cardinals in 1995. One bad year isn't enough to completely ruin this guy. But if he has a second bad year, his career will be over.

	AB	R	HR	RBI	SB	BA	$
1994 Oakland AL	198	23	3	20	7	.222	4
1995 St. Louis NL	118	11	3	9	0	.144	-
1996 Projection >>>	184	20	4	17	4	.202	-

HENCE, SAM - OF - BR - Age 25
The Indians' number one sandwich pick in 1990 has absolutely no concept of the strike zone. He has never posted double figures in homers or steals, a no-no for an outfield prospect.

HENDERSON, RICKEY - OF - BR - Age 37
The greatest player of his generation, and still very productive, Henderson misses playing time due to injuries (not due to a lack of desire, despite what Tony LaRussa might think), otherwise he's a fine player. May have finally outdone peoples expectations: his actual achievements at this point are probably higher than people's perceptions of those achievements.

	AB	R	HR	RBI	SB	BA	$
1994 Oakland AL	296	66	6	20	22	.260	17
1995 Oakland AL	407	67	9	54	32	.300	27
1996 Projection >>>	447	84	11	51	32	.282	23

HERMANSEN, CHAD - SS - BR - Age 18
How good is the Pirates' first-round draft pick in 1995? So good that managers in both the short-season Class A New York-Penn League and Rookie-level Gulf Coast League selected him as their leagues' best prospect - and he was only 17 years old. He may eventually move to third base but the ultra-poised Hermansen figures to be a power-hitting threat in the big leagues - perhaps in the not-to-distant future.

HERNANDEZ, CARLOS - C - BR - Age 28
As long as he stays with the Dodgers, Hernandez has a chance to be the Charley Silvera or Bill Plummer of the 90's. His minor league statistics suggest that he is a much better hitter than he has shown so far, but he won't get a chance to show anything trapped behind Piazza.

	AB	R	HR	RBI	SB	BA	$
1994 Los Angeles NL	64	6	2	6	0	.219	-
1995 Los Angeles NL	94	3	2	8	0	.149	-
1996 Projection >>>	102	6	2	9	0	.220	-

HERNANDEZ, JOSE M. - OF - BR - Age 26
Hernandez hit for surprising power in 1996 - 28 extra-base hits in just 245 at-bats. It was the first time he'd reach double-digits in homers at any professional level. He's a good utility player who can fill-in anywhere on the infield, but his playing time will be cut by the return of Ryne Sandberg.

	AB	R	HR	RBI	SB	BA	$
1994 Chicago NL	132	18	1	9	2	.242	1
1995 Chicago NL	245	37	13	40	1	.245	6
1996 Projection >>>	221	33	5	31	2	.247	2

HERRERA, JOSE - OF - BL - Age 23
A prototype of the "tools" player so beloved of scouts, Herrera has a monster throwing arm and is a decent power-speed combination. He will likely have a major-league job by 1997 (he has yet to play at Triple-A), but is not likely to be particularly productive in the majors, based on his minor-league career. Think Grade B Devon White with half the steals and minus the Gold Glove.

	AB	R	HR	RBI	SB	BA	$
1995 Huntsville AA	358	37	6	45	9	.282	

	AB	R	HR	RBI	SB	BA	$
1995 Oakland AL	70	9	0	2	1	.243	-
1996 *Projection* >>>	127	13	1	12	2	.244	-

HIATT, PHIL - 3B/OF - BR - Age 26
Hiatt, who has big league power, came to Detroit from Kansas City late in the season. Plate discipline, injuries, and attempts to jump him past Triple-A have hindered him. Hiatt needs another year or two in the minors before he surfaces as a platoon outfielder.

	AB	R	HR	RBI	SB	BA	$
1994 Memphis AA	400	57	17	66	12	.300	
1995 Detroit AL	113	11	4	12	1	.204	0
1996 *Projection* >>>	101	10	3	12	1	.224	-

HIDALGO, RICHARD - OF - BR - Age 20
Hidalgo's 1995 numbers were not overly impressive (.266-14-59-8 at Double-A), but he projects as a major league superstar. He has exceptional tools and just needs more time to refine his skills. Rated by Baseball America as the fourth best prospect in the Texas League in 1995, Hidalgo should arrive to stay as the Astros' rightfielder sometime in 1997 at the age of 22.

HIGGINS, KEVIN - 1B - BL - Age 29
He is a poor hitter whose best shot at a major league job is as a utility infielder.

HIGGINSON, BOB - OF - BL - Age 25
Higginson broke into the Detroit lineup in '95 with an excellent first half, displaying surprising power and patience for a rookie and playing well in left field. His production declined in the second half, and he must show he can handle the rigors of a full season. Higginson will play right field in '96 if Danny Bautista isn't ready or if Phil Nevin is ready for left field - down the road he will compete with Nevin in left.

	AB	R	HR	RBI	SB	BA	$
1995 Detroit AL	410	61	14	43	6	.224	6
1996 *Projection* >>>	433	64	15	48	6	.244	8

HILL, GLENALLEN - OF - BR - Age 31
Handed a regular job for the first time in his career, Hill responded with a solid season with his 24 homers and 25 steals. Hill is a prime candidate for a falloff in 1996: he is already in his thirties, and is coming off career highs in HR, RBI and steals.

	AB	R	HR	RBI	SB	BA	$
1994 Chicago NL	269	48	10	38	19	.297	21
1995 San Francisco NL	497	71	24	86	25	.264	26
1996 *Projection* >>>	507	76	23	84	28	.264	24

HILL, LEW - OF - BB - Age 26
A raw power-speed source who is moving slowly up the Yankees farm ladder. Hill will have to improve his K/W ratio.

HINZO, TOMMY - 2B - BB - Age 31
Hinzo's last chance to play in the majors ended with the decision not to open with replacement players. His basestealing ability has waned over the last couple of seasons.

HOCKING, DENNY - SS - BB - Age 25
Hocking either will be a good backup infielder in the major leagues or a marginally successful regular. He has stayed healthy and earned a shot in Minneapolis, and the signs for '96 point toward him joining the major league club in a reserve role.

	AB	R	HR	RBI	SB	BA	$
1994 Minnesota AL	31	3	0	2	2	.323	0
1995 Salt Lake AAA	397	51	8	75	12	.282	
1995 Minnesota AL	25	4	0	3	1	.200	-
1996 *Projection* >>>	190	22	3	29	10	.244	4

HOILES, CHRIS - C - BR - Age 31
Power-hitting catcher Chris Hoiles slumped badly early in the season. He was overswinging, trying to prove that he was worth the millions of dollars from his big new contract. Finally finding the groove around the All-Star game, he pulled a hamstring requiring time on the disabled list. Hoiles finally came around to hit a solid .294 in the second half.

	AB	R	HR	RBI	SB	BA	$
1994 Baltimore AL	332	45	19	53	2	.247	12
1995 Baltimore AL	352	53	19	58	1	.250	9
1996 *Projection* >>>	419	63	24	70	1	.270	13

HOLBERT, AARON - SS - BR - Age 23
The slick-fielding Holbert is highly regarded by the Cardinals. He showed some power in his first year at Triple-A where he batted .257-9-40 with fourteen steals for Louisville. Holbert could make the final jump to the majors in 1996.

HOLBERT, RAY - SS - BR - Age 25
Holbert stumbled through his first season in the majors, hitting poorly and not displaying his usual defensive expertise. He can earn a utility infield role for the Padres, but he'll have to show more glove to keep the job in 1996. Holbert won't hit much in any case.

	AB	R	HR	RBI	SB	BA	$
1994 San Diego NL	5	1	0	0	0	.200	-
1995 San Diego NL	73	11	2	5	4	.178	0
1996 *Projection* >>>	92	14	2	5	5	.222	-

HOLIFIELD, RICK - OF - BL - Age 26
Holifield has teased the Blue Jays and now the Phillies with glimpses of tape measure home run power and blazing speed in between extended slumps featuring frequent strikeouts. His star rose with a scintillating Arizona Fall League campaign following the 1994 season, and then fell in 1995 when he failed at both Triple-A and Double-A. The Phils will be reluctant to give up on a player with such natural power/speed ability, but at his age, there must be a short-term payoff - he'll likely start 1996 at Triple-A.

HOLLANDSWORTH, TODD - OF - BL - Age 22
One of the many young Dodger outfield prospects, Hollandsworth made the team out of spring training and was a semi-regular early until injuries effectively ended his season. In the minors, Hollandsworth displayed good power and speed, and he is young enough to develop. His biggest problem will be playing time - the Dodgers have even better outfield prospects (Karim Garcia and Roger Cedeno) coming up behind him.

	AB	R	HR	RBI	SB	BA	$
1994 Albuquerque AAA	505	80	19	91	15	.285	
1995 Los Angeles NL	103	16	5	13	2	.233	2
1996 *Projection* >>>	297	40	7	35	3	.263	5

HOLLINS, DAMON - OF - BR - Age 21
Hollins' production took a dip last year in his Double-A debut with the Greenville Braves. But with 41 homers in the last two full pro seasons, Hollins remains a potential power source for Atlanta.

HOLLINS, DAVE - 3B/1B - BB - Age 29
Injuries and the addition of Charlie Hayes and Gregg Jefferies pushed Hollins out of Philadelphia in 1995. He was a bust for Boston, too, getting hurt less than a week after joining the Red Sox. Hollins has been a decent power hitter for a number of years, but he'll be lucky to start 1996 on a major league bench.

	AB	R	HR	RBI	SB	BA	$
1994 Philadelphia NL	162	28	4	26	1	.222	2
1995 Philadelphia NL	205	46	7	25	1	.229	2
1995 Boston AL	13	2	0	1	0	.154	-
1996 *Projection* >>>	335	69	10	47	1	.252	6

HOOD, DENNIS - OF - BR - Age 31
Hood has been in the minors for 10 years showing some power and stealing as many as 43 bases in a season. He was in the Braves and Mariners organizations getting as high as Triple-A. He's playing out the string in independent ball.

HORN, SAM - DH/1B - BL - Age 32
Horn still has tremendous power, but a lackluster showing in his September callup didn't help his chances of returning to the majors. His only position is as a DH.

HORNE, TYRONE - OF - BL - Age 25
Horne had a solid year at Class AA Harrisburg. He'll have to do better this year or get lost in the shuffle of Montreal's many outfield prospects.

HOSEY, DWAYNE - OF - BB - Age 29
The 1994 American Association Player of the Year finally got his shot at the big leagues after he joined the Red Sox at the end of the year. The Royals released him from Triple-A Omaha despite another good season at the plate where he again hit for average while showing good power and speed. Hosey acquitted himself well for the Red Sox and will have a chance at a platoon role in 1996.

	AB	R	HR	RBI	SB	BA	$
1995 Omaha AAA	271	59	12	50	15	.295	
1995 Boston AL	68	20	3	7	6	.338	3
1996 *Projection* >>>	156	22	6	17	6	.278	4

HOSEY, STEVE - OF - BR - Age 26
The Angels' Steve Hosey spent most of his pro baseball career in the Giants organization where he had two good years in Triple-A hitting around .290, with 15 homers, and stealing a few bases. On switching to the Angels Triple-A club, his production has decreased substantially, and he even went back to Double-A for a time. Hosey is not a prospect, and at most, he would be a fill-in 4th or 5th outfielder in the majors.

HOUSTON, TYLER - 1B - BL - Age 25
Houston has been trying to avoid the tag of first-round draft pick bust since 1989. He's no longer a catcher. He did improve his power production in his third trip through Richmond.

HOWARD, CHRIS - C - BR - Age 30
Not to be confused with White Sox farm pitcher Chris Howard who was at Nashville in 1993. Now he's stuck behind Dan Wilson.

	AB	R	HR	RBI	SB	BA	$
1994 Seattle AL	25	2	0	2	0	.200	-
1995 Tacoma AAA	268	33	4	31	0	.243	
1996 *Projection* >>>	70	6	1	8	0	.222	-

HOWARD, DAVID - SS/2B - BB - Age 29
It took a platoon-crazed manager to find a successful role for David Howard, letting Howard produce his best season ever as the righthanded half of a second base platoon. Still one of baseball's weakest hitters, Howard is an excellent and versatile fielder who can help a team in a utility role. It's a testament to how lame the Royals offense is when a "hitter" like Howard is given 255 at-bats.

	AB	R	HR	RBI	SB	BA	$
1994 Kansas City AL	83	9	1	13	3	.229	1
1995 Kansas City AL	255	23	0	19	6	.243	3
1996 *Projection* >>>	209	20	1	19	5	.242	0

HOWARD, MATT - SS/2B - BR - Age 28
Matt Howard is a shortstop and second baseman in the Orioles system who was formerly in the Dodgers organization. He has proven that he can hit Double-A and Triple-A pitching. Howard doesn't have any power, but he has stolen as many as 50 bases in a season in the minors.

HOWARD, THOMAS - OF - BB - Age 31
Howard made the most of his opportunity when Deion Sanders sprained his ankle in May. By the time Deion was ready to return, the Reds figured out that the only thing Deion could do better than Howard was get endorsements and cover wide receivers. Howard is not a great player, but his strengths (speed, defense, and hitting lefthanded) make him an ideal platoon centerfielder.

	AB	R	HR	RBI	SB	BA	$
1994 Cincinnati NL	178	24	5	24	4	.264	6
1995 Cincinnati NL	281	42	3	26	17	.302	13
1996 Projection >>>	222	32	4	23	9	.283	6

HOWITT, DANN - 1B/OF - BL - Age 32
This minor league journeyman power hitter was once Mark McGwire's chief minor league competition in the A's chain. He's now a certified nomad who had appeared in the majors in six straight seasons before falling short in 1995, when he toiled at Triple-A in the Indians' system. Howitt has a pro body at 6'5", 205, but has a big, looping swing that has been proven ineffective at the big league level. He will once again have to scramble for a minor league job in 1996, as the Indians have younger prospects who need a place to play.

HUBBARD, MIKE - C - BR - Age 25
The Cubs are extremely high on Hubbard, especially after his good campaign in his first year at triple-A. He's solid defensively behind the plate with a good arm and a decent release. He hits for average and is developing some power.

	AB	R	HR	RBI	SB	BA	$
1995 Chicago NL	23	2	0	1	0	.174	-

HUBBARD, TRENT - OF - BR - Age 31
When Hubbard was recalled from Triple-A Colorado Springs in late August last year, he was leading the Pacific Coast League in both hitting and steals. He provided a spark for the Rockies coming off the bench and during his occasional starts in center field. Hubbard could possibly stick with the Rockies in 1996 as the fifth outfielder; however, his age and the possible return of Eric Young to the outfield make this a longshot.

	AB	R	HR	RBI	SB	BA	$
1994 Colorado NL	25	3	0	3	0	.280	-
1995 Colorado Springs AAA	480	102	12	66	37	.340	
1995 Colorado NL	58	13	3	9	2	.310	2
1996 Projection >>>	101	16	3	14	4	.288	2

HUDLER, REX - OF/IF - BR - Age 35
The versatile hustling Rex Hudler played six positions last year, but mostly at second, appearing in 52 games. His style of play is reminiscent of Kirk Gibson or Mickey Hatcher, and it's a pleasure to watch him play. Hudler turned it up a notch in the second half, hitting a solid .276, but about all you can expect from him at his age is .250-260.

	AB	R	HR	RBI	SB	BA	$
1994 California AL	124	17	8	20	2	.298	6
1995 California AL	223	30	6	27	13	.265	10
1996 Projection >>>	203	27	7	27	8	.258	5

HUFF, MICHAEL - OF - BR - Age 32
Huff lost playing time to Shawn Green and to the disabled list, and when he did play, he fell back to the level he had shown with the White Sox in the early 1990s. Huff takes a walk sometimes but has no real specialty to earn him playing time. The Blue Jays dropped him from their 40-man roster during the winter, giving him the chance to sign with another team.

	AB	R	HR	RBI	SB	BA	$
1994 Toronto AL	207	31	3	25	2	.304	7
1995 Toronto AL	138	14	1	9	1	.232	-
1996 Projection >>>	162	20	2	15	2	.265	1

HUGHES, KEITH - OF - BL - Age 32
Journeyman Hughes has had limited major league stints for four different teams. He has good power against lefthanders and is a decent fielder. Despite a respectable 1995 season, Hughes has little chance of earning a big league job.

HUGHES, TROY - OF - BR - Age 25
Hughes struggled noticeably in his first year above Double-A in 1994, but recovered his batting stroke after his demotion from Richmond. Hughes has decent power and some speed, but he'll have to learn to hit breaking balls to get much farther.

HULETT, TIM - 3B/2B - BR - Age 36
The utility infielder's long and winding carer brought him briefly to St. Louis last season. He played poorly, was released and finished the year with Texas' Triple-A Oklahoma City farm club. The end is near.

	AB	R	HR	RBI	SB	BA	$
1994 Baltimore AL	92	11	2	15	0	.228	0
1995 St. Louis NL	11	0	0	0	0	.182	-

HULSE, DAVID - OF - BL - Age 28
Maybe there's a surprise in store, but Hulse has struggled now for two years, and I don't see it getting any better. With playing time, however, Hulse could steal 35 bases or more.

	AB	R	HR	RBI	SB	BA	$
1994 Texas AL	310	58	1	19	18	.255	12
1995 Milwaukee AL	339	46	3	47	15	.251	11
1996 Projection >>>	332	52	2	36	17	.256	9

HUMPHREYS, MIKE - OF - BR - Age 28
Good talent, but he's starting to look like a career minor leaguer with 85 major league at bats (the last one in 1993).

HUNDLEY, TODD - C - BB - Age 26
After a career year in 1995, Hundley is ready for more of the same in 1996. Simply stated, he has moved beyond the platoon role with which he began the season a year ago. By getting to the majors very early, on the strength of unusual defensive prowess, Hundley put up some early hitting stats that didn't indicate his potential. What you see from 1995 is what you get.

	AB	R	HR	RBI	SB	BA	$
1994 New York NL	291	45	16	42	2	.237	9
1995 New York NL	275	39	15	51	1	.280	10
1996 Projection >>>	390	55	19	64	2	.270	11

HUNTER, BRIAN L. - OF - BR - Age 25
After a spectacular season at Triple-A Tucson in 1994, Hunter was expected to start the 1995 season in Houston. However, he was a victim of the shortened spring training and started the season back in Tucson. When he was recalled in June, he provided an immediate spark and became one of the top baserunning threats in the league. He was slowed by injuries in the second half, but has established himself as the Astros' centerfielder and leadoff hitter for the foreseeable future.

	AB	R	HR	RBI	SB	BA	$
1994 Houston NL	24	2	0	0	2	.250	-
1995 Houston NL	321	52	2	28	24	.302	16
1996 Projection >>>	444	63	3	40	29	.298	20

HUNTER, BRIAN R. - 1B - BR - Age 28
The next Hector Villanueva batted only 79 times in 1995 due to a problem hamstring which he pulled at every opportunity. Hitting for power is Hunter's only skill (half of his career hits are for extra bases) and he is young enough to help a team given the opportunity. He probably won't get that opportunity with the Reds.

	AB	R	HR	RBI	SB	BA	$
1994 Cincinnati NL	256	34	15	57	0	.234	9
1995 Cincinnati NL	79	9	1	9	2	.215	0
1996 Projection >>>	75	9	3	14	0	.223	-

HUNTER, TORII - OF - BB - Age 20
The first of Minnesota's four first-round draft picks in '93. Projected as a power-speed package and center fielder.

HURST, JIMMY - OF - BR - Age 24
Hurst, a 6-6, 225-pound package of power, had trouble making contact in Class A, but nothing compared to what he experienced in Double-A. He effectively played his way out of the lineup with the White Sox farm at Birmingham.

HUSKEY, BUTCH - 3B - BR - Age 24
Huskey made solid advances mentally and physically in 1995. The International League MVP is clearly major league

ready for whatever the Mets can find for him in 1996. A crowd around third base and a minor wrist injury were his only problems going into the winter.

	AB	R	HR	RBI	SB	BA	$
1994 Norfolk AAA	474	59	10	57	16	.228	
1995 Norfolk AAA	394	66	28	87	8	.284	
1995 New York NL	90	8	3	11	1	.189	-
1996 *Projection* >>>	228	24	8	38	4	.250	4

HUSON, JEFF - SS/2B - BL - Age 31
Huson is a hustling utility infielder that Orioles Manager Phil Regan took a liking to, giving him playing time in various capacities. He produced, albeit in a modest fashion, even stealing a few bases. But Davey Johnson became the new Orioles manager, so Huson's future with the team was unclear. Huson may hook on with another team needing a versatile veteran hustling utility man.

	AB	R	HR	RBI	SB	BA	$
1994 Oklahoma City AAA	302	47	1	27	18	.301	
1995 Baltimore AL	161	24	1	19	5	.248	
1996 *Projection* >>>	193	29	2	22	5	.234	1

HYERS, TIM - SS - BL - Age 24
The Padres selected first baseman Tim Hyers from the Blue Jays in the 1993 Rule V draft. He's had some solid years in the minors, and could mature into a good hitter with power.

	AB	R	HR	RBI	SB	BA	$
1994 San Diego NL	118	13	0	7	3	.254	1
1995 Las Vegas AAA	259	46	1	23	0	.290	
1996 *Projection* >>>	124	12	0	7	1	.238	-

HYZDU, ADAM - OF - BR - Age 23
The former number one draft pick (by San Francisco in 1990) and Cincinnati native, Hyzdu (pronounced HIGHS-dew) was acquired by the Reds after failing to develop into a power hitter in the Giants system. Hyzdu turned in a decent half season in AA Chattanooga and is young enough to continue to improve.

IBANEZ, RAUL - C - BL - Age 23
The Mariners are loaded with catcher prospects. this one hit 20 homers at Class-A in 1995.

IBARRA, JESUS - 1B - BB - Age 23
MVP of the low Class-A Midwest League, Ibarra led the league in homers, was second in RBI, and drew plenty of walks. He has no speed, but shows good defense at first base. Ibarra is worth keeping an eye on.

INCAVIGLIA, PETE - OF - BR - Age 31
This one-dimensional hitter failed in his Japanese Leagues stint for the Chiba Lotte Marines, hitting below .200. It's hard to imagine that Inky's inability to put the ball in play and lack of conditioning went over well in Japan. Incaviglia may return to the US, but will have to battle for a reserve outfield role.

INGRAM, GAREY - 3B - BR - Age 25
Ingram also has played second base and the outfield, but he doesn't hit righthanded pitching well enough for anything more than a part-time role with the Dodgers. He is not surehanded at third base.

	AB	R	HR	RBI	SB	BA	$
1994 Los Angeles NL	78	10	3	8	0	.282	1
1995 Los Angeles NL	55	5	0	3	3	.200	-
1996 *Projection* >>>	70	8	1	5	2	.238	-

INGRAM, RICCARDO - OF - BR - Age 29
Ingram is an eight year pro who turned on the power at Salt Lake City this year, collecting 57 extra base hits, after several years of decent production for the Detroit organization. Ingram has improved as a hitter, and he has a future as a pinch hitter or a platoon DH.

JACKSON, BO - OF/DH - BR - Age 33
Bo knows retirement.

JACKSON, DAMIAN - SS - BR - Age 22
Jackson was on the fast track after a solid 1994 Double-A season as a 20-year old, but a subpar 1994 Arizona Fall League campaign necessitated a 1995 return to Double-A, where he stagnated. Jackson is a wild swinger (103 whiffs in 1995) who needs to learn to swing down on the ball to more effectively utilize his excellent speed (132 steals in four pro seasons). Defensively, he has great range but has a maddening tendency to botch the routine play.

JACKSON, DARRIN - OF - BR - Age 32
Yet another fading outfielder whose career was revived by a year in rightfield at Comiskey Park, Jackson spent 1995 as one of the Seibu Lions better power threats. He has expressed an interest in returning to the US and would be a fine platoon player who can hit .280 with occasional power.

JACKSON, JEFF - OF - BR - Age 24
The legend of the "Guy Picked Before Frank Thomas" continued to grow. He has struck out once every three at bats in his six-year pro career.

JACKSON, JOHN - OF - BL - Age 29
Jackson is a weak-bat singles-type of hitter who can steal some bases.

JACKSON, RYAN - OF - BL - Age 24
The Marlins' 1994 seventh round pick was named the best batting prospect and most exciting player in the Class-A Midwest League in 1995. Jackson does have a smooth lefthanded swing with gap power and a good eye, but he's essentially a college graduate playing with kids a year removed from high school. The Marlins will likely jump him to Double-A in 1996 - expect him to struggle against the stronger competition.

JACOBS, FRANK - 1B - BL - Age 28
Despite the distraction of playing for four different teams last season, Jacobs had the best power production of his four-year career. He'll be forever known as a former Notre Dame tight end. For now, he'd settle for being known as a Montreal Expo.

JAHA, JOHN - 1B - BR - Age 29
He showed grit and determination in coming back from a dreadful 1994 campaign. Inconsistency is a trait, and we might be in the midst of a player experiencing the good year-bad year syndrome. If so, 1996 will be a bummer.

	AB	R	HR	RBI	SB	BA	$
1994 Milwaukee AL	291	45	12	39	3	.241	8
1995 Milwaukee AL	316	59	20	65	2	.313	15
1996 *Projection* >>>	387	67	20	67	2	.275	13

JAMES, CHRIS - OF - BR - Age 33
An aging, veteran hitter, James was infrequently used by the Royals before he joined the Red Sox pennant drive - his fourth team in three seasons. He can pop an occasional homer, but he's weak in most areas of the game. James refused a minor league assignment to become a free agent at season's end; he'll battle for a pinch-hitting role in 1996.

	AB	R	HR	RBI	SB	BA	$
1994 Texas AL	133	28	7	19	0	.256	3
1995 Two Teams	82	8	2	8	1	.268	0
1996 *Projection* >>>	127	19	4	16	1	.248	0

JAMES, DION - OF - BL - Age 33
About as overlooked as anyone who has hit .304 over the last five years in the majors, James quietly became important after the Yankees jettisoned Luis Polonia in late 1995. He can play left field, first base or DH, pinch hit, and even steal a base. Much as Buck Showalter made use of these diverse talents, a new manager offers hope that this veteran off-the-bench type can remain valuable.

	AB	R	HR	RBI	SB	BA	$
1995 New York AL	209	22	2	26	4	.287	5
1996 *Projection* >>>	190	20	1	24	4	.287	3

JAVIER, STAN - OF - BB - Age 32
Javier has made the most of his return to Oakland. He's aging and will never steal 36 bases in a season again.

	AB	R	HR	RBI	SB	BA	$
1994 Oakland AL	419	75	10	44	24	.272	24
1995 Oakland AL	442	81	8	56	36	.278	26
1996 Projection >>>	398	69	7	49	25	.276	19

JEFFERIES, GREGG - 1B - BB - Age 28
Based on a first glance at Jefferies' 1995 numbers, one might conclude that he had an excellent season. However, he fell well short of his established production level of the previous two seasons, padded his stats with a late season run after the Phils dropped out of the race. He was nagged by a persistent hamstring injury, which drained him of his speed, the one attribute which sets him apart from the rest of the first base population. He's still in his prime, and should rack up another .300 season in 1996, with more steals - he will never steal 30 again, however.

	AB	R	HR	RBI	SB	BA	$
1994 St. Louis NL	397	52	12	55	12	.325	25
1995 Philadelphia AL	480	69	11	56	9	.306	18
1996 Projection >>>	545	77	14	69	16	.310	24

JEFFERSON, REGGIE - DH - BB - Age 27
Jefferson spent most of the year on the disabled list, but was a key player when replacing Jose Canseco during his injury. He's a switch-hitter in name only; Jefferson is a much better hitter against righthanded pitching. He'll only get a bench role for the Red Sox, but would be excellent in a platoon first base role somewhere else, hitting over .300 with occasional power.

	AB	R	HR	RBI	SB	BA	$
1994 Seattle AL	162	24	8	32	0	.327	8
1995 Boston AL	121	21	5	26	0	.289	3
1996 Projection >>>	186	28	8	34	0	.295	5

JENNINGS, DOUG - 1B - BL - Age 31
The ex-Cub, ex-A's pinch hitter may have earned a return to the majors with a big season at Indianapolis, leading the team in doubles, homers, RBI and walks. There's no opportunity in Cincinnati, but Jennings could contribute in another situation.

JENNINGS, LANCE - C - BR - Age 24
A fine defensive catcher with a good arm, Jennings hasn't taken a step forward in three years and has barely hit his weight above Class A. Jennings strikes out too often for a low power hitter.

JENNINGS, ROBIN - OF - BL - Age 24
Jennings stepped up to the Cubs' Double-A farm at Orlando and had the best power season of his four-year career. He has a right field arm, but does not have base-stealing speed. His sweet swing should get him to Iowa, and possibly to Chicago, this season. He was the best hitter in the 1995 Arizona Fall League.

JENSEN, MARCUS - C - BB - Age 23
The Giants' catcher of the future, his hitting continued to improve at Double-A in 1995. He has no power or speed, but is probably a better hitter than Kirt Manwaring. Jensen should make the majors in 1997.

JETER, DEREK - SS - BR - Age 22
A first round pick who's blossomed fully, Jeter is major league ready. After he filled in capably for an injured Tony Fernandez in 1995, there was a telling moment when Fernandez finally came off the DL (after talking for some time about being 100% healthy). In his first game back, Fernandez played second base with Jeter at short.

	AB	R	HR	RBI	SB	BA	$
1994 Albany AA	122	17	2	13	12	.377	
1994 Columbus AAA	126	25	3	16	10	.349	
1995 Columbus AAA	486	96	2	45	20	.317	
1995 New York AL	48	5	0	7	0	.250	-
1996 Projection >>>	388	66	4	57	12	.274	12

JETER, SHAWN - OF - BL - Age 29
Good runner and a good outfielder, Jeter surfaced with the White Sox in 1992.

JOHNS, KEITH - SS - BR - Age 24
Another potential Gold Glove shortstop in the Cardinals farm system, Johns took a big step forward at the plate in 1995. He added 52 points to his batting average with more walks than strikeouts while advancing to Double-A for the first time. Johns has little power, but can get to the majors quickly if he can continue his progress for Louisville in 1996.

JOHNSON, BRIAN D. - C - BR - Age 28
Johnson is a good back-up catcher. He hit well in a short stretch in June: in six starts going 10 for 23 with three doubles, two home runs, and eight RBI. He hit a nice .286 in the second half albeit in only 98 at-bats.

	AB	R	HR	RBI	SB	BA	$
1994 San Diego NL	93	7	3	16	0	.247	1
1995 San Diego NL	207	20	3	29	0	.251	2
1996 *Projection* >>>	179	16	3	26	0	.255	0

JOHNSON, CHARLES - C - BR - Age 24
After a disappointing offensive first half of his rookie season, Johnson batted over .300 with extra base power in the second half. Defensively, he was nothing less than the best defensive catcher in the NL, throwing out 42.7% of opposing basestealers. Now that Johnson has apparently gotten his bearings offensively, he is primed for a breakout season in 1996. Expect Johnson to ascend to the All Star level sometime in the next two seasons.

	AB	R	HR	RBI	SB	BA	$
1994 Florida NL	11	5	1	4	0	.455	0
1995 Florida NL	315	40	11	39	0	.251	6
1996 *Projection* >>>	417	56	15	54	0	.246	6

JOHNSON, ERIK - 2B - BR - Age 30
This journeyman infielder had a fine year for the Pirates' Triple-A Calgary farm club in 1995. He played in nine games for San Francisco in 1993-94 and could resurface in the majors if someone is short a utility infielder.

JOHNSON, HOWARD - 3B - BB - Age 35
Johnson got a few key hits as a pinch-hitter for the Cubs in 1995, but is essentially washed up as a pro. He'll be lucky to snare a Triple-A contract in 1996.

	AB	R	HR	RBI	SB	BA	$
1994 Colorado NL	227	30	10	40	11	.211	10
1995 Chicago NL	169	26	7	22	1	.195	1
1996 *Projection* >>>	133	19	6	19	3	.206	0

JOHNSON, LANCE - OF - BL - Age 32
Johnson suddenly turned on the power in the second half of 1995. After seven career homers in seven-and-a-half years in the majors, he connected for ten in the last half of the year, slugging over .700. Of course, he still stole a bagful of bases and finished second to Kenny Lofton with twelve triples, so the great speed is still there. Johnson is considered a good defensive centerfielder but is probably overrated since he plays too deep; he robs some extra-base hits, but lets too many singles fall in front of him. Look for more of the same speed and defense from Johnson in 1996, but don't expect the same kind of power.

	AB	R	HR	RBI	SB	BA	$
1994 Chicago AL	412	56	3	54	26	.277	24
1995 Chicago AL	607	98	10	57	40	.306	35
1996 *Projection* >>>	573	87	7	59	33	.298	25

JOHNSON, MARK - C - BL - Age 20
Johnson was the 1994 first-round draft choice of the White Sox. He's considered a strong defensive catcher.

JOHNSON, MARK - 1B - BL - Age 28
Johnson was the talk of spring training for the Pirates last year with his tape-measure homers. He hit some blasts in Pittsburgh but they came too infrequently and he ended the season on Triple-A Calgary's disabled list with a broken

thumb. He's 28 years old and had spent three straight seasons in Double-A before last year. One senses that last season was as good as it'll ever get.

	AB	R	HR	RBI	SB	BA	$
1995 Pittsburgh NL	221	32	13	28	5	.208	5
1996 Projection >>>	189	28	9	24	4	.211	1

JOHNSON, MATT - SS - BR - Age 25
When he did play, he did little to make anyone take notice. He has almost no power and doesn't make much contact. Johnson will be lucky to stay at Double-A in 1996.

JOHNSON, RUSS - SS - BR - Age 23
Johnson was the Southeastern Conference Player of the Year at LSU in 1994 and began his professional career at Double-A Jackson in 1995 (.248-9-53-10). He is the top shortstop prospect in the Astro organization. Johnson has some power and speed and could have a chance to move up to the majors by 1997 if Orlando Miller moves to third base.

JONES, ANDRUW - OF - BR - Age 19
Just what the Braves need: another budding superstar outfielder. It will take another couple of years for this youngster to reach major league productivity, but when he arrives he will be a huge success. Right now it's too early even to guess at a limit of Jones' big potential. He can do it all.

JONES, CHIPPER - 3B - BB - Age 23
The injury-delayed emergence of Jones as a quality major league hitter was finally realized in 1995 as he put up numbers worthy of Rookie-of-the-Year consideration. He has a quick bat, growing power and slings just enough leather to succeed at third base. Jones is very young and very good; he's ready to have a breakout year in 1996 or 1997.

	AB	R	HR	RBI	SB	BA	$
1994			Did Not Play				
1995 Atlanta NL	524	87	23	86	8	.265	19
1996 Projection >>>	528	92	26	88	8	.288	22

JONES, CHRIS - OF - BR - Age 30
Jones became a Dallas Green favorite in 1995, with a productive mixture of pinch hitting and starting against southpaws. Although limited to part time duty, it was probably Jones' career year. If the Mets are serious about developing their budding stars in the outfield and at first base, they will have to give them all real chances to hit lefties, meaning less time for Jones.

	AB	R	HR	RBI	SB	BA	$
1994 Colorado NL	40	6	0	2	0	.300	-
1995 New York NL	182	33	8	31	2	.280	
1996 Projection >>>	161	28	6	25	3	.270	3

JONES, DAX - OF - BR - Age 25
He might have a career as a fourth or fifth outfielder, but Jones has little power, decent but not great speed, and won't hit for average in the majors.

JONES, JAIME - OF - BL - Age 19
The Marlins snatched the San Diego high school phenom with their 1995 first round draft choice. He was considered to be the best all around hitter - including the eligible collegians - in his draft class. He has all the tools - power, speed, an excellent right field throwing arm. The only question is his ability to adjust to the wooden bat - keep a close eye on him at Class-A in 1996 - he has a scary upside.

JONES, KEITH - OF - BL - Age 24
Jones can hit for average, has excellent speed and a decent glove. His biggest problem in 1995 with Double-A Arkansas was a scuffle involving fans at a game in Wichita, for which Jones was given a 30-day suspension by the Texas League. He didn't return to Arkansas after the incident. His status with the Cardinals organization at the end of 1995 was unclear.

JONES, TERRY - OF - BR - Age 25
Jones is one of those slap-hitting fast guys, on the order of Kenny Lofton, Otis Nixon and Brett Butler. He'll probably move from Double-A to Triple-A in the Rockies organization in 1996. Jones stole 51 bases at New Haven in 1995, but his plate discipline needs to improve.

JONES, TIM - SS - BL - Age 33
This veteran utilityman was Indians' Triple-A second baseman. Has managed to cram less than a season's worth of major league at-bats into six years. He has no bat and the best he can hope for is a 25th-man role on someone's major league roster.

JORDAN, BRIAN - OF - BR - Age 29
The multi-talented Jordan finally blossomed into the player the Cardinals hoped he would become, posting a 20-20 season and giving promise that a 30-30 season could be in the offing. He has everything you want: power, speed and defense. The former Atlanta Falcons defensive back has finally gotten football completely out of his blood. He turned down an offer from the Oakland Raiders last September and signed a three-year, baseball-only deal with the Cardinals.

	AB	R	HR	RBI	SB	BA	$
1994 St. Louis NL	178	14	5	15	4	.258	5
1995 St. Louis NL	490	83	22	81	24	.296	28
1996 *Projection* >>>	508	76	20	83	21	.288	24

JORDAN, KEVIN - 2B - BR - Age 26
As if the rookie needed any additional pressure, Phils' owner Bill Giles explained the late season departure of old hand Mariano Duncan by declaring that Jordan was a better player than Duncan. Maybe someday soon. Jordan, like Duncan, has impressive power for a middle infielder, and to a fault, loves to swing the bat. He doesn't have Duncan's speed, but is similar defensively. He only hit .048 against major league righthanders (1 for 21), but could earn a platoon role with Mickey Morandini.

	AB	R	HR	RBI	SB	BA	$
1995 Scranton WB AAA	410	61	5	60	3	.310	
1995 Philadelphia NL	54	6	2	6	0	.185	-
1996 *Projection* >>>	108	12	1	12	0	.232	-

JORDAN, RICKY - 1B - BR - Age 30
Jordan has quickly diminished from a regular first baseman for the Phillies to a pinch-hitter, to a bad Triple-A player. Since he simply won't take a pitch, Jordan will have to hit more than the .222-2-9 season he posted at Triple-A Vancouver. He's not done yet, but he's very close.

	AB	R	HR	RBI	SB	BA	$
1994 Philadelphia NL	220	29	8	37	0	.282	7
1996 *Projection* >>>	75	10	3	12	0	.260	-

JORGENSEN, RANDY - 1B - BL - Age 23
Jorgensen was the California League's best defensive first baseman, but hasn't shown he can hit. He has played the outfield, but doesn't have much speed.

JORGENSEN, TERRY - 3B - BR - Age 29
After contending for the Twins' major league third base job for several years, Jorgensen officially cemented his journeyman status with a mediocre Triple-A season in the Marlins' organization. Despite his impressive 6'4", 213 lbs., build, Jorgensen does not generate much extra base power, and he might have to find another organization for 1996, as the Marlins would like to take a look at Lou Lucca at Triple-A. He'll find a job and hang around for a while, with little chance for eventual major league success.

JOSE, FELIX - OF - BB - Age 30
Felix came to the Royals spring training camp overweight and out of shape. He hit and fielded poorly, ran the bases slowly and earned a benching; when his attitude became unbearable Jose was released. A tryout with the Cubs was an abject failure and Jose was completely out of work by June. He can still play ball, but only if he can overcome a severe ego problem and get himself back into playing shape.

	AB	R	HR	RBI	SB	AVG	$
1995 Kansas City AL	30	2	0	1	0	.133	-

JOYNER, WALLY - 1B - BL - Age 33
Another season of low power and high batting average kept Joyner among the lower half of the league's first basemen. For the Royals his RBI production was important; his controlled swing results in base hits, but not many extra bases. 500 plate appearances in 1995 forced the Royals to extend his contract, but they put him on the trade block.

	AB	R	HR	RBI	SB	BA	$
1994 Kansas City AL	363	52	8	57	3	.311	16
1995 Kansas City AL	465	69	12	83	3	.310	17
1996 Projection >>>	516	73	13	81	3	.304	18

JUSTICE, DAVID - OF - BL - Age 29
He just can't seem to string together any consistent offensive production. Sometimes he's a good line drive hitter, other times he's hitting for power, and sometimes he's not hitting much at all. For the Braves offense to succeed, Justice has to step forward and be the kind of hitter his fluid swing says he can be. He's capable of league-leading power numbers, if he can only be more consistent at the plate.

	AB	R	HR	RBI	SB	BA	$
1994 Atlanta NL	352	61	19	59	2	.313	20
1995 Atlanta NL	411	73	24	78	4	.253	15
1996 Projection >>>	484	84	28	89	4	.272	18

KARKOVICE, RON - C - BR - Age 32
Karkovice is one of baseball's very best defensive catchers; he throws very well. He has become a useful hitter, within limits; he draws some walks and has some power to offset his low batting average and numerous strikeouts. He can't catch more than 125 games or he breaks down, so a quality backup catcher is needed to support Karkovice.

	AB	R	HR	RBI	SB	BA	$
1994 Chicago AL	207	33	11	29	0	.213	3
1995 Chicago AL	323	44	13	51	2	.217	4
1996 Projection >>>	345	50	15	52	2	.217	3

KARROS, ERIC - 1B - BR - Age 28
Karros turned in an "Age 27" breakout year, setting career highs in almost everything. He took more walks, and also struck out more while posting a batting average 44 points over his career average. Karros is extremely durable, missing only eight games in the last three seasons. I would not expect him to maintain the MVP candidate level he reached in 1995, but I would not expect him to crash to his 1994 level either.

	AB	R	HR	RBI	SB	BA	$
1994 Los Angeles NL	406	51	14	46	2	.266	12
1995 Los Angeles NL	551	83	32	105	4	.298	27
1996 Projection >>>	584	79	27	91	3	.270	18

KATZAROFF, ROBBIE - OF - BR - Age 27
A true minor league journeyman. He's a fine Double-A player, who slashes line drives to all fields, consistently makes contact, is willing to take a walk, and who is an accomplished basestealer. Unfortunately, he just doesn't have the physical tools to excel at the next level. A seventh minor league season with a fifth organization could be in the offing.

KEENE, ANDRE - 1B - BL - Age 25
Keene plays poor defense, is too old to be stuck at Class A, and is reputed to be a head case, but he has some power and is as patient a hitter as you'll find. He's not much of a prospect at this point, but could have one surprising season at the major-league level in his late twenties, if he ever makes the majors.

KELLNER, FRANK - SS - BB - Age 29
Kellner has split time between Triple-A Tucson and Double-A Jackson for the past four years and will probably continue to do so for the remainder of his career.

KELLY, MIKE - OF - BR - Age 25
Kelly's limited playing time was primarily due to the addition of Lonnie Smith as the Braves' primary righthanded bat

off of the bench. Kelly still chases too many bad pitches, as evidenced by his 49 Ks in just 137 at-bats - he struck out at a similar rate in Richmond. While he has some power and decent speed, Kelly's playing time won't increase until his batting eye improves.

	AB	R	HR	RBI	SB	BA	$
1994 Atlanta NL	77	14	2	9	0	.273	1
1995 Atlanta NL	137	26	3	17	7	.190	2
1996 Projection >>>	125	23	3	15	4	.232	0

KELLY, PAT - 2B - BR - Age 28
A superb athlete with an injury bug that rivals Geronimo Pena's for persistence, it was a wrist ligament that took Kelly out for five weeks and put him through an 0-for-23 slump when he returned in 1995. By year end, utilityman Randy Velarde had taken the second base job away. Now if Kelly could just stay healthy, if if if ...

	AB	R	HR	RBI	SB	BA	$
1994 New York AL	286	35	3	41	6	.280	10
1995 New York AL	270	32	4	29	8	.237	5
1996 Projection >>>	343	41	5	42	9	.256	6

KELLY, ROBERTO - OF - BR - Age 31
Once an intriguing power/speed combination, Kelly is now more notable for his odyssey around the National League, playing for four teams in two years. He has now been traded for Paul O'Neill, Deion Sanders, Tony Tarasco, and Henry Rodriguez, among others. One reason for his frequent trades is that he has become, as Bill James puts it, a Juan Samuel. Kelly has a little power, but not enough to hit in the middle of the lineup. He has some speed, but doesn't walk enough to hit at the top of the lineup. He can play a key defensive position (centerfield) but not very well. Kelly is not going to keep any of the Dodger outfield prospects out of the lineup if they have a strong spring.

	AB	R	HR	RBI	SB	BA	$
1994 Cincinnati - Atlanta NL	434	73	9	45	19	.293	23
1995 Two Teams	504	58	7	57	19	.278	17
1996 Projection >>>	534	71	9	59	22	.285	20

KENDALL, JASON - C - BR - Age 21
The Pirates' top pick in the 1992 draft, Kendall emerged as a potential All-Star catcher last season as he was named MVP of the Double-A Southern League. His defensive abilities are already major-league caliber and now he's learning to hit. Kendall should be the Pirates' starting catcher this year and for many years to come.

	AB	R	HR	RBI	SB	BA	$
1995 Carolina AA	429	87	8	71	10	.326	
1996 Projection >>>	209	31	4	30	2	.256	2

KENDALL, JEREMY - OF - BR - Age 24
After ranking second in the minors in 1994 with 62 stolen bases, his major league aspirations were dealt a severe blow when he suffered a badly broken arm in the first week of the 1995 season, costing him most of the campaign. After his return, his timing was way off, and he performed abysmally with the bat, striking out every third at bat. Though the blazing speed remains, he must quickly make up for lost time in 1996 to rate an eventual chance at a big league backup job.

KENNEDY, DARRYL - C - BR - Age 27
Kennedy is a capable receiver who hasn't hit well enough to advance past Double-A. He looks a lot like a career minor leaguer at this point.

KENT, JEFF - 2B - BR - Age 28
Although his full-year numbers remained consistent with his 1993-1994 level, Kent was steadier in 1995, with fewer/shorter streaks and slumps. With enough power to be a productive cornerman, Kent may shift to third base in '96. If he stays at second, he will be one of the best hitters at the position.

	AB	R	HR	RBI	SB	BA	$
1994 New York NL	415	53	14	68	1	.292	17
1995 New York NL	472	65	20	65	3	.278	15
1996 Projection >>>	533	72	21	79	3	.282	17

KESSINGER, KEITH - SS - BB - Age 29
Kessinger struggled at Triple-A Iowa after he got a leg infection late in the season. Don's son got a brief cup of coffee with the Reds in 1993. The Cubs have probably given up on the "good-field, no-hit" Kessinger.

KEY, JEFF - OF - BL - Age 21
To date, Key has not justified his high draft status (Phils' fourth round pick in 1993), as he has yet to rise above Class-A. He has shown power possibilities, and has a 6'1", 200 lbs., body, but he has been overaggressive, posting a 180/47 strikeout/walk ratio over the past two seasons. For Key to have a material shot at future major league duty, he needs to become more patient, or he will be eaten up by the pitching at higher levels.

KIESCHNICK, BROOKS - OF - BL - Age 23
The Cubs' top prospect, Kieschnick led the American Association with 23 homers for Triple-A Iowa. A 1993 top draft pick out of Texas, he has a ton of power, but needs to be more selective at the plate - he strikes out way too much. In the outfield, he has an incredible arm. The Cubs will move him along quickly; look for Kieschnick in Wrigley this year.

KILLEEN, TIM - C - BL - Age 25
The Padres obtained catcher Tim Killeen from the Oakland A's who drafted him out of the University of Iowa. He has shown power in the minors, but he has a big swing striking out 30 per cent of the time, a figure that he reaches every year indicating that he is not improving.

KIMBERLIN, KEITH - SS - BB - Age 29
Formerly a Tigers prospect, Kimberlin is a speedy spray hitter who gets the most out of his ability. In the event of an injury to Kevin Stocker, Kimberlin and Kim Batiste are about the only alternatives.

KING, ANDRE - OF - BR - Age 22
The Braves second round pick in 1993, King is a speedy Jamaican who has yet to advance past A-ball. He had almost the same year for Durham in 1995 that he had at Macon in 1994; low power, good speed with a ton of whiffs. King needs to show better plate discipline if he hopes to advance, now in the White Sox system.

KING, BRETT - SS - BR - Age 23
You can't steal first base, which pretty much ensures that this speedster won't make the majors.

KING, JEFF - 3B/1B - BR - Age 31
Just when you want to write him off, King rebounds with a good season. It happened again last year as King came back from a horrible 1994. He can be very good and he can be very bad. Which will King be in '96? Flip a coin.

	AB	R	HR	RBI	SB	BA	$
1994 Pittsburgh NL	339	36	5	42	3	.263	8
1995 Pittsburgh NL	445	61	18	87	7	.265	16
1996 Projection >>>	504	62	14	83	6	.253	11

KINGERY, MIKE - OF - BL - Age 35
Kingery's base salary of $600,000 in 1995 makes him an attractive package for the Rockies in 1996 in an otherwise high-priced outfield. His numbers declined substantially from those he posted in 1994, but his hustle, defensive skills and gritty determination make him an excellent fourth outfielder, notwithstanding his advancing age. Kingery became a free agent after the 1995 season.

	AB	R	HR	RBI	SB	BA	$
1995 Colorado NL	350	66	8	37	13	.269	11
1996 Projection >>>	300	51	6	35	8	.281	9

KIRALY, JEFF - 1B - BL - Age 22
Kiraly was the South Atlantic League's best defensive first baseman in his second season in the league in 1994, but he neither makes contact nor hits for power.

KIRBY, WAYNE - OF - BL - Age 32
Kirby's 1994 platoon role diminished into a 1995 fourth outfielder role as Manny Ramirez developed into a full-time

bomber. Kirby is above average defensively, and has retained a significant portion of his speed despite his advancing age. With minor leaguer Brian Giles a cheaper, more talented alternative, Kirby will be hard pressed to retain a job in Cleveland in 1996. He is a veteran presence who should fill a similar role elsewhere in 1996, with double-digit steal potential.

	AB	R	HR	RBI	SB	BA	$
1994 Cleveland AL	191	33	5	23	11	.293	12
1995 Cleveland AL	188	29	1	14	10	.207	3
1996 Projection >>>	135	21	2	13	6	.246	1

KLESKO, RYAN - OF - BL - Age 24
Only an injury and early season slump prevented Klesko from having a truly spectacular year; Klesko hit .331 and slugged .680 over the last four months of the year. Instead he had to settle for an unexpectedly good batting average, fine power and improving defensive skills. Klesko will be the Braves regular leftfielder in 1996; expect big things from this budding star.

	AB	R	HR	RBI	SB	BA	$
1994 Atlanta NL	245	42	17	47	1	.278	12
1995 Atlanta NL	329	48	23	70	5	.310	19
1996 Projection >>>	452	69	28	86	5	.300	21

KMAK, JOE - C - BR - Age 32
Kmak is a second string catcher at best; he's really just a Triple-A extension of the major league bench. Kmak hit just .173 for Triple-A Iowa in 1995 and will have to battle for any major league time he gets.

	AB	R	HR	RBI	SB	BA	$
1995 Chicago NL	53	7	1	6	0	.245	-

KNOBLAUCH, CHUCK - 2B - BR - Age 27
Knoblauch erased any remaining doubts about his game in '95 with a masterful campaign. He was extremely consistent as he led Minnesota in walks, set career highs in home runs and stolen bases, and played a Gold Glove caliber second base. Among the majors' second basemen, he ranks alongside Carlos Baerga and Craig Biggio, and is only a level below Roberto Alomar.

	AB	R	HR	RBI	SB	BA	$
1994 Minnesota AL	445	85	5	51	35	.312	35
1995 Minnesota AL	538	107	11	63	46	.333	41
1996 Projection >>>	590	106	9	65	46	.310	32

KNAPP, MIKE - C - BR - Age 31
Catcher Mike Knapp has spent 10 years in the minors, about five of them in Triple-A, without getting a call up to the show. He usually gets a job with an organization needing a fill-in catcher, temporarily playing in the high minors until a younger prospect is ready, or when one is promoted.

KNORR, RANDY - C - BR - Age 27
When Pat Borders left, Knorr had his chance to take over as the regular catcher and didn't take it. His throwing arm is inadequate and now his hitting seems to have disappeared. Knorr may be in the majors in 1996, but not likely as an everyday player.

	AB	R	HR	RBI	SB	BA	$
1994 Toronto AL	124	20	7	19	0	.242	3
1995 Toronto AL	132	18	3	16	0	.212	-
1996 Projection >>>	151	22	5	21	0	.225	-

KOELLING, BRIAN - 2B - BR - Age 26
The Phils acquired Koelling from the Reds for Mariano Duncan late in the 1995 season. He is a quick, slick-fielding middle infielder with no power or selectivity at the plate. He hits for a decent average in the minors, but would be totally overmatched at the major league level, as he was in his brief 1993 trial with the Reds. He should settle in as a perennial Triple-A player in the intermediate future.

KONERKO, PAUL - C - BR - Age 20
Konerko was the 1994 first-round draft pick by the Dodgers, who apparently have tired of choosing pitchers as number one busts. They lured the high school star away from Arizona State.

KOPRIVA, DAN - 3B - BR - Age 26
Having torn up Winston-Salem for more than a year, Kopriva earned a promotion to Double-A Chattanooga where he matched his career average of .281, but with little power. Unless he can pick up his run production, he's not a prospect.

KOSCO, BRYN - 3B - BL - Age 29
Kosco is your basic power hitter who strike out too much. He's an average fielder and the Cubs haven't given up on him yet, but he needs to have a great season in 1996 to have any chance at the majors.

KOSLOFSKI, KEVIN - OF - BL - Age 29
Long-time Royals prospect Koslofski platooned at Triple-A New Orleans in 1995, hitting just .212 with 100 strikeouts in 312 at-bats. He has "career minor leaguer" written all over him.

KOWITZ, BRIAN - OF - BL - Age 26
Kowitz was a career minor leaguer before earning a 10-game promotion to Atlanta last season. He contributes to his team by getting on base by hook or crook, stealing occasionally and playing good defense.

	AB	R	HR	RBI	SB	BA	$
1995 Atlanta NL	24	3	0	3	0	.167	-

KREMBLAS, FRANK - 3B/2B - BR - Age 29
A utility player who can play any position, Kremblas was mainly used as a reserve for Triple-A Indianapolis before being demoted to Double-A Chattanooga. He has a great work ethic, but is on the downhill side of his career.

KREMERS, JIMMY - C - BL - Age 30
This journeyman has traversed five organizations in his eight pro seasons and even managed 73 major league at bats (with only eight hits) as a Brave in 1990. His 1995 outpost was the Marlins' Double-A Charlotte affiliate, where he was a platoon catcher and designated hitter. His always suspect bat is not improving - he is a .239 career hitter with decent power who strikes out 22% of the time. He may have drawn his last pro paycheck.

KREUTER, CHAD - C - BB - Age 31
Too many good young Mariner catchers for Kreuter to be much of a factor. He had his career year in Detroit a couple years ago and is now strictly a third stringer if he remains on a major league roster.

	AB	R	HR	RBI	SB	BA	$
1994 Detroit AL	170	17	1	19	0	.224	-
1995 Seattle AL	75	12	1	8	0	.227	-
1996 Projection >>>	79	10	1	9	0	.239	-

KREVOKUCH, JIM - 3B - BR - Age 26
A scrappy utility infielder who has never played above Double-A, Krevokuch was slated to be on the Pirates' opening-day roster if replacement ball had lasted. That was his best hope at ever appearing in a major-league game.

KRUK, JOHN - 1B - BL - Age 35
Kruk gave up his gardening career to return for part of the 1995 season. He proved that he could still hit, but was so badly out of shape that he faded badly over the season and retired in August. It's back to the garden for one of the game's most enjoyable characters...

	AB	R	HR	RBI	SB	BA	$
1994 Philadelphia NL	255	35	5	38	4	.302	10
1995 Chicago AL	159	13	2	23	0	.308	3

LADELL, CLEVELAND - OF - BR - Age 25
The second time around was much better for Ladell at Double-A Chattanooga. He reached career highs in batting average and stolen bases. He'll need to succeed in Triple-A this year to have a chance with the Reds.

LAKER, TIM - C - BR - Age 26
A long-time favorite of Expos manager Felipe Alou, Laker went back to Triple-A Ottawa in 1994 and had an outstanding season. He returned to the majors in 1995 and didn't do so well. However, Alou has made it clear that he wants Laker to replace Darrin Fletcher as the Expos' starting catcher in 1996.

	AB	R	HR	RBI	SB	BA	$
1995 Montreal NL	141	17	3	20	0	.234	1

LAMPKIN, TOM - C - BL - Age 32
Lampkin had one of the more narrow job descriptions in the majors in 1995, as the number two lefty-hitting backup catcher for the Giants. He could conceivably aspire to moving up to the number one lefty-hitting backup catcher for some team.

	AB	R	HR	RBI	SB	BA	$
1995 San Francisco NL	76	8	1	9	2	.276	1
1996 Projection >>>	72	7	1	8	1	.236	-

LANDRUM, CEDRIC - OF - BL - Age 32
Landrum started the 1995 campaign as a replacement player, then was retained at Triple-A after the non-settlement. He played irregularly, stole enough bases to keep his reputation, and provided Colorado Springs with some slap-hitting on their way to the Pacific Coast League championship. Landrum gave us the "Cedric Landrum" principle when he stole 27 bases in 86 at-bats, thus proving that you must back out pinch running stats when analyzing a hitter's full-season potential. Landrum played in Coors Field for two spring training replacement games in 1995; that's as close as he'll get to "The Show" in Colorado as he was given an unconditional release after the season.

LANDRUM, TITO - OF - BR - Age 25
Landrum hits for power, including clubbing home runs in back-to-back games for Double-A San Antonio in 1995. But, his power numbers aren't good enough to balance his low batting average. He's a decent fielder with a good arm. Landrum needs more time at the Double-A level.

LANE, BRIAN - 3B/SS - BR - Age 26
The acquisition of Willie Greene put a wet blanket on Lane's career in Cincinnati. A one-time prospect who has faded, Lane will need a great deal of luck to reach the majors.

LANKFORD, RAY - OF - BL - Age 28
Just when it seemed his star was fading fast, Lankford turned it around and had a very good year for St. Louis. He probably won't turn into the superstar that many projected when he was younger but Lankford is a first-rate player with good power and speed. Fearing his salary will reach the $4 million level in 1996, the Cardinals may look to deal Lankford in the right package.

	AB	R	HR	RBI	SB	BA	$
1994 St. Louis NL	416	89	19	57	11	.267	20
1995 St. Louis NL	483	81	25	82	24	.277	27
1996 Projection >>>	541	97	23	81	21	.275	24

LANSING, MIKE - SS - BR - Age 27
A solid second baseman with some power and good speed, Lansing is capable of surpassing his decent numbers of 1995. He turns 28 in April and is just entering his prime. He figures to become one of the best all-around second basemen in baseball and the Expos would be wise to loosen their purse strings to keep this guy.

	AB	R	HR	RBI	SB	BA	$
1994 Montreal NL	394	44	5	35	12	.266	13
1995 Montreal NL	467	47	10	62	27	.255	19
1996 Projection >>>	515	55	9	59	25	.270	18

LARKIN, BARRY - SS - BR - Age 31
If the MVP means "most indispensible player on a pennant contender" Larkin would win every year. The only thing surprising about Larkin's season was his stolen base total, which topped his career high by 11. His only weakness used to be staying healthy, but in the last two seasons he has missed only 17 games. Due to his late start (he didn't make the majors until he was 23) Larkin probably needs five more good seasons to merit Hall of Fame consideration.

	AB	R	HR	RBI	SB	BA	$
1994 Cincinnati NL	427	78	9	52	26	.279	26
1995 Cincinnati NL	496	98	15	66	51	.319	39
1996 *Projection* >>>	511	94	13	65	32	.293	27

LARREGUI, ED - OF - BR - Age 23
A second round pick in 1989, Larregui lacks both power and good contact hitting.

LATHAM, CHRIS - OF - BB - Age 22
Latham is a streaky hitter with some pop, but his power numbers were disappointing for Double-A San Antonio. He can hit for average, too, which should get him to back Triple-A in 1996.

LAVALLIERE, MIKE - C - BL - Age 35
"Spanky" LaValliere is still a fine catcher with good mechanics and a good arm; he handles pitchers very well. Strictly a singles hitter, he has a good batting eye, but is very slow due to bad knees. LaValliere is fine as a second string catcher, but probably has a 150 at-bat limit on his odometer.

	AB	R	HR	RBI	SB	BA	$
1994 Chicago AL	139	6	1	24	0	.281	2
1995 Chicago AL	98	7	1	19	0	.245	0
1996 *Projection* >>>	98	6	1	17	0	.261	-

LAWTON, MATT - OF - BL - Age 24
Lawton is a lefty hitting outfielder who can hit at the top of the batting order. He played well in '95 at Double-A as he hit .269 with 26 stolen bases and earned a September callup. Lawton would earn a regular role if he started to hit for power. He should make the major leagues to stay by '97.

	AB	R	HR	RBI	SB	BA	$
1995 New Britain AA	412	75	13	54	26	.269	
1995 Minnesota AL	60	11	1	12	1	.317	1
1996 *Projection* >>>	141	23	3	20	4	.260	2

LEACH, JALAL - OF - BL - Age 27
Leach's prospect status slipped. He has struck out more than 100 times in each of his four full seasons as a pro, and his home run and stolen base totals both have been dropping.

LEARY, ROB - 1B - BL - Age 24
The Pirates discovered Leary playing in the Hawaiian Winter League following the 1994 season and signed him away from the independent Northern League. He's young with power potential and rates keeping an eye on.

LeBRON, JUAN - OF - BR - Age 19
The Royals' top pick of 1995, LeBron came from a Puerto Rican high school. The Royals believe he's a pure hitter, but are worried about his defense. Since he hit .177 in rookie ball, striking out once for every four at-bats, they probably should worry about his hitting, too.

LEDESMA, AARON - 3B - BR - Age 24
Just what the Mets need: another solid infield candidate. Ledesma went to the 1995 Arizona Fall League to fine-tune his skills -- most likely in preparation for becoming trade bait. He can be an OK major leaguer in the right situation, but not a star -- and he doesn't fit into the Mets crowded picture unless some bodies get moved.

	AB	R	HR	RBI	SB	BA	$
1995 Norfolk AAA	201	26	0	28	6	.299	
1995 New York NL	33	4	0	3	0	.242	-
1996 *Projection* >>>	64	9	0	6	0	.242	-

LEE, DEREK - OF - BL - Age 29
Lee hit .325 at Birmingham in 1991, but just spent his third year in Triple-A. He has some power and base-stealing speed, but is future is mostly behind him now.

LEE, DERREK - 3B - BR - Age 20
Derrick Lee is one of the Padres' top prospects. He is moving up very nicely and could mature into a 30-homer per year hitter in the majors. He's an excellent hitter who should be able to cut down on the strikeouts when he gets more experience and plate discipline. He may be with the Angels in September or in 1997.

LEE, MANUEL - SS - BB - Age 30
Dumped by Texas after the 1994 season as the Rangers made room for rookie shortstop Benji Gil, Lee hooked on with the Cardinals last season. He was dogged by injuries all season and appeared in just one game. Lee, who has underachieved his whole career, might hook on somewhere as a utility infielder. Then again, he might not. Either way, he'll never be a starter again.

LEGREE, KEITH - OF - BL - Age 24
Legree, a former University of Louisville basketball player, has played little in four years of pro baseball. A breakthrough year similar to Tony Clark's is highly unlikely.

LEIUS, SCOTT - 3B/SS - BR - Age 30
Leius had a decent year, as he reached base an acceptable amount despite a low average. The acquisition of Ron Coomer casts some doubt on his role for '96, as Coomer is a better hitter, while Leius has the edge defensively. Expect a better average from Leius in fewer at bats.

	AB	R	HR	RBI	SB	BA	$
1994 Minnesota AL	350	57	14	49	2	.246	10
1995 Minnesota AL	372	51	4	45	2	.247	4
1996 Projection >>>	298	44	6	38	1	.246	3

LEMKE, MARK - 2B - BB - Age 30
Lemke served as the Braves infield glue, showing his usual good defense and steady hitting. He always provides a lot of the "little" things on offense, like bunting, a good OBP, and clutch contact hitting. Lemke will remain the Braves regular second sacker for most of 1996, but he will soon be pressured for playing time by Tony Graffanino or Marty Malloy.

	AB	R	HR	RBI	SB	BA	$
1994 Atlanta NL	350	40	3	31	0	.294	8
1995 Atlanta NL	399	42	5	38	2	.253	5
1996 Projection >>>	406	44	4	38	1	.252	3

LENNON, PATRICK - OF - BR - Age 27
Lennon is an outfielder who, like Lee Tinsley, is a former first round pick who has played for both Seattle and Boston. He hit well in limited duty at Triple-A for the Twins in '95, and has enough speed and power to be an asset on a big league bench.

LEONARD, MARK - OF - BL - Age 31
This perennial prospect had a wonderful minor-league season for the gazillionth year in a row, and for the gazillionth year in a row was not given a legitimate chance to prove himself at the major-league level. You have to beware of players in their thirties who have little chance of getting any playing time in the majors, and it may be too late for Leonard at this point, but it must be noted that Leonard is still fully capable of having a fine offensive season with a major-league team.

	AB	R	HR	RBI	SB	BA	$
1994 San Francisco NL	11	2	0	2	0	.364	-
1995 San Francisco NL	21	4	1	4	0	.190	-

LESHER, BRIAN - OF - BR - Age 25
Lesher led Double-A Huntsville in homers with 19. Lesser-known than teammate Jose Herrera, but a better hitter, Lesher is a marginal sleeper, worth watching.

LEVIS, JESSE - C - BL - Age 27
Levis is obviously heading nowhere in the Indians' chain. Despite clearly demonstrating that he can hit for average, with excellent patience, at the major league level, doubts about his defense and size (5'9", 180 lbs.) have reduced him to an afterthought in the system's eyes. He could fit in somewhere - probably not in Cleveland - as a third catcher/lefthanded bat off the bench. It's at least as likely that he will settle in for the long haul at the Triple-A level.

	AB	R	HR	RBI	SB	BA	$
1995 Cleveland AL	18	1	0	3	0	.333	-

LEWIS, ANTHONY - OF - BL - Age 25
Lewis has excellent power, and hit 16 of his 24 homers in the second half of the season for Double-A Arkansas after being hurt during the early part of the year. A six-year minor league free agent after 1995, Lewis is likely to move on to another organization for 1996. His power impresses scouts.

LEWIS, DARREN - OF - BR - Age 28
After showing some improvement in 1994, Lewis regressed in 1995. Lewis is a terrible hitter, whose only positive is stolen base ability (18 of 20 in 1995) but his on-base percentage (.311) is clearly unacceptable for a leadoff hitter. Davey Johnson was the first manager to realize this, limiting Lewis to the role of righthanded half of a centerfield platoon and defensive replacement.

	AB	R	HR	RBI	SB	BA	$
1994 San Francisco NL	451	70	4	29	30	.257	22
1995 Two Teams	472	66	1	24	32	.250	14
1996 Projection >>>	496	70	3	32	35	.253	16

LEWIS, MARK - 3B - BR - Age 26
Lewis is a classic example of a player who was perceived as failure at the major league level despite a ridiculously brief opportunity. After two decent seasons at a very young age, Lewis was shuttled between AAA and Cleveland, replaced by Jim Thome, then traded to the Reds for failed first round pick Tim Costo. Davey Johnson used him as the righthanded half of a third base platoon/pinch hitter and Lewis responded with his best season. Lewis has never shown much power or speed but the combination of high average, good strike zone judgement, and good defense make him a useful player

	AB	R	HR	RBI	SB	BA	$
1994 Cleveland AL	73	6	1	8	1	.205	-
1995 Cincinnati NL	171	25	3	30	0	.339	6
1996 Projection >>>	181	24	4	29	1	.287	3

LEWIS, T.R. - OF/DH - BR - Age 24
T.R. Lewis plays, first, third, and the outfield. He is a good hitter who could hit about .250 in the majors. It's unlikely that Lewis will get much playing time for the parent Orioles as they plan to use more established veterans.

LEYRITZ, JIM - 1B/C - BR - Age 32
Showing some decline at age 32, Leyritz remained one of the better hitters capable of handling backstop chores in 1995. Even when he was younger, stamina was an issue, so reserve duty and utility work including first base and outfield are on the horizon for Leyritz in 1996. Staying in New York looked uncertain during the winter.

	AB	R	HR	RBI	SB	BA	$
1994 New York AL	249	47	17	58	0	.265	12
1995 New York AL	264	37	7	37	1	.269	5
1996 Projection >>>	234	37	9	42	1	.262	5

LIEBERTHAL, MIKE - C - BR - Age 24
The Phils' top pick in 1990 will never be a full-time player in the majors due to a lack of size (6'0", 179 lbs.) and offensive ability. However, he is fundamentally sound behind the plate, calls a solid game and has an adequate arm. He also makes consistent contact and gets solid licks against lefties. His defensive superiority gives him the edge over Lenny Webster in the battle for the 1996 backup role.

	AB	R	HR	RBI	SB	BA	$
1994 Philadelphia NL	79	6	1	5	0	.266	0
1995 Scranton WB AAA	278	44	6	42	1	.281	
1995 Philadelphia NL	47	1	0	4	0	.255	-
1996 Projection >>>	165	14	2	16	0	.261	-

LIND, JOSE - 2B - BR - Age 31
Jose Lind was released by the Royals and signed by the Angels to shore up the infield playing second following the

injury to shortstop Gary DiSarcina. It didn't work out and he was released. Lind was never much of a hitter, and his lack of run production for the Angels was not a surprise.

	AB	R	HR	RBI	SB	BA	$
1994 Kansas City AL	290	34	1	31	9	.269	9
1995 Two Teams	140	9	0	7	0	.236	-
1996 *Projection* >>>	140	13	0	11	1	.238	-

LINDEMAN, JIM - OF - BR - Age 34
Lindeman can still hit for power, but the market for 34 year old first basemen is pretty weak. He could hang on for a couple of years in the minors.

LINDSEY, DOUG - C - BR - Age 28
Lindsey will never hit enough to be a major league asset. He has a career .220 batting average after eight minor league seasons.

LIRIANO, NELSON - 2B - BB - Age 31
Liriano was one of the few bright spots in the Pirates' dismal 1995 season, having a fine season as a backup infielder, primarily at second base. He's a true pro and figures to have a few more good years left as a bench player.

	AB	R	HR	RBI	SB	BA	$
1994 Colorado NL	255	39	3	31	0	.255	3
1995 Pittsburgh NL	259	29	5	38	2	.286	7
1996 *Projection* >>>	189	25	3	25	2	.276	2

LIS, JOE - 2B - BR - Age 27
Lis saw his average drop but his power numbers reach new highs at Triple-A last year. He can hit for average and has nice extra base potential, especially for an infielder. At twenty-seven, he could post good numbers as a late arriver.

LISTACH, PAT - SS - BR - Age 28
Hard to tell what's up here. Chances are he's never going to play as well as he did in his rookie year.

	AB	R	HR	RBI	SB	BA	$
1994 Milwaukee AL	54	8	0	2	2	.296	0
1995 Milwaukee AL	334	35	0	25	13	.219	4
1996 *Projection* >>>	284	32	0	21	11	.228	2

LITTON, GREG - OF - BR - Age 31
Erstwhile major leaguer Litton hit .309 at Triple-A Tacoma in 1995. He does nothing special but can be a useful bench player in the majors.

LIVINGSTONE, SCOTT - 3B/DH - BL - Age 30
Scott Livingstone is a singles-hitter who can pop an occasional home run. He usually hits for a good average when he plays, but doesn't produce very many RBI. He is a third baseman, but got into 43 games at first base last year, as the Padres' rookie prospects couldn't produce, hitting .361 in 144 at-bats in the second half including a streak of 34-for-84 (.405). Livingstone is a valuable bench player who can do a good job playing regularly if needed.

	AB	R	HR	RBI	SB	BA	$
1994 Detroit - San Diego	203	11	2	11	2	.266	3
1995 San Diego NL	196	26	5	32	2	.337	8
1996 *Projection* >>>	248	26	3	30	2	.284	4

LOCKETT, RON - 1B/OF - BL - Age 26
Lockett has graduated to Triple-A Scranton-Wilkes Barre, seemingly by default. His incredible shrinking on-base percentage hasn't been above .300 since 1991, and both his power and speed have steadily diminished. The end appears to be near for the Phils' 1990 8th-round draft pick.

LOCKHART, KEITH - OF - BL - Age 31
Yet another of the Royals old "rookies" rescued from the minor league scrap heap, Lockhart had an outstanding year in every respect. Besides leading the Royals in batting average, Lockhart showed good range at second base and had decent speed and power. By year's end he was the team's most productive hitter in the second spot in the order.

He's the leading candidate for regular play at second base in 1996, but a risk to return to more mundane offensive performance.

	AB	R	HR	RBI	SB	BA	$
1994 San Diego NL	43	4	2	6	1	.209	0
1995 Kansas City AL	274	41	6	33	8	.321	12
1996 *Projection* >>>	280	35	5	31	4	.278	5

LoDUCA, PAUL - C - BR - Age 23
LoDuca was an outstanding player in college, but has struggled in pro ball and last year at Double-A San Antonio was no exception. His basic skills behind the plate are poor.

LOFTON, KENNY - OF - BL - Age 28
Is it possible for a leadoff hitter to bat .310 and lead the league in steals and still be a disappointment? Kenny Lofton raised the stakes so high with his mammoth 1994 season that he was just that in 1995. Lofton was overaggressive at the plate, posting career lows in walks (40) and OBP (.362). Nevertheless, Lofton remains one of the most exciting players in baseball, and will remain the game's premier leadoff hitter if he relearns the boundaries of the strike zone. He is still able to steal at will, and should remain a .300 hitter and 60 base stealer in the intermediate term.

	AB	R	HR	RBI	SB	BA	$
1994 Cleveland AL	459	105	12	57	60	.349	55
1995 Cleveland AL	481	93	7	53	54	.310	39
1996 *Projection* >>>	574	118	9	64	61	.315	42

LONG, KEVIN - OF - BL - Age 29
Long had a good season for Double-A Wichita after being demoted from Triple-A Omaha. He hits for average, but has no power. Long gets on base a lot, and is pretty fair on the basepaths, but he's probably on the downhill side of his career.

LONG, RYAN - 3B - BR - Age 23
Long was a legitimate prospect for the Royals, but had a disappointing 1995 season at Double-A Wichita. His batting average dropped 30 points, as he struggled in every offensive aspect following a good 1994 campaign at Class A Wilmington. Long has shown occasional power, but hit only five homers last season, with two coming in one game.

LONG, TERRENCE - 1B/OF - BL - Age 20
Long was the Mets' second first-round draft pick in 1994. He showed good power in the Appalachian League, where he played mostly outfield to take advantage of his speed.

LONGMIRE, TONY - OF - BL - Age 27
Longmire was an offensive force in the first half of the 1995 season before being sidelined by a broken navicular (wrist) bone. This is the single slowest healing bone in the body, and almost surely will result in a permanent loss of power. Longmire's dominance of lefties (.524 average) prior to the injury was particularly eye-opening, but will likely never be witnessed again. Despite excellent straight-ahead speed, Longmire has never stolen many bases nor played particularly well defensively.

	AB	R	HR	RBI	SB	BA	$
1994 Philadelphia NL	139	10	0	17	2	.237	1
1995 Philadelphia NL	104	21	3	19	1	.356	4
1996 *Projection* >>>	130	18	2	20	2	.281	1

LOPEZ, JAVIER - C - BR - Age 25
Lopez hit for expected power but a much better batting average, adding 70 points in 1995. His defense is still erratic and his poor strike zone judgment will slow his development as a hitter. But, Lopez remains one of the best hitting young catchers in baseball and he's just reaching his peak - look for impressive power numbers in 1996.

	AB	R	HR	RBI	SB	BA	$
1994 Atlanta NL	277	27	13	35	0	.245	7
1995 Atlanta NL	333	37	14	51	0	.315	13
1996 *Projection* >>>	410	47	18	61	0	.292	12

LOPEZ, LUIS - 2B - BB - Age 25
At best, Luis Lopez is a .250 hitter, but he doesn't have any power or speed. The Padres' reserve middle infielder tore a ligament in his elbow in May missing the rest of the 1995 season. His future role is as a utility infielder.

	AB	R	HR	RBI	SB	BA	$
1994 San Diego NL	235	29	2	20	3	.277	5
1995 San Diego NL			Did Not Play - Injured				
1996 Projection >>>	121	14	1	11	1	.270	-

LOPEZ, LUIS - OF - BR - Age 31
Lopez first graduated to Triple-A in 1989 at the age of 24, but has only mustered 88 major league at bats since then. Though he slipped to .266 in 1995, he has a minor league average over .300 in over 4700 at bats. He is a clear example of the career minor leaguer who will positively never get an extended major league trial. He's a free swinger with extra-base power, but must get out of the Indians' organization to even rate a remote shot at a future major league cup of coffee.

LORETTA, MARK - SS - BR - Age 24
A fine fielder, Loretta made significant strides in his second year at Triple-A New Orleans, earning a September recall to the big leagues for the first time. Loretta is a one of the Brewers best prospects and can be expected to compete for a regular role in the major leagues in 1996. Despite his .286-7-79 season for New Orleans there are still questions about whether Loretta will hit enough in the majors.

	AB	R	HR	RBI	SB	BA	$
1995 New Orleans AAA	479	48	7	79	8	.286	
1995 Milwaukee AL	50	13	1	3	1	.260	-
1996 Projection >>>	104	20	2	18	3	.264	1

LOTT, BILLY - OF - BR - Age 25
Marginal Dodger outfield prospect who hit well in a limited playing time at Albuquerque.

LOVULLO, TOREY - 2B - BB - Age 30
Remember this guy - one of the many "greatest players ever seen" by Sparky Anderson? Lovullo actually had a rather excellent Triple-A season in 1995, combining excellent plate discipline with uncommon power for a middle infielder. His ability to play several positions makes him an excellent Triple-A rainy day policy, and the void behind Carlos Baerga in the Indians' organization increases the chances that the Indians will continue to pay the premiums. He is basically Rene Gonzales, Jr.

	AB	R	HR	RBI	SB	BA	$
1994 Seattle AL	72	9	2	7	1	.222	0
1995 Buffalo AAA	474	84	16	61	3	.255	
1996 Projection >>>	67	8	1	6	1	.238	-

LOWERY, TERRELL - OF - BR - Age 25
A ruptured Achilles tendon ended Lowery's season before it started. The former Loyola Marymount basketball star had been a highly regarded prospect, but will probably need a year at Triple-A in 1996. With a full recovery, Lowery would be a legitimate centerfielder with excellent speed and developing power. Lowery was slated to play in the Arizona Fall League.

LUCCA, LOU - 3B - BR - Age 25
Lucca sure doesn't look like a prospect, with his stocky 5'11", 210 lbs., build, his questionable bat speed and lack of pedigree (32nd round draftee), but he keeps on plugging. He has solid strike zone knowledge, and gap power. He should be the Marlins' Triple-A third baseman in 1996, but that could be his ceiling. Both his relatively high age for a prospect and his lack of tools could conspire against him.

LUCE, ROGER - C - BR - Age 26
Luce is a terrific defensive catcher, with a great arm. The rap has always been that Luce couldn't hit.

LUKACHYK, ROB - OF - BL - Age 27
Lukachyk played his first complete Triple-A season in 1995, with his fourth organization. He became a minor league free agent again, offering his wares to any team needing a spare part with a little speed, a little pop in his bat and a little defensive ability.

LUKE, MATT - OF - BL - Age 25
Baseball America's poll voted Luke the Florida State League's best power prospect, and he continued to power the ball in the Eastern League. His arm is strong enough to play right field.

LUTZ, BRENT - C - BR - Age 25
After a solid year in 1994, he couldn't repeat the feat and will hope for another chance at Double-A. Even though he has been a base stealer, he's not a very fast runner and strikes out often. For now, he's a fringe player.

LUZINSKI, RYAN - C - BR - Age 22
A first round sandwich draft pick in 1992, Greg's son Ryan hit .336 at the Dodgers Class A Vero Beach in 1995. Luzinski is a good power hitting prospect who may have to move to another position before he reaches the majors.

LYDEN, MITCH - C - BR - Age 31
Lyden is a good catcher who hits for average and power. He entered the history books on June 16, 1993, when he homered in his first major league at-bat at Wrigley Field as a member of the Florida Marlins. However, the Marlins weren't impressed and he garnered only nine more at-bats with Florida. Despite limited playing time for Triple-A Omaha in 1995 due to injuries, Lyden had another good season, his tenth straight year above Class A.

LYDY, SCOTT - OF - BR - Age 27
Lydy didn't hit during his first trip to the majors in 1993, and will apparently never get a second chance. He's a fourth outfielder at best, although he would be a good one. If he played for the Rockies people would think he was a star.

LYONS, BARRY - C - BR - Age 35
Lyons is a second string catcher who is really more of an extra hitter than defensive replacement. He hits well enough to play first base or even DH occasionally, but he's a bad catcher who can't throw. Lyons has some power and could win a right-handed pinch-hitting role somewhere in 1996.

	AB	R	HR	RBI	SB	BA	$
1995 Chicago AL	64	8	5	16	0	.266	1
1996 *Projection* >>>	73	10	2	11	0	.238	-

GOT A QUESTION? CALL JOHN BENSON LIVE

Your Question - Your Roster - Your Situation

Let the top analyst in the business help you!!

1-900-773-7526

$2.49/minute

1 pm to 11 pm Eastern Time - 7 days a Week

MAAS, KEVIN - DH/1B - BL - Age 31
Maas looked like a perfect fit for the Twins, who wanted to replace Kent Hrbek, until they decided to audition some younger players. He could still latch on as pinch hitter/DH, and is only 31 years old, so he's not done yet.

	AB	R	HR	RBI	SB	BA	$
1995 Minnesota AL	57	5	1	5	0	.193	-

MABRY, JOHN - OF - BL - Age 25
Mabry excited the St. Louis faithful last season by hitting .300 as a rookie. However, it was more of a case of a guy looking better than he was because he was on a bad team. Mabry has a strong arm, which was wasted in his move from outfield to first base, but only decent average and no speed. His offense isn't what you're looking for from a first baseman or outfielder. The Cardinals have also had thoughts about moving him to third.

	AB	R	HR	RBI	SB	BA	$
1994 St. Louis NL	23	2	0	3	0	.304	-
1995 St. Louis NL	388	35	5	41	0	.307	10
1996 Projection >>>	380	34	6	42	0	.280	6

MACFARLANE, MIKE - C - BR - Age 31
A free agent acquisition before the 1995 season, Macfarlane gave the Red Sox good power, a low batting average and hard-nosed play behind the plate, just as expected. Macfarlane has been one of the more reliable hitters at catcher and can again be counted on for a sub-.250 average, 15-20 homers and 50-70 RBI.

	AB	R	HR	RBI	SB	BA	$
1994 Kansas City AL	314	53	14	47	1	.255	10
1995 Boston AL	364	45	15	51	2	.225	6
1996 Projection >>>	416	58	18	61	2	.239	7

MACK, QUINN - OF - BL - Age 30
Shane's younger brother had a decent minor league season, batting .265 with 3 home runs and 11 stolen bases. Darren Bragg is light years ahead of Mack to be a regular in the Mariners outfield.

MACK, SHANE - OF - BR - Age 32
To avoid the risk of a missed payroll resulting from the strike extending long into the 1995 season, Shane Mack signed a big contract with the Yomiuri Giants in the Japanese Central League. Usually hitting around .300 in the majors, Mack had difficulty bringing his average up to .250 in the Japanese league.

MAGADAN, DAVE - 3B/1B - BL - Age 33
Magadan had a solid year as a platoon third baseman for Houston in 1995. Without any power or speed, his major asset is his excellent plate discipline which has produced a career on base average of .390 (.428 in 1995). He does not have enough power to hold a regular job at first or third base and is not likely to receive as much playing time or hit as well in 1996.

	AB	R	HR	RBI	SB	BA	$
1994 Florida NL	211	30	1	17	0	.275	2
1995 Houston NL	348	44	2	51	2	.313	10
1996 Projection >>>	276	35	1	35	1	.276	3

MAGEE, WENDELL - OF - BR - Age 23
The Phils' 1994 12th round pick has an athletic, 6'0", 225 lbs., body, and is a consistent line drive machine who has yet to show power befitting someone of his size. His speed and defense are also unremarkable - his bat should carry him to a starting Triple-A role in 1996, and he could be the first outfielder summoned to the majors. Improvement in either the power or speed department will be necessary for him to be a productive starting major leaguer.

MAHAY, RON - OF - BL - Age 24
Mahay gained notoriety by being the first replacement player recalled to the majors. It was a lot of fuss for five games played by a guy coming off a .278 season in the Florida State League. Mahay spent most of last season with the Red Sox Double-A farm at Trenton. Defense is his strength.

	AB	R	HR	RBI	SB	BA	$
1995 Boston AL	20	3	1	3	0	.200	-

MAKAREWICZ, SCOTT - C - BR - Age 29
Makarewicz has spent seven years in the Astro system and has established himself as a career minor leaguer.

MAKSUDIAN, MIKE - 1B/C - BL - Age 29
A good 25th man, Maksudian can catch in an emergency. He hits for some power, takes walks, and has a fine attitude. He probably will stick somewhere in 1996.

MALAVE, JOSE - OF - BR - Age 24
In what could have been Malave's rookie season with the Red Sox, instead of cheers he heard "overweight" and "bad attitude." He started slowly, and finished fast, to thrust himself into Boston's outfield/DH picture for sure in '96. Defensively, he took a step backwards last year.

MALDONADO, CANDY - OF - BR - Age 35
Maldonado still has some pop in his bat, and he can crush a mistake pitch. He'll play another season or two as a reserve before he calls it a career.

	AB	R	HR	RBI	SB	BA	$
1994 Cleveland AL	92	14	5	12	1	.196	1
1995 Texas AL	190	28	9	30	1	.263	4
1996 Projection >>>	159	23	8	24	1	.232	1

MALLOY, MARTY - 2B - BL - Age 23
Mark Lemke has settled in at second base for the Braves in recent years because of his steady defense; Malloy may soon challenge Lemke based on the same qualifications. But, Malloy can up the ante because he's a decent hitter, too. He's got good strike-zone judgment, a little power and above average speed to go along with his award winning glove. Watch Malloy's progress at Triple-A Richmond in 1996 to see how much he'll make Lemke sweat.

MANAHAN, TONY - 3B - BR - Age 27
Manahan was signed by the Phils as a minor league free agent prior to 1995, to hold the fort for one season prior to Scott Rolen's long-awaited arrival at Triple-A Scranton-Wilkes Barre. Manahan makes fairly consistent line drive contact, but does not have the power one desires in a corner infielder. A Mariners' number one pick, he now appears to have little or no chance of ever playing in the majors. He will likely relocate to another organization in 1996.

MANTO, JEFF - 3B/1B - BR - Age 31
After years of battling and failed trials, Jeff Manto finally earned a starting third base job last year. He slammed 12 homers in 26 games, but soon came down with a bad hamstring injury, and was never the same afterwards. Manto has shown that he can hit major league pitching with power, especially the second and third-line pitchers who tend to make mistakes that he crushes. But he has some defensive shortcomings, and his best role may be as a DH and part time player.

	AB	R	HR	RBI	SB	BA	$
1994 Rochester AAA	444	81	31	100	3	.297	
1995 Baltimore AL	254	31	17	38	0	.256	7
1996 Projection >>>	214	26	10	32	0	.254	3

MANWARING, KIRT - C - BR - Age 30
Manwaring is a terrible hitter with a good defensive reputation, which ensures that he will have lots of useless at-bats. He has no power, no speed, a career average of .247, and is now past his prime.

	AB	R	HR	RBI	SB	BA	$
1994 San Francisco NL	316	30	1	29	1	.250	3
1995 San Francisco NL	379	21	4	36	1	.251	4
1996 Projection >>>	432	32	4	41	1	.248	2

MARINI, MARC - OF - BL - Age 26
Marini is a consistent line drive hitter with gap power who has averaged 30 doubles per season over four pro campaigns. Marini doesn't have the home run power or plus speed that one looks for in a starting major league outfielder, and he is way too old to have accumulated only 85 Triple-A at bats. He looks like a major league extra outfielder at best, assuming he can escape the Indians' system. You could be seeing his namein Triple-A box scores for years to come.

MARRERO, ELIESER - C - BR - Age 22
Marrero is a power-hitting catching prospect in the Cardinals' chain who is clearly the best catcher in the Cardinals' farm system.

MARRERO, ORESTE - 1B - BL - Age 26
Minor league journeyman who last appeared in the majors in 1993 (for 32 games) with Montreal. He set career highs in home runs and RBI in 1995, but unfortunately for him it was at AA San Antonio, where he was named to the Texas League post season All-Star team as DH. He is not a prospect.

MARSH, TOM - OF - BR - Age 30
He's tough - but not particularly talented. He swings at everything (eight walks in 265 career major league plate appearances), is suspect defensively, but has occasional long ball power. The Phils' macho players and manager love him, but will have a hard time justifying his presence should better backup options present themselves

	AB	R	HR	RBI	SB	BA	$
1994 Philadelphia NL	18	3	0	3	0	.278	-
1995 Philadelphia NL	109	13	3	15	0	.294	
1996 Projection >>>	144	18	4	20	0	.258	0

MARSHALL, JASON - SS - BR - Age 25
Marshall has been used on a limited basis in his last three seasons, which doesn't bode well for his future considering last season was his first above Class A. He's a fine utility player - at the minor league level.

MARTIN, AL - OF - BL - Age 28
Martin seemingly has the makings of a star with power and speed. However, injuries have held him back. If he's going to make good on his star potential, now is the time because he isn't getting any younger.

	AB	R	HR	RBI	SB	BA	$
1994 Pittsburgh NL	276	48	9	33	15	.286	17
1995 Pittsburgh NL	439	70	13	41	20	.282	18
1996 Projection >>>	460	76	14	48	21	.283	18

MARTIN, CHRIS - SS/2B - BR - Age 28
Somewhere there may be a major league utility job with Martin's name on it. Defensively, he's probably best at second base, but he also has played the other infield positions and is fast enough to play the outfield. He wouldn't hit enough to help much, but he wouldn't be an automatic out. Martin's eye-catching statistic from 1995 with the Expos' top farm at Ottawa: an 86 percent success rate on steals.

MARTIN, JIM - OF - BL - Age 25
The Dodgers are really high on Martin, but he's error prone in the field. He has excellent speed on the bases, but he needs to exhibit more power if he is going to make it Los Angeles.

MARTIN, NORBERTO - 2B/SS - BB - Age 29
Martin is a decent utility player who can fill in anywhere on the infield or outfield. A line drive hitter, Martin has a little speed, but not much power. He doesn't hit well enough or have a good enough glove to be a regular, although he's better as a second baseman. Martin will again be a White Sox utility player in 1996.

	AB	R	HR	RBI	SB	BA	$
1994 Chicago AL	131	19	1	16	4	.275	4
1995 Chicago AL	160	17	2	17	5	.269	4
1996 Projection >>>	154	19	2	17	5	.272	2

MARTINDALE, RYAN - C - BR - Age 27
Martindale was injured for most of 1995, and lost his place in line as a contender for the Indians' big league backup job. He has shown offensive skills in only one of his five pro seasons, and though he has decent defensive skills and a prototype body (6'3", 215), he has been surpassed by Brook Fordyce, who will shortly be followed by Einar Diaz. Martindale will likely move on to another organization in 1996, and has little chance of making it to the majors.

MARTINEZ, CARLOS - 1B/DH - BR - Age 30
Veteran Carlos Martinez has a major league career batting average of .265 in 1369 at-bats, including hitting ace Randy Johnson for 14 for 31 or a .452 clip. The Angels found him wanting last year and waived him in July, but his solid bat should enable him to get a part time job somewhere.

	AB	R	HR	RBI	SB	BA	$
1995 California AL	61	7	1	9	0	.180	-

MARTINEZ, CHITO - OF - BL - Age 30
A hitless, 15 at-bat stint for Baltimore in 1993 was Martinez's last major league shot. In 1995 he was released from Triple-A Colorado Springs after a .155-4-6 performance that featured 32 strikeouts in 110 at-bats. He's still young enough to get another shot, but Martinez might be better off in Japan.

MARTINEZ, DAVE - OF - BL - Age 31
The White Sox have a knack for rejuvenating careers of fading outfielders. Martinez didn't get to play much until John Kruk retired and Devereaux was dealt to Atlanta, but he more than made up for lost time with a great second half. He played a lot more at first base after Frank Thomas suffered a minor injury and showed a surprisingly good glove there. Martinez was one of the few bright spots for the White Sox in 1995 and will have an important role again in 1996.

	AB	R	HR	RBI	SB	BA	$
1994 San Francisco NL	235	23	4	27	3	.247	4
1995 Chicago AL	303	49	5	37	8	.307	11
1996 Projection >>>	247	35	5	29	5	.279	5

MARTINEZ, DOMINGO - 1B - BR - Age 28
As a platoon first-baseman for Triple-A Louisville Martinez continued to strike out at a prodigious rate in 1995. He has some power and can be a pinch-hitter in the majors. In the meantime, he'll play in the high minors and continue to strike out regularly.

MARTINEZ, EDDY - SS - BR - Age 18
Martinez is another shortstop from the world's shortstop factory, San Pedro de Macoris, Dominican Republic. Only 18, he's one of the best prospects in the Orioles farm system.

MARTINEZ, EDGAR - 1B - BR - Age 33
As a full time DH, Martinez responded with an MVP-type year. 1995 was the first time in many years Martinez remained healthy. He should hit very well for at least two more years. In 1996, expect somewhat less than 1995 and you'll enjoy him.

	AB	R	HR	RBI	SB	BA	$
1994 Seattle AL	326	47	13	51	6	.285	16
1995 Seattle AL	511	121	29	113	4	.356	31
1996 Projection >>>	495	93	22	90	4	.310	23

MARTINEZ, FELIX - SS - BB - Age 21
"El Gato" is generally characterized as the Royals' shortstop of the future. He's a superb fielder with incredible range and a decent hitter. The emotional Martinez' biggest drawback is that his throws can often be wild. His chances of making it to the majors with Kansas City may depend on the his ability to hit for average. Martinez is still a few years away, but time is definitely on his side.

MARTINEZ, RAMON - 2B - BB - Age 26
Martinez is an adequate infielder who hits for average. Last year, he had his best professional season, hitting .275-3-51 for Double-A Wichita.

MARTINEZ, SANDY - C - BL - Age 23
He arrived in the major leagues out of necessity and looked more comfortable than expected. He has a big swing without the power and is perhaps a little too agressive for his own good. He has the best throwing arm of any catcher that was in the Toronto organization last year and will now have a chance to be an everyday catcher in the majors.

	AB	R	HR	RBI	SB	BA	$
1995 Knoxville AA	144	14	2	22	0	.229	

	AB	R	HR	RBI	SB	BA	$
1995 Toronto AL	191	12	2	25	0	.241	
1996 *Projection* >>>	180	12	2	22	0	.230	-

MARTINEZ, TINO - 1B - BL - Age 28
He's been hot since the second half of 1994 and hasn't cooled yet. Expect him to stay close to 25+ homer levels for the next two or three years.

	AB	R	HR	RBI	SB	BA	$
1994 Seattle AL	329	42	20	61	1	.261	14
1995 Seattle AL	519	92	31	111	0	.293	22
1996 *Projection* >>>	529	83	29	98	0	.278	19

MARX, TIM - C - BR - Age 27
Marx is a decent catching prospect in the Pirates' system but he stands behind Jason Kendall and Angelo Encarnacion. He could make it to the majors as a backup catcher but it will likely have to be in another organization.

MARZANO, JOHN - C - BR - Age 33
Marzano made the American Association All-Star team, and had a cameo appearance in the majors. He could conceivably get a few major league at bats as a backup.

MASHORE, DAMON - OF - BB - Age 26
This aging prospect came back from injuries to hit .300 with 17 steals for Triple-A Edmonton. He could be a decent fourth outfielder in the majors.

MASHORE, JUSTIN - OF - BR - Age 24
Mashore's unfamiliarity with the concept of the strike zone continued last year, when he couldn't stick all season with the Tigers' Triple-A team at Toledo. He can run and play some defense, but he doesn't have enough power to help a team when he strikes out 100 times a season.

MASSARELLI, JOHN - OF - BR - Age 30
The nine-year minor league vet split his 1995 season between the Marlins' and Indians' Triple-A affiliates. He is a free-swinging spray hitter who has accumulated 273 pro steals with a success rate of over 80%. Lack of any significant batting skills, plus his status as a former replacement player, minimizes his chances of ever playing in the majors. Look for him to continue hopscotching around the minor leagues.

MASSE, BILLY - OF - BR - Age 29
An exceptional minor league hitter who hasn't had a chance in the majors. He led the International League with 82 walks in '93. Could be a role player for some team. If so, he'd be good for some extra homers and steals. He just spent his fourth year stuck at Triple-A Columbus in 1995.

MASTELLER, DAN - 1B/OF - BL - Age 28
Masteller received an extended shot at the first base job after Scott Stahoviak was injured. He is a good contact hitter and can help in a platoon role, but he needs to hit at least .280 to have value.

	AB	R	HR	RBI	SB	BA	$
1995 Salt Lake AAA	152	25	4	18	4	.303	
1995 Minnesota AL	198	21	3	21	1	.237	1
1996 *Projection* >>>	164	17	2	17	1	.247	-

MATHENY, MIKE - C - BR - Age 25
Matheny was voted the American Association's best defensive catcher in 1994. In his big-league trial in 1994, he was better than the Brewers' other catchers in throwing out base-stealers, but still not very good at 24 percent.

	AB	R	HR	RBI	SB	BA	$
1994 New Orleans AAA	177	20	4	21	1	.220	
1994 Milwaukee AL	53	3	1	2	0	.226	-
1995 Milwaukee AL	166	13	0	21	2	.247	1
1996 *Projection* >>>	235	19	1	29	2	.242	0

MATOS, FRANCISCO - 2B - BR - Age 26
The Pirates signed Matos away from Oakland as a six-year free agent and he had a good season at Triple-A Calgary in 1995. He is an outstanding fielder and makes decent contact. Matos could have a career as a utility infielder.

MATTINGLY, DON - 1B - BL - Age 34
Back problems (which Mattingly will never use as an excuse, and won't even mention unless pressed to admit they have existed) changed this .330, 30-homer hitter into a mere .300 hitter who is also a defensive gem and one of the last great team leaders.

	AB	R	HR	RBI	SB	BA	$
1994 New York AL	372	62	6	51	0	.304	12
1995 New York AL	458	59	7	49	0	.288	9
1996 Projection >>>	309	44	5	38	0	.293	6

MAURER, RON - 2B - BR - Age 27
Maurer has been a part-time player since leaving the California League in 1991. He has performed solidly, but not spectacularly, the last three seasons at Albuquerque. He doesn't have specific skills such as speed or power that would interest the Dodgers.

MAXWELL, PAT - 2B - BL - Age 26
Maxwell is a survivor, a 1991 29th round Indians' pick who has endured five nondescript minor league seasons. Maxwell makes consistent contact, but hits for a mediocre average with no power. He is surehanded defensively, and can play second base, shortstop and third base. He appears to have reached the upper limit of his potential - though the Triple-A second and third base jobs appear open to competition, the Indians can find somebody better on the six-year free agent list.

MAY, DERRICK - OF - BL - Age 27
May performed well in a platoon role for the Astros after coming from Milwaukee in a trade in June. He has been a consistent .280 hitter in his four year major league career. If he develops the power that might be expected from someone his size, he could become a full time player.

	AB	R	HR	RBI	SB	BA	$
1994 Chicago NL	345	43	8	51	3	.284	12
1995 Milwaukee AL	113	15	1	9	0	.248	-
1995 Houston NL	206	29	8	41	5	.301	10
1996 Projection >>>	467	62	11	72	7	.284	14

MAYNE, BRENT - C - BL - Age 27
"Play me every day and I'll hit .300" said Mayne; well, more like .250, and he needed a furious sprint at the end of the season to get there. Mayne is a low-average, no power catcher who is in the lineup for his defense. A poor hitter against lefties, Mayne would benefit from a platoon arrangement, but he was the Royals everyday catcher at the end of 1995 and should continue in that role for 1996.

	AB	R	HR	RBI	SB	BA	$
1994 Kansas City AL	144	19	2	20	1	.257	2
1995 Kansas City AL	307	23	1	27	0	.251	1
1996 Projection >>>	310	28	2	31	1	.252	1

McBRIDE, CHARLIE - OF - BR - Age 22
"Gator" McBride was relegated solely to outfield duty for Class A Durham in 1995 after playing all over the park in 1994. A late round, 1993 draft pick, McBride lost 100 points off of his team-leading batting average the previous year. He has some power and some speed, but fans too much and really is without a true position. He'll have to hit more than .238 to make it solely as a hitter.

McCALL, ROD - 1B - BL - Age 24
McCall began 1995 as a seemingly unwanted Indians' prospect dispatched to the independent Bakersfield club in the Class-A California League. A career .226 hitter prior to 1995, he dazzled by hitting for both extreme power and average, albeit in a hitters' league. The 1990 9th round pick has intriguing possibilities (he's 6'7", 220), but the loaded Indians' organization will likely have a difficult time finding room for the six-year minor league free agent.

McCARTY, DAVID - OF/1B - BR - Age 26
McCarty could be the 1996 poster child for the Could Surprise Foundation. A former first-round draft pick, McCarty never got along with Tom Kelly at Minnesota and posted disappointing numbers with the Twins. After being traded to the Giants in midseason last year, McCarty tore up Pacific Coast League pitching. The Giants' firstbase situation is muddled, McCarty seems to have a good relationship with his new club, and he'll be 26 years old in 1996. He needs regular playing time to prove himself, and he has yet to live up to his advance notices.

	AB	R	HR	RBI	SB	BA	$
1994 Minnesota AL	131	21	1	12	2	.260	1
1995 Minnesota AL	55	10	0	4	0	.218	
1995 San Francisco NL	20	1	0	2	1	.250	-
1996 *Projection* >>>	204	29	2	31	3	.240	1

McCLAIN, SCOTT - 3B - BR - Age 23
McClain has some power, but has to improve his overall hitting before he can become a candidate for the Orioles third base job. McClain began last year on a hitting tear in Triple-A, leading the league in home runs in early May. But the pitchers caught up with him leading to a demotion back to Double-A. His defense is good, and he knows the strike zone, but he needs to make some adjustments to become a better hitter to make any further progress towards the majors.

McCLENDON, LLOYD - OF/1B - BR - Age 37
After eight years as a useful right-handed bat off the bench for the Reds, Cubs and Pirates, McClendon spent 1995 in the same role at Triple-A Buffalo. He's always been a good pinch-hitter, but, at age 37, McClendon is probably finished.

McCONNELL, CHAD - OF - BR - Age 25
The Phillies' 1992 1st round pick has had a disappointing, injury-riddled pro career to date. His 1995 Double-A campaign was his most promising, as he showed moderate longball potential, though he continued to be overly aggressive at the plate and less than stellar in the field. Maintenance of his 1995 power numbers at Triple-A in 1996 could propel him into the race for a big league backup role.

McCOY, TREY - 1B/DH - BR - Age 29
McCoy can hit. Unfortunately, he can't field and he's extremely slow on the bases, both of which, along with his age, will limit McCoy's opportunities for advancement. McCoy had bone chips removed from his right elbow in 1994.

McCRACKEN, QUINTON - OF - BR - Age 26
It would be easy to explain McCracken's success at Triple-A Colorado Springs last year as the result of park effects -- if he hadn't started his second season at New Haven with an average 79 points better than in 1994. The Rockies' center field prospect is an exceptional base stealer who could help them diversify their attack away from Coors Field.

McDAVID, RAY - OF - BL - Age 24
Although he has shown some power in the minors, Ray McDavid is perceived by some observers as a fast base-stealing threat. He spent two years in the hitter-friendly Triple-A Pacific Coast League hitting around .265, equivalent to about .220 in the majors.

	AB	R	HR	RBI	SB	BA	$
1994 San Diego NL	28	2	0	2	1	.250	-
1995 Las Vegas AAA	166	28	5	27	7	.271	
1995 San Diego NL	17	2	0	0	1	.176	-
1996 *Projection* >>>	222	19	5	40	5	.238	2

McDONALD, JASON - SS/2B - BB - Age 24
With Class A Modesto, McDonald led all minor leaguers with 70 steals. He also led all minor leaguers with 110 walks. He's a fascinating prospect, well worth keeping an eye on.

McDOWELL, ODDIBE - OF - BL - Age 33
McDowell arose like a phoenix from the ashes in 1994, showing good speed and enough of everything else to be a

strong candidate to make the Rangers' roster. McDowell is no longer a major league caliber centerfielder, however, so he'll compete for a job as an extra outfielder.

McEWING, JOE - OF - BR - Age 23
The speedy McEwing started the 1995 season back at St. Pete, and advanced from there, even with his poor results.

McFARLIN, JASON - OF - BL - Age 25
Hit .337 with walks and eight steals for Double-A Shreveport. Worth watching, but he's been in AA forever, and the Giants have plenty of other outfield prospects.

McGEE, WILLIE - OF - BB - Age 37
McGee made a remarkable comeback from a serious injury suffered in 1994, eventually grabbing the Red Sox centerfield job. He hit .476 in a brief tune-up at Pawtucket, then gave Boston an aggressive leadoff hitter who revitalized their flagging offense. It was a wholly unexpected flashback to McGee's productive days with the Cardinals, but McGee will still have to battle for a big league job wherever he goes in 1996.

	AB	R	HR	RBI	SB	BA	$
1994 San Francisco NL	156	19	5	23	3	.282	6
1995 Boston AL	200	32	2	15	5	.285	4
1996 Projection >>>	190	27	3	18	5	.277	3

MCGINNIS, RUSS - C/1B - BR - Age 32
McGinnis has been in the minors for 11 years. He got a cup of coffee with the Rangers in 1992, getting into 14 major league games. A poor defensive catcher, McGinnis' power represents the bulk of his value as a player. He is simply an extra bat stored at Triple-A and would serve only as a pinch-hitter or part-time DH if he returns to the majors.

McGRIFF, FRED - 1B - BL - Age 32
McGriff failed to reach the 30 homer mark for the first time since 1987 and his other offensive totals reflect an overeagerness to jump start a flagging Braves offense. He owns a keen batting eye and is one of the National League's most consistent power threats. Don't be surprised by a return of the "Crime Dog" in 1996; he's still a 40 homer, 120 RBI threat.

	AB	R	HR	RBI	SB	BA	$
1994 Atlanta NL	424	81	34	94	7	.318	34
1995 Atlanta NL	528	85	27	93	3	.280	21
1996 Projection >>>	560	97	34	106	5	.292	26

McGRIFF, TERRY - C - BR - Age 32
Last seen hanging on at Triple-A Toledo, near the end.

McGUIRE, RYAN - 1B - BL - Age 24
McGuire improved his .305 career average for three minor league seasons by finishing second in the Eastern League batting race. He is also an accomplished fielder, but the Red Sox would like to see a little more power.

McGWIRE, MARK - 1B - BR - Age 32
When he plays, McGwire is one of the best hitters in baseball. When you consider on base percentage, McGwire becomes especially valuable. He was healthy in 1995; if he was ever traded to a hitters' park, he could set records.

	AB	R	HR	RBI	SB	BA	$
1994 Oakland AL	135	26	9	25	0	.252	4
1995 Oakland AL	317	75	39	90	1	.274	19
1996 Projection >>>	279	48	24	54	1	.271	11

McKNIGHT, JEFF - SS - BB - Age 33
Back in 1993 McKnight was in the right place at the right time to get a major league shot, but his opportunities are behind him now. Never more than a fair hitter, anyway.

McLEMORE, MARK - OF - BB - Age 31
McLemore was an important cog in the Ranger offense while filling in for injured leftfielder Juan Gonzalez in 1995; once Gonzalez returned McLemore shifted back to second base. McLemore has a good batting eye, has hit at least

.257 and stolen at least 20 bases in each of the last three seasons, and he plays second base better than he is usually given credit for. A very competitive player, McLemore is one of the better unsung regulars in baseball.

	AB	R	HR	RBI	SB	BA	$
1994 Baltimore AL	343	44	3	29	20	.257	15
1995 Texas AL	467	73	5	41	21	.261	15
1996 *Projection* >>>	380	56	4	35	14	.259	9

McMILLON, BILL - OF - BL - Age 24
The Marlins jumped McMillon over a level to Double-A in 1995, and all he did was win the sportswriters' version of the Eastern League MVP Award. Undersized at 5'11", 172 lbs., McMillon nevertheless is a line drive machine who possesses solid gap power, refuses to swing at bad pitches. and is able to steal the occasional base. He has the offensive skills to be an eventual major league platooner or extra outfielder perhaps by 1997.

McMULLEN, JON - 1B - BL - Age 22
McMullen lost the bulk of his 1995 season to shoulder surgery. Considered to have the highest upside of Phils' first base prospects entering the season, McMullen is a strapping (6'0", 240 lbs.) lefthanded power hitter, who did show improved plate discipline before he was sidelined by the injury. He needs to watch his weight, which has fluctuated wildly in the past, prove his shoulder is healthy, and then leapfrog Dan Held, who had a fine year in his absence.

MCNABB, BUCK - OF - BL - Age 23
McNabb was a second round draft choice by the Astros out of high school in 1991 and has moved up a level each year. However, he has no power and will have to hit for a higher average to be given a shot in the major leagues.

McNAIR, FRED - 1B - BR - Age 26
This seven year minor league veteran finally tasted Double-A success in 1995 at Reading in the Phils' organization. He's a free-swinging longballer with a prototypical power body. However, he is much too old to have just reached Double-A, and does not appear to have the bat speed to do significant damage against big league pitching. Look for him to fill the rosters of Double or Triple-A teams for the foreseeable future.

McNAMARA, JIM - C - BL - Age 30
McNamara is a journeyman minor league catcher. He can't hit a lick and was out of baseball in 1995.

McNEELY, JEFF - OF - BR - Age 26
This notoriously slow starter joined the Cardinals in the Luis Alicea deal over the winter. His regular season wasn't spectacular, but he was phenomenal in the post season. He was the best defensive outfielder in the American Association. However, McNeely is a longshot to make it to the majors with St. Louis.

McRAE, BRIAN - OF - BB - Age 28
Unlike previous seasons when McRae faded in the second half, he gave the Cubs a full season of fantastic defensive play and steady hitting. The Cubs really want to bring him back for 1996; he'll hit near the top of the order and play centerfield.

	AB	R	HR	RBI	SB	BA	$
1994 Kansas City AL	436	71	4	40	28	.273	24
1995 Chicago NL	580	92	12	48	27	.288	24
1996 *Projection* >>>	597	90	13	55	30	.282	25

McREYNOLDS, KEVIN - OF - BR - Age 36
Hobbled by leg injuries, McReynolds would have played even less for the Mets, if they hadn't given up Vince Coleman to get him. Unless there's a serious physical turnaround, McReynolds is done.

MEADE, PAUL - 3B - BB - Age 27
The 1991 9th-round Indians' draftee finally graduated above Single-A for the first time in 1994, a concern at his age. A free swinger with little power, only his versatility and ability to switch-hit have kept him in the hunt this long. Little chance for a big league future.

MEARES, PAT - SS - BR - Age 27
Meares played well in '95, hitting twelve home runs and improving defensively despite committing eighteen errors.

He still needs to improve his plate discipline, as he drew only fifteen walks all year. Meares might well be a player who needed the offensive explosion of the last few years to establish himself.

	AB	R	HR	RBI	SB	BA	$
1994 Minnesota AL	229	29	2	24	5	.266	6
1995 Minnesota AL	390	57	12	49	10	.269	13
1996 Projection >>>	394	54	9	46	9	.267	10

MEJIA, ROBERTO - 2B - BR - Age 23

At the tender age of 23, Mejia has the Rockies are completely baffled. Is he about to mature and play to his well-documented potential, or has he become a burned-out head case? 1995 provided few answers, as he was demoted to Triple-A Colorado Springs in June following a horrid start. He hit for average (but not power) in the Springs, but was never penciled in as a starter on a consistent basis. 1996 will likely be either Mejia's breakout year or his last chance in the Rockies organization.

	AB	R	HR	RBI	SB	BA	$
1994 Colorado NL	116	11	4	14	3	.241	3
1995 Colorado Springs AAA	143	18	2	14	0	.294	
1995 Colorado NL	52	5	1	4	0	.154	-
1996 Projection >>>	235	24	7	24	4	.239	2

MELENDEZ, DAN - 1B - BL - Age 25

A good fielder, Melendez began the 1995 season at Double-A San Antonio with an extremely hot bat, then fought through mid-season injuries that caused him to taper off to a .261-7-59 season. He has exhibited some power, but needs another year in Double-A before moving up.

MELUSKEY, MITCH - C - BB - Age 22

The Indians' 1992 #12 pick struggles offensively. He was stuck at A-ball in 1995.

MELVIN, BOB - C - BR - Age 34

Melvin's just a backup, and a weak-hitting one at that.

MENDENHALL, KIRK - SS - BR - Age 28

Mendenhall is a weak hitter who can play all of the infield positions.

MERCED, ORLANDO - 1B/OF - BL - Age 29

Merced is a solid, though not spectacular, major-league hitter. He hit for average with decent power in 1995. He seemed to grow up a lot last season and has a few better years ahead of him.

	AB	R	HR	RBI	SB	BA	$
1994 Pittsburgh NL	386	48	9	51	4	.272	12
1995 Pittsburgh NL	487	75	15	83	7	.300	20
1996 Projection >>>	536	78	15	84	6	.292	18

MERCEDES, HENRY - C - BR - Age 26

Mercedes is a great defensive catcher, but as a major league hitter, he's still just a great defensive catcher. He spent the last third of the season in Kansas City, but he will never be more than a backup unless his bat improves significantly. Look for him to begin the 1996 season at Triple-A Omaha, with a chance for a late-season callup -- maybe earlier if injuries dictate. Mercedes has decent speed for a catcher.

	AB	R	HR	RBI	SB	BA	$
1995 Kansas City AL	43	7	0	9	0	.256	-

MERCEDES, LUIS - OF - BR - Age 28

Mercedes stands as an example of what can happen when you let attitude get in the way of potential. Despite his obvious talent as a hitter, he has bounced around the high minors from one organization to another because he is uncoachable. Mercedes got just 84 at-bats for Triple-A Calgary in 1995 and is on his way out of pro ball.

MERULLO, MATT - DH/C - BL - Age 30

Merullo is a good backup catcher. He makes contact, is a .265 hitter, and is durable. He has made it to the majors just shy of thirty years old and has some productive years left.

	AB	R	HR	RBI	SB	BA	$
1994 Cleveland AL	10	1	0	0	0	.100	-
1995 Minnesota AL	195	19	1	27	0	.282	2
1996 *Projection* >>>	138	13	1	18	0	.273	-

MEULENS, HENSLEY - OF - BR - Age 28
Meulens was one of the top power hitters in Japan for the second straight year as he helped the Yakult Swallows to a Central League title. He'd be a good power hitting reserve if he returns to the US majors.

MIESKE, MATT - OF - BR - Age 28
His career (albeit without the stops) is starting to resemble Brad "The eternal prospect" Komminsk. Mieske's getting a bit old to be considered a prospect. He doesn't have much of a future.

	AB	R	HR	RBI	SB	BA	$
1994 Milwaukee AL	259	39	10	38	3	.259	9
1995 Milwaukee AL	267	42	12	48	2	.251	7
1996 *Projection* >>>	295	46	13	49	3	.254	7

MILLAR, KEVIN - 1B - BR - Age 24
Millar was an exceptional all-around offensive performer at Class-A Brevard County in the Marlins' chain in 1995, hitting for average with gap power, and exhibiting excellent patience at the plate (70 walks). However, it is very difficult to get excited about any prospect who doesn't reach Double-A before age 24 - to put it another way, this guy is eight months and six days older than Manny Ramirez. Millar should get a crack at Double-A pitching in 1996 - he projects as a major league extra man at best.

MILLARES, JOSE - 1B - BR - Age 28
Millares has not hit much in the minors. Thus, his upward growth is very limited, especially because he plays third, considered to be a power position.

MILLER, BARRY - 1B - BL - Age 27
He's a career minor-leaguer who might have reached the end of even that career.

MILLER, BRENT - 1B - BL - Age 25
Miller was the 19th pick overall in the June 1990 draft. He showed some long ball power in the Orioles farm system, but they ran out of patience and released him in early 1994 and he never surfaced in 1995.

MILLER, DAVID - 1B - BL - Age 22
A power hitting lefty from Clemson, Miller was the Indians' first round pick in 1995. He was considered to be a reach, as Baseball America had pegged him as the #53 prospect in the draft. He signed late, and will begin his pro career in 1996 in Class A. He has a powerful build at 6'4", 200, but bear in mind that he is a year older than established top prospect Richie Sexson, who will start 1996 in Double-A.

MILLER, KEITH - 3B/OF - BR - Age 32
For the second year in a row, Miller got just 15 big league at-bats; he can't stay healthy for a whole month, let alone a whole season. When last in the majors for an extended period of time, he had some speed, but a poor glove kept him from earning a regular role. Miller is a long shot to ever spend another year in the majors.

	AB	R	HR	RBI	SB	BA	$
1994 Kansas City AL	15	1	0	0	0	.133	-
1995 Kansas City AL	15	2	1	3	0	.333	-

MILLER, ORLANDO - SS - BR - Age 27
Miller hit better than expected in his rookie year in Houston before being sidelined for the remainder of the season in mid-August with what was first believed to be a minor knee injury. He should be back at full strength in 1996, but his durability has to be questioned. Miller is oversized for a shortstop and could be moved to third base at some point. He will have difficulty hitting for average unless he improves his plate discipline.

	AB	R	HR	RBI	SB	BA	$
1994 Houston NL	40	3	2	9	1	.325	1

	AB	R	HR	RBI	SB	BA	$
1995 Houston NL	324	36	5	36	3	.262	6
1996 *Projection* >>>	236	26	4	28	2	.256	2

MILLETTE, JOE - SS - BR - Age 29
His 88 major league at bats without an extra-base hit are 11 short of the all-time mark. Surehanded defensively but a zero offensively, his major league days appear to be behind him.

MILLIARD, RALPH - 2B - BR - Age 22
Milliard cemented his status as one of the finest minor league prospects at his position with a fine season at Double-A in 1995. He did so despite skipping a level, and he was named the premier defensive second baseman in the Eastern League by league managers. He did slump somewhat in the season's second half, but remains a prototypical top of the order hitter, drawing scores of walks, stealing bases, and showing surprising power for someone so small (5'10", 160 lbs.). He'll be at Triple-A in 1996, but Quilvio Veras has laid claim to the major league job, and megaprospect Luis Castilla is hot on his heels - he is a strong candidate for a position change or a trade.

MILNE, DARREN - OF - BR - Age 25
Milne is a weak hitter who needs to improve if he is to make further progress towards the majors.

MIRABELLI, DOUG - C - BR - Age 25
Mirabelli hit .302 with walks but no homers for Double-A Shreveport. He's a backup at best.

MIRANDA, GEOVANY - 3B - BR - Age 26
Miranda has no professional homers in seven seasons. Enough said.

MITCHELL, KEITH - OF - BR - Age 26
Mitchell could be an excellent reserve outfielder in the right organization A member of the 1991 and 1992 Braves World Series teams, he has good power, but might be a better candidate for the proposed U.S. Baseball League than to make it back to the majors.

MITCHELL, KEVIN - OF - BR - Age 34
Mitchell hit .300 for the Fukuoka Daiei Hawks in Japan in 1995, but battled injuries and team management for much of the year. He'll likely return to the States again in 1996, but would probably have to settle for a platoon role. He's still a fine power hitter and could be a very productive player in right situation in 1996.

MITCHELL, TONY - OF - BB - Age 25
Mitchell is a big powerhitting outfielder obtained by the Astros from the Cleveland organization. Since he has never been above the Double-A level in seven minor league seasons, he is not a major league prospect. He has struck out in over 25% of his career at-bats.

MOLER, JASON - 3B/C - BR - Age 26
Not long ago, Moler was a high level catching prospect in the Phils' organization. He was moved to third base in 1994 because of a supposedly awkward throwing motion, althouth he did throw out a high proportion of baserunners. In his second year at Double-A in 1995, Moler's season, and possibly his career, was short-circuited by a broken leg. Moler does have an excellent eye and power potential, but even if healthy, he will now be left in megaprospect Scott Rolen's wake.

MOLITOR, PAUL - DH - BR - Age 39
Though he finished up strong, Molitor suffered his worst season since 1984 and he spent parts of the year considering retirement. His bat speed has not slowed much and he makes contact as much as always. The Blue Jays bought out the option on his contract in October, making him a free agent heading into the winter. With only 211 hits remaining until 3,000, Molitor will probably stay in baseball a bit longer.

	AB	R	HR	RBI	SB	BA	$
1994 Toronto AL	454	86	14	75	20	.341	36
1995 Toronto AL	525	63	15	60	12	.270	17
1996 *Projection* >>>	549	82	16	75	17	.298	24

MOLINA, IZZY - C - BR - Age 24
Yet another weak hitting minor league catcher in the A's organization, Molina did nothing offensively last season to

advance his care. He will hit the occasional homerun, but otherwise there's not much to rave about.

MONDESI, RAUL - OF - BR - Age 25
Mondesi turned in a fine power/speed season, and missed only five games despite numerous injuries. He still doesn't walk much, but he improved his strikeout to walk ratio from five-to-one to three-to-one. Mondesi's arm and power are his obvious assets, but don't overlook his speed - he was an 87% base stealer in 1995 (27 of 31), his highest total since 1990 in Class A.

	AB	R	HR	RBI	SB	BA	$
1994 Los Angeles NL	434	63	16	56	11	.306	24
1995 Los Angeles NL	536	91	26	88	27	.285	30
1996 *Projection* >>>	553	89	23	84	23	.292	28

MONDS, WONDERFUL - OF - BR - Age 23
A very late 1993 draft pick (50th round), Monds was wonderful in name only. While he improved his batting average for Class A Durham, his speed is still his only asset. Monds is far too aggressive at the plate; he's not much of a prospect.

MONELL, JOHNNY - OF/DH - BB - Age 30
Monell is a former Mexican League star who was slated to be a replacement player. He is a high average hitter with some power, but his defensive limitations may make it hard for him to move beyond Triple-A.

MONTGOMERY, RAY - OF - BR - Age 26
The Astros tried to convince Montgomery to become a replacement player but he resisted and went on to have his best season, splitting time between Triple-A and Double-A. His .301 batting average, 21 homers and 92 RBIs were career highs for his six years in the Astro system. He could enhance his chances to make it to the majors as a spare outfielder if he has a strong showing in the Arizona Fall League.

MONTOYO, CHARLIE - 3B - BR - Age 31
Montoyo is the quintessential example of the famously successful minor leaguer who will simply never get an extended shot in the majors. At 5'11", 170 lbs., he is unimpressive phyically, he desn't hit for average or power, and has only average speed. However, he walks constantly, and has a superb nine year minor league career on-base percentage of .402. With the Phils' best prospects converging on Triple-A in 1996, a change of scenery could be in his immediate future.

MONZON, JOSE - C - BR - Age 27
Catcher Jose Monzon has been in the minors for eight years hitting a career .240 with essentially no power. He was in the Blue Jay system for six years. Looking at his overall record, it's unlikely that he will get to the show unless he turns things around quickly.

MOORE, KERWIN - OF - BB - Age 25
After several minor league seasons with eye-popping steals and walks totals, Moore slipped at Triple-A last season. A football player in high school, Moore is a late-bloomer in baseball who will never hit for average. After last year, his prospects have dimmed, but he's still worth watching. Think "Gary Pettis."

MOORE, MIKE - OF - BR - Age 25
Moore, a 1992 first-round draft pick out of UCLA, has had difficulty making contact.

MOORE, VINCE - OF - BL - Age 24
Proceeds of the Fred McGriff trade, Moore was overmatched in Double- AA, and needs to improve his hitting to move up.

MORA, MELVIN - OF - BR - Age 24
Mora is one of the many young players signed by the Astros out of Venezuela. Speed has been his biggest asset as he has moved up through the organization (.298-3-45-22 at Double-A in 1995). With limited power, he will have to hit for a higher average to reach the majors.

MORANDINI, MICKEY - 2B - BL - Age 29
Playing everyday for the first time in his career, Morandini did not embarrass himself in the leadoff role vacated by the injured Lenny Dykstra, showing Dykstra-like doubles power, but lacking the requisite base-stealing ability one desires in a leadoff man. He still cannot hit lefties (.229 in 1995), and could possibly find himself again in a platoon situation should Kevin Jordan impress in the spring. 1995 was as good as it will get for Morandini.

	AB	R	HR	RBI	SB	BA	$
1994 Philadelphia NL	274	40	2	26	10	.292	11
1995 Philadelphia NL	494	65	6	49	9	.283	13
1996 Projection >>>	500	67	5	48	11	.277	12

MORDECAI, MIKE - SS/2B - BB - Age 28
Mordecai reprised his brief 1994 role in the majors, serving as a defensive replacement and erstwhile pinch-hitter. He has a good glove but isn't really much of a major league hitter, despite his success in just 79 big league at-bats. Mordecai has proven he can fill a bench role in the majors and will do so for the Braves in 1996.

	AB	R	HR	RBI	SB	BA	$
1994 Atlanta NL	4	1	1	3	0	.250	-
1995 Atlanta NL	75	10	3	11	0	.280	1
1996 Projection >>>	75	10	3	10	0	.262	-

MORILLO, CESAR - SS - BB - Age 22
Not a highly regarded prospect, Morillo hits for a decent average but offers little else besides an above average glove. His progress has been slow, but he's still young enough to keep moving.

MORMAN, RUSS - 1B/OF - BR - Age 32
This minor league journeyman had another in a long line of fine Triple-A seasons in 1995, and spent the season's last two months successfully plugging some of the Marlins' injury-related holes. He is a free swinger with longball power who could conceivably be useful in a limited full season role. However, the Marlins got him through waivers after season's end, and he once again became a minor league free agent. He'll likely be on the first sack for someone's Triple-A club in 1996.

	AB	R	HR	RBI	SB	BA	$
1994 Florida NL	33	2	1	2	0	.212	-
1995 Florida NL	72	9	3	7	0	.278	1
1996 Projection >>>	56	7	2	6	0	.247	-

MORRIS, BOBBY - 2B - BL - Age 23
Hal's brother advanced to a higher Class A level in 1995 and retained his good batting average and speed, hitting .308 with 22 steals. Morris has good strike-zone judgment and is a fine line drive hitter. The Cubs continue to be concerned about his defense, though, so he may end up at third base or first base after advancing to a higher level in 1996.

MORRIS, HAL - 1B - BL - Age 30
Morris' first half was a disaster as he battled a recurrent hamstring problem, but a strong second half made his final stats respectable. Morris is like Mark Grace as a hitter, featuring a very high average and mediocre to poor power for a first baseman. His biggest weaknesses are an inability to hit lefties and durability. Morris is free agent and unlikely to return to the Reds.

	AB	R	HR	RBI	SB	BA	$
1994 Cincinnati NL	436	60	10	78	6	.335	25
1995 Cincinnati NL	359	53	11	51	1	.279	10
1996 Projection >>>	463	66	12	72	3	.304	16

MORROW, TIMMIE - OF - BR - Age 26
Morrow is a good defensive outfielder who may not hit well enough to advance.

MOTA, ANDY - 2B - BR - Age 30
Probably a career minor leaguer, Mota isn't a spectacularly good hitter and his glove work is suspect.

MOTA, GARY - OF - BR - Age 25
After his 1992 MVP season at Class A Asheville, Mota missed most of 1993 with an injury and didn't play well enough at Double-A in 1994 or 1995 to regain his status as a top prospect in the Houston organization. Time is running out.

MOTA, JOSE - 2B - BB - Age 31
This Royals replacement player has always been able to hit for average, and even steal a base or two, but he can no longer be considered a legitimate prospect because of his age. He appeared in 17 games for San Diego in 1991, and was called up by the Royals in '95, but appeared in only one game before suffering an injury. He hit .382 for Triple-A Omaha before his promotion.

MOTA, SANTO - SS - BR - Age 22
Mota is a lithe shortstop in the Cardinals' farm system. He has yet to get past Class A in five seasons. He has decent speed and a good glove, though he isn't exactly on the fast track to St. Louis.

MOTTOLA, CHAD - OF - BR - Age 24
Considered one of the Reds top prospects at the beginning of the year, Mattola's stock is falling after a mediocre year in AAA. Mottola is a power hitting rightfielder with a good arm and some speed but he definitely needs more seasoning before he can make the jump to the majors. He was the Reds #1 pick in 1992.

MOUTON, JAMES - OF - BR - Age 27
Mouton made a modest improvement in his second major league season in Houston, but still hasn't shown he can hit well enough to claim a regular job. His biggest asset is his speed which is good for 25 stolen bases as a part time player. He appears headed for a platoon role again in 1996.

	AB	R	HR	RBI	SB	BA	$
1994 Houston NL	310	43	2	16	24	.245	15
1995 Houston NL	298	42	4	27	25	.262	13
1996 *Projection* >>>	331	46	4	25	27	.267	13

MOUTON, LYLE - OF - BR - Age 26
Mouton joined the White Sox as the player to be named later in the Jack McDowell trade. He started off well at Triple-A Nashville, then showed good pop in his bat as the White Sox regular rightfielder in August and September. He looks physically like Frank Thomas; not as big, but much faster. Mouton is not a great outfielder, but will be a regular in left or right field in 1996.

	AB	R	HR	RBI	SB	BA	$
1995 Nashville AAA	267	40	8	41	10	.296	
1995 Chicago AL	179	23	5	27	1	.302	5
1996 *Projection* >>>	252	33	6	37	2	.278	5

MUCKER, KELCEY - OF/DH - BL - Age 21
Turned down offers to play football, basketball or baseball at Indiana and accepted $300,000 to sign with the Twins, who made him their fourth pick in the first round of 1993's draft.

MUELLER, BILL - 3B - BB - Age 25
Someone give this man a job! Mueller's minor-league career looks a lot like that of Edgar Martinez, another thirdbaseman who didn't get a legitimate major-league shot until he was 27 years old. Mueller hits for average, walks a lot, and has "doubles-power." He doesn't steal much or hit many homers, and has been stuck behind Matt Williams on the Giants' depth chart. If Williams (or Mueller) is traded, Bill Mueller is ready to have a breakout season in the majors, but he has only spent half-a-season at Triple-A and may not even make the majors for another year. It's worth keeping an eye out for this guy.

MULLIGAN, SEAN - C - BR - Age 25
Padres catching prospect Sean Mulligan has proven that he's a solid minor league hitter, and he will be competing for the back-up catching job in 1996. But the Padres may feel that he needs to play in Triple-A to stay sharp rather than spend his time on the bench.

MUNOZ, OMER - 2B - BR - Age 30
A career minor-league utilityman, Munoz was a replacement player in the Pirates' camp last spring but missed his

only chance to play in the big leagues when the strike ended. He's a nice man, who has managerial aspirations.

MUNOZ, ORLANDO - 2B - BB - Age 24
After spending 1994 in Triple-A, Angels shortstop Orlando Munoz slipped back to Double-A last year. He is a very weak hitter.

MUNOZ, PEDRO - OF - BR - Age 27
Munoz enjoyed the best year of his career in '95 as he reached career highs in almost every category. As long as he stays healthy he can produce sixty to seventy RBI per year. There is always the danger of a wild swinger's average going through the floor.

	AB	R	HR	RBI	SB	BA	$
1994 Minnesota AL	244	35	11	36	0	.295	10
1995 Minnesota AL	376	45	18	58	0	.301	13
1996 Projection >>>	440	54	20	66	0	.292	14

MURPHY, MIKE - OF - BR - Age 24
A 1990 sixth round pick, Murphy abandoned switch hitting in 1992, with positive results. He has excellent speed (33 steals in 1993) and hit 29 doubles at Single-A Spartanburg, but he needs to improve his discipline at the plate (only 35 walks in 544 plate appearances). He dropped back to Class A in 1995 however, slowing his progress.

MURRAY, CALVIN - OF - BR - Age 24
The exemplary "tools" player who has never performed up to expectations, Murray's career has stalled in the mid-minors, and he is unlikely at this point to ever become a star in the majors. He can steal bases and play defense, but probably won't hit enough to hold a job in the bigs.

MURRAY, EDDIE - DH - BB - Age 40
Murray continued on his consistent, relentless path towards first ballot Hall of Fame selection with a monstrous 1995 season. Murray recorded a career high batting average in 1995, and recorded his incredible 19th straight season with 75 or more RBI - including two strike seasons. He split 1996 between 1B and DH, and should be expected to fill the same role in 1996. His 1995 resurgence interrupted what had been an orderly four-year decline in productivity.

	AB	R	HR	RBI	SB	BA	$
1994 Cleveland AL	433	57	17	76	8	.254	18
1995 Cleveland AL	436	68	21	82	5	.323	22
1996 Projection >>>	457	62	18	77	3	.271	13

MURRAY, GLENN - OF - BR - Age 25
Murray hasn't panned out as Red Sox general manager Dan Duquette expected when he brought him along from Montreal. Sure, he's hit 25 home runs both years at Pawtucket, but with averages and RBI totals. And his defense has deteriorated. With Jose Malave and Wes Chamberlain flanking him, Murray was part of the worst defensive outfield of our time.

MYERS, GREG - C - BL - Age 29
Angels catcher Greg Myers appears to be injury prone as he usually gets injured one way or another every year. When healthy, he can hit .250-10-60 over a full season. Myers may revert to a back-up role if rookie phenom Todd Greene develops as expected.

	AB	R	HR	RBI	SB	BA	$
1994 California AL	126	10	2	8	0	.246	0
1995 California AL	273	35	9	38	0	.260	
1996 Projection >>>	327	38	10	41	0	.257	4

MYERS, ROD - OF - BL - Age 23
Not to be confused with the Royals pitcher of the same name, Myers is a pure hitter who had his best professional season for Double-A Wichita in 1995, leading the Texas League with 153 hits. A speedy outfiedler who is also handy with the leather and possesses a good arm, Myers biggest problem is that the Royals are over-stocked with young, talented outfielders who hit from the left side. He is still a good candidate to eventually make it to the big leagues.

MYROW, JOHN - OF - BR - Age 24
After his first two pro seasons, Myrow was considered one of the Rockies' best prospects. He tarnished that reputation in his Double-A debut at New Haven. On the plus side is his base-stealing judgment.

NAEHRING, TIM - 3B - BR - Age 29
Well, you always knew he could hit; staying healthy was the only real question. Naehring shifted to third base and turned in his finest season yet. With a good glove, some power and a high batting average, Naehring can be a successful third sacker in the major leagues. He's got one full season under his belt. Can he go for two in a row?

	AB	R	HR	RBI	SB	BA	$
1994 Boston AL	297	41	7	42	1	.276	8
1995 Boston AL	433	61	10	57	0	.307	12
1996 Projection >>>	430	60	10	58	1	.286	11

NATAL, BOB - C - BR - Age 30
Natal is a passable defensive catcher who has always hit in the minors, but then has been plagued by a slow bat in the majors. He also gets himself out quite often by swinging at bad pitches. With the lack of Marlins' catching prospects, Natal will again be in a dogfight for the backup position, barring a free agent acquisition. With Charles Johnson on the verge of stardom, there won't be many at bats left over even if Natal wins the backup job.

	AB	R	HR	RBI	SB	BA	$
1994 Florida NL	29	2	0	2	1	.276	-
1995 Florida NL	43	2	2	6	0	.233	-
1996 Projection >>>	63	2	1	6	1	.239	-

NAVARRO, TITO - SS - BR - Age 25
Navarro is a slick fielder with good speed.

NEAL, MIKE - 2B - BR - Age 24
The Indians' 1993 16th round pick from LSU had a fine season at Double-A Canton-Akron, ranking among league leaders with 71 walks, and adding solid defense. A natural shortstop, Neal has a chance to reach the majors as a utilityman, but doesn't have nearly enough tools to be a regular. Second base is one of the least fortified positions in the Indians' system, which should enable Neal to start in Triple-A, where he will be only a heartbeat away from a major league audition.

NEEL, TROY - 1B - BL - Age 30
Neel made it to the Japanese League World Series for the Orix Blue Wave in 1995; he fell one short of the homer crown with 27, but hit just .244. Should Neel return to the States, he would best serve a team in a platoon role and would hit for a low batting average, but decent power.

NELSON, BRYANT - SS - BB - Age 22
Nelson was Houston's 44th round draft choice in 1993 but has moved close to the head of his class after two solid seasons. A contact hitter who was switched from the outfield to shortstop, he has alot of work ahead of him on defense. He was selected by Baseball America as the ninth best prospect in the Florida State League in 1995 and was nominated by the Astros to play in the Arizona Fall League.

NEVERS, TOM - SS - BR - Age 24
Nevers was the Astros No. 1 draft choice in 1990. After progressing in each of his first four years, he has stalled at the Double-A level. Nevers needs a breakthrough year in 1996 to merit future consideration.

NEVIN, PHIL - 3B - BR - Age 25
A steal for the Tigers, Nevin was acquired from the Astros for Mike Henneman and was quickly inserted into left field. He will share time there with Bob Higginson in '96, and could play some in right as well. Nevin was inconsistent with Houston, but he still has a chance to be eighty percent of the player Kevin McReynolds was.

	AB	R	HR	RBI	SB	BA	$
1995 Tucson AAA	223	31	7	41	2	.291	
1995 Houston NL	60	4	0	1	1	.117	
1995 Dertoit AL	96	9	2	12	0	.219	-
1996 Projection >>>	175	20	3	22	2	.238	0

NEWFIELD, MARC - OF/1B - BR - Age 23
Newfield is a top prospect who was the key player coming to the Padres from Seattle in the Andy Benes trade. He has good power and has the potential to develop into a 30-homer per-year hitter.

	AB	R	HR	RBI	SB	BA	$
1994 Seattle AL	38	3	1	4	0	.184	-
1995 Seattle AL	85	7	3	14	0	.188	
1995 San Diego NL	55	6	1	7	0	.309	
1996 *Projection* >>>	303	33	9	44	0	.268	5

NEWSON, WARREN - OF - BL - Age 31
Newson has never had a chance to play regularly, despite a career OBP over .400 and respectable power. He hit .235 for the White Sox in 1995, then moved over to play leftfield in Seattle after Darren Bragg lost the job. He hit .292 for the Mariners but still lost his job to Vince Coleman. Newson can be a fine platoon outfielder if given a chance.

	AB	R	HR	RBI	SB	BA	$
1994 Chicago AL	102	16	2	7	1	.255	1
1995 Chicago-Seattle AL	157	34	5	15	2	.261	2
1996 *Projection* >>>	153	31	4	14	2	.267	2

NEWSTROM, DOUG - 3B - BL - Age 24
Newstrom, the Dodgers' seventh-round draft pick in 1993, moved from third base back to the position he played at Arizona State. He has a good batting eye, but may not have enough power to be a major league corner infielder.

NIEVES, MELVIN - OF - BB - Age 24
Melvin Nieves is a power-hitting switch hitter that the Padres management expect to develop into a Mike Schmidt-type of hitter any day now. Blessed with great raw power, he needs to learn the strike zone better and how to make more consistent contact. Nieves hit two grand slams last year, and had an excellent September, so the outlook for his emerging into an offensive force is brighter than it has been.

	AB	R	HR	RBI	SB	BA	$
1994 San Diego NL	19	2	1	4	0	.263	-
1995 San Diego NL	234	32	14	38	2	.205	4
1996 *Projection* >>>	222	30	13	36	1	.254	4

NILSSON, DAVE - OF - BL - Age 26
Nilsson posted decent full season numbers even though he missed about half of it with a wierd tropical disease. In his prime and could be due for a breakout this year.

	AB	R	HR	RBI	SB	BA	$
1994 Milwaukee AL	397	51	12	69	1	.275	14
1995 Milwaukee AL	263	41	12	53	2	.278	9
1996 *Projection* >>>	500	70	18	89	3	.288	17

NIXON, OTIS - OF - BB - Age 37
If Nixon is slowing down with age, it certainly isn't apparent. He is the prototypical leadoff hitter, and can be counted on to hit in the high .200s, score runs and be in the top five leaguewide in steals. Nixon is one of the best in baseball in bunting for a base hit.

	AB	R	HR	RBI	SB	BA	$
1994 Boston AL	398	60	0	25	42	.274	29
1995 Texas AL	589	87	0	45	50	.295	34
1996 *Projection* >>>	537	81	0	38	39	.286	22

NIXON, TROT - OF - BL - Age 21
The back injury which ended his 1994 season early also wrecked his 1995 campaign. A full recovery will be necessary before Nixon can show the good power and defense which made him a centerfield prospect for the Red Sox.

NOBOA, JUNIOR - 2B - BR - Age 31
This versatile, erstwhile major leaguer toiled for Triple-A Rochester in 1995, hitting just .100. Noboa has never had much power or speed, but has often been a useful pinch-hitter in the majors. He'll hang around for awhile and try out

with yet another team in 1996; Noboa has already been with eight different organizations since signing as a sixteen-year old phenom in 1981.

NOKES, MATT - C - BL - Age 32
Following his release from the Yankees in 1995, Nokes joined the Rockies via a minor league contract. After a short (and unremarkable) stint at Triple-A Colorado Springs, Nokes was called up, reportedly over Manager Don Baylor's objections; it was hoped Nokes would provide some left-handed stick as Girardi's backup. An injury caused by a home-plate collision soon ended this experiment. Nokes, a free agent at the end of 1995, may still have enough left to provide a team some left-handed power, but he'll need more than the 130 AB's he's averaged the last three years to prove it.

NORMAN, LES - OF - BR - Age 27
One of 19 rookies used by the 1995 Royals, Norman's a solid outfielder and a good hitter. Despite being a late round draft pick (1991, 25th round), the Royals have always thought highly of Norman, naming him their Minor League Player of the Year in 1993. A spray hitter with occasional power, he got little playing time at the major league level in 1995, but hit .284-9-33 in four months for Triple-A Omaha.

	AB	R	HR	RBI	SB	BA	$
1995 Kansas City AL	40	6	0	4	0	.225	-

NORTHRUP, KEVIN - OF - BR - Age 26
Northrup is a line-drive hitter with gap power who hit .309 at Class AA Harrisburg before finishing the season at Class AAA Edmonton. He is a good-looking player but could be hurt by the glut of outstanding outfield prospects in the Expos' farm system.

NUNEVILLER, TOM - OF - BR - Age 26
Once promising career was sidetracked by a serious knee injury in 1992. His power and speed haven't been the same since and Triple-A seems to be the upper boundary for the Phils' 1990 5th-round pick who spent 1995 at Class-A Clearwater.

NUNEZ, RAMON - 1B/OF - BR - Age 23
This Dominican started out at shortstop but gradually migrated to first base where he displayed modest power for Double-A Greenville in 1995. He's not highly regarded by the Braves.

NUNEZ, ROGEILO - C - BB - Age 25
A six-year minor league free agent, Nunez provides some experience behind the plate and works well with pitchers. Though he's a solid defensive catcher, he struggles at the plate. Nunez is not prospect, but is still a useful guy to have in the organization.

NUNNALLY JON - OF - BL - Age 24
A Rule Five draft pick from Cleveland, Nunnally emerged from a bench role to become a regular rightfielder by virtue of some first half homers. Possessed of good power, but a frequent strikeout victim, Nunnally was second in homers for the Royals. His production dropped sharply in the second half, though (.180 with no homers in his last 100 at-bats), and his immediate future will include some seasoning in the high minors.

	AB	R	HR	RBI	SB	BA	$
1995 Kansas City AL	303	51	14	42	6	.244	8
1996 Projection >>>	295	49	12	44	6	.248	7

OBANDO, SHERMAN - OF/DH - BR - Age 26
In 1995, Sherman Obando made the Orioles coming out of spring training and it was thought that he would platoon with Harold Baines at DH and play some occasional outfield. But he lost his power swing and looked like a singles hitter, soon being demoted to Triple-A where he hit well but his power stroke didn't return. His defense in the outfield and at first base is pathetic. The Orioles still have some hope that Obando will emerge as a 30-homer hitter, but he has to find consistent power to stick in the majors.

	AB	R	HR	RBI	SB	BA	$
1994 Rochester AAA	403	67	20	69	1	.330	
1995 Rochester AAA	324	42	9	53	1	.296	
1995 Baltimore AL	38	0	0	3	1	.263	-
1996 Projection >>>	190	18	1	22	5	.270	2

O'BRIEN, CHARLIE - C - BR - Age 34
Good defense and occasional power are O'Brien's hallmarks. He's one of the league's better second string catchers and will have a similar role for a few more years.

	AB	R	HR	RBI	SB	BA	$
1994 New York NL	152	24	8	28	0	.243	4
1995 Atlanta NL	198	18	9	23	0	.227	2
1996 *Projection* >>>	216	22	7	25	0	.222	-

OCHOA, ALEX - OF - BR - Age 24
Speed, power, and the famous "blink" trade in which the Orioles added Ochoa at the last minute to the package that brought Bobby Bonilla to Baltimore for the 1995 pennant race, will have fans watching Ochoa with much anticipation. So far he's produced more "all-the-tools" scouting raves than big numbers (career year: .301 average, 14 homers, 82 RBI and 28 steals at Double-A in 1994). 1996 will bring both opportunity and spotlight.

	AB	R	HR	RBI	SB	BA	$
1995 Rochester AAA	336	41	8	46	17	.274	
1995 Norfolk AAA	123	17	2	15	7	.309	
1995 New York NL	37	7	0	0	1	.297	-
1996 *Projection* >>>	333	67	8	44	9	.273	10

O'CONNER, KEVIN - OF - BL - Age 26
O'Connor continued his slow rise through the Braves system with a .222-4-14 season at Triple-A Richmond in 1995. He has a good batting eye and above average speed; he's also a good defensive outfielder. Still, O'Conner needs a much better year to get noticed.

OFFERMAN, JOSE - SS - BB - Age 27
Offerman's solid offensive year was obscured by his horrendous defense, which sent him to the bench during the stretch run. His 35 errors in 119 games translates to 48 over a 162 game season. A tremendous base stealer in the minors, Offerman's speed has disappeared the last two years in the majors, with only four steals in 191 games. Offerman's strike zone judgment makes him an excellent number two hitter, but he probably needs a trade and a position change to reach his potential.

	AB	R	HR	RBI	SB	BA	$
1994 Los Angeles NL	243	27	1	25	2	.210	-
1995 Los Angeles NL	429	69	4	33	2	.287	8
1996 *Projection* >>>	451	66	3	39	7	.267	8

O'HALLORAN, GREG - 1B - BL - Age 27
Finally reached the majors in 1994 after a steady but unspectacular five-year jaunt through the Blue Jays' organization. Last seen playing in independent ball in 1995.

O'LEARY, TROY - OF - BL - Age 26
Hitting for average and slugging .491, O'Leary was one of the Red Sox most pleasant surprises in 1995. He has decent speed and was a better outfielder than he was given credit for. He'd still be better in a platoon, but O'Leary should get another shot at a regular outfield job with Boston in 1996.

	AB	R	HR	RBI	SB	BA	$
1994 Milwaukee AL	66	9	2	7	1	.273	1
1995 Boston AL	399	60	10	49	5	.308	14
1996 *Projection* >>>	404	60	10	48	5	.286	11

OLERUD, JOHN - 1B - BL - Age 27
Not many people can hit .291 and call it a disappointing season. In Olerud's case, he has become more tentative at the plate than ever and isn't swinging as quickly as he did in his batting title year. With his big salary, Olerud's going to play everyday but he should be in his prime and hasn't posted the expected numbers.

	AB	R	HR	RBI	SB	BA	$
1994 Toronto AL	384	47	12	67	1	.297	16
1995 Toronto AL	492	72	8	54	0	.291	10
1996 *Projection* >>>	548	79	15	80	0	.303	18

OLIVA, JOSE - 3B - BR - Age 25
Oliva's big swing resulted in a few homers but far too many strikeouts. When the Braves tired of his whining about Chipper Jones starting ahead of him at third base they dealt him to the Cardinals last August. Starved for power, the Cardinals are thinking of starting him at first or third this season. That's yet another bad decision by a franchise that used to be one of the game's best.

	AB	R	HR	RBI	SB	BA	$
1994 Atlanta NL	59	9	6	11	0	.288	2
1995 Two Teams	183	15	7	20	0	.142	-
1996 *Projection* >>>	148	14	6	18	0	.216	-

OLIVER, JOE - C - BR - Age 30
Oliver came back with a vengeance. He's OK as long as he sees enough lefthanded pitching to offset his ineptitude against righties.

	AB	R	HR	RBI	SB	BA	$
1994 Cincinnati NL	19	1	1	5	0	.211	-
1995 Milwaukee AL	337	43	12	51	2	.273	9
1996 *Projection* >>>	222	23	6	26	1	.234	0

OLMEDA, JOSE - 2B - BB - Age 27
Olmeda converted from second base to the outfield, but didn't hit enough while striking out too much. He also played shortstop for Double-A Greenville with the same marginal results. Olmeda is too old to be at Double-A and is starting to look like a career minor leaguer.

O'NEILL, PAUL - OF - BL - Age 33
The 1994 batting champion had another good year in '95 despite a wrist injury and a trip to the DL. During the Seattle - New York playoff, it was downright amusing to hear the conventional media talk about O'Neill's progress under Lou Piniella in Cincinnati; escaping that person and that place were major factors in O'Neill's emergence as a top hitter. For 1996: more of the same success.

	AB	R	HR	RBI	SB	BA	$
1994 New York AL	368	68	21	83	5	.359	30
1995 New York AL	460	82	22	96	1	.300	19
1996 *Projection* >>>	505	85	23	95	3	.308	23

OQUENDO, JOSE - SS/2B - BB - Age 32
Once a utility man extrordinaire, Oquendo hasn't had a good season since 1989 and his four-year, $8-million deal with the Cardinals expired at the end of last season. Plagued by injuries throughout the life of that contract, Oquendo says he feels good enough to play a few more years. If that's the case, he's going to have to take a large paycut and start producing a little more.

	AB	R	HR	RBI	SB	BA	$
1994 St. Louis NL	129	13	0	9	1	.264	0
1995 St. Louis NL	220	31	2	17	1	.209	-
1996 *Projection* >>>	210	27	1	16	1	.233	-

ORDONEZ, REY - SS - BB - Age 24
With a glove and moves like Ozzie Smith, and a bat like Mario Mendoza, Ordonez is today's epitome of good-field, no-hit shortstops. His presence in 1995 will help all Mets pitchers. Ordonez would have been in the majors in September 1995 if not for 40-man roster exposure problems. In the beginning he will be a void in the batting order, but he does have a tendency to make contact, and thus can become a 50-RBI guy when he matures.

ORIE, KEVIN - SS - BR - Age 23
A 1993 sandwich pick (for the loss of Greg Maddux), Orie has a quick, powerful bat but is still several years off.

ORSULAK, JOE - OF - BL - Age 33
Orsulak keeps beginning every year with no clear role and ending up with a major share of outfield time. With age he has lost a step in the field and become strictly a platooner at the plate, and with the Mets youth movement under way, he will likely play even less.

	AB	R	HR	RBI	SB	BA	$
1994 New York NL	292	39	8	42	4	.260	9
1995 New York NL	290	41	1	37	1	.283	5
1996 *Projection* >>>	230	32	3	29	2	.270	3

ORTIZ, BO - OF - BR - Age 25
Outfielder Bo Ortiz had a good year in 1994 with Bowie in the tough Eastern League, but he struggled last year in the Double-A Texas League where he should have feasted. Ortiz is not progressing very well, and he must become a stronger hitter if he is to move up.

ORTIZ, JAVIER - OF - BR - Age 33
Ortiz hit just .167 for Triple-A Nashville in 1995, his twelfth minor league season - and maybe his last.

ORTIZ, JUNIOR - C - BR - Age 36
This veteran catcher with over 11 years of major league experience is winding down his career. He saw limited action in 1995 for Triple-A Nashville.

ORTIZ, LUIS - 3B - BR - Age 25
Ortiz is rapidly approaching the make-or-break point in his career. He has hit well for average, but lacks power and speed. Ortiz is a major defensive liability at third base, but doesn't generate enough offense to play first or to DH. His prospects for significant playing time in the majors are questionable.

	AB	R	HR	RBI	SB	BA	$
1994 Boston AL	18	3	0	6	0	.167	-
1995 Texas AL	108	10	1	18	0	.231	-
1996 *Projection* >>>	202	20	3	34	0	.265	1

ORTIZ, RAY - OF - BL - Age 27
A career minor-leaguer who hasn't done much in the last three years to get anyone's attention. He's no prospect.

ORTON, JOHN - C - BR - Age 30
Sub-.200 batting averages the last two years have run this former Angels "catcher of the future" out of baseball.

OSIK, KEITH - C/3B - BR - Age 27
Osik regained stature as a decent prospect in the Pirates' organization last season with a good year at Triple-A Calgary after serving as a replacement player in spring training. He can play every position on the field and could fashion a major-league career as a 25th man.

OTANEZ, WILLIS - 3B - BR - Age 22
Otanez has discovered surprising power for a player listed at 150 pounds, and has nothing more to prove in Class A..

OTERO, RICKY - OF - BB - Age 23
Youth and speed are Otero's big assets. His biggest liability is the growing crowd in the Mets outfield, loaded with future stars.

	AB	R	HR	RBI	SB	BA	$
1995 Norfolk AAA	295	37	1	23	16	.268	
1995 New York NL	51	5	0	1	2	.137	-
1996 *Projection* >>>	62	7	0	5	3	.244	-

OWEN, SPIKE - SS - BB - Age 34
Spike Owen's hitting .310 in 1994 was a fluke, and he returned to his normal level last year. Actually .225 is 21 points below his career .246, but he was hobbled with a shoulder problem last year. He was found wanting as a shortstop replacing the injured Gary DiSarcina. Owen has a limited role of part time third baseman and pinch hitter, and is very vulnerable to being replaced by a younger and more versatile player.

	AB	R	HR	RBI	SB	BA	$
1994 California AL	268	30	3	37	2	.310	9
1995 California AL	218	17	1	28	3	.229	1
1996 *Projection* >>>	170	18	1	17	1	.234	-

OWENS, BILLY - 1B - BB - Age 24
First baseman Billy Owens hit well in the pitching-tough Double-A Eastern League last year, earning a promotion to Triple-A. While not yet ready to dislodge Rafael Palmeiro, Owens can get closer with a good season in Triple-A in 1996, and he may earn a September call-up.

OWENS, ERIC - SS - BR - Age 25
Owens established himself as a significant prospect in 1995, winning the American Association MVP despite missing the last few weeks of the season due to a torn right ACL ligament. He led the league in runs scored, stolen bases, was second in batting average and slugged .492. Owens is considered a below average second baseman but the breadth of his offensive skills should get him a chance in the majors soon, perhaps as an outfielder.

OWENS, JAYHAWK - C - BR - Age 27
Owens reputation before last season was "good catch - no hit." He proved the critics wrong at the Triple-A level in 1995 prior to his August 1st recall when Matt Nokes went down with an injury. Owens played in 18 games for the Rocks down the stretch, providing some clutch hits which belied his .244 average. He's likely to start the 1996 campaign as Girardi's backup and see substantial playing time.

	AB	R	HR	RBI	SB	BA	$
1994 Colorado NL	12	4	0	1	0	.250	-
1995 Colorado Springs AAA	221	47	12	48	2	.294	
1995 Colorado NL	45	7	4	12	0	.244	1
1996 *Projection* >>>	114	21	5	22	0	.260	1

PAGLIARULO, MIKE - 3B - BL - Age 36
Pagliarulo's playing time came at the expense of an injury to Dean Palmer. Pagliarulo has lost a step defensively, and his bat seemed slow. He may be good for one or two more years as a utility player.

	AB	R	HR	RBI	SB	BA	$
1995 Texas AL	241	27	4	27	0	.232	1
1996 *Projection* >>>	113	12	2	12	0	.228	-

PAGNOZZI, TOM - C - BR - Age 33
Once one of baseball's most underrated catchers, Pagnozzi suffered through another injury-plagued season in 1995 with the Cardinals. His knees are shot and his bat has slowed. His best bet of sticking around a few more years is to swallow his pride, take a hefty pay cut and land a job as a backup somewhere. A savvy veteran, he could help someone as a number two catcher.

	AB	R	HR	RBI	SB	BA	$
1994 St. Louis NL	243	21	7	40	0	.272	7
1995 St. Louis NL	219	17	2	15	0	.215	-
1996 *Projection* >>>	283	23	5	31	0	.241	0

PALMEIRO, ORLANDO - OF - BL - Age 27
Palmeiro is a small and fast base-stealing outfielder who has hit decently in Triple-A for the past two years. He has no home-run power. In the majors, he could be an excellent bench player and a fill-in outfielder, pinch runner, and pinch hitter.

	AB	R	HR	RBI	SB	BA	$
1995 California AL	20	3	0	1	0	.350	-

PALMEIRO, RAFAEL - 1B - BL - Age 31
Palmeiro is one of the best hitters in baseball, and he loves to hit balls over the scoreboard in Camden Yards. He would have many more RBI, but the lead-off and second hitters batting ahead of him are far from the league leaders in on-base percentage. Palmeiro should hit even better in 1996 because he has power hitter Bobby Bonilla batting behind him, rather than the weaker and slump-prone Cal Ripken.

	AB	R	HR	RBI	SB	BA	$
1994 Baltimore AL	436	82	23	76	7	.319	28
1995 Baltimore AL	554	89	39	104	3	.310	28
1996 *Projection* >>>	587	99	33	107	7	.312	29

PALMER, DEAN - 3B - BR - Age 27
In early June, Palmer suffered a torn left bicep muscle that effectively ended his season, although he returned in late September and tore scar tissue from the surgery. He is expected to recover fully by next season. Palmer was off to a torrid start, and may have finally broken through as a hitter.

	AB	R	HR	RBI	SB	BA	$
1994 Texas AL	342	50	19	59	3	.246	13
1995 Texas AL	119	30	9	24	1	.336	6
1996 Projection >>>	518	94	32	96	6	.270	21

PAPPAS, ERIK - C - BR - Age 29
Always a respectable minor leaguer behind the plate and with the bat, Pappas came up woefully short in his most recent (1994) shot in the majors. He settled in with the Marlins' Triple-A club in Charlotte in 1995, and continued his career pattern of hitting for a low average, but with good power and an excellent eye. At best, he will be involved in a battle for the Marlins' backup catcher job in 1996 - more likely, it will be back to Triple-A for this minor league journeyman.

PAQUETTE, CRAIG - 3B - BR - Age 27
Paquette's stats read like the offspring of Todd Benzinger and Cory Snyder in a bad year. Paquette's ridiculous 88/12 K/BB ratio in 1995 actually represented an improvement over his previous career totals. His 283 at-bats last year offer definitive proof that Tony LaRussa is no longer a genius. He has no business on a major league roster.

	AB	R	HR	RBI	SB	BA	$
1994 Oakland AL	49	0	0	0	1	.143	-
1995 Oakland AL	283	42	13	49	5	.226	7
1996 Projection >>>	251	32	10	38	4	.227	3

PAREDES, JOHNNY - 2B - BR - Age 33
Back in 1987 he was a good prospect with the Expos: high average, high speed. Now over the hill.

PARENT, MARK - C - BR - Age 34
The long-time backup catcher had the season of his life with the Pirates last season, seeing significant playing time after Don Slaught got hurt and setting career highs in almost every category. Traded to the Cubs last Aug. 31st, he'll never have another season like 1995 but should stick around a few more years as a backup because he is one of the game's true professionals.

	AB	R	HR	RBI	SB	BA	$
1995 Two Teams	265	30	18	38	0	.234	7
1996 Projection >>>	165	18	8	25	0	.233	0

PARKER, RICK - OF - BR - Age 33
Journeyman outfielder who hits for average and not much else. He managed to get another cup of coffee (his fifth) in the majors in 1995, this time pinch hitting for the Dodgers. The chances for a sixth are not good.

PARRA, FRANKLIN - SS - BB - Age 24
Speedy Parra is a good minor league utility player who has spent a seven years with the Rangers but doesn't look to be in their long range plans.

PARRISH, LANCE - C - BR - Age 39
Parrish was as surprised as anyone that he played as much as he did. The power is not what it once was and he never was a contact hitter. Close to retirement, he could be worth having around to teach a young catcher.

	AB	R	HR	RBI	SB	BA	$
1994 Pittsburgh NL	126	10	3	16	1	.270	2
1995 Toronto AL	178	15	4	22	0	.202	-
1996 Projection >>>	114	10	3	14	1	.213	-

PATTERSON, JOHN - 2B - BB - Age 29
He hit .205 in 1995 as a backup. Patterson can't hit, is too old to be considered a prospect, and won't play enough to get many steals.

	AB	R	HR	RBI	SB	BA	$
1994 Pittsburgh NL	240	36	3	32	13	.238	9
1995 San Francisco NL	205	27	1	14	4	.205	-
1996 *Projection* >>>	241	33	2	23	8	.222	1

PAYTON, JAY - OF - BR - Age 22
To use Gerry Hunsicker's three-word scouting report: "born to hit." Payton didn't get a September callup because of 40-man roster problems, but his chance of being in the opening day lineup is still good.

	AB	R	HR	RBI	SB	BA	$
1995 Binghampton AA	357	59	14	54	16	.345	
1995 Norfolk AAA	196	33	4	30	11	.240	
1996 *Projection* >>>	232	33	5	44	6	.280	6

PEARSON, EDDIE - 1B - BB - Age 22
An injury laid waste Pearson's 1995 season, but he did come back in time to get in his first 50 games at the Double-A level. The White Sox are expecting the 6-3, 225-pounder to increase his power as he matures. They'd also like to see better defense.

PECORILLI, ALDO - 1B - BR - Age 25
The Braves obtained Pecorilli from the Cardinals organization before last season. By devastating the Southern League, Pecorilli earned a promotion to join his boyhood pal Kevin Grijak with Triple-A Richmond. Pecorilli's greatest need is a position; it may help his chances that he has done some catching.

PEGUES, STEVE - OF - BR - Age 27
Pegeus spent his first full season in the majors last year with the Pirates. He has some skills, a decent bat and some speed. However, he doesn't do anything well enough to warrant being more than a fifth outfielder in the big leagues. Being dropped from the Pirates roster a week after the 1995 season wasn't a real good sign for his future.

	AB	R	HR	RBI	SB	BA	$
1994 Pittsburgh NL	36	2	0	2	1	.361	0
1995 Pittsburgh NL	171	17	6	16	1	.246	2
1996 *Projection* >>>	131	12	4	12	1	.252	-

PELTIER, DAN - OF - BL - Age 27
Peltier doesn't field well enough to play in the outfield and doesn't hit with enough power to be a major league first baseman. At his best, Peltier is a Jack Daugherty type of hitter.

PEMBERTON, RUDY - OF - BR - Age 26
Pemberton, a young Dominican outfielder, has shown marked improvement since the Tigers signed him in '87. He has a chance to develop into a good fourth outfielder in the big leagues, and at this point is more polished than future right fielder Danny Bautista. Pemberton still will have to fight hard for playing time in '96.

	AB	R	HR	RBI	SB	BA	$
1995 Detroit AL	30	3	0	3	0	.300	-

PENA, GERONIMO - 2B - BB - Age 29
For years, the Cardinals have insisted that Pena has the talent to become one of the game's premier second baseman. However, it's hard to ever develop that talent when you're always on the disabled list. The Cardinals have finally come to the realization that it's not going to happen with Pena and will look in another direction for a second baseman.

	AB	R	HR	RBI	SB	BA	$
1994 St. Louis NL	213	33	11	34	9	.254	11
1995 St. Louis NL	101	20	1	8	3	.267	1
1996 *Projection* >>>	193	33	6	24	7	.259	4

PENA, TONY - C - BR - Age 38
Pena was again a godsend, holding the fort for the Indians' as Sandy Alomar made his annual pilgrimage to the disabled list. Though his throwing skills have deteriorated, he certainly knows how to call a game and handle a young pitching staff. Offensively, he is no longer the automatic out that he was in his final seasons as a fulltimer in Boston. He sprays the ball around while swinging at everything, and can still drive the ball on occasion - just ask the Bosox.

He is a low-risk backup who will likely return in a reserve role somewhere in 1996.

	AB	R	HR	RBI	SB	BA	$
1994 Cleveland AL	112	18	2	10	0	.295	2
1995 Cleveland AL	263	25	5	28	1	.262	3
1996 *Projection* >>>	195	20	4	19	1	.244	0

PENDLETON, TERRY - 3B - BB - Age 35
Just when it appeared that Pendleton was fading into the sunset of his career, he bounced back with a representative season with the Marlins. Though he should not be batting in the middle third of anyone's order at this stage of his career, Pendleton hit for average and decent extra base power, and mashed lefties at a .336 clip.

	AB	R	HR	RBI	SB	BA	$
1994 Atlanta NL	309	25	7	30	2	.252	6
1995 Florida NL	513	70	14	78	1	.290	16
1996 *Projection* >>>	509	62	13	70	2	.269	11

PENN, SHANNON - 2B - BB - Age 26
Penn is a good defensive second baseman whose talents are better suited to Triple-A than the majors. He does have the speed to become a pinch runner, and the glove for a utility role.

PENNYFEATHER, WILLIAM - OF - BR - Age 27
A great athlete who once was a wide receiver at Syracuse, Pennyfeather hasn't been able to transfer all that ability to the baseball field. He can run and catch but cannot hit breaking junk. He's a fifth outfielder at best.

PEREZ, DANNY - OF - BR - Age 25
Perez didn't generate much power last season playing in his hometown, El Paso, but everything else pointed toward considering him one of the better prospects in the Milwaukee organization.

PEREZ, EDDIE - C - BR - Age 27
Perez may be growing impatient waiting for the Braves to unload Charlie O'Brien. Perez approaches O'Brien's defensive ability, and is a much better hitter against both righthanded and lefthanded pitching.

	AB	R	HR	RBI	SB	BA	$
1995 Atlanta NL	13	1	1	4	0	.308	-

PEREZ, EDUARDO - 3B/1B - BR - Age 26
Perez failed in two trials with the Angels, but they are still optimistic that he will develop into a consistent producer. Playing regularly, he could hit .250-.260 with 10 homers and 12 stolen bases, adequate numbers but still not the offensive force expected from the third base slot.

	AB	R	HR	RBI	SB	BA	$
1994 California AL	129	10	5	16	3	.209	2
1995 California AL	71	9	1	7	0	.169	-
1996 *Projection* >>>	190	19	5	22	3	.231	0

PEREZ, JHONNY - SS - BR - Age 19
Yes he really spells it that way. Perez is a high speed, high average hitter on his way up.

PEREZ, NEIFI - SS - BB - Age 21
The most important factor to remember with Perez is his age. Any player who can reach Triple-A even briefly as a teen-ager has to be a top prospect. Despite a slow start, he became far more than an automatic out at bat, even showing some power. There never was any doubt about his defense. The Rockies may even allow him another year to develop.

PEREZ, ROBERT - OF - BR - Age 26
He had a fantastic year at Triple-A and has now hit over .290 three straight minor league seasons. Perez is extremely aggressive but is a good contact hitter. Entering the winter, he appeared to have a shot at landing a 1996 spot in the major leagues.

	AB	R	HR	RBI	SB	BA	$
1994 Toronto AL	8	0	0	0	0	.125	-

	AB	R	HR	RBI	SB	BA	
1995 Syracuse AAA	502	70	9	67	7	.343	
1996 *Projection* >>>	136	20	3	19	0	.270	0

PEREZ, TOMAS - SS - BB - Age 22
As a Rule 5 draft pick, he had to spend the entire season in the majors and played well in limited work. His stance is very similar to Roberto Alomar's although he swings wildly and at just about everything. Having spent the required year on the major league roster, he can now be sent to Triple-A. If Roberto Alomar were to sign elsewhere, Perez would get some consideration.

	AB	R	HR	RBI	SB	BA	$
1995 Toronto AL	98	12	1	8	0	.245	-
1996 *Projection* >>>	117	14	2	9	0	.255	-

PERONA, JOE - C - BR - Age 26
1995 was Perona's third in Class AA. Unfortunately, he had a worse year at the plate, slipping from a respectable .269 down to a poor .147. He needs to improve his hitting.

PERRY, GERALD - 1B - BL - Age 35
Perry's lone value for the past several seasons has been his ability to pinch hit. He stopped doing that last season and the Cardinals released him. Good pinch hitters are hard to find and he's likely to get one more chance to salvage his career with another team this spring.

	AB	R	HR	RBI	SB	BA	$
1994 St. Louis NL	77	12	3	18	1	.325	3
1995 St. Louis NL	79	4	0	5	0	.165	-
1996 *Projection* >>>	65	7	1	9	1	.237	-

PERRY, HERBERT - 1B/3B - BR - Age 26
Perry established himself as a solid major league line-drive bat with gaps power in 1996. When Dave Winfield, Eddie Murray and Paul Sorrento all suffered injuries in 1995, Perry capably stepped in and kept the Indians' juggernaut moving forward. He especially grinds lefties (.344 in 1995), and will likely slide neatly into the righthanded DH role manned by Winfield in 1995. He is not your typical 30 homer first baseman, and is therefore unlikely to become a star - expect 280 highly professional at bats in 1996.

	AB	R	HR	RBI	SB	BA	$
1994 Cleveland AL	9	1	0	1	0	.111	-
1995 Cleveland AL	162	23	3	23	1	.315	1
1996 *Projection* >>>	284	60	6	40	2	.294	7

PETAGINE, ROBERTO - 1B - BL - Age 24
After two outstanding seasons in the high minors, it was expected that Roberto Petagine would evolve into a major league hitting machine. Given a shot at the starting first base job, he struggled at bat and was benched. But he only got 124 at-bats, and he may yet emerge as a good major league hitter.

	AB	R	HR	RBI	SB	BA	$
1994 Tucson AAA	247	53	10	44	3	.316	
1995 San Diego NL	124	15	3	17	0	.234	1
1996 *Projection* >>>	307	35	9	39	0	.266	4

PETERSON, CHARLES - OF - BR - Age 21
When the Pirates drafted this outfielder in the first round in 1993 out of a South Carolina high school, they warned that his skills were very raw and would probably need five years in the minor leagues. He has accelerated that timetable, though, finishing last season in Double-A. He has good power potential and outstanding speed. With the Pirates sorely needing impact hitters, he could well be in the majors by 1997.

PETERSEN, CHRIS - SS - BR - Age 25
He has six home runs in four pro seasons(four of them coming in 1995), and has never batted above .226, including a career low .212 in 1995.

PHILLIPS, J.R. - 1B - BL - Age 25
Given 285 at-bats at the major league level, J.R. flopped bigtime, losing his job to journeyman Mark Carreon. Phillips

can hit home runs, but that is the extent of his offensive contributions. His minor-league numbers were unimpressive in the context of his league, and he is an extreme longshot to last in the majors.

	AB	R	HR	RBI	SB	BA	$
1994 San Francisco NL	38	1	1	3	1	.132	-
1995 San Francisco NL	231	27	9	28	1	.195	1
1996 *Projection* >>>	173	19	7	21	1	.212	-

PHILLIPS, TONY - 3B/OF - BB - Age 36
The Angels were very pleased with Phillips, who was a very valuable part of the Angels offense, the sparkplug leading off and getting on base to set the table for the big hitters. Now getting up in years, he hasn't slowed down much, setting a career high with 27 homers last year. However, looking deeper into last year's stats, there are a couple of bad signs: Phillips struck out a career high 135 times; and in the second half last year, he slumped badly, hitting only .235 and striking out almost 30 per cent of the time with his 84 strikeouts far exceeding his 50 walks, whereas he usually walks more than he strikes out.

	AB	R	HR	RBI	SB	BA	$
1994 Detroit AL	438	91	19	61	13	.281	24
1995 California AL	525	119	27	61	13	.261	19
1996 *Projection* >>>	511	105	14	62	12	.260	15

PIAZZA, MIKE - C - BR - Age 27
Piazza turned in a sensational season despite injuries that cost him 32 games. Bench and Campanella hit 45 homers in a good year, but did they ever hit .346? Lombardi won a batting title and regularly hit about 14 homers a year. Piazza's late start may be the only reason that keeps him out of the Hall of Fame. In 1995, there were whispers about his defense, and possibly moving him to another position but that doesn't seem likely, at least in 1996. The logical positions (first base and left field) are or will be taken and third base is a difficult transition for a catcher (although Joe Torre did it and hit .363 one year.)

	AB	R	HR	RBI	SB	BA	$
1994 Los Angeles NL	405	64	24	92	1	.319	26
1995 Los Angeles NL	434	82	32	93	1	.346	28
1996 *Projection* >>>	518	90	33	110	1	.327	29

PICHARDO, SANDY - 2B - BL - Age 21
The Mets have made a commitment to middle-infield defense. Down the line behind Edgardo Alfonzo is Pichardo. He also can run.

PICO, BRANDON - OF - BL - Age 21
Still just a pup, Pico lacks a good batting eye or great speed. He has a little power as shown in his 4 homers and 27 doubles in 1995 at Class A Wilmington.

PIRKL, GREG - 1B - BR - Age 25
Talented but unproven and injured most of 1995, Pirkl is unlikely to break into this lineup. The best factor a player can have going for him, other than pure talent, is someone in the front office watching his career with interest.

	AB	R	HR	RBI	SB	BA	$
1994 Seattle AL	53	7	6	11	0	.264	2
1995 Seattle AL	17	2	0	0	0	.235	-

PLANTIER, PHIL - OF - BL - Age 27
In July, the Astros dealt slugger Phil Plantier back to the Padres for a couple of non-prospect minor league pitchers, indicating how his value has gone down. But it was only in 1993 that he hit 34 home runs with 100 RBI, and at age 27, Plantier is your prototypical low-average slugger, and he can't hit southpaws worth a darn, so .250 is about the best you can expect.

	AB	R	HR	RBI	SB	BA	$
1994 San Diego NL	341	44	18	41	3	.220	8
1995 San Diego NL	216	33	9	34	1	.255	5
1996 *Projection* >>>	335	47	17	50	2	.252	7

POLCOVICH, KEVIN - SS - BR - Age 25
Considered nothing more than a fringe prospect by the Pirates before last season, Polcovich emerged in 1995. He doesn't appear to have the necessary skills to be a starting major-league shortstop but now looks like he'll make it as a utility infielder.

POLONIA, LUIS - OF - BL - Age 31
A reduced role for the Yankees precipitated his escape to the Braves where he provided speed, defense, experience and an extra lefty bat off the bench. Polonia could be a regular again, but not for any team with established outfielders. He probably won't return to the Braves; his role in 1996 depends upon where he ends up - don't count on more than about 20 steals unless he's guaranteed a starting job.

	AB	R	HR	RBI	SB	BA	$
1994 New York AL	350	62	1	36	20	.311	21
1995 NY AL - Atlanta NL	291	43	2	17	13	.261	7
1996 Projection >>>	381	60	2	28	22	.281	14

POSADA, JORGE - C - BB - Age 24
Who needs a switch-hitting catcher with decent power, outstanding defensive skills including a very strong arm? Just about every team in the majors. Posada will likely spend much of 1996 up with the Yankees, beginning a long and productive career.

POSE, SCOTT - OF - BL - Age 29
Pose had such a great spring training with the first edition of the Florida Marlins that he was in their opening day lineup. It wasn't long before he was back in Triple-A, and has been with three other organizations' top farm teams since. He was a minor league free agent again during the off-season. He's strictly insurance for a team needing a temporary singles-hitting player who can get on base, steal occasionally and play some defense.

POUGH, PORK CHOP - 1B - BR - Age 26
Formerly of the Indians, "Pork Chop" Pough joined the Red Sox as a six-year minor league free agent. He has good power, but strikes out far too much to be a real prospect. He's a bench player if he ever gets to the big leagues.

POWELL, DANTE - OF - BR - Age 22
A first-round draft pick of the Giants in 1994, Powell struggled in his first full professional season, yet still hit ten homers and stole 43 bases playing his home games in a pitchers' park. He's still at least two years away, but remains intriguing.

POZO, ARQUIMEDEZ - 2B - BR - Age 22
Pozo can hit for both power and average, and he's also a good fielder. He hit .300 with ten homers for Tacoma in 1995, earning a one at-bat visit to the majors. This young second baseman will soon join Alex Rodriguez to form the best young double play combination in the majors.

	AB	R	HR	RBI	SB	BA	$
1995 Tacoma AAA	450	57	10	62	3	.300	
1996 Projection >>>	206	24	3	25	1	.270	2

PRATT, TODD - C/1B - BR - Age 29
The ex-Phillie is a decent second string catcher who is easily replaced by any of the other available second string catchers that inhabit the major league fringe every year.

	AB	R	HR	RBI	SB	BA	$
1994 Philadelphia NL	102	10	2	9	0	.196	-
1995 Chicago NL	60	3	0	4	0	.133	-
1996 Projection >>>	55	4	1	5	0	.210	-

PRATTE, EVAN - 2B - BB - Age 27
Pratte is a versatile infielder who can play second, third, and shortstop. He spent the past three years in Double-A, but he still needs to improve his hitting.

PRIDE, CURTIS - OF - BL - Age 27
His story is certainly inspirational, overcoming deafness to reach the major leagues. However, Pride hasn't produced much the past two seasons and the Expos have plenty of other good young outfielders. At age 27, his best bet now

is to stick around somewhere as a fifth outfielder.

	AB	R	HR	RBI	SB	BA	$
1995 Ottawa AAA	154	25	4	24	8	.279	
1995 Montreal NL	63	10	0	2	3	.175	
1996 Projection >>>	73	12	0	2	3	.225	-

PRINCE, TOM - C - BR - Age 31
The journeyman catcher got another chance to show he can't hit major league pitching when Piazza was injured early in the season. He did hit decently at Albuquerque for the second straight season. The Dodgers will need a better reason than Prince to consider moving Piazza to another position.

PRITCHETT, CHRIS - 1B - BL - Age 26
Although this first baseman has hit decently in the minors through Triple-A, he has not hit strongly enough to warrant getting a call-up or other attention. Pritchett hits like a minor-league version of Mike Aldrete.

PUCKETT, KIRBY - OF - BR - Age 35
After a slow start, Puckett picked up the pace and turned in good final numbers. Then in late September a Dennis Martinez fastball broke his jaw, an injury from which it is difficult to regain aggressiveness at the plate. Puckett should be able to do it. He has at least five years of productivity left, and has reportedly decided to stay in Minneapolis for the Twins' rebuilding.

	AB	R	HR	RBI	SB	BA	$
1994 Minnesota AL	439	79	20	112	6	.317	30
1995 Minnesota AL	538	83	23	99	3	.314	23
1996 Projection >>>	557	87	22	102	4	.300	22

PULLIAM, HARVEY - OF - BR - Age 28
Pulliam never really had a chance with the Royals, who preferred their outfielders fast. The Rockies, however, like outfielders who can hit. And that's exactly what Pulliam did at Colorado Springs to earn a brief promotion to the big club. He's a good outfielder, but his arm limits him to left field.

	AB	R	HR	RBI	SB	BA	$
1995 Colorado Springs AAA	407	90	25	91	6	.327	
1995 Colorado NL	5	1	1	3	0	.400	-

PYE, EDDIE - 2B - BR - Age 29
Pye is a career minor leaguer who hits for average and not much else. His .295 average at Albuquerque was his worst there in four seasons. In two late season trials with the Dodgers he is 1 for 18. He is too old to be considered a prospect.

	AB	R	HR	RBI	SB	BA	$
1995 Los Angeles NL	8	0	0	0	0	.000	-

QUINLAN, TOM - 3B - BR - Age 28
Former Blue Jays prospect Quinlan led Triple-A Salt Lake City with 17 homers and 88 RBI. His problem has always been, and remains, strikeouts; he fanned 124 times in 466 at-bats in 1995, typical of his nine year pro career. Quinlan has a chance to earn a bench role for a weaker major league team; he'll bide his time at Triple-A in the meantime.

RAABE, BRIAN - 2B - BR - Age 28
A contact hitter extraordinaire, Raabe has struck out just 95 times in six seasons on the Twins farm. He can play a utility role for a major league team, and is capable of hitting .270.

	AB	R	HR	RBI	SB	BA	$
1995 Salt Lake City AAA	440	88	3	60	15	.305	
1995 Minnesota AL	14	4	0	1	0	.214	-

RADZIEWICZ, DOUG - 1B/OF - BL - Age 26
Class AA is usually where the prospects and suspects are separated. One suspects Radziewicz is no longer a prospect as he hit .233 for the Cardinals' Class AA Arkansas farm club in 1995.

RAINES, TIM - OF - BB - Age 36
Raines can still hit, but the White Sox are really down on him due to his miserable fielding. He still can't judge a fly

ball after fifteen years in the majors and his dizzy outfielding cost them some games over the last few years. They were looking to dump Raines and his $4.5 million salary. He has very little time left as a regular in the majors.

	AB	R	HR	RBI	SB	BA	$
1994 Chicago AL	384	80	10	52	13	.266	17
1995 Chicago AL	502	81	12	67	13	.285	18
1996 *Projection* >>>	490	84	11	62	14	.280	17

RALEIGH, MATT - 3B - BR - Age 25
Still at Class-A at 25. At his age, an advance to the majors is very unlikely.

RAMIREZ, ALEX - OF - BR - Age 21
Despite his relative youth and solid 1994 power numbers, the Indians chose to send Ramirez to independent Bakersfield in the Class A California League in 1995. Known for his power, Ramirez uncharacteristically hit for average with only doubles power, resulting in a promotion to Double-A, where he will most likely spend 1996. His insistence on swinging at most everything - he had a 100/23 K/BB ratio in 1995 - caused him to struggle there. The Indians aren't quite sure that his 5'11", 176, body will retain its power all the way up the ladder. He will struggle to advance further without enhancing his plate discipline.

RAMIREZ, J.D. - 2B - BR - Age 29
Ramirez is a little second baseman who can't seem to get above Double-A. Although he is small, he can occasionally jack the ball over the fence. At age 29, still not in the majors, Ramirez looks like a career minor leaguer.

RAMIREZ, MANNY - OF - BR - Age 23
His progress intensified in 1995, as he raised his average against righties by over 70 points to .275, and feasted on lefties at a .407 clip. Ramirez is extremely disciplined at the plate for such a youngster, and can drive the ball 450 feet to all fields. He is set to explode, and will be the next Indian to crush 50 homers in a season.

	AB	R	HR	RBI	SB	BA	$
1994 Cleveland AL	290	51	17	60	4	.269	15
1995 Cleveland AL	484	85	31	107	6	.308	26
1996 *Projection* >>>	529	99	34	116	7	.309	29

RAMIREZ, OMAR - OF - BR - Age 25
He's a gap hitter with a good eye and decent speed, but he has been passed by as the Indians' readiest outfield prospect.

RAMOS, EDDIE - 1B - BR - Age 23
Ramos was voted the the Midwest League's best defensive first baseman in 1994, but didn't improve his offense a bit in his third season in the league - a .114 batting average in 105 plate appearances says it all.

RAMOS, JOHN - DH - BR - Age 30
After batting .308 for both Columbus and the Yankees in 1991, Ramos appeared to have a bright future as a catcher. Injuries, however, set him back. He's now a power hitter who could play in the field only at first base.

RAMOS, KEN - OF - BL - Age 28
Ramos is a veteran minor league outfielder who consistently hits for average and steals some bases (.315-3-47-14 at Houston's Triple-A affiliate in 1995). However, he doesn't have any power. It appears that he will not get a shot at the majors because there are too many outfielders ahead of him.

RAMSEY, FERNANDO - OF - BR - Age 30
A great defensive outfielder with blazing speed, Ramsey has never been able to hit enough to stick in the majors; in his eight-year career he has registered just big league 18 games. He may have turned some heads with his .310-5-45 performance at Triple-A Nashville in 1995, including hitting .360 with runners in scoring position. Ramsey will start 1996 in Triple-A, but could get a look as a reserve outfielder.

RANDA, JOE - 3B - BR - Age 26
Randa has succeeded at every minor league level - both in the field and at the plate - but struggled in his major league debut for the Royals in 1995. Bouncing between Kansas City and Triple-A Omaha prevented Randa from getting into

a good groove last year. Randa's bat might be a little weak at this point but he has the glove to play third base regularly in the majors right now, a job he may have in the spring.

	AB	R	HR	RBI	SB	BA	$
1995 Omaha AAA	233	33	8	33	2	.275	
1995 Kansas City AL	70	6	1	5	0	.171	-
1996 *Projection* >>>	222	22	7	22	1	.247	1

RAPPOLI, PAUL - OF - BL - Age 24
He can play center field, and with his speed and batting eye could be an effective leadoff hitter.

RATLIFF, DARYL - OF - BR - Age 26
Once considered a top prospect in the Pirates' organization, Ratliff fell off the face of the Earth for a few years but bounced back with a good year at Triple-A Calgary in 1995. If he does make it to the majors, it will be as no more than a fifth outfielder.

RAVEN, LUIS - 3B - BR - Age 27
Raven came out of nowhere in 1994 and hit 31 home runs in the minors, getting a great deal of attention. But the Triple-A pitchers caught up with him last year, and he struggled mightily.

READY, RANDY - 1B - BR - Age 36
One of the game's nicest guys, Ready overcame personal tragedy to become a handy utility player. He retired after 23 games for the Phillies in 1995; look for Ready as a coach - and a good one.

	AB	R	HR	RBI	SB	BA	$
1994 Philadelphia NL	42	5	1	3	0	.381	1
1995 Philadelphia NL	29	3	0	0	0	.138	-

REBOULET, JEFF - SS/3B - BR - Age 31
Reboulet played very well in '95, raising his average for the third consecutive year while stabilizing the Twins infield defense. There isn't a lot of glory in his role, but he can play. He will face a challenge for his job in '96 from Brian Raabe and Mitch Simons.

	AB	R	HR	RBI	SB	BA	$
1994 Minnesota AL	189	28	3	23	0	.259	2
1995 Minnesota AL	216	39	4	23	1	.292	4
1996 *Projection* >>>	249	41	4	27	1	.269	3

REDINGTON, TOM - 3B - BR - Age 27
Redington had a solid year in the Class A California League in 1995 showing some power, but he's fallen a long way from top prospect status four years ago.

REDMOND, MIKE - C - BR - Age 24
Redmond is a nondescript Marlins' farmhand who is adequate defensively behind the plate and possesses little in the way of offensive skills. He does make consistent contact - he has struck out only 62 times in 681 at bats over the last two seasons. With the lack of viable catching prospects in the upper levels of the Marlins' chain, Redmond could still be in line for a promotion to Triple-A in 1996. That is likely the extent of his upward potential.

REED, JEFF - C - BL - Age 33
Veteran lefty-hitting catchers always seem to find a job somewhere. Unfortunately, Reed can't hit for average or power, so while he may have a job with a major-league team, he won't be more than a reserve.

	AB	R	HR	RBI	SB	BA	$
1994 San Francisco NL	103	11	1	7	0	.175	-
1995 San Francisco NL	113	12	0	9	0	.265	0
1996 *Projection* >>>	131	14	1	10	0	.235	-

REED, JODY - 2B - BR - Age 33
Veteran Jody Reed did an adequate job playing second for the Padres last year. His days of hitting in the .270-290 range appear to be over.

	AB	R	HR	RBI	SB	BA	$
1994 Milwaukee AL	399	48	2	37	5	.271	9
1995 San Diego NL	445	58	4	40	6	.256	7
1996 *Projection* >>>	512	64	4	46	6	.263	7

REESE, CALVIN - SS - BR - Age 22
"Pokey" Reese is an extremely well regarded prospect, based almost entirely on his defense and age. He struggled in his first year at Triple-A, hitting only .238 and missing time with a broken ankle but was still rated as the 4th best prospect in the American Association by Baseball America. Reese displayed power and speed at Double-A and has more time than he needs to develop as Barry Larkin isn't going anywhere soon.

REEVES, GLENN - OF - BR - Age 22
One of a wave of Australian prospects entering the pros in recent seasons, Reeves signed with the Marlins in 1993. He possesses little power or speed, but has a well developed knowledge of the strike zone for such a youngster. The Marlins hope that his physical skills will catch up with the mental in 1996 at Double-A. Only a near-term increase in power will propel him to the front of the pack of Marlin outfield prospects.

REIMER, KEVIN - OF/DH - BL - Age 31
A teammate of Kevin Mitchell for the Fukuoka Daiei Hawks in 1995, Reimer didn't produce the kind of power or batting average usually expected from US players in Japan. He might return to the States, but he'd have to fight for a reserve outfield/DH role in the majors.

RELAFORD, DESI - SS - BB - Age 22
Showed great speed in 1994 Arizona Fall League, but overall Relaford is just short of discipline and experience.

RENDINA, MIKE - 1B - BL - Age 25
Rendina spent the past three years in Double-A, where his offensive production declined from a solid .282-10-77 down to .224-3-12.

RENTERIA, EDGAR - SS - BR - Age 20
Renteria made a quantum leap in 1995, going from a player known more for his relative youth than for his production, to a solid all-around prospect. The Marlins' shortstop of the not-too-distant future was in the Double-A Eastern League, following a season in which he hit for average with decent power to the gaps and excellent speed. Defensively, he is a 6'1", 172, gazelle who was overshadowed in his league by the Red Sox' incomparable Nomar Garciaparra. He has been the youngest starter in his league every year of his career, and he is likely one year away from seriously challenging Kurt Abbott for the big league job.

REYNOLDS, HAROLD - 2B - BB - Age 35
Since the Mariners gave up on Reynolds a couple of years ago, he hasn't been anywhere very long. Last year, the Royals picked him up as a mid-season insurance policy when Chico Lind went AWOL. He failed to hit and was released after a .202-1-11 performance at Triple-A Omaha. Switch-hitting Reynolds hits much better from the right side. He'll probably be retired by the time spring training starts in 1996.

RHODES, KARL - OF - BL - Age 27
"Tuffy" hit little in brief major league stints for the Cubs and Red Sox, but showed both power and speed in half a season for Triple-A Pawtucket. It's beginning to look like the Astros and Royals were right about Rhodes not being a major league talent. In 1996, he'll start the year at Triple-A and wait for an opening on a major league roster where he can serve as a fourth outfielder.

	AB	R	HR	RBI	SB	BA	$
1994 Chicago NL	269	39	8	19	6	.234	6
1995 Boston AL	41	4	0	3	0	.098	-
1996 *Projection* >>>	70	10	2	5	1	.210	-

RICHARDSON, JEFF - IF - BR - Age 30
Richardson's pursuit of a return to the major leagues ended after just 18 at-bats for Triple-A Calgary. This career minor leaguer is probably finished.

RICHARDSON, SCOTT - OF - BR - Age 25
Richardson is a good leadoff hitter because he draws walks and steals bases. Unless he can hit for a higher average, he's not going much farther in the game.

RIGGS, ADAM - 2B - BR - Age 23
Riggs hit .362 with 24 homers in his second year in the Dodgers farm system. He stayed at Class-A all of 1995.

RILES, ERNEST - IF - BL - Age 35
A veteran of nine major league seasons and six organizations, Riles hit a very weak .189 for the Red Sox in 1993, his last in the majors. He attempted a comeback and didn't make it.

RILEY, MARQUIS - OF - BR - Age 25
Riley is a speedy base-stealing outfielder being groomed as a lead-off hitter. But he hit only .262 in the hitter-friendly Pacific Coast League last year, and he needs to improve. Riley is a singles hitter with no power.

RIOS, ARMANDO - OF - BL - Age 24
Rios had an outstanding season for Class A San Jose, including 34 doubles and 51 steals. Named to Baseball America's California League All-Star team. He's still a long ways from the majors, and old for a Class A prospect.

RIOS, EDDIE - 2B - BR - Age 23
Rios platooned with Miguel Cairo for Double-A San Antonio in 1995. A great fielder who makes very few errors, Rios always puts the ball in play as a hitter. In the right organization, he would be a front-line prospect.

RIPKEN, BILLY - 2B - BR - Age 31
After his years of caddying for his brother in Baltimore and a couple more uninspiring years in Texas, most had forgotten that Billy Ripken actually possessed some baseball skills of his own. Ripken had a solid 1995 campaign as the Indians' Triple-A shortstop, hitting for average with doubles power and making consistent contact.

	AB	R	HR	RBI	SB	BA	$
1994 Texas AL	81	9	0	6	2	.309	1
1995 Cleveland AL	17	4	2	3	0	.412	-

RIPKEN, CAL - SS - BR - Age 35
Ripken's streak continues, but the pressure of breaking Lou Gehrig's record is gone. Ripken is slump prone, and went into one in the second half last year, hitting only .226, but fortunately he maintained his power stroke with 10 homers and 51 RBI. He works very hard to get out of his slumps, taking extra batting practice, hitting off batting tees, and tinkering with his stance and mechanics.

	AB	R	HR	RBI	SB	BA	$
1994 Baltimore AL	444	71	13	75	1	.315	21
1995 Baltimore AL	550	71	17	88	0	.262	12
1996 Projection >>>	582	80	18	94	1	.266	14

RIVERA, DAVID - SS - BB - Age 26
Rivera has good speed but is a career .252 hitter in the low minors. The Twins have better players ahead of him.

RIVERA, LUIS - 2B/SS - BR - Age 32
Rivera's career peak came with the Red Sox in 1991 when he hit .258 and got into 129 games.

RIVERA, RUBEN - OF - BR - Age 22
Rivera's luggage has an eventual destination of "Right Field, Yankee Stadium." He's simply the Yankees best outfield prospect and possibly the one of the top five prosects in the league. He's probably still a year away, but is improving both his on-base skills and power hitting as he advances up the farm ladder. Rivera hit 24 home runs and stole 24 bases before a late 1995 callup.

ROBERSON, KEVIN - OF - BB - Age 28
Roberson strikes out too much to be an effective regular player. He's behind Ozzie Timmons and Scott Bullett in the Cubs' outfield pecking order. Roberson will be lucky to make the majors in 1996.

	AB	R	HR	RBI	SB	BA	$
1994 Chicago NL	55	8	4	9	0	.218	0
1995 Chicago NL	38	5	4	6	0	.184	0

ROBERTS, BIP - 2B - BB - Age 32
Roberts had another injury-filled year playing in only 73 games. He missed many games due to a strained right-quadriceps muscle, and later broke his shin bone when hit by a ball. He's a major offensive force when healthy, but every year some different injury gets him.

	AB	R	HR	RBI	SB	BA	$
1994 San Diego NL	403	52	2	31	21	.320	24
1995 San Diego NL	296	40	2	25	20	.304	14
1996 *Projection* >>>	398	53	2	32	25	.286	15

ROBERTS, LONELL - OF - BB - Age 24
Roberts is a base-stealer, pure and simple, with 252 thefts in seven pro seasons. The Blue Jays know he could steal even more if he would cut down his swing and hit the ball on the ground instead of in the air. Chuck Carr did it; perhaps Roberts can too.

ROBERTSON, MIKE - 1B - BL - Age 25
Robertson is a solid defensive first baseman with a great work ethic. He's a better hitter than his 1995 batting average (.248) indicates, and he has power (19 HRs). Unless Chicago moves the Big Hurt to DH, his best opportunity is as a utility guy - or with another organization.

ROBERTSON, ROD - 2B/SS- BB - Age 28
Robertson is an older minor-league utility infielder and outfielder in the Orioles organization. Previously, he was in the Phillies, Tigers, and Cubs organizations. He has a good bat for Triple-A with a little power, and he can steal a base occasionally.

ROBINSON, DON - OF - BL - Age 24
Yet another lefty outfielder in the Braves organization, Robinson has some power and a little speed, but is far too aggressive at the plate. In his first year above Class A, Robinson reduced his strikeout rate slightly but still fanned once in every five at bats. Robinson needs to show increased patience and better defense to advance much farther.

RODRIGUEZ, ALEX - SS - BR - Age 20
Be Patient! He's still more baby than Babe, but he should be the number one guy this season.

	AB	R	HR	RBI	SB	BA	$
1994 Seattle AL	54	4	0	2	3	.204	-
1995 Seattle AL	142	15	5	19	4	.232	3
1996 *Projection* >>>	399	40	11	47	13	.262	11

RODRIGUEZ, CARLOS - 2B - BL - Age 28
Rodriguez played his way back from injury rehab to Boston, briefly. He's an OK infielder whose best offensive skill is getting on base. He's a Triple-A insurance-type player.

	AB	R	HR	RBI	SB	BA	$
1994 Boston AL	174	15	1	13	1	.287	3
1995 Boston AL	30	5	0	5	0	.333	-

RODRIGUEZ, HENRY - OF - BL - Age 28
Acquired from the Dodgers for Roberto Kelly last May, Rodriguez was quickly sidelined with a broken leg and didn't get a chance to show the Expos much. He has a good bat with power potential but time is running out at age 28. His window of opportunity for grabbing a starting job in the major leagues has likely closed.

	AB	R	HR	RBI	SB	BA	$
1994 Los Angeles NL	306	33	8	49	0	.268	8
1995 Montreal NL	138	13	2	15	0	.239	0
1996 *Projection* >>>	139	15	3	19	0	.247	-

RODRIGUEZ, IVAN - C - BR - Age 24
Rodriguez has established himself as one of the best young hitters in baseball; the fact that he is also a top defensive catcher makes him all the more remarkable. Rodriguez' durability is increasing with age and he should continue to improve as a hitter.

	AB	R	HR	RBI	SB	BA	$
1994 Texas AL	363	56	16	57	6	.298	19
1995 Texas AL	492	56	12	67	0	.303	14
1996 *Projection* >>>	502	63	15	72	3	.299	16

RODRIGUEZ, STEVE - 2B - BR - Age 25
The Tigers took Steve away from Boston's Rodriguez factory. The former Pepperdine U. star is an extremely heady player, and a sure-handed fielder. His negatives are his size (5-8, 170) and his inability to hit righthanders. He'll have to improve against righties; there's not much call for platoon second basemen.

	AB	R	HR	RBI	SB	BA	$
1995 Detroit AL	39	5	0	0	2	.179	-

RODRIGUEZ, TONY - 3B - BR - Age 25
In his first full year at Triple-A, Rodriguez hit for a slightly better average than usual (a career high .268, compared to a career .234 mark), but was otherwise the same kind of low-power hitter he's always been. He has an above average glove and could reach the big leagues as a utility player, as long as he keeps hitting a little bit.

RODRIGUEZ, VICTOR - 3B - BR - Age 19
The Marlins' #2 pick in 1994 out of Guayama, Puerto Rico. A defensive wizard, he hit the ground running offensively with the Marlins' rookie league club in Melbourne, Florida. Watch his development closely.

RODRIGUEZ, VIC - 3B - BR - Age 33
Give him credit for perseverance; Rodriguez has been in the minor leagues for 19 seasons after signing as a sixteen year-old in 1977 - and all for 28 major league at-bats. He was a bit player for Triple-A Pawtucket in 1995. Obviously, Rodriguez is a career minor leaguer.

ROGERS, LAMARR - 2B - BR - Age 24
Rogers showed some improvement in his second year with the Rockies' Double-A farm. His batting average went up 17 points, he walked enough to be a viable leadoff candidate and he went from a sub-.500 base stealer to a .750 percentage. If he can produce in Triple-A this year, he may have a shot.

ROHDE, DAVE - IF - BB - Age 31
Rohde is a veteran Triple-A infielder who has failed to hit in three major league trials. After a mediocre year in 1995 (.276-0-20-2), he can't expect another chance.

ROHRMEIER, DAN - OF/DH - BR - Age 30
Long-time White Sox and Royals prospect Rohrmeier topped out at Double-A before joining the Reds late in 1994. He wasn't any different in 1995, posting his usual high batting average and marginal power at Chattanooga, but showing little in a brief Triple-A fling. Rohrmeier is a career minor leaguer.

ROJAS, ROBERTO - OF - BL - Age 25
Rojas is a weak singles hitter who needs dramatic improvement in his hitting to move upward to the majors. He can steal bases.

ROLEN, SCOTT - 3B - BR - Age 20
The long dormant Phils' farm system is ready to produce its first premier prospect in ages. Rolen has it all - a consistent line drive bat with developing home run power, excellent range and surehandedness in the field with a cannon arm, and an air of confidence which should enable him to be a team leader in the majors. He's fully recovered from a 1995 broken wrist, and is just one Triple-A season away from a long run in Philly.

ROLISON, NATE - 1B - BL - Age 19
The Marlins were absolutely thrilled to find the high school player generally regarded as having the most power available in the second round of the 1995 draft. The Marlins sweetened their offer to him enough to induce him to back

out of a college commitment to Miami. The 6'5", 210, prodigy showed only gap power in the spacious Gulf Coast League ballparks, but he is the frontrunner for the Class-A first base job in 1996 - watch him closely.

ROMERO, MANDY - C - BB - Age 28
After seven seasons in the Pirates organization, Romero played at Double-A Wichita team in 1995 and had a great season. Though Romero has shown glimpses of power in the past, his 21 home runs in 1995 were a career best. He has shown he can play after eight seasons in the minors, but time is running out; he looks like a career minor leaguer.

ROMERO, WILLIE - OF - BR - Age 21
Romero was injured in the last half of the season at Double-A San Antonio. An exciting outfielder, he has some power and good speed on the bases. Romero could use another year in Double-A before moving up.

RONAN, MARC - C - BL - Age 26
Ronan is a solid defensive catcher who was platooned at Triple-A Louisville in 1995. He was a surprise late-season callup to St. Louis in 1994, but has shown little to warrant returning to the big leagues.

ROPER, CHAD - 3B - BR - Age 22
Roper slipped in his second season in the Florida State League, but rebounded nicely in 1995 at Double-A New Britain where he hit 11 homers and drove in 61.

ROSE, BOBBY - IF/OF - BR - Age 29
Once an Angel second base prospect, Rose has played in Japan for several years. He hit for a good average last year, even showing a little power.

ROSKOS, JOHN - C - BR - Age 21
The Marlins' 1995 Class-A catcher is a muscled 5'11", 198, power hitter who will see many of the long doubles he hit last year become homers at higher levels. His defensive ability behind the plate is uncertain, and he may find himself transferred to a corner infield position within the next two years. Roskos, the Marlins' 1993 number two pick, has a chance to develop into a major league power hitter, though his big league debut is at least two years away.

ROSSY, RICO - 2B - BR - Age 32
Infielder Rossy is a 10-year minor-league veteran, playing in a number of organizations. He spent parts of 1992 and '93 with the Royals as a utility infielder hitting .216 in 236 at-bats. His best hope for more major league playing time is as a utility man and pinch runner.

ROWLAND, RICH - C - BR - Age 29
After winning the catching job at the end of the 1994 season, Rowland looked to be the Red Sox starting backstop for 1995. Mike Macfarlane wrecked those plans and Rowland turned in a forgettable year, mostly for Triple-A Pawtucket. In the right role Rowland could produce 8-12 homers, but with a low batting average and marginal defense.

	AB	R	HR	RBI	SB	BA	$
1994 Boston AL	118	14	9	20	0	.229	3
1995 Boston AL	29	1	0	1	0	.172	-

RUMFIELD, TOBY - 1B - BR - Age 23
Last season showed that Rumfield's 29 home runs at Winston-Salem in 1994 were the product of a park effect. He has totaled just 20 long balls in his four other seasons. He hasn't played as many as 100 games in any of those four. Rumfield is painfully slow, and has to hit with power to be able to play.

RUNDELS, MATT - 2B - BR - Age 25
Lingering strike effects put Rundels on the Triple-A Ottawa roster, but the Expos soon demoted him to Harrisburg. In his third tour of duty there, he showed his best power, but struck out 112 times. He has enough speed to steal a base and play the outfield, so he could have an outside shot at a utility job in a couple of years.

RUPP, BRIAN - 1B - BR - Age 24
He didn't hit at Class A St. Petersburg. Simply put, he's not much of a prospect.

RUSSO, PAUL - 3B - BR - Age 26
Veteran minor-leaguer Russo was formerly in the Twins organization where he couldn't make the parent club despite big holes at the major league level. He was in the Padres organization last year. He's not considered to be a prospect, and Triple-A may be his peak level.

SABO, CHRIS - 3B/1B - BR - Age 34
There were few players who saw their career take a sharper nose dive in 1995 than Sabo. When he wasn't hurt, he spent almost the entire season in the minors. After they traded Todd Zeile early last season, the Cardinals thought Sabo would be their answer at first base. That experiment lasted only five games, which very well could have been Sabo's swan song.

	AB	R	HR	RBI	SB	BA	$
1994 Baltimore AL	258	41	11	42	1	.256	8
1995 Two Teams	84	10	1	11	3	.238	1

SAENZ, OLMEDO - 3B - BR - Age 25
Saenz is a good player, just a little inconsistent. He's got a good RBI bat, reacts well around third base and has a cannon arm. Although he runs the bases like a catcher, Saenz should make it in the majors.

SAGMOEN, MARC - OF - BL - Age 24
Sagmoen split time between Double-A and Triple-A, and struggled offensively for the first time in his pro career. In the low minors, Sagmoen had hit for average with moderate power. His batting stance has been compared to Don Mattingly's. He has an outside chance to reach the majors, but will likely spend 1996 at Triple-A.

SALMON, TIM - OF - BR - Age 27
Salmon had another outstanding year, breaking the 30-homer barrier for the second time. He hit a great .362-18-59 in the second half, nearly carrying the Angels to a division championship. The great second half indicates that even better things can be expected from Salmon, say breaking the 100 RBI barrier and winning a batting championship or even a triple crown.

	AB	R	HR	RBI	SB	BA	$
1994 California AL	373	67	23	70	1	.287	19
1995 California AL	537	111	34	105	5	.330	30
1996 Projection >>>	541	106	34	104	4	.312	29

SAMUEL, JUAN - 1B/OF - BR - Age 35
Samuel has completed his career transition to role player, and has shown that he still has some life in his bat. He is a defensive liability, but should have another year or two of decent totals left.

	AB	R	HR	RBI	SB	BA	$
1994 Detroit AL	136	32	5	21	5	.309	8
1995 Kansas City AL	205	31	12	39	6	.263	9
1996 Projection >>>	172	29	9	29	5	.253	5

SANCHEZ, REY - SS - BR - Age 28
Sanchez is a steady player whose offensive value is mostly tied to his batting average. He's an aggressive hitter who doesn't walk or strikeout much and has little power or speed. Sanchez is a good enough shortstop, but a better second baseman. With Shawon Dunston expected to leave Chicago as a free agent, Sanchez would move to shortstop to accomodate Ryne Sandberg's return.

	AB	R	HR	RBI	SB	BA	$
1994 Chicago NL	291	26	0	24	2	.285	5
1995 Chicago NL	428	57	3	27	6	.278	8
1996 Projection >>>	206	24	1	14	2	.280	1

SANCHEZ, YURI - SS - BL - Age 22
Sanchez is a young shortstop prospect who has not hit for average, as he has played against older competition in the minors. He should fashion a career of part time major league duty by virtue of his good speed and defense.

SANDBERG, RYNE - 2B - BR - Age 36
Contrary to previous denials, Sandberg decided to return from retirement, the second "No. 23" in Chicago to return; I wonder if he'll wear number 45 when he comes back. Sandberg has really been a shadow of his former self on the field in recent years, so don't expect much in his return. He'll play at second base regularly in 1996, no matter how rusty he looks.

	AB	R	HR	RBI	SB	BA	$
1994 Chicago NL	223	36	5	24	2	.238	3
1996 Projection >>>	496	58	8	64	5	.269	10

SANDERS, DEION - OF - BL - Age 28
Once again in 1995, Deion demonstrated that he is a better football player than baseball player. He has never played 100 games in a season, never reached double-digits in home runs, never had more than 28 RBI (oddly, he has totaled exactly 28 RBI four seasons in a row) and his career batting average is .264. There is also a chance Deion will take a year off from baseball.

	AB	R	HR	RBI	SB	BA	$
1994 Two Teams	375	58	4	28	38	.283	29
1995 Two Teams	343	48	6	28	24	.268	14
1996 Projection >>>	416	61	7	33	34	.274	19

SANDERS, REGGIE - OF - BR - Age 28
Sanders has always been a good player, but in 1995, he improved his one weakness (strike zone judgement) and as a result set career highs in almost everything. Sanders, Raul Mondesi, and Sammy Sosa are extremely similar players (power hitters who can run and play defense) and it will be interesting to see which one emerges as the dominant NL right fielder of the 90's.

	AB	R	HR	RBI	SB	BA	$
1994 Cincinnati NL	400	66	17	62	21	.263	25
1995 Cincinnati NL	484	91	28	99	36	.306	38
1996 Projection >>>	534	96	29	104	35	.289	35

SANDERS, TRACY - OF - BL - Age 26
Sanders was a top power prospect before last season, when he took too many pitches. He is not a good defensive outfielder, and now he's a suspect.

SANTANGELO, F.P. - 3B/OF - BB - Age 28
In his seventh professional season, Santangelo finally made it to Montreal and did a good job as a utility player. He hit better in the majors than he did in the minors and that was an aberration. However, Santangelo can play any position on the field and Expos manager Felipe Alou loves that kind of versatility.

	AB	R	HR	RBI	SB	BA	$
1995 Ottawa AAA	267	37	2	25	7	.255	
1995 Montreal NL	98	11	1	9	1	.296	1
1996 Projection >>>	188	20	2	17	3	.266	1

SANTANA, RUBEN - 2B - BR - Age 26
If Santana had played in the Pacific Coast League in 1995, instead of getting a thrid year at Double-A, his numbers would actually have been more impressive. Now he's somewhat obscure, and he's also being passed by Arquimedez Pozo on the road to the majors.

SANTIAGO, BENITO - C - BR - Age 31
Santiago turned out to be one of the better bargains signed out of Camp Homestead despite missing several weeks due to elbow surgery. His season turned out to be the opposite of his image as an erratic offensive and defensive player - Santiago commited only two errors all year, and set career highs in on-base and slugging average. Santiago was never as good as his press, but he appears to have resurrected a career that appeared almost over in 1993.

	AB	R	HR	RBI	SB	BA	$
1994 Florida NL	337	35	11	41	1	.273	10
1995 Cincinnati NL	266	40	11	44	2	.286	9
1996 Projection >>>	368	47	13	52	3	.260	8

SASSER, MACKEY - C/OF - BL - Age 33
After spending most of 1994 in Mexico, Sasser made the Pirates' opening-day roster as the third-string catcher last season. He was released in mid-May and was not heard from again. His career appears over.

	AB	R	HR	RBI	SB	BA	$
1995 Pittsburgh NL	26	1	0	0	0	.154	-

SAUNDERS, DOUG - 2B - BR - Age 26
Saunders surfaced with the Mets in 1993 but spent 1994 and 95 back in the minors. He can hit fairly well for a middle infielder, but the overall package of offense/defense isn't quite major league caliber.

SAVARY, SCOTT - OF - BR - Age 23
Savary is an excellent hustling team player who could move up quickly with solid hitting.

SAX, STEVE - OF/DH - BR - Age 36
Injuries took their toll on this 1981 Rookie of the Year and he retired after 46 at-bats in 1994.

SAWKIW, WARREN - DH - BB - Age 28
Had the strike not ended before last season, Sawkiw might have been a star. The Northern League expatriate pounded replacement pitching. Against the real stuff with Toronto's top two farm teams, Sawkiw came down to earth -- hard. If any organization cares, he's a minor league free agent.

SBROCCO, JON - 2B - BL - Age 25
He hit .301 with steals for Class A San Jose. He displays good defense, old for a prospect, and there are better second basemen in the organization.

SCARSONE, STEVE - 3B/1B - BR - Age 29
Always a decent utility infielder, Scarsone blossomed as Matt Williams' replacement during Matt's injury. Multi-position players with some pop in their bat will always find a job, but Scarsone may be overvalued by people who make the mistake of projecting his limited-play numbers from 1995 into a full season. Will never be a fulltime regular.

	AB	R	HR	RBI	SB	BA	$
1994 San Francisco NL	103	21	2	13	0	.272	1
1995 San Francisco NL	233	33	11	29	3	.266	7
1996 Projection >>>	129	20	3	13	1	.262	0

SCHALL, GENE - OF/1B - BR - Age 25
The Phils' 1991 fourth round pick had a quite inauspicious major league debut in September 1995. With the bat, he only managed two extra base hits (both doubles) in 65 at bats, after consistently reaching the gaps while hitting for average in his minor league career. Of even more concern was his cluelessness afield - he dropped balls that weren't even in the dirt at first base, and had that deer-in-the-headlights look in the outfield. Though there is still hope for his bat, he must become adequate at one position to warrant a spot on an NL roster as a backup.

	AB	R	HR	RBI	SB	BA	$
1995 Scranton WB AAA	320	52	12	63	3	.313	
1995 Philadelphia NL	65	2	0	5	0	.231	-
1996 Projection >>>	128	19	4	20	1	.256	0

SCHOFIELD, DICK - SS - BR - Age 33
Schofield was released by the Dodgers in May and retired. But the Angels were desperate following the injury to Gary DiSarcina and signed the 12-year veteran in August. The prototypical good-field-no-hit shortstop, he didn't help the Angels. It's likely Schofield will retire for good.

	AB	R	HR	RBI	SB	BA	$
1994 Toronto AL	325	38	4	32	7	.255	8
1995 California AL	30	1	0	2	0	.200	-

SCHU, RICK - 3B - BR - Age 34
Schu put together a nice Triple-A season after returning from Japan, but it's probably a little too late to expect a return to the majors.

SCHUNK, JERRY - SS - BR - Age 30
The journeyman infielder toiled in his tenth minor league campaign without a major league appearance in 1995. Despite his lack of offensive value, he is certainly what you would call a contact hitter - he has never had as many as 40 walks or strikeouts in any season. Schunk has simply been marking time in the Marlins' organization until their wide array of middle infield talent began to reach Triple-A. Schunk's run is likely at its end.

SCHWAB, CHRIS - OF - BR - Age 21
The Expos envisioned Schwab as a big-time power prospect when they made him their top draft pick in 1993. However, he has struggled mightily in making the conversion from the aluminum to wood bat and is years away from the big leagues.

SCOTT, GARY - 3B - BR - Age 27
Scott used to be a good prospect in the Cubs organization but is now just bench help at Triple-A. And he wasn't much help for Triple-A Richmond in 1995, hitting .151 before being released.

SEE, LARRY - DH/1B - BR - Age 35
Minor-league veteran Larry See has become a player-coach, and will likely move to full time coaching in the near future. Like the movies' Crash Davis, he spent 15 years in the minors and hit over 150 home runs, and was called up to the show for 26 games in 1986 and 1988.

SEEFRIED, TATE - 1B - BL - Age 23
Seefried is literally a hit-or-miss player. To advance to the majors, he'll need to cut down on his long swing that gives pitchers handy holes to hit. Even swinging at half-speed, Seefried has enough power to hit home runs.

SEFCIK, KEVIN - SS/2B - BR - Age 25
Sefcik gets the most out of his limited natural ability, making all of the routine plays at shortstop and third base, making consistent contact, and running the bases well. However, the 1993 33rd round draftee does no one single thing well enough to stand out as a prospect. He will be a candidate for a major league utility spot in the short term future, as the Phils are woefully thin at shortstop within the organization. He is the leading candidate to play shortstop at Triple-A in 1996.

	AB	R	HR	RBI	SB	BA	$
1995 Philadelphia NL	4	1	0	0	0	.000	-

SEGUI, DAVID - 1B - BB - Age 29
Traded from the Mets to the Expos in June, Segui stepped in for the injured Cliff Floyd at first base and had a fine season. He doesn't have the home run power you want from a first baseman but he is a good hitter who gets his share of extra-base hits. Expos manager Felipe Alou is pushing management hard to lock Segui up to a long-term deal. Segui, unlike many players, likes playing in Montreal.

	AB	R	HR	RBI	SB	BA	$
1994 New York NL	336	46	10	43	0	.241	6
1995 NY - Montreal NL	456	68	12	68	2	.309	16
1996 Projection >>>	505	73	15	72	2	.295	16

SEITZER, KEVIN - 1B/3B - BR - Age 34
Seitzer has talked of retiring. His decent batting average is about the only positive note in an otherwise light offense.

	AB	R	HR	RBI	SB	BA	$
1994 Milwaukee AL	309	44	5	49	2	.314	12
1995 Milwaukee AL	492	56	5	69	2	.311	14
1996 Projection >>>	469	57	7	68	3	.290	12

SELBY, BILL - 3B - BL - Age 25
In his third Carolina League season, Selby saw his career take off. He even hit with gap power in the Eastern League, where pitchers worked him carefully. His arm is an asset.

SERVAIS, SCOTT - C - BR - Age 28
Servais is a good defensive catcher despite not having a good arm. He hit for surprising power - 12 homers and 12 doubles in just 175 at-bats - after his mid-season acquisition from Houston; don't extrapolate those numbers into a

30-homer season, though, as Servais isn't capable of that kind of power for a full season. He's the Cubs number one catcher going into 1996.

	AB	R	HR	RBI	SB	BA	$
1994 Houston NL	251	27	9	41	0	.195	2
1995 Houston - Chicago NL	264	38	13	47	2	.265	9
1996 Projection >>>	319	40	12	54	1	.239	4

SEXSON, RICHIE - 1B - BR - Age 21
Sexson graduated from intriguing to dominating in 1995 in the Class-A Carolina League. Sexson needs to refine his strike zone judgement, but that's the only chink in the armor. He is likely to begin 1996 at Double-A, with a midseason promotion to Triple-A a possibility.

SHABAZZ, BASIL - OF - BR - Age 24
The Cardinals top draft pick of 1991 washed out of their organization and wound up hitting .216 at Double-A in 102 at-bats at Double-A El Paso. As a first round draft pick, Shabazz has to be considered a huge flop.

SHARPERSON, MIKE - 2B - BR - Age 34
An aging infielder, Sharperson played hard for Triple-A Richmond and was rewarded with a brief return to the big leagues in 1995. He still has a little speed and a decent batting eye, but he's not really a big league talent any longer. Sharperson's future is as Triple-A roster filler.

	AB	R	HR	RBI	SB	BA	$
1995 Atlanta NL	7	1	0	2	0	.143	-

SHAVE, JON - 2B - BR - Age 28
Shave's best chance at a big league career ended when he was struck in the throat by a line drive in spring training of 1994. After emergency surgery to repair a fractured larynx he returned to play at Triple-A Oklahoma City. However, his career may be in jeopardy as Shave has hit just .217 over the last two years.

SHEAFFER, DANNY - C - BR - Age 34
After a bazillion years of bouncing around the minors, Sheaffer has finally established himself as a decent number two catcher. He wasn't great in 1995 but he was certainly an upgrade over backup Cardinal catchers of recent seasons. He should be able to hang on for another year or two as a productive reserve.

	AB	R	HR	RBI	SB	BA	$
1994 Colorado NL	110	11	1	12	0	.218	-
1995 St. Louis NL	208	24	5	30	0	.231	2
1996 Projection >>>	203	23	4	28	0	.233	1

SHEFF, CHRIS - OF - BR - Age 25
Sheff excelled in his second Double-A season in 1995, combining power with excellent selectivity at the plate and above average speed on the bases. His numbers have consistently improved as he has advanced through the Marlins' organization. However, his relatively advanced age suggests that he has very limited major league potential. Expect Sheff to begin 1996 in Triple-A, with a chance for eventual major league bench duty.

SHEFFIELD, GARY - OF - BR - Age 27
For the second straight season, injuries prevented National League pitchers from having to face the wrath of Sheffield over a full season. Despite missing more than half of an already shortened season, he was four homers and a steal away from a 20/20 season. His absence cost the Marlins a potential run at .500 or even an outside shot a wildcard spot. Sheffield clubs lefties and righties (over .320 against each), makes consistent contact for a power hitter and has developed excellent strike zone knowledge. He is a major hazard to himself in right field, but if he remains healthy, he will be the premier candidate for NL MVP honors in 1996.

	AB	R	HR	RBI	SB	BA	$
1994 Florida NL	322	61	27	78	12	.276	26
1995 Florida NL	213	46	16	46	19	.324	19
1996 Projection >>>	450	86	30	97	27	.300	32

SHELTON, BEN - OF - BR - Age 26
A former high draft pick (second round, 1987) by the Pirates, Shelton failed as a Twins minor-league first basemen

before winding up as Double-A Trenton's DH where he hit just .186. He was hurt all of 1994 and has never had a really good year above Class A. Shelton's star has faded.

SHERMAN, DARRELL - OF - BL - Age 28
Sherman rebouned from a terrible year in 1994 to hit .257 with 19 steals for Triple-A Tacoma in 1995. He doesn't really fit into the Mariners' future plans, though. Sherman could serve as a fifth outfielder/pinch-runner on a major league bench.

SHIPLEY, CRAIG - 3B/SS - BR - Age 33
Shipley filled a platoon role at third base for Houston in 1995. The best he can hope for is to do the same in 1996. He can play every infield position and hit about .260 which gives him somevalue as a utility player.

	AB	R	HR	RBI	SB	BA	$
1994 San Diego NL	240	32	4	30	6	.333	13
1995 Houston NL	232	23	3	24	6	.263	5
1996 Projection >>>	226	25	3	25	6	.268	4

SHORES, SCOTT - OF - BR - Age 24
The Phils' 1994 5th round pick, like many other Phils' prospects, was much older than the players at his level (Class-A) in 1995. Shores has gaps power and well above average speed, but is a wild swinger with little knowledge of the strike zone. If he is to have a major league future, he must explode through Double and Triple-A quite rapidly - in no more than one and a half seasons. Don't bet on that happening - Shores appears to have a major league future as no more than an extra man/pinch runner.

SHUMPERT, TERRY - 2B - BR - Age 29
Shumpert rode the bench for a couple of months in Boston, then platooned for Triple-A Pawtucket. He didn't hit much at either locale, though he continued to steal bases successfully. Shumpert can't hit enough to stay in the majors and would only get a reserve role if recalled; he'd still be able to steal a few bases even in a backup role, though.

	AB	R	HR	RBI	SB	BA	$
1994 Kansas City AL	183	28	8	24	18	.240	14
1995 Boston AL	47	6	0	3	3	.234	0

SIDDALL, JOE - C - BL - Age 28
Siddall has an excellent throwing arm, but can't hit a lick. This Canadian's playing days may be near an end, for the Expos left him off their 40-man roster, making him a minor league free agent.

	AB	R	HR	RBI	SB	BA	$
1995 Montreal NL	10	4	0	1	0	.300	-

SIERRA, RUBEN - OF/DH - BB - Age 30
In a trade of two unhappy campers, the Yankees got by far the better end of the deal that gave up Danny Tartabull for Sierra. Call him sullen if you must, but the fact is: Sierra collected 44 RBI after August 1 and hit .291 after September 1 (Tartabull: 7 RBI for comparison). And Sierra is still young enough to put together a really big season or two before he fades.

	AB	R	HR	RBI	SB	BA	$
1994 Oakland AL	426	71	23	92	8	.268	23
1995 Oakland - NY AL	479	73	19	86	5	.263	15
1996 Projection >>>	535	82	24	101	9	.261	18

SILVESTRI, DAVE - 2B - BR - Age 28
Though he was touted as a top prospect and put up good minor-league numbers, the Yankees never gave him a chance. He got a new opportunity with the Expos last season and played decently. He's really not a shortstop though and, at age 28, will probably settle into a utility role.

	AB	R	HR	RBI	SB	BA	$
1994 New York AL	18	3	1	2	0	.111	-
1995 NY AL - Montreal NL	93	16	3	11	2	.226	1
1996 Projection >>>	112	19	4	14	2	.244	0

SIMMONS, NELSON - OF - BB - Age 32
No one had a better replacement spring than this veteran outfielder did with the Pirates. Though he can hit, he is too slow and too much of a defensive liability to ever play in the real majors again.

SIMMS, MIKE - 1B - BR - Age 29
Simms finally showed that he could hit major league pitching in his fifth trial with the Astros. He is not strong enough defensively or consistent enough with the bat to hold a starting job, but he is a useful power hitter in a reserve role.

	AB	R	HR	RBI	SB	BA	$
1994 Houston NL	12	1	0	0	1	.083	-
1995 Houston NL	121	14	9	24	1	.256	4
1996 Projection >>>	118	13	5	21	1	.246	0

SIMONS, MITCH - 2B - BR - Age 27
This minor league infielder had a good year at Triple-A Salt Lake City, hitting .325 with 32 stolen bases. Simons would make a good role player in the majors, and will soon compete for a utility role in Minnesota.

SIMONTON, BENJI - OF - BR - Age 23
The powerful outfielder made it to Double-A in 1995. His stock has risen in the Giants' organization. He could be a good one, but first needs to prove himself at higher levels.

SINGLETON, CHRIS - OF - BL - Age 23
Singleton has lots of speed, but is still not particularly impressive at the plate, even after two seasons in the Class A California League. A former football player who is still learning how to play baseball, could be a late bloomer for that reason. Limited prospects.

SINGLETON, DUANE - OF - BL - Age 23
A raw, developing talent, who is still year or two away from being a real contributor.

	AB	R	HR	RBI	SB	BA	$
1995 New Orleans AAA	355	48	4	29	31	.268	
1996 Projection >>>	133	23	1	16	7	.261	2

SISCO, STEVE - 2B - BR - Age 26
Sisco has always been able to hit and last year was no exception as he hit .301 at Double-A Wichita in his first season above Class A. An experiment as an outfielder ended early due to a broken ankle. Sisco isn't likely to be a major league regular, but could get some time as a reserve. He'll advance as far as his bat takes him.

SKEELS, MARK - OF - BB - Age 26
An 18th-round pick in 1992, Skeels hasn't hit much in two years of A-ball, but he's from Stanford, is a switch-hitter and draws an awful lot of walks.

SLAUGHT, DON - C - BR - Age 37
Slaught had another typical year with the Pirates in 1995. He hit over .300 and spent a good portion of the season on the disabled list. His days as a starting catcher are certainly over but he could hang around as a good backup for another year or two.

	AB	R	HR	RBI	SB	BA	$
1994 Pittsburgh NL	240	21	2	21	0	.288	4
1995 Pittsburgh NL	112	13	0	13	0	.304	1
1996 Projection >>>	214	21	2	23	0	.286	2

SMILEY, RUEBEN - OF - BL - Age 27
Smiley appeared at Triple-A for the Padres and Double-A for the Royals, but was unimpressive, hitting a combined .230. Good speed is his best asset and he had hit .300 as recently as 1994. Still, Smiley is too old to be at Double-A. His best shot in the majors would be as a pinch-runner/fifth outfielder.

SMITH, BOBBY - 3B - BR - Age 21
Smith turned heads in the Arizona Fall League with the same skills he's shown in four pro seasons -- some power,

some speed, some defensive ability. He could move up to Triple-A Richmond this season, and could help hasten Chipper Jones' move to the outfield in 1997 or '98.

SMITH, BUBBA - 1B - BR - Age 26
If there wasn't a Hector Villanueva, Smith would be a folk hero. He is listed -- sympathetically, it seems -- at 225 pounds. He's instantly recognizable to fans in bush-league towns; he's played only 83 games above Class A because he's never averaged better than .243 in Double-A. When he hits the ball, it can go a long way. No prospect, but a lot of fun to watch.

SMITH, CHRIS - 3B - BR - Age 22
Baseball America tabbed Smith as a high school All-American in 1989. He slowed his progress by hitting a poor .261 in the hitter-friendly Texas League in 1994, but he is still young and could improve and move up quickly.

SMITH, DWIGHT - OF - BL - Age 32
His position says "OF", but he usually had "PH" next to his name in the box score. Smith gave the Braves timely hitting off of the bench in 1995. He's got a few years left as a pinch hitter.

	AB	R	HR	RBI	SB	BA	$
1994 Baltimore AL	196	31	8	30	2	.281	7
1995 Atlanta NL	131	16	3	21	0	.252	1
1996 *Projection* >>>	124	18	4	18	1	.271	1

SMITH, ED - 3B - BR - Age 26
The consummate journeyman - he has played nine years in the White Sox, Brewers, Cubs, and most recently, the Indians' chain without ever making it past Double-A. He has a powerful build at 6'4", 220, and has hit for home run power in his last three seasons, but his bat would certainly be too slow to move any higher. Defensively, he is willing to play anywhere, but is barely adequate at third base, first base and outfield. His time is almost up.

SMITH, GREG - SS/2B - BB - Age 28
Second-baseman Smith is a weak hitter. Except for three short call-ups in 1989-91, he has been in the minors for 11 years. He fills a role of playing a position until a younger prospect develops.

SMITH, IRA - OF - BR - Age 28
Smith is a talented hitter with excellent base-stealing speed. Originally in the Dodger organization, he was a Rule V draft pick in 1992. He could have been called up to the Padres last year, but he was a replacement player and Padres management had a concern about the players' reaction.

SMITH, LONNIE - OF/DH - BR - Age 40
Smith retired before he could get that fourth World Series ring - one year before his Braves finally won it all.

SMITH, MARK - OF - BR - Age 25
The Orioles are disappointed that outfielder Mark Smith has not developed into the strong authoritative hitter they expected. Getting his first real taste of major league ball last year, he hit a weak .231, about what was expected after almost three years in Triple-A without showing much improvement. On the Orioles, Smith looks like a 4th or 5th outfielder.

	AB	R	HR	RBI	SB	BA	$
1994 Baltimore AL	7	0	0	2	0	.143	-
1995 Rochester AAA	364	55	12	66	7	.277	
1995 Baltimore AL	104	11	3	15	3	.231	1
1996 *Projection* >>>	164	16	4	23	2	.236	0

SMITH, MATT - 1B - BL - Age 19
The Royals first round pick of 1994, Smith was also an accomplished pitcher in high school. He hasn't shown much with the bat, yet, hitting a combined .228 in two pro seasons; most recently he hit .226-6-46 for Class A Springfield. The Royals are grooming him as a middle-of-the-order power threat. He's a long way from the big leagues.

SMITH, MIKE - 2B - BR - Age 25
Smith is a blue-collar second baseman who won a triple crown while playing college ball at Indiana University. He

hit .257-16-64 with 16 steals for Double-A Tulsa in 1995, his first year above A-ball, and has a good batting eye. Smith's bat is the key to how far he'll advance.

SMITH, OZZIE - SS - BB - Age 41
After ten seasons, Smith finally succumbed to a torn rotator cuff last season and underwent surgery. Like the entire Cardinal organization, Smith had a miserable 1995. However, he's still in great shape and insists his shoulder will hold up long enough to allow him to play another two or three years. You can't bet against The Wizard.

	AB	R	HR	RBI	SB	BA	$
1994 St. Louis NL	381	51	3	30	6	.262	8
1995 St. Louis NL	156	16	0	11	4	.199	-
1996 Projection >>>	320	40	1	25	7	.246	3

SNOPEK, CHRIS - 3B - BR - Age 25
The White Sox really like the way Snopek blossomed in 1995. He was second in the American Association in batting average and on-base percentage. He's obviously ready for the majors, but where should he play? He's a good third baseman and also played some shortstop at Triple-A Nashville last year, although he probably can't handle that position in the bigs. Don't be surprised to see the White Sox move Robin Ventura to accomodate Snopek's advance to the big leagues. Snopek will play somewhere regularly in 1996. He won't ride the major league bench, and he should be good for a .280 BA and 12-15 homers if he returns to the minors.

	AB	R	HR	RBI	SB	BA	$
1994 Birmingham AA	365	58	6	54	9	.263	
1995 Nashville AAA	393	56	12	55	2	.323	
1995 Chicago AL	68	12	1	7	1	.324	1
1996 Projection >>>	136	24	3	15	2	.264	1

SNOW, J.T. - 1B - BB - Age 28
The Angels and ex-GM Whitey Herzog are very pleased that J.T. Snow has finally developed into an aggressive and very productive hitter. He didn't let a very hot first half carry his seasonal statistics. His second half was an excellent .274-12-49, a good indicator that a 25-homer and 100-RBI year may be on the horizon in 1996.

	AB	R	HR	RBI	SB	BA	$
1994 California AL	223	22	8	30	0	.220	2
1995 California AL	544	80	24	102	2	.289	20
1996 Projection >>>	503	69	21	87	2	.272	16

SNYDER, CORY - 3B/OF - BR - Age 33
Hitting a combined .240 at Triple-A (Pawtucket and Las Vegas) won't get you back to the big leagues any time soon. Snyder was released twice in 1995. He could still smack a homer or two if he gets back, but don't count on it.

SOJO, LUIS - 2B/SS - BR - Age 30
Sojo always finds a way to get playing time with his mixture of speed, defense and line drive hitting.

	AB	R	HR	RBI	SB	BA	$
1994 Seattle AL	213	32	6	22	2	.277	6
1995 Seattle AL	339	50	7	39	4	.289	9
1996 Projection >>>	323	48	7	36	4	.274	7

SOLOMON, STEVE - OF - BL - Age 25
In his first venture above Single-A, Solomon showed why he had been promoted so slowly by the Phillies. After hitting for a consistently high average with doubles power in A-ball, Solomon's bat was clearly too slow against Double-A pitchers. Though he bats lefthanded and has above average speed, Solomon has appeared to reach the apex of his minor league progress. At best, he will return to Double-A in 1996.

SORRENTO, PAUL - 1B - BL - Age 31
Sorrento evolved into the most fearsome bottom-of-the-order platooner in baseball in 1995. He is a strapping, streaky power hitter who tailed off drastically at the end of 1995, and who is overmatched by lefties (.163 in 1995). If Herbert Perry was a lefty, Sorrento last year would have been in considerable peril - as it is, expect Sorrento to continue to be a .250-.270 hitting one-dimensional power threat, if he stays in Cleveland.

	AB	R	HR	RBI	SB	BA	$
1994 Cleveland AL	322	43	14	62	0	.280	13
1995 Cleveland AL	323	50	25	79	1	.235	11
1996 *Projection* >>>	300	44	15	65	1	.253	7

SOSA, SAMMY - OF - BR - Age 27
Sosa's a very athletic player, but his stats are padded with numerous flashy, meaningless homers that hide his frequent dumb plays. He'll earn a great deal of money on the free agent market; while the Cubs would like to have him back they won't break the bank to do it. Wherever he plays in 1996 he'll hit homers, steal bases - and make some spetacular blunders.

	AB	R	HR	RBI	SB	BA	$
1994 Chicago NL	426	59	25	70	22	.300	35
1995 Chicago NL	564	89	36	119	34	.268	37
1996 *Projection* >>>	589	89	35	108	34	.276	34

SPARKS, GREG - 1B - BL - Age 32
Twelve seasons, nine organizations and just 136 games above Double-A. That's because he has yet to hit his weight (185) in Triple-A. He's from baseball's Sparks family, so he knows the game and provides an experienced hitter. He was -- what else? -- a minor league free agent after last season.

SPEARMAN, VERN - OF - BL - Age 26
A leadoff prospect, Spearman needs to bring the rest of his game up near the level of his speed.

SPEHR, TIM - C - BR - Age 29
His primary value to the Expos has been as a pinch runner and defensive replacement for starting catcher Darrin Fletcher. He gets few at bats and doesn't do much with them. His 1995 season was cut short due to testicular cancer surgery.

	AB	R	HR	RBI	SB	BA	$
1994 Montreal NL	36	8	0	5	2	.250	0
1995 Montreal NL	35	4	1	3	0	.257	-

SPIERS, BILL - 2B - BL - Age 29
Spiers was a solid-hitting shortstop on the rise before back surgery felled him in 1991. Since then he's never been the same, and more recently has had shoulder woes leading to throwing errors. The future is in doubt.

	AB	R	HR	RBI	SB	BA	$
1994 Milwaukee AL	214	27	0	17	7	.252	4
1995 New York NL	72	5	0	11	0	.208	-
1996 *Projection* >>>	81	9	0	8	2	.237	-

SPIEZIO, SCOTT - 3B - BB - Age 23
He's an interesting prospect, who hits gobs of doubles and the occasional homer. He stole ten bases in 1995, and is willing to take a walk. He made the Double-A Southern League All-Star team and should be pushing Jason Giambi for a major league job by 1997.

SPRAGUE, ED - 3B - BR - Age 28
Sprague finally became the player the Blue Jays hoped he would be, reaching career highs in homers, RBI, runs scored, walks and slugging percentage. He's still a big swinger and crowds the plate but his power gets better each year. He will be the everyday third baseman, perhaps for a long time.

	AB	R	HR	RBI	SB	BA	$
1994 Toronto AL	405	38	11	44	1	.240	7
1995 Toronto AL	521	77	18	74	0	.244	9
1996 *Projection* >>>	516	65	16	68	1	.244	8

SPRINGER, STEVE - 2B/3B - BR - Age 35
Springer is a career minor leaguer who spent ten rather undistinguished seasons in Triple-A.

STAHOVIAK, SCOTT - 3B/1B - BL - Age 26
Injuries hampered an otherwise promising first season for Stahoviak. He had sewn up the first base job by midsummer, and enters '96 as the favorite at the position. As a hitter, he can produce .270-20-75 totals, provided the Twins break him in slowly versus lefthanders (.077 in '95).

	AB	R	HR	RBI	SB	BA	$
1994 Salt Lake AAA	437	96	13	94	6	.318	
1995 Minnesota AL	263	28	3	23	5	.266	3
1996 Projection >>>	270	28	4	30	4	.273	4

STAIRS, MATT - OF - BL - Age 27
Stairs had his contract sold to a Japanese team partway through the year, but the deal fell through and he remained with Triple-A Pawtucket where he had a good year. He has some power and can hit for a good average. Weak defense will keep Stairs confined to a platoon or bench role; he can be a useful reserve outfielder/pinch-hitter for a major league team.

	AB	R	HR	RBI	SB	BA	$
1995 Pawtucket AAA	317	44	9	61	10	.309	
1995 Boston AL	88	8	1	17	0	.261	-
1996 Projection >>>	92	12	2	18	0	.270	-

STANKIEWICZ, ANDY - 2B - BR - Age 31
Stankiewicz is a borderline major league utility player. He gives a strong effort, but his tools are limited. He is not likely to get significant playing time. The Astros sent Stankiewicz outright to Triple-A after the 1995 season.

	AB	R	HR	RBI	SB	BA	$
1994 Houston NL	54	10	1	5	1	.259	0
1995 Houston NL	52	6	0	7	4	.115	-
1996 Projection >>>	59	9	0	7	3	.190	-

STANLEY, MIKE - C - BR - Age 32
A finger injury got Stanley off to a slow start in '95, but he recovered to hit .275 with 11 homers and 49 RBI after the All-Star break. The good strike zone judgment and raw power are still there, even if the batspeed is down a fraction of a second. Heck, how many catchers had a .368 on base percentage and slugged over .500 in the second half of '95? Mike Piazza, and, er, ah ... you get the idea.

	AB	R	HR	RBI	SB	BA	$
1994 New York AL	290	54	17	57	0	.300	15
1995 New York AL	399	63	18	83	1	.268	12
1996 Projection >>>	433	66	20	81	1	.274	13

STATON, DAVID - 1B - BR - Age 27
Power-hitting Staton missed a golden opportunity to grab a wide-open first base job in San Diego in 1994 by hitting .182 with just six RBI. In 1995 he led Triple-A New Orleans with 19 homers, but continued to strikeout frequently - 96 Ks in 325 at-bats. In any weak organization he has a chance to win a part-time role as a first-baseman/designated hitter. As a big league hitter he would pop a few homers, and strike out a ton.

	AB	R	HR	RBI	SB	BA	$
1994 San Diego NL	66	6	4	6	0	.182	-
1995 New Orleans AAA	325	42	19	46	0	.252	

STEFANSKI, MIKE - C - BR - Age 26
Stefanski swings the bat better than other Brewers minor league catchers, but his age makes him a marginal prospect. He also has played third base.

STEINBACH, TERRY - C - BR - Age 34
Steinbach has the same season every year: average around .275, 10-15 homers, no speed. He's getting older and will eventually start to slide; when this happens, the dropoff may seem severe, since he is not as good a hitter as his reputation to begin with. Still, he's as sure a bet as any 34-year-old catcher.

	AB	R	HR	RBI	SB	BA	$
1994 Oakland AL	369	51	11	57	2	.285	14
1995 Oakland AL	406	43	15	65	1	.278	11
1996 Projection >>>	438	51	14	64	2	.268	10

STEVENS, LEE - OF - BL - Age 28
In his second season in Japan, Stevens hit .247 with 23 homers and 70 RBI for the Kintetsu Buffaloes. He'd be a lefty pinch-hitter if he were to return to the US.

STEVERSON, TODD - OF - BR - Age 24
Detroit selected this former first round pick from Toronto in the Rule Five draft before the season, then lost him to the disabled list for most of the year. He has a chance to be a factor in Detroit's future outfield, as he has some power and speed and can hit .260. Steverson will spend '96 at Triple-A and then enter the Tigers' crowded outfield derby.

	AB	R	HR	RBI	SB	BA	$
1995 Detroit AL	42	11	2	6	2	.262	0

STEWART, ANDY - 1B/C - BR - Age 25
Stewart is a fairly versatile player whose hitting has improved vastly over the last two seasons. Last season, he fought through some injuries and still put together a respectable season. Because he can play behind the plate, at first base, or in the outfield, Stewart may have a place as a major league reserve.

STEWART, SHANNON - OF - BR - Age 22
After showing great speed and an excellent eye at Double-A, Stewart got the callup in September to replace the injured Devon White. He's a very fast runner and is extremely patient for his age... similar to a young Rickey Henderson. If White were no longer in Toronto, Stewart would get consideration as the regular center fielder.

	AB	R	HR	RBI	SB	BA	$
1995 Knoxville AA	498	89	5	55	42	.287	
1995 Toronto AL	38	2	0	1	2	.211	-

STILLWELL, KURT - 2B/SS - BB - Age 30
Once upon a time, Stillwell was considered as good a prospect as Barry Larkin. Now he is hanging on for one more chance at major league meal money - his last appearance in the bigs was with California in 1993.

STINNETT, KELLY - C - BR - Age 26
The emergence of Todd Hundley as a strong hitter from both sides of the plate, combined with Stinnett's weak second half, changed their relationship from platooners to clear number one and clear number two. And now defensive gem Alberto Castillo is on the way.

	AB	R	HR	RBI	SB	BA	$
1994 New York NL	150	20	2	14	2	.253	2
1995 New York NL	196	23	4	18	2	.219	1
1996 Projection >>>	151	19	3	14	1	.230	-

STOCKER, KEVIN - SS - BB - Age 26
Stocker was a major disappointment in 1995 for the Phils, both offensively and defensively. At the plate, he was an overanxious free swinger, in direct contrast to the disciplined maturity he displayed in his first two pro seasons. In the field, he is laid back and lets the the ball play him, making many sloppy errors. He generally lost confidence, and was the biggest of many 1995 disappointments in the eyes of the Phils' coaching staff. His job is not in danger - he is simply not as good as he was in 1993-94, and not as bad as he was in 1995.

	AB	R	HR	RBI	SB	BA	$
1994 Philadelphia NL	271	38	2	28	2	.273	5
1995 Philadelphia NL	412	42	1	32	6	.218	1
1996 Projection >>>	444	52	2	38	5	.251	4

STOVALL, DAROND - OF - BB - Age 23
Stovall is a power hitter who strikes out too much to be considered a strong prospect at this time.

STRANGE, DOUG - 2B - BB - Age 31
The numbers game reduced Strange to a bit part in the Mariners pennant drive. He gave them good pinch-hitting and versatile defensive play. Strange is no more than a reserve, but a good one.

	AB	R	HR	RBI	SB	BA	$
1994 Texas AL	226	26	5	26	1	.212	1

	AB	R	HR	RBI	SB	BA	$
1995 Seattle AL	155	19	2	21	0	.271	1
1996 Projection >>>	136	16	2	17	1	.245	-

STRAWBERRY, DARRYL - OF - BL - Age 34
If three home runs and 13 RBI can be called a comeback, Strawberry had one in 1995. It's more telling, however, to look at the .265, .237, .140 and .239 trail of batting averages that Strawberry left during his years with the Dodgers and Giants in 1991-1994 and 17-homer total in the last four years combined. As a platoon DH or pinch hitter there may be some latent value, but the glove and legs haven't improved in the nine years since Darryl was a 30/30 man.

	AB	R	HR	RBI	SB	BA	$
1994 San Francisco NL	92	13	4	17	0	.239	1
1995 New York AL	87	15	3	13	0	.276	1
1996 Projection >>>	227	36	8	36	0	.246	2

STRICKLAND, CHAD - C - BR - Age 24
Strickland is an outstanding defensive catcher with a great arm. However, he has shown very little with the bat. He began the year with Triple-A Omaha, then finished the season as a second string catcher for Double-A Wichita. Scouts are high on Strickland's prowess behind the plate - if his bat shows any signs of life he'd get a quick ticket to the big leagues.

STRITTMATTER, MARK - C - BR - Age 26
Strittmatter's hitting for the most part has held him down to Double-A in the Rockies organization. He's a good catcher, and he's not an automatic out because he can draw a walk. His offensive statistics should look better at Triple-A Colorado Springs, and he might get a chance as a major league backup.

STUBBS, FRANKLIN - OF/1B - BL - Age 34
Stubbs performed well as a role player for the Tigers in '95, yet will likely have to search for another job in '96. He needs to produce more than the two home runs he managed in '95 to entice a potential employer; Stubbs is facing retirement.

	AB	R	HR	RBI	SB	BA	$
1995 Detroit AL	116	13	2	19	0	.250	0

STYNES, CHRIS - 2B/3B - BR - Age 23
The latest heir apparent to the Royals second base job, Stynes was acquired in the David Cone deal prior to the 1995 season and split time between Triple-A and the major league bench. Stynes was sometimes awkward at second base; he was originally a third baseman. A late-season surge helped raise his Omaha batting line to .275-9-42. Stynes could win a platoon role as early as 1996.

	AB	R	HR	RBI	SB	BA	$
1995 Omaha AAA	306	51	9	42	4	.275	
1995 Kansas City AL	35	7	0	2	0	.171	-
1996 Projection >>>	145	20	2	18	2	.242	0

SURHOFF, B.J. - 3B/OF - BL - Age 31
1995 was a season to savor, and has a chance to be repeated.

	AB	R	HR	RBI	SB	BA	$
1994 Milwaukee AL	134	20	5	22	0	.261	3
1995 Milwaukee AL	415	72	13	73	7	.320	19
1996 Projection >>>	435	71	12	73	7	.290	16

SUTKO, GLENN - C - BR - Age 27
Sutko showed some power hitting in the Southern League in 1992, but since then he's gone steadily downward, finishing with a .208 average on the Brewers farm in 1995.

SUTTON, LARRY - 1B - BL - Age 25
Sutton spent the majority of the 1995 season on the disabled list with an arm injury, which seemed to hamper his timing at the plate once he returned to Double-A Wichita in mid-July. Though he's a great defensive first baseman, he also has some power and can hit for average. By the end of last season, Sutton was hitting much better than indicated by his .269-5-32 line.

SVEUM, DALE - 1B - BB - Age 32
Sveum hit 25 homers for Milwaukee in 1987 but that seems like 100 years ago. He had an OK season for the Pirates' Triple-A Calgary farm club last year and still has hopes of getting back to the majors as a utility infielder. Those hopes are fading, though.

SWANN, PEDRO - OF - BL - Age 25
Swann has hit very well during the last three seasons with Double-A Greenville. His defense and the glut of outfield prospects in the Braves organization have held him back. Swann would have a better chance with another team.

SWEENEY, MARK - 1B - BL - Age 26
Sweeney finally reached Triple-A in 1994 and got a September call-up in 1995 to St. Louis. He's shown signs of power and can hit for average.

	AB	R	HR	RBI	SB	BA	$
1995 Vancouver AAA	226	48	7	59	3	.345	
1995 Louisville AAA	76	15	2	22	2	.368	
1995 St. Louis NL	77	5	2	13	1	.273	1
1996 *Projection* >>>	147	20	3	28	3	.273	2

SWEENEY, MIKE - C - BR - Age 22
Sweeney never played above Class-A until a September callup to the majors. His catching skills need further development, but he has good potential as a hitter. Sweeney won the Carolina League batting championship in 1995 with his .310-18-53 effort and has shown a superior batting eye. Considering the need for a good hitting catcher in Kansas City, Sweeney is on the fast track to the majors but he'll first have to prove himself at Double-A Wichita in 1996.

	AB	R	HR	RBI	SB	BA	$
1995 Kansas City AL	4	1	0	0	0	.250	-

TACKETT, JEFF - C - BR - Age 30
This veteran of the Baltimore organization can chip in a .250 average and some good defense behind the plate. Tackett won't take the starting job from John Flaherty, but is more than capable of filling in as his backup.

TALANOA, SCOTT - OF - BR - Age 26
After four minor league seasons of putting up solid power numbers, Talanoa slipped in his first trip to Triple-A in 1995.

TARASCO, TONY - OF - BL - Age 25
Acquired from Atlanta as part of the Marquis Grissom trade last spring, Tarasco had a fine first half for the Expos in his first shot at playing reguarly in the major leagues. Then, he faded terribly in the second half. That raised serious questions about all the hype he received while coming up through the Braves' system. He could be a good player but it's doubtful he'll become a superstar.

	AB	R	HR	RBI	SB	BA	$
1994 Atlanta NL	132	16	5	19	5	.273	6
1995 Montreal NL	438	64	14	40	24	.249	16
1996 *Projection* >>>	425	61	14	42	22	.263	16

TARTABULL, DANNY - OF/DH - BR - Age 33
This perennially underrated slugger had his worst season ever in 1995. However, he's still capable of a 25-homer season. Watch the wires during the offseason for reports on Tartabull's health and status: if ends up in a hitters' park, he could be Comeback Player of the Year, if he ends up hurt and miserable, he could be on the bench in 1996 and then out of baseball in a year.

	AB	R	HR	RBI	SB	BA	$
1994 New York AL	399	68	19	67	1	.256	14
1995 NY - Oakland AL	280	34	8	35	0	.236	3
1996 *Projection* >>>	276	41	11	42	0	.246	4

TATUM, JIM - 1B/3B/C - BR - Age 28
Tatum has bounced back and forth between the Rockies and their Triple-A affiliate so often the last three years that he probably has the 70-mile route between Denver and Colorado Springs committed to memory. His efforts to become

an effective backup catcher at the major league level were thwarted by the emergence of Jayhawk Owens, and his primary pinch-hitter status was subsumed by John Vander Wal. Tatum's Triple-A numbers, where he got regular playing time, were solid in 1995, but his major league value is rapidly fading.

	AB	R	HR	RBI	SB	BA	$
1995 Colorado NL	34	4	0	4	0	.235	-

TAUBENSEE, EDDIE - C - BL - Age 27
What should have been his breakout year was derailed when the Reds signed Benito Santiago. Taubensee matched Santiago in nearly every offensive category, but Santiago got most of the starts when both were healthy. Taubensee is still young and has 20 home run potential if he ever gets a full time chance.

	AB	R	HR	RBI	SB	BA	$
1994 Cincinnati NL	187	29	8	21	2	.283	7
1995 Cincinnati NL	218	32	9	44	2	.284	8
1996 Projection >>>	254	36	9	43	2	.280	6

TAVAREZ, JESUS - OF - BB - Age 25
With the injuries to Chuck Carr and Gary Sheffield, Tavarez got an extended audition as a Marlins' starting outfielder in 1995. He possesses excellent speed and is wonderful defensively, but he possesses absolutely no power and swings at too many bad pitches to be an effective leadoff hitter. He's basically a switch-hitting Carr with a slightly better bat and less raw speed. The Marlins were expected to open the coffers for a free agent center fielder, which would leave Tavarez as their fourth outfielder.

	AB	R	HR	RBI	SB	BA	$
1994 Florida NL	39	4	0	4	1	.179	-
1995 Charlotte AAA	140	15	1	8	7	.300	
1995 Florida NL	190	31	2	13	7	.289	4
1996 Projection >>>	310	50	2	22	11	.272	7

TAYLOR, REGGIE - OF - BL - Age 19
The Phils' 1995 top pick was generally thought to the fastest runner and best all around athlete among high schoolers in the draft. He had a rocky pro debut, evoking memories of former failed Phils' top draft pick Jeff Jackson, but was still named the number three prospect in the Rookie level Appalachian League by Baseball America. Amid his low average and high strikeout rate, however, were a bunch of triples and steals, and a calculated abandon on the bases reminiscent of Kenny Lofton. Watch his progress closely.

TAYLOR, SAM - OF - BL - Age 27
He has increased his home runs every year while his batting average drops. At this point, he doesn't appear to have much of a major league future. Taylor was playing out the string in 1995 on an independent team.

TAYLOR, WILL - OF - BB - Age 27
Once going places as a base stealer, now just going, going - gone.

TEDDER, SCOTT - OF - BL - Age 29
Tedder draws a spectacular amount of walks every year, but that is his only marker. Six home runs in seven pro seasons.

TETTLETON, MICKEY - C/1B/OF - BB - Age 35
Juan Gonzalez' bad back forced Tettleton to play the outfield on two bad knees for the last two months of the 1995 season. Tettleton responded with a typical Mickey Tettleton season: low average, good power and over 100 walks for the fifth time in six years. With successful offseason knee surgery, there isn't any reason Tettleton can't do it again in 1996. He isn't likely to be anything but an emergency catcher at this point in his career.

	AB	R	HR	RBI	SB	BA	$
1994 Detroit AL	339	57	17	51	0	.248	10
1995 Texas AL	429	76	32	78	0	.238	13
1996 Projection >>>	484	78	27	80	0	.233	10

TEXIDOR, JOSE - OF - BR - Age 24
Despite his being named to the Texas League All-Star team, Texidor is not a highly regarded prospect, which may

account for his willingness to become a replacement player. Texidor is a decent minor league hitter, but that's about it.

THOMAS, BRIAN - OF - BL - Age 24
An adequate fielder who can play anywhere in the outfield, Thomas had a respectable .269-4-35 season for Double-A Tulsa. However, the Rangers think he's capable of a lot more as a hitter. Thomas will spend 1996 at Triple-A Oklahoma City.

THOMAS, FRANK - 1B - BR - Age 27
Thomas played hurt for much of the 1995 season, he ran into a wall chasing a foul pop up. Still, in a "down" year he placed among league leaders in many offensive categories. Thomas is simply a bad fielder who should become a full-time DH in the not-too-distant future. But, there is no better pure hitter in baseball.

	AB	R	HR	RBI	SB	BA	$
1994 Chicago AL	399	106	38	101	2	.353	37
1995 Chicago AL	493	102	40	111	3	.308	28
1996 Projection >>>	544	122	45	127	3	.321	35

THOMAS, GREG - 1B - BL - Age 23
The 1993 9th-round Indians' draftee was a major disappointment at Single-A Kinston, batting around .200, albeit with good power. The Tribe isn't ready to give up on him just yet, but a return trip to Single-A looked like a certainty after 1995. His stock has dropped significantly in the past year.

THOMAS, KEITH - OF - BR - Age 27
Last year was outfielder Keith Thomas's third full year in Double-A. He's a very fast base stealer, but he has trouble hitting as indicated by his batting average hovering around .240 in all three years. At age 27, Thomas will have to improve quickly to make progress to the majors, or else drop out of baseball.

THOMAS, SKEETS - OF - BR - Age 27
Personal problems hindered the performance of this Cardinals' replacement player. Thomas has opposite field power but strikes out frequently. His hustle at Triple-A Louisville was called into question in 1995. Thomas' brother plays football in the NFL.

THOME, JIM - 3B - BL - Age 25
Jim Thome has arrived as one of the most devastating offensive forces in all of baseball. Now, all the Indians need to do is realize this fact, and give him bigger role in their offense. His only offensive shortcoming entering 1995 was his inability to hit lefthanded pitching - he remedied that flaw in 1995, batting a respectable .275 against southpaws. He hits for average with extreme power and excellent plate discipline - he is a better offensive player than Geroge Brett was at a similar point in his career.

	AB	R	HR	RBI	SB	BA	$
1994 Cleveland AL	321	58	20	52	3	.268	15
1995 Cleveland AL	452	92	25	73	4	.314	21
1996 Projection >>>	525	105	30	91	5	.310	27

THOMPSON, FLETCHER - 2B - BL - Age 27
His career was sidetracked by an injury which caused him to miss the entire 1992 season. Thompson has not yet hit well enough to have any chance for a major league opportunity. He finished 1995 playing for an independent team.

THOMPSON, JASON - 1B - BL - Age 25
First baseman Jason Thompson has raw power, much of it undisciplined as shown by his striking out nearly 30 per cent of the time last year in Double-A.

THOMPSON, MILT - OF - BL - Age 37
Thompson is a veteran who has appeared in the National League in each of the last 12 years. He is very popular with his teammates and, in what may have been the last week of his career, contributed to two Astro victories in the wild card drive by scoring the only run in a 1-0 game and hitting a pinch home run in the last game of the season.

	AB	R	HR	RBI	SB	BA	$
1994 Houston NL	241	34	4	33	9	.274	10

	AB	R	HR	RBI	SB	BA	$
1995 Houston NL	132	14	2	19	4	.220	1
1996 *Projection* >>>	134	17	2	19	3	.251	0

THOMPSON, ROBBY - 2B - BR - Age 33

A second consecutive poor season for this aging, injury-plagued infielder suggests he may be nearing the end of the line. He won't steal bases any more, has had only one season with a batting average over .271, medium power in his best years. Thompson was one of the best secondbasemen in the league only three years ago.

	AB	R	HR	RBI	SB	BA	$
1994 San Francisco NL	129	13	2	7	3	.209	0
1995 San Francisco NL	336	51	8	23	1	.223	1
1996 *Projection* >>>	318	46	8	24	1	.234	1

THOMPSON, RYAN - OF - BR - Age 28

The cycle continues year after year: Thompson a learns a compact swing, generates more power, hits home runs, and then begins making the wildly looping undisciplined swings again. And now he's gone through elbow ligament and hamstring woes. And here come Carl Everett, Alex Ochoa and company. Thompson still has speed and power, but he looked about done in New York when last season ended.

	AB	R	HR	RBI	SB	BA	$
1994 New York NL	334	39	18	59	1	.225	8
1995 New York NL	267	39	7	31	3	.251	5
1996 *Projection* >>>	300	40	11	41	3	.240	4

THURMAN, GARY - OF - BR - Age 31

Thurman hit .300 and stole 22 bases to earn a recall for the Mariners in 1995. Desperately searching for a leftfielder and leadoff hitter, Seattle decided Thurman wasn't a good fit after just 13 games, despite his hitting .320 and stealing five bases. He obviously earned another chance to be a reserve major league outfield, but it will have to be with another organization in 1996.

TIMMONS, OZZIE - OF - BR - Age 25

Timmons put together a decent rookie campaign in 1995, serving as a reserve outfielder. He has some power and speed, but is probably best cast as a fourth outfielder. His immediate future depends upon the return of Luis Gonzalez and Sammy Sosa. Timmons could platoon in left or right field with Scott Bullett in 1996.

	AB	R	HR	RBI	SB	BA	$
1995 Chicago NL	171	30	8	28	3	.263	5
1996 *Projection* >>>	115	20	5	19	2	.263	1

TINGLEY, RON - C - BR - Age 36

Tingley played well in '95, hitting .333 against lefthanders and throwing out a better percentage of basestealers than the starter, John Flaherty. He is still the type of marginal veteran who could lose his job if he has a poor spring and would be a backup backstop for any major league team.

	AB	R	HR	RBI	SB	BA	$
1994 Chicago AL	57	4	1	2	0	.158	-
1995 Detroit AL	124	14	4	18	0	.226	0
1996 *Projection* >>>	84	9	2	12	0	.195	-

TINSLEY, LEE - OF - BB - Age 27

Tinsley shot out of the gate quickly, but the luster had faded by mid-season and he lost his regular job to Willie McGee and Dwayne Hosey. His batting line over the final two months of 1995, .239-1-12-5, is very close to his career line prior to last season. Tinsley has lost his regular job but could hold down a reserve outfield spot and provide decent speed off of the bench.

	AB	R	HR	RBI	SB	BA	$
1994 Boston AL	144	27	2	14	13	.222	7
1995 Boston AL	341	61	7	41	18	.284	16
1996 *Projection* >>>	264	48	5	31	13	.262	8

TOKHEIM, DAVE - OF - BL - Age 26

The Phils' 1991 number seven pick is a lefthanded line drive hitter who does not possess the power nor the speed one looks for in a starting major league outfielder. He also falls short in other areas such as plate discipline and defensive ability which would give him an edge in the race for a big league backup spot. His status as a southpaw is all that sets him apart from the competition - he is an average Triple-A player, at best.

TOMBERLIN, ANDY - OF - BL - Age 29
Tomberlin gave the Athletics an occasional homer as a reserve outfielder in 1995. It was his third short major league stint with as many organizations since 1993. Tomberlin can hit enough to fill a reserve outfield/pinch-hitter role.

	AB	R	HR	RBI	SB	BA	$
1994 Boston AL	36	1	1	1	1	.194	-
1995 Oakland AL	85	15	4	10	4	.212	1

TORRES, PAUL - OF - BR - Age 25
An average fielder with good power, Torres joined the Cardinals via the Todd Zeile trade. Scouts were disappointed with his play at Double-A Arkansas, where he hit .225-10-33 following a .298-10-45 performance at Double-A Orlando.

TOVAR, EDGAR - SS - BR - Age 22
His outstanding defense carried him from short-season A-ball to Double-A in less than a year. Scouts say his glove will get him to the major leagues, probably as a second baseman.

TOWNLEY, JASON - C - BR - Age 26
Townley played more than he has since 1990 and showed a touch of power in his second season at Triple-A.

TOWNSEND, CHAD - 1B - BL - Age 24
Townsend is a free swinging lefty who was the Indians' primary Double-A first baseman in 1995. He has a pro body (6'5", 222), but the 1992 14th round draftee has huge holes in his swing and gets himself out on a regular basis. He is quite slow, even by relaxed first baseman standards. Townsend may have reached his apex with the Tribe, as he is about to be overtaken by megaprospect Richie Sexson.

TRAMMELL, ALAN - SS/3B - BR - Age 38
Trammell finished his historic career with the Tigers as a still useful player, hitting lefthanders well and playing sturdy defense. An outstanding all around shortstop for over a decade, he will certainly reach the Hall of Fame, perhaps in his first year of eligibility. The following projection is purely "what if he plays?"

	AB	R	HR	RBI	SB	BA	$
1994 Detroit AL	292	38	8	28	3	.267	8
1995 Detroit AL	223	28	2	23	3	.269	3
1996 Projection >>>	213	29	4	22	3	.260	2

TRAMMELL, BUBBA - OF - BR - Age 24
Good power at Class-A, but getting up there in age.

TREADWAY, JEFF - 2B/3B - BL - Age 33
Treadway retired from the Expos last September in the midst of a dreadful season. He toiled without fanfare for Cincinnati, Atlanta, Cleveland, Los Angeles and Montreal but was a real pro.

	AB	R	HR	RBI	SB	BA	$
1994 Los Angeles NL	67	14	0	5	1	.299	0
1995 LA - Montreal NL	67	6	0	13	0	.209	-

TREDAWAY, CHAD - 2B - BB - Age 23
Tredaway has been slowed by injuries since hitting .300 as an All-Star at Williamsport in the New York-Penn League in 1992. He doesn't have great raw skills, but makes good contact and plays good defense. Tredaway is a utility infielder prospect at best.

TREMIE, CHRIS - C - BR - Age 26
Tremie is a third string catcher, at best, who can't even hit in the minors; note his career .202 batting average in the minor leagues. He's a good defensive catcher, but would have to be the best fielding catcher ever to justify his poor hitting. Tremie will return to the minors again in 1996.

	AB	R	HR	RBI	SB	BA	$
1995 Chicago AL	24	0	0	0	0	.167	-

TUBBS, GREG - OF - BR - Age 33
A long-time minor leaguer, Tubbs has almost no chance of ever getting back to the majors.

TUCKER, MICHAEL - OF - BL - Age 24
Tucker lost the leftfield job, then put on a hitting display for Triple-A Omaha and was recalled as a part of the Royals August 11th roster purge. An uppercut swing helps him hit for power but also contributed to his high strikeout rate. Tucker is a much more confident and aggressive hitter and will again have the leftfield job to start 1996; he's expected to carry a large part of the Royals offense once he fully develops.

	AB	R	HR	RBI	SB	BA	$
1995 Omaha AAA	275	37	4	28	11	.305	
1995 Kansas City AL	177	23	4	17	2	.260	2
1996 *Projection* >>>	388	52	10	40	4	.270	8

TUCKER, SCOOTER - C - BR - Age 29
Tucker bounced through three organizations in 1995, Houston to Cleveland to Atlanta; at least they were all winning teams. He's not much of a hitter, but is a passable catcher. Tucker has very little chance of getting more than 50 major league at-bats in any season.

	AB	R	HR	RBI	SB	BA	$
1995 Cleveland AL	27	3	1	1	0	.074	-

TURANG, BRIAN - OF - BR - Age 28
A 1994 elbow injury slowed Turang's career just as he was beginning to get some playing time in the big leagues. He has good speed and can pop an occasional homer. Turang will have to move on to another organization to get another shot and he'll have to do better than his .240-1-18 performance at Triple-A Tacoma in 1995.

TURCO, FRANK - OF/2B - BR - Age 27
Turco is a career minor leaguer with almost no chance of reaching the majors.

TURNER, CHRIS - C - BR - Age 27
Turner is a weak hitting Angels catcher. Playing full time he could hit .240-5-50.

	AB	R	HR	RBI	SB	BA	$
1994 California AL	149	23	1	12	3	.242	1
1995 California AL	10	0	0	1	0	.100	-

TWARDOSKI, MIKE - 1B - BL - Age 31
Former Indians farmhand, about what you would expect from a minor league first baseman: can hit .280 with 10+ home runs in a good, full season.

TYLER, BRAD - 2B - BL - Age 27
Last year was Tyler's second in Triple-A, but he didn't improve his hitting much as he hit for almost the same average, around .260. But he showed some power for the first time with 17 homers, and he showed a good eye leading the league with 71 walks. Unfortunately, he is very weak defensively, and can't play second in the majors. Tyler is not in the Orioles plans as they are looking to others to plug their second base hole.

UNROE, TIM - 3B - BR - Age 25
Unroe followed up a 1994 season in which he led the Texas league in hits, runs scored and RBI with a .261-6-45 performance for Triple-A New Orleans and also got to the major leagues for the first time. He's a fair prospect who should win at least a part-time role with the Brewers in 1996; look for marginal power and a batting average around .240 in 250 at-bats.

VALDEZ, PEDRO - OF - BL - Age 22
Has been playing pro ball for four years, despite his youth. Valdes is far too young to forget about.

VALENTIN, JOHN - SS - BR - Age 29
More than any other player, Valentin's emergence as the league's best hitting shortstop boosted the Red Sox offense into a fearsome unit. His 27 homers in 1995 were more than he had hit in his entire career before last year. He's not one of the better defensive shortstops, but his hitting places Valentin among the league's shortstop elite.

	AB	R	HR	RBI	SB	BA	$
1994 Boston AL	301	53	9	49	3	.316	13
1995 Boston AL	520	108	27	102	20	.298	31
1996 Projection >>>	524	99	21	92	15	.295	25

VAIENTIN, JOSE - C - BB - Age 20
The Twins' catcher of the future, young Valentin has some excellent front line strengths: ability to hit for average, power hitting, and defensive prowess. A smaller build (5'10", 190) than the prototypical catcher is his only weakness.

VALENTIN, JOSE - SS - BB - Age 26
Valentin fell back after a promising rookie year. Jose has some power and should get get his BA up into the .240-.250 range.

	AB	R	HR	RBI	SB	BA	$
1994 Milwaukee AL	285	47	11	46	12	.239	15
1995 Milwaukee AL	338	62	11	49	16	.219	11
1996 Projection >>>	363	65	12	54	16	.236	11

VALLE, DAVE - C - BR - Age 35
Valle has settled into the role of backup catcher, and should be able to remain there for a couple more years. Valle's all right behind the plate, but he has never been much of a hitter.

	AB	R	HR	RBI	SB	BA	$
1994 Two Teams	112	14	2	10	0	.232	-
1995 Two Teams	75	7	0	5	1	.240	-

VALRIE, KERRY - OF - BR - Age 27
Valrie has a substantial amount of raw talent, including a good arm and great speed. He led Triple-A Nashville in runs scored, hits and doubles, but also in strikeouts. Valrie can get to the big leagues, but only as a reserve outfielder.

VAN BURKLEO, TY - 1B - BL - Age 32
Van Burkleo spent all of 1995 at Triple-A, where his numbers were pedestrian and his playing time was limited by the strong season put forth by Jay Gainer. The talent of Gainer, John Vander Wal and Andres Galarraga, along with his advanced age limit Van Burkleo's big league potential.

VANDERWAL, JOHN - 1B/OF - BL - Age 29
Vander Wal emerged as an outstanding pinch-hitter for the Rockies in 1995, setting the major league record for most pinch hits in a season. His time in the field will be limited so long as Galarraga remains with the Rockies, but his defensive skills make him an adequate backup. Vander Wal's status as one of the few left-handed hitters on the team will gain him extra plate appearances over the course of the 1996 season.

	AB	R	HR	RBI	SB	BA	$
1994 Colorado NL	110	12	5	15	2	.245	3
1995 Colorado NL	101	15	5	21	1	.347	5
1996 Projection >>>	136	19	6	23	2	.294	3

VAN SLYKE, ANDY - OF - BL - Age 35
A degenerative back condition has reduced Van Slyke to a shell of his former self, especially in the power hitting department. After posting slugging percentages between .439 and .507 in eight of the nine seasons between 1985 and 1993, he has dropped way off to .358 and .343 in the past two seasons. He never learned how to hit lefties, against whom he hit .200 in 1995. He still plays the game full throttle, and was 14 for 14 stealing bases in 1994-95, but he just doesn't have enough remaining skills to compensate for his loss of power - his days as a full time player are over.

	AB	R	HR	RBI	SB	BA	$
1994 Pittsburgh NL	374	41	6	30	7	.246	8
1995 Two Teams	277	32	6	24	7	.224	4
1996 Projection >>>	227	26	4	21	5	.240	1

VARGAS, HECTOR - 2B - BR - Age 29
At this stage of his career, Vargas is an itinerant minor league veteran. He was brought in to fill a hole in the depleted Texas minor league system. Vargas' chances of playing in the majors are very slim.

VARITEK, JASON - C - BB - Age 24
This much sought after college star from Georgia Tech finally signed a pro contract and began his career with a .224-10-44 season for Double-A Port City. The Mariners would like to push him quickly through their system, but he'll have to cut down on the whiffs to reach the majors; Varitek struck out 126 times in 352 at-bats in 1995. He's a raw talent and has a lot of work to do.

VARSHO, GARY - OF - BL - Age 34
Varsho is a very limited offensive player who remains in the majors only because of his ability to play above average defense at all three outfield positions and the fact that he bats lefthanded. He has absolutely no pop in his bat, and is not particularly selective, either - there is absolutely no need for him to occupy a valuable major league roster spot any longer, despite his love for the game and strength in its fundamentals.

	AB	R	HR	RBI	SB	BA	$
1994 Pittsburgh NL	82	15	0	5	0	.256	-
1995 Philadelphia NL	103	7	0	11	2	.252	0
1996 Projection >>>	113	12	0	11	1	.236	-

VATCHER, JIM - OF - BR - Age 29
Vatcher is an older minor-league veteran who got into 87 major league games with 109 at-bats in 1990-92. He hits decently in the minors, with 8 or 10 homers per year, but he has no speed. Vatcher is one of the many older veteran players at Triple-A who wait for the call from the majors, and then usually playing a part time fill-in role when somebody gets injured.

VAUGHN, GREG - OF/DH - BR - Age 30
Injuries and poor plate discipline have steadily eroded his value. Good for 20 homers and some steals, but the batting average is brutal.

	AB	R	HR	RBI	SB	BA	$
1994 Milwaukee AL	370	59	19	55	9	.254	17
1995 Milwaukee AL	392	67	17	59	10	.224	10
1996 Projection >>>	437	73	20	67	9	.239	11

VAUGHN, MO - 1B - BL - Age 28
Vaughn came into his own with a marvelous 1995 MVP-candidate season, setting several personal bests and leading the Red Sox in most power hitting categories. He tied Albert Belle for the league lead in RBI, hit .300 for the second straight year and even stole some bases. Vaughn no longer has to bow to Frank Thomas; this popular team leader was the AL's best first baseman in 1995.

	AB	R	HR	RBI	SB	BA	$
1994 Boston AL	394	65	26	82	4	.310	26
1995 Boston AL	550	98	39	126	11	.300	32
1996 Projection >>>	571	96	37	118	8	.302	30

VELANDIA, JORGE - SS - BR - Age 21
Young shortstop Jorge Velandia tarnished his reputation as a defensive whiz last year as he made 31 errors in 66 games in Triple-A. Thus far, he hasn't shown much of a bat or any speed.

VELARDE, RANDY - OF/SS - BR - Age 33
Velarde's 1995 season carried him all the way from Homestead free agent to regular second baseman in a dramatic playoff. "Bronco" is most valuable for his multiposition flexibility and will find a utility role elsewhere in 1996.

	AB	R	HR	RBI	SB	BA	$
1994 New York AL	280	47	9	34	4	.279	10
1995 New York AL	367	60	7	46	5	.278	9
1996 Projection >>>	308	50	7	38	4	.271	7

VELASQUEZ, EDGARD - OF - BR - Age 20
Hitting .300 with power at High Class- A in 1995 put Velasquez on the prospect map.

VELASQUEZ, GUILLERMO - 1B - BL - Age 27
In 1993 Velasquez lost his regular first base job with the Padres, then dropped back to Double-A in 1994. He hit .250 with one homer for Triple-A Ottawa before his release. Velasquez will have to scramble for another chance in 1996.

VELEZ, JOSE - OF - BB - Age 22
A good hitter with some speed, Velez platooned at Arkansas in 1995. He has decent power (.421 slugging average), but needs more time to develop it. Look for Velez back in Double-A in 1996.

VENTURA, ROBIN - 3B - BL - Age 28
Ventura had another great year in 1995, giving the White Sox steady hitting and defense. He's really a better third baseman than his error count might show as Frank Thomas doesn't help him much at first base. Ventura may move to first base to accomodate Chris Snopek's advance to the major leagues and to replace Thomas' poor defense.

	AB	R	HR	RBI	SB	BA	$
1994 Chicago AL	401	57	18	78	3	.282	19
1995 Chicago AL	492	79	26	93	4	.295	21
1996 Projection >>>	529	82	25	97	4	.278	19

VERAS, QUILVIO - 2B - BB - Age 25
Veras paced the NL in steals, and has become one of baseball's foremost leadoff men. Very few rookies come down the pike and walk more than they whiff in their first big league season. He also appears to have the potential to be an excellent defensive second baseman. He's on his way to becoming an All Star.

	AB	R	HR	RBI	SB	BA	$
1994 Norfolk AAA	457	71	0	43	40	.249	
1995 Florida NL	440	86	5	32	56	.261	27
1996 Projection >>>	528	98	5	43	51	.270	28

VESSEL, ANDREW - OF - BR - Age 21
Vessel is the Rangers' top hitting prospect. He is expected to develop into a solid power hitter, but is probably at least two years away from the big leagues.

VIDRO, JOSE - OF - BB - Age 21
Vidro is a good-looking second base prospect who had a decent year at Class A West Palm Beach in 1994 and 1995. He will likely start the 1996 season at Class Double-A, the level were we'll get a real read on his major-league potential.

VILLANUEVA, HECTOR - C - BR - Age 31
Villanueva lost the battle of the bulge (around his waist) and is probably finished with professional ball in the states. Look for him to return to the Mexican Leagues.

VINA, FERNANDO - 2B - BL - Age 26
Once promising for his speed and defense, Vina has been passed on and is now a backup player at best..

	AB	R	HR	RBI	SB	BA	$
1994 New York NL	124	20	0	6	3	.250	1
1995 Milwaukee AL	288	46	3	29	6	.257	5
1996 Projection >>>	251	40	2	22	6	.252	3

VIRGILLO, GEORGE - 2B - BB - Age 25
Formerly in the Expo organization, second baseman George Virgillio is now in the Orioles system. He has trouble hitting minor league pitching.

VITIELLO, JOE - 1B/OF - BR - Age 25
One of the better young prospects that few people have even heard of, Vitiello bounced between Triple-A Omaha and the big league club, hitting well at both sites. The 1994 American Association batting champion, Vitiello put on a power display down the stretch as he started to pull more pitches. Vitiello could eventually be a decent power hitter

as a first baseman or rightfielder. Look for Vitiello to gradually earn more playing time in 1996, then become the Royals' regular first baseman in 1997.

	AB	R	HR	RBI	SB	BA	$
1995 Omaha AAA	229	33	12	42	0	.279	
1995 Kansas City AL	130	13	7	21	0	.254	2
1996 *Projection* >>>	306	31	13	48	0	.277	7

VIZCAINO, JOSE - SS/3B/2B - BB - Age 28
A career year in 1995 raised Vizcaino's stock at a time when super-fielder Rey Ordonez was becoming major league ready. The force of someone who can field like a young Ozzie Smith is unstoppable, but Vizcaino has earned more than a one-year caddy role if he stays with the Mets.

	AB	R	HR	RBI	SB	BA	$
1994 New York NL	410	47	3	33	1	.256	5
1995 New York NL	509	66	3	56	8	.287	13
1996 *Projection* >>>	441	56	3	44	5	.278	8

VIZQUEL, OMAR - SS - BB - Age 28
Vizquel was brought east to Cleveland to be their defensive rock and an occasional stolen base threat - not to be a hitter. He has delivered, fulfilling the Tribe's expectations. Vizquel reached a career high in walks in 1995, and has greatly evolved as a basestealer, converting 74% of his attempts successfully as an Indian, after managing a success rate of barely over 50% as a Mariner. One or two more years for Vizquel, before minor leaguers Damian Jackson and Enrique Wilson mount a serious challenge to his job.

	AB	R	HR	RBI	SB	BA	$
1994 Cleveland AL	286	39	1	33	13	.273	12
1995 Cleveland AL	542	87	6	56	29	.266	22
1996 *Projection* >>>	502	76	5	51	24	.263	16

VOIGT, JACK - OF - BR - Age 29
Voigt is a role player whose versatility, defense and pinch-hitting could keep him on a major league roster.

	AB	R	HR	RBI	SB	BA	$
1994 Baltimore AL	141	15	3	20	0	.241	1
1995 Texas AL	63	9	2	8	0	.175	-

WACHTER, DEREK - OF - BR - Age 25
A year after hitting 22 home runs in the California League in 1993, Wachter showed little power even though he hit for average in 1994 and 95. He has a long swing, and has to guard against pitchers' getting inside on him. Wachter is a so-so outfielder.

WAKAMATSU, DON - C - BR - Age 33
An experienced knuckleball catcher, Wakamatsu spent 1995 at Double-A Canton-Akron where he hit .266-4-23 in a reserve role. He's made 18 career appearances in the big leagues, but won't likely make another as he's not a very good hitter. Wakamatsu is a career .258 hitter in the minors.

WALBECK, MATT - C - BB - Age 26
It hasn't been pretty, but Walbeck showed some life with the bat in '95 as he held up his end defensively. Walbeck will never be an offensive star, but he is a .260 hitter who could develop a little power, and he catches a good game. He will keep his job in '96.

	AB	R	HR	RBI	SB	BA	$
1994 Minnesota AL	338	31	5	35	1	.204	0
1995 Minnesota AL	393	40	1	44	3	.257	4
1996 *Projection* >>>	410	40	3	45	2	.260	4

WALKER, HUGH - OF - BL - Age 26
A 1988 first round pick who didn't develop, Walker was last seen hanging on in Independent ball in 1995.

WALKER, LARRY - OF - BL - Age 29
Walker is one of the most complete players in the game today, but he goes about his business quietly and without self-promotion. He gives his full effort to every play, every day. His attractiveness to the Rockies was enhanced by the fact that he is a left-handed power hitter. Watch for more balls flying off Walker's potent bat into the right field porch in Coors Field in 1996.

	AB	R	HR	RBI	SB	BA	$
1994 Montreal NL	395	76	19	86	15	.322	32
1995 Colorado NL	494	96	36	101	16	.306	33
1996 Projection >>>	528	101	33	109	19	.301	32

WALKER, SHON - OF - BL - Age 21
Walker set the single-season high school home run record in Kentucky in 1993 then was a supplemental first-round draft pick of the Pirates that June. He has not shown much power in pro ball and the Pirates feel he is at least four years away from the majors. Walker did steal bases last season, though, which was surprising.

WALKER, TODD - 2B - BL - Age 22
Walker is the Twins' best prospect, a potential .300 hitter and a decent defensive second sacker who also has the makeup of a future star. He hits with enough power (21 homers in '95) to play third base, and he might have to if Minnesota can sign Chuck Knoblauch.

WALLACH, TIM - 3B/1B - BR - Age 38
Wallach returned to earth after his stunning comeback season in 1994 and was contemplating retirement at the end of the season. He can still play a little, he lacks the versatility one would like in a bench player and the odds of him staying healthy for a full season are slim.

	AB	R	HR	RBI	SB	BA	$
1994 Los Angeles NL	414	68	23	78	0	.280	19
1995 Los Angeles NL	327	24	9	38	0	.266	6
1996 Projection >>>	257	27	7	36	0	.244	1

WALTERS, DAN - C - BR - Age 29
Walters' career continues to go in reverse; in two years he has fallen from a prospective major league starter to a Triple-A reserve. He'll move on to another site for 1996 with only a remote shot as a backup catcher in the majors.

WALTON, JEROME - OF - BR - Age 30
Walton turned in his second straight fine year as a pinch-hitter/reserve outfielder. Not known for his power, he slugged .525 and chipped in 10 steals. Davey Johnson is a genius at picking the spots for his reserve players, so it is questionable if Walton can be as effective playing for Ray Knight.

	AB	R	HR	RBI	SB	BA	$
1994 Cincinnati NL	68	10	1	9	1	.309	1
1995 Cincinnati NL	162	32	8	22	10	.290	9
1996 Projection >>>	138	26	5	19	7	.277	4

WARD, TURNER - OF - BB - Age 30
The quintessential fourth outfielder. Always starts out fast and fades before May is over.

	AB	R	HR	RBI	SB	BA	$
1994 Milwaukee AL	367	55	9	45	6	.232	8
1995 Milwaukee AL	129	19	4	16	6	.264	4
1996 Projection >>>	139	20	4	18	4	.240	1

WARNER, MIKE - OF - BL - Age 24
Warner jumped all the way to Triple-A Richmond, but hit just .206. He had been a consistent .300 hitter at lower levels, also showing an excellent batting eye. Warner still has the good batting eye and decent speed, too; he'll get another chance to show both at Richmond in 1996.

WASZGIS, BJ - C - BR - Age 25
Waszgis is a catcher in the Orioles' system who has shown a good bat with some power in the minors.

WATKINS, PAT - OF - BR - Age 23
After a 27 home run/31 steal season at hitter haven Winston Salem, Watkins' power and speed totals dropped considerably in his first season at AA Chattanooga. A first round supplemental pick in 1993, Watkins is considered to be an excellent defensive outfielder and is being groomed as a leadoff hitter.

WAWRUCK, JIM - OF - BL - Age 25
The Orioles' Jim Wawruck is a smooth hitting outfielder with a little power, and he steals bases. He has shown that he can hit Triple-A pitching, and will compete for a job with the Orioles in 1996, but the competition is tough.

WEBSTER, LENNY - C - BR - Age 31
Webster swings a lusty bat for a backup catcher, but is among the worst throwing catchers in baseball, as he threw out only seven of 55 (12.7%) basestealers in 1995. He can hit a mistake fastball a long way, but his lack of defensive skills were exposed in Darren Daulton's absence in 1995 - look for Mike Lieberthal to seize his job in 1996, with Webster likely latching on as a backup elsewhere.

	AB	R	HR	RBI	SB	BA	$
1994 Montreal NL	143	13	5	23	0	.273	3
1995 Philadelphia NL	150	18	4	14	0	.267	2
1996 *Projection* >>>	172	19	5	20	0	.265	1

WEBSTER, MITCH - OF - BB - Age 36
It should be the end of the line for the veteran reserve, whose best year was in 1987 playing for Montreal.

	AB	R	HR	RBI	SB	BA	$
1994 Los Angeles NL	84	16	4	12	1	.274	2
1995 Los Angeles NL	56	6	1	3	0	.179	-

WEDGE, ERIC - 1B/C - BR - Age 28
Wedge is a former catcher who has found a power stroke the last couple of seasons, when he has seen his most extensive action. The one-dimensional player was a minor league free agent.

WEGER, WES - 2B/SS - BR - Age 25
A top prospect as El Paso's shortstop in 1993, Weger is Triple-A New Orleans' second baseman.

WEHNER, JOHN - 3B - BR - Age 28
Wehner, who has spent parts of the last five seasons with the Pirates, had his best major-league year in 1995. The .308 batting average was an aberration but Wehner is a valuable bench player as he can play every position on the field.

	AB	R	HR	RBI	SB	BA	$
1994 Pittsburgh NL	4	1	0	3	0	.250	-
1995 Pittsburgh NL	107	13	0	5	3	.308	-
1996 *Projection* >>>	180	21	1	18	5	.262	1

WEINKE, CHRIS - 1B - BL - Age 23
Weinke got his promotion to Triple-A last year and failed to show that he is ready for the major leagues. He strikes out too often for someone who probably will never hit 20 home runs and he's got too many prospects ahead of him right now.

WEISS, WALT - SS - BB - Age 32
Weiss is the heart and soul of the Rockies' defense, and is in large part responsible for the Rockies going from the worst defensive team in the league in 1993 to one of the best in 1995. His batting stats look lukewarm, but he was in the league's top ten in OBP in 1995. Weiss became an unrestricted free agent after the 1995 season, but has moved to the Denver area and wanted to remain with the Rockies.

	AB	R	HR	RBI	SB	BA	$
1994 Colorado NL	423	58	1	32	12	.251	9
1995 Colorado NL	427	65	1	25	15	.260	8
1996 *Projection* >>>	516	73	1	34	14	.259	8

WHITAKER, LOU - 2B - BL - Age 38
Trivia question: who finished their career with more career hits, Whitaker or Alan Trammell? It's Sweet Lou with 2370, to Trammell's 2320. Whitaker was an above average player even in '95, his last season, and he should be elected to the Hall of Fame without much difficulty. The following projection is strictly "if he played."

	AB	R	HR	RBI	SB	BA	$
1994 Detroit AL	322	67	12	43	2	.301	14
1995 Detroit AL	249	36	14	44	4	.293	11
1996 Projection >>>	240	38	8	35	3	.265	5

WHITE, BILLY - 2B - BR - Age 27
White, a former star shortstop at Villanova, came up in the Cubs organization with Gary Scott. While Scott was failing in the big leagues, White has spent the last four years, the last two in the Colorado organization, as a so-so Double-A player.

WHITE, DERRICK - 1B - BR - Age 26
White had a decent year as Detroit's Triple-A first baseman in '95. He doesn't have the potential to advance beyond being a good minor leaguer, however.

	AB	R	HR	RBI	SB	BA	$
1995 Detroit AL	48	3	0	2	1	.188	-

WHITE, DEVON - OF - BB - Age 33
White was having a decent year when he fouled a ball off his foot, breaking a bone and ending his season at the end of August. He had virtually the same numbers as in the strike-shortened 1994 season. The speed has not returned to where it was a few years ago. Entering the winter, White was a free agent who was not certain of returning to Toronto. His glove ensures he will remain a regular, even if his stolen bases do not return.

	AB	R	HR	RBI	SB	BA	$
1994 Toronto AL	403	67	13	49	11	.270	18
1995 Toronto AL	427	61	10	53	11	.283	15
1996 Projection >>>	517	81	14	62	15	.278	18

WHITE, JASON - 1B - BR - Age 26
Tore up Class A pitching for Modesto, slipped a bit at Double-A but still hit eight homers in 167 at-bats. He's at least two years away, but worth watching.

WHITE, JIMMY - OF - BL - Age 23
White is young enough to have a chance, but there are several outfield prospects ahead of him in the organization. He slipped in 1995, playing on three Class-A teams and one Double-A squad. All of his numbers were down, including stolen bases. He needs a big 1996 in order to move up.

WHITE, RONDELL - OF - BR - Age 24
White had a fine 1995 in his first full major-league season and is clearly a star of the future in Montreal. He is a lot like former Expo center fielder Marquis Grissom in the fact that the type of player he will become depends on where manager Felipe Alou places him in the batting order. If he stays in the leadoff spot, he'll be a high-average hitter with a good number of steals. If he hits lower, he'll be an RBI guy with pretty good home run power. Either way, he's going to be a good one. Bet on him being a power guy.

	AB	R	HR	RBI	SB	BA	$
1994 Montreal NL	97	16	2	13	1	.278	2
1995 Montreal NL	474	87	13	57	25	.295	24
1996 Projection >>>	529	95	14	65	24	.292	24

WHITEN, MARK - OF - BB - Age 29
Whiten was a disaster in Boston, but was a lifesaver in Philadelphia late in 1995 as the team's only power threat. Whiten is not a tremendously savvy ballplayer - he will swing at pitches early in the count when his team is behind in the late innings, and is infatuated with his strong throwing arm, more errors than assists. However, if you throw him a mistake, he will hit it nine miles. He will always experience greater success in the fastball-laden National League, but will never develop into the All Star slugger he is purported to be.

	AB	R	HR	RBI	SB	BA	$
1994 St. Louis NL	334	57	14	53	10	.293	19
1995 Two Teams	320	51	12	47	8	.241	9
1996 *Projection* >>>	477	76	19	74	13	.263	17

WHITMORE, DARRELL - OF - BL - Age 27
It took a while, but the mainstream baseball media has finally gotten the message that Whitmore is not a top prospect. Whitmore enjoyed banner seasons at Triple-A in the offense-laden Pacific Coast League in 1993 and 1994, but got himself out on a regular basis in the majors by swinging at bad pitches. Despite his excellent athletic background (starting defensive back at West Virginia), Whitmore has never exhibited speed either on the bases or in the field. He missed the bulk of 1995 with inflammation in his throwing shoulder, and appears to have reached the end of the major league line.

	AB	R	HR	RBI	SB	BA	$
1994 Florida NL	22	1	0	0	0	.227	-
1995 Florida NL	58	6	1	2	0	.190	-

WIDGER, CHRIS - C - BR - Age 24
Talented enough to play in the Arizona Fall League in 1994. Still needs work and could end up in the minors most of the year. Definitely a solid prospect.

	AB	R	HR	RBI	SB	BA	$
1994 Jacksonville AA	388	58	16	59	8	.260	
1995 Tacoma AAA	174	29	9	21	0	.276	
1995 Seattle AL	45	2	1	2	0	.200	-

WILKERSON, CURTIS - IF - BB - Age 34
After logging more than a decade in the major leagues as a realiable utility infielder, the clock appeared to run out on Curtis Wilkerson last season after 18 at-bats at Triple-A Tacoma. He might find work in 1996 but time and injuries have eroded his skills.

WILKINS, RICK - C - BL - Age 28
Wilkins had a sensational year in 1993 with 30 home runs and a batting average of .303. Hampered by an injury which has now been corrected by surgery, he hasn't come close to this level of production in the last two years. Wilkins was acquired by the Astros from the Cubs in a mid-season trade in 1995. He faces a critical year in 1996 if he is to have the type of career that was anticipated two years ago.

	AB	R	HR	RBI	SB	BA	$
1994 Chicago NL	313	44	7	39	4	.227	5
1995 Houston NL	202	30	7	19	0	.203	0
1996 *Projection* >>>	367	55	13	44	2	.239	5

WILLARD, JERRY - C - BL - Age 36
Willard has spent parts of eight seasons in the majors as a third string catcher, but moved over to first base for Triple-A Tacoma in 1995, where he hit .268 with nine homers and 47 RBI in a part-time role. Willard is near the end of his long career, but could return to the big leagues for one last hurrah as a lefty pinch-hitter.

WILLIAMS, BERNIE - OF - BB - Age 27
Hitting .370 in his final 165 at bats of 1995, Williams put an exclamation mark on his breakthrough season. And now with a manager who likes the stolen base, Williams can actually get better in 1996. More power and more speed wouldn't be a big surprise.

	AB	R	HR	RBI	SB	BA	$
1994 New York AL	408	80	12	57	16	.289	23
1995 New York AL	563	93	18	82	8	.307	23
1996 *Projection* >>>	590	100	17	83	13	.297	24

WILLIAMS, CARY - OF - BR - Age 28
After five years on the Phillies farm, Williams has a little power, a little speed and a powerful arm. He has never hit for average.

WILLIAMS, EDDIE - 1B/C - BR - Age 31
Aches and pains, especially a year-long hamstring strain, hampered Eddie Williams last year, holding him to only 270 at-bats. Furthermore, his .270 is deceptive as he hit only .234 in the second half as the pitchers caught up with him.

	AB	R	HR	RBI	SB	BA	$
1994 San Diego NL	175	32	11	42	0	.331	11
1995 San Diego NL	296	35	12	47	0	.260	7
1996 Projection >>>	223	30	11	40	0	.262	5

WILLIAMS, GEORGE - C - BB - Age 26
All the signs are there for a breakout season. Williams has hit well at all three minor-league levels, making the Pacific Coast League All-Star team at catcher in 1995, he hit well in his short stay with Oakland, and he's 26 years old. Switch-hitting catchers who can hit for average and power, with walks, are rare. His defense gets a bad rap, and a shoulder injury in 1994 may limit his playing time behind the plate, but if he gets at-bats, George Williams will hit.

	AB	R	HR	RBI	SB	BA	$
1995 Edmonton AAA	290	53	13	55	0	.310	
1995 Oakland AL	79	13	3	14	0	.291	1
1996 Projection >>>	200	34	6	34	0	.270	3

WILLIAMS, GERALD - OF - BR - Age 29
On a team that didn't have such a love for big-name free agents, Gerald Williams could have been an everyday outfielder contributing 20 homers and 20 steals per year in addition to his sterling defense. On the Yankees he has been a mere spot-starter, pinch hitter/runner and late-inning defenseman with a great arm. In that role he can remain useful for years.

	AB	R	HR	RBI	SB	BA	$
1994 New York AL	86	19	4	13	1	.291	3
1995 New York AL	182	33	6	28	4	.247	4
1996 Projection >>>	196	37	7	30	4	.253	4

WILLIAMS, JUAN - OF - BL - Age 23
A .313 average at Double-A Greenville earned Williams a mid-year promotion. He's for real.

WILLIAMS, KEITH - OF - BR - Age 23
Coming on strong, Williams hit .300 at both Double-A and Triple-A in 1995. Has shown power at every level, and should make the majors by 1997. He's not a superstar, and his defense is suspect.

WILLIAMS, MATT - 3B - BR - Age 30
Enormous power once again in 1995, and appeared to be completely recovered from his midseason injury. Will hit many more homeruns in his career, but his .336 average should be considered a fluke.

	AB	R	HR	RBI	SB	BA	$
1994 San Francisco NL	445	74	43	96	1	.267	28
1995 San Francisco NL	283	53	23	65	2	.336	19
1996 Projection >>>	506	89	38	104	1	.284	23

WILLIAMS, REGGIE - OF - BB - Age 20
Williams is a good average, no power hitter who had shown good speed in the past, but stole only 6 bases in 1995 at Albuquerque. He is not likely to get a long chance with the Dodgers in 1996.

	AB	R	HR	RBI	SB	BA	$
1995 Los Angeles NL	11	2	0	1	0	.091	-

WILLIAMSON, ANTONE - 3B - BL - Age 22
The Brewers first round draft pick in 1994 is considered one of their best prospects. He led Double-A El Paso with 90 RBI while hitting .309. Williamson has developing power, but his hitting needs to be kept in perspective as El Paso is a notorious hitters' park. A much better test of his mettle as a prospect will be his 1996 season at Triple-A New Orleans.

WILSON, BRANDON - SS - BR - Age 27
Wilson has good speed, draws some walks, plays solid defense, and has a winning attitude, but won't move anywhere unless he hits. One good season away from the majors.

WILSON, CRAIG - SS - BR - Age 25
This Craig Wilson, not to be confused with the one who once played for St. Louis and Kansas City and was at Toledo last year, is now the top shortstop prospect in the White Sox organization -- supplanting the departed Brandon Wilson. Craig had the best of his three pro seasons at Double-A Birmingham. He has little power or speed, but can field and draw a walk.

WILSON, CRAIG - IF/OF - BR - Age 31
This veteran infielder's career is winding down, but he was able to assemble a respectable year for Triple-A Toledo in '95.

WILSON, DAN - C - BR - Age 27
Last year Wilson was 26...with experience. Bingo! He broke through rather nicely. While he should hit with more power as he matures, .278 is about as good as it will ever get given the demands of being a catcher.

	AB	R	HR	RBI	SB	BA	$
1994 Seattle AL	282	24	3	27	1	.216	0
1995 Seattle AL	399	40	9	51	2	.278	9
1996 Projection >>>	425	41	8	51	2	.258	5

WILSON, DESI - OF - BL - Age 27
Wilson is an OK hitter with more speed than the average firstbaseman, but he is already 27 years old and still stuck at Double-A. Limited prospect.

WILSON, ENRIQUE - SS - BB - Age 20
The Indians stole Wilson from the Twins following the 1993 season in a trade for minor league pitcher Shawn Bryant. Wilson puts the ball in play (his 38 whiffs in 1995 were a career high), runs the bases with reckless abandon and hits the ball with surprising extra-base authority for someone so small. He only needs to develop some patience at the plate to become a "can't miss" all-around shortstop prospect. He will start 1996 at Double-A - don't be surprised if he leapfrogs Damian Jackson and gets a clear shot at the Cleveland job in 1997.

WILSON, NIGEL - OF - BL - Age 26
Wilson was the first pick by the Marlins in the expansion draft, but never panned out due to horrendous strike zone judgement. A solid power hitter, Wilson turned in a good season at Indianapolis except for the one area he must improve - his strikeout to walk ratio was almost 7 to 1. In 23 major league at bats, Wilson is hitless with 15 strikeouts. Despite this weakness, Wilson may get a chance to compete for the left field job if Ron Gant signs elsewhere.

	AB	R	HR	RBI	SB	BA	$
1995 Indianapolis AAA	304	53	17	51	5	.313	

WILSON, POOKIE - OF - BL - Age 25
Like Mookie Wilson, the Pookster is a lefthanded batter with good speed, little power and absolutely no plate discipline. However, this Wilson is unlikely to ever reach the majors - his performance dropped off significantly upon his arrival at Double-A in 1995, especially in the speed categories. With a barrage of younger, better prospects coming up through the Marlins' chain, Wilson's pro future could be in jeopardy.

WILSON, PRESTON - 3B - BR - Age 21
Playing near home in Columbia, Mookie Wilson's stepson was one of four Bombers who struck out more than 100 times. He remains a power prospect, and has some speed.

WILSTEAD, RANDY - 1B - BL - Age 28
Wilstead doesn't have quite enough power to be a major-league first baseman.

WIMMER, CHRIS - 2B - BR - Age 25
A fomer Olympian with a fine glove, Wimmer can steal the occasional base and is the heir-apparent to Robby Thompson with the Giants. On the other hand, he hit only .263 with two homers in the offense-heavy Pacific Coast League, and has an even better prospect, Jay Canizaro, nipping at his heels. He's more likely to resemble Jose Lind than Ryne Sandberg.

WINFIELD, DAVE - DH - BR - Age 44
Of all of the Indians' free agent acquisitions prior to the 1995 season, the Winfield signing was the only failure. Expected to be the Indians' righthanded DH, injuries and a slow bat kept Winfield from having any impact. To make matters worse, he pouted when he was left off the postseason roster, and turned it into the only clubhouse-dividing issue of the season.

	AB	R	HR	RBI	SB	BA	$
1994 Minnesota AL	294	35	10	43	2	.252	8
1995 Cleveland AL	115	11	2	4	1	.191	-

WITKOWSKI, MAT - 2B - BR - Age 26
His 1993 season at AAA Las Vegas (.283-1-35-10 in a hitters' haven) typified this player -- unspectacular. He could challenge for the Padres' second base job, but he really doesn't offer anything more than Jeff Gardner.

WITT, KEVIN - 3B-SS - BL - Age 20
Witt was the final player chosen in the 1994 draft's first round, by the Blue Jays. He's a former tennis player who was a high school star in Jacksonville who hasn't led anyone to believe he still has a major league future.

WOLAK, JERRY - OF - BR - Age 25
Streak-hitter Wolak had five homers and ten RBI in three games for Triple-A Nashville in 1995, finishing the year at .229-14-63. Wolak can play any outfield position, but is a jack of all trades (and master of none). He frequently plays out of position and his good speed can't always save him.

WOLFE, JOEL - OF - BR - Age 25
An exciting baserunner with interesting potential if he plays firstbase (corner infielders with steals being a rarity), but Wolfe still needs to prove himself at Triple-A. He hasn't overwhelmed anyone in the lower minors, and he's old for a prospect. He's a longshot a best.

WOLFF, MIKE - OF - BR - Age 25
Angel outfielder Mike Wolff has spent the past two years in Double-A, hitting around .300, with a dozen home runs and stolen bases each year. He needs to step it up a notch to make substantial progress towards the majors.

WOMACK, TONY - SS - BL - Age 26
In 1993, this speedy middle infielder was the Pirates' minor-league player of the year. After spending all of 1994 in Triple-A, he wound up back in Double-A last season. Suffice it to say, his career is not exactly headed in the right direction.

WOOD, JASON - 3B - BR - Age 26
A weak bat and advancing age would seem to doom this infielder to a career in the minor leagues. Said to have a fine glove and better attitude, if that helps.

WOOD, TED - OF - BL - Age 28
Wood had some solid seasons in the Giants organization without winning a job in San Francisco. The last three seasons have been OK with the Expos' Triple-A farm at Ottawa. The minor league free agent can be insurance as an outfielder, first baseman and lefthanded batter.

WOODS, TYRONE - OF - BR - Age 26
Tyrone Woods is a first baseman and outfielder who hits well in Double-A, but can't get above .261 in Triple-A. His future is limited.

WOODSON, TRACY - 3B - BR - Age 33
In 1995, Woodson was a fan-favorite for Triple-A Louisville, leading the team with 18 homers and 76 RBI; he slugged .469 and also stole 12 bases. A member of the 1988 World Series champion Dodgers, Woodson has only briefly appeared in the majors over the last five years. Look for Woodson to finish his career in the minors, or perhaps jump to Japan.

WOOTEN, SHAWN - 3B - BR - Age 23
Wooten had a respectable year in his second full season of pro ball, but he needs to improve his batting eye.

WORTHINGTON, CRAIG - 3B - BR - Age 30
Worthington is a fine defensive third baseman who cannot consistently hit major league pitching. His continued presence in the major leagues depends upon a team's willingness to carry an extra glove man on the bench.

	AB	R	HR	RBI	SB	BA	$
1995 Indianapolis AAA	277	48	9	41	1	.318	
1995 Texas AL	86	5	3	8	0	.233	-
1996 *Projection* >>>	88	5	3	8	0	.233	-

WRIGHT, RON - 1B - BR - Age 20
Wright smashed 32 homers in his second pro season but stayed at the Braves Class-A Macon team all of 1995.

WRONA, RICK - C - BR - Age 32
Wrona was acquired to help Triple-A Louisville past some injuries, appearing in just sixteen games. He was released when other catchers returned to health. Wrona is a backup Triple-A catcher at best.

YAN, JULIAN - 1B - BR - Age 30
Yan looks older than his listed age and lighter than his listed weight, but he had the best of his 10 minor league seasons in his first year in the Montreal organization. He set the season home run record for its three-year-old Ottawa Triple-A farm.

YELDING, ERIC - IF/OF - BR - Age 31
Just five years ago Yelding stole 64 bases for the Astros. Since then he has lost his regular major league job, then lost his platoon role, then was demoted to the minors; finally, in 1995, he split the year between Double-A Canton-Akron and Triple-A Buffalo. Good speed is Yelding's only asset and it's just not enough.

YOUNG, DMITRI - 3B - BB - Age 22
One of the Cardinals' top prospects since his first round selection in the 1991 draft, Young hits for both average and power. Unfortunately, he has no position, having been tried also at first base. Young had trouble at Double-A Arkansas in 1995, drawing a 30-day suspension after fighting with fans at a game in Wichita.

YOUNG, ERIC - 2B - BR - Age 28
"EY" started the 1995 season as a spot player in the crowded Rockies outfield, and batted under .175. He returned to second base after a two-year absence when Roberto Mejia was sent to Triple A in June, and his batting average soared. Young will never win a Gold Glove as an infielder, but his speed and hustle.

	AB	R	HR	RBI	SB	BA	$
1994 Colorado NL	228	37	7	30	18	.272	16
1995 Colorado NL	366	68	6	36	35	.317	24
1996 *Projection* >>>	333	59	6	35	30	.290	18

YOUNG, ERNIE - OF - BR - Age 26
Young is an OK prospect, but he's too old to be a star. He used to steal bases, doesn't do that anymore. If he gets a full season at the major-league level in 1995, he could hit 20 homers, but is otherwise mediocre.

	AB	R	HR	RBI	SB	BA	$
1994 Oakland AL	30	2	0	3	0	.067	-
1995 Edmonton AAA	347	70	15	72	2	.277	
1995 Oakland AL	50	9	2	5	0	.200	-
1996 *Projection* >>>	147	22	5	28	0	.254	1

YOUNG, KEVIN - 1B - BR - Age 26
Voted by league managers as the best prospect in the Triple-A American Association in 1992, Young has never had consistent success in three years with the Pirates. The guy has some skills but never seems to put it all together. He looks like a man in desperate need of a change of scenery.

	AB	R	HR	RBI	SB	BA	$
1994 Pittsburgh NL	122	15	1	11	0	.205	-
1995 Calgary AAA	163	24	8	34	6	.356	
1995 Pittsburgh NL	181	13	6	22	1	.232	2
1996 *Projection* >>>	308	30	8	39	1	.248	3

ZAMBRANO, EDDIE - 1B/OF - BR - Age 30
A major leaguer as recently as 1994 when he hit six homers for the Cubs, Zambrano dropped all the way to Double-A Trenton in 1995. He hit just .145 and is now contemplating what to do for his second career.

ZAUN, GREGG - C - BB - Age 24
Zaun is a good defensive catcher but can't hit much. Although he did hit .293 in Triple-A last year, it was in only 140 at-bats, and it was his second year at the same level. Unless he matures and develops some power or an aggressive bat, his best chance of major league time is a backup role. He's a good "rah-rah" guy lifting team spirits, and that may help him stick.

	AB	R	HR	RBI	SB	BA	$
1995 Rochester AAA	140	26	6	18	0	.293	
1995 Baltimore AL	104	18	3	14	1	.260	1
1996 *Projection* >>>	155	27	4	20	2	.251	1

ZEILE, TODD - 3B - BR - Age 30
Despite wanting to come to Wrigley, Zeile had a bad half-season there. His .227-9-30 performance for the Cubs reflects the thumb injury he played with for much of the season. Zeile's hustle was appreciated by Cubs' brass and they want him back for 1996.

	AB	R	HR	RBI	SB	BA	$
1994 St. Louis NL	415	62	19	75	1	.267	16
1995 Chicago NL	426	50	14	52	1	.246	8
1996 *Projection* >>>	509	67	19	76	2	.256	11

ZINTER, ALAN - C/1B - BB - Age 27
Zinter, a former first-round draft choice by the Mets as a catcher, hasn't made it to the majors, but not for a lack of effort. He has been in double figures in home runs the last four years, but in triple figures in strikeouts the last five. He was a minor league free agent.

ZOSKY, EDDIE - SS - BR - Age 28
This Blue Jays' number one pick moved to the Marlins in 1996, and became firmly entrenched in his journeyman status. Though he is a solid defensive player, he couldn't beat out Mario Diaz for a major league spot, and he has evolved into an automatic out offensively. Zosky swings at everything, has little speed and poor baserunning judgement, and has little power. He has a chance to sneak into the last spot on the Marlins' roster in 1996, but that is his ceiling as a major leaguer. He will soon be overrun by the avalanche of Marlins' middle infield prospects that are on the way.

	AB	R	HR	RBI	SB	BA	$
1995 Florida NL	5	0	0	0	0	.200	-

ZUBER, JON - 1B/OF - BL - Age 26
Zuber enjoyed another line drive filled season at Triple-A Scranton-Wilkes Barre in 1995 and was named as the best defensive first baseman in the International League. However, Zuber does not possess the extra base power one looks for in a first sacker, and therefore projects as no better than a pinch hitter and defensive replacement at the major league level. Zuber could earn that role in Philadelphia sometime in 1996.

ZUPCIC, BOB - OF - BR - Age 29
Afforded numerous major league opportunities in Boston because of his 1987 second round draftee status, Zupcic has proven that he has marginal major league skills. He spent 1995 at Triple-A in the Marlins chain, and showed decent extra base power. His above average defensive ability at all three outfield positions is his only possible ticket back to the majors - he wasn't recalled despite a rash of injuries to Marlin big league regulars. He is likely now entrenched as Triple-A roster filler for the foreseeable future.

ABBOTT, JIM - TL - Age 28
The Angels were in a pennant chase and acquired Jim Abbott to put them over the top. He pitched effectively for them, but he alone couldn't pull them out of their team slump. Abbott is talented, tough, and just needs to throw his curve for strikes to be a big winner. Scouts say Abbott has lost a mile or two per hour off his fastball, but the main issue is the curve being precise enough. Given a tiny shift in precision, he could go a long way around the success/confidence cycle. Winning 15 or even 20 games would be possible in the right situation.

	W	SV	ERA	IP	H	BB	SO	B/I	$
1994 New York AL	9	0	4.55	160	167	64	90	1.44	7
1995 Two Teams	11	0	3.70	197	209	64	86	1.39	12
1996 Projection >>>	12	0	4.02	222	232	76	105	1.39	12

ABBOTT, KYLE - TL - Age 28
Abbott will likely be remembered mainly for his hard-luck 1-14 campaign for the Phils in 1992 and as the man who first turned then Japanese League teammate Hideo Nomo onto the idea of giving American baseball a shot. Abbott returned to the Phils in 1995 and was a serviceable lefthanded reliever in the season's first half before undergoing season-ending shoulder surgery. Abbott has no job security with the Phils. He's squarely on the major league fringe.

	W	SV	ERA	IP	H	BB	SO	B/I	$
1995 Philadelphia NL	2	0	3.81	28	28	16	21	1.57	0
1996 Projection >>>	1	0	3.82	19	19	11	14	1.55	-

ABBOTT, PAUL - TR - Age 28
Erstwhile major leaguer Abbott led Triple-A Iowa with 127 strikeouts while going 7-7 in 1995. His fastball is good enough for Triple-A, but that's the best he can do. Abbott has entered the journeyman phase of his career in the minors.

	W	SV	ERA	IP	H	BB	SO	B/I	$
1994 Omaha AAA	4	0	4.87	57	57	45	48	1.78	
1995 Iowa AAA	7	0	3.67	115	104	64	127	1.46	

ACEVEDO, JUAN - TR - Age 25
Named the 1994 Eastern League player of the year for his 17 wins at New Haven, his fastball is in the low 90s. He also has a splitter, curveball and changeup. Acevedo got cheated out of a September callup by the '94 strike, but then found himself in the majors on opening day '95 because the longest winter in history had taken a physical toll on some veteran major leaguers. He was predictably hammered while with the Rockies. The move to the Mets will mean less opportunity initially but a much better chance for success when he reaches the majors again, which he will.

	W	SV	ERA	IP	H	BB	SO	B/I	$
1995 Colorado NL	4	0	6.44	65	82	20	40	1.56	-
1996 Projection >>>	3	0	4.94	50	64	11	30	1.49	-

ACRE, MARK - TR - Age 27
The heir apparent to Eck the past few years, Acre took a step backward in 1995, posting an ERA more than a run higher than any in his professional career at any level. However, there were bright spots, as Acre increased his K/IP ratio while reducing his BB/IP ratio. He has lost the confidence of his pitching coach, but with a good spring Acre could impress any new bosses who might come his way. He still has potential to be a closer.

	W	SV	ERA	IP	H	BB	SO	B/I	$
1994 Tacoma AAA	1	6	1.88	28	24	11	31	1.20	
1994 Oakland AL	5	0	3.41	34	24	23	21	1.37	3
1995 Oakland AL	1	0	5.71	52	52	28	47	1.54	-
1996 Projection >>>	3	1	5.04	50	45	29	41	1.49	0

ADAMS, TERRY - TR - Age 23
Not many have heard of Adams, who streaked all the way from Double-A Orlando through Triple-A Iowa to the Cubs, collecting 25 saves along the way. He has become more of a strikeout pitcher since he began working exclusively in relief, and he has pretty good stuff. Adams is considered a future closer who will pitch as a the Cubs main setup man in 1996.

	W	SV	ERA	IP	H	BB	SO	B/I	$
1995 Iowa AAA	0	5	0	6	3	2	10	0.79	
1995 Chicago NL	1	1	6.50	18	22	10	15	1.78	-
1996 Projection >>>	3	4	4.43	62	64	28	52	1.48	1

ADAMS, WILLIE - TR - Age 23
A former first round draft pick, Adams pitched extremely well at Double-A and didn't embarrass himself in the offense heaven of the Pacific Coast League. He's still a year away, but an interesting prospect.

	W	SV	ERA	IP	H	BB	SO	B/I	$
1995 Edmonton AAA	2	0	4.37	68	73	15	40	1.30	

ADAMSON, JOEL - TL - Age 24
Adamson is a crafty lefty whom the Marlins obtained from the Phillies in the Danny Jackson trade on the day of the expansion draft. Adamson does not throw hard, but is extremely precise, as he has walked only 2.3 batters per nine innings over his entire pro career. His ticket to the majors is the fact that he throws lefthanded - he could earn a situational bullpen role, but nothing better.

	W	SV	ERA	IP	H	BB	SO	B/I	$
1995 Charlotte AAA	8	0	3.29	115	113	20	80	1.16	

ADKINS, STEVE - TL - Age 31
Once a highly regarded Yankees prospect, Adkins is trying to get another shot at the majors. He shared the closer's job at Triple-A last year, but his best chance of making the majors is as a lefthanded pitcher used in special situations. He blew some saves and lost seven games last year.

AGUILERA, RICK - TR - Age 34
Aguilera's oft-rumored trade finally went down in 1995; he joined the Red Sox in time to help them to a division crown in 1995. He doesn't throw quite as hard as he used to, but he still has great control of an above-average split-finger fastball. Aguilera remained healthy all year and remained near the top of American League closers; there's no reason to expect he won't be a top flight closer again in 1996.

	W	SV	ERA	IP	H	BB	SO	B/I	$
1994 Minnesota AL	1	23	3.63	44	57	10	46	1.50	29
1995 Minnesota - Boston AL	3	32	2.60	55	46	13	52	1.08	37
1996 Projection >>>	3	33	3.06	63	61	14	60	1.19	40

AHEARNE, PAT - TR - Age 26
Despite advancing steadily up the Tigers' minor league ladder as a starter, Ahearne does not figure to have much of a big league career. Look for a series of brief call-ups instead.

	W	SV	ERA	IP	H	BB	SO	B/I	$
1995 Toledo AAA	7	0	4.70	139	165	37	54	1.45	
1995 Detroit AL	0	0	11.70	10	20	5	4	2.50	-

AHERN, BRIAN - TR - Age 27
Gradual minor league progress stunted at Double-A. May be better in relief role; he doesn't quite have starter stamina, or enough pitches to go through the order a second and third time.

AKERFELDS, DARREL - TR - Age 33
Akerfelds has had minimal major league experience, with 1990 being his best year when he appeared in 71 games with the Phillies going 5-2 with three saves, and a 3.77 ERA in 93 innings. Since then he has drifted through several teams, trying to make a comeback.

ALBERRO, JOSE - TR - Age 26
Alberro had an opportunity to shine in a wide-open major league bullpen and failed to impress. Alberro throws hard, but doesn't have good enough location to get big league hitters out. His live arm will probably give him another chance to stick.

	W	SV	ERA	IP	H	BB	SO	B/I	$
1995 Oklahoma City AAA	4	0	3.35	77	73	27	55	1.29	
1995 Texas AL	0	0	7.40	20	26	12	10	1.84	-

ALDRED, SCOTT - TL - Age 27
Aldred, a lefthander, came up through the Tiger system until the Rockies selected him in the expansion draft. Back where he started last year, he succeeded as a reliever at Class A and Double-A. Aldred could eventually resurface in the majors as a situational reliever.

ALEXANDER, GERALD - TR - Age 28
Acquired from Texas, Alexander was released by the Orioles in spring training. He was a starter and reliever for the Rangers in 1991 posting a 5.24 ERA in 89 innings. He spent four years in Triple-A.

ALFONSECA, ANTONIO - TR - Age 23
The Marlins skipped Alfonseca a level to Double-A in 1995, with positive results. After pitching out of the bullpen in low A-ball in 1994, he was very difficult to hit as a starter in 1995, though his control was spotty and he was susceptible to the big inning. The hard thrower does not have particularly good stamina, and will likely have to contend for a major league middle relief role down the road. He will be ticketed for Triple-A in 1996.

ALLEN, RONNIE - TR - Age 25
Allen is another Phils' high round pick (number 3 in 1991) who is going nowhere. After he dominated Single-A hitters (who were three years younger than he was) in his first two pro seasons, his statistics have come to this: almost as many walks as whiffs; and an ERA crowding seven.

ALMANZAR, CARLOS - TR - Age 22
Almanzar is a control pitcher who bears watching because he jumped from Rookie ball to Double-A and had some success after moving to the bullpen. He may not have a good enough strikeout pitch to make it.

ALSTON, GARVIN - TR - Age 24
Alston showed marked improvement the second time around in both the California and Eastern leagues. He was a sometime closer last season, and a definite strikeout pitcher. With any Triple-A success this year, he could be with the Rockies in '97.

ALVAREZ, TAVO - TR - Age 24
Alvarez has always been touted as a pitcher of great promise but got hit hard in his first taste of the major leagues with the Expos in 1995. He's overweight and has been dogged by injuries throughout his career. That's not exactly the recipe for future stardom.

	W	SV	ERA	IP	H	BB	SO	B/I	$
1994			Did Not Play						
1995 Montreal NL	1	0	6.75	37	46	14	17	1.62	-
1996 *Projection* >>>	4	0	4.24	98	111	31	49	1.45	-

ALVAREZ, WILSON - TL - Age 26
Alvarez reported to 1995 spring training out of shape and his pitching suffered for it early in the season. He turned his season around once he got back into shape and finished strong. Alvarez throws hard and has great stuff, so he should be a winner if he can stay fit.

	W	SV	ERA	IP	H	BB	SO	B/I	$
1994 Chicago AL	12	0	3.45	161	147	62	108	1.29	18
1995 Chicago AL	8	0	4.32	175	171	93	118	1.51	4
1996 *Projection* >>>	12	0	3.89	207	194	100	140	1.42	11

ANDERSEN, LARRY - TR - Age 42
Numerous injuries over the last two years reduced Andersen's effectiveness and he finally retired after five outings at Double-A Reading. He'll be missed by the sportswriters, especially as he could always be counted on for a clever quip.

ANDERSON, BRIAN - TL - Age 23
Anderson had a rough year last season, and he was removed from the rotation during the Angels stretch run for the division title. For a lefty, it's unusual that left handed hitters hit him very well, over .300 every year. He is still learning how to pitch in the majors, and he relies on control to be effective with his five below-average pitches. Anderson could quickly turn things around to be a very effective pitcher, but it frequently takes control pitchers several years to develop.

	W	SV	ERA	IP	H	BB	SO	B/I	$
1994 California AL	7	0	5.22	101	120	27	47	1.45	3
1995 California AL	6	0	5.87	99	110	30	45	1.40	0
1996 *Projection* >>>	7	0	4.96	145	164	40	71	1.41	2

ANDERSON, JIMMY - TL - Age 20
The Pirates drafted this left-hander in the ninth round in 1994 from a Virginia high school and he's on the fast track, finishing up last season with Pittsburgh's Class A Lynchburg farm club. His stuff is pretty good, highlighted by a 90-MPH fastball and a sharp slider. However, his poise and pitching aptitude are what stand out. He could get to the major leagues very quickly.

ANDERSON, MIKE - TR - Age 29
Anderson was Triple-A Iowa's most consistent starter in 1995, going 7-9 and holding opponents to a respectable batting average. It was an encouraging year, but Anderson looks like one of those pitchers who simply can't make that last jump to the major leagues.

	W	SV	ERA	IP	H	BB	SO	B/I	$
1995 Iowa AAA	7	0	3.46	171	156	69	123	1.31	

ANDERSON, PAUL - TR - Age 27
Anderson is a middle relief power pitcher who was a legitimate Cardinals' prospect until 1994 when he struggled at Double-A Arkansas. He returned to Arkansas in 1995 and showed some improvement, but, at his age, he's going to have to be really impressive to regain prospect status.

ANDERSON, SCOTT - TR - Age 33
Originally slated to be the replacement Royals' Opening Day starter, Anderson instead became a midseason callup. He didn't pitch badly, but he didn't blow anyone away, either. He is no prospect; however, his strong work ethic makes him a good role model for an organization focusing on youth. Last seen in the majors with Montreal in 1990.

	W	SV	ERA	IP	H	BB	SO	B/I	$
1995 Omaha AAA	5	0	4.17	73	63	16	47	1.08	
1995 Kansas City AL	1	0	5.33	25	29	8	6	1.46	-

ANDUJAR, LUIS - TR - Age 23
Andujar overcame 1994 arm trouble to become the Southern League's Pitcher of the Year in '95. He won his last 12 decisions, including a no-hitter, then pitched effectively for the White Sox in September. He'll need to show better control of his offspeed pitches to stay in the White Sox rotation this season.

	W	SV	ERA	IP	H	BB	SO	B/I	$
1995 Chicago AL	2	0	3.26	30	26	14	9	1.33	1
1996 *Projection* >>>	4	0	4.44	55	49	27	40	1.39	1

APPIER, KEVIN - TR - Age 28
The ace of the Royals staff, Appier set the league on fire for the first half. Tendinitis and a tired arm due to a four-man rotation dulled his great fastball and hard slider and he finished the year in a slump. It was the second straight year he has experienced arm problems. While Appier remains one of the league's best pitchers, his continuing health problems are a cause for caution.

	W	SV	ERA	IP	H	BB	SO	B/I	$
1994 Kansas City AL	7	0	3.83	155	137	63	145	1.29	13
1995 Kansas City AL	15	0	3.89	201	163	80	185	1.21	19
1996 *Projection* >>>	13	0	3.90	225	201	96	204	1.32	16

AQUINO, LUIS - TR - Age 30
Competent when healthy, but often hurt, Aquino hit the DL almost immediately after coming to the Giants.

	W	SV	ERA	IP	H	BB	SO	B/I	$
1994 Florida NL	2	0	3.73	50	39	22	22	1.20	3
1995 Two Teams	0	2	5.10	42	57	13	26	1.66	-
1996 *Projection* >>>	1	1	4.71	31	35	12	17	1.52	-

ARCHER, KURT - TR - Age 27
Pitching well in middle/long relief in 1994 with AA El Paso. He got five wins, nine saves and 58 strikeouts in 77 innings. Still working out of the pen in '95, after a promotion to Triple-A, he produced this respectable line:

	W	SV	ERA	IP	H	BB	SO	B/I	$
1995 New Orleans AAA	2	2	3.25	61	57	17	41	1.22	

ARMSTRONG, JACK - TR - Age 31
Armstrong hasn't been healthy for two years and hasn't been a good pitcher since his lone All-Star appearance in 1990. He used to throw hard, but was somewhat wild. It's hard to believe Armstrong would still be effective after such a long period of relative inactivity.

	W	SV	ERA	IP	H	BB	SO	B/I	$
1996 Projection >>>	2	0	5.48	45	49	17	23	1.46	-

ARNOLD, JAMIE - TR - Age 22
Arnold's progress slowed last year. He was promoted during last season from A ball to Double-A, but had a losing record at each level. He averaged barely a strikeout every three innings in the Southern League, and has fallen behind a number of other Braves prospects.

AROCHA, RENE - TR - Age 30
After doing a decent job as the Cardinals' closer in 1994, Arocha was bumped to a set-up role last season as Tom Henke became the bullpen ace. Though he has an assortment of about eight pitches which would seemingly make him a better starter, he likes closing. If Henke retires, Arocha will get first crack at the job and should excel. His only drawback is that he was injured a lot last season.

	W	SV	ERA	IP	H	BB	SO	B/I	$
1994 St. Louis NL	4	11	4.01	83	94	21	62	1.39	15
1995 St. Louis NL	3	0	3.99	49	55	18	25	1.48	0
1996 Projection >>>	2	1	4.14	55	61	16	33	1.40	0

ARRANDALE, MATT - TR - Age 25
In his third pro season, Arrandale advanced to Double-A for the first time in 1995. Pitching in Arkansas proved to be a big adjustment for the crafty curveball specialist. He was used primarily in long relief and showed good control. Arrandale is not a top prospect.

ARTEAGA, IVAN - TR - Age 24
Arteaga's 1995 season ended after 34 innings because of a frayed labrum in his shoulder. He underwent arthroscopic surgery during the off-season. He should start this season no higher than Double-A New Haven.

ASHBY, ANDY - TR - Age 28
Ashby has posted some impressive statistics for two years in a row, but his won-lost record is only so-so as he is a victim of some tough breaks. With some better luck, Ashby could come through with a very good year like 15-6 with an ERA below 3.00.

	W	SV	ERA	IP	H	BB	SO	B/I	$
1994 San Diego NL	6	0	3.40	164	145	43	121	1.14	15
1995 San Diego NL	12	0	2.94	192	180	62	150	1.26	15
1996 Projection >>>	12	0	2.92	211	199	65	160	1.25	19

ASHWORTH, KYM - TL - Age 19
In the Dodgers' talented Kiddie Corps, Ashworth was the youngest pitcher to reach the Texas League. The Australian shows pitching savvy with a curve and changeup, and his fastball is expected to improve as he gains maturity and strength.

ASSENMACHER, PAUL - TL - Age 35
In what has to be an alltime record, Assenmacher had more appearances than innings pitched for the fourth season in a row in 1995. Assenmacher uses a sweeping overhand curveball to frustrate lefthanded hitters (.163 in 1995) and was the top lefty in the Indians' setup committee. He is the consummate role player - he can continue to lose velocity gradually and still remain somewhat effective for a few more years. However, he is no threat to close games at this stage in his career.

	W	SV	ERA	IP	H	BB	SO	B/I	$
1994 Chicago AL	1	1	3.55	33	26	13	29	1.18	3
1995 Cleveland AL	6	0	2.82	38	32	12	40	1.15	5
1996 Projection >>>	5	1	3.11	45	38	16	44	1.18	6

ASTACIO, PEDRO - TR - Age 26
Astacio was dropped from the rotation in mid-season and pitched mostly in middle relief. His ERA, baserunners per game, strikeout, and walk rates were all similar to last season. His only weakness was gopher balls, allowing 12 in 104 innings. Astacio could easily regain his spot in the rotation - at the end of the season Kevin Tapani was the most notable competition for the fifth spot in the rotation.

	W	SV	ERA	IP	H	BB	SO	B / I	$
1994 Los Angeles NL	6	0	4.29	149	142	47	108	1.27	7
1995 Los Angeles NL	7	0	4.24	104	103	29	80	1.27	4
1996 *Projection* >>>	10	0	3.86	165	159	49	122	1.26	9

ATKINSON, NEIL - TL - Age 25
Workhorse Atkinson struggled in his first Double-A season at Wichita, and was eventually demoted during the Wranglers playoff drive. He pitched better in limited action for Class-A Wilmington. Atkinson had been a strikeout pitcher at lower levels but had less success in Double-A in 1995.

AUCOIN, DEREK - TR - Age 26
Aucoin is a big guy (6-7, 226 lbs.) whom the Expos desperately would like to have succeed because he is from Montreal. He was a hard-throwing middle reliever in Double-A, then helped Ottawa win the International League playoffs and pitched very well in the Arizona Fall League.

AUGUST, DON - TR - Age 32
August found success in the Mexican League, but no longer seems able to cut it north of the border.

AUSANIO, JOE - TR - Age 30
An eight-year pro, Ausanio had the stuff to be a minor league closer but is just another arm in the majors. Improved control could help him advance to the level of setup man, but he also has downward possibilities going into 1996.

	W	SV	ERA	IP	H	BB	SO	B / I	$
1994 New York AL	2	0	5.17	15	16	6	15	1.40	0
1995 New York AL	2	1	5.73	37	42	23	36	1.73	-
1996 *Projection* >>>	1	0	5.01	32	35	17	27	1.62	-

AUSTIN, JAMES - TR - Age 32
Strong righty with effective slider, but too many walks to be a star.

AVERY, STEVE - TL - Age 25
A second straight disappointing season has gotten some Braves fans down on Avery. But, Braves management is still convinced he has star potential. He was extremely inconsistent in 1995, never knowing from one start to the next what kind of stuff he was going to have. As is often the case with young lefties, once Avery fine tunes his good fastball and slider, he's going to become one of the league's best pitchers.

	W	SV	ERA	IP	H	BB	SO	B / I	$
1994 Atlanta NL	8	0	4.04	151	127	55	122	1.20	11
1995 Atlanta NL	7	0	4.67	173	165	52	141	1.25	4
1996 *Projection* >>>	11	0	4.14	203	186	61	159	1.22	10

AYALA, BOBBY - TR - Age 26
He blew it as closer and is now a longshot for the closer role. His arm is sound but his mechanics are shaky. Don't give up on him especially with Charlton's history of arm trouble.

	W	SV	ERA	IP	H	BB	SO	B / I	$
1994 Seattle AL	4	18	2.86	56	42	26	76	1.20	29
1995 Seattle AL	6	19	4.44	71	73	30	77	1.45	21
1996 *Projection* >>>	5	12	4.31	82	81	39	81	1.47	14

AYRAULT, BOB - TR - Age 29
Briefly looked good in a trial with the Phillies, but since 1990 he has generally struggled in repeated shots at the majors.

BACKLUND, BRETT - TR - Age 26
The right-hander had a chance to win a spot in the Pirates' starting rotation in the spring of 1993, one year after being

drafted from the University of Iowa. He has done little since, though, and his name is never mentioned by the Pirates anymore. If he ever gets to the big leagues, he'll be a Rick Reed-type pitcher.

	W	SV	ERA	IP	H	BB	SO	B/I	$
1995 Calgary AAA	2	0	5.22	50	59	9	29	1.36	

BADOREK, MIKE - TR - Age 26
Badorek began the season in awesome fashion, going 7-0 for Double-A Arkansas. Then a midseason elbow injury slowed him - his ERA climbed and he lost his last five decisions. Nevertheless, 1995 is considered a breakthrough season; he should advance to Triple-A Louisville in 1996.

BAILEY, CORY - TR - Age 25
Bailey was the 1995 American Association Rolaids Relief Man winner for Triple-A Louisville. He led the league with 25 saves despite giving up his ace relief role for the last six weeks of the season; it was his fourth straight season with at least nineteen saves, the last three in Triple-A. He has talent, but his command could be his downfall as illustrated by his walk total (30 walks in 59 innings). Bailey is a marginal prospect.

	W	SV	ERA	IP	H	BB	SO	B/I	$
1995 Louisville AAA	5	25	4.55	59	51	30	49	1.37	
1995 St. Louis NL	0	0	7.36	3	2	2	5	1.09	-
1996 *Projection* >>>	1	1	4.95	36	46	11	30	1.57	-

BAILEY, ROGER - TR - Age 25
Bailey made the jump from Double-A New Haven in 1994 to the majors in 1995 due in part to a Rockies pitching staff that was decimated by injuries. He's not overpowering, and is dependent upon pitch placement for his success. Bailey needs to improve his strikeout ratio to contend for a starter's role in 1996.

	W	SV	ERA	IP	H	BB	SO	B/I	$
1995 Colorado NL	7	0	4.98	81	88	39	33	1.57	-
1996 *Projection* >>>	4	0	4.94	84	90	39	50	1.53	-

BAKER, DEREK - TR - Age 23
The Mets reliever at Class-A Pittsfield posted a 1.59 ERA on the way to a one win/11 save season in 1994.

BAKER, SCOTT - TL - Age 25
An impressive starter at the Double-A level, Baker dropped off at Triple-A in 1995. He lacks a knockout pitch and is unlikely to succeed at the major-league level.

	W	SV	ERA	IP	H	BB	SO	B/I	$
1995 Edmonton AAA	4	0	5.28	107	123	46	56	1.58	
1995 Oakland AL	0	0	9.82	3	5	5	3	2.72	-

BAKKUM, SCOTT - TR - Age 25
Bakkum pitched at Double-A and Triple-A in 1995 with an ERA under 2.00 at both levels.

	W	SV	ERA	IP	H	BB	SO	B/I	$
1995 Pawtucket AAA	1	2	1.71	26	27	7	15	1.07	

BALDWIN, JAMES - TR - Age 24
Baldwin started 1995 in the White Sox rotation, but couldn't throw strikes and was quickly sent back to Triple-A Nashville where he didn't pitch much better. He's still a good strikeout pitcher who just needs to harness that excellent fastball in order to succeed in the majors.

	W	SV	ERA	IP	H	BB	SO	B/I	$
1994 Nashville AAA	12	0	3.72	162	144	83	156	1.40	
1995 Nashville AAA	5	0	5.85	95	120	44	89	1.72	
1995 Chicago AL	0	0	12.89	14	32	9	10	2.80	-
1996 *Projection* >>>	2	0	5.77	44	56	17	30	1.66	-

BANKHEAD, SCOTT - TR - Age 32
A solid middle reliever in 1992-93 after some success as a starter with the Mariners in the late 1980's, Bankhead has lost just enough velocity to slip into the questionable category for 1996.

	W	SV	ERA	IP	H	BB	SO	B/I	$
1994 Boston	3	0	4.54	37	34	12	25	1.22	2
1995 Edmonton AAA	1	1	7.85	18	28	7	15	1.91	
1995 New York AL	1	0	6.00	39	44	16	20	1.28	-

BANKS, JIM - TR - Age 26
Banks had an excellent 1994 season in Class A Modesto and has proven he can strike out more than a batter an inning at the A level. Given a chance at Double-A in 1995, he delivered so-so work out of the pen (two wins, two saves, and a 4.73 ERA).

BANKS, WILLIE - TR - Age 27
The former Twins' number one pick bounced around the National League (Cubs, Dodgers and Marlins) in 1995, and will take his act to Philly in 1996. Banks has tantalized all of his employers with glimpses of his hard fastball and deceptive straight change, but he appeared very confused on the mound for most of 1995. An audience with Phils' pitching coach Johnny Podres could work wonders - Banks is a prime 1996 comeback candidate.

	W	SV	ERA	IP	H	BB	SO	B/I	$
1994 Chicago NL	8	0	5.40	138	139	56	91	1.41	1
1995 Three Teams	2	0	5.66	90	106	58	62	1.82	-
1996 *Projection* >>>	8	0	4.32	155	159	72	107	1.49	-

BAPTIST, TRAVIS - TL - Age 24
He wasn't bad as a starter at Triple-A but didn't do enough to make anyone take notice. He'd need a better year at Syracuse to earn a call-up.

	W	SV	ERA	IP	H	BB	SO	B/I	$
1995 Syracuse AAA	3	0	4.33	79	83	32	52	1.46	

BARBER, BRIAN - TR - Age 23
Barber is a prime example of how organizations will give their top draft picks every chance in the world. He has done little since being a first-round pick in 1991. However, he ended last season in the Cardinals' starting rotation. He has provided little evidence that he is close to being a winning major-league starter.

	W	SV	ERA	IP	H	BB	SO	B/I	$
1994 Louisville AAA	4	1	5.38	85	79	46	95	1.46	
1995 St. Louis NL	2	0	5.22	29	31	16	27	1.60	-
1996 *Projection* >>>	5	0	4.77	130	128	70	120	1.52	-

BARCELO, MARC - TR - Age 24
Barcelo struggled badly at Triple-A Salt Lake City after he came off of a great year at Double-A. He must prove he's healthy; it's hard to believe he's the same highly regarded prospect we saw in '94. Barcelo will be at least a setup man in the major leagues.

	W	SV	ERA	IP	H	BB	SO	B/I	$
1995 Salt Lake AAA	8	0	7.05	143	214	59	63	1.91	

BARFIELD, JOHN - TL - Age 31
Barfield has spent the last two years in the minors after parts of two seasons with Texas. He's a finesse pitcher who could earn a long relief role as a major league lefty, but he's barely a Triple-A pitcher at this point.

BARK, BRIAN - TL - Age 27
Primarily a starter in the Braves organization, Bark was released and signed with the Red Sox. He was successful in his first long-term exposure as a closer at Pawtucket, and pitched well in spots for Boston. He's a little (5-9) overachiever whose fast ball also may be a bit short for the big leagues.

	W	SV	ERA	IP	H	BB	SO	B/I	$
1994 Richmond-Pawtucket AAA	4	0	4.76	127	128	51	87	1.40	
1995 Pawtucket AAA	5	7	2.99	72	63	31	43	1.30	

BARNES, BRIAN - TL - Age 29
Barnes is at the stage of his career where he could show up almost anywhere as a spare lefthander on a major league or Triple-A staff. Since the end of the 1993 season, he has been in the Montreal, Cleveland, Los Angeles, Florida,

Detroit and Boston organizations. He can still get a strikeout when he needs one, but he has trouble against righthanders.

	W	SV	ERA	IP	H	BB	SO	B/I	$
1994 Los Angeles NL	0	0	5.89	18	22	19	10	2.24	-
1995 Pawtucket AAA	7	0	4.23	106	107	30	90	1.29	

BARTON, SHAWN - TL - Age 32

The man who won't go away, Barton pitched well at Triple-A and was called up by the Giants to fill the one-out lefty role in the bullpen. He held lefties to a .242 average, so he'll probably get a job again in 1996, but is otherwise uninteresting.

	W	SV	ERA	IP	H	BB	SO	B/I	$
1995 San Francisco NL	4	1	4.26	44	37	19	22	1.27	2
1996 *Projection* >>>	2	1	4.27	44	39	20	22	1.33	1

BATCHELOR, RICHARD - TR - Age 28

After a couple of disappointing years in the minors, Batchelor buckled down for an excellent '95 season at Triple-A Louisville. A middle reliever with a good breaking ball, he may have worked his way back into prospect status. Still, 28-year-olds should already have several major league seasons under their belts if they are truly going to be stars.

	W	SV	ERA	IP	H	BB	SO	B/I	$
1995 Louisville AAA	5	0	3.28	85	85	16	61	1.19	

BATISTA, MIGUEL - TR - Age 25

Batista never translated his terrific velocity into solid performance in his five years in the Expos' chain, and then slid farther down the slope in a miserable 1995 season with the Marlins' Triple-A affiliate. A fastball pitcher with a deteriorating fastball does not have a long shelf life - expect Batista to fade out of sight in relatively short order.

	W	SV	ERA	IP	H	BB	SO	B/I	$
1994				Did Not Play					
1995 Charlotte AAA	6	0	4.80	116	118	60	58	1.53	

BAUER, MATT - TL - Age 26

Bauer has been a middle or set-up reliever through most of his five minor league seasons. Despite pitching well last season at Toledo, he was sent down to Double-A Jacksonville. Time is running out, but after all he is lefthanded.

BAUTISTA, JOSE - TR - Age 31

It seemed like a smart pickup for the Giants, but Bautista was plagued by the longball, giving up 24 homers in only 100 innings, putting his career in danger. He gets bombed as a starter, and won't get saves as a reliever.

	W	SV	ERA	IP	H	BB	SO	B/I	$
1994 Chicago NL	4	1	3.89	69	75	17	45	1.33	4
1995 San Francisco NL	3	0	6.44	100	120	26	45	1.46	-
1996 *Projection* >>>	1	0	5.37	39	44	11	20	1.41	-

BAXTER, BOB - TL - Age 27

Finally made it past Single A in 1994, going 11-3 for Double-A Harrisburg. But then at Triple-A in '95 he was unimpressive.

	W	SV	ERA	IP	H	BB	SO	B/I	$
1995 Ottawa AAA	5	0	3.92	101	125	25	39	1.49	

BEATTY, BLAINE - TL - Age 31

Beatty continues to be a big winner in the Reds' high minors, pitching for Triple-A Indianapolis in 1995; he has posted a 21-8 record and a 2.70 ERA over the last two years. He's too old to be a prospect and has been overlooked as the Reds have turned to younger, harder-throwing prospects when they needed emergency starters. Beatty has had two brief major league stints with the Mets in 1989 and 1991, and can return to the majors again as a fifth starter if he can find the right situation.

BECK, ROD - TR - Age 27

Beck clearly has lost something. Not only did he blow ten saves last season, but his K/IP ratio is in decline at an early age. He's still valuable as long as he has the stopper's job, but is slipping at this point. Watch the transaction wires during the offseason; if he goes to a team that needs a closer, or if the Giants make no moves to acquire a replacement for him so he will get saves.

	W	SV	ERA	IP	H	BB	SO	B/I	$
1994 San Francisco NL	2	28	2.77	48	49	13	39	1.27	33
1995 San Francisco NL	5	33	4.45	58	60	21	42	1.39	29
1996 *Projection* >>>	4	35	3.67	68	67	20	53	1.28	32

BECKETT, ROBBIE - TL - Age 23
Beckett looks like another one of those wild lefthanders, taking years to find himself and achieve consistent effectiveness. He strikes out a lot of hitters, averaging more than one per inning, but he walks as many as he whiffs. Beckett can become another Mitch Williams.

BEDROSIAN, STEVE - TR - Age 38
The aging veteran has reached the end of the line after a forgettable 1995 campaign. Bedrosian hasn't thrown hard for a long time; he had been getting by on good movement and working against a hitter's timing. The finesse act didn't work so well in 1995 and Bedrosian is probably finished for good.

	W	SV	ERA	IP	H	BB	SO	B/I	$
1994 Atlanta NL	0	0	3.33	46	41	18	43	1.28	1
1995 Atlanta NL	1	0	6.11	28	40	12	22	1.86	-

BEECH, MATT - TL - Age 24
The Phils' 1994 seventh round pick was aggressively promoted to Double-A Reading in his first full pro season. His velocity is not exceptional, but he has excellent movement on his sinking fastball, and his strikeout rate did not fall off markedly after his promotion. Beech does not project as a top line major league starter, but he should earn an audition in the majors by late 1997. He should be a viable Triple-A starter by the end of 1996.

BELCHER, TIM - TR - Age 34
He's on the downside of a decent career, but he should find a job somewhere if not Seattle. He'll offer an occasional good outing. His past reputation will make his perceived value greater than it should be.

	W	SV	ERA	IP	H	BB	SO	B/I	$
1994 Detroit AL	7	0	5.89	162	192	78	76	1.67	-
1995 Seattle AL	10	0	4.52	179	188	88	96	1.55	4
1996 *Projection* >>>	11	0	4.95	210	227	98	110	1.55	-

BELINDA, STAN - TR - Age 29
Belinda found new life in the Boston bullpen by keeping his good fastball down in the strike zone. He temporarily grabbed the closer role after Ken Ryan lost it and before Rick Aguilera was acquired. While Belinda's closer days are probably behind him, he can still succeed in a setup role, as long as he can keep that fastball down.

	W	SV	ERA	IP	H	BB	SO	B/I	$
1994 Kansas City AL	2	1	5.14	49	47	24	37	1.45	1
1995 Boston AL	8	10	3.10	69	51	28	57	1.13	19
1996 *Projection* >>>	4	4	3.73	75	61	30	60	1.22	10

BELL, ERIC - TL - Age 32
Bell is a 12 year minor league veteran who first reached Triple-A in 1986, and has had six separate big league trials with three clubs. Bell is Triple-A roster filler, just hanging around waiting to fill someone's situational relief need. Don't expect him to get another major league summons.

	W	SV	ERA	IP	H	BB	SO	B/I	$
1995 Calgary AAA	13	0	3.90	161	177	47	87	1.39	

BELTRAN, RICO - TL - Age 26
A crafty lefty with a nasty screwball, Beltran is also an excellent hitter who often pinch-hit for Triple-A Louisville in 1995. Beltran has good stuff, but lack of consistency holds him back.

	W	SV	ERA	IP	H	BB	SO	B/I	$
1995 Louisville AAA	8	0	5.21	129	156	34	92	1.47	

BENE, BILL - TR - Age 28
A hard-throwing first round draft pick in 1988, Bene spent time at both Double and Triple A in the Dodgers farm system. He played well at Double A, but got shelled at Triple A.

BENES, ALAN - TR - Age 24
Andy's younger brother is a can't-miss prospect. He would have been in the majors last year with St. Louis had he not spent part of the year fighting injuries. He threw two complete-game three-hitters in the playoffs for Triple-A American Association champions Louisville, then joined the big league Cardinals' rotation in September. The Cardinals' top pick in 1993, Benes will bring his good fastball to Busch Stadium in 1996.

	W	SV	ERA	IP	H	BB	SO	B/I	$
1995 Louisville AAA	4	0	2.41	56	37	14	54	0.91	
1995 St. Louis NL	1	0	8.44	16	24	4	20	1.75	-
1996 *Projection* >>>	10	0	4.42	98	120	22	91	1.44	5

BENES, ANDY - TR - Age 28
The AL was a disaster for Benes. He pitched well at times, especially down the stretch. Benes is a thouroughbred with the ability to raise his game, but must find the consistency to be termed great. Can he raise his game this year? Yes, count on it. If he goes back to the NL he's even more interesting.

	W	SV	ERA	IP	H	BB	SO	B/I	$
1994 San Diego NL	6	0	3.86	172	155	51	189	1.20	12
1995 San Diego NL	4	0	4.17	118	121	45	126	1.40	
1995 Seattle AL	7	0	5.86	63	72	33	45	1.67	4
1996 *Projection* >>>	11	0	4.36	218	215	81	213	1.36	10

BENITEZ, ARMANDO - TR - Age 23
Benitez has a fastball that lights up the radar guns. But the combination of immaturity and inexperience must be overcome before he can be a major league closer. Benitez gets very rattled when giving up a key hit or blowing a game, and it often takes him a week to get over such things.

	W	SV	ERA	IP	H	BB	SO	B/I	$
1994 Bowie AA	8	16	3.14	71	41	39	106	1.12	
1995 Baltimore AL	1	2	5.66	47	37	37	56	1.55	0
1996 *Projection* >>>	1	4	4.44	49	36	33	52	1.41	3

BENNETT, ERIK - TR - Age 27
Bennett was acquired by the Astros from the Angels system in a minor league deal in 1995. He was exclusively a starter for five years but has pitched primarily as a middle reliever at the Triple-A level the past two seasons. He has not yet established the credentials to compete for a major league job. He had a good year in the hitter-friendly Triple-A Pacific Coast League in 1994.

	W	SV	ERA	IP	H	BB	SO	B/I	$
1995 Two AAA Teams	9	3	4.42	73	71	32	63	1.41	

BENNETT, JOEL - TR - Age 26
Bennett solidified his status as a bona fide strikeout pitcher in 1994. He did struggle after his promotion to Triple-A, so he'll need to prove himself there before he can pitch in Boston. His curve is his best pitch.

	W	SV	ERA	IP	H	BB	SO	B/I	$
1995 Pawtucket AAA	2	0	5.84	77	91	45	50	1.77	

BENNETT, ROB - TR - Age 25
Bennett won ten games at Double-A in 1995. He has good control, but should still be considered a marginal prospect.

BERE, JASON - TR - Age 24
Bere pitched about as bad as he possibly could while still pitching in the major leagues in 1995. His control was horrible; his 106 walks allowed were second only to Al Leiter in the American League. Bere will have to go back to the minors in 1996 to learn how to throw strikes.

	W	SV	ERA	IP	H	BB	SO	B/I	$
1994 Chicago AL	12	0	3.81	141	119	80	127	1.40	12
1995 Chicago AL	8	0	7.19	137	151	106	110	1.88	-
1996 *Projection* >>>	6	0	4.43	125	110	80	105	1.52	1

BERGMAN, SEAN - TR - Age 25
Bergman emerged in '95 as Detroit's best hope for immediate help in the starting rotation. Along with Greg Gohr, Bergman generates more strikeouts than the youngsters now pitching for the Tigers, and he has decent control. Expect two or three seasons of mixed results from Bergman while the Detroit farm system develops their future rotation; he has a 50-50 chance to be a starter in five years.

	W	SV	ERA	IP	H	BB	SO	B/I	$
1994 Detroit AL	2	0	5.60	17	22	7	12	1.64	-
1995 Detroit AL	7	0	5.12	135	169	67	86	1.75	-
1996 *Projection* >>>	7	0	5.17	185	233	83	117	1.71	-

BERTOTTI, MIKE - TL - Age 26
Bertotti was forced along from Double-A Birmingham to Triple-A Nashville and up to the big leagues despite relatively poor performances at each level; he got worse with each promotion, too. The White Sox once had high hopes for this strikeout pitcher, but it doesn't look like he's going to make it in the majors.

	W	SV	ERA	IP	H	BB	SO	B/I	$
1995 Nashville AAA	2	0	8.72	32	41	17	35	1.82	
1995 Chicago AL	1	0	12.56	14	23	11	15	2.37	-

BERUMEN, ANDRES - TR - Age 24
Berumen began last season with the Padres. He's a reliever who walks nearly a hitter per inning, a weakness that sent him back to Triple-A. The walks have contributed to some high ERA's in Triple-A and the majors, jeopardizing his major-league career.

	W	SV	ERA	IP	H	BB	SO	B/I	$
1995 San Diego NL	2	1	5.68	44	37	36	42	1.66	-
1996 *Projection* >>>	1	1	5.10	31	26	24	29	1.60	-

BEVIL, BRIAN - TR - Age 24
A strikeout pitcher with a strong fastball, Bevil struggled at both Double-A Wichita and Triple-A Omaha in 1995, posting an ERA much higher than in any of his previous four seasons. Of greater concern was his dropping strikeout rate, from seven per nine innings in 1994 to just four per nine innings at Omaha. Bevil needs a year at Double-A to regroup.

BIELECKI, MIKE - TR - Age 36
Good work at Richmond earned Bielecki a trip back to the majors in a relief role in 1994. He's well past the days when he could succeed in a starting role. Bielecki never threw especially hard to begin with, and arm trouble over the last two years hasn't helped. There's little room in the majors for fading 36-year-old righthanded finesse pitchers.

	W	SV	ERA	IP	H	BB	SO	B/I	$
1994 Atlanta NL	2	0	4.00	27	28	12	18	1.48	0
1995 California AL	4	0	5.97	75	80	31	45	1.48	-

BIRKBECK, MIKE - TR - Age 35
After washing out as a starter with the Brewers in the late 1980's, Birkbeck became a fixture with the Triple-A Richmond Braves. A move to the Mets farm got him a 1995 callup with attention-getting results that should earn him another look, somewhere in the majors, in 1996.

	W	SV	ERA	IP	H	BB	SO	B/I	$
1994 Richmond AAA	13	0	2.73	164	145	46	143	1.16	
1995 New York NL	0	0	1.63	27	22	2	14	0.87	3
1996 *Projection* >>>	2	0	3.84	52	53	18	26	1.37	0

BLACK, BUD - TL - Age 38
This veteran lefty has finally hung up his spikes after fifteen years in the majors, finishing with a career 121-116 mark. Black helped the Indians usher in their younger future stars and has a future as a pitching coach.

Benson's Baseball Player Guide: 1996

	W	SV	ERA	IP	H	BB	SO	B/I	$
1994 San Francisco NL	4	0	4.47	54	50	16	28	1.21	3
1995 Cleveland AL	4	0	6.85	47	63	16	34	1.68	-

BLAIR, DIRK - TR - Age 26
Long relief specialist Blair had another good year for Double-A Greenville, earning a promotion to Triple-A Richmond where he struggled through eight appearances. Blair has excellent control (eleven walks in 62 innings at Greenville), but allows too many hits for a non-strikeout pitcher. He's a distant prospect at best.

BLAIR, WILLIE - TR - Age 30
The Padres signed this veteran on the recommendation of Tony Gwynn, who videotapes and studies pitchers in great detail to keep one step ahead of them. Blair moved into the starting rotation replacing the traded Andy Benes and pitched well with some good outings including a stretch of allowing only three runs in four starts. He came through with his career-best 4.34 ERA and his first winning season with a 7-5 record. Blair may have finally found the secret to pitching success, albeit a modest success.

	W	SV	ERA	IP	H	BB	SO	B/I	$
1994 Colorado NL	0	3	5.79	77	98	39	68	1.76	-
1995 San Diego NL	7	0	4.34	114	112	45	83	1.38	2
1996 Projection >>>	7	0	4.76	136	151	45	102	1.44	-

BLAZIER, RON - TR - Age 24
It took Blazier until his sixth pro season to finally make it to Double-A in 1995. After starting for five seasons, Blazier comfortably settled into his role as Eastern League champion Reading's setup man. He averaged two innings per outing, striking out a batter per inning with a strikeout/walk ratio of better than three to one. His high 80's fastball retains its velocity much better when it only travels once around the batting order. Another plus is his protoypical pitcher's body (6'6", 215 lbs.). Blazier could challenge for a deep bullpen role in Philadelphia sometime in 1996.

BLOMDAHL, BEN - TR - Age 25
Blomdahl improved significantly upon being converted to relief in his second Triple-A season. He struggled in his first big league season and is not a power pitcher, placing him in the group of young hurlers who have some lumps ahead of them before they settle down. Blomdahl is one of the better qualified candidates for Detroit's bullpen in '96.

	W	SV	ERA	IP	H	BB	SO	B/I	$
1995 Toledo AAA	5	3	3.54	56	55	13	39	1.21	
1995 Detroit AL	0	1	7.77	24	36	13	15	2.01	-
1996 Projection >>>	1	1	4.88	46	50	19	28	1.51	-

BLUMA, JAMIE - TR - Age 23
This guy is the real deal. Bluma led Double-A Wichita with 22 saves before finishing the year as Triple-A Omaha's closer. Formerly a star for national baseball-powerhouse Wichita State University, Bluma throws hard and has displayed excellent control. He stumbled a few times in Omaha, but should begin 1996 there before moving to Kansas City later in the year. Bluma is being groomed to close games for the Royals.

	W	SV	ERA	IP	H	BB	SO	B/I	$
1995 Omaha AAA	0	4	3.04	23	21	14	12	1.48	

BOCHTLER, DOUG - TR - Age 25
Doug Bochtler's roles in the minors and majors have been set-up and middle relief. After some poor years in Triple-A, he surprised everybody last year with a fine season with the Padres as he took over and solidified the set-up role. Bochtler held hitters to a very low .239.

	W	SV	ERA	IP	H	BB	SO	B/I	$
1995 San Diego NL	4	1	3.57	45	38	19	45	1.26	3
1996 Projection >>>	4	1	3.68	70	59	30	68	1.27	4

BOEHRINGER, BRIAN - TR - Age 26
Boehringer is capable of better than he showed in his 1995 major league light-up. His main problem is that the Yankees are about as well stocked as any team with good up-and-coming pitchers.

	W	SV	ERA	IP	H	BB	SO	B/I	$
1995 Columbus AAA	8	0	2.77	104	101	31	58	1.27	

BOEVER, JOE - TR - Age 35
Boever's offspeed offerings grew increasingly appetizing to AL hitters in '95; his season unraveled as the Tigers' did. He still notched a good number of strikeouts, giving hope of another comeback. Boever is under contract for another season in Detroit, but he's kind of risky at this point.

	W	SV	ERA	IP	H	BB	SO	BP	$
1994 Detroit AL	9	3	3.98	81	80	37	49	1.44	
1995 Detroit AL	5	3	6.39	98	128	44	71	1.74	-
1996 Projection >>>	4	1	5.38	90	105	39	61	1.61	-

BOHANON, BRIAN - TL - Age 27
Bohanon received more duty in '95 with the Tigers than he was ready for, but this was nothing new for the erratic but promising lefthander. With his selection of breaking balls, Bohanon is capable of retiring lefthanders when pitching out of the bullpen (.250 opposition batting average in '95). As long as he's healthy, Detroit will probably keep him in long relief.

	W	SV	ERA	IP	H	BB	SO	B/I	$
1994 Texas AL	2	0	7.23	37	51	8	26	1.58	-
1995 Detroit AL	1	1	5.54	105	121	41	63	1.54	-
1996 Projection >>>	3	1	4.91	108	133	27	65	1.48	0

BOLTON, RODNEY - TR - Age 27
Bolton is one of those great minor league pitchers who simply can't make the jump to the bigs. Compare his minor league career record of 67-30 and 2.41 ERA to his big league record of 2-8, 7.69 ERA. Bolton's finesse style just doesn't fool major league hitters - he needs a trade to get a more substantial shot in the majors, but don't count on success.

	W	SV	ERA	IP	H	BB	SO	B/I	$
1994 Nashville AAA	7	0	2.56	116	108	35	63	1.23	
1995 Chicago AL	0	0	8.18	22	33	14	10	2.14	-
1996 Projection >>>	0	0	5.90	41	50	24	25	1.80	-

BOLTON, TOM - TL - Age 33
A veteran situational lefty with several years of major league experience, Bolton lacks dominant stuff. He has been a consistent pitcher but is a marginal major leaguer at best.

	W	SV	ERA	IP	H	BB	SO	B/I	$
1994 Baltimore AL	1	0	5.40	23	29	13	12	1.80	-
1995 Nashville AAA	5	0	4.43	101	106	31	82	1.35	

BONES, RICKY - TR - Age 26
If the Brewers have a staff ace, Bones is the guy. He had a strong first half in 1994, but the batters seem to have caught on since then.

	W	SV	ERA	IP	H	BB	SO	B/I	$
1994 Milwaukee AL	10	0	3.43	170	166	45	57	1.24	19
1995 Milwaukee AL	10	0	4.63	200	218	83	77	1.51	4
1996 Projection >>>	12	0	5.05	197	219	70	72	1.47	1

BORBON, PEDRO - TL - Age 28
Borbon filled his expected role as a middle reliever in his first full season in the big leagues. His stuff isn't good enough for him to be much more than he was in 1995, but that will be sufficient for the Braves current needs.

	W	SV	ERA	IP	H	BB	SO	B/I	$
1994 Richmond AAA	3	4	2.79	80	66	41	82	1.33	
1995 Atlanta NL	2	2	3.09	32	29	17	33	1.44	2
1996 Projection >>>	2	3	3.02	44	40	23	43	1.44	3

BORLAND, TOBY - TR - Age 26
Borland emerged as one of the more durable relievers in the National League in 1995, routinely being counted upon to keep the Phils in ballgames after short outings from their mediocre starters. He is a sidearmer who throws a sinking fastball and slider which are very difficult to catch - he had 12 wild pitches in 74 innings in 1995. He is murder on righthanders and will likely be used again as a situational setup man in 1996, though he can still be counted on for the occasional three-inning save.

	W	SV	ERA	IP	H	BB	SO	B/I	$
1994 Scranton AAA	4	4	1.68	53	36	21	61	1.06	
1994 Philadelphia NL	1	1	2.36	34	31	14	26	1.31	3
1995 Philadelphia NL	1	6	3.77	74	81	37	59	1.59	3
1996 *Projection* >>>	1	4	3.45	64	68	28	51	1.48	3

BOROWSKI, JOE - TR - Age 24
Borowski is a reliever with a solid minor league record. He has an outstanding slider and is a strong candidate for the Orioles' bullpen as a set-up man or middle reliever.

	W	SV	ERA	IP	H	BB	SO	B/I	$
1995 Baltimore AL	0	0	1.23	7	5	4	3	1.23	0
1996 *Projection* >>>	1	0	4.92	44	47	15	22	1.41	-

BOSIO, CHRIS - TR - Age 31
Bosio had some good outings in 1995, but overall failed to stage a complete comeback. He lacks his old consistency, but is not washed up.

	W	SV	ERA	IP	H	BB	SO	B/I	$
1994 Seattle AL	4	0	4.32	125	137	40	67	1.42	5
1995 Seattle AL	10	0	4.92	170	211	69	85	1.65	0
1996 *Projection* >>>	10	0	4.95	184	220	76	97	1.61	-

BOSKIE, SHAWN - TR - Age 29
Veteran Shawn Boskie has been a starter and reliever with a number of major league teams, including three clubs in 1994. That in itself is a hidden clue about the quality of his pitching. As a starter, he has a career ERA over 5.00 as he is homer-prone. He is more effective as a reliever. The Angels used him as a starter last year, with modest success, but he came down with an inflamed elbow.

	W	SV	ERA	IP	H	BB	SO	B/I	$
1994 Three Teams	4	0	5.06	90	92	30	61	1.35	3
1995 California AL	7	0	5.64	111	127	25	51	1.36	2
1996 *Projection* >>>	3	0	5.76	80	90	23	43	1.41	-

BOTTALICO, RICKY - TR - Age 26
Bottalico was one of the most dominating relievers in baseball in 1995, but like Troy Percival of the Angels, he went unnoticed because he was used primarily as a setup man. Bottalico held batters to a .167 average, with an amazing hits/innings ratio. He has a live fastball, but his out pitch is a devastating overhand curve that he will throw in any situation. Unlike most closers, he has a two inning arm. He needs to hone his control somewhat, but he should claim the closer role sometime in 1996 and hold it for many years.

	W	SV	ERA	IP	H	BB	SO	B/I	$
1994 Reading AA	2	22	2.53	42	29	10	51	0.91	
1994 Scranton AAA	3	3	8.87	22	32	22	22	2.42	
1995 Philadelphia NL	5	1	2.46	87	50	42	87	1.05	11
1996 *Projection* >>>	4	4	3.00	88	55	43	87	1.11	12

BOTTENFIELD, KENT - TR - Age 27
This righthander has had opportunities to establish himself in the majors and has fallen short, and his '95 season at Triple-A doesn't suggest a potential change in this pattern.

	W	SV	ERA	IP	H	BB	SO	B/I	$
1994 San Francisco NL	3	1	6.15	26	33	10	15	1.63	-
1995 Toledo AAA	5	1	4.54	136	148	55	68	1.49	

BOUCHER, DENIS - TL - Age 28
At a pitchers' park in Ottawa, Boucher has struggled for the last two seasons, posting a combined 4.33 ERA with as many walks as strikeouts. For a non-strikeout pitcher, he doesn't have especially good command. Boucher is a distant hope to become the "native-son" star the Expos had hoped.

	W	SV	ERA	IP	H	BB	SO	B/I	$
1994 Montreal NL	0	0	6.75	18	24	7	17	1.66	-
1995 Ottawa AAA	2	0	5.69	55	65	31	22	1.74	

BOURGEOIS, STEVE - TR - Age 23
Bourgeois was the Texas League Pitcher of the Year in 1995; he also pitched well in a handful of starts at Triple-A. He's not an overpowering pitcher, but the Giants need help in their rotation, and he may get a chance. However, he was a replacement during the strike, and the Giants' players took a hard stand against any such callups, which complicates Bourgeois' status with the team.

	W	SV	ERA	IP	H	BB	SO	B/I	$
1995 Phoenix AAA	1	0	3.38	34	38	13	23	1.48	

BOVEE, MIKE - TR - Age 22
The Royals are high on Bovee; he was the club's minor league pitcher of the year in 1994 after going 13-4 with a 2.65 ERA for Class-A Wilmington. He's a curveball specialist who occasionally fights his control; his 72 Ks for Double-A Wichita in 1995 were the fewest of his pro career. Bovee needs to keep his weight under control and have a better season when he returns to Double-A in 1996.

BOWEN, RYAN - TR - Age 28
Bowen has hurt virtually every part of his body in his pro baseball career - arms, legs, hips, you name it. When healthy, he has been hit hard. Still, the big fastball remains after all that adversity. Bowen doesn't have much of a clue where the ball is going, but he is clearly capable of striking out nearly a batter per inning. The Marlins will likely give him a shot at making their 1996 rotation, but his power repertoire looks better suited for the bullpen.

	W	SV	ERA	IP	H	BB	SO	B/I	$
1994 Florida NL	1	0	4.94	47	50	19	32	1.46	-
1995 Florida NL	2	0	3.78	16	23	12	15	2.10	-
1996 Projection >>>	3	0	4.50	47	52	25	40	1.64	-

BOWERS, SHANE - TR - Age 24
Twins prospect Bowers produced a 2.16 ERA and had a strikeout/walk ratio over 3:1 at Class A in 1995. Still a long way to go, but looks promising.

BOZE, MARSHALL - TR - Age 24
After going 30-12 in 1992 and '93, Boze struggled in his Triple-A debut in '94 and did only a little better in his second try in 1995. At this point he would have a hard time making it in the majors.

	W	SV	ERA	IP	H	BB	SO	B/I	$
1995 New Orleans AAA	3	1	4.27	111	134	45	47	1.61	

BRADFORD, TROY - TR - Age 27
Bradford made it to Double-A in his fifth pro season, with no great success. This formerly promising hurler has seen little action after 1993 arm surgery.

BRANDENBURG, MARK - TR - Age 25
Brandenburg has succeeded at every minor league level, but was hittable in a late-season callup. Brandenburg is a sidearming control specialist who, with further experience and refinement, has some chance to turn into Mark Eichhorn. He was slated to pitch in the Arizona Fall League.

	W	SV	ERA	IP	H	BB	SO	B/I	$
1995 Texas AL	0	0	5.93	27	36	7	21	1.57	-
1996 Projection >>>	2	0	5.05	40	51	9	31	1.51	-

BRANTLEY, CLIFF - TR - Age 27
A former second-round draft choice who showed promise in 1992 but then had three lost seasons.

BRANTLEY, JEFF - TR - Age 32
Brantley turned in his second straight good year for the Reds, saving 28 games in 32 opportunities. Brantley relies on an excellent splitter and gives up very few hits. He has decent control but gave up more home runs than you would like out of a closer (11 in 70 innings). He will remain the primary Cincinnati closer (at least until Hector Carrasco develops).

	W	SV	ERA	IP	H	BB	SO	B/I	$
1994 Cincinnati NL	6	15	2.48	65	46	28	63	1.13	25
1995 Cincinnati NL	3	28	2.82	70	53	20	62	1.04	31
1996 *Projection* >>>	5	28	2.90	86	66	29	76	1.11	33

BREWER, BILLY - TL - Age 27
Brewer's worst season ever resulted in a demotion to A-ball. Expected to be a hard-throwing lefty setup man in the Royals bullpen, he couldn't get the ball over the plate in most outings and when he did it was hit hard. Look for Brewer to go to the high minors to work on his stuff. He'll return to the majors someday as lefty relievers are in great demand.

	W	SV	ERA	IP	H	BB	SO	B/I	$
1994 Kansas City AL	4	3	2.56	38	28	16	25	1.14	9
1995 Kansas City AL	2	0	5.56	45	54	20	31	1.63	-
1996 *Projection* >>>	2	1	4.43	41	41	18	28	1.44	0

BREWER, NEVIN - TR - Age 24
Originally drafted as a starting pitcher, Brewer moved to the bullpen in 1994, then split time between the pen and the rotation at Double-A Wichita in 1995. Brewer struck out a batter per inning in the low minors his first two seasons, but didn't enjoy that kind of success in 1995. He needs another year in the minors before taking a middle innings relief role in Kansas City.

BREWINGTON, JAMIE - TR - Age 24
He had never pitched above Class A before 1995, but was called up by the Giants after pitching OK at Double-A Shreveport. Brewington didn't embarrass himself with the Giants, but he has control trouble and needs a year at Triple-A. If the Giants force him into the majors in 1996, he'll have a rough year.

	W	SV	ERA	IP	H	BB	SO	B/I	$
1995 San Francisco NL	6	0	4.54	75	68	45	45	1.50	0
1996 *Projection* >>>	3	0	4.70	51	48	31	30	1.56	-

BRINK, BRAD - TR - Age 31
A long reliever/swingman for the Giants and Athletics Triple-A franchises in 1995, Brink hasn't been the same pitcher since suffering extensive injuries in 1990. He could eventually return to the majors, but he doesn't really throw hard enough to be anything more than a tenth or eleventh pitcher on a big league staff.

	W	SV	ERA	IP	H	BB	SO	B/I	$
1994 Phoenix AAA	7	0	4.15	128	140	41	79	1.41	-
1995 Two AAA Teams	2	0	6.29	68	79	46	48	1.82	-

BRISCOE, JOHN - TR - Age 28
A member of the "if he can learn to throw strikes, he'll be a star" brigade, Briscoe has struck out almost a hitter per inning in the majors, but has walked more men than he has struck out.

	W	SV	ERA	IP	H	BB	SO	B/I	$
1994 Oakland AL	4	1	4.01	49	31	39	45	1.42	4
1995 Oakland AL	0	0	8.35	18	25	21	19	2.51	-
1996 *Projection* >>>	2	0	5.80	36	32	33	34	1.84	-

BRITO, MARIO - TR - Age 29
The long-time farm hand played with Milwaukee's Triple A team getting six wins and 11 saves in 58 innings pitched, throwing 74 strikeouts in 1994.

BROCAIL, DOUG - TR - Age 28
Brocail was a spot starter and long reliever with Houston in 1995 after being acquired from San Diego as part of the big twelve player trade. He is not a hard thrower despite his impressive size. He should get an opportunity as a fifth starter.

	W	SV	ERA	IP	H	BB	SO	B/I	$
1994 San Diego NL	0	0	5.82	17	21	5	11	1.53	-
1995 Houston NL	6	1	4.19	77	87	22	39	1.41	2
1996 *Projection* >>>	4	0	4.41	72	82	21	38	1.42	-

BROCK, CHRIS - TR - Age 26
Brock had a dreadful year as a middle reliever and occasional starter for Triple-A Richmond in 1995, going 2-8 with a 5.40 ERA. He lacks a major league fastball and his other pitches aren't anything special. He'll have to have a much better year at Triple-A in 1996 to even get noticed in the well-stocked Braves farm system.

	W	SV	ERA	IP	H	BB	SO	B/I	$
1995 Richmond AAA	2	0	5.40	60	68	27	43	1.59	

BROCK, RUSSELL - TR - Age 26
The curveballer was impressive at both Class AA and AAA in '94, and had the confidence of the Oakland organization. But then in 1995 he struggled and lost his starter's role.

	W	SV	ERA	IP	H	BB	SO	B/I	$
1995 Edmonton AAA	1	1	6.87	55	75	31	44	1.93	

BROHAWN, TROY - TL - Age 22
This lefty posted a 1.65 ERA in eleven Class A starts. He's a strikeout pitcher and has good control. He's considered as a solid future prospect.

BRONKEY, JEFF - TR - Age 30
Another Brewer rehab case, Bronkey just hasn't been able to stay healthy. But he is talented.

	W	SV	ERA	IP	H	BB	SO	B/I	$
1994 Milwaukee AL	1	1	4.35	20	20	12	13	1.55	-
1995 Milwaukee AL	0	0	3.65	12	15	6	5	1.70	-
1996 *Projection* >>>	1	1	4.01	32	35	16	17	1.58	-

BROSNAN, JASON - TL - Age 28
Brosnan has been up and down throughout the Dodgers' organization as a swingman, never spending any season in one place. He had a great season at Double-A San Antonio in 1995 after he moved to the bullen. Brosnan has the look of a career minor leaguer who can be found in the high minors for any team, anywhere.

BROSS, TERRY- TR - Age 30
Bross helped lead the Yakult Swallows to the Central Japanese League title in 1995, going 14-5 with a 2.29 ERA. He's a tall (6'9") righthander who made two brief appearances in the US major leagues in the early 1990's. Should Bross return to the majors he could be successful in a righthanded setup role.

BROW, SCOTT - TR - Age 27
Brow continued to struggle with his control and doesn't throw hard enough to offset his shortcomings. He'll be lucky to return to Triple-A.

	W	SV	ERA	IP	H	BB	SO	B/I	$
1994 Toronto AL	0	2	5.90	29	34	19	15	1.83	-
1995 Syracuse AAA	1	0	9.00	31	52	18	14	2.26	

BROWN, KEITH - TR - Age 32
He had four brief trials with Cincinnati, but hasn't won a major league game since '88. Never has thrown hard. Has good control, but allows too many hits.

BROWN, J. KEVIN - TR - Age 31
Kevin Brown is a sinker-slider pitcher with the nastiest slider in baseball. Last year was pretty much a lost year for him as he started slowly because of the short spring training, and then injured his thumb trying to catch a line drive barehanded. He also had some tough luck because the Oriole bullpen blew a few wins for him. But Brown finished strong, going 5-3 with a 3.36 ERA, providing the optimism that he will return to win 20 as he did back in 1992.

	W	SV	ERA	IP	H	BB	SO	B/I	$
1994 Texas AL	7	0	4.82	170	218	50	123	1.58	1
1995 Baltimore AL	10	0	3.60	172	155	48	117	1.18	16
1996 *Projection* >>>	12	0	4.01	211	219	60	145	1.32	14

BROWN, KEVIN D. - TL - Age 30
Still the wrong Kevin Brown.

BROWN, MICHAEL - TL - Age 24
After failing to develop as a power-hitting first baseman, Brown was recalled by the Pirates from Double-A Carolina last September and converted into a left-handed pitcher. He looks the part but time will tell if he can make the transition.

BROWN, TIM - TR - Age 27
He pitched a seven-inning perfect game in 1993, his sixth year as a pro, but except for that game he's far from perfect and remained stuck at Triple-A in 1995.

	W	SV	ERA	IP	H	BB	SO	B/I	$
1995 Syracuse AAA	3	0	6.27	74	95	28	54	1.65	

BROWN, WILLARD - TR - Age 23
Brown is a young hard throwing starter with a lot of potential. He found Double-A a little rough last year, but the Angels hope he can make the necessary adjustments to move up the ladder to Anaheim.

BROWNING, TOM - TL - Age 35
The surprising thing is that Browning even got back to pro ball in 1995 after breaking his arm while throwing a pitch in 1994. He was plagued by injuries all year, though, and was very ineffective in two starts for the Royals. He'll hang around for a few more years, but it's hard to believe Browning can ever succeed in the majors again.

	W	SV	ERA	IP	H	BB	SO	B/I	$
1994 Cincinnati NL	3	0	4.20	40	34	13	22	1.16	2
1995 Kansas City AL	0	0	8.10	10	13	5	3	1.80	-

BROWNSON, MARK - TR - Age 20
Brownson played well in his first season in Rookie ball with four wins, three saves, a 1.66 ERA, and 72 srtrikeouts in 54 innings pitched. Obviously has high potential.

BRUMLEY, DUFF - TR - Age 25
A sinker/slider pitcher, Brumley has been ineffective above Double-A. He has posted good strikeout totals in past minor league seasons, but is probably at the end of his brief career.

BRUMMETT, GREG - TR - Age 28
Brummett is a breaking-ball pitcher the Red Sox acquired from Minnesota last season. He also has pitched for Wichita State and San Francisco.

BRUNDAGE, DAVE - TL - Age 31
Longtime Seattle outfielder couldn't hit, converted to pitcher, and got a few saves in 1994. Walks too many, but an interesting story nonetheless.

BRUSKE, JIM - TR - Age 31
Once an outfielder with the Indians, Bruske pitched just three professional innings before 1990, then advanced slowly through four organizations before finally reaching the majors at age 30. He throws hard enough to succeed, but without much command of his pitches. Bruske can be a middle reliever for a big league club in 1996, but he'll have to battle many other younger prospects for the chance.

	W	SV	ERA	IP	H	BB	SO	B/I	$
1995 Los Angeles NL	0	1	4.50	10	12	4	5	1.60	-

BRYANT, SHAWN - TL - Age 26
Bryant's value has fallen to the point where he can hope only to latch on as a situational lefty.

	W	SV	ERA	IP	H	BB	SO	B/I	$
1995 Salt Lake AAA	4	0	4.88	48	62	16	27	1.63	

BUCKELS, GARY - TR - Age 30
St. Louis farmhand got a cup of coffee in 1994 and did pretty well. He saw time in the Arizona Fall League and got a good look in spring training but then faltered upon returning to Louisville. Picked up by the Tigers, he did much better at Triple-A.

	W	SV	ERA	IP	H	BB	SO	B/I	$
1994 Louisville AAA	7	2	3.26	77	69	21	69	1.16	
1994 St. Louis NL	0	0	2.25	12	8	7	9	1.25	0
1995 Toledo AAA	2	0	2.15	46	37	20	38	1.24	

BUCKLEY, TRAVIS - TR - Age 25
Formerly Rangers property, Buckley has been inconsistent in the high minors. Scouts like his good fastball and slider, but he needs more minor league time to hone his stuff. Buckley will return to Triple-A Indianapolis in 1996 with a shot at a mid-season promotion.

BULLINGER, JIM - TR - Age 30
Bullinger had a pretty good year but that 12-8 record is about the best you can reasonably expect from this curveball specialist. He suffered through a bad August slump after a great first half in 1995. Bullinger is an ex-shortstop who only converted to pitching in the minor leagues in 1989, so his arm doesn't have as much mileage as you might find on most thirty-year old pitchers. He's a ten-game winner at best, though, and is in danger of losing his rotation spot.

	W	SV	ERA	IP	H	BB	SO	B/I	$
1994 Chicago NL	6	2	3.60	100	87	34	72	1.21	10
1995 Chicago NL	12	0	4.14	150	152	65	93	1.45	4
1996 Projection >>>	10	0	4.10	160	167	65	104	1.45	1

BULLINGER, KIRK - TR - Age 26
Sinkerball pitcher Kirk doesn't throw as hard as his brother Jim, the Cubbie pitcher. He came over to the Expos after toiling in the Cardinals' farm system for several years and advance to Double-A for the first time; Bullinger went 5-3 with seven saves and a 2.42 ERA at Harrisburg in 1995. He once saved 33 games at a lower Class-A site, providing further proof of the lack of importance that can be placed upon saves accumulated in the lower minors - especially by Cardinals minor leaguers.

BUNCH, MELVIN - TR - Age 24
Bunch reached the majors for the first time in 1995, despite a relatively poor season for him. He doesn't throw especially hard but has fine control. Unfortunately, Bunch lacks major league stuff and will be relegated to a career of mostly Triple-A pitching interspersed with spot work for major league teams desperate for bullpen arms.

	W	SV	ERA	IP	H	BB	SO	B/I	$
1995 Omaha AAA	1	0	4.57	65	63	20	50	1.28	
1995 Kansas City AL	1	0	5.63	40	42	14	19	1.40	-
1996 Projection >>>	1	0	5.70	34	38	12	16	1.48	-

BURBA, DAVE - TR - Age 29
Burba was wasted in the San Francisco bullpen setting up Rod Beck even after the entire Giants rotation hit the DL. Acquired by the Reds in the Deion Sanders trade, Burba was shifted to the rotation where he promptly reeled off seven wins, helped by the best run support on the team. Burba's four pitch repertoire is much more suited to starting and he combines a high strikeout rate with the highest groundball to flyball ratio on the team (almost 2 to 1). Despite his success, his starting role is not entirely secure - the Reds have six qualified starters if Jose Rijo returns healthy in 1996.

	W	SV	ERA	IP	H	BB	SO	B/I	$
1994 San Francisco NL	3	0	4.38	74	59	45	84	1.41	1
1995 Two Teams	10	0	3.97	106	90	51	96	1.32	6
1996 Projection >>>	9	0	4.10	155	131	78	150	1.35	4

BURGOS, ENRIQUE - TL - Age 30
This guys throws heat! Nevertheless, at age 30 he's only been given 13.1 innings at the major league level (with 18

strikeouts!), posting an ERA of almost 9.00 in those few innings. So we can assume he will never become the next Lee Smith.

	W	SV	ERA	IP	H	BB	SO	B/I	$
1994 Omaha AAA	1	19	2.88	56	44	33	68	1.37	
1995 Phoenix AAA	2	2	6.14	58	63	40	77	1.76	
1995 San Francisco NL	0	0	8.64	8	14	6	12	2.40	-

BURGOS, JOHN - TL - Age 28
Shaping up to be a career minor leaguer. He had a decent baserunner per inning ratio in 1994 at Chattanooga and Single A Charleston. Stayed at Double-A in 1995, with a 2.78 ERA but only three wins and no saves.

BURKE, JOHN - TR - Age 26
This first-ever Rockies amateur draft pick (1992) recovered admirably in 1995 from an almost complete loss of pitching control a year earlier. He was dogged by injuries almost all of the 1995 season, however. If he's at full strength this spring and remains healthy, Burke should see at least limited action with the Rockies.

	W	SV	ERA	IP	H	BB	SO	B/I	$
1995 Colorado Springs AAA	7	1	4.55	87	79	48	65	1.46	

BURKETT, JOHN - TR - Age 31
Burkett raised fans' expectations with his misleading 22-7 record in 1993, which was largely an illusion created by excellent run support. He is, and always was, a durable, reliable starter with top notch control but quite nondescript stuff. He has allowed more than a hit per inning in four of his six seasons, and that should become the norm as his power decreases through his early 30's. Burkett can be expected to deliver a workmanlike (some would say mediocre) performance befitting a number three or four starter.

	W	SV	ERA	IP	H	BB	SO	B/I	$
1994 San Francisco NL	6	0	3.62	159	176	36	85	1.33	9
1995 Florida NL	14	0	4.30	188	208	57	126	1.41	5
1996 *Projection* >>>	14	0	4.02	217	244	60	135	1.40	5

BURLINGAME, BEN - TR - Age 26
Despite a 9-2 record and 3.53 ERA, Burlingame spent yet another full year at Double-A Orlando. He moved from the starting rotation to the bullpen at mid-season with encouraging results. He's too old to still be at Double-A and needs a good year at Triple-A in 1996 to be considered a prospect.

BURLINGAME, DENNIS - TR - Age 26
Despite a poor start for AA Greenville, Burlingame eventually moved up to AAA Richmond and also moved to the bullpen. A finesse pitcher, Burlingame walks too many batters to succeed in the majors at this point.

BURROWS, TERRY - TL - Age 27
Burrows is a lefty swingman with so-so stuff. He has to be extremely fine with his control to succeed. Burrows' biggest problem in 1995 was an inability to get lefthanded hitters out, which doesn't bode well for his immediate future.

	W	SV	ERA	IP	H	BB	SO	B/I	$
1995 Texas AL	2	1	6.45	44	60	19	22	1.77	-
1996 *Projection* >>>	1	1	5.82	45	63	13	22	1.68	-

BUSBY, MIKE - TR - Age 23
Busby has progressed slowly through the Cardinals farm system, usually needing a full year to master each level. He has an above average fastball and slider but lost most of 1994 to an elbow injury. Busby displayed good control and a low opponent batting average in 20 starts at Double-A Arkansas in 1995 and six Triple-A starts at Louisville. He's not a great prospect, but the Cardinals will give him a long look in spring training in 1996.

	W	SV	ERA	IP	H	BB	SO	B/I	$
1995 Louisville AAA	2	0	3.29	38	28	11	26	1.02	

BUSHING, CHRIS - TR - Age 28
The former Red reliever gets plenty of strikeouts but doesn't have overpowering velocity. He missed almost all of the 1994 season with injuries.

BUSSA, TODD - TR - Age 23
Since 1991 Bussa was a nondescript journeyman in the Tigers' system, but he was virtually unhittable as the Marlins' low A-ball closer in 1995, allowing just over four hits per nine innings. However, he was way too old to be pitching at that level, he doesn't throw particularly hard, and his 5'11", 170, frame is not a classic pitcher's build. Still, anyone who performs as he did in 1995 needs to be watched closely the following season.

BUTCHER, MIKE - TR - Age 29
Over the years, Butcher failed in numerous chances to be the Angels closer. He was also erratic in a set-up role, and it tells you something when the Angels released him during their September stretch run for the division title.

	W	SV	ERA	IP	H	BB	SO	B/I	$
1994 California AL	2	1	6.67	29	31	23	19	1.82	
1995 California AL	6	0	4.73	51	49	31	29	1.57	1
1996 Projection >>>	1	1	5.11	33	32	21	20	1.60	-

BYRD, PAUL - TR - Age 25
Norfolk coach Bob Apodaca convinced Byrd to give up his over-the-head windup and go with a simple hands-in-front stretch delivery. Suddenly the sinking fastball and assorted curve, slurve and changeup repertoire began to hit spots with precision, and Byrd jumped from so-so minor leaguer to useful major leaguer just like that. Needs to keep that fine control to remain effective in 1996.

	W	SV	ERA	IP	H	BB	SO	B/I	$
1994 Charlotte AAA	2	1	3.93	36	33	11	15	1.20	
1995 New York NL	2	0	2.05	22	18	7	26	1.14	2
1996 Projection >>>	2	1	2.88	44	38	16	43	1.22	4

BYRDAK, TIM - TL - Age 22
A great curveball is Byrdak's best asset, and it helped him go 11-5 with a 2.16 ERA for Class-A Wilmington in 1995. He allowed too many homers, but should advance to Double-A Wichita in 1996. Byrdak is a marginal prospect at this point.

CABRERA, JOSE - TR - Age 24
The righty's stock has dropped significantly after a disappointing season at Single-A Kinston, where he battled for the league lead in losses. Still he got a promotion to Double-A in 1995 and held his own with a 3.28 ERA and another good strikeout/walk ratio, making his overall track record more upward-pointing.

CADARET, GREG - TL - Age 34
Veteran lefty reliever Cadaret has bounced around in seven organizations over the past four years. He pitched well in Triple-A last year, and there are always jobs for lefty relievers. Thus Cadaret may get another job in the majors, probably as a lefty set-up man and situational reliever.

	W	SV	ERA	IP	H	BB	SO	B/I	$
1994 Two Teams	1	2	4.73	40	41	33	29	1.85	-
1995 Las Vegas AAA	3	0	5.88	52	56	22	52	1.50	

CAIN, TIM - TR - Age 26
Red Sox farmhand Cain pitched at Double-A and Triple-A in 1995 and held up fine at the higher level.

	W	SV	ERA	IP	H	BB	SO	B/I	$
1995 Pawtucket AAA	4	4	2.28	27	24	8	19	1.16	

CAMPBELL, KEVIN - TR - Age 31
Campbell is late bloomer who washed out of the Twins' organization after just nine innings in '95. He can still chip in a few good innings if the right manager finds a place for him.

	W	SV	ERA	IP	H	BB	SO	B/I	$
1994 Minnesota AL	1	0	2.92	24	20	5	15	1.01	2
1995 Tacoma AAA	3	1	3.67	49	50	14	34	1.31	
1995 Minnesota AL	0	0	4.66	9	8	5	5	1.34	-

CAMPBELL, MIKE - TR - Age 32
A veteran of parts of five seasons in the majors for three different teams, Campbell had a fine year for Triple-A Iowa

in 1995, going 9-3 with a 2.45 ERA. He has spent ten years in Triple-A and is only an emergency major leaguer at best.

	W	SV	ERA	IP	H	BB	SO	B/I	$
1995 Iowa AAA	9	0	2.45	102	93	29	88	1.19	

CANDIOTTI, TOM - TR - Age 38
1995 was another typical Tom Candiotti year in Los Angeles, featuring a poor record given his ERA and terrible run support (3.5 runs per game). He had the dubious honor of being the number one victim of the dubious Dodger defense, giving up a total of 19 unearned runs. He is a knuckleballer, so there is no reason to expect a decline in 1996, and as a free agent he may escape the Dodgers and their non-support.

	W	SV	ERA	IP	H	BB	SO	B/I	$
1994 Los Angeles NL	7	0	4.12	153	149	54	102	1.33	7
1995 Los Angeles NL	7	0	3.50	190	187	58	141	1.29	9
1996 Projection >>>	10	0	3.70	214	208	68	154	1.29	11

CARLSON, DAN - TR - Age 26
Carlson has led three different minor leagues in wins and has now spent almost three years at Triple-A, but has yet to pitch in the majors, even in an organization desperate for pitching help. He certainly deserves his chance, although he will never be a superstar.

	W	SV	ERA	IP	H	BB	SO	B/I	$
1994 Phoenix AAA	13	1	4.64	151	173	55	117	1.50	
1995 Phoenix AAA	9	0	4.27	132	138	66	93	1.54	

CARLYLE, KENNY - TR - Age 26
Carlyle had some solid years in the lower minors, but struggled at higher levels in 1993 and 1994. Working mainly as a starter again in 1995, Carlyle leveled off at 8-8, and right now what you see is what you get. Further improvement is unlikely, so it's a question of opportunity whether he ever gets to the majors.

	W	SV	ERA	IP	H	BB	SO	B/I	$
1995 Toledo AAA	8	0	4.33	124	139	44	63	1.47	

CARMAN, DON - TL - Age 36
Hasn't been a good pitcher since 1986, but lefties keep getting try-outs. During the mid 1980's I had a young man working for me, who had been a lefty pitcher with the University of Connecticut. Nothing special, he had trouble reaching 70 MPH on the radar gun at a country fair. Nonetheless, every six months or so, someone would call and ask if we would come for a try-out. It went on for years. Probably still going on.

CARMONA, RAFAEL - TR - Age 23
Carmona earned his first big league opportunity with outstanding work at Double-A Port City in 1995. He was less effective for Seattle and Triple-A Tacoma, but he remains a highly regarded righthanded relief prospect. Carmona has fashioned high strikeout rates throughout his three pro years and could start 1996 in the Mariners bullpen.

	W	SV	ERA	IP	H	BB	SO	B/I	$
1995 Tacoma AAA	4	0	5.06	48	52	19	37	1.48	
1995 Seattle AL	2	1	5.66	47	55	34	28	1.87	-
1996 Projection >>>	2	0	5.15	39	44	22	25	1.70	-

CARPENTER, BRIAN - TR - Age 25
In his third pro season, Carpenter moved from the rotation to swingman and setup relief pitching for the Cardinals, winning a promotion to Double-A Arkansas. He's really nothing special and is too old to be a true prospect.

CARPENTER, CHRIS - TR - Age 21
Disappointing in Double-A but still throwing hard, he's got a great fastball and one of the best curves in the Blue Jays organization. He is intimidating at 6-5, 225 lbs and at his age he has a long time to develop. He'll probably spend 1996 working things out at Double-A Knoxville.

CARPENTER, CRIS - TR - Age 30
Triple-A Louisville's most valuable pitcher in 1995, Carpenter returned to the Cardinals' organization after two years with Florida and Texas. He isn't overpowering but instead uses an intelligent mix of pitches. In 1996, Carpenter could

be in a major league bullpen as a middle innings guy or he could go back to Triple-A.

	W	SV	ERA	IP	H	BB	SO	B/I	$
1994 Texas AL	2	5	5.03	59	69	20	39	1.51	6
1995 Louisville AAA	2	5	2.43	66	59	20	41	1.19	

CARRARA, GIAVANNI - TR - Age 28
Called up to replace the traded David Cone, he didn't do enough to get a very long look. He was wild high and outside much of the time and didn't show the fastball he needs to have to stay in the major leagues. At his age, he should start the season at Triple-A until there's a requirement for an emergency starter.

	W	SV	ERA	IP	H	BB	SO	B/I	$
1995 Toronto AL	2	0	7.21	48	64	25	27	1.83	-
1996 *Projection* >>>	1	0	5.72	44	61	14	24	1.71	-

CARRASCO, HECTOR - TR - Age 26
After a fine debut in 1994, Carrasco did not develop much in 1995. He lost seven games, blew four of nine save opportunities, and averaged 4.7 walks per nine innings. Carrasco relies on a good fastball and hard slider, but needs to develop more consistency before he can be trusted with the closer role.

	W	SV	ERA	IP	H	BB	SO	B/I	$
1994 Cincinnati NL	5	6	2.24	56	42	30	41	1.28	13
1995 Cincinnati NL	2	5	4.12	87	86	46	64	1.51	3
1996 *Projection* >>>	3	5	3.58	83	76	43	60	1.44	5

CARTER, ANDY - TL - Age 27
The fact that Carter could not stick with the lefty-hungry Phillies in 1995 speaks volumes about his major league future. Despite his size (6'5", 220 lbs.), Carter is a soft-tosser who relies on a deceptive delivery and needs pinpoint control to be effective - his control has been anything but in recent years. He might be the only player ever to be thrown out of his major league debut (for hitting Tony Gwynn with a pitch). Carter is not on the short list to make the Phils' 1996 staff.

	W	SV	ERA	IP	H	BB	SO	B/I	$
1994 Philadelphia NL	0	0	4.46	34	34	12	18	1.34	
1995 Scranton AAA	1	0	4.35	20	17	13	18	1.46	
1995 Philadelphia NL	0	0	6.14	7	4	2	6	0.82	-

CARTER, JOHN - TR - Age 24
There was a major divergence of opinion regarding Carter's upside potential entering the 1995 season. Many were swayed by his 17-7 1993 low A-ball campaign, in which he was one of his league's older starting pitchers, and wasn't particularly overpowering. Predictably, he struggled at Double-A Canton-Akron in 1994. The debate is now seemingly moot, as Carter underwent Tommy John surgery after an early 1995 elbow injury, robbing him of an essential developmental season. By the time Carter returns, he will have been bypassed by several younger, better prospects.

CARTER, LARRY - TR - Age 30
Rose to the majors in 1992, but his 1993 season was shortened by injury.

CASIAN, LARRY - TL - Age 30
A mediocre lefty reliever, Casian had a good year split between Triple-A Iowa and the Cubs. He's a journeyman at best.

	W	SV	ERA	IP	H	BB	SO	B/I	$
1994 Two Teams	1	1	7.35	49	73	16	20	1.82	
1995 Chicago NL	1	0	1.93	23	23	15	11	1.63	0
1996 *Projection* >>>	2	1	4.73	42	50	15	19	1.55	-

CASTILLO, FRANK - TR - Age 27
Castillo returned very strong from injuries which wrecked most of his 1994 season. He's not a hard thrower but knows how to pitch and how to set up hitters. Castillo is an intelligent control pitcher who can be a consistent ten or twelve game winner in the big leagues.

	W	SV	ERA	IP	H	BB	SO	B/I	$
1994 Chicago NL	2	0	4.30	23	25	5	19	1.30	0

	W	SV	ERA	IP	H	BB	SO	B/I	$
1995 Chicago NL	11	0	3.21	188	179	52	135	1.23	14
1996 *Projection* >>>	10	0	3.60	190	186	52	136	1.25	12

CASTILLO, JUAN - TR - Age 25
Castillo was acquired by the Astros from the Mets in the Pete Harnisch trade. He was very disappointing in ten starts at Triple-A Tucson, but fared better in twelve starts after being sent down to Double-A Jackson. He needs a strong year in 1996 to earn a shot at the majors. Steady progress up the Mets farm earned Castillo a brief major league trial in 1994.

CASTILLO, TONY - TL - Age 33
Everyone, including his manager, said that he was getting saves because there wasn't anyone else. He doesn't throw hard enough to be a prototypical closer but did everything an effective pitcher should do. Castillo will be a lefty setup man. With 8 blown saves in 21 opportunities, he's not likely to be used in many save situations in 1996.

	W	SV	ERA	IP	H	BB	SO	B/I	$
1994 Toronto AL	5	1	2.51	68	66	28	43	1.38	8
1995 Toronto AL	1	13	3.22	72	64	24	38	1.21	17
1996 *Projection* >>>	3	5	3.20	70	64	23	39	1.24	11

CASTRO, NELSON - TR - Age 24
Primarily a setup man, Castro has the rubber arm to log a lot of bullpen innings. He briefly advance to Triple-A Albuquerque for the first time after a consistent season at Double-A San Antonio. Castro could be in the majors by 1997, probably as a long man out of the bullpen.

CEDENO, BLAS - TR - Age 23
Cedeno was switched to the bullpen in Double-A in 1994 after being used as a starter in Single-A in 1993. He took to his new role very well and had a solid year. In '95 he stayed at Double-A with a respectable 3.46 ERA working mainly in middle relief. His biggest asset: youth.

CENSALE, SILVIO - TL - Age 24
The Phils' 1993 tenth round draftee bounced back with an exceptional season at Class-A Piedmont after losing the entire 1994 season to injury. He is a hard thrower who has regained most of his velocity and possesses solid control for a power pitcher. However, he could ill afford to lose that 1994 season, as he was already older than most of his league peers.

CHAPIN, DARRIN - TR - Age 30
Once a fringe major leaguer, Chapin has struggled mightily in his last two Triple-A campaigns. He's a journeyman reliever who has reached the end of his journey.

CHARLTON, NORM - TL - Age 33
Piniella picked him off the the Phillies junk pile and loves him. He's as tough and smart a competitor as you'll find, and he pitched like it was 1990 for Seattle. He'll close for Piniella until his arm falls apart, which unfortunately has been Norm's tendency.

	W	SV	ERA	IP	H	BB	SO	B/I	$
1994 Philadelphia NL				Did Not Play					
1995 Philadelphia NL	2	0	7.36	22	23	15	12	1.73	
1995 Seattle AL	2	14	1.51	47	23	16	58	0.83	20
1996 *Projection* >>>	3	19	3.28	51	33	22	52	1.10	25

CHAVEZ, TONY - TR - Age 25
With 16 saves at Single A in 1994, Chavez got some exposure at Double-A and Triple-A in 1995 but spent most of the year still in A-ball and needs more time to succeed at the higher levels. He better hurry.

CHITREN, STEVE - TR - Age 28
Chitren has twice been considered a closer candidate, first in Oakland, then in Baltimore. Since he lost the pop on his fastball, Chitren has struggled at Triple-A Rochester. In 1995 he threw just four innings before quitting for the year. He'll have to regain the velocity on his fastball or he's done.

CHOUINARD, BOB - TR - Age 23
Chouinard had a good season for Double-A Huntsville where he won 14 games. He has excellent control, but his mediocre strikeout/innings ratio suggests he is still beneath several other young pitchers on the Oakland depth chart. He'still young with plenty of time to improve and is at least two years away from the majors.

CHRISMAN, JIM - TR - Age 25
Royals farmhand had a good 1994 in relief at Single A Wilmington with 8 saves and a 1.91 ERA. Needs to step it up to get to the next level, but is behind Enrique Burgos.

CHRISTIANSEN, JASON - TL - Age 26
This hard-throwing lefty had a good first half for the Pirates as a rookie in 1995 but struggled mightily after the break when his curveball left him. He had good hits-per-innings and control numbers in the minors and should develop into an above-average set-up reliever.

	W	SV	ERA	IP	H	BB	SO	B / I	$
1995 Pittsburgh NL	1	0	4.15	56	49	34	53	1.48	-
1996 Projection >>>	3	1	4.10	64	56	35	60	1.42	1

CHRISTMAN, SCOTT - TL - Age 24
Chicago's number one pick in 1993 has pitched well in the low minors despite a poor record (largely due to a lack of offensive and defensive support). The Sox corrected some mechanical flaws in Christman's delivery and he improved as the year progressed. He's still years away, having struggled (6.39 ERA) in 12 starts at Double-A in 1995.

CHRISTOPHER, MIKE - TR - Age 32
Christopher is the perfect example of a pitcher who does not beat himself. He seized his first extended shot at the major leagues in '95 after spending a decade in the minor leagues. Christopher won each of his four decisions and stranded 30 of the 33 runners he inherited. He should pitch 50 capable innings for the Tigers in '96.

	W	SV	ERA	IP	H	BB	SO	B / I	$
1995 Detroit AL	4	1	3.82	61	71	14	34	1.40	4
1996 Projection >>>	3	1	3.88	50	58	12	28	1.40	2

CIMORELLI, FRANK - TR - Age 25
Since moving to the bullpen full time in 1992, Cimorelli has totaled 17 saves. He's just another pitcher in a crowd of middle reliever/setup men.

CLARK, DERA -TR - Age 30
Clark is an older pitcher who has spent five rather undistinguished years in Triple-A as a set-up man or middle reliever. Triple-A appears to be the highest he can go.

CLARK, MARK - TR - Age 27
Clark garnered some attention with his 11-3 1994 campaign, which was largely the product of generous run support. The myth of Mark Clark was exposed in 1995, as lefties hit him at a .318 clip, and he continued to be vulnerable to the gopher ball (60 homers in 497 career innings). The curveball specialist was left off of the postseason roster, signifying his loss of rank in the organization. He has a plus curveball which is tough on righties, so he might have a future as a situational bullpen righty.

	W	SV	ERA	IP	H	BB	SO	B / I	$
1994 Cleveland AL	11	0	3.82	127	133	40	60	1.36	12
1995 Cleveland AL	9	0	5.27	124	143	42	68	1.48	2
1996 Projection >>>	5	0	4.67	111	123	35	57	1.42	1

CLARK, TERRY - TR - Age 35
Pitching in organized ball since 1979, Clark has spent almost nine years in Triple-A. Last year, he got the mid-season call from the Orioles because the phenoms in their bullpen had trouble getting guys out. Clark pitched very well, but

struggled in September. He's a capable middle reliever, but not much else.

	W	SV	ERA	IP	H	BB	SO	B/I	$
1995 Two Teams	2	1	3.59	42	43	20	20	1.48	2
1996 Projection >>>	2	1	3080	33	33	16	20	1.48	1

CLAYTON, ROYAL - TR - Age 30
Long time Yankee farm hand had a decent year in 1994. Clayton had 12 wins and five saves, but still averaged over one hit per inning.

CLEMENS, ROGER - TR - Age 33
The Rocket struggled through injuries in a disappointing season in 1995. He still has great stuff, though he was often inconsistent with it. Clemens was talking retirement in 1995, particularly if he got the World Series ring he covets so much. Boston's quick elimination in the first round of the playoffs should mean Clemens will be back again in 1996; look for a big rebound.

	W	SV	ERA	IP	H	BB	SO	B/I	$
1994 Boston AL	9	0	2.85	170	124	71	168	1.14	24
1995 Boston AL	10	0	4.18	140	141	60	132	1.44	7
1996 Projection >>>	15	0	3.69	190	172	81	180	1.33	16

CLONTZ, BRAD - TR - Age 24
This hard thrower jumped directly from a Double-A Southern League All-Star berth in 1994 into a big league set-up role in 1995. He saved a few games early in the season before Braves management finally handed the closer's job to Mark Wohlers. Clontz has a good fastball and will be a very successful set-up man for the 1996 Braves, and he could eventually become a closer in his own right for another team farther down the road.

	W	SV	ERA	IP	H	BB	SO	B/I	$
1995 Atlanta NL	8	4	3.65	69	71	22	55	1.35	8
1996 Projection >>>	5	2	3.54	47	48	15	37	1.35	4

COCHRAN, JAMIE - TR - Age 27
Cochran paid for his record-setting 46-save 1993 season with an elbow injury that limited his activity last year.

COGGIN, DAVE - TR - Age 19
The Phillies' signed their first round sandwich pick despite the fact that many clubs considered him unsignable due to his commitment to play football at Clemson University. Coggin has a devastating 95 MPH fastball and a prototypical pitcher's body (6'3", 190 lbs.). Coggin struggled with his control in his pro debut in Rookie ball, but he showed the seeds of a solid repertoire. If he secures a rotation spot in a full season league in 1996, he could soon find himself on the fast track to the majors.

COLE, VICTOR - TR - Age 28
Cole is the first Russian player in American professional baseball in many decades, but he's not much more than a human interest story. He really hasn't pitched well above Double-A and has bounced around from one organization to another over the last few years. He's a journeyman minor leaguer at best.

COLEMAN, BILLY - TR - Age 27
In his fourth pro season, Coleman made great strides, overpowering Sally League batters in 1994. Given a shot at Double-A later in '94 and again in '95, he had serious control problems and now has a cloudy future.

COLON, BARTOLO - TR - Age 20
Colon emerged as one of the finest pitching prospects in all of baseball with a dominant season at high A-ball Kinston (Carolina League) in the Indians' organization. He was cited for having the league's best fastball and was named the circuit's best pitching and overall prospect. He brings it at 95 MPH with pinpoint control, and greatly improved his curve and changeup in the past season. He was shut down as a precaution in late July with a bone bruise on his pitching elbow. Colon will start 1996 at Double-A and should continue his rapid ascent.

COMBS, PAT - TL - Age 29
The Phillies top draft pick of 1988 finally washed out of their system after going 4-4 with a 5.43 ERA at Triple-A Scranton/Wilkes-Barre. He hooked on with the Brewers Triple-A affiliate in New Orleans to finish the year, but wasn't

any better there. Combs' promising debut in 1989 in his first pro season, when he jumped all the way from Class A to the majors to post go 4-0 in six starts is only a distant memory now.

	W	SV	ERA	IP	H	BB	SO	B / I	$
1994 Scranton AAA	6	0	6.29	137	167	75	70	1.76	
1995 New Orleans AAA	1	0	5.40	15	19	13	10	2.14	

COMPRES, FIDEL - TR - Age 30
A career minor leaguer, Compres has been waiting ten years. A change in organizations (from the Cardinals to the Padres) didn't help, so he may never make it.

CONE, DAVID - TR - Age 33
The "have gun, will travel" of the major league pitching profession, Cone has matured mentally without losing any of his live arm velocity or fine control of his big fastball and splitter. He's durable, has the stuff for blow-'em-away strikeouts, and now uses his defense wisely too. In the past he has struggled in April and then come on strong in the warm weather.

	W	SV	ERA	IP	H	BB	SO	B / I	$
1994 Kansas City AL	16	0	2.94	171	130	54	132	1.07	29
1995 Toronto - New York AL	18	0	3.57	229	195	88	191	1.24	23
1996 Projection >>>	20	0	3.36	240	199	89	194	1.20	30

CONNER, SCOTT - TR - Age 24
Although reliever Scott Conner had only a so-so ERA in Double-A last year, he didn't give up very many hits, and he got a lot of strikeouts. He's developing nicely and could be in the Orioles bullpen soon.

CONNERS, CHAD - TR - Age 24
A young reliever at Single A Winston-Salem. Conners got 11 saves and a pair of wins with a 1.18 ERA and a 0.80 in 1994.

CONVERSE, JIM - TR - Age 24
Converse hasn't developed beyond the Triple-A level and was worse than that in 1995; his combined Triple-A ERA was 5.61 for Tacoma and Omaha and he wasn't any better for the Royals or Mariners in the big leagues. His stuff is pretty pedestrian. Converse will have to take a significant stride forward if he's ever to become a big league regular.

	W	SV	ERA	IP	H	BB	SO	B / I	$
1994 Seattle AL	0	0	8.69	48	73	40	39	2.32	-
1995 Seattle-Kansas City AL	1	1	6.56	23	28	16	14	1.89	-
1996 Projection >>>	2	1	5.80	38	40	22	27	1.63	-

COOK, ANDY - TR - Age 28
Cook pitched better in relief the last two years than he had as a starter, but he's still not a real prospect.

	W	SV	ERA	IP	H	BB	SO	B / I	$
1995 Columbus AAA	2	2	3.36	56	53	19	28	1.28	

COOK, DENNIS - TL - Age 33
Cook pitched decently for Texas, his fifth major league team. He should have a few more seasons as a bullpen lefty in him. Cook has to keep the ball low or it leaves the park (one homer every 6.1 innings).

	W	SV	ERA	IP	H	BB	SO	B / I	$
1994 Chicago AL	3	0	3.55	33	29	14	26	1.30	-
1995 Two Teams	0	2	4.53	57	63	26	53	1.54	1
1996 Projection >>>	2	1	4.39	58	61	25	50	1.47	0

COOKE, STEVE - TL - Age 26
Cooke's 1995 season was ruined by nerve damage and bursitis in his shoulder. However, he was scheduled to pitch winter ball in the Dominican Rebuplic and hoped to be 100 percent by spring training. He had a solid rookie year in 1993 then slumped in 1994 as he hid the shoulder problem. He's a good bet to come back and win 10-12 games.

	W	SV	ERA	IP	H	BB	SO	B / I	$
1994 Pittsburgh NL	4	0	5.02	134	157	46	74	1.51	-

	W	SV	ERA	IP	H	BB	SO	B/I	$
1995			Did Not Play						
1996 Projection >>>	10	0	4.71	152	170	49	87	1.44	-

COPPINGER, ROCKY - TR - Age 22
Big (6-5 and 240 lbs.) Coppinger rocketed through the Orioles' minor league system last year, beginning the year at Single-A, making some starts in Double-A, and finishing at Triple-A. He is a power pitcher with a good fastball and a power slider. He is also a smart pitcher who understands hitters, and he could be pitching in Camden Yards sometime in 1996.

	W	SV	ERA	IP	H	BB	SO	B/I	$
1995 Rochester AAA	3	0	1.04	34	23	17	19	1.16	

CORBIN, ARCHIE - TR - Age 28
A hard-throwing right-hander who has never been able to harnass his ability, Corbin nearly made the Pirates' opening-day roster as a non-roster invitee in the spring of 1994 but has been dogged by arm problems and inconsistency since.

	W	SV	ERA	IP	H	BB	SO	B/I	$
1994 Buffalo AAA	0	0	4.76	22	14	18	23	1.41	
1995 Calgary AAA	1	1	8.56	61	76	55	54	2.15	

CORMIER, RHEAL - TL - Age 28
Acquired with Luis Alicea in an off-season deal with the Cardinals, Cormier gave Boston the best year of his career while shuttling between long relief and the starting rotation. He can't really throw hard enough for a closer and lacks the stamina to be an effective starter, so a long relief job is ideal for Cormier and his sinker. Look for him to again fill an important relief role in 1996.

	W	SV	ERA	IP	H	BB	SO	B/I	$
1994 St. Louis NL	3	0	5.45	39	40	7	26	1.18	1
1995 Boston AL	7	0	4.07	115	131	31	69	1.41	6
1996 Projection >>>	7	0	4.31	109	121	26	65	1.36	5

CORNELIUS, REID - TR - Age 25
After making Team USA in 1998, Cornelius has had a career featuring mainly arm problems. After moving to the Mets farm in 1995, Cornelius finally stayed healthy long enough to produce his best pro stats ever, capped with ten starts in the majors. If the Mets find him a rotation spot, he could be one of the big surprises of 1996.

	W	SV	ERA	IP	H	BB	SO	B/I	$
1995 Norfolk AAA	8	0	1.67	81	73	24	50	1.20	
1995 New York NL	3	0	5.54	66	75	30	39	1.59	-
1996 Projection >>>	6	0	4.97	116	133	43	68	1.52	-

CORNETT, BRAD - TR - Age 27
He spent his few significant innings repeating all the mistakes he had shown in 1994 with the Blue Jays. He wasn't throwing hard and was wild high and inside to the few hitters he faced in Toronto. At his age, his stock has dropped significantly from where it was a few years ago.

	W	SV	ERA	IP	H	BB	SO	B/I	$
1994 Toronto AL	1	0	6.68	31	40	11	22	1.65	-
1995 Syracuse AAA	0	0	4.91	11	13	4	3	1.55	
1995 Toronto AL	0	0	9.00	5	9	3	4	2.40	-

CORPS, EDWIN - TR - Age 23
Corps won thirteen games for Double-A Shreveport, but didn't pitch very well. His awful K/IP ratio is ominous; he's at least two years away, if he ever makes it.

CORREA, RAMSER - TR - Age 25
Correa was the closer at Double-A San Antonio in 1995 but was inconsistent. The big guy throws heat, but often has control problems. He needs a reliable breaking pitch.

CORSI, JIM - TR - Age 34
Corsi is an aging one-out righty still coming back from a serious shoulder injury in 1993.

	W	SV	ERA	IP	H	BB	SO	B/I	$
1994 Edmonton AAA	0	0	4.50	22	29	10	15	1.77	
1995 Oakland AL	2	2	2.20	45	31	26	26	1.27	6
1996 Projection >>>	1	1	3.06	30	21	18	18	1.29	2

COSTELLO, FRED - TR - Age 30
Aging prospect showed little in Phoenix last season, and must be considered a longshot at this point.

COURTRIGHT, JOHN - TL - Age 25
The player the Twins received for David McCarty, Courtright is a lefthander who has started throughout his career, including at Triple-A Salt Lake for Minnesota. He will try to become the next Mark Guthrie.

	W	SV	ERA	IP	H	BB	SO	B/I	$
1994 Indianapolis AAA	9	0	3.55	142	144	46	73	1.34	
1995 Salt Lake AAA	3	0	6.80	84	108	36	42	1.70	

COX, DANNY - TR - Age 36
After his worst season in the major leagues, there was talk that perhaps he has begun his exit. Cox wasn't throwing nearly as hard as he has the previous few years and was unusually wild. Entering the winter, his future with the Blue Jays looked cloudy.

	W	SV	ERA	IP	H	BB	SO	B/I	$
1994 Toronto AL	1	3	1.45	18	7	7	14	0.75	7
1995 Toronto AL	1	0	7.40	45	57	33	38	2.00	-
1996 Projection >>>	1	0	5.62	31	32	18	27	1.64	-

CRABTREE, TIM - TR - Age 26
Crabtree arrived in the major leagues and had a very good debut. Called by some the closer of the future, he now has all of the elements required for that role except for a convincing fastball, which he continues to develop. He proved enough to start 1996 in the majors at least.

	W	SV	ERA	IP	H	BB	SO	B/I	$
1995 Toronto AL	0	0	3.09	32	30	13	21	1.34	1
1996 Projection >>>	2	1	3.67	54	51	22	35	1.34	3

CRAWFORD, CARLOS - TR - Age 24
Crawford's progress stagnated somewhat in 1995. He couldn't cut it as a Triple-A reliever and was sent back to Double-A, where he approximated his 1994 success as a starter. He would appear to be best suited for a starting role, but the quickest road to Cleveland would be through the bullpen. He needs a change of scenery, and in any event should not be expected to make a significant major league impact.

CRAWFORD, JOE - TL - Age 25
Mets farmhand Crawford pitched in Double-A ball posting a 2.23 ERA and then at Triple-A, not missing a beat.

	W	SV	ERA	IP	H	BB	SO	B/I	$
1995 Norfolk AAA	1	0	1.93	18	9	4	13	0.70	

CREEK, DOUG - TL - Age 27
After four seasons as a struggling starter in the Cardinals' farm system, Creek moved to the bullpen and wound up spending September in St. Louis. He turned his career around last season and his starting days are likely over. He's a little old at 27 but lefties often develop late. Creek should have a career as a bullpen specialist.

	W	SV	ERA	IP	H	BB	SO	B/I	$
1995 Louisville AAA	3	0	3.23	30	20	21	29	1.34	
1996 Projection >>>	1	0	3.96	35	30	20	52	1.44	-

CREEK, RYAN - TR - Age 23
Creek was Houston's 34th round draft choice in 1992 but has moved toward the head of the class. He led the Double-A Jackson staff with nine wins and 120 strikeouts. He has a chance to reach the majors if he continues the progress he has shown in his first three years.

CROGHAN, ANDY - TR - Age 26
Made the jump from Single A to Double-A Albany in the reliever role. Croghan had a 1.72 ERA, 16 saves, and 38 strikeouts in 37 innings pitched at Class A in 1994 but has looked more vulnerable at Triple-A.

	W	SV	ERA	IP	H	BB	SO	B/I	$
1995 Columbus AAA	1	4	3.60	25	21	22	22	1.72	

CROMWELL, NATE - TL - Age 27
The Astros selected southpaw Cromwell from the Padres in the Rule V draft, but found him wanting and returned him. Except for his ERA, his minor league statistics like strikeouts and hits per inning all look good, indicating some upward potential.

CROSS, JESSE - TR - Age 28
Cross was the epitome of a workhorse last season. He also won his final six decisions to lead Syracuse's run to the playoffs. If Darren Hall hadn't come through in the Toronto bullpen, Cross might have been an alternative. He still has a chance with a major league club needing pitching.

CUMMINGS, JOHN - TL - Age 26
A failed starter in Seattle, Cummings was converted to a lefty setup role by the Dodgers and pitched well in a limited trial. He is a control pitcher and there is no reason to expect him to expand his role in 1996.

	W	SV	ERA	IP	H	BB	SO	B/I	$
1994 Seattle AL	2	0	5.63	64	66	37	33	1.61	-
1995 Seattle AL	0	0	11.81	5	8	7	4	2.81	
1995 Los Angeles NL	3	0	3.00	39	38	10	21	1.23	0
1996 *Projection* >>>	2	0	3.80	57	65	13	30	1.36	1

CUNNANE, WILL - TR - Age 22
Cunnane exploded onto the scene with an amazing 1994 season, when he posted a 1.43 ERA at Class A Kane County. The Marlins jumped him a level to Double-A Portland in 1995 and he continued to pitch well. He throws a hard, straight fastball with extreme precision, though he was much more hittable in 1995. Cunnane appears to have a major league future, though his repertoire might be better suited for the bullpen. In any event, expect a full Triple-A campaign as a starter in 1997.

CURTIS, CHRIS - TR - Age 24
Curtis needs a third pitch to be effective as a starter and doesn't have the dominant stuff that a closer needs. Curtis could be tried in long relief, but he doesn't appear to be much of a prospect.

	W	SV	ERA	IP	H	BB	SO	B/I	$
1995 Oklahoma City AAA	3	5	5.00	77	81	39	40	1.56	

CZAJKOWSKI, JIM - TR - Age 32
Czajkowski led Triple-A Colorado Springs with 17 saves in 1995. He's not an especially hard thrower, though, and walks too many batters to be successful in a setup role. Czajkowski's best bet to return to the majors will be as a middle reliever.

	W	SV	ERA	IP	H	BB	SO	B/I	$
1994 Colorado NL	0	0	4.15	8	9	6	2	1.73	-
1995 Colorado Springs AAA	3	17	5.06	83	90	52	56	1.70	

DAAL, OMAR - TL - Age 24
Apparently Daal is being groomed as a lefty specialist. In 99 games with Los Angeles, he has thrown a total of 69 innings. He was pretty terrible in that role in 1995 with a 7.20 ERA and will have some competition in 1996 from newly-acquired John Cummings and Mark Guthrie.

	W	SV	ERA	IP	H	BB	SO	B/I	$
1994 Los Angeles NL	0	0	3.29	13	12	5	9	1.24	-
1995 Albuquerque AAA	2	1	4.05	53	56	26	46	1.53	
1995 Los Angeles NL	4	0	7.20	20	29	15	11	2.20	-

DALTON, MIKE - TL - Age 33
When he didn't get a callup at the end of a strong 1992 season, Dalton fell into the career minor leaguer stereotype.

D'AMICO, JEFF - TR - Age 20
D'Amico, a Milwaukee first-round draft pick in 1993, has not played pro ball. He signed late in '93, and last June underwent surgery to remove a bone spur from his right elbow.

D'ANDREA, MIKE - TR - Age 26
Too old to be reaching Double-A for the first time, as D'Andrea did in 1995, he also had a rather forgettable year, going 3-6 with a 4.88 ERA as a long reliever and spot starter. D'Andrea has a good fastball, but not much else, and he just can't get it past hitters in the high minors. He'll get another chance in Greenville in 1996.

DARENSBOURG, VIC - TL - Age 25
This little lefty (5'10", 165 lbs.) had a chance to make the Marlins' 1995 roster as a reliever, but he lost the whole season to extensive elbow surgery. The Marlins are second-guessing their strategy to use him as a starter at Double-A Portland in 1994 to "build up his arm strength". He needs velocity to be effective - if he isn't whiffing batters in the spring, his career is in jeopardy. When healthy, he gobbles up righties - if the elbow's sound he'll start 1996 at Triple-A Charlotte.

DARLING, RON - TR - Age 35
Yale alumnus Darling had his moments during 1995 but got released in August nonetheless. A second comeback (his 1994 revival was a success) now appears unlikely. Dave Duncan and Tony LaRussa did everything they could, and it wasn't enough to get through two years.

	W	SV	ERA	IP	H	BB	SO	B/I	$
1994 Oakland AL	10	0	4.50	160	162	59	108	1.38	-
1995 Oakland AL	4	0	6.23	104	124	46	69	1.64	-
1996 Projection >>>	7	0	5.35	155	172	61	101	1.50	-

DARWIN, DANNY - TR - Age 40
Darwin has lost quite a bit of velocity and now has to try to fool hitters. Last season, very few were fooled and his career may be over.

	W	SV	ERA	IP	H	BB	SO	B/I	$
1994 Boston AL	7	0	6.30	75	101	24	54	1.65	
1995 Two Teams	3	0	7.45	99	131	31	58	1.64	-

DARWIN, JEFF - TR - Age 26
Another one of the Mariners' tall relievers, Darwin was the righthanded closer for Triple-A Tacoma in 1995, his second straight year in that role. Darwin could earn a shot in the topsy-turvy Mariners bullpen in 1996.

	W	SV	ERA	IP	H	BB	SO	B/I	$
1995 Tacoma AAA	7	12	2.70	63	51	21	51	1.14	
1996 Projection >>>	1	1	4.12	30	37	4	8	1.38	1

DASPIT, JAMIE - TR - Age 26
Daspit is a tall righthander with an intimidating fastball who has pitched with some success for two years in the Astro system after being acquired from the Dodger organization. In 1995 he was used exclusively in middle relief at Triple-A Tucson. He was removed from the 40-man major league roster in mid-season and is not expected to compete for a major league job in 1996.

DAVIS, MARK - TL - Age 35
Former NL Cy Young winner (1989) Davis tossed just nine innings at Triple-A Charlotte in 1995. He made the Marlins major league roster in September but didn't pitch.

DAVIS, RAY - TR - Age 23
A very late pick in 1991 (61st round), Davis had an up-and-down year as a starter for Double-A Arkansas in 1995. His good fastball sometimes betrays him and he has poor control in the strike zone, making the pitches too fat. An emotional pitcher, Davis sometimes loses his concentration. He should return to Double-A in 1996.

DAVIS, STORM - TR - Age 34
Davis hasn't been an effective major league pitcher for about five years. He was cut by the Reds after five useless innings at Triple-A Indianapolis in 1995 and may finally be finished for good.

DAVIS, TIM - TR - Age 25
If healthy, Davis could deliver a big season. He looked good as a starter in spring training in 1995.

	W	SV	ERA	IP	H	BB	SO	B/I	$
1994 Seattle AL	2	2	4.01	49	57	25	28	1.66	2
1995 Tacoma AAA	0	0	5.40	13	15	4	13	1.43	
1995 Seattle AL	2	0	6.38	24	30	18	19	2.00	-
1996 *Projection* >>>	5	0	4.75	90	90	48	60	1.53	-

DAVISON, SCOTT - TR - Age 25
Out of pro baseball for two years, this former infielder quickly jumped through the Mariners system from lower Class A ball in 1994 to the majors in 1995. He's been a big strikeout pitcher in his 104 professional innings, fanning 110. In 1995 he struck out 50 in 40.2 innings while saving ten games for Double-A Port City. Davison will be one of many righthanders battling for a spot role in the Mariners' bullpen in 1996.

	W	SV	ERA	IP	H	BB	SO	B/I	$
1995 Seattle AL	0	0	6.23	4	7	1	3	1.85	

DEBRINO - ROB - TR - Age 22
Minnesota's ace at Class A Fort Wayne racked up 11 saves and 58 strikeouts in 72 innings pitched.

DEDRICK, JIM - TR - Age 27
An emergency opening in the Orioles' bullpen got Dedrick to the majors for the first time. His control was a mess in the short major league stint, but he had a marvelous campaign for Triple-A Rochester, going 4-0 with a 1.77 ERA in a long relief/spot starter role. Dedrick will have a chance to win a spot as the last guy in the Orioles' bullpen again in 1996.

	W	SV	ERA	IP	H	BB	SO	B/I	$
1995 Baltimore AL	0	0	2.35	7	8	6	3	1.83	-

DEJESUS, JAVI - TL - Age 24
Flame thrower with a 0.93 ERA and 55 strikeouts in 39 innings of work in 1994.

DEJESUS, JOSE - TR - Age 31
This big righthander throws hard and has had a couple of good seasons in the majors. 1995 was not one of them, however, as DeJesus struggled through his worst season at Triple-A Omaha. He still brings the heat, but often has no idea where it's going. DeJesus has never completely recovered from a complete tear of his rotator cuff in 1992.

DELAHOYA JAVIER - TR - Age 26
A five-year vet of the Dodgers' farm system Delahoya was victimized at Double-A Portland, in the Marlin chain, resulting in a demotion to Single-A. Has a very live arm, evidenced by the fact that he has struck out more than a batter per inning pitched in his pro career. He must make a major impression in 1995, as the Marlins' best starting pitcher prospects are in the process of passing him.

DE LA MAZA, ROLAND - TR - Age 24
In an extremely quiet, inconspicuous manner, Delamaza has fashioned a 30-8 record in his first three pro seasons. However, he does not rank that high on the list of Indians' starting pitching prospects. He has only adequate velocity, but does have impeccable control. He'll get another shot at Double-A Canton-Akron in 1996 - don't expect him to make a major league impact.

DeLaROSA, FRANCISCO - TR - Age 30
Dela Rosa is a typical ex-prospect who has been in several organizations. He filled several roles at Triple-A Louisville in 1995, but wasn't impressive in any of them. Dela Rosa was a free agent acquisition from the Taiwanese Leagues after the 1994 season.

	W	SV	ERA	IP	H	BB	SO	B/I	$
1995 Louisville AAA	2	0	4.06	115	104	38	66	1.24	

DELEON, JOSE - TR - Age 35
Few players have ever fashioned a longer major-league career (13 years) based more on promise than production. The Expos picked up DeLeon midway through last season to help in the bullpen and he was hit hard. They gladly let him leave as a free agent but someone else will give him a shot in 1996. Why? Because he has so much potential ... even at age 35.

	W	SV	ERA	IP	H	BB	SO	B/I	$
1994 Chicago AL	3	2	3.36	67	48	31	67	1.18	0
1995 Chicago AL	5	0	5.19	67	60	28	53	1.30	
1995 Montreal NL	0	0	7.56	8	7	7	12	1.68	-
1996 Projection >>>	3	0	5.04	62	52	32	55	1.35	-

DE LOS SANTOS, MARIANO - TR - Age 25
His status as a prospect dimmed last season as he was dropped off the 40-man roster in midseason. De Los Santos has an exceptional changeup but his fastball and breaking stuff are ordinary at best. He also constantly battles weight problems, which doesn't help his cause.

DeLUCIA, RICH - TR - Age 31
Selected by the Cardinals from Baltimore in the Rule Five Draft, this former Seattle prospect had his best season in 1995. He excelled in middle relief but don't expect his role to expand into closing anytime soon. Likely, his 1995 season was more of a fluke than anything.

	W	SV	ERA	IP	H	BB	SO	B/I	$
1994 Indianapolis AAA	5	19	2.30	43	22	24	52	1.06	
1994 Cincinnati NL	0	0	4.22	10	9	5	15	1.31	
1995 St. Louis NL	8	0	3.39	82	63	36	76	1.21	7
1996 Projection >>>	5	0	3.80	64	53	30	62	1.29	3

DESHAIES, JIM - TL - Age 35
The definitive lefty finesse pitcher, Deshaies hasn't been effective for years. His 20.25 ERA in two appearances for the Phillies is representative of his slide into obscurity.

	W	SV	ERA	IP	H	BB	SO	B/I	$
1994 Minnesota AL	6	0	7.39	130	170	54	78	1.72	
1995 Philadelphia NL	0	0	20.25	5	15	1	6	3.00	-

DESILVA, JOHN - TR - Age 28
Formerly in the Tigers and Dodger organizations, DeSilva was acquired by the Orioles on the recommendation of manager Phil Regan who was impressed with him in winter ball. Hard throwing DeSilva has struggled as a starter and may be better off in the bullpen

	W	SV	ERA	IP	H	BB	SO	B/I	$
1994 Albuquerque AAA	3	1	7.83	66	90	27	39	1.74	
1995 Rochester AAA	11	0	4.18	150	156	51	82	1.37	
1995 Baltimore AL	1	0	7.27	8	8	7	1	1.73	-
1996 Projection >>>	1	0	4.96	33	35	17	19	1.58	-

DESSENS, ELMER - TR - Age 24
The Pirates purchased Dessens' contract from the Mexican League after the 1994 season and he baffled hitters in the Double-A Southern League last season. He's not a hard thrower but has outstanding control and a good feel for pitching. He will likely start 1996 in Triple-A but could come to the majors quickly.

DETTMER, JOHN - TR - Age 26
Dettmer started nine games for the Rangers in 1994 and went 0-6. Used as a starter and reliever at Triple-A Rochester, he had a so-so year. He has a good fastball and slider and may be better suited as a reliever. Dettmer has a good shot at making the Orioles bullpen as a middle reliever and mop-up man.

	W	SV	ERA	IP	H	BB	SO	B/I	$
1994 Texas AL	0	0	4.33	54	63	20	27	1.54	-
1995 Rochester AAA	4	1	4.68	82	98	16	46	1.38	-
1996 *Projection* >>>	1	0	4.55	31	37	11	15	1.55	-

DEWEY, MARK - TR - Age 31
When healthy, Dewey is a pretty good pitcher in a one-out righty role. In 1989, he led the California League in saves. If the Giants reduce their budget by trading Rod Beck, Dewey is a longshot candidate to pick up some saves.

	W	SV	ERA	IP	H	BB	SO	B/I	$
1994 Pittsburgh NL	2	1	3.68	51	61	19	30	1.56	1
1995 San Francisco NL	1	0	3.13	31	30	17	32	1.48	0
1996 *Projection* >>>	2	1	3.34	46	47	20	36	1.48	1

DIAZ, RALPH - TR - Age 26
Won nine games at AA Harrisburg in 1994, but has now struggled (ERA over six) in two lengthy trials at Triple-A. Must be regarded as a longshot.

DIBBLE, ROB - TR - Age 32
He's now just trying to hang on. Dibble is nowhere near what he used to be.

	W	SV	ERA	IP	H	BB	SO	B/I	$
1994 Cincinnati NL			Did Not Play						
1995 Two Teams	1	1	7.18	26	16	46	26	2.38	-

DICKSON, LANCE - TL - Age 26
Despite a myriad of injuries, Dickson has good stuff and control, and is still young enough to have a career. He broke his hand trying to bunt early in 1994 and later underwent shoulder surgery. Expected to be healthy this season, Dickson will begin at Iowa.

DIPINO, FRANK - TL - Age 39
Released by the Royals at 1993's end, DiPino had little command of his pitches in very short Kansas City stint and was unremarkable at AAA Omaha in 1993. May be finished, but lefties have a way of turning up on major league rosters.

DIPOTO, JERRY - TR - Age 27
Coming back from thyroid cancer, DiPoto became the Mets bullpen workhorse in 1995. He's basically a direct hard thrower with a fastball and slider but now uses a splitfinger effectively too. In a crowded pen his role is necessarily limited, but he can perform any relief role, included that of closer when needed.

	W	SV	ERA	IP	H	BB	SO	B/I	$
1994 Cleveland AL	0	0	8.04	15	26	10	9	2.30	-
1995 New York NL	4	2	3.78	78	77	29	49	1.36	4
1996 *Projection* >>>	3	2	3.82	65	64	25	46	1.36	3

DISHMAN, GLENN - TL - Age 25
Dishman was a rookie last year, and he took his lumps learning his craft in the bigs. Considering both his minor and major league pitching last year, he pitched a lot of innings and was noticeably tired in late August and September when he lost the zip on his fastball and got hit hard. He has a good change-up and excellent control, and he should be in the Padres rotation in 1996. Dishman was impressively consistent and a very cool-under-pressure pitcher in Triple-A, both characteristics that should help be a winner in the majors.

	W	SV	ERA	IP	H	BB	SO	B/I	$
1995 San Diego NL	4	0	5.01	97	104	34	43	1.42	-
1996 *Projection* >>>	6	0	4.71	131	137	44	58	1.38	-

DIXON, STEVE - TL - Age 26
The minors are littered with former Cardinals' farmhands who once had high saves counts but can't make the jump to the major leagues. Dixon did well enough at Triple-A Iowa in 1995, going 6-3 with a 2.85 ERA and leading the team with 53 appearances. He can still get a shot as a situational lefty in a major league bullpen, but he'll never again save twenty games in a season and is no closer candidate.

	W	SV	ERA	IP	H	BB	SO	B/I	$
1995 Iowa AAA	6	0	2.85	41	34	19	38	1.30	
1996 *Projection* >>>	1	1	5.10	32	35	11	16	1.44	-

DODD, ROBERT - TL - Age 23
The Phils' 1994 14th round draft pick is a crafty lefthander who advanced rapidly in his first full pro season, finishing up in the bullpen of the Double-A champion Reading Phillies. Overall he doesn't quite measure up to his competition, which includes Carlton Loewer, Ryan Nye, Matt Beech and Rich Hunter, among others, but Dodd could find a niche as one of the only viable lefthanded relief prospects in the Phils' organization. Look for him to be the lefthanded setup man at Double-A in 1996.

DOHERTY, JOHN - TR - Age 28
Doherty stabilized his career in '95, as he brought his ERA down from '94 while working in long relief for Detroit. He can retire a righthanded hitter (.249 opponent batting average in '95) and has stayed healthy, offering hope that he can forge a career as a reliever. Don't look for Doherty to succeed until the Tigers start to receive more innings from their starters, thus lightening his workload.

	W	SV	ERA	IP	H	BB	SO	B/I	$
1994 Detroit AL	6	0	6.48	101	139	26	28	1.63	-
1995 Detroit AL	5	6	5.10	113	130	37	46	1.48	6
1996 *Projection* >>>	3	4	4.92	104	111	26	51	1.32	6

DOOLAN, BLAKE - TR - Age 27
Doolan posted gaudy numbers for a reliever at Double-A Reading, earning 11 wins and 16 saves. He led all Eastern League pitchers in wins through May 1995 - the Phils magically scored runs every time he entered a tie game. Don't believe the numbers. 1995 was his third shot at Double-A, and the first in which he experienced any level of success. He did not possess the stuff to get the ball past Double-A hitters, and will reach his Triple-A ceiling in 1996.

DOORNEWEERD, DAVID - TR - Age 23
The Pirates' second-round pick in the 1991 draft (out of high school), he was impressive early with his advanced knowledge of pitching. However, Doorneweerd has struggled since being drafted and had arm problems. He's still young, so it's too early to give up on him.

DORLARQUE, AARON - TR - Age 26
Dorlarque was outstanding in his first two pro seasons, but hasn't had as much success in the higher minors. His strikeout count has dipped with each promotion and in 1995 he had a lot of trouble retiring righthanded batters at Triple-A Omaha - not a good sign for a righthanded reliever. Dorlarque needs a big year in 1996 to re-establish himself as a prospect.

	W	SV	ERA	IP	H	BB	SO	B/I	$
1995 Omaha AAA	2	4	4.24	40	38	15	24	1.32	

DOUGHERTY, JIM - TR - Age 28
Dougherty is a sidewheeling righthander who was a successful closer in all four of his minor league seasons. He is not overpowering and has trouble with lefthanded batters. He was a useful middle reliever with Houston in 1995 and is likely to continue in that role.

	W	SV	ERA	IP	H	BB	SO	B/I	$
1995 Houston NL	8	0	4.92	67	76	25	49	1.50	1
1996 *Projection* >>>	5	0	4.73	63	68	20	46	1.40	-

DOYLE, IAN - TR - Age 24
Doyle was shut down last year after just eight mostly ineffective games. He had two good seasons as a closer in A ball.

DRABEK, DOUG - TR - Age 33
Drabek had a disappointing season in 1995, posting, by far, the highest ERA of his career. Without an overpowering fastball, he must rely on changing speeds and pinpoint control to be effective. At times he was able to do this but, more often than not, he was hit hard. He came back strong in 1994 after a bad year in 1993 but, the odds are against it happening again in 1996.

	W	SV	ERA	IP	H	BB	SO	B/I	$
1994 Houston NL	12	0	2.84	164	132	45	121	1.07	23
1995 Houston NL	10	0	4.77	185	205	54	143	1.40	1
1996 *Projection* >>>	13	0	4.05	218	218	61	163	1.28	10

DRAHMAN, BRIAN - TR - Age 29
For the first time in five seasons, Drahman did not pitch in the majors. He was effective, but not dominant, as a part-time closer in Triple-A. Drahman could still surface as a long man in somebody's bullpen, but the likelihood of any major impact is very slight.

	W	SV	ERA	IP	H	BB	SO	B/I	$
1994 Florida NL	0	0	6.23	13	15	6	7	1.62	2
1995 Two AAA Teams	2	4	2.83	35	39	15	22	1.55	-
1996 *Projection* >>>	1	0	5.07	31	34	13	17	1.52	-

DREIFORT, DARREN - TR - Age 23
The first pitcher drafted in June of 1993, Dreifort rocketed to the major leagues for six saves in 1994, then blew out his elbow and missed the entire 1995 season. With a full recovery he'd have to be considered a closer candidate in Los Angeles in 1996 or 1997.

	W	SV	ERA	IP	H	BB	SO	B/I	$
1994 Los Angeles NL	0	6	6.21	29	45	15	22	2.07	1
1996 *Projection* >>>	1	2	4.52	30	33	12	23	1.50	0

DRESSENDORFER, KIRK - TR - Age 26
Shoulder surgery in 1992 has reduced this 1990 first round sandwich pick by the Athletics to a shell of his former self. He has thrown just 56.2 innings over the last four years and hasn't won a game since 1991, when he last appeared in the big leagues. Dressendorfer has a lot to prove, particularly in regards to his stamina.

DREWS, MATT - TR - Age 21
Drews, the Yankees' first-round draft pick in 1993, turned in an impressive pro debut last season. Drews' best pitch is a low-90s fastball. He should arrive in New York in 1997 or '98.

DREYER, STEVE - TR - Age 26
Dreyer suffered through shoulder and elbow problems in 1995, then was outrighted off the major league roster when he refused to play winter ball. Dreyer is a control specialist who has not been able to pitch effectively at the major league level. He is still young enough to put his career back together, but will need a change of organization and sustained health in order to do it.

DRISKILL, TRAVIS - TR - Age 24
The Indians' 1993 4th-round pick from Texas Tech was a dominant closer for Single-A Columbus in the Sally League. In 1994 he chalked up 35 saves, gave up far less than a hit per inning pitched, and averaged close to 12 strikeouts per nine innings pitched. The Indians' envision him as a potential future closer, and would like to see him advance more quickly than he did in 1995, when he gave up a hit per inning and yielded a 4.66 ERA after moving up to Double-A Canton-Akron.

DRUMRIGHT, MIKE - TR - Age 22
The Tigers' first round pick out of Wichita State in '95, Drumright has the raw ability one looks for in a starter, and he pitched well at Class A and Double-A in '95. Drumright does need at least a full season at Double-A, but he should reach the majors in '96. He looks like Detroit's future ace.

DUBOIS, BRIAN - TL - Age 29
After a history of arm problems, DuBois wore out the Orioles patience and was released in late June 1994. But he was signed by the Phillies and had a solid year in the minors. He had the "Tommy John" surgery on his elbow three years ago and had a fair '95 season on an extension of the major league bench. Key asset: that "TL".

	W	SV	ERA	IP	H	BB	SO	B/I	$
1995 Scranton AAA	1	1	4.56	51	58	25	48	1.62	

DUKE, KYLE - TL - Age 26
Duke did not progress at a rate at all close to what the Rockies had hoped for in 1994.

DUNNE, MIKE - TR - Age 33
The Rookie of the Year in a galaxy long ago and far away (National League, 1987), Dunne spent most of last season on the disabled list.

DURAN, ROBERTO - TL - Age 23
He played well at Class A Bakersfield, posting six wins, 10 saves and 86 strikeouts in 61 innings pitched.

DYER, MIKE - TR - Age 29
The one-time Minnesota prospect capped his comeback from circulatory problems in his shoulder by spending all of last year with the Pirates, his first full season in the majors. He throws 95 MPH but his slider is eractic and he has no off-speed pitch. He'll struggle to hang on as a middle reliever.

	W	SV	ERA	IP	H	BB	SO	B/I	$
1994 Buffalo AAA	3	12	2.34	34	33	16	26	1.41	
1994 Pittsburgh NL	1	4	5.87	15	15	12	13	1.76	2
1995 Pittsburgh NL	4	0	4.34	74	81	30	53	1.49	0
1996 Projection >>>	3	2	4.51	57	61	24	41	1.49	0

ECKERSLEY, DENNIS - TR - Age 41
Eckersley could probably pitch another ten years in a one-out righty role, but the great Eck can no longer get lefties out. He'll pitch one more year at the most.

	W	SV	ERA	IP	H	BB	SO	B/I	$
1994 Oakland AL	5	19	4.26	44	49	13	47	1.40	26
1995 Oakland AL	4	29	4.83	50	53	11	40	1.27	30
1996 Projection >>>	4	19	4.90	59	72	16	49	1.48	19

EDDY, CHRIS - TL - Age 26
Eddy would probably rather forget 1995 altogether. A Rule Five draftee by Oakland, Eddy made a few appearances in the majors, not fooling anyone, then was returned to the Royals where he had a horrible season split between Double-A Wichita and Triple-A Omaha. While lefties often get more opportunities than their righthanded counterparts, Eddy's chances are running out.

EDENFIELD, KEN - TR - Age 29
Edenfield has been very successful as a reliever in the minors, posting a very good record almost every year. He got his first taste of the majors last year, and he should be able to move into the Angels bullpen in 1996 as a middle reliever, set-up and mop-up man.

	W	SV	ERA	IP	H	BB	SO	B/I	$
1995 Vancouver AAA	7	0	3.45	60	56	25	44	1.35	
1995 California AL	0	0	4.26	12	15	5	6	1.58	-
1996 Projection >>>	1	0	4.42	33	39	12	16	1.55	-

EDENS, TOM - TR - Age 35
Edens pitched well for Iowa but was rarely used in important game situations, even in Triple-A. He's an intelligent junkball pitcher who gets hitters out with mediocre offspeed stuff. Edens will have to fight for a spot on a major league roster.

	W	SV	ERA	IP	H	BB	SO	B/I	$
1994 Two Teams	5	1	4.33	54	59	18	39	1.43	
1995 Iowa AAA	2	1	3.46	41	36	17	28	1.27	
1995 Chicago NL	1	0	6.00	3	6	3	2	3.00	-

EDMONDSON, BRIAN - TR - Age 23
Edmondson is a control pitcher without any outstanding pitches. He had a winning record but a rough year in Class AA in 1994, and will have difficulty winning at higher levels unless he shows more improvement. Moving to the Mets farm means facing tougher competition for promotions. He was 7-11 with a 4.76 ERA for Binghamton in 1995.

EDWARDS, WAYNE - TL - Age 31
Edwards moved to his fourth organization in as many seasons with a forgettable half-season at Triple-A Albuquerque. He throws pretty hard, but with poor control and has been plagued by the home-run ball in recent years. Edwards will have trouble finding a new venue in 1996.

EGGERT, DAVID - TL - Age 26
Eggert was a strikeout machine in the Midwest League in 1993, but found the going much tougher after a promotion to the Florida State League.

EGLOFF, BRUCE - TR - Age 30
Former Cleveland prospect spent 1993 trying to come back from rotator cuff operations.

EHLER, DAN - TR - Age 21
Ehler, the Marlins' 1993 thrid round pick, is a control specialist who has been unable to blow the ball past Class-A hitters at this point in his pro career. The Marlins envisioned a power pitcher when they drafted him, based on the 6'3", 180 lbs, frame he brought straight out of high school. Unless additional power materializes, Ehler should be expected to struggle at Double-A Portland in 1996. At this point, he has not established himself as a major league prospect.

EICHHORN, MARK - TR - Age 35
Eichhorn spent last season rehabbing from off-season rotator cuff surgery, and he was sorely missed in the Orioles' bullpen. The sidearmer's role is set-up relief, going an inning at most. Some pitchers have difficulty coming back from rotator cuff surgery, and those like Orel Hershiser that do come back to be effective often take a few years to regain their skills.

	W	SV	ERA	IP	H	BB	SO	B / I	$
1994 Baltimore AL	6	1	2.15	71	62	19	35	1.14	13
1995			Did Not Play						
1996 *Projection* >>>	3	0	2.80	37	34	10	19	1.18	4

EILAND, DAVE - TR - Age 29
On the strength of 30 very promising innings back in 1990, Eiland has managed to hang around the fringes of the major leagues ever since. His career 5.28 ERA gives a pretty fair picture of his total results.

	W	SV	ERA	IP	H	BB	SO	B / I	$
1994 Columbus AAA	9	0	3.58	140	141	33	84	1.24	
1995 New York AL	1	0	6.30	10	16	3	6	1.90	-

EISCHEN, JOEY - TL - Age 25
Once a hot prospect as a starter in the Expos' farm system, Eischen had not pitched well above Double-A and was dealt to the Dodgers mid-season in 1995. He is a strikeout pitcher who had struggled with his control and also surrendered too many homers. But, in 1995 he allowed just one homer in over fifty innings at Triple-A and in the majors. Eischen's prospects of obtaining a short-relief lefty job in the Dodger bullpen are relatively good in 1996.

	W	SV	ERA	IP	H	BB	SO	B / I	$
1995 Albuquerque AAA	3	2	0.00	16	8	3	14	0.67	
1995 Los Angeles NL	0	0	3.10	20	19	11	15	1.48	-
1996 *Projection* >>>	1	1	3.81	31	30	16	23	1.51	0

ELARTON, SCOTT - TR - Age 20
Elarton was a first round draft choice by Houston in 1994 and was very impressive in his first professional season. His second year was not as successful but he remains on a fast track toward the majors. He has a plus 90 fastball, a curve, a straight change and great makeup. At 6'7" and 225 pounds, Elarton is an imposing figure on the mound and he could get a look in the majors as early as September 1997.

ELDRED, CAL - TR - Age 28
An arm injury means Eldred is a big question mark for 1996, despite him being one of the Brewer's best long-term pitching hopefuls, with a great curveball.

	W	SV	ERA	IP	H	BB	SO	B / I	$
1994 Milwaukee AL	11	0	4.68	179	158	84	98	1.35	11

	W	SV	ERA	IP	H	BB	SO	B/I	$
1995 Milwaukee AL	1	0	3.42	23	24	10	18	1.44	0
1996 Projection >>>	3	0	4.60	45	41	19	27	1.33	1

ELLIOTT, DON - TR - Age 27
Elliott is a big, hard throwing reliever who experienced some shoulder and elbow problems last year. In the minors, he averaged nearly one strikeout per inning, a good sign for a rookie prospect. Elliott has a good shot to make the Padres' bullpen in 1996.

	W	SV	ERA	IP	H	BB	SO	B/I	$
1995 Las Vegas AAA	1	1	4.50	8	8	4	2	1.50	
1996 Projection >>>	1	0	3.88	31	29	18	25	1.51	-

ELLIS, ROBERT - TR - Age 25
After just 12 Double-A starts in 1993, Ellis scuffled at Nashville last year and went two months without a win. A big man with a good fastball and curve, Ellis has not racked up an overwhelming number of strikeouts during his career, but had improved at each stop until 1994. He went on the disabled list in late July, but a healthy return is expected..

	W	SV	ERA	IP	H	BB	SO	B/I	$
1995 Nashville AAA	1	0	2.18	20	16	10	9	1.26	

EMBREE, ALAN - TL - Age 26
Embree has made a successful recovery from 1993 elbow ligament transplant surgery this former prospect has now become a viable major league reliever. Triple-A American Association managers cited him for having the best fastball in the league and he was named the sixth best prospect in the league at season's end. He struggled with his control in his late-season trial with the Indians, but still held lefties to a .217 average. Expect Embree to quickly maneuver into the primary lefthanded setup role in Cleveland.

	W	SV	ERA	IP	H	BB	SO	B/I	$
1995 Cleveland AL	3	1	5.11	24	23	16	23	1.58	1
1996 Projection >>>	2	3	4.70	44	41	26	41	1.52	2

ERICKS, JOHN - TR - Age 28
A one-time first-round draft choice of St. Louis, the hard-throwing Ericks finally made it to the majors with the Pirates last season. He has finally recovered from 1992 reconstructive elbow surgery and pitched better as a starter than his numbers indicated last year. He throws 95 MPH and has outstanding poise. He could very well be a late bloomer but his rebuilt shoulder will always be a concern.

	W	SV	ERA	IP	H	BB	SO	B/I	$
1995 Pittsburgh NL	3	0	4.58	106	108	50	80	1.49	-
1996 Projection >>>	6	0	4.47	135	137	60	102	1.46	-

ERICKSON, SCOTT - TR - Age 28
Trading Erickson to the Orioles was thought to be a match made in heaven as the Orioles' good defense and natural grass field were perfect for the sinker-baller. The Orioles also tightened up his motion, a move that increased his velocity by 4-5 MPH. He had a good record with the Orioles and showed great improvement. Erickson can easily become a big winner again, even a 20 game winner.

	W	SV	ERA	IP	H	BB	SO	B/I	$
1994 Minnesota AL	8	0	5.44	144	173	59	104	1.61	-
1995 Two Teams	13	0	4.81	196	213	67	106	1.43	7
1996 Projection >>>	13	0	4.80	215	236	73	127	1.44	5

ESHELMAN, VAUGHN - TL - Age 27
This rookie opened the season pitching very well in the Red Sox' rotation, then spent the rest of the year either hurt or in the minors. He throws a good fastball, offset by a changeup, but was inconsistent with both after the first two weeks of the season. Eshelman could eventually win a spot in Boston's rotation, but should open 1996 in the bullpen.

	W	SV	ERA	IP	H	BB	SO	B/I	$
1995 Boston AL	6	0	4.85	81	86	36	41	1.49	1
1996 Projection >>>	4	0	4.67	75	76	29	38	1.40	1

ESTES, SHAWN - TL - Age 23
The first round pick of the Mariners in 1991, Estes came out of nowhere to post mindboggling numbers at Class A

San Jose. He then came through with a 2.01 ERA in four starts at Double-A, and pitched well despite a high ERA in three late starts for the Giants at the end of the season. He would seem to need more seasoning, but is well worth keeping an eye on.

	W	SV	ERA	IP	H	BB	SO	B/I	$
1995 San Francisco NL	0	0	6.75	17	16	5	14	1.21	-
1996 *Projection* >>>	2	0	4.87	49	47	17	40	1.30	-

ETTLES, MARK - TR - Age 30
Ettles rose quickly to the majors in 1993, but has sunk back just as quickly. he was released after posting a 7.82 ERA in a brief stint at Triple-A Las Vegas in 1995. Ettles is close to being finished as a pro.

EVANS, BART - TR - Age 25
The 1994 Carolina League Pitcher of the Year struggled horribly in his first taste of Double-A ball, going 0-4 with a 10.46 ERA in seven starts at Wichita. He was quite a bit better back at Class Wilmington, with a 2.89 ERA; he really turned his year around after moving to the bullpen. Evans has a blazing fastball, but not very good control. He'll try again at Double-A in 1996, this time in a relief role.

EVANS, DAVE - TR - Age 28
Evans spent four years in the Seattle system before signing a minor league contract with the Astros in 1995. He has made the transition from starter to middle reliever to closer. He is not on a track that is leading to a major league opportunity.

EVANS, SEAN - TR - Age 25
Evans struggled last season in his first taste of Double-A. The Pirates like his arm, though, and he'll get another chance this year.

EVERSGERD, BRYAN - TL - Age 27
This left-hander put up some phenomenal numbers while coming up through the St. Louis farm system. After spending 1994 with the Cardinals, he was dealt to Montreal in the Ken Hill trade last spring. He's a finesse lefty who hasn't done much on the major league level. At best, he will be the type of guy who hangs around as a second or third left-hander in a major league bullpen.

	W	SV	ERA	IP	H	BB	SO	B/I	$
1994 St. Louis NL	2	0	4.52	67	75	20	47	1.40	
1995 Ottawa AAA	6	2	2.38	53	49	26	45	1.42	
1995 Montreal NL	0	0	5.14	21	22	9	8	1.48	-
1996 *Projection* >>>	1	0	4.80	43	46	15	25	1.45	-

EYRE, SCOTT - TL - Age 23
Acquired from Texas this spring for Esteban Beltre, Eyre has struck out about a man an inning each of his three pro seasons. He throws hard and has excellent control. He'll probably go to high class-A in 1995.

FAINO, JEFF - TL - Age 23
Faino is a southpaw reliever formerly in the Red Sox system, now with the Orioles. Left handed relievers are always in demand, so Faino may be in the Orioles bullpen in 1996 or '97 if he continues to be effective.

FAJARDO, HECTOR - TR - Age 25
What a curious case this right-hander with the live arm is, having been placed on the suspended list three times in the past two seasons. He never showed up for spring training, citing family problems in Mexico. Texas traded him to the Expos during the 1995 season. When Montreal tried to call him up to the majors, he refused and was released. Once again to make sure you have it right, he refused a *promotion* to the majors not a *demotion*. Go figure.

	W	SV	ERA	IP	H	BB	SO	B/I	$
1994 Texas AL	5	0	6.91	83	95	26	45	1.45	-
1995 Ottawa AAA	0	0	4.11	15	18	6	9	1.57	
1995 Texas AL	0	0	7.80	15	19	5	9	1.60	-
1996 *Projection* >>>	2	0	5.14	45	53	14	25	1.48	-

FALTEISEK, STEVE - TR - Age 24
Expos farmhand Falteisek, after getting a 2.95 ERA in Double-A, moved on to Triple A and did even better.

	W	SV	ERA	IP	H	BB	SO	B/I	$
1995 Ottawa AAA	2	0	1.17	23	17	5	18	0.96	

FARMER, HOWARD - TR - Age 30
Six-year Expos farmhand, he surfaced in Montreal in 1990, did poorly in four starts, and has been essentially the same pitcher ever since, although he works out of the pen more now.

FARR, STEVE - TR - Age 39
Farr announced his retirement last year, a few months before it would likely have been forced upon him. He was expected to at least help with the Sox' closing duties, but proved to be unsteady from the time he was acquired, and Ken Ryan took the job exclusively.

	W	SV	ERA	IP	H	BB	SO	B/I	$
1994 Two Teams	2	4	5.72	28	41	18	20	2.08	2

FARRAR, TERRY - TL - Age 26
A lefthander acquired by the Pirates in the late-season 1993 trade that sent Lonnie Smith to Baltimore, Farrar missed most of last season with arm problems. He is considered a marginal prospect at best, but he'll be given every chance since he's a lefty.

FARRELL, JOHN - TR - Age 33
Farrell is Triple-A filler material at this point in his career, coming full circle to complete his baseball life with the Indians' organization that gave him his big league start. Farrell has churned out innings and worked with youngsters like Julian Tavarez, Chad Ogea and Albie Lopez during the past two seasons. His stuff is mediocre, even by Triple-A standards. There is virtually no potential for upward mobility.

	W	SV	ERA	IP	H	BB	SO	B/I	$
1994 Cleveland AL	1	0	9.00	13	16	8	10	1.85	-
1995 Buffalo AAA	11	0	4.54	184	198	61	92	1.41	
1995 Cleveland AL	0	0	3.86	4	7	0	4	1.50	-

FASSERO, JEFF - TL - Age 33
After starting the season 7-0, Fassero lost 14 of his last 20 decisions in 1995. He has outstanding stuff and is one of the best-kept secrets in baseball. However, a major falling out with Expos pitching coach Joe Kerrigan is said to have triggered Fassero's downfall. His chances of returning to form in 1996 are much better somewhere outside of Montreal.

	W	SV	ERA	IP	H	BB	SO	B/I	$
1994 Montreal NL	8	0	2.99	138	119	40	119	1.15	16
1995 Montreal NL	13	0	4.33	189	207	74	164	1.49	2
1996 *Projection* >>>	13	0	3.88	201	206	75	175	1.40	6

FERMIN, RAMON - TR - Age 23
It took four years for Fermin to get out of Class A, and he didn't overwhelm in his first season at Double-A. He's still young enough to improve but a longshot in any event.

	W	SV	ERA	IP	H	BB	SO	B/I	$
1995 Oakland AL	0	0	13.50	1	4	1	0	3.75	-

FERNANDEZ, ALEX - TR - Age 26
An on-going arbitration case affected Fernandez's attitude in 1995; he pressed too much and wasn't sharp in the first half. He relaxed in the second half and had much better results. He's an emotional pitcher who can get into long streaks, both good and bad. Fernandez is only 26 years old but has already spent the better part of the last six years in the big leagues; he's an excellent long-term prospect who could win 22 games in a good year.

	W	SV	ERA	IP	H	BB	SO	B/I	$
1994 Chicago AL	11	0	3.86	170	163	50	122	1.25	17
1995 Chicago AL	12	0	3.80	203	200	65	159	1.30	15
1996 *Projection* >>>	16	0	3.57	218	210	62	164	1.25	23

FERNANDEZ, SID - TL - Age 33
Many thought Fernandez was finished when the Orioles cut him loose in mid-1995 after his second bad season in the AL. The Phils took note of his still high strikeout rate, and gave him a chance. He became one of the most dominant NL starters following his signing. He held lefties to an amazing .100 average as a Phil, and struck out 11 batters per nine innings. He throws a 90 MPH rising fastball and changes speeds effectively - but his flaws include vulnerability to the gopher ball and the stolen base (he allowed 20 of each in 93 innings). He is also a consistent injury risk because of poor conditioning.

	W	SV	ERA	IP	H	BB	SO	B/I	$
1994 Baltimore AL	6	0	5.15	115	109	46	95	1.34	5
1995 Baltimore AL	0	0	7.39	28	36	17	31	1.89	
1995 Philadelphia NL	6	0	3.34	64	48	21	79	1.07	2
1996 Projection >>>	9	0	3.80	166	149	65	165	1.29	8

FERRY, MIKE - TR - Age 26
Ferry is a once-hot prospect who appears to have topped out in Double-A. He is a pitcher in the Bob Tewksbury mold, allowing very few walks (1.5 per 9 innings) and many hits (10.9 per 9 innings). Control pitchers like Ferry usually have to wait forever to get a chance at the majors.

FESH, SEAN - TL - Age 23
Fesh is a young lefty reliever whose best shot at making the majors is as a set-up man and situational reliever.

	W	SV	ERA	IP	H	BB	SO	B/I	$
1995 Two AAA Teams	3	1	2.81	51	64	19	25	1.62	

FETTERS, MIKE - TR - Age 31
There's no reason to think he won't be the closer again in 1996. He's not a classic closer as he doesn't have the great strikeout ability, but he does get the job done with his sinker.

	W	SV	ERA	IP	H	BB	SO	B/I	$
1994 Milwaukee AL	1	17	2.54	46	41	27	31	1.48	23
1995 Milwaukee AL	0	22	3.38	34	40	20	33	1.73	20
1996 Projection >>>	1	19	3.82	49	50	27	38	1.58	19

FINLEY, CHUCK - TL - Age 33
Finley has lost some velocity on his fastball, and his ERA was over 4.00 for the second year in a row. He makes up for the lower velocity by being craftier. Finley's days as sub-3.00 ERA pitcher are over, and he is now a workhorse-type pitching .500 ball in 200-plus innings.

	W	SV	ERA	IP	H	BB	SO	B/I	$
1994 California AL	10	0	4.32	183	178	71	148	1.36	12
1995 California AL	15	0	4.21	203	192	93	195	1.40	12
1996 Projection >>>	15	0	4.40	219	209	91	195	1.37	11

FINNVOLD, GAR - TR - Age 27
A sixth round, 1990 draft pick, Finnvold spent almost the entire season on the disabled list, pitching just once at Triple-A Pawtucket in 1995. He's a control specialist and not a good prospect.

FLEMING, DAVE - TL - Age 26
Fleming is still searching for the command which let him go 29-15 in 1992-3. He has some good stuff, but all too often makes one very hittable pitch to each batter; he paid the price with 19 homers allowed in just 80 innings - Ouch! He was considerably better after leaving the Mariners for Kansas City. Fleming will serve as a lefty long reliever/swingman.

	W	SV	ERA	IP	H	BB	SO	B/I	$
1994 Seattle AL	7	0	6.46	117	152	65	65	1.85	-
1995 Omaha AAA	1	0	3.38	16	17	7	8	1.50	-
1995 Seattle - Kansas City AL	1	0	5.96	80	84	53	40	1.71	-
1996 Projection >>>	5	0	5.94	120	135	66	62	1.68	-

FLENER, HUCK - TL - Age 27
He was ordinary at Triple-A last year but should get a brief look in spring training as a starting pitcher.

	W	SV	ERA	IP	H	BB	SO	B/I	$
1994				Did Not Play					
1995 Syracuse AAA	6	0	3.94	134	131	41	83	1.28	

FLETCHER, PAUL - TR - Age 29
Fletcher has bounced around the Phils' organization for eight seasons. He does not throw particularly hard and doesn't have particularly good control.

	W	SV	ERA	IP	H	BB	SO	B/I	$
1995 Philadelphia NL	1	0	5.40	13	15	9	10	1.80	-

FLORENCE, DON - TL - Age 29
In his eighth year in the minors, Florence moved to the Mets farm, where he was encouraged to throw more two-seam sinkers. The results: he reached a new high level and found himself in the majors before year-end.

	W	SV	ERA	IP	H	BB	SO	B/I	$
1995 New York NL	3	0	1.50	12	17	6	5	1.92	0
1996 *Projection* >>>	1	0	3.96	34	43	12	14	1.62	-

FLORIE, BRYCE - TR - Age 25
Florie was a starter in the minors until converted to relief in 1994. He's a slider-sinker type of pitcher reminding some observers of Billy Swift. He's looking to get hitters to hit ground balls.

	W	SV	ERA	IP	H	BB	SO	B/I	$
1995 San Diego NL	2	1	3.01	68	49	38	68	1.28	4
1996 *Projection* >>>	1	1	3.21	50	36	26	49	1.25	3

FORDHAM, TOM - TL - Age 21
Lefties with a good changeup often succeed. Fordam split 1995 between Class-A and Double-A

FORNEY, RICH - TR - Age 24
Last year was Forney's second in Double-A, but unfortunately, it was his worst. He's a young starter with below average stuff struggling to become an effective pitcher.

FORTUGNO, TIMOTHY - TL - Age 33
The Angels acquired this lefty reliever from the White Sox in the Jim Abbott trade. He's a veteran of 10 minor-league seasons, pitching effectively here and there, and 76 games in the majors. Fortugno's role is lefty set-up, middle relief and mop-up man.

	W	SV	ERA	IP	H	BB	SO	B/I	$
1994 Cincinnati NL	1	0	4.20	30	32	14	29	1.53	-
1995 Vancouver AAA	1	1	1.54	11	8	4	7	1.03	
1995 California AL	1	0	5.59	38	30	19	24	1.27	0
1996 *Projection* >>>	1	0	5.13	39	34	20	28	1.38	-

FOSSAS, TONY - TL - Age 38
Fossas is the definitive one-batter lefty reliever. But he's awfully good at it and had a tremendous year for the Cardinals in 1995. As long as he can get a tough lefty out, there's a place for him in the major leagues.

	W	SV	ERA	IP	H	BB	SO	B/I	$
1994 Boston AL	2	1	4.76	34	35	15	31	1.47	-
1995 St. Louis NL	3	0	1.47	36	28	10	40	1.05	5
1996 *Projection* >>>	2	0	3.05	43	37	13	44	1.18	3

FOSTER, KEVIN - TR - Age 27
Foster's first full season in the big leagues produced favorable results. An aggressive pitcher, he relies mostly on a good fastball, but also allows a lot of homers because he challenges hitters; sometimes not a good combination in Wrigley's friendly confines. Foster is a useful third or fourth starter who can be counted on for 200 innings per year.

	W	SV	ERA	IP	H	BB	SO	B/I	$
1994 Chicago NL	3	0	2.89	81	70	35	75	1.30	6
1995 Chicago NL	12	0	4.51	167	149	65	146	1.28	6
1996 *Projection* >>>	9	0	3.79	136	140	49	126	1.39	4

FOULKE, KEITH - TR - Age 23
The California League All-Star dominated Class A hitters in 1995 and is worth keeping an eye on.

FOX, CHAD - TR - Age 25
Despite a terrible year at Double-A Chattanooga, Fox is considered one of the Reds better long term pitching prospects. Fox was a 23rd round pick in 1992 and features a good fastball (considered the best in the organization by Baseball America). The Reds sent him to the Arizona Fall League following the 1995 season.

FRANCO, JOHN - TL - Age 35
A strong finish in 1995 confirmed Franco's return to the top tier of NL relievers, proving that his league-leading save total in '94 wasn't all just management discretion giving him every possible save. Franco is past his prime but still highly effective.

	W	SV	ERA	IP	H	BB	SO	B/I	$
1994 New York NL	1	30	2.70	50	47	19	42	1.32	35
1995 New York NL	5	29	2.44	51	48	17	41	1.27	29
1996 *Projection* >>>	4	32	2.70	60	57	21	48	1.31	31

FRANEK, TOM - TR - Age 25
Drafted in the 5th round by the Phils in 1993, Franek hasn't pitched badly, walking less than two batters per nine innings in his first two seasons, with a five to one strikeout/walk ratio in 1994. The problem is the slow development track on which he has been placed.

FRASCATORE, JOHN - Age 26
The Cardinals have long raved about Frascatore's great arm. He throws as hard as any starting pitcher in their organization. However, he will also be 26 by opening day. If he's really that good, why have the Cardinals still not given him a shot in their rotation?

	W	SV	ERA	IP	H	BB	SO	B/I	$
1995 Louisville AAA	2	5	3.95	82	89	34	55	1.50	-
1995 St. Louis NL	1	0	4.41	32	39	16	21	1.68	-
1996 *Projection* >>>	2	0	4.22	58	65	26	37	1.57	-

FRASER, WILLIE - TR - Age 31
Fraser keeps getting chances in the major leagues and doing nothing with them, even though he's now 31 years old. If he were a left-hander, there might be an explanation. But he's not. Go figure.

	W	SV	ERA	IP	H	BB	SO	B/I	$
1994 Florida NL	2	0	5.84	12	20	6	7	2.11	-
1995 Montreal NL	2	2	5.61	25	25	9	12	1.32	1
1996 *Projection* >>>	1	1	4.98	33	32	12	15	1.35	-

FREDRICKSON, SCOTT - TR - Age 28
Fredrickson rebounded from a disappointing 1994 with a good year as a setup reliever at Triple-A Colorado Springs, winning eleven games in relief. His 3.45 ERA is particularly good in the Rocky Mountains' thin air, but his control remains a problem. Fredrickson will battle several other Rockies' long relief candidates for a major league bullpen role in 1996.

	W	SV	ERA	IP	H	BB	SO	B/I	$
1995 Colorado Springs AAA	11	4	3.45	75	70	47	70	1.55	

FREEMAN, MARVIN - TR - Age 32
Freeman started 1995 with high hopes after being the Rockies' most effective starter in 1994, but was basically ineffective the entire season. He pitched at least seven innings in only one start and uncharacteristically had control trouble. His season ended early with arthroscopic elbow surgery. When healthy Freeman has good power and outstanding movement on his pitches.

	W	SV	ERA	IP	H	BB	SO	B/I	$
1994 Colorado NL	10	0	2.80	112	113	23	67	1.21	14
1995 Colorado NL	3	0	5.89	94	122	41	61	1.73	-
1996 *Projection* >>>	6	0	5.33	114	135	42	72	1.56	-

FREY, STEVE - TL - Age 32
Frey has pitched only 269 innings in 283 career appearances. After going most of the season without a viable lefty in their pen, the Phils turned to Frey in September, and used him virtually every day, with solid results. He is not overpowering or physically imposing (5'9", 170 lbs.), but will continue to linger in the majors in his limited role. The Phils would like him back in 1996.

	W	SV	ERA	IP	H	BB	SO	B/I	$
1994 San Francisco NL	1	0	4.94	31	37	15	20	1.68	-
1995 Seattle AL	0	0	4.76	11	16	6	7	2.34	
1995 Two NL Teams	0	1	2.12	17	10	4	7	0.82	1
1996 Projection >>>	1	2	3.77	37	37	16	20	1.43	1

FRIETAS, MIKE - TR - Age 26
Frietas was out for over a year with an arm injury. He's a skinny guy who can back and pitched as a middle reliever and set-up man posting a mediocre record in Double-A last year.

FRITZ, JOHN - TR - Age 27
The Brewers could use more arms, and Fritz showed definite improvement in 1995 after two lackluster seasons near the top of the Angels farm system. He won 20 games in the Midwest League back in 1992 but has converted to relief.

	W	SV	ERA	IP	H	BB	SO	B/I	$
1995 New Orleans AAA	6	1	3.97	81	70	42	56	1.38	

FROHWIRTH, TODD - TR - Age 33
Which hand does he froh wirth? The right, of course. Other than being the subject of a bad play on words, submariner Frohwirth is a veteran of eight major league seasons for three teams, but has recently been Triple-A roster filler. He's still a decent pitcher and would have been opportunities in a less-well-stocked farm system. Frohwirth could compete for a setup or middle relief role in the right major league situation.

	W	SV	ERA	IP	H	BB	SO	B/I	$
1994 Boston AL	0	1	10.80	26	40	17	13	2.14	-
1995 Buffalo AAA	0	3	3.34	32	31	12	33	1.33	

FRONIO, JASON - TR - Age 26
The converted reliever advanced slowly through Indians' chain, not arriving at Double-A until 1994. He was downright unhittable at Single-A, but has been unable to get similar results at higher levels (7.22 ERA at Double-A in 1995).

FYHRIE, MIKE - TR - Age 26
Basically, Fyhrie is the model of consistency in a starting pitcher. He's not flashy, but gets the job done. However, he has struggled in promotions to Triple-A in the last two seasons. He'll advance to Triple-A Omaha again in 1996, but this finesse pitcher needs a good year this time around to get a shot at a major league opportunity.

	W	SV	ERA	IP	H	BB	SO	B/I	$
1994 Omaha AAA	6	0	5.72	85	100	33	37	1.55	
1995 Omaha AAA	3	0	4.45	60	71	14	39	1.41	

GADDY, BOB - TL - Age 29
A 1989 41st round draftee who should be thrilled to still be earning a paycheck for playing a game, Gaddy was strafed at Triple-A in the Phils' organization in 1995. He is a lefty with very marginal stuff and mediocre control. He had some success as a setup reliever earlier in his career, and a short-term mopup role necessitated by injuries in the majors appears to be the most he can hope for at this stage.

	W	SV	ERA	IP	H	BB	SO	B/I	$
1995 Scranton AAA	5	0	6.28	86	100	56	42	1.82	

GAILLARD, EDDY - TR - Age 25
Gaillard led higher Class A Lakeland with 25 saves and a sparkling 1.31 ERA in 1995, his first full season in the bullpen, then advanced to Double-A Jacksonville by season's end. Still, he's too old to be pitching in Class A and he has a lot to prove in the higher minors - there's a large difference between Class A and Double-A hitters. If Gaillard proves himself in Double-A in 1996 then he'd be a prospect for a major league bullpen role by 1997.

GAJKOWSKI, STEVE - TR - Age 26
A six-year minor leaguer, Gajkowski has advanced slowly to finally reach Triple-A for the first time in 1995. A sinker/slider pitcher he doesn't get a log of strikeouts but has decent control and can win a middle relief role in 1996.

GAKELER, DAN - TR - Age 31
Former Tiger farmhand Gakeler made four terrible starts at Triple-A Pawtucket and was released. He's likely finished after a twelve year pro career.

GALLAHER, KEVIN - TR - Age 27
Gallaher is a late blooming power pitcher who has been regarded as a prospect by the Astros. His 1995 season was largely lost to arm problems, but he was throwing well at the end of the season and was nominated to pitch in the Arizona Fall League. If he shows improvement in his control and off speed pitches, Gallaher should compete for a major league job in 1996.

GAMEZ, BOB - TL - Age 27
Gamez had some success at the Class A level, although he wasn't promoted beyond A ball until his sixth year as a pro. For two years now, he has been hit pretty hard at AAA Phoenix, and looks no closer to the majors than he did two years ago. Like so many pitching careers have been affected the last two years, however, maybe the majors will come down to Gamez' level if he can't move up to theirs.

	W	SV	ERA	IP	H	BB	SO	B/I	$
1995 Phoenix AAA	3	2	5.59	66	76	27	41	1.56	

GARAGOZZO, KEITH - TL - Age 26
Garagozzo spent time between Double and Triple A in the Yankee farm system. The former starter at Double A saw time out of the bullpen at Triple A.

GARCES, RICH - TR - Age 24
The bulky (6'0", 215++lbs.) righthander was once the premier closer prospect in baseball, but he nearly ate himself out of the sport. He still throws quite hard and is particularly tough on righties, but since the Cubs and Marlins both saw fit to let him go in 1995 (the Marlins waived him after season's end), one cannot be too optimistic about his major league future. However, he is still young and can still bring it - if he controls his weight, he could help someone in a bullpen role.

	W	SV	ERA	IP	H	BB	SO	B/I	$
1994 Nashville AA	4	3	3.72	77	70	31	76	1.31	
1995 Two Teams	0	0	4.44	24	25	11	22	1.48	-
1996 Projection >>>	1	0	4.60	31	32	13	28	1.44	-

GARCIA, APOLINAR - TR - Age 28
He has pitched well for two consecutive seasons at Double-A Canton-Akron as a spot starter/middle reliever. However, Garcia has been stuck in neutral since 1990, and he has only pitched 35 innings above Double-A in seven pro seasons. He has the look of a career minor leaguer, despite his 3.5 to one strikeout/walk ratio over the past three seasons.

GARCIA, JOSE - TR - Age 23
The Dodgers have soured on this lanky side-arm pitcher after another poor showing at Triple-A Albuquerque. His delivery is smooth and effortless, but hitters also seemed to hit him effortlessly in 1995.

GARCIA, RAMON - TR - Age 26
The White Sox liked Garcia so much in 1991, they brought him up before Wilson Alvarez. The enchantment wore off, however. Garcia was not recalled again and was released at the end of 1993. He's still young enough to surface somewhere in 1995.

GARCIA, VICTOR - TR - Age 29
From 1988 to 1991 Garcia could do no wrong; he swept through all five levels of the Reds farm system in just four years. In 1992 he couldn't do anything right, and in 1993 he slipped back to A-ball as a setup man.

GARDINER, MIKE - TR - Age 30
Inconsistency has plagued this veteran righthander throughout his attempts to gain footing in the major leagues. He did not show any signs of progress in '95.

	W	SV	ERA	IP	H	BB	SO	B/I	$
1994 Detroit AL	2	5	4.14	58	53	23	31	1.30	9
1995 Toledo AAA	0	0	4.41	16	19	13	10	1.96	
1995 Detroit AL	0	0	14.59	12	27	2	7	2.35	-

GARDNER, CHRIS - TR - Age 27
Gardner made a brief appearance with the Astros in 1991 and was on the 40-man roster in spring training last year. However he had arm problems and was very ineffective in 1995. He appears to have missed his chance for a major league career.

	W	SV	ERA	IP	H	BB	SO	B/I	$
1994 Tucson AAA	3	0	6.10	72	95	32	33	1.75	
1995 Tucson AAA	1	0	8.54	26	43	19	6	2.36	

GARDNER, MARK - TR - Age 34
For the second straight year, Gardner entered the season on thin ice with the Marlins, but wound up taking a regular turn due to a rash of injuries to other starters. He is a curveball specialist who is able to get the key strikeout, but he is undone by allowing homers.

	W	SV	ERA	IP	H	BB	SO	B/I	$
1994 Florida NL	4	0	4.87	92	97	30	57	1.38	1
1995 Florida NL	5	1	4.49	102	109	43	87	1.49	0
1996 *Projection* >>>	3	0	4.75	86	93	33	65	1.47	-

GARRELTS, SCOTT - TR - Age 34
The former NL ERA champ has never been the same since serious arm troubles in the early 1990's. Garrelts called it quits after nine forgettable outings at Triple-A Omaha in 1995.

GASPAR, CADE - TR - Age 22
Gaspar, Detroit's first round pick from Pepperdine University in '94, has an excellent curveball and a future in the Tigers' rotation. He was not outstanding at Class A in '95, yet pitched well enough to justify his club's investment.

GAVAGHAN, SEAN - TR - Age 26
A sixteenth round draft choice out of the U. of Richmond in '92, Gavaghan sped through Class A his first two pro summers before settling down at Double-A Nashville in 1994. He did fine again at Double-A in 1995 but couldn't make the next step.

	W	SV	ERA	IP	H	BB	SO	B/I	$
1995 New Britain AA	2	1	2.20	28	18	10	30	0.98	
1995 Salt Lake AAA	1	5	5.51	47	53	31	28	1.78	

GEEVE, DAVE - TR - Age 26
Geeve had made steady progress through the Texas system, posting 4:1 strikeout to walk ratios in four seasons. In 1995, his progress was stunted when he got hit hard at both Double- and Triple-A. Geeve will get another full season in the minors to get back on track.

GENTILE, SCOTT - TR - Age 25
Gentile was Montreal's ace reliever at A West Palm Beach. In 1994 he had 26 saves and 90 strikeouts in 66 innings of work. In 1995 he spent the whole year at Double-A Harrisburg, chipping in 11 saves while holding his own with a 3.44 ERA, much less than a hit per inning, and a strikeout/walk ratio over 3:1. Watch this guy.

GIBBS, PAUL - TR - Age 25
Flamethrowing reliever who has struck out about twelve (yes, twelve) batters per nine innings in his first three pro seasons. ERA has consistently been below 2.00. How deep is the Indians system? He wasn't even the closer at Class A Columbus.

GIBSON, PAUL - TL - Age 36
This journeyman keeps bouncing around and always has a chance to wind up in the majors again because he's a left-handed reliever. He finished last season with the Pirates' Triple-A Calgary farm club after being released by Toronto. He isn't in the plan of a rebuilding Pittsburgh club but can land somewhere.

	W	SV	ERA	IP	H	BB	SO	B/I	$
1994 Two Teams	1	0	4.97	29	26	17	21	1.48	-
1995 Calgary AAA	0	1	3.72	19	21	9	17	1.56	

GILMORE, JOEL - TR - Age 26
The massive (6'-6", 230 lb.) righty put up solid numbers for four years after being drafted in 1991's 33rd round. The Phils chose not to promote him above Class A, and 1995 showed why: a 6.25 ERA at Double-A Reading, turning his career path to Sioux Falls in Independent ball.

GIVENS, BRIAN - TL - Age 30
Twelve year minor-league veteran Givens finally broke through to the majors due to the desperation of the Brewers to find a starting pitcher. He was hardly a revelation, but Givens did well enough to earn another chance in 1996. Givens was once a hard thrower, but injuries wrecked most of 1990 to 1993 and he is just now beginning to throw hard again. Control has always been his biggest problem.

	W	SV	ERA	IP	H	BB	SO	B/I	$
1995 Milwaukee AL	5	0	4.95	107	116	54	73	1.59	0
1996 Projection >>>	3	0	4.95	72	78	36	49	1.58	-

GLAVINE, TOM - TL - Age 30
Another fine season as one of baseball's top lefty starters was somewhat overshadowed by Glavine's role in the off-season labor negotiations. His candid, but ill-advised commentary on the relative importance of ballplayers made Glavine a lightning rod for criticism of overpaid, selfish, arrogant athletes. On the ballfield, Glavine's excellent sinker again induced a lot of grounders and helped him reduce his ERA to almost a full run better than 1994.

	W	SV	ERA	IP	H	BB	SO	B/I	$
1994 Atlanta NL	13	0	3.97	165	173	70	140	1.47	8
1995 Atlanta NL	16	0	3.08	198	182	66	127	1.25	17
1996 Projection >>>	17	0	3.20	218	210	78	150	1.32	16

GLINATSIS, GEORGE - TR - Age 27
Glinatsis got as far as the majors in 1994, but regressed in 1995, going a combined 5.81 ERA while going 7-9 in 26 starts at Triple-A Tacoma and Double-A Port City. A late-round 1991 draft pick, Glinatsis is not a highly regarded prospect and would have to make remarkable progress to get noticed.

GOETZ, BARRY - TR - Age 27
Goetz got the first six starts of his six-year career in 1995. He seems destined to finish his career as a minor leaguer.

	W	SV	ERA	IP	H	BB	SO	B/I	$
1995 Oklahoma City AAA	4	1	5.72	89	97	49	46	1.63	

GOHR, GREG - TR - Age 28
Gohr was Detroit's top starting prospect heading into the '93-'94 seasons before he spent most of the '95 season on the disabled list. He returned impressively in September and might be prepared for a regular turn in the Tigers' rotation in '96. Gohr will eventually compete with Sean Bergman for a starters spot.

	W	SV	ERA	IP	H	BB	SO	B/I	$
1994 Detroit AL	2	0	4.50	34	36	21	21	1.68	-
1995 Detroit AL	1	0	0.87	10	9	3	12	1.16	1
1996 Projection >>>	3	0	3.93	84	85	43	69	1.53	1

GOLDSMITH, GARY - TR - Age 24
Although he had a losing record overall, Goldsmith had a solid year in both Class A and AA in 1994. Spending a whole year at Double-A in 1995, however, he was less impressive (4-7 with a 4.61 ERA). His biggest asset now is that there isn't much pitching talent ahead of him in the Tigers organization.

GOMES, WAYNE - TR - Age 23
The Phils' 1993 top pick was a closer in college, but has been a starter in his last two minor league seasons. His control has been very spotty, but he throws a blazing 95 MPH heater along with improving breaking stuff and has consistently posted high strikeout totals. However, he has averaged less than five innings per start due to the high pitch counts resulting from his wildness. Unless he improves in that area, he will not develop into a top major league starter. He is a quality Triple-A season away, however, from a meaningful bullpen role with the Phils, leading to his eventual promotion to closer.

GOMEZ, PAT - TL - Age 28
A one-out lefty who has excelled in that role in the past, Gomez has also suffered from control difficulties. Last year his control difficulties continued, while lefties hit .381 against him. He's unlikely to advance beyond the one-out stage.

	W	SV	ERA	IP	H	BB	SO	B / I	$
1994 San Francisco NL	0	0	3.78	33	23	20	14	1.29	0
1995 San Francisco NL	0	0	5.14	14	16	12	15	2.00	-
1996 *Projection* >>>	1	0	4.42	31	28	21	22	1.59	-

GONZALES, FRANK - TL- Age 28
This lefthander showed marked improvement for Detroit upon a full conversion to relief in his fourth season at Triple-A Toledo. Gonzales has earned a shot with the Tigers in '96 and is well qualified for spot duty.

	W	SV	ERA	IP	H	BB	SO	B / I	$
1995 Toledo AAA	3	0	3.31	51	43	17	54	1.17	

GOODEN, DWIGHT - TR - Age 31
"Where have you gone, Joe DiMaggio?" New York's last best hero is back in New York. The arm is fine, and there are many great games left in Gooden if he can just find a way to get baseball back near the top of his priorities list. Potentially a big surprise for all those who have been focused solely on his off-the-field events.

	W	SV	ERA	IP	H	BB	SO	B / I	$
1994 New York NL	3	0	6.32	41	46	15	40	1.48	-
1995				Did Not Play					
1996 *Projection* >>>	10	0	4.75	155	155	50	129	1.32	7

GORDON, TOM - TR - Age 28
It's becoming more clear every year that Gordon is unable to take that next step forward to stardom. Just when you think he's got his excellent curve under control he'll go out and walk five guys in the first two innings - it drives you nuts to watch him pitch. Fine run support helped him achieve his .500 record; he wasn't nearly that good.

	W	SV	ERA	IP	H	BB	SO	B / I	$
1994 Kansas City AL	11	0	4.35	155	136	87	126	1.44	9
1995 Kansas City AL	12	0	4.43	189	204	89	119	1.55	5
1996 *Projection* >>>	11	0	4.83	208	215	108	148	1.55	-

GORECKI, RICK - TR - Age 22
The hard-throwing Gorecki was one of the youngest pitchers in the Pacific Coast League last season, and he figures to be again in 1995. He has a future, but there is no need to rush him.

GOTT, JIM - TR - Age 36
Gott, who set the Pirates' single-season save record with 34 in 1988, returned to the Pirates last season to serve as young closer Dan Miceli's mentor. However, it wasn't a happy homecoming. He was on the disabled list three times before finally having reconstructive shoulder surgery in September. The Pirates released him at the end of the season and even the always-optimistic Gott admits his career is probably over.

	W	SV	ERA	IP	H	BB	SO	B / I	$
1994 Los Angeles NL	5	2	5.95	36	46	20	29	1.82	-
1995 Pittsburgh NL	2	3	6.03	31	38	12	19	1.61	0

GOZZO, MAURO -TR - Age 30
Gozzo was released after six mediocre outings at Triple-A Iowa. He was once a marginal prospect for the Mets and Indians, but never had great stuff and is now likely finished with pro ball.

GRACE, MIKE - TR - Age 25
After battling through two lost seasons (1992-93) due to arm miseries, Grace clawed his way back to Double-A, where he dominated in 1995, and enjoyed two respectable major league starts before disaster struck. Grace had major shoulder surgery in late September, and his future is quite murky. Grace doesn't throw particularly hard, but has solid control and is very tough on righties - he is like Paul Quantrill with a little more power. Unfortunately for the Phils, he could go down as the second coming of Dave Downs - look it up.

	W	SV	ERA	IP	H	BB	SO	B/I	$
1995 Scranton AAA	2	0	1.59	17	17	2	13	1.16	
1995 Philadelphia NL	1	0	3.18	11	10	4	7	1.26	0

GRAHE, JOE - TR - Age 28
Following reconstructive surgery in 1994, Grahe signed a minor league contract with the Rockies and was brought up last May. He was routinely bombed as a short reliever, but made several effective starts before going on the DL for most of July and August. His short-lived career as a closer is - thankfully - a distant memory.

	W	SV	ERA	IP	H	BB	SO	B/I	$
1994 California AL	2	13	6.65	43	68	18	26	1.98	10
1995 Colorado NL	4	0	5.08	56	69	27	27	1.69	-
1996 *Projection* >>>	2	0	5.33	43	56	20	22	1.75	-

GRANGER, JEFF - TL - Age 24
A former Texas A & M star, Granger has failed to live up to the high hopes the Royals had for him when he became their top draft pick in 1993 (fifth pick overall). He has shown glimpses of brilliance, but has mostly been pedestrian. A stint on the disabled list slowed his progress at Double-A Wichita in 1995, but he began to pitch better as the season wound down; he was especially effective in the Texas League playoffs. Granger's future depends upon his consistency.

GRANT, MARK - TR - Age 32
Yet another aging, former major leaguer at Triple-A Iowa in 1995, Grant made eleven decent starts, going 5-2 with a 3.13 ERA. More importantly, he vastly improved his usually spotty control, striking out four times as many batters as he walked. Still, Grant's chances of a return to the majors have to be considered remote at best.

	W	SV	ERA	IP	H	BB	SO	B/I	$
1995 Iowa AAA	5	0	3.13	69	58	10	38	0.99	

GRAVES, DANNY - TR - Age 22
The Indians' fourth round draft pick in 1994 had a solid pro debut in 1995, allowing all of five earned runs in 70 innings split between three levels. He was named the best relief prospect in the high A-ball Carolina League by circuit managers. However, his ability to strike out batters greatly diminished as he moved up. His velocity is average, but he has pinpoint control and an excellent breaking ball repertoire. Look for him to spend 1996 at Triple-A Buffalo as the closer and show up in the majors in 1997 as a middleman. He does not have big league closer written all over him.

GRAY, DENNIS - TL - Age 26
With his second straight bad season in Double-A, he is now trying to hang on. Once a coveted starting prospect, he has had the same control problems for five straight years.

GREEN, OTIS - TL - Age 32
Minor league outfielder 1983-1990. Tried pitching in 1991 and did well at Single-A and Double-A but has struggled since at higher levels (5.76 ERA with no saves working from the pen for Triple-A Tacoma in 1995).

GREEN, TYLER - TR - Age 26
There were two Tyler Greens in 1995 - the durable All Star who led the NL in complete games at the break, and the scared stiff, hopeless version who didn't win a game the rest of the way. Green has the physical tools to be a major league winner, but he is a mental wreck. This facet of his game had landed him in Manager Jim Fregosi's doghouse in 1994 Spring Training. His knuckle curve is effective in short bursts - Green could be a viable short reliever, a role which would insulate him from his tendency to overanalyze.

	W	SV	ERA	IP	H	BB	SO	B/I	$
1995 Philadelphia NL	8	0	5.31	140	157	66	85	1.59	-
1996 *Projection* >>>	5	0	5.31	95	106	44	57	1.58	-

GREENE, RICH - TR - Age 25
This big former first round pick and US Olympic closer showed improvement in '95 in his third attempt at Double-A. In his defense, the Tigers hardly broke Greene in slowly after drafting him. Greene has the arm to reach the major leagues, and will move up as quickly as his control will allow.

GREENE, TOMMY - TR - Age 28
Greene remains in a Catch-22 situation with the Phillies - arm exams continue to show no major structural problems, but Greene insists that his arm hurts too much for him to cut loose. Late in 1995, the Phils adopted a "throw till it blows" stance towards Greene, and he was thrashed on a regular basis. He has not been dominant since early in the 1993 season - his fastball is now long gone, and his control will never be good enough to sustain him through in a "finesse" phase.

	W	SV	ERA	IP	H	BB	SO	B/I	$
1994 Philadelphia NL	2	0	4.54	35	37	22	28	1.65	-
1995 Scranton AAA	3	0	2.22	28	18	6	19	0.85	
1995 Philadelphia NL	0	0	8.29	33	45	20	24	1.93	-
1996 *Projection* >>>	2	0	5.62	58	63	29	45	1.60	-

GREER, KEN - TR - Age 28
Greer is another aging prospect who parlayed a decent Triple-A season into a few innings with the Giants. He's still unlikely to have much of a major-league career.

	W	SV	ERA	IP	H	BB	SO	B/I	$
1995 Phoenix AAA	5	1	3.98	63	65	19	41	1.33	
1995 San Frnacisco NL	0	0	5.25	12	15	5	7	1.67	

GRIFFITHS, BRIAN - TR - Age 27
Had a dominant season in A-ball in 1991, but found the going tougher in Double-A. Still a prospect for now.

GRIMM, JOHN - TR - Age 25
Grimm is a hard throwing closer who had an outstanding year in Class A last year. He gets a lot of strikeouts, averaging more than one per inning. Keep an eye on him.

GRIMSLEY, JASON - TR - Age 28
One way of determining that the Cleveland Indians had indeed arrived in 1995 was that Mr. Grimsley's presence was no longer required in their starting rotation. His startling curve ball is simply too good - it breaks too much and is rarely a strike, and is quite difficult for catchers to handle. He will likely remain as Triple-A insurance for the Indians or another club - in fact, his control was downright exemplary after his early 1995 demotion.

	W	SV	ERA	IP	H	BB	SO	B/I	$
1994 Cleveland AL	5	0	4.57	82	91	34	59	1.51	2
1995 Buffalo AAA	5	0	2.91	68	61	19	40	1.18	
1995 Cleveland AL	0	1	6.09	34	37	32	25	2.03	-
1996 *Projection* >>>	2	1	5.18	62	68	37	44	1.71	-

GROOM, BUDDY - TL - Age 30
Groom was hit hard in a 1995 season split between the Tigers and Marlins. Without precise control, Groom is a batting practice pitcher - lefties and righties in both leagues hit over .300 against him in 1995, as he walked 32 hitters in 56 innings. He is not a prime lefty bullpen candidate because he is not a strikeout pitcher, but he apparently thinks highly of the opportunities with the Marlins as he accepted an outright assignment to Triple-A rather than becoming a free agent.

	W	SV	ERA	IP	H	BB	SO	B/I	$
1994 Detroit AL	0	1	3.94	32	31	13	27	1.38	
1995 Detroit AL	1	1	7.52	40	55	26	23	1.99	

	W	SV	ERA	IP	H	BB	SO	B/I	$
1995 Florida NL	1	0	7.20	15	26	6	12	2.13	-
1996 Projection >>>	1	1	6.48	55	72	28	36	1.84	-

GROSS, KEVIN - TR - Age 34
Gross was unaccountably horrid during the first two-thirds of the season (7.37 ERA in late July), but finished fairly strong. His primary problem was the longball - only rookie Brad Radke allowed more homers in the A.L. Gross was, as usual, durable and healthy, and should find himself in someone's rotation in 1996, where he should improve on his dreadful 1995 numbers.

	W	SV	ERA	IP	H	BB	SO	B/I	$
1994 Los Angeles NL	9	1	3.60	157	162	43	124	1.30	12
1995 Texas AL	9	0	5.54	183	200	89	106	1.57	-
1996 Projection >>>	11	0	4.79	210	225	84	139	1.47	3

GROSS, KIP - TR - Age 31
Gross became the first American pitcher to lead the Japanese Pacific League in victories as he won sixteen for the Nippon Ham Fighters while posting a 3.04 ERA. He had appeared briefly for the Reds and Dodgers from 1990 to 1993. Gross would be a fringe major leaguer in the States, but has apparently become a reliable starting pitcher in Japan.

GROTT, MATT - TL - Age 28
Grott is a marginal prospect who received a brief cup of coffee with the Reds when John Roper was placed on the DL in early May. Grott has turned in three good years at Indianapolis as a swing man, allowing less than a hit per inning with a 3-to-1 strikeout to walk ratio in 1995. Chuck McElroy had a terrible 1995, so Grott could be in the picture for a lefthanded setup role for 1996.

	W	SV	ERA	IP	H	BB	SO	B/I	$
1995 Indianapolis AAA	7	2	4.24	114	99	24	74	1.08	

GRUNDT, KEN - TL - Age 26
The Rockies signed Grundt, a former Giants farmhand, out of the Northern League. He was promoted twice last season, reaching Triple-A. He never has started a game in his pro career, and has been used in save situations. If the strikeout pitcher can come through this time at Colorado Springs, he could reach the big time.

GRZANICH, MIKE - TR - Age 23
Grzanich was converted to a relief role in his fourth season in the Astro system. He was selected by the Astros to pitch in the Arizona Fall League. He needs a breakthrough season in 1996 to earn a shot at the majors.

GUARDADO, EDDIE - TL - Age 25
Guardado did not have a bad year, as he stayed healthy and stifled lefthanded hitters (.223 opponent batting average). The Twins appear to have enough young starters to keep him in the bullpen. He's not yet a reliable pitcher, but he's getting there quickly.

	W	SV	ERA	IP	H	BB	SO	B/I	$
1994 Minnesota AL	0	0	8.47	17	26	4	8	1.76	-
1995 Minnesota AL	4	2	5.12	91	99	45	71	1.58	1
1996 Projection >>>	3	1	4.94	78	90	35	56	1.60	-

GUBICZA, MARK - TR - Age 33
Gubicza has the longest running career of any AL pitcher with one club, dating back to the Royals lone World Championship in 1985. He's a finesse pitcher now; shoulder problems stole his fastball a few years ago. But, he is a much more complete pitcher now and can succeed in a No. 2 or No. 3 starter role for a few more years. Gubicza needs a lot of bullpen help as he's not capable of throwing more than about six innings per start.

	W	SV	ERA	IP	H	BB	SO	B/I	$
1994 Kansas City AL	7	0	4.50	130	158	26	59	1.42	6
1995 Kansas City AL	12	0	3.75	213	222	62	81	1.33	15
1996 Projection >>>	12	0	3.89	209	229	55	87	1.36	14

GUETTERMAN, LEE - TL - Age 37
Guetterman relies on a sinkerball and gets into serious problems when he leaves his pitches high in the strike zone.

Guetterman must have perfect control to succeed, which he didn't in 1995.

	W	SV	ERA	IP	H	BB	SO	B/I	$
1995 Seattle AL	0	1	6.88	17	21	11	11	1.88	-

GUILFOYLE, MICHAEL - TL - Age 27
Guilfoyle has pitched pretty well the last three seasons in Double-A, but the Tigers have not promoted him beyond that level. He has a moving fastball, and can be an effective set-up man as long as he throws strikes.

GUNDERSON, ERIC - TL - Age 30
Although Gunderson produced excellent results in his brief callup with the Mets in 1994, he's on the wrong side of that thin dividing line which separates minor league stars from major league success. His fastball is just a little short on velocity, and he doesn't have any big out pitch. A move to the Red Sox didn't change that basic fact.

	W	SV	ERA	IP	H	BB	SO	B/I	$
1994 Norfolk AAA	3	1	3.68	36	25	17	31	1.15	
1995 New York NL	1	0	3.70	24	25	8	19	1.36	
1995 Boston AL	2	0	5.11	12	13	9	9	1.78	1
1996 *Projection* >>>	2	0	4.22	29	29	14	21	1.51	-

GUTHRIE, MARK - TL - Age 30
The veteran reliever was acquired from Minnesota during the season and was used in his familiar lefty specialist role, throwing only 19.2 innings in 24 games with the Dodgers. Guthrie's last good year was 1992.

	W	SV	ERA	IP	H	BB	SO	B/I	$
1994 Minnesota AL	4	1	6.14	51	65	18	38	1.62	-
1995 Minnesota AL	5	0	4.46	42	47	16	48	1.49	
1995 Los Angeles NL	0	0	3.66	19	19	9	19	1.42	1
1996 *Projection* >>>	5	0	3.86	66	77	17	63	1.44	1

GUTIERREZ, JIM - TR - Age 25
Last season was Gutierrez's third at Double-A Jacksonville, this time in the Detroit organization. The Tigers also moved him to the bullpen, and he pitched effectively (a career-best ERA). To succeed in Triple-A this year, he'll have to move the ball around. He is not a strikeout pitcher.

GUZMAN, JOSE - TR - Age 32
Guzman's surgically repaired right shoulder again broke down under the strain of too many innings. He pitched just 19.2 innings in 1994 and hasn't thrown a pitch in organized ball since. He had a few good seasons in the majors, but isn't likely to return.

GUZMAN, JUAN - TR - Age 29
It didn't seem possible that Guzman could be worse than he was in 1994 but that's exactly what he was with career-lows in virtually every category. His control has always been a problem but now his fastball has slowed some as well. Guzman will start the season with another chance to prove that he can get back to being a good major league starter but is running out of time.

	W	SV	ERA	IP	H	BB	SO	B/I	$
1994 Toronto AL	12	0	5.68	147	165	76	124	1.64	0
1995 Toronto AL	4	0	6.32	135	151	73	94	1.66	-
1996 *Projection* >>>	9	0	5.90	175	192	92	135	1.62	-

HAAS, DAVE - TR - Age 30
Haas injured his shoulder early last season. He was released by the Tigers following five games on rehab with Class A Lakeland. Haas was a reliever with Detroit in 1991-92.

HABYAN, JOHN - TR - Age 32
Middle reliever and set-up man Habyan had some good years with the Yankees and Cardinals, but he was erratic last year with the Angels, blowing games with wild pitches and the like. Right handed hitters also got to him at a .293 clip, much higher than the .244 over his career. Middle relievers like Habyan can have bad years and bounce right back the next year.

	W	SV	ERA	IP	H	BB	SO	B/I	$
1994 St. Louis NL	1	1	3.23	47	50	20	46	1.48	2
1995 St. Louis NL	3	0	2.88	40	32	15	35	1.16	
1995 California AL	1	0	4.13	32	36	12	25	1.47	5
1996 *Projection* >>>	3	1	3.70	75	73	28	64	1.35	4

HALL, DARREN - TR - Age 31
After being the surprise closer in 1994, Hall was disappointing last year, spending a lot of time on the disabled list. He wasn't throwing hard and was wild high. In October, the Blue Jays dropped him from their 40-man roster, making him eligible to sign with any team. At his age and given his limited major league experience, his immediate future is probably as a middle reliever.

	W	SV	ERA	IP	H	BB	SO	B/I	$
1994 Toronto AL	2	17	3.41	31	26	14	28	1.26	23
1995 Toronto AL	0	3	4.41	16	21	9	11	1.84	1
1996 *Projection* >>>	1	1	4.61	30	31	15	24	1.52	-

HAMILTON, JOEY - TR - Age 25
The talented Hamilton could develop into one of the best pitchers in baseball very soon. He throws five pitches: a good fastball, and an excellent sinker and slider, but a so-so curve and change-up, and he can control all of them. He also has the necessary poise and pitching smarts. Taking it all together, the good stuff and excellent control, with the poise and smarts lead to a big winner, like possibly 18 to 20 wins very soon.

	W	SV	ERA	IP	H	BB	SO	B/I	$
1994 San Diego NL	9	0	2.98	108	98	29	61	1.17	13
1995 San Diego NL	6	0	3.08	204	189	56	123	1.20	14
1996 *Projection* >>>	14	0	3.15	204	188	55	121	1.19	20

HAMMAKER, ATLEE - TL - Age 38
It's hard to believe he's still around, but this 1983 NL ERA leader keeps getting back to the majors, most recently for 13 relief appearances with the White Sox in 1995. Maybe this time his 12.79 ERA will finally lead to his retirement.

HAMMOND, CHRIS - TL - Age 30
Hammond is among the most predictable of all major league starters. You can count on him to rank among league pitching leaders through June, at which point he is injured, and then roughed up miserably after his return. Hammond has fine-tuned his control to the point that he can spin the occasional 90-pitch, Greg Maddux-like outing when he is in early season mode. He is amazing at holding runners - basestealers were zero for seven when attempting to steal on him. He should remain a stable, unspectacular number three or four starter for the time being.

	W	SV	ERA	IP	H	BB	SO	B/I	$
1994 Florida NL	4	0	3.07	73	79	23	40	1.39	4
1995 Florida NL	9	0	3.80	161	157	47	126	1.27	8
1996 *Projection* >>>	9	0	3.90	159	163	50	113	1.34	5

HAMPTON, MIKE - TL - Age 23
Hampton was Houston's most consistent starter in 1995 after spending the 1994 season as a reliever. Hampton is not overpowering but he throws hard enough to set up his other pitches, all of which are of major league quality. He missed almost a month on the disabled list with a minor arm problem but he was sound late in the season. He has remarkable maturity for his age and should have a productive career ahead of him.

	W	SV	ERA	IP	H	BB	SO	B/I	$
1994 Houston NL	2	0	3.70	41	46	16	24	1.50	0
1995 Houston NL	9	0	3.35	150	141	49	115	1.26	10
1996 *Projection* >>>	10	0	3.30	188	183	64	138	1.31	12

HANCOCK, CHRISTOPHER - TL - Age 26
It took Hancock almost five years to get past Class A, and now he's been at AA for more than two years without impressing. Tall lefthanded pitchers get as many chances as anyone, but Hancock's may have finally run out.

HANCOCK, LEE - TL - Age 28
A lefty who has bounced back and forth between the rotation and bullpen, Hancock finally got his first major-league

shot with the Pirates last September. He is nothing spectacular but did a solid job in his major-league debut. Pirates manager Jim Leyland loves to have three lefties in his bullpen and Hancock put himself in position to gain the third spot in 1996.

	W	SV	ERA	IP	H	BB	SO	B/I	$
1995 Calgary AAA	6	0	5.07	113	146	27	49	1.52	
1995 Pittsburgh NL	0	0	1.93	14	10	2	6	0.86	1

HANCOCK, RYAN - TR - Age 24
Hancock is a former Brigham Young University quarterback who opted for baseball. Pitching for Midland in the tough Double-A Texas League, Hancock had an excellent first half last year, going 6-2 with a 3.65 ERA, an excellent ERA considering the situation. But he struggled in the 2nd half, getting hit hard. He has a good 93-MPH fastball and slider.

HANEY, CHRIS - TL - Age 27
Haney appeared to finally be delivering on his promising potential when a bulging disk in his back made it too painful for him to continue pitching in 1995. He wasn't able to throw his fastball effectively or snap off his slider or curve with enough break. September surgery was deemed successful and he pitched winter ball to rebuild his arm strength. Look for Haney to start 1996 in the Royals rotation; he could be a pleasant surprise if he can retain his success from 1995.

	W	SV	ERA	IP	H	BB	SO	B/I	$
1994 Kansas City AL	2	0	7.31	28	36	11	18	1.66	-
1995 Kansas City AL	3	0	3.65	81	78	33	31	1.37	4
1996 *Projection* >>>	6	0	4.57	135	140	55	60	1.44	2

HANSELL, GREG - TR - Age 25
Part of the Kevin Tapani deal, this tall righthander will have a chance to win a bullpen spot in '96. Hansell thrived once converted to relief in '94, and although he didn't pitch especially well in '95, he should develop into a good setup man in a couple of years. Keep an eye on him for '97.

	W	SV	ERA	IP	H	BB	SO	B/I	$
1995 Two AAA Teams	4	1	6.14	48	64	10	32	1.53	
1995 Los Angeles NL	0	0	7.45	19	29	6	13	1.81	-
1996 *Projection* >>>	1	0	5.40	31	44	9	21	1.71	-

HANSEN, BRENT - TR - Age 25
In the ghetto that was the Red Sox lower minors, Hansen was 11-24 in his first three pro seasons. Last year, even though he was demoted briefly to Double-A from Pawtucket, Hansen equaled his wins total. He consistently pitched deep into games by throwing strikes. He lacks only punchout power.

	W	SV	ERA	IP	H	BB	SO	B/I	$
1995 Pawtucket AAA	7	0	4.29	92	90	23	50	1.23	

HANSON, ERIK - TR - Age 30
Staying healthy all year helped Hanson have his best season since 1990. He has good control of an excellent curveball, although he was less effective in the second half of 1995. The Red Sox will look for Hanson to be their number two starter in 1996; while he'll probably still be above average in most respects, don't expect him to again post a 15-5 record.

	W	SV	ERA	IP	H	BB	SO	B/I	$
1994 Cincinnati NL	5	0	4.11	122	137	23	101	1.30	6
1995 Boston AL	15	0	4.24	186	187	59	139	1.32	13
1996 *Projection* >>>	13	0	4.12	199	207	58	153	1.33	13

HARIKKALA, TIM - TR - Age 24
Harikkala was promoted twice in 1994 and reached the majors briefly in 1995. Because he is not a strikeout pitcher, he will struggle more at higher levels. His 3+ innings with the Mariners looked like batting practice, but he's got the craft and poise to merit another look.

	W	SV	ERA	IP	H	BB	SO	B/I	$
1995 Tacoma AAA	5	0	4.24	146	151	55	73	1.41	

HARKEY, MIKE - TR - Age 29
With an outstanding fastball, Harkey was once a top pitching prospect with the Cubs. But several shoulder injuries took their toll, and the Cubs eventually gave up on him. He began last year in the Oakland rotation, but was later waived. A's pitching coach Dave Duncan is one of the best, but he didn't see much potential in Harkey. Harkey was signed by the Angels, then desperate for a starter. He was soon relegated to the Angels bullpen, and he appears better suited to middle and long relief.

	W	SV	ERA	IP	H	BB	SO	B/I	$
1994 Colorado NL	1	0	5.79	91	125	35	39	1.75	-
1995 California AL	8	0	5.44	127	155	47	56	1.59	-
1996 Projection >>>	4	0	5.51	135	169	48	59	1.61	-

HARNISCH, PETE - TR - Age 29
Trying to shift from pure power pitcher to use more finesse after shoulder soreness had sidelined him in 1994, Harnisch nonetheless ran into shoulder miseries again in 1995. Offseason surgery left him a question mark going into spring training.

	W	SV	ERA	IP	H	BB	SO	B/I	$
1994 Houston NL	8	0	5.40	95	100	39	62	1.46	0
1995 New York NL	2	0	3.68	110	111	24	82	1.23	4
1996 Projection >>>	6	0	4.07	136	134	40	100	1.28	5

HARRAH, DOUG - TR - Age 26
Harrah has pitched well as a setup man and sometime closer in two years with the Cubs' Double-A farm at Orlando, blossoming with a 1.94 ERA in 1995 but getting no promotion anyway. Toby Harrah's nephew, he served in the Persian Gulf War; even taking that minor delay into consideration, it's obvious that the Cubs are moving him along very, very patiently.

HARRIGER, DENNY - TR - Age 26
Last year was Harriger's second year in Triple-A. He improved his record somewhat, but he was still a very hittable pitcher. If he was a good pitcher, he would have been in the majors by now. Still the Padres think enough of Harriger to protect him on their 40-man roster.

	W	SV	ERA	IP	H	BB	SO	B/I	$
1995 Las Vegas AAA	9	0	4.07	177	187	60	97	1.40	

HARRIS, BRYAN - TL - Age 24
The Angels switched Harris to a relief role last year, his third in professional ball. He was hit hard, but it was in the tough Double-A Texas League. After averaging nearly a strikeout per inning in his first two years, the K's weren't nearly as easy to come by at the higher Double-A level, and Harris must adjust to becoming a pitcher rather than a thrower.

HARRIS, DOUG - TR - Age 26
This Oriole farm hand is a starter struggling to become an effective winning pitcher. Thus far, it's been an uphill battle.

HARRIS, GENE - TR - Age 31
The Phils traded Harris to the Orioles where he soon came down with an arm problem requiring surgery. He posted 23 saves as the Padres' closer in 1993, his best year ever. The Orioles are his sixth organization in seven years, a sign that he has some talent, but there may be some other problems. Harris was released by the O's in October.

	W	SV	ERA	IP	H	BB	SO	B/I	$
1994 Two Teams	1	1	7.60	23	34	12	19	1.94	-
1995 Two Teams	2	0	4.30	23	23	9	13	1.39	0
1996 Projection >>>	1	0	5.10	31	35	15	21	1.60	-

HARRIS, GREG A. - TR - Age 40
Finally left for dead after being released by Boston and the Yankees in 1994, Harris bounced back to have a fine season as a set-up reliever for the Expos last season. The ambidextrous Harris even got to achieve his lifelong dream of pitching left-handed in a game during the final week of the season. He's 40 now but you can never count him out. Maybe he has 10 more years remaining as a lefty.

	W	SV	ERA	IP	H	BB	SO	B/I	$
1994 Two Teams	3	2	7.99	50	64	26	48	1.78	-
1995 Montreal NL	2	0	2.61	48	45	16	47	1.26	3
1996 *Projection* >>>	2	1	4.56	41	42	17	39	1.45	-

HARRIS, GREG W. - TR - Age 32
Harris pitched poorly in his limited time with the Twins, marking the second straight year he has struggled. His best talent, a sharp curve, suggests he can contribute in some role to a bullpen, and we might see him resurface in '96.

	W	SV	ERA	IP	H	BB	SO	B/I	$
1994 Colorado NL	3	1	6.65	130	154	52	82	1.58	-
1995 Minnesota AL	0	0	8.82	32	50	16	21	2.02	-
1996 *Projection* >>>	7	1	4.96	202	205	65	142	1.33	-

HARRIS, PEP - TR - Age 23
Harris fell off the Indians' minor league closer fast track in 1995, as he had to settle for a setup role following his promotion to Triple-A. Unlike his competition (Paul Shuey and Alan Embree), Harris does not throw particularly hard, and while his control is only average, he has an uncanny knack for wriggling out of jams. Harris will likely spend 1996 in Triple-A and should not be expected to make a significant major league impact.

HARRIS, REGGIE - TR - Age 27
A Rule Five pick in December 1989, the A's were able to keep Harris by disabling him for the first half of 1990, while he pitched rehab in the minors. The walks were a minor nuisance with Oakland in 1991, but have a become a major block in his career now. Harris is a good hard thrower but hasn't made any progress in four years.

HARRISON, BRIAN - TR - Age 27
Harrison moved to the bullpen last summer, his worst season as a pro. He really lacks any outstanding pitch and had trouble with Triple-A hitters in 1995. He has a long way to go and looks like a career minor leaguer at this point.

HART, JASON - TR - Age 24
Cubs prospect Hart pitched in Single-A and Double-A in 1995 getting a 2.21 ERA and a 2.12 ERA, respectively, while maintaining a very good strikeout/walk ratio.

HARTGRAVES, DEAN - TL - Age 29
Hartgraves spent nine largely undistinguished seasons in the Astro minor league system before achieving modest success as a limited role reliever in the majors in 1995. He should be competing for the same position in 1996.

	W	SV	ERA	IP	H	BB	SO	B/I	$
1994 Tucson AAA	7	3	5.07	97	106	36	54	1.45	
1995 Houston NL	2	0	3.22	36	30	16	24	1.27	1
1996 *Projection* >>>	2	1	3.34	70	59	32	46	1.30	4

HARTLEY, MIKE - TR - Age 34
One of several righthanders the Red Sox tried out in 1995, Hartley was found wanting and released. He throws a good splitter, but is a fringe major leaguer at this point. Hartley finished last season with the Orioles and will be looking for work in 1996.

	W	SV	ERA	IP	H	BB	SO	B/I	$
1995 Two AAA Teams	1	1	3.43	57	51	14	51	1.13	
1995 Baltimore - Boston AL	1	0	5.14	14	13	3	6	1.14	0

HARTSOCK, JEFF - TR - Age 29
Yet another failed Dodger pitching prospect, he had a couple of good years in the Dodgers' chain, then was traded to the Cubs for Steve Wilson in 1991. He made four relief appearances for Chicago in 1992, hasn't been back to the majors since and probably never will be.

	W	SV	ERA	IP	H	BB	SO	B/I	$
1994 Louisville AAA	1	0	6.21	33	41	14	16	1.65	

HARVEY, BRYAN - TR - Age 32
It didn't take long - one appearance - for Harvey to suffer his annual elbow injury in 1995. The Marlins have assembled

an excellent organization in a short period of time, but they will forever rue the decision not to deal Harvey elsewhere for a package of top prospects while they had the chance. Clearly, Harvey is too much of a risk to warrant an investment of prime dollars. He will again attempt to air it out in spring training, but unlike last season, the closer job belongs to Robb Nen, no matter what.

	W	SV	ERA	IP	H	W	SO	B/I	$
1994 Florida NL	0	6	5.23	10	12	4	10	1.55	5
1995 Florida NL				Injured					

HASSINGER, BRAD - TR - Age 28
Converted from a starting role to the bullpen in 1992, Hassinger has good control, but lacks major league stuff. He's simply minor league roster filler.

HATHAWAY, HILLY - TL - Age 26
Hathaway had several trials with the Angels back in 1992 and '93. He didn't pitch very well then and is now trying to get another shot with the Padres. He didn't pitch very well as a Triple-A starter last year. Hathaway would have a better chance of making the majors as a reliever.

	W	SV	ERA	IP	H	BB	SO	B/I	$
1994 Las Vegas AAA	2	0	6.25	95	121	48	68	1.77	
1995 Las Vegas AAA	4	0	6.22	63	76	27	37	1.62	

HAWBLITZEL, RYAN - TL - Age 24
Hawblitzel appeared to be a can't-miss prospect after winning 15 games in the hitters' park at Winston-Salem in 1991. Thus far, he has missed. Last season was the best of his three at Triple-A Colorado Springs. He throws strikes, but not strikeouts, so consequently he has been hit hard.

	W	SV	ERA	IP	H	BB	SO	B/I	$
1995 Colorado Springs AAA	5	0	4.55	83	88	17	40	1.27	

HAWKINS, LaTROY - TR - Age 23
Hawkins will be a steady starter, although he may not win many games for the '96 Twins. He has a good fastball and a good change up, reminding some of Ramon Martinez. Hawkins is not overpowering and will have to gain some experience around the league before he is on solid ground. The former Indiana high school basketball star will be worth the wait.

	W	SV	ERA	IP	H	BB	SO	B/I	$
1995 Salt Lake AAA	9	0	3.55	144	150	40	74	1.32	
1995 Minnesota AL	2	0	8.67	27	39	12	9	1.89	-
1996 *Projection* >>>	4	0	6.10	136	200	42	65	1.78	-

HAYNES, HEATH - TR - Age 27
Haynes is an unsung, aging prospect who had a disastrous 1995 season at Triple-A and may have seen his window of opportunity close.

	W	SV	ERA	IP	H	BB	SO	B/I	$
1995 Edmonton AAA	2	0	6.27	18	21	11	13	1.72	

HAYNES, JIMMY - TR - Age 23
Haynes got it all together in the second half in Triple-A, earning a promotion to the Orioles. He was very impressive with the O's, reminding a few observers of Mike Mussina. He throws a good fastball mixing it with two different curveballs. Haynes has the stuff and the poise to succeed as the Orioles' fourth or fifth starter.

	W	SV	ERA	IP	H	BB	SO	B/I	$
1995 Rochester AAA	12	0	3.29	167	162	49	140	1.26	
1995 Baltimore AL	2	0	2.25	24	11	12	22	0.96	3
1996 *Projection* >>>	3	0	3.76	90	89	31	83	1.33	4

HEATHCOTT, MIKE - TR - Age 26
He began the season at Double-A, but slumped seriously and in August was sent to the Carolina League, where he continued to sag. With poor control, he's not a strikeout pitcher and he's not a prospect.

HEBLE, KURT - TR - Age 27
Heble tried to rebound from a bad season in 1994 and was even worse last year. It's tough to give up on a guy with his strikeout-to-inning ratio but he's not getting results and isn't young enough to count as a prospect any longer. He proved a few years ago that he can be an effective minor league pitcher but that's all so far.

HEFLIN, BRONSON - TR - Age 24
Heflin opened the eyes of Phils' brass by striking out an amazing 84 batters in only 61 innings as the closer at Class-A Clearwater. Not much was expected of Heflin, a 1994 37th round pick, but he possesses decent velocity and has impeccable control. He was among the older players in the Florida State League in 1995, and a clearer barometer of his future potential will be his likely 1996 turn as Double-A closer.

HELLING, RICH - TR - Age 25
Helling continued to struggle, both at Triple-A and in his second major league stint. Helling's best pitch has been his slider, but he couldn't get hitters out consistently with it last season. The Texas system is largely devoid of pitching prospects, so Helling will continue to get every chance to turn it around. He was slated to pitch in the Arizona Fall League.

	W	SV	ERA	IP	H	BB	SO	B/I	$
1994 Texas AL	3	0	5.88	52	62	18	25	1.54	-
1995 Oklahoma City AAA	4	0	5.33	109	132	41	80	1.58	
1995 Texas AL	0	0	6.57	12	17	8	5	2.03	-
1996 Projection >>>	4	0	4.67	80	83	26	61	1.36	-

HENDERSON, KENNY - TR - Age 23
Milwaukee's number one pick in 1991, Henderson rejected the Brewers offer and instead took a scholarship to play for the Hurricanes.

HENDERSON, ROD - TR - Age 25
Henderson, the Expos' first draft choice in 1992, has seen his career progress stalled by injuries and a premature recall to Montreal in '94. Last year he was pitching well at times with Double-A Harrisburg. Henderson can keep batters off balance by mixing his fastball with a sharp-breaking curve. He is a prospect.

HENKE, TOM - TR - Age 38
Henke switched over to the National League last season and was overpowering at age 37. He again established himself as one of the game's best closers after an off year with Texas in 1994. However, Henke was leaning towards retirement at the end of last season. If he decides to come back for one more season with the Cardinals, there's no reason to expect he can't have another big year.

	W	SV	ERA	IP	H	BB	SO	B/I	$
1994 Texas AL	3	15	3.79	38	33	12	39	1.18	22
1995 St. Louis NL	1	36	1.82	54	42	18	48	1.11	36
1996 Projection >>>	2	35	2.75	60	48	20	57	1.13	35

HENNEMAN, MIKE - TR - Age 34
Henneman was acquired from Detroit in August to be the Astro closer down the stretch. He was largely successful before faltering in a couple of key games in the last week of the season. He can still be a useful closer if he elects not to retire.

	W	SV	ERA	IP	H	BB	SO	B/I	$
1994 Detroit AL	1	8	5.19	34	43	17	27	1.73	7
1995 Detroit AL	0	18	1.53	29	24	9	24	1.13	
1995 Houston NL	0	8	3.00	21	21	4	19	1.19	26
1996 Projection >>>	1	23	3.00	56	55	19	46	1.33	21

HENNIS, RANDY - TR - Age 30
This righthander made a promising debut with the Astros in late 1990 before missing most of the last three years with arm problems.

HENRY, BUTCH - TL - Age 27
Just when he was continuing his emergence as a fine left-handed starting pitcher with the Expos, Henry's 1995 season

ended with elbow ligament transplant surgery. It is indeed a serious operation and Henry will miss part or all of 1996. While others have come back from the "Tommy John" surgery, you can never be sure. Montreal tried to sneak him through waivers at the end of last season and Boston grabbed him as a reclamation project.

	W	SV	ERA	IP	H	BB	SO	B/I	$
1994 Montreal NL	8	1	2.43	107	97	20	70	1.09	16
1996 Projection >>>	2	0	3.45	51	52	14	30	1.30	2

HENRY, DOUG - TR - Age 32
In Puerto Rican winter ball a year ago, Henry came up with two new reliable pitches, a slider and a forkball, to go with his big fastball. Thus he became a better pitcher than he was while getting 61 saves for Milwaukee in 1991-1993 "I'm all the way back," Henry said at the end of '95, and he really is now a creditable game finisher capable of getting saves for any team that needs a closer.

	W	SV	ERA	IP	H	BB	SO	B/I	$
1994 Milwaukee AL	2	0	4.60	31	32	23	20	1.76	-
1995 New York NL	3	4	2.96	67	48	25	62	1.09	9
1996 Projection >>>	3	3	3.52	64	53	29	54	1.27	5

HENRY, DWAYNE - TR - Age 34
Henry returned to the major leagues in '95 after one season in Japan with the Chunichi Dragons. He has always had a good arm, and he displayed some control at Triple-A before a mildly successful September callup. Pitchers such as Henry can thrive only in a low pressure role, and his best assignment would be to set up another closer.

	W	SV	ERA	IP	H	BB	SO	B/I	$
1995 Toledo AAA	1	11	3.35	48	43	24	52	1.39	
1995 Detroit AL	1	5	6.23	8	11	10	9	2.42	3
1996 Projection >>>	2	5	5.25	33	34	22	28	1.70	2

HENRY, JON - TR - Age 27
Henry has spent two years trying to make the jump from Double-A to Triple-A, and the PCL has proved too difficult. He dominated at Nashville in '94, going 8-1, 2.93, before being hit hard at Salt Lake City. Henry could contribute to the Twins' bullpen some day.

HENTGEN, PAT - TR - Age 27
After two very good seasons, Hentgen finally struggled in 1995. He doesn't go to his fastball as often as in the past and he can't seem to keep his pitches down in the strike zone as he did in 1993 and 1994. He will be a regular starter and is a good bet to rebound in 1996.

	W	SV	ERA	IP	H	BB	SO	B/I	$
1994 Toronto AL	13	0	3.40	174	158	59	147	1.24	21
1995 Toronto AL	10	0	5.11	200	236	90	135	1.62	-
1996 Projection >>>	14	0	4.44	231	247	99	165	1.50	5

HEREDIA, GIL - TR - Age 30
Heredia does whatever the Expos ask: start, mop up, set up or close. And he does a solid job. He certainly isn't a star but has been reliable for the Expos and a valuable guy to have on the pitching staff.

	W	SV	ERA	IP	H	BB	SO	B/I	$
1994 Montreal NL	6	0	3.46	75	85	13	62	1.30	6
1995 Montreal NL	5	1	4.31	119	137	21	74	1.33	3
1996 Projection >>>	6	1	4.06	118	135	21	80	1.32	4

HEREDIA, JULIAN - TR - Age 26
Hard throwing reliever Julian Heredia has had some good years in the minors, and he made the Triple-A All-Star team last year. He's a candidate for the Angels' bullpen.

	W	SV	ERA	IP	H	BB	SO	B/I	$
1995 Vancouver AAA	5	10	3.63	74	69	23	65	1.24	

HEREDIA, WILSON - TR - Age 24
Heredia joined the Marlins' organization in late 1995 after toiling in the Rangers' minor leagues for over four seasons. He is a lean righty (6'0", 165 lbs.) with a live, somewhat straight, fastball. Primarily a reliever with the Rangers, the

Marlins envision him as a starter despite his slender frame. Expect Heredia to earn a spot in the Marlins' Triple-A rotation in 1995, with a midseason promotion a possibility. Any major league future would more likely be as a reliever, due to his size and rather one-dimensional repertoire.

	W	SV	ERA	IP	H	BB	SO	B/I	$
1995 Texas AL	0	0	3.75	12	9	15	6	2.00	-

HERMANSON, DUSTIN - TR - Age 23
The flame-throwing Hermanson was the Padres' first round draft pick in 1995. His outstanding fastball and slider enabled him to establish himself very quickly, and he began last season with the parent club. But he was a little shaky and in need of more minor-league experience. Hermanson has the tools and make-up to be a top closer.

	W	SV	ERA	IP	H	BB	SO	B/I	$
1995 Las Vegas AAA	0	11	3.50	36	35	29	42	1.78	
1995 San Diego NL	3	0	6.82	31	35	22	19	1.80	-
1996 Projection >>>	2	1	3.92	42	46	27	33	1.75	-

HERNANDEZ, FERNANDO - TR - Age 24
Hernandez is a starter who has struggled in Double-A for the past two years. But he strikes out a lot of hitters indicating some potential. The Padres like his live arm, and they are working with him to improve his mechanics to get better control and consistency.

HERNANDEZ, JEREMY - TR - Age 29
This righthanded workhorse was a Marlins' lifesaver in early 1994, after an injury to Bryan Harvey and before the emergence of Robb Nen, before he lost a full calendar year due to a bulging disk in his neck. He showed layers of rust in his brief comeback in late 1995. He needs to regain the bite on his sinker to recapture his previous effectiveness. No matter how good a pitcher is, it is extremely difficult to regain top form after missing the bulk of two seasons - don't count on a stellar performance from Hernandez in 1996.

	W	SV	ERA	IP	H	BB	SO	B/I	$
1994 Florida NL	3	9	2.70	23	16	14	13	1.29	12
1995 Florida NL	0	0	11.57	7	12	3	5	2.14	-
1996 Projection >>>	2	1	4.73	36	37	16	22	1.46	-

HERNANDEZ, ROBERTO - TR - Age 31
Hernandez was inconsistent all year, specifically having control problems in the strike zone. He has good stuff and a great strikeout ratio, but gives up too many hard hit balls in clutch situations. Hernandez is in serious danger of losing his role as closer.

	W	SV	ERA	IP	H	BB	SO	B/I	$
1994 Chicago AL	4	14	4.91	47	44	19	50	1.32	19
1995 Chicago AL	3	32	3.92	59	63	28	84	1.54	32
1996 Projection >>>	4	31	4.02	68	68	29	85	1.41	34

HERNANDEZ, XAVIER - TR - Age 30
After a disastrous 1994 with the Yankees, Hernandez returned to his more familiar setup role in 1995 with mixed results for the Reds. He vultured seven wins with good strikeout and walk totals, but his ERA was a lofty 4.60. Hernandez relies primarily on a splitter and was effective against righties, but struggled against lefties.

	W	SV	ERA	IP	H	BB	SO	B/I	$
1994 New York AL	4	6	5.85	40	48	21	37	1.73	6
1995 Cincinnati NL	7	3	4.60	90	95	31	84	1.40	4
1996 Projection >>>	7	5	4.62	87	92	32	82	1.42	4

HERSHISER, OREL - TR - Age 37
Mr. October - The Pitcher experienced a major career resurgence in 1995, as his move to the mighty Indians seemingly added some life to his fastball. Though he is mainly just a six or seven inning pitcher at this stage in his career, his guile and savvy gives his team a chance to win whenever he takes the mound. Though lefites largely have their way with him, he held righties to a miniscule .196 average. Hershiser will be hard pressed to match his 1995 performance, but he will likely remain an innings-eating number 3 or 4 starter in the short term, with lots of cheap wins the result of pitching for the Indians' juggernaut.

	W	SV	ERA	IP	H	BB	SO	B/I	$
1994 Los Angeles NL	6	0	3.79	135	146	42	72	1.39	6
1995 Cleveland AL	16	0	3.87	167	151	51	111	1.21	17
1996 *Projection* >>>	15	0	3.81	191	184	63	119	1.29	17

HIBBARD, GREG - TL - Age 31
Hibbard gets by on great control; he rarely fans more than four per nine innings. He was injured midway through 1994 and hasn't been able to pitch since. Because he was never a hard thrower to begin with, Hibbard could make a return to the majors should he heal completely.

HICKERSON, BRYAN - TL - Age 32
Hickerson joined the Rockies from the Cubs just before the trading deadline last year. After only a few appearances, he had so endeared himself to Rockies fans that they would routinely shriek "NO!!!" in unison when Hickerson trotted in from the bullpen. He needs to vastly cut down the number of hits, homers and walks given up in order to find a roster position elsewhere in 1996.

	W	SV	ERA	IP	H	BB	SO	B/I	$
1994 San Francisco NL	4	1	5.40	98	118	38	59	1.59	-
1995 Colorado NL	3	1	8.57	48	69	28	40	2.02	-
1996 *Projection* >>>	2	0	6.44	43	55	19	29	1.73	-

HIGUERA, TEDDY - TL - Age 37
Higuera tried a comeback with the Padres last season, but was cut in spring training. He never recovered following the rotator cuff surgery.

HILLEGAS, SHAWN - TR - Age 30
Ex-major leaguer made a brief attempt to hang on with an Independent team in 1995; didn't make it.

HILJUS, ERIK - TR - Age 23
Santa Claus comes to Santa Clara (Calif.), Hilus' hometown, on his birthday. The 6'-5" righthander made good progress in the Florida State, but he still needs better control of his plus fastball. He's the leader of a wave of pitchers coming up behind the Pulsipher-Isringhausen-Roberts class at Binghamton, where Hiljus struggled in ten starts (going 2-4 with a 5.86 ERA) in 1995.

HILL, ERIC - TR - Age 28
A 43rd round pick in 1989, Hill toiled for three consecutive years at Double-A Reading, posting ERA's above 4.00 each season (not exactly the recipe for major league success). However, in his first full season out of the pen in 1994, he struck out nearly a batter per inning with a 2.5:1 strikeout/walk ratio. He's still a longshot to reach the majors, and was only fair in his first exposure to Triple-A.

	W	SV	ERA	IP	H	BB	SO	B/I	$
1995 Scranton AAA	4	2	4.30	23	24	9	16	1.44	

HILL, KEN - TR - Age 30
While Hill was putting together his 16-5 1994 campaign with the Expos, most observers overlooked the major deterioration in his K/BB ratio. Hill's fastball has lost a ton of steam since the 1992 season, his true peak. His conditioning and work ethic have also been called into question. Hill's mediocre control, easily overlooked when he had a strikeout pitch, consistently gets him into trouble now. Hill's elite days are over, though he could have a limited shelf life as a fourth starter.

	W	SV	ERA	IP	H	BB	SO	B/I	$
1994 Montreal NL	16	0	3.32	154	145	44	85	1.22	18
1995 St. Louis NL	6	0	5.06	110	125	45	50	1.54	
1995 Cleveland AL	4	0	3.98	74	77	32	48	1.46	4
1996 *Projection* >>>	10	0	4.68	195	214	84	104	1.53	1

HILL, MILT - TR - Age 30
The Pirates' organization has become a haven for pitchers rebounding from arm operations. While some of the gambles have worked out for the Pirates, this former Cincinnati prospect didn't particular glorify himself last season.

He'll probably get one last shot somewhere this season but he's past the age of becoming anything more than a long reliever.

	W	SV	ERA	IP	H	BB	SO	B/I	$
1994 Two Teams	1	0	6.94	35	48	17	26	1.86	-
1995 Calgary AAA	0	1	4.90	60	69	14	31	1.37	
1996 *Projection* >>>	1	0	6.72	35	47	16	26	1.80	-

HILL, TYRONE - TL - Age 23
Hill, the Brewers' 1991 first-round draft pick underwent shoulder surgery last June, and is expected to miss at least have of this season.

HILLMAN, ERIC - TL - Age 29
Hillman is a tall lefty like Randy Johnson, but the resemblance ends there. Hillman is a sinker/slider pitcher who needs to keep the ball down, which he didn't do well in 1994 and then took his stuff to Japan for a workout.

HITCHCOCK, STERLING - TL - Age 24
In 1995 Hitchcock was more wanted by other organizations than he was by the Yankees, but in the end he was a key player in the September surge of New York into the postseason. Hitchcock features a good live heater and also uses a two-seam sinking fastball and a straight change plus an assortment of sliders and splitter/forkballs. He's especially well-suited to pitching at Yankee Stadium.

	W	SV	ERA	IP	H	BB	SO	B/I	$
1994 New York AL	4	2	4.20	49	48	29	37	1.56	4
1995 New York AL	11	0	4.70	168	155	68	121	1.33	9
1996 *Projection* >>>	8	0	4.53	167	156	72	121	1.36	6

HOEME, STEVE - TR - Age 28
The 6-6, 230-pound Hoeme's career peaked in 1993, when he had 19 saves at Wichita. Last season he pitched with limited success in the Red Sox organization, his fourth, reaching Triple-A for the first time. He's a minor league free agent again, and may show up somewhere, but not in the majors.

HOFFMAN, TREVOR - TR - Age 28
Hard-throwing Padre closer Hoffman pitched the latter part of last year with shoulder pain, and, following the season, he underwent arthroscopic surgery to clean out his rotator cuff. The Padres expect Hoffman to be healed and ready for spring training.

	W	SV	ERA	IP	H	BB	SO	B/I	$
1994 San Diego NL	4	20	2.57	56	39	20	68	1.05	29
1995 San Diego NL	7	31	3.88	53	48	14	52	1.17	31
1996 *Projection* >>>	7	34	3.43	69	57	21	72	1.14	35

HOLDRIDGE, DAVID - TR - Age 27
Holdridge was a starter earlier in his minor league career, converted to relief in 1994. He's a much better reliever than he was a starter.

	W	SV	ERA	IP	H	BB	SO	B/I	$
1995 Vancouver AAA	0	1	4.61	13	18	7	13	1.83	

HOLLINS, JESSIE - TR - Age 26
The once-promising reliever has pitched one inning in the last two seasons due to a torn rotator cuff.

HOLLINS, STACY - TR - Age 23
Gradually working his way through the minors, Hollins had impressed at every stop until he got bombed in seven starts in the Triple-A Pacific Coast League. He needs at least one more year, but is still an interesting prospect.

HOLMAN, BRAD - TR - Age 28
Brian Holman's younger brother. Brad was signed by the Royals out of Auburn, but released during spring training 1991. The Mariners got steady results from Holman at Class A Eugene and AA Jacksonville (2.57 ERA and almost 4:1 strikeout/walk ratio in 1992). Holman attracted attention in the 1992 Arizona Fall League but has since bounced

around the Mariners, Orioles and Rockies farm systems.

HOLMAN, SHAWN - TR - Age 31
Holman is the kind of pitcher who looks better warming up in the bullpen than he does on the mound. In his one major league shot with the Tigers in 1989, he couldn't throw strikes. He has pitched 10 seasons in five organizations (61-62 career record), and was a minor league free agent during the off-season.

	W	SV	ERA	IP	H	BB	SO	B/I	$
1995 Albuquerque AAA	5	5	5.13	79	107	39	60	1.85	

HOLMES, DARREN - TR - Age 29
Holmes again led the Rockies in saves in 1995, but was more set-up man than closer late in the year. When he's "on," he has one of the best overhand curveballs in baseball, but when he's not, each appearance is truly an adventure. He starts a new two-year contract with the Rockies in 1996 and will probably share the closer role.

	W	SV	ERA	IP	H	BB	SO	B/I	$
1994 Colorado NL	0	3	6.35	28	35	24	33	2.08	
1995 Colorado NL	6	14	3.24	66	59	28	61	1.31	16
1996 Projection >>>	3	14	3.81	64	58	28	61	1.36	13

HOLT, CHRIS - TR - Age 24
Holt is a big righthander who has moved steadily up through the Astro system in his four year career. His strong point is control, he has maintained a strikeout to walk ratio over 3.3 for his career. If he continues to progress, he should get an opportunity to compete for a starting spot in the majors in 1997.

	W	SV	ERA	IP	H	BB	SO	B/I	$
1994 Jackson AA	10	0	3.45	167	169	22	111	1.14	
1995 Tucson AAA	5	0	4.10	118	155	32	69	1.58	

HOLZEMER, MARK - TL - Age 26
In 1993 and '94, Holzemer was a poor starter in Triple-A and for the Angels. Switched to relief last season, he pitched much more effectively, and is now a candidate for a 1996 job in the Angels bullpen doing just about everything except closing.

	W	SV	ERA	IP	H	BB	SO	B/I	$
1994 Vancouver AAA	5	0	6.60	117	144	58	77	1.72	
1995 California AL	0	0	5.40	8	11	7	5	2.22	-
1996 Projection >>>	1	0	5.11	36	40	17	22	1.58	-

HONEYCUTT, RICK - TL - Age 41
A long-time lefty short relief craftsman, Honeycutt hasn't had a year without a save since 1991. His basic mission, should he choose to keep it, is to get out one or two lefty batters in a tight situation.

	W	SV	ERA	IP	H	BB	SO	B/I	$
1994 Texas AL	1	1	7.20	25	37	9	18	1.84	-
1995 Two Teams	5	2	2.96	45	39	10	21	1.08	8
1996 Projection >>>	2	1	3.91	39	38	10	20	1.25	2

HOOK, CHRIS - TR - Age 27
A righthander bullpen specialist who held lefties to a .210 average and vultured five wins, but righties clubbed him, suggesting he will never rise above the specialist stage of his career.

	W	SV	ERA	IP	H	BB	SO	B/I	$
1995 San Francisco NL	5	0	5.50	52	55	29	40	1.61	-
1996 Projection >>>	3	0	5.24	35	37	19	27	1.59	-

HOPE, JOHN - TR - Age 25
Hope has had elbow and shoulder operations during his career but shows flashes of ability when healthy. He has an outstanding curveball and used it to baffle Triple-A Pacific Coast League hitters last season at Calgary. He's a starter all the way and has problems getting loose in the bullpen. For some inexplicable reason, the Pirates used him as a reliever in his brief callup last season. He needs to move on to another organization.

	W	SV	ERA	IP	H	BB	SO	B/I	$
1994 Pittsburgh NL	0	0	5.79	14	18	4	6	1.57	-

	W	SV	ERA	IP	H	BB	SO	B/I	$
1995 Calgary AAA	7	0	2.79	80	76	11	41	1.08	
1995 Pittsburgh NL	0	0	30.86	2	8	4	2	5.14	-
1996 Projection >>>	2	0	4.88	55	60	22	23	1.49	-

HORSMAN, VINCE - TL - Age 29
The Twins thought they had added some bullpen depth by obtaining Horsman before the start of the season. He managed just nine innings with them and will have to improve markedly to earn another big league job.

	W	SV	ERA	IP	H	BB	SO	B/I	$
1994 Oakland AL	0	0	4.91	29	29	11	20	1.36	-
1995 Salt Lake AAA	1	0	10.38	13	23	4	10	2.08	

HOSTETLER, MIKE - TR - Age 25
A 1994 leg injury set back Hostetler's career. His .500 record last year was better than it would seem, for the Greenville Braves finished 24 games under. He was hurt by 24 home run balls. He'll have to prove himself in Triple-A to get a major league shot.

HOWARD, CHRIS - TL - Age 30
Howard pitched effectively in Boston's bullpen in 1994, but found himself back in the minors after straining a forearm muscle last spring. The Rangers signed him in September after the Red Sox designated him for assignment. Howard is tough on lefthanders, so he can be an effective spot reliever.

	W	SV	ERA	IP	H	BB	SO	B/I	$
1995 Pawtucket AAA	3	0	3.92	20	25	4	19	1.15	
1995 Texas AL	0	0	0.00	4	3	1	2	1.00	-
1996 Projection >>>	1	0	3.77	34	33	12	19	1.31	0

HOWE, STEVE - TL - Age 38
For the second time in three years, Howe suffered from a mixture of unfavorable publicity, limited usage affecting his sharpness, and overall inconsistency, The good news is that he's been resilient and made a terrific comeback from similar circumstances in 1994. Physically he remains sound and just needs frequent work to break into the success/confidence cycle again; without that opportunity, however, it could be another long hard year in '96.

	W	SV	ERA	IP	H	BB	SO	B/I	$
1994 New York AL	3	15	1.80	40	28	7	18	0.88	26
1995 New York AL	6	2	4.96	49	66	17	28	1.69	2
1996 Projection >>>	3	4	3.99	51	58	14	26	1.41	5

HOWRY, BOBBY - TR - Age 22
Howry made the California League All-League team, but was probably only the third-best starter on his team. He's worth watching.

HOY, PETE - TR - Age 29
Once right behind Ken Ryan in the Red Sox depth charts, Hoy has sunk to the Independent league level.

HRUSOVSKY, JOHN - TR - Age 25
A major strikeout pitcher at the Single-A level, Hrusovsky has been hit hard at higher levels (most recently a 7.11 ERA at Double-A Canton-Akron) so you probably won't have to deal with the spelling or pronunciation of his name on a major league roster any time soon.

HUBBS, DAN - TR - Age 25
Overall Hubbs had a pretty good season at Double-A San Antonio, posting an impressive 3.3-to-1 strikeout to walk ratio. He'll advance to the Pacific Coast League in 1996 as a long reliever.

HUBER, JEFF - TL - Age 25
Huber was the bullpen ace for San Diego's AA Wichita farm club and is still advancing.

HUDEK, JOHN - TR - Age 29
Hudek established himself as the Astros' closer in 1994 and began the 1995 season impressively in the same role.

However, he suffered an unusual injury which required the removal of a rib and ended his season. The prognosis for a complete recovery is good. If he is able to regain his overpowering fastball, his only effective pitch, he has a good chance to regain his role as Houston's closer.

	W	SV	ERA	IP	H	BB	SO	B / I	$
1994 Houston NL	0	16	2.97	39	24	18	39	1.07	20
1995 Houston NL	2	7	5.40	20	19	5	29	1.20	6
1996 Projection >>>	1	2	5.00	36	27	13	43	1.12	2

HUDSON, JOE - TR - Age 25
Hudson earned his first major league callup with an excellent performance for Double-A Trenton where he tied for the team lead with eight saves. He doesn't throw very hard but has good command and improving control. Hudson isn't likely to be a big league closer, but can be useful in a setup role.

	W	SV	ERA	IP	H	BB	SO	B / I	$
1995 Boston AL	0	1	4.11	46	53	23	29	1.65	-
1996 Projection >>>	1	1	4.11	31	36	15	20	1.65	-

HUISMAN, RICK - TR - Age 26
Huisman came to the Royals in the mid-August Pat Borders trade with Houston. He pitched pretty effectively at Triple-A in 1995, but still needs more minor league seasoning. Huisman was mostly missing high with his good fastball; once he gets it under control he could get a chance as a setup man in the majors, or even a shot as a closer.

HUNTER, BOBBY - TR - Age 27
Despite their pitching woes and Hunter's impressive numbers, the Pirates never gave Hunter a call. Scouts simply don't believe he has major league stuff.

HUNTER, JIM - TR - Age 31
Still a marginal prospect at the end of 1992, Hunter is now just a reserve arm stored on the Triple-A roster, at best.

HUNTER, RICH - TR - Age 21
The Phils' 1993 14th round pick was no less than the Greg Maddux of the minor leagues, going 20-2 (including the Double-A playoffs) in a season spanning three minor league levels. Hunter's fastball maxes out around 85 MPH, but he can throw it on a dime. He also has a solid curve and a drop-dead changeup. In his first Double-A start, he pitched a one-hitter through seven innings in a pennant race while Blue Angels planes from a nearby air show buzzed the field. He will eventually be a number two or three starter for the Phils and should debut sometime in 1997. He'll begin 1996 at Double-A.

HURST, JAMES - TL - Age 28
The Orioles needed starting pitching in late August and called up Hurst from their Triple-A club. They quickly learned that Hurst was a former replacement player with the Rangers and immediately released him.

	W	SV	ERA	IP	H	BB	SO	B / I	$
1995 Two AAA Teams	1	5	7.20	50	73	26	43	1.98	

HURST, JONATHAN - TR - Age 29
After extensive labor in farm systems, Hurst has now had two shots at the majors, one in 1992 with the Expos and one last year with the Mets. He hasn't helped himself in those brief trials and will have some trouble getting another.

HURTA, BOB - TL - Age 30
He averaged over a strikeout per inning in 1992 at Jackson, but failed to challenge in a wide open competition for the Astros' lefty reliever job in 1993 and 1994. He may not get another chance.

HURTADO, EDWIN - TR - Age 26
Hurtado's ERA last year was misleading in that he actually threw the ball relatively well. With a nice sinking fastball and a good changeup, Hurtado's problem is allowing hitters too many high fastballs. If he shows better command in spring training, he could be a starter again in 1996. In the minors, he had a reputation for having the best control in the organization.

	W	SV	ERA	IP	H	BB	SO	B/I	$
1995 Toronto AL	5	0	5.45	77	81	40	33	1.56	-
1996 *Projection* >>>	3	0	5.12	52	42	37	22	1.51	-

HUTCHINS, JASON - TR - Age 26
Control problems plagued Hutchins, especially after his promotion to Double-A.

HUTCHESON, DAVID - TR - Age 24
Hutcheson won 14 games in 1994, but had more difficulty in his first full Double-A season at Orlando, giving up hits, walks and especially home runs (23) at an accelerated rate.

HUTTON, MARK - TR - Age 26
Hutton is a promising hard-thrower (mid-90's fastball) who just needs to keep the ball over the plate and stay healthy to be successful. Although he was limited to 11 starts in 1995, Yankees trade talks often involve other teams asking about Hutton.

	W	SV	ERA	IP	H	BB	SO	B/I	$
1994 Columbus AAA	2	3	3.63	34	31	12	27	1.24	
1995 Columbus AAA	2	0	8.43	52	64	24	23	1.68	

IGNASIAK, MIKE - TR - Age 30
Another possibility for some saves if Fetters stumbles, Ignasiak is a good hard thrower who often looks impressive but is plagued by wildness.

	W	SV	ERA	IP	H	BB	SO	B/I	$
1994 Milwaukee AL	3	0	4.53	47	51	13	24	1.34	2
1995 New Orleans AAA	1	0	2.50	18	9	8	19	0.95	
1995 Milwaukee AL	4	0	5.90	39	51	23	26	1.89	-
1996 *Projection* >>>	2	1	4.98	51	56	21	30	1.53	-

ILSLEY, BLAISE - TL - Age 31
Ilsley lingers in pro baseball after 11 seasons because of impeccable control - and he's a lefty. He hasn't allowed less than a hit per inning since 1987 - he just slops it up there and lets you put it in play. Everybody except O.J. pitched for the Phils in 1995, and yet Ilsley was not called up from Triple-A. He's just another journeyman nearing the end of his journey.

	W	SV	ERA	IP	H	BB	SO	B/I	$
1995 Scranton AAA	8	0	3.88	185	210	34	102	1.32	

INGRAM, TODD - TR - Age 28
Ingram pitched reasonably well in Double-A ball in the Oakland and Toronto organizations, but was a disaster after moving to the Red Sox farm at Trenton during last season. He just didn't throw strikes. Don't look for him in the majors.

INNIS, JEFF - TR - Age 33
Innis is on the downhill side of a long career as a middle innings reliever. He doesn't throw especially hard and hasn't been in the majors since 1993. He's strictly Triple-A bench filler at this point.

ISRINGHAUSEN, JASON - TR - Age 23
In late 1995 David Segui called Isringhausen simply "the best pitcher in the National League for being tough to hit." The dominant repertoire is founded on a curve that can hit spots precisely, a real major league fastball and an effective straight change. Maintaining last year's numbers will be a challenge, but Isringhausen in the real deal with a bright future.

	W	SV	ERA	IP	H	BB	SO	B/I	$
1995 New York NL	9	0	2.81	93	88	31	55	1.28	8
1996 *Projection* >>>	14	0	3.34	189	179	65	112	1.29	14

JACKSON, DANNY - TL - Age 34
Jackson was the clearly the biggest free-agent flop of 1995, though it wasn't all his fault. He was still recovering from thyroid cancer surgery when last season began, then suffered a season-ending ankle injury just as he started pitching well. The Cardinals didn't waste their money, though. There are few greater competitors in the game than Jackson and he's resurrected his career before.

	W	SV	ERA	IP	H	BB	SO	B / I	$
1994 Philadelphia NL	14	0	3.26	179	183	46	129	1.28	18
1995 St. Louis NL	2	0	5.90	100	120	48	52	1.68	-
1996 *Projection* >>>	8	0	4.41	164	179	59	101	1.45	-

JACKSON, MIKE - TR - Age 31
Jackson is a brilliant but somewhat fragile setup man who features an excellent fastball and hard slider. He missed the first month with shoulder tendinitis but was Cincinnati's most effective reliever after his return. He could close if given the opportunity, but he has never received a chance at the glamour job despite seven good years as a setup man.

	W	SV	ERA	IP	H	BB	SO	B / I	$
1994 San Francisco NL	3	4	1.49	42	23	11	51	0.80	12
1995 Cincinnati NL	6	2	2.39	49	38	19	41	1.16	7
1996 *Projection* >>>	5	3	2.88	59	41	25	56	1.13	9

JACOBSEN, JOE - TR - Age 24
Jacobsen pitched well in relief at both A Vero Beach and AA San Antonio in the Dodgers farm system. He could get some saves on the major league level in a few years. He still has Rudy Seanez and Greg Hansell ahead of him.

JACOME, JASON - TL - Age 25
Jacome's fastball tops out at 84 MPH, so he has to get by on smoke and mirrors. It was enough for once around the National League in 1994, but he got lit up in five NL starts for the Mets in 1995 and was dealt to Kansas City. For the Royals he fooled 'em once around the block but was roundly pounded the second time around the league. Jacome has now run out of major leagues, so he'll have to develop some new pitch(es) or he'll quickly be finished as a big league pitcher.

	W	SV	ERA	IP	H	BB	SO	B / I	$
1994 New York NL	4	0	2.67	54	54	17	30	1.31	5
1995 New York NL	0	0	10.29	21	33	15	11	2.29	-
1995 Kansas City AL	4	0	5.36	84	101	21	39	1.45	-
1996 *Projection* >>>	4	0	5.45	134	162	44	66	1.54	-

JAMES, MIKE - TR - Age 28
A rookie in the Angels bullpen last year, James did his job well as a middle reliever and mop-up man, typical low pressure situations where a rookie can be worked in. It's remarkable that except for saves, James's statistics like runners allowed per nine innings, opponents' batting average, and others, look almost like Lee Smith's.

	W	SV	ERA	IP	H	BB	SO	B / I	$
1995 California AL	3	1	3.88	55	49	26	36	1.36	3
1996 *Projection* >>>	3	2	3.69	60	55	29	39	1.40	4

JANICKI, PETE - TR - Age 25
Janicki was the Angels first round draft pick in 1992, but breaking his elbow two years in a row slowed his progress until last year, his first full season without an injury. He pitched very effectively in Class-A, and was promoted to Triple-A late in the season. Janicki is the Angels' top pitching prospect, and he is likely to be pitching for the Angels sometime in 1996.

	W	SV	ERA	IP	H	BB	SO	B / I	$
1995 Vancouver AAA	1	0	7.03	48	64	23	34	1.79	

JANZEN, MARTY - TR - Age 22
The pitching-poor Blue Jays organization received a real boost last season when it acquired Janzen in the David Cone trade. He advanced from A ball to Double-A without a drop in strikeout ratio. The most encouraging sign was that he

completed two of his seven starts at Knoxville after just one complete game in his first 57. Janzen should be in Triple-A this year, and could reach the majors.

JARVIS, KEVIN - TR - Age 26
After racing through the minors in three years, Jarvis has struggled at the major league level the last two seasons. He started 1995 as the fifth starter but was sent back to Indianapolis in July, where he pitched well the rest of the year. Jarvis features the standard four pitches and has shown good control in the minors but the Cincinnati rotation will be much tougher to crack in 1996 than it was in 1995.

	W	SV	ERA	IP	H	BB	SO	B/I	$
1994 Cincinnati NL	1	0	7.13	17	22	5	10	1.53	-
1995 Indianapolis AAA	4	0	4.45	60	62	18	37	1.32	
1995 Cincinnati NL	3	0	5.70	79	91	32	33	1.56	-
1996 *Projection* >>>	4	0	4.88	79	92	31	34	1.55	-

JARVIS, MATT - TL - Age 24
Jarvis is a starter/reliever struggling to get things together to get the call from the Orioles. He was hit hard last year.

JEAN, DOMINGO - TR - Age 27
The Rangers took a chance on Jean, and it was obvious that he is not the pitcher that he was prior to missing the 1994 season with arm injuries. Jean is as wild as ever, but has not regained the velocity he once had.

	W	SV	ERA	IP	H	BB	SO	B/I	$
1994			Did Not Play						
1995 Oklahoma City AAA	3	1	6.14	88	102	61	72	1.86	

JEFFCOAT, MIKE - TL - Age 36
Desperation by the Marlins brought on by injuries returned lefty Jeffcoat to the majors, despite his lack of major league stuff. Jeffcoat really hasn't been the same since an elbow injury in 1992 and even then he was barely capable of getting major league hitters out. Jeffcoat joined Omaha in August as roster filler. It's a wonder that he has held out this long: Jeffcoat's career is nearly finished.

JIMINEZ, MIGUEL - TR - Age 27
Since two brief appearances in the major leagues in 1993-4, Jiminez has taken large steps backwards. He hasn't been able to get out Triple-A hitters for the last two years. In particular Jiminez has little concept of the strike zone, having averaged nearly a walk per inning over the last few years. Until he can find the plate Jiminez will never get back to the big leagues.

JOHNS, DOUG - TL - Age 28
Johns has posted good ERAs in the offense-happy Pacific Coast League for two straight years, leading that league in ERA in 1994. However, he is old for a prospect, has never been overpowering, and while he held AL batters to a .226 average last season, Johns walked more batters than he struck out.

	W	SV	ERA	IP	H	BB	SO	B/I	$
1995 Oakland AL	5	0	4.61	54	44	26	25	1.29	3
1996 *Projection* >>>	4	0	4.58	74	73	23	34	1.30	2

JOHNSON, BARRY - TR - Age 26
Johnson has been pitching well, but in limited middle-relief roles, the last three seasons for the White Sox Double-A affiliate at Birmingham. Unless he shows he can handle a bigger role in Triple-A, he's not a prospect.

JOHNSON, CHRIS - TR - Age 27
Johnson had his best year since moving to the bullpen in 1993. He has been in three organizations in nine seasons without advancing past Double-A (with the Cubs' Orlando farm the last three years). He was a minor league free agent, and not expected to attract much attention.

JOHNSON, DANE - TR - Age 33
Johnson had a great second half for Triple-A Nashville in 1995, leading the team with 15 saves. His live fastball and split-finger pitch are an effective combination, but nine years in the minors, two in Taiwan and one as a coach at Lamar

University haven't taught him the value of throwing strikes consistently. Time has nearly run out on this former second round draft pick (Blue Jays, 1984).

	W	SV	ERA	IP	H	BB	SO	B/I	$
1995 Nashville AAA	4	15	2.41	56	48	28	51	1.36	
1996 Projection >>>	1	1	5.09	32	39	15	20	1.69	-

JOHNSON, DAVE - TR - Age 36
Ex-Oriole Johnson worked his way back to the majors with the pitching-poor Tigers. He has had shoulder surgery. Even as a healthy youngster, he usually had a high ERA.

JOHNSON, JEFF - TL - Age 29
Johnson was a sensation when he produced a 4-1 record with a 1.88 ERA immediately after his callup in 1991, a classic lesson why a 4-1 record doesn't mean a darn thing. When you get excited about this pitcher or that pitcher who is 4-1 in May 1994, stop and think about Jeff Johnson.

JOHNSON, JUDD - TL - Age 29
Johnson is too old to be a prospect. For two years he was a lefty long relief man in Richmond's bullpen. He doesn't throw hard enough to close games and lacks enough stamina to start them. Despite a good ERA at Triple-A, Johnson has a questionable major league future, although moving to the Twins organization in 1995 (3.43 ERA for Salt Lake) put him in a less competitive arena for major league consideration.

JOHNSON, RANDY - TL - Age 32
Of all major league starting pitchers, only Greg Maddux is clearly better. In the AL Johnson's in a class of his own. He's still improving and the bouts of mechanical problems seem to grow shorter. His walks peaked in 1991 at 152. They've gone down dramatically every year since.

	W	SV	ERA	IP	H	BB	SO	B/I	$
1994 Seattle AL	13	0	3.19	172	132	72	204	1.19	23
1995 Seattle AL	18	0	2.48	214	159	65	294	1.05	33
1996 Projection >>>	19	0	2.77	230	172	83	299	1.11	37

JOHNSTON, SEAN - TL - Age 25
Johnston has been a winner in the minors (38-20 in four seasons), including last year at Double-A Birmingham, but may not throw hard enough to make it to the majors with the White Sox.

JOHNSTON, JOEL - TR - Age 29
Johnston has spent brief portions of the last five seasons with three different major league clubs, most recently four innings for Boston in 1995. A 6.59 ERA at Triple-A Pawtucket hastened his release and he finished the year with Triple-A Colorado Springs. As with many hard throwers, Johnston has control problems and won't get a longer big league shot until he harnesses it.

	W	SV	ERA	IP	H	BB	SO	B/I	$
1994 Buffalo AAA	0	2	5.14	14	8	14	11	1.57	
1995 Two AAA Teams	2	0	5.96	22	26	12	14	1.68	

JOHNSTONE, JOHN - TR - Age 27
Just as Johnstone was settling into his best opportunity to secure a major league middle relief role, he was struck down by an elbow injury. Though he was primarily a starter in the minors, he showed promise in a late 1994 relief stint with the Marlins' Triple-A affiliate, where he used his plus fastball to shut down righthanded hitters. While he lingered on the sidelines, nondescript pitchers such as Terry Mathews and Randy Veres earned key bullpen roles. Even if Johnstone's elbow is healthy, he will never again have such a golden big league opportunity.

	W	SV	ERA	IP	H	BB	SO	B/I	$
1996 Projection >>>	1	0	4.88	30	35	17	28	1.72	-

JONES, BARRY - TR - Age 33
Jones got thrashed in the bigs for the second straight season, although he continues to impress whenever demoted to the minors.

JONES, BOBBY - TL - Age 23
The Rockies acquired Jones from the Milwaukee organization. He wasn't ready for a jump from A ball to Triple-A, but pitched well after a demotion to Double-A New Haven. He is a power pitcher, but lacks the other two sure-fire ingredients for success: a pitcher-friendly home park and height (he's 6-0).

JONES, BOBBY - TR - Age 26
The Mets opening day starter a year ago, Jones will likely slide into a third or fourth slot as bigger talents emerge -- even if he's there again on opening day this year. Jones is a classic heady pitcher with a large repertoire, fine control, and the ability to battle in games when he doesn't have his best stuff.

	W	SV	ERA	IP	H	BB	SO	B/I	$
1994 New York NL	12	0	3.15	160	157	56	80	1.33	14
1995 New York NL	10	0	4.19	195	209	53	127	1.33	6
1996 Projection >>>	12	0	3.82	206	213	60	123	1.33	9

JONES, CALVIN - TR - Age 32
Jones has established himself as a viable closer at the Triple-A level, last year with the Pawtucket Red Sox. He sometimes has trouble with control, particularly forkballs that dive into the dirt.

JONES, DOUG - TR - Age 38
Jones had a solid season as the Orioles closer last year, but new O's Manager Davey Johnson prefers an overpowering closer, so Jones will most likely be closing elsewhere in 1996. He is an effective closer whose best pitch is a change-up. Jones is prone to a few bad outings every year, especially if he gets too much rest between appearances. The bad days inflate his statistics.

	W	SV	ERA	IP	H	BB	SO	B/I	$
1994 Philadelphia NL	2	27	2.17	54	55	6	38	1.13	35
1995 Baltimore AL	0	22	5.01	46	55	16	42	1.52	19
1996 Projection >>>	1	15	4.94	63	76	18	48	1.50	13

JONES, JIMMY - TR - Age 31
A former high draft pick in 1982 - taken ahead of Dwight Gooden - Jones spent most of 1995 on the disabled list with the Yomiyuri Giants in Japan. He last appeared in the US major leagues with Montreal in 1993. Jones has never lived up to his vast potential.

JONES, STACY - TR - Age 28
One of several marginal relievers who got saves for Triple-A New Orleans in 1995, Jones has been an effective Double-A pitcher for years, but really has not accomplished very much at higher levels. He got a cup of coffee with the Orioles in 1991, which may turn out to be his career highlight. Should he return to the big leagues he'd be a middle relief/situational specialist.

	W	SV	ERA	IP	H	BB	SO	B/I	$
1994 Shreveport AA	3	34	2.39	64	73	12	64	1.32	
1995 New Orleans AAA	3	6	3.02	47	51	12	39	1.33	

JONES, TODD - TR - Age 27
Hard-throwing Jones had taken over the closer role from John Hudek when Mike Henneman was added for the pennant stretch drive. Jones has the strikeout ability desired in a relief ace, but has recently had some control problems. Obviously, save opportunities are at the discretion of the manager, but Jones would appear to have an inside track to regain the closer job should Henneman retire as expected.

	W	SV	ERA	IP	H	BB	SO	B/I	$
1994 Houston NL	5	5	2.72	72	52	26	63	1.07	15
1995 Houston NL	6	15	3.07	99	89	52	96	1.41	17
1996 Projection >>>	5	12	3.26	102	96	46	94	1.40	14

JORDAN, RICARDO - TL - Age 25
Jordan struggled in the major leagues but has enjoyed enough success in the minors to get another look in the spring. With the Blue Jays, he didn't show much of the great fastball he possesses. With Tony Castillo likely moving back to the lefty setup role, Jordan's chances were slim, but not impossible, of returning to the majors in 1996.

	W	SV	ERA	IP	H	BB	SO	B/I	$
1995 Syracuse AAA	0	0	6.57	12	15	7	17	1.78	
1995 Toronto AL	1	1	6.60	15	18	13	10	2.02	-
1996 *Projection* >>>	1	3	4.78	34	36	18	26	1.59	1

JUDEN, JEFF - TR - Age 25
A huge (6'8", 265 lbs.) righthander, Juden has pretty good stuff, but not very good control of it. He has walked 4.3 batters per nine innings in parts of four years in the majors. Still, 1995 was his most successful year as he made ten starts for Philadelphia and went 6-4 with a 4.10 ERA for Triple-A Scranton/Wilkes-Barre. Juden will have a chance to crack the Phillies jumble of a starting rotation in 1996.

	W	SV	ERA	IP	H	BB	SO	B/I	$
1994 Philadelphia NL	1	0	6.18	27	29	12	22	1.48	-
1995 Philadelphia NL	2	0	4.02	62	53	31	47	1.34	1
1996 *Projection* >>>	9	0	4.10	190	169	92	145	1.37	3

JUHL, MIKE - TL - Age 26
A smallish lefty with good control, Juhl had walked only 38 batters in four years, but in 1995 after his first promotion above A-ball, found out what patient hitters look like, almost doubling his career walk total in one year.

KAISER, JEFF - TL - Age 35
Like many veteran lefties past their prime years, Kaiser was able to find major league work in 1993. He is (to understate the case) not a prospect.

KAMIENIECKI, SCOTT - TR - Age 31
For years Kamieniecki kept beginning each year in the pen and then winning a spot in the starting rotation when someone else got injured. In 1995 he was handed a spot, but then missed almost half the year with an elbow strain. Kamieniecki finished strong and looks OK for 1996. He will never be a staff ace, but he's a steady presence good enough for any team.

	W	SV	ERA	IP	H	BB	SO	B/I	$
1994 New York AL	8	0	3.76	117	115	59	71	1.48	7
1995 New York AL	7	0	4.01	89	83	49	43	1.48	4
1996 *Projection* >>>	9	0	3.92	145	140	74	76	1.47	6

KARCHNER, MATT - TR - Age 28
Twice a Rule Five draft pick, Karchner is being groomed as a potential closer by the White Sox. He had a marvelous 1995 campaign, leading Triple-A Nashville with fifteen saves and a 1.45 ERA. The White Sox like the way he challenges hitters and he has fine control, too. Karchner didn't back down in his first big league trial late in 1995; he'll have a chance at a setup role - or more - in 1996.

	W	SV	ERA	IP	H	BB	SO	B/I	$
1995 Chicago AL	4	0	1.69	32	33	12	24	1.41	3
1996 *Projection* >>>	3	1	3.55	33	34	12	25	1.38	2

KARL, SCOTT - TL - Age 24
Inclusion in the Arizona Rookie League in 1994 indicates the Brewers have high hopes for Karl. He still needs a lot of work at this point. Drafted in the sixth round in '92, out of the University of Hawaii. Karl throws only a mid-80s fastball, but gets batters to beat balls into the ground with his changeup and curve.

	W	SV	ERA	IP	H	BB	SO	B/I	$
1995 Milwaukee AL	6	0	4.14	124	141	50	59	1.54	3
1996 *Projection* >>>	4	0	4.14	84	93	33	40	1.51	1

KARP, RYAN - TL - Age 25
Karp is a breaking ball specialist who has been able to post reasonable strikeout totals despite the lack of a plus fastball. An angular (6'4", 205 lbs.) lefty, he was dominant in Class-A, but needed two seasons to master Double-A, and had mixed results in his first crack at Triple-A in 1995. At his age, his biggest plus is his status as a southpaw - he will be a longshot in the race for the Phils' 1996 fifth starter role and could also be a fit as a middleman in the pen.

	W	SV	ERA	IP	H	BB	SO	B/I	$
1995 Scranton AAA	7	0	4.20	81	81	31	73	1.38	
1996 Projection >>>	1	0	4.62	36	28	28	36	1.56	-

KARSAY, STEVE - TR - Age 24
He missed the entire 1995 season due to injury. Watch him carefully for at least one year after he returns, if he does return. He was a good pitcher before the injuries.

	W	SV	ERA	IP	H	BB	SO	B/I	$
1994 Oakland AL	1	0	2.57	28	26	8	15	1.21	2
1996 Projection >>>	2	0	3.84	38	36	13	22	1.29	1

KAUFMAN, BRAD - TR - Age 23
Kaufman had a few bad games in Double-A last year, inflating his statistics. His fastball hits the radar gun at 95 MPH, and he has a good slider. He strikes out almost one hitter per inning on average, a good sign for a minor league pitcher.

KEAGLE, GREG - TR - Age 24
Keagle is a starter who struggled in Double-A in 1994 and in Triple-A last year. In Triple-A, he walked more than he struck out, indicating that he is not quite ready for prime time. Keagle was traded to the Mariners as the player-to-be-named in the Andy Benes deal.

	W	SV	ERA	IP	H	BB	SO	B/I	$
1995 Las Vegas AAA	7	0	4.28	75	76	42	49	1.56	

KELING, KOREY - TR - Age 27
Keling has pitched as both a starter and a reliever in Double-A for the past two years. He improved greatly last year, and his 3.46 ERA at Midland in the Texas League, a hitter's paradise, is outstanding. He will likely start in Triple-A in 1996, and may get called to the Angels to help the bullpen.

KELLEY, RICH - TL - Age 25
Kelley was a starter and reliever last year in Double-A with mixed success. He had some good years in the lower minors, and it remains to be seen if he can be successful in the higher minors and the majors.

KELLY, JOHN - TR - Age 28
Kelly is a former St. Louis farmhand, now toiling for Detroit, who notched a few seasons of high save totals despite a lack of velocity. His good year for Detroit's Double-A club in '95 guarantees him little except an eventual shot at the major leagues. Kelly is another example of why minor league saves mean little toward major league bullpen success.

KENDRENA, KEN - TR - Age 25
Moving from the Florida organization to Montreal's, Kendrena pitched better after an in-season promotion to Double-A. He's strictly a middle reliever/set-up man, and not really a prospect.

KETCHEN, DOUG - TR - Age 27
Ketchen has completed six years in the Astro system without establishing credentials as a major league prospect. He was hit hard in his first exposure at the Triple-A level in 1995.

KEY, JIMMY - TL - Age 34
Key's rotator cuff acted up again in 1995, taking the Yanks ace out for the season. Now it's a question how much, if at all, Key can pitch in 1996. Whatever he can do, it is likely to be good quality. Key has a long history of strong comebacks raising hope for one more.

	W	SV	ERA	IP	H	BB	SO	B/I	$
1994 New York AL	17	0	3.27	168	177	52	97	1.36	20
1995 New York AL	1	0	5.64	30	40	6	14	1.53	-
1996 Projection >>>	6	0	3.63	98	105	25	58	1.33	7

KEYSER, BRIAN - TR - Age 29
Desperation set in for the White Sox in 1995, forcing Keyser into their major league rotation. He's not really a major league pitcher; his Triple-A success in recent years belies his lack of talent. Keyser is barely a marginal major leaguer.

	W	SV	ERA	IP	H	BB	SO	B/I	$
1995 Chicago AL	5	0	4.97	92	114	27	48	1.53	1
1996 *Projection* >>>	3	0	5.16	62	77	18	32	1.53	-

KIEFER, MARK - TR - Age 27
Kiefer did fine for a rookie set up man. He has a strong fastball and a good mix of breaking pitches.

	W	SV	ERA	IP	H	BB	SO	B/I	$
1994 Milwaukee AL	1	0	8.43	10	15	8	8	2.16	-
1995 New Orleans AAA	8	0	2.82	70	60	19	52	1.13	
1995 Milwaukee AL	4	0	3.44	49	37	27	41	1.30	4
1996 *Projection* >>>	3	0	3.93	48	39	27	39	1.37	1

KIELY, JOHN - TR - Age 31
Kiely has previously spent parts of three seasons in Detroit, but has since been slowed by injury, pitching just 25 innings the last two years. He's a fringe minor league pitcher at this point, with little prospect of returning to the big leagues.

KILE, DARRYL - TR - Age 27
After his excellent 1993 season, Kile faltered so badly in the next two years that he was sent to the minors for a month. He has a fastball in the nineties and one of the best curveballs in baseball. However, he lacks consistent command of his pitches and he easily loses his self confidence. If he ever gets it all together, Kile could still be an outstanding major league pitcher.

	W	SV	ERA	IP	H	BB	SO	B/I	$
1994 Houston NL	9	0	4.57	147	153	82	105	1.59	0
1995 Tucson AAA	2	0	8.51	24	29	12	15	1.69	
1995 Houston NL	4	0	4.96	127	114	73	113	1.47	-
1996 *Projection* >>>	8	0	4.66	165	156	89	134	1.49	-

KILGO, RUSTY - TL - Age 29
Signed as a free agent in 1992, Kilgo led the Southern League in saves in 1995. He is too old to be considered a serious prospect, but he posted a 4.7 to 1 strikeout to walk ratio and will get a second chance at Triple-A Indianapolis in 1996. The Reds are desperate for lefthanded relievers.

KILGUS, PAUL - TL - Age 34
The soft-throwing journeyman made his way back to the majors with the Cardinals in 1993, but he couldn't stay healthy. He was once a promising starter for Texas, however, at this point his best bet is to continue his major league career as the 10th or 11th pitcher somewhere.

KING, KEVIN - TL - Age 27
A tall (6'4") control pitcher, King has never pitched well above Double-A ball and hasn't made any progress since two short appearances for the Mariners in 1993-4. He had a 3.77 ERA for Double-A Port City in 1995, but struggled in Triple-A, posting a 7.56 ERA while allowing 33 hits in 17 innings. If King makes it back to the big leagues it would be as a situational lefthander.

	W	SV	ERA	IP	H	BB	SO	B/I	$
1996 *Projection* >>>	1	0	6.10	31	38	15	16	1.70	-

KIPPER, BOB - TL - Age 31
Kipper was last up with the Twins in 1992, as a lefty setup man and middle reliever behind Mark Guthrie and Gary Wayne. These specialists are supposed to be safe, but Kipper wasn't. Future looks gloomy.

KIRKREIT, DARON - TR - Age 23
The Indians' 1993 number one pick was considered to be among their finest upper minor league starting pitching prospects entering 1995, but control and injury problems set back his progress significantly. The 6'6", 225 lbs., righty possesses an above average fastball, slider and curve, but he didn't throw any of them consistently for strikes at Double-A Canton-Akron. In two years, he is now 5-14 with an ERA of 5.92 at that level. Kirkreit will have to overcome his Double-A phobia in 1996 before any further advancement. Bartolo Colon and Casey Whitten have clearly passed him in the eyes of Indians' brass.

KISER, GARLAND - TL - Age 27
Terrific in the low minors 1989-1991. Still stuck in the minors but still young enough to make it.

KLINE, STEVE - TL - Age 23
Kline had a bittersweet 1995, missing a healthy chunk of the season with elbow problems, then skipping over a level to Double-A Canton-Akron without being overmatched. Kline was a strikeout pitcher at low Class-A Columbus in 1994. His loss of power in 1995 was partially due to the injury, and partially due to the fact that his average fastball couldn't overmatch higher classification hitters. Still, he averaged over six innings per start in cementing a Triple-A rotation spot for 1996. His major league future could be in the bullpen.

KLINGENBECK, SCOTT - TR - Age 25
Acquired from Baltimore for Scott Erickson, Klingenbeck has given up more than a hit per inning for the last two years and hasn't yet had the benefit of a full year at Triple-A. The Twins shouldn't have been surprised to see him struggle in a variety of roles in '95. His good control will secure him a future as a long reliever or swingman in '96.

	W	SV	ERA	IP	H	BB	SO	B/I	$
1995 Baltimore-Minnesota AL	2	0	7.12	79	101	42	42	1.79	-
1996 Projection >>>	2	0	5.44	57	70	25	30	1.68	-

KLINK, JOE - TL - Age 34
"Colonel" Klink was a lefty situational reliever for Triple-A Buffalo in 1995, getting an occasional save and generally pitching pretty well. He won't get a second look with the Indians, but would have a chance to win a one-out lefty role for a weaker major league club.

	W	SV	ERA	IP	H	BB	SO	B/I	$
1995 Buffalo AAA	2	8	3.00	39	31	15	32	1.18	

KLOEK, KEVIN - TR - Age 24
After his second year at AA El Paso, the Brewers sent him to the Arizona Fall League in 1994 to see if he was ready to move up. The result: a third year at El Paso in 1995, no better than his previous tries.

KNACKERT, BRENT - TR - Age 26
A Rule Five pick in 1989, has been stuck at Double-A since spending a year in Seattle. The Mets got a 2.30 ERA and 11 saves out of him at Binghamton in 1995, raising fresh new hopes.

KNOWLES, GREG - TR - Age 27
At age 26 last year, Knowles was a little old to be a reliever in Double-A. He didn't pitch particularly well last year, and unless he turns things around quickly, his future is limited.

KNUDSEN, KURT - TR - Age 29
Knudsen has below average stuff and hasn't been effective in his brief major league appearances, despite seven saves for the Tigers from 1992 to 1994. He can get Triple-A hitters out, but can get his pitches past big league hitters. It's unlikely that he'll get another change in the majors.

KOLLER, JERRY - TR - Age 23
Koller has been a workmanlike number three-type starter the past two seasons with the Double-A Greenville Braves. He was not helped by his home park's small dimensions, but he wouldn't get a break in Atlanta either. He'd be better off, but not a star, in another organization.

KONIECZKI, DOM - TL - Age 26
If Konieczki could throw strikes, he would be a prospect. He can blow away hitters, especially lefthanders. He has never started a game in five pro seasons, but hasn't been a regular closer since 1992.

KONUSZEWSKI, DENNIS - TR - Age 25
The fact that Konuszewski was called up from Double-A Carolina for a brief spell last August is an indictment of the Pirates' pool of pitching talent. Though he has a live arm, he has little idea of how to pitch and needs at least two more seasons in the minors.

KOTARSKI, MIKE - TL - Age 25
Kotarski, who throws hard but not always over the plate, improved significantly in his second try at Double-A. If he can do the same with Triple-A Colorado Springs this season, he may have a shot with the Rockies.

KOTES, CHRIS - TR - Age 26
Time is running out on Kotes, who pitched well neither as a starter nor as a reliever with Toronto's Double-A farm at Knoxville.

KRAMER, TOM - TR - Age 28
A big season at Double-A Chattanooga wasn't enough for the Reds to protect Kramer on their 40-man roster. He spent all of 1993 with the Indians, and went 7-3 including a shutout. Kramer throws gas, and seems to have harnessed the control trouble that knocked him out of the majors. With the state of pitching in today's majors, he should be worthy of a shot.

KRIVDA, RICK - TL - Age 26
Krivda looks like a younger version of Jamie Moyer. He has below average stuff, relying on changing speeds and location to be effective. He was a consistent winner in the minors, leading the league in strikeouts. But he is home-run prone, and at best, will be a fifth starter or a reliever.

	W	SV	ERA	IP	H	BB	SO	B/I	$
1995 Baltimore AL	2	0	4.54	75	76	25	53	1.34	2
1996 Projection >>>	2	0	4.65	51	51	18	36	1.36	0

KROON, MARC - TR - Age 22
Kroon is a top Padres pitching prospect with an outstanding arm and a blazing fastball hitting the radar guns in the 95-97 MPH range. He gets a lot of strikeouts, plus he gave up less than an average of one hit per inning last year. Collectively, such statistics usually indicate that a minor-league pitcher has a good chance of success in the majors, although he needs to improve his slider and change-up.

KRUEGER, BILL - TL - Age 37
Kreuger's baseballological clock is ticking, but he's a lefty so he might actually land somewhere.

	W	SV	ERA	IP	H	BB	SO	B/I	$
1994 Two Teams	3	0	6.38	60	68	24	47	1.52	-
1995 Tacoma AAA	5	0	4.26	50	52	9	39	1.20	
1995 Two Teams	2	0	6.18	27	50	8	16	2.10	-
1996 Projection >>>	2	0	5.83	38	52	13	27	1.71	-

KUTZLER, JERRY - TR - Age 31
Kutzler made seven starts for the White Sox in 1990, and since then has been a consistent Triple-A pitcher. He balanced a hot start in 1995 with a really awful stretch in June, then settled down to his usual level of performance. He's a Triple-A pitcher at best.

	W	SV	ERA	IP	H	BB	SO	B/I	$
1995 Omaha AAA	8	4	4.02	103	128	27	45	1.50	

LACY, KERRY - TR - Age 23
As is often the case with star closers from the low minors, Lacy has been unable to achieve the same degree of dominance in Double-A. Lacy will probably move up to Triple-A Oklahoma City, where he needs more work on controlling his breaking pitches.

LANCASTER, LES - TR - Age 33
Another of the aging, veteran relievers who filled Triple-A Buffalo's bullpen in 1995, Lancaster had the kind of season you would expect from a journeyman minor leaguer. He was a big winner a year earlier, going 14-3 out of Triple-A Syracuse's bullpen in 1994. Lancaster would have an outside shot at a return to the big leagues with a weaker team.

	W	SV	ERA	IP	H	BB	SO	B/I	$
1994 Syracuse AAA	14	3	3.61	89	95	25	69	1.34	
1995 Buffalo AAA	4	0	4.31	87	90	19	69	1.24	

LANE, AARON - TL - Age 24
This southpaw reliever had a very good season in Double-A last year. He could be a set-up man in the Orioles bullpen in 1996 or '97.

LANGSTON, MARK - TL - Age 35
Langston had an off-year as he pitched with shoulder pain for the latter two months of the season. Earlier, he experienced elbow tightness. But he was lucky and received very good run support from the Angels' hitters, averaging over seven runs per game. It was the second year in a row that he has experienced troublesome ailments and ERA's over 4.00. It could be that his below-4.00 ERA years are over, and with that, the yearly 16-18 wins.

	W	SV	ERA	IP	H	BB	SO	B/I	$
1994 California AL	7	0	4.68	119	121	54	109	1.47	4
1995 California AL	15	0	4.63	200	212	64	142	1.38	10
1996 *Projection* >>>	14	0	4.46	211	216	73	161	1.37	10

LaPOINT, DAVE - TL - Age 36
LaPoint pitched for the Twins' Triple-A franchise in 1993, hoping to make a comeback. He didn't.

LARKIN, ANDY - TR - Age 22
Larkin endured a lost season in 1995 as a result of elbow problems and back spasms. He had established himself as a top prospect in 1994, as he featured a 90 MPH fastball and a sharp curve while posting a strikeout/walk ratio of nearly five to one at low A-ball Kane County. In his limited 1995 Double-A run, he was quite difficult to hit, though his strikeout rate was down. He should open 1996 in Triple-A, and if his health is sound and he retains his velocity, he should be a viable candidate for the Marlins' rotation in 1997.

LA ROSA, MARK - TL - Age 27
West Palm Beach's bullpen ace, La Rosa overpowered Florida State League batters. If he does well at Double-A in 1995, he could be in the majors in 1996.

LAWRENCE, SEAN - TL - Age 25
Lawrence struggled last season in his first taste of Double-A. However, the Pirates like his arm and he'll get another chance at Carolina this season.

LAYANA, TIM - TR - Age 32
This soft-tossing journeyman reliever has fallen as far as A-ball in 1994, then posted a horrible 8.50 ERA while allowing two baserunners per inning at a pitchers' park in Ottawa. Once a middle reliever in the Reds' major league bullpen, Layana can no longer even retire Triple-A hitters.

LEACH, TERRY - TR - Age 42
Underwent a wrist-to-elbow ligament transplant in September. Leach vows a return despite his age. As with most righty submariners, could probably make a living retiring righthanded batters almost indefinitely.

LEAHY, PAT - TR - Age 25
The Marlins' 1992 sixth-round pick ventured above Single-A for the first time in 1994, with disastrous results. A massive (6-6, 245) righty who can be tough on righthanded hitters, he's remained unimpressive above Class A.

LEARY, TIM - TR - Age 37
Any team that needs Leary to fill out its rotation is in big trouble. Given the sorry state of pitching in the big leagues, Leary will probably get another call from somebody in 1995.

LEE, JEREMY - TR - Age 21
The third of four Toronto first-round draft picks in '93, and the second of three pitchers. He also was the only one who signed early enough to pitch in the minors in 1994, because he accepted a relatively meager $165,000 bonus. Another big one, at 6'7".

LEE, MARK - TL - Age 31
Lee was promoted from Triple-A during the season as the Orioles bullpen needed some new arms. He's a set-up man and a situational reliever, frequently brought in to get a lefthanded hitter out. The Orioles plan to strengthen their

bullpen for 1996, so Lee may be looking for a job.

	W	SV	ERA	IP	H	BB	SO	B/I	$
1994 Iowa AAA	1	10	3.38	61	69	21	42	1.47	
1995 Baltimore AL	2	1	4.86	33	31	18	27	1.47	1
1996 Projection >>>	1	1	5.10	31	30	16	25	1.48	-

LEFTWICH, PHIL - TR - Age 26
Leftwich was first called up to the Angels in 1993 and showed good promise going 4-6 with a solid 3.79 ERA. But he had a disappointing year in 1994, making 20 starts with a 5-10 record. Last year was almost a complete loss as he underwent surgery on his pitching shoulder, missing most of the season. The outlook for 1996 is unclear, and he will most likely spend some time in the minors to re-establish himself.

	W	SV	ERA	IP	H	BB	SO	B/I	$
1994 California AL	5	0	5.68	114	127	42	67	1.48	0
1995 Vancouver AAA	2	0	3.19	36	28	9	25	1.01	
1996 Projection >>>	3	0	5.40	56	61	20	31	1.45	-

LEGAULT, KEVIN - TR - Age 25
Legault had the best of his four minor league seasons working out of the bullpen for Minnesota's Double-A farm at New Britain going 6-1 with three saves. He can pitch to spots, and could earn a spot with a Twins team needing pitching. Watch him in Triple-A in 1996.

LEIPER, DAVE - TL - Age 33
After being out of the majors for five years and surviving a life-threating blood clot in his shoulder, Leiper returned with Oakland in 1994. He was dealt to Montreal midway through last season and did a fine job as a set-up man. He has pitched better than ever the last two years and figures to have some more good seasons left as a lefty specialist out of the bullpen.

	W	SV	ERA	IP	H	BB	SO	B/I	$
1994 Tacoma AAA	1	4	2.05	26	25	8	24	1.25	
1994 Oakland AL	0	1	1.93	18	13	6	14	1.02	3
1995 Oakland AL	1	0	3.57	22	23	13	10	1.59	-
1995 Montreal NL	0	2	2.86	22	16	6	12	1.00	3
1996 Projection >>>	1	2	3.34	38	33	16	21	1.28	3

LEITER, AL - TL - Age 30
After eight years of promise, Leiter finally had his good season. His fastball has always been his biggest asset and he didn't suddenly gain control last year. He kept the ball down and has now become effective against both righty and lefty hitters. Leiter entered the winter as a free agent and both Boston and Florida were said to be in hot competition with the Jays for his services.

	W	SV	ERA	IP	H	BB	SO	B/I	$
1994 Toronto AL	6	0	5.08	111	125	65	100	1.70	-
1995 Toronto AL	11	0	3.64	183	162	108	153	1.48	10
1996 Projection >>>	11	0	4.04	181	171	106	152	1.53	5

LEITER, MARK - TR - Age 32
Leiter led the Giants in wins and innings pitched, working solely as a starting pitcher, and deserved the kudos which accompanied his results. Nevertheless, he is not a staff ace, despite the Giants' needs in that area, but rather a surprisingly useful third or fourth starter.

	W	SV	ERA	IP	H	BB	SO	B/I	$
1994 California AL	4	2	4.72	95	99	35	71	1.41	6
1995 San Francisco NL	10	0	3.82	195	185	55	129	1.23	11
1996 Projection >>>	10	1	3.89	183	177	53	124	1.26	10

LEON, DANNY - TR - Age 28
After a good season at AA Tulsa in 1992, Leon hasn't done much to impress. Poor control is holding him back.

LESKANIC, CURT - TR - Age 27
Leskanic started his first complete major league season as a middle reliever and ended it as the Rockies' most

effective closer. He is durable (led the NL in appearances) and unafraid to challenge hitters with his fastball (led NL relievers in strikeouts). Eccentric Leskanic shaves his arm to cut down on wind resistance; he's a good bet to emerge as the primary closer in 1996.

	W	SV	ERA	IP	H	BB	SO	B/I	$
1994 Colorado NL	1	0	5.64	22	27	10	17	1.66	-
1995 Colorado NL	6	10	3.40	98	83	33	107	1.18	16
1996 *Projection* >>>	5	15	3.60	81	73	28	82	1.25	17

LEVINE, ALAN - TR - Age 27
After his career Triple-A record as a starter fell to 0-4, Levine was demoted to the bullpen at Double-A Birmingham. He is a strikeout pitcher whose fastball and curve could be good enough to make him a candidate as closer with the White Sox Triple-A team at Nashville this year.

LEWIS, JIM - TR - Age 26
Lewis is a finesse righty snatched by the Indians from the Astros in the Rule 5 draft following the 1994 season. He is an eminently hittable pitcher who cannot sneak his fastball past high minor league hitters. He is a watered down version of 1995 Triple-A teammate Joe Roa, who went 17-3 in 1995. Roa is no lock to be a major league contributor, so that should give one an idea as to where Lewis stands.

	W	SV	ERA	IP	H	BB	SO	B/I	$
1995 Buffalo AAA	6	1	3.64	94	101	25	50	1.34	

LEWIS, RICHIE - TR - Age 30
Lewis is a curveball specialist who will throw his hook to anyone, on any count. Lewis has historically struggled with his control and has had trouble retiring lefthanded hitters. Ironically, after a season in which he made some progress on both of those fronts, he was removed from the Marlins' 40-man roster and became a free agent. He sits squarely on the major league fringe.

	W	SV	ERA	IP	H	BB	SO	B/I	$
1994 Florida NL	1	0	5.67	54	62	38	45	1.85	-
1995 Charlotte AAA	5	0	3.20	59	50	20	45	1.19	
1995 Florida NL	0	0	3.75	36	30	15	32	1.25	0
1996 *Projection* >>>	1	0	4.45	55	53	30	47	1.52	-

LEWIS, SCOTT - TR - Age 30
Lewis pitched horribly in his short stint with the Angels in 1994 before he got hurt. He started 1995 on the Mariners farm and then moved on to the Red Sox Pawtucket franchise, working a total of only 14 innings in his comeback campaign.

LIEBER, JON - TR - Age 25
Few pitchers have had a quicker fall than Lieber. He went from being the Pirates' opening-night starter last season to being a batting practice pitcher for Triple-A Calgary. The Pirates got a little carried away with his average rookie season in 1994 and dubbed him the ace of the staff. He crumbled under the expectations and will now try to piece his career back together. At the very best, he'll be a No. 4 starter.

	W	SV	ERA	IP	H	BB	SO	B/I	$
1994 Pittsburgh NL	6	0	3.73	108	116	25	71	1.30	7
1995 Calgary AAA	1	0	7.01	77	122	19	34	1.84	
1995 Pittsburgh NL	4	0	6.32	72	103	14	45	1.62	-
1996 *Projection* >>>	5	0	5.06	95	118	20	60	1.46	-

LILLIQUIST, DEREK - TL - Age 30
1995 represents the worst end of a three-year downward trend for Lilliquist. He recorded nearly as many homers as strikeouts before his mid-season release; he hooked on with the Dodgers' Triple-A Albuquerque franchise to finish the year. Lilliquist could still re-surface as a situational lefty, but his days as a successful setup man are long gone.

	W	SV	ERA	IP	H	BB	SO	B/I	$
1994 Cleveland AL	1	1	4.91	29	34	8	15	1.43	1
1995 Albuquerque AAA	0	5	2.70	13	18	3	9	1.58	
1995 Boston AL	2	0	6.26	23	27	9	9	1.57	-
1996 *Projection* >>>	1	0	5.02	31	35	10	15	1.46	-

LIMA, JOSE - TR - Age 23
Lima showed some control and poise during his first extended shot at the majors. He has worked his way up through the Tiger farm system steadily despite compiling losing records. Lima is another young Tiger who should eventually find a niche in the bullpen when Detroit's young starting pitching prospects reach the majors.

	W	SV	ERA	IP	H	BB	SO	B/I	$
1995 Detroit AL	3	0	6.11	73	85	18	37	1.41	-
1996 *Projection* >>>	6	0	5.83	146	168	35	78	1.39	-

LINTON, DOUG - TR - Age 31
Linton allowed eight of his 18 major league earned runs on eight straight batters to start a June game against the Indians; Paul Sorrento capped the scoring with a homer; his ERA for the season was 4.03 outside of that inning. He doesn't have great stuff so he has to nibble at the corners to win. A career 6.48 ERA is a reflection of Linton's success at finessing big league hitters. He's Triple-A roster filler at best.

	W	SV	ERA	IP	H	BB	SO	B/I	$
1994 New York NL	6	0	4.47	50	74	20	29	1.87	-
1995 Omaha AAA	7	0	4.40	108	129	24	85	1.42	
1995 Kansas City AL	0	0	7.25	22	22	10	13	1.45	-
1996 *Projection* >>>	3	0	5.79	37	47	16	22	1.70	-

LIRA, FELIPE - TR - Age 23
This young Venezuelan showed potential in '95 as he shifted between the bullpen and the rotation, keeping the opposition off balance. Lira's best role is in long relief, yet the Tigers will probably need him in the rotation in '96.

	W	SV	ERA	IP	H	BB	SO	B/I	$
1995 Detroit AL	9	1	4.31	146	151	56	89	1.42	8
1996 *Projection* >>>	6	0	4.46	165	170	64	100	1.42	4

LISTER, MARTY - TL - Age 23
Houston acquired Lister from Cincinnati in the Eddie Taubensee trade. He pitched in relief his first three years when he averaged over one strikeout per inning each season and recorded 32 saves in 1993. He was converted to a starter in his first exposure at the Double-A level in 1995 but achieved only modest success. He is still young and needs a breakthrough year.

LIVERNOIS, DEREK - TR - Age 28
For someone who's been in the minors for nine years, he's still fairly young. Running out of chances.

LLOYD, GRAEME - TL - Age 28
If healthy, he's good for a few saves from the left side, but as a closer he lacks the big strikeout pitch, being basically a sinker/slider groundball pitcher.

	W	SV	ERA	IP	H	BB	SO	B/I	$
1994 Milwaukee AL	2	3	5.17	47	49	15	31	1.36	4
1995 Milwaukee AL	0	4	4.50	32	28	8	13	1.13	4
1996 *Projection* >>>	2	4	4.55	48	46	13	25	1.23	5

LOAIZA, ESTEBAN - TR - Age 24
Of the many young pitchers the Pirates have tried out in recent seasons, Loaiza has the best chance of being something special. He throws 95 MPH, has a good slider, a developing changeup and superb mechanics. The only thing he lacks is intensity. Once he acquires some killer instinct, he will be a big winner.

	W	SV	ERA	IP	H	BB	SO	B/I	$
1995 Pittsburgh NL	8	0	5.16	172	205	55	85	1.51	-
1996 *Projection* >>>	9	0	4.93	187	217	58	92	1.47	-

LOEWER, CARLTON - TR - Age 22
The Phils' 1994 number one pick made his pro debut in 1995, and worked his way up to Double-A Reading by season's end. Loewer doesn't have a single dazzling pitch, but has a well-rounded repertoire inclding a fastball, curve and changeup. He struggled with his control upon his arrival at Double-A, and has been known to nibble around the edges of the plate, while doubting his ability to effectively challenge hitters. He has a prototype body (6'6", 220 lbs.) and a

knack for escaping jams, but he must develop an imposing mound presence to complete the package. He could start 1996 at Triple-A - he needs some polish and doesn't appear to be a future stud at this point.

LOISELLE, RICH - TR - Age 24
Loiselle was acquired by Houston from San Diego as part of the Phil Plantier trade. His minor league numbers in the Padre system are not particularly impressive, but he is considered a possible prospect. He pitched in only two games after the trade because of an injury. Loiselle needs a big year at Triple-A in 1996 to get in line for a major league opportunity.

	W	SV	ERA	IP	H	BB	SO	B/I	$
1995 Two AAA Teams	2	0	5.97	37	44	13	20	1.52	

LOMON, KEVIN - TR - Age 24
Steadily progressing through the Braves system, Lomon has quietly moved in position to challenge for a major league job. He's not an overpowering hurler and has to have good control to be successful. With an organization less well-stocked than the Braves, Lomon would have a better chance to immediately reach the big leagues. The Mets are perhaps a bit less stocked, but Lomon will have to be superb to hang on with them in '96.

	W	SV	ERA	IP	H	BB	SO	B/I	$
1995 Richmond AAA	1	1	3.00	60	62	32	52	1.57	
1995 Atlanta NL	0	0	6.75	9	17	5	6	2.36	-

LONG, JOEY - TL - Age 25
Long has pitched with some success in the minors, and has a shot at making the Padres as a set-up man and situational reliever. It helps that he's a lefty as reliable lefties are always in demand. Long pitched in the Arizona Fall League over the winter, usually an indicator that a team is high on a prospect.

LONG, STEVE - TR - Age 26
This Marlins' Triple-A starter/reliever was an excellent Single-A pitcher, but his average stuff has not held up well at higher levels. Long experienced his greatest pro success as a reliever in 1991, but a return to the pen in '95 hasn't added much hope of his making it in the majors at this point.

	W	SV	ERA	IP	H	BB	SO	B/I	$
1995 Charlotte AAA	5	4	5.96	74	71	46	46	1.58	

LONG, TONY - TL - Age 24
Replacement player Long is a big reliever with a good fastball who had a decent season for Double-A Arkansas in 1995. Long is young enough to advance but his status as a replacement player might complicate his future.

LOONEY, BRIAN - TL - Age 26
The Red Sox obtained Looney, a former Boston College hockey player, from the Montreal organization. He throws a good assortment of breaking pitches, but his fastball lacks zip. He has confounded both organizations because his results the last three seasons have seemed to fall short of his talent.

	W	SV	ERA	IP	H	BB	SO	B/I	$
1995 Pawtucket AAA	4	0	3.49	100	106	33	78	1.38	
1996 *Projection* >>>	2	0	4.96	55	62	20	34	1.49	-

LOPEZ, ALBIE - TR - Age 24
Lopez had a clear shot at the 1995 Tribe rotation, but blew it with a poor spring training. He struggled with his control over the first half of the season, but gathered himself and finished strong, dominating at times in a late-season major league trial. He held lefties to a miniscule .122 average in the majors, a solid indicator of his still immense potential. The hard thrower has fallen behind Chad Ogea in the Indians' pecking order, and will have to rely on the misfortune of others to gain a 1996 rotation spot. He could be prime trade bait, and should prove himself as a viable number four major league starter by season's end.

	W	SV	ERA	IP	H	BB	SO	B/I	$
1994 Cleveland AL	1	0	4.24	17	20	6	18	1.53	-
1995 Buffalo AAA	5	0	4.44	101	101	51	82	1.50	
1995 Cleveland AL	0	0	3.13	23	17	7	22	1.04	1
1996 *Projection* >>>	5	0	3.92	138	124	52	124	1.27	9

LORRAINE, ANDREW - TL - Age 23
The Angels' best pitching prospect, Lorraine, was obtained by the White Sox in the Jim Abbott trade. He'll have an excellent chance to make the rotation in Chicago next year.

	W	SV	ERA	IP	H	BB	SO	B/I	$
1994 Vancouver AAA	12	0	3.42	142	156	34	90	1.34	
1994 California AL	0	0	10.61	18	30	11	10	2.20	-
1995 Nashville AAA	4	0	6.00	39	51	12	26	1.62	
1996 Projection >>>	5	0	4.54	136	150	53	78	1.49	1

LOWE, DEREK - TR - Age 22
Lowe was Seattle's eighth-round draft pick in 1992. The big guy (6-6) is strong enough to go out every five days, but more often than not he has taken his lumps. If he can develop a better fastball, he may have a chance.

LOWE, SEAN - TR - Age 23
Lowe was inconsistent at Double-A Arkansas in 1995 after steady advancement in previous seasons. The Cards' first round 1992 draft pick will get another look in the Texas League in 1996.

LOYND, MIKE - TR - Age 31
Loynd is a former Ranger who joined the Braves as a free agent. He's a decent pitcher but wasn't much of a threat to crack the Atlanta rotation.

LUEBBERS, LARRY - TR - Age 26
Luebbers had a cup of coffee with the Reds in 1993 but has been bombed in his last two minor league seasons. In 1995, he posted a 10-6 record in Double-A despite 4.5 walks per game and a 4.65 ERA. He is not a prospect.

LUKASIEWICZ, MARK - TL - Age 23
The 6-7 Lukasiewicz, a 1993 supplemental first-round draft pick by the Blue Jays, made his pro debut last season. He didn't throw his mid-90s fastball for strikes often enough.

LYNCH, JOHN - TR - Age 24
At press time, Lynch was leading all of professional baseball in tackles, as a starting safety for the 1993 Tampa Bay Bucs. A second-round pick in 1992 out of Stanford, he throws serious gas, but has walked almost a batter per inning in his limited pro experience. He could eventually be a number one starter, but not if he keeps using that valuable right arm trying to tackle guys like Barry Sanders.

MABERRY, LOUIS - TR - Age 25
The hard-throwing Maberry missed the first part of last season, and wasn't effective when he returned.

MacDONALD, BOB - TL - Age 30
Although he peaked back in 1991 with Toronto, MacDonald remains a lefty capable of throwing strikes -- and that can mean a major league job in the bullpens of the late 1990's.

	W	SV	ERA	IP	H	BB	SO	B/I	$
1996 Projection >>>	1	0	4.86	31	34	15	28	1.56	-

MACHADO, JULIO - TR - Age 29
Big talent with big legal problems. Has been trying to get out of Venezuela for three years.

MADDUX, GREG - TR - Age 29
An unprecedented fourth straight Cy Young award barely describes how well Maddux has pitched during the 1990s. He has been far and away the best pitcher on the planet for more than two years by throwing four different pitches with excellent precision and great timing instead of just trying to blow away every hitter. Since he's never missed a start due to injury and hitters haven't figured him out yet, it's hard to predict anything but continued dominance by Maddux in 1996.

	W	SV	ERA	IP	H	BB	SO	B/I	$
1994 Atlanta NL	16	0	1.56	202	150	31	156	0.90	42

	W	SV	ERA	IP	H	BB	SO	B/I	$
1995 Atlanta NL	19	0	1.63	209	147	23	181	0.81	41
1996 *Projection* >>>	20	0	2.32	233	185	36	191	.095	43

MADDUX, MIKE - TR - Age 34
Greg's older brother began the year in the Pirates' bullpen before moving on to Boston where he was a successful swingman. He throws several different pitches; although none is outstanding, he can be very effective if he can change speeds and hit corners. Maddux will again fill an important bullpen role wherever he pitches in 1996.

	W	SV	ERA	IP	H	BB	SO	B/I	$
1994 New York NL	2	2	5.11	44	45	13	32	1.32	2
1995 Pittsburgh NL	1	0	9.00	9	14	3	4	1.89	-
1995 Boston AL	4	1	3.61	89	86	15	65	1.13	8
1996 *Projection* >>>	4	2	4.26	93	94	21	66	1.24	7

MADURO, CALVIN - TR - Age 21
Maduro couldn't win early in the season with Class A Frederick, then he went on a winning streak that earned a promotion to Double-A Bowie. He couldn't win there because his control deserted him. But Maduro can pitch. He has a fastball and a hard slider, with which he can get both strikeouts and double-play grounders. He could follow, or surpass, Rocky Coppinger's success.

MAGEE, BO - TL - Age 27
Reliever Bo Magee struggled in Double-A last year, walking almost one batter per inning. He also struck out almost one batter per inning. Taken all together, Magee needs to improve his control to become a more reliable and effective pitcher.

MAGNANTE, MIKE - TL - Age 30
Magnante spent another year bouncing between Triple-A and the majors, this time with a little more success. He's a finesse artist who can make an occasional spot start, if necessary, but his role is and will be as a lefty long reliever.

	W	SV	ERA	IP	H	BB	SO	B/I	$
1994 Kansas City AL	2	0	4.60	47	55	16	21	1.51	0
1995 Kansas City AL	1	0	4.23	44	45	16	28	1.38	1
1996 *Projection* >>>	2	0	4.35	53	57	18	29	1.41	0

MAGRANE, JOE - TL - Age 31
After being released by the Angels last spring, Magrane went to Las Vegas and worked with former pitching coach Guy Hansen, who recommended him to Kevin Malone, then the Expos' general manager. Magrane, who has had elbow and shoulder problems, started slowly at Ottawa, then was a key in the Lynx drive to the International League title. Magrane, a minor league free agent, could end up wherever Malone is in '96.

	W	SV	ERA	IP	H	BB	SO	B/I	$
1995 Ottawa AAA	3	0	4.84	67	69	31	37	1.49	
1996 *Projection* >>>	2	0	5.30	48	54	20	20	1.56	-

MAHOMES, PAT - TR - Age 25
Mahomes took his demotion to the bullpen in stride and pitched well enough to give hope for the future. The Twins will need all the hope they can get in '96, and Mahomes can help the bullpen by setting up new closer Dave Stevens. Minnesota would be wise to leave him in a relief role.

	W	SV	ERA	IP	H	BB	SO	B/I	$
1994 Minnesota AL	9	0	4.73	120	121	62	53	1.53	4
1995 Minnesota AL	4	3	6.37	94	100	47	67	1.56	-
1996 *Projection* >>>	5	2	5.16	118	116	55	70	1.45	1

MALDONADO, CARLOS - TR - Age 29
Maldonado was pounded at AAA Tacoma in 1994, and has shown little in his various major league callups.

MALLICOAT, ROB - TL - Age 31
Once the brightest pitching prospect in the Astros' organization, Mallicoat missed the entire 1993 season with a rotator cuff problem. Released and his career appears to be over.

MANNING, LEN - TL - Age 24
The Phillies' 1994 44th round pick dominated the low A-ball South Atlantic League in 1995, giving up well under a hit per inning and posting an impressive strikeout/walk ratio (154/58). However, one would expect such a performance from a pitcher hurling against hitters three to four years his junior. Manning has only ordinary stuff and will likely be severely challenged once he reaches Double-A, possibly sometime in 1996.

MANON, RAMON - TR - Age 28
In eight minor league seasons in three organizations he has won 10 games twice, including '93. Pitched one game with the Rangers in '90.

MANSUR, JEFF - TL - Age 25
On a team with an excellent pitching staff, Mansur's second season in the Southern League was a disaster.

MANTEI, MATT - TR - Age 22
The Marlins plucked Mantei from the Mariners' organization in the Rule 5 draft following the 1994 season, and kept him in the majors all season (including a long stint on the disabled list) despite the fact that he had never previously pitched above low A-ball. Mantei throws serious gas, but needs more exposure against minor leaguers before he can be expected to successfully function in a significant bullpen role. Expect him to markedly improve his control at Triple-A in 1996, then assume a top major league setup role by 1997.

	W	SV	ERA	IP	H	BB	SO	B/I	$
1995 Florida NL	0	0	4.73	13	12	13	15	1.88	-

MANUEL, BARRY - TR - Age 30
Scouts see "95" on their radar guns, and fall in love with Manuel. He has spent most of the last four seasons in Triple-A, including the last two as a starter, with only slight success. He was a minor league free agent, and he'll keep getting chances as long as he keeps his fastball.

	W	SV	ERA	IP	H	BB	SO	B/I	$
1994 Rochester AAA	11	4	5.48	139	161	58	107	1.56	
1995 Ottawa AAA	5	1	4.59	127	125	50	85	1.37	

MANZANILLO, JOSIAS - TR - Age 28
Overloaded with righty setup men, the Mets cut Manzanillo loose in 1995, but the Yankees found him a useful arm in the pen during their late-season surge. He's past the prime form he showed in 1994, but with just a little shift toward finer control and working more directly, he can still be a useful middle-inning reliever.

	W	SV	ERA	IP	H	BB	SO	B/I	$
1994 New York NL	3	2	2.66	47	34	13	48	0.99	8
1995 New York NL	1	0	7.88	16	18	6	14	1.50	-
1995 New York AL	0	0	2.08	17	19	9	11	1.62	-
1996 Projection >>>	2	1	4.80	45	44	19	39	1.39	0

MANZANILLO, RAVELO - TL - Age 32
After improbably leading the Pirates in appearances as a 30-year-old rookie in 1994, Manzanillo was back in the minors by mid-May in 1995 and spent most of the season on Triple-A Calgary's disabled list with shoulder problems. His 15 minutes of fame on the mound have expired but he'll always be remembered as the man who claimed he had 26 brothers and 11 sisters.

	W	SV	ERA	IP	H	BB	SO	B/I	$
1994 Pittsburgh NL	4	1	4.14	50	45	42	39	1.74	0
1995 Calgary AAA	0	0	12.75	12	23	10	2	2.75	

MARQUEZ, ISIDRO - TR - Age 30
A side-arm delivery that is especially tough on righthanders got Marquez a brief taste of the majors in 1995 in the middle of a marginal season for Triple-A Nashville. His good fastball is complemented by sweeping off-speed stuff and he has the kind of arm that can endure a lot of innings from the bullpen. Marquez would be a long reliever should he return to the big leagues in 1996.

	W	SV	ERA	IP	H	BB	SO	B/I	$
1995 Nashville AAA	7	4	4.75	72	80	27	57	1.49	

MARRIOTT, MIKE - TR - Age 19
The Marlins figure that they got a fourth round steal in the 1995 draft, as Marriott was ranked as the #60 prospect in the entire draft by Baseball America. A series of off-field problems, most notably poor grades, shortened his final high school season and scared other clubs away. Marriott throws extremely hard, has a prototypical 6'3", 205 lbs., body, and has a bulldog mentality on the mound. He signed late and was overpowering in rookie ball, albeit with poor control. Marriott will likely spend 1996 at Low A-ball - if he matures as a person, he could advance very quickly.

MARSHALL, RANDY - TL - Age 29
Marshall, who appeared to be an up-and-comer after winning 20 games in Class A in 1990, now seems to be a late bloomer, with a 12-5 record in Triple-A over the last three seasons. He returned to the Tigers' organization with Toledo last year, and was one of the International League's ERA leaders. He throws strikes. Still, if Detroit didn't protect him on its 40-man roster, you have to wonder.

	W	SV	ERA	IP	H	BB	SO	B/I	$
1995 Toledo AAA	7	0	2.30	109	99	29	67	1.17	

MARTIN, JEFF - TR - Age 23
Hasn't pitched above Class A in three seasons, but has pitched well at that level since converting to the bullpen and is a marginal prospect.

MARTIN, JERRY - TR - Age 24
Martin began the 1995 season on the Rangers' 40-man roster, which ultimately hurt his development as he missed spring training because of the strike. He subsequently struggled at Double-A Tulsa. Martin has good stuff; look for him to rebound in 1996, pitching in the high minors with a chance for a late season promotion to the majors.

MARTINEZ, CALEB - TL - Age 19
The Phils' took a calculated risk when they drafted Martinez in the sixth round in 1995 shortly after he had been seriously injured in an auto accident. He was considered a potential number one pick prior to the accident, and his selection will be a coup if his pitching shoulder, injured in the accident, fully recovers. Martinez will make his pro debut in 1996, quite likely in short season Rookie ball. He is another of the increasing number of Cuban expatriates making a dent in American baseball.

MARTINEZ, DENNIS - TR - Age 40
El Presidente again bamboozled AL hitters with his array of breaking stuff. His control ranked among baseball's best, but he is finding it increasingly difficult to sneak his fastball past hitters. He's not through yet. The fact that he pitched best against lefthanded hitters (.229 opponent batting average), indicates that his stuff is still downright nasty. His career will likely end by his choice, not the Indians'. If he wants to, he can be the Tribe ace again in 1996, and the strength of the club will prop up his win totals very deep into his decline phase.

	W	SV	ERA	IP	H	BB	SO	B/I	$
1994 Cleveland AL	11	0	3.52	176	166	44	92	1.19	21
1995 Cleveland AL	12	0	3.08	187	174	46	99	1.18	21
1996 Projection >>>	14	0	3.30	223	208	55	119	1.18	27

MARTINEZ, FRANKIE - TR - Age 27
Martinez is a middle reliever who may have been overmatched at Triple-A Louisville in 1995. He enjoyed some success there, but obviously needs more polish; Martinez is a marginal prospect at best.

	W	SV	ERA	IP	H	BB	SO	B/I	$
1995 Louisville AAA	2	0	3.61	52	60	21	23	1.55	

MARTINEZ, JESUS - TL - Age 22
A consistent starter, Martinez has pretty good stuff. His good fastball sets up off-speed pitches that he uses to retire batters. Martinez's good year at Double-A San Antonio will mean a promotion to Triple-A Albuquerque in 1996.

MARTINEZ, JOHNNY - TR - Age 23
Martinez stepped into the void created by phenom Danny Graves' promotion to become the late season closer for the high A-ball Carolina League champion Kinston Indians. Martinez is a slender righthander (6'3", 168 lbs.) who has an average fastball which he can locate with extreme precision. However, it is very difficult to get excited about a

player who has played just six high A-ball games at his age. Martinez will quickly become lost in the deep sea of bonafide Indians' relief prospects.

MARTINEZ, JOSE - TR - Age 25
Martinez had a terrible year in 1994 in Double-A, but improved greatly last year in Triple-A. The 4.75 ERA is good for the hitter-friendly Pacific Coast League.

	W	SV	ERA	IP	H	BB	SO	B / I	$
1994 San Diego NL	0	0	6.75	12	18	5	7	1.92	0
1995 Las Vegas AAA	6	0	4.75	151	156	44	64	1.32	
1996 Projection >>>	1	0	5.70	68	78	27	40	1.55	-

MARTINEZ, PEDRO A - TL - Age 27
Martinez was an important part of the twelve player trade between San Diego and Houston in December 1994. However, he was a major disappointment in Houston after two impressive years in San Diego. When he didn't do any better after being sent down to Triple-A Tucson, he was traded back to San Diego. He should be happier in San Diego and needs to show something in 1996 to save his career.

	W	SV	ERA	IP	H	BB	SO	B / I	$
1994 San Diego NL	3	3	2.90	68	52	49	52	1.48	6
1995 Tucson AAA	1	2	6.62	34	44	13	21	1.68	
1995 Houston NL	0	0	7.40	20	29	16	17	2.18	-
1996 Projection >>>	2	1	4.21	46	44	32	37	1.64	-

MARTINEZ, PEDRO J - TR - Age 24
A funny thing happened to Pedro Martinez last season in his second year with the Expos. He lost his reputation as a headhunter and started earning respect as one of the finest young starting right-handed pitchers in baseball. Yes, he is willing to throw inside but he also has dominating stuff and should be a big winner for years to come. He does have a tendency to fade some in August-September.

	W	SV	ERA	IP	H	BB	SO	B / I	$
1994 Montreal NL	11	1	3.42	144	115	45	142	1.11	18
1995 Montreal NL	14	0	3.51	194	158	66	174	1.15	17
1996 Projection >>>	15	1	3.48	203	169	72	189	1.19	19

MARTINEZ, RAMIRO - TR - Age 24
A 1992 fourth round draft pick, Martinez made good progress in his first exposure to Double-A hitters in 1994 but hasn't advanced much since then. Martinez uses an excellent changeup to set up a decent fastball, and he still has some time to develop.

MARTINEZ, RAMON - TR - Age 28
Do not be deceived by Martinez' glittering win/loss record in 1995. His ERA improved slightly, but his walk rate increased, his strikeout rate declined slightly and he had the best run support on the team (5.3 runs per game). He is a two pitch pitcher (fastball, changeup) and is a slightly better than league average starter who benefits from a favorable park and support.

	W	SV	ERA	IP	H	BB	SO	B / I	$
1994 Los Angeles NL	12	0	3.97	170	160	56	119	1.27	13
1995 Los Angeles NL	17	0	3.66	206	176	81	138	1.25	15
1996 Projection >>>	14	0	3.84	212	189	81	142	1.27	12

MASTERS, DAVE - TR - Age 31
Long-time Giants farmhand, never made it to San Francisco and won't likely make it anywhere.

MATHEWS, T.J. - TR - Age 26
Many scouts, including one who knows Mathews quite well, insists he doesn't have major-league stuff. However, he saved two games for the Cardinals last season as a September callup (the only other pitcher on the staff other than Tom Henke to record a save). And he has had good minor-league ERA numbers, so you can't take him too lightly.

	W	SV	ERA	IP	H	BB	SO	B / I	$
1995 St. Louis NL	1	2	1.52	29	21	11	28	1.08	4
1996 Projection >>>	2	2	3.64	61	53	23	58	1.24	4

MATHEWS, TERRY - TR - Age 31
With Bryan Harvey and Jeremy Hernandez sidelined by injury, Mathews made the Marlins' pitching staff by default in 1995. However, the breaking ball craftsman had a fine season in middle relief, with excellent control and just enough bite on his breaking stuff to get key strikeouts. He shut down both righties (.240) and lefties (.227), though his ERA was deceptively low, as he did allow a high 13 of 34 inherited runners to score. After a long, unspectacular minor league career, Mathews has seemingly carved a niche as a serviceable ninth or tenth pitcher on a major league staff.

	W	SV	ERA	IP	H	BB	SO	B/I	$
1994 Florida NL	2	0	3.35	43	45	9	21	1.26	2
1995 Florida NL	4	3	3.38	82	70	27	72	1.17	8
1996 Projection >>>	3	2	3.80	74	66	22	57	1.19	5

MATHILE, MIKE - TR - Age 27
Moving up steadily through the Expos and Reds organizations from short-season A-ball to Triple-A since 1990, Mathile just needs to be healthy to get a crack at the majors in 1996. He's a soft tosser with fine control.

	W	SV	ERA	IP	H	BB	SO	B/I	$
1995 Indianapolis AAA	0	0	2.51	28	22	8	16	1.05	

MATTHEWS, MIKE - TL - Age 22
Sadly, the verdict appears to be in regarding the return of the Indians' 1992 number two draftee from 1993 rotator cuff surgery. Though his arm appears to be sound, he has struggled with his conditioning and control, and must battle to last five innings in most starts. The Indians will not give up on him since he's a southpaw and was one of the Double-A Eastern League's younger starters in 1995. He's a longshot to make the bigs, and will likely have to return to Double-A Canton-Akron in 1996.

MATTSON, ROB - TR - Age 29
The Padres signed Mattson out of the replacement player pool. At age 28, a starting pitcher is considered rather old to be in Double-A. But he had a solid but not outstanding record and made the Double-A All-Star team.

MAUSER, TIM - TR - Age 29
Mauser had a good year in relief with the Padres in 1994, but spent most of last year in Triple-A where he had a poor year. He's a middle reliever. Mauser was a six-year free agent, and he was let go by the Padres following the season.

	W	SV	ERA	IP	H	BB	SO	B/I	$
1994 San Diego NL	2	2	3.49	49	50	19	32	1.41	4
1995 Las Vegas AAA	3	0	4.80	50	63	20	32	1.64	

MAXCY, BRIAN - TR - Age 24
Immediately after the trade of closer Mike Henneman, Manager Sparky Anderson appointed Brian Maxcy as the new Tiger closer. But that lasted only a few outings as Maxcy had trouble getting guys out. His best roles are set-up man or middle relief.

	W	SV	ERA	IP	H	BB	SO	B/I	$
1995 Detroit AL	4	0	6.88	52	61	31	20	1.76	-
1996 Projection >>>	3	1	5.33	35	43	14	16	1.62	-

MAY, DARRELL - TL - Age 23
May has a consistent pattern of overachievement. A low draft pick, he won 28 games in 1993 and '94. Last season, two factors hampered his effectiveness. He gave up 18 home runs in the Southern League, but still was promoted to Triple-A Richmond, and eventually to Atlanta, because Greenville's batters supported him with only 14 runs in his eight losses. The slightly built May could challenge Pedro Borbon for a bullpen job by the end of this season.

	W	SV	ERA	IP	H	BB	SO	B/I	$
1995 Richmond AAA	4	0	3.71	51	53	16	42	1.36	

MAYSEY, MATT - TR - Age 29
Maysey has had brief stints in the majors with Montreal and Milwaukee but he spent last season filling out the roster with the Pirates' Triple-A Calgary pitching staff. Though expansion has diluted pitching talent throughout baseball, it's still not weak enough for Maysey to make it back.

	W	SV	ERA	IP	H	BB	SO	B/I	$
1995 Calgary AAA	8	1	5.50	103	122	44	71	1.61	

McANDREW, JAMIE - TR - Age 28
The son of Jim McAndrew, this kid has some talent and is worth a look, despite missing all of 1994 after undergoing surgery.

	W	SV	ERA	IP	H	BB	SO	B/I	$
1994			Did Not Play						
1995 Milwaukee AL	2	0	4.71	36	37	12	19	1.35	0
1996 *Projection* >>>	1	0	4.82	39	40	14	20	1.39	-

McCARTHY, GREG - TL - Age 27
McCarthy the entire 1992 season at Class A Kinston without giving up a run (23 games, 27 1/3 innings). Since then, he has barely made it past Double-A because he has walked nearly a batter an inning. Last year his fastball was marginally successful with Birmingham, the White Sox Double-A farm.

McCARTHY, TOM - TR - Age 34
McCarthy hasn't been around forever -- quite. But last season was the former Red Sox and White Sox reliever's ninth in Triple-A, with the Dodgers' Albuquerque farm. It also may have been the last for the minor league free agent.

	W	SV	ERA	IP	H	BB	SO	B/I	$
1995 Albuquerque AAA	3	0	6.00	48	61	22	28	1.73	

McCASKILL, KIRK - TR - Age 34
McCaskill has made a good transition to the bullpen in recent years. He still throws a good curveball, but has lost his set up role and won't be used in pressure situations any longer. McCaskill is on the downhill side of a steep slope.

	W	SV	ERA	IP	H	BB	SO	B/I	$
1994 Chicago AL	1	3	3.42	52	51	22	37	1.39	6
1995 Chicago AL	6	2	4.89	81	97	33	50	1.60	2
1996 *Projection* >>>	4	2	4.90	88	101	35	56	1.54	0

McCLURE, BOB - TL - Age 41
The much-maligned lefty has lasted this long only because he can get lefthanders out. He's forty and was released by an expansion team.

McCREADY, JIM - TR - Age 26
Though not overpowering, McCready blossomed in his first season exclusively in the bullpen; he held his own in Double-A in 1994 and at Triple-A in '95.

	W	SV	ERA	IP	H	BB	SO	B/I	$
1995 Norfolk AAA	0	0	2.01	40	41	20	21	1.52	

McCULLERS, LANCE - TR - Age 32
Once a top reliever with San Diego, McCullers has suffered through years of injuries (including blood clot surgery) and minor league obscurity but never made it back. Looks like the end.

McCURRY, JEFF - TR - Age 26
McCurry had a horrible rookie season as a Pirates' reliever last season, giving up more than a hit per inning with more walks than strikeouts. He had put up some good save totals in the lower minors but certainly doesn't look much like a major-league pitcher.

	W	SV	ERA	IP	H	BB	SO	B/I	$
1995 Pittsburgh NL	1	1	5.02	61	82	30	27	1.84	-
1996 *Projection* >>>	1	1	5.02	41	53	18	20	1.72	-

McDILL, ALLEN - TL - Age 24
McDill looked great at Double-A Wichita after he came to the Royals in a July trade from the Mets. Batters hit just over .200 against him, but he's susceptible to the home run ball. McDill will get a chance to make the big club in the spring, but should return to the minors in 1996.

McDONALD, BEN - TR - Age 28
Following a strong 1994 season, the optimistic expectation for 1995 was 20 wins, but the season was pretty much a loss for Big Ben McDonald as he came down with shoulder tendinitis. He is now more of a complete pitcher than the

rare-back-and-throw guy he was a few years ago. With a few breaks McDonald can win 20, but he is prone to a few very bad outings every year that inflate his other statistics.

	W	SV	ERA	IP	H	BB	SO	B/I	$
1994 Baltimore AL	14	0	4.06	157	151	54	94	1.30	16
1995 Baltimore AL	3	0	4.16	80	67	38	62	1.31	4
1996 *Projection* >>>	9	0	3.99	142	127	56	98	1.29	10

McDOWELL, JACK - TR - Age 30
McDowell's 90+ fastball and sharp splitter make him a dominant force who can carry a team when he's right. Two years of slow starts followed by long hot streaks have hidden McDowell's peak ability behind some so-so numbers. He finished '95 with some stiffness in his back, but the Yankees still thought he was worth pursuing.

	W	SV	ERA	IP	H	BB	SO	B/I	$
1994 Chicago AL	10	0	3.73	181	186	42	127	1.26	18
1995 New York AL	15	0	3.93	217	211	78	157	1.33	16
1996 *Projection* >>>	17	0	3.81	249	247	77	175	1.30	21

McDOWELL, ROGER - TR - Age 35
McDowell was second in the American League in appearances, displaying a rubber arm and generally keeping the ball in the park. That performance probably earned McDowell another season in the primary righthanded setup role with his sinkerball and assorted junk, legal and otherwise.

	W	SV	ERA	IP	H	BB	SO	B/I	$
1994 Los Angeles NL	0	0	5.23	41	50	22	29	1.74	-
1995 Texas AL	7	4	4.02	85	86	34	49	1.41	8
1996 *Projection* >>>	3	2	4.25	70	74	30	41	1.49	2

McELROY, CHUCK - TL - Age 28
After a good year in 1994 as the lefty setup man for Davey Johnson, he was hit hard in 1995. Lefthanders hit .283 and slugged .533 against him in 1995. There aren't any lefthanded relievers in the Reds system ready for the majors, so the Reds may import some competition for the job in 1996.

	W	SV	ERA	IP	H	BB	SO	B/I	$
1994 Cincinnati NL	1	5	2.34	57	52	15	38	1.16	11
1995 Cincinnati NL	3	0	6.02	40	46	15	27	1.51	-
1996 *Projection* >>>	3	2	4.31	56	60	19	37	1.40	1

McFARLIN, TERRIC - TR - Age 26
In his second year in relief in Triple-A, McFarlin improved his record over 1994, showing some consistency and reliability. He's a candidate for the Padres' bullpen as a middle and long reliever.

	W	SV	ERA	IP	H	BB	SO	B/I	$
1995 Las Vegas AAA	7	7	3.96	122	120	59	85	1.46	

McGARITY, JEREMY - TR - Age 25
He's considered to have one of the better arms in the organization but the Cardinals don't know whether to use him as a starter or out of the bullpen. He's expected to make the jump to AA Arkansas and the Cardinals figure to get a better read on his potential at a higher level.

McGEHEE, KEVIN - TR - Age 27
McGehee had a good year in Triple-A in 1993, but he has struggled in Triple-A for the past two years. Other prospects have passed him by, and he's beginning to look more and more like he's peaked in Triple-A.

	W	SV	ERA	IP	H	BB	SO	B/I	$
1994 Rochester AAA	10	0	4.76	149	165	35	89	1.34	
1995 Rochester AAA	11	0	5.83	126	150	33	84	1.44	

McMICHAEL, GREG - TR - Age 29
McMichael's fleeting role as a closer shouldn't be viewed as a serious failure; he still had a nice season as a righthanded setup man. McMichael's breaking stuff is a good complement to Mark Wohlers' power pitching. McMichael will continue to have an important bullpen job as long as he keeps throwing strikes.

	W	SV	ERA	IP	H	BB	SO	B/I	$
1994 Atlanta NL	4	21	3.84	58	66	19	47	1.45	24
1995 Atlanta NL	7	2	2.79	80	64	32	74	1.19	9
1996 *Projection* >>>	4	2	3.10	71	62	26	63	1.24	7

McMURTRY, CRAIG - TR - Age 36
In a controversial move, McMurtry returned to the majors in 1995 after a four year absence. He had been slated to be the ace of the Houston replacement staff, and while his promotion was justified based on his exceptional record at Triple-A Tucson, it did not sit well with his teammates. After a strong outing in his first appearance, McMurtry couldn't get anybody out and he was sent outright to Tucson after the season.

	W	SV	ERA	IP	H	BB	SO	B/I	$
1995 Houston NL	0	0	7.84	10	15	9	4	2.32	-

MEACHAM, RUSTY - TR - Age 28
1995 was easily the worst season of Meacham's career and a whole lot worse than it looks on paper. He was actually demoted to the minors immediately before playoff rosters were announced, thereby removing him from any chance at post-season play. That demotion said a lot about Meacham's future in Kansas City. He can still pitch in the big leagues, but will have to fight for a job in 1996.

	W	SV	ERA	IP	H	BB	SO	B/I	$
1994 Kansas City AL	3	4	3.73	50	51	12	36	1.24	9
1995 Kansas City AL	4	2	4.98	59	72	19	30	1.54	2
1996 *Projection* >>>	3	1	4.84	46	53	13	26	1.44	0

MEADOWS, BRIAN - TR - Age 20
Meadows was the Marlins' number three pick in 1994. Meadows throws hard, but straight, and was surprisingly hittable at low A-ball Kane County in 1995. His control is probably too good - he must learn how to more effectively manipulate the edges of the strike zone. Despite the slight 1995 setback, Meadows remains a solid prospect because of his stuff, his size (6'4", 210 lbs.) and his relative youth compared to other starters at his level.

MECIR, JIM - TR - Age 25
Experience as a minor leaguer does not often translate to a similar role in the majors. It does make Mecir a player to keep on your list for the future. Today he's a longshot chance at major league saves.

MELENDEZ, JOSE - TR - Age 30
A talented, but oft-injured pitcher, Melendez has spent parts of five years in the majors, but really didn't pitch well in 1995. If he can stay healthy Melendez has a chance to return to the majors.

	W	SV	ERA	IP	H	BB	SO	B/I	$
1994 Boston AL	0	0	6.06	16	20	8	9	1.71	-
1995 Omaha AAA	3	0	4.89	35	44	14	30	1.66	

MENDOZA, REYNOL - TR - Age 25
After missing nearly all of 1994 with arm problems, Mendoza bounced back with an above average season at Double-A Portland. He possesses average velocity, but no longer possesses the precision for which he was noted prior to the injury. At his age, it is a negative sign that he has never pitched in Triple-A. Mendoza will likely advance to Triple-A Charlotte in 1996, but doesn't have a material chance of denting the Marlins' major league rotation.

MENENDEZ, TONY - TR - Age 31
Aging has-been who gets his share of saves in the minors but doesn't get chances for any in the majors.

	W	SV	ERA	IP	H	BB	SO	B/I	$
1995 Phoenix AAA	5	13	3.92	64	67	32	61	1.54	

MENHART, PAUL - TR - Age 27
After missing all of 1994, Menhart arrived in the major leagues in what should have been a minor league comeback season. When he's wild, he misses high and inside to lefthanded hitters. He'll get a look as a starting pitcher in the spring. He threw a one-hitter against the Orioles last summer... and lost on a Mike Mussina shutout.

	W	SV	ERA	IP	H	BB	SO	B/I	$
1995 Toronto AL	1	0	4.92	78	72	47	50	1.51	-
1996 Projection >>>	3	0	4.97	69	63	38	44	1.46	-

MERCADO, HECTOR - TL - Age 21
Mercado is a big lefthander who has shown some promise at times in his four years in the Astro system, but needs more consistency. He is still young and needs a breakthrough year.

MERCEDES, JOSE - TR - Age 25
Well regarded, Mercedes pitched well in the minors, and the major league experience should add to his confidence.

	W	SV	ERA	IP	H	BB	SO	B/I	$
1994 Milwaukee AL	2	0	2.32	31	22	16	11	1.23	3
1995 Milwaukee AL	0	0	9.82	7	12	8	6	2.73	-

MERCKER, KENT - TL - Age 28
Mercker wasn't really as bad as his 7-8 record might indicate. He usually pitched pretty well, but seemed to make just one too many bad pitches just before leaving the game; he needs to rely more on his good fastball instead of making mistakes with fat breaking balls. Mercker's peripheral numbers are very much in line with his career stats, so a rebound to 1993-4 form would be no surprise in 1996.

	W	SV	ERA	IP	H	BB	SO	B/I	$
1994 Atlanta NL	9	0	3.45	112	90	45	111	1.20	11
1995 Atlanta NL	7	0	4.15	143	140	61	102	1.41	2
1996 Projection >>>	11	0	3.87	160	146	68	129	1.34	6

MERRIMAN, BRETT - TR - Age 29
The ace of Portland's bullpen became a joker in the Twins' deck in 1994. He couldn't throw strikes in his major league debut, and remains on the fringe of the major leagues.

MESA, JOSE - TR - Age 29
Mesa used his lively heater, placing it with precision he never possessed as a starter, to post one of the best years ever by a reliever. Of course, his is a great job - lots of leads to protect, a crew of excellent setup men allowing him the luxury of never having to pitch more than one inning, with very few inherited runners (nine all year). However, don't expect him to come close to repeating 1995 - he will still get tons of save opportunities, but there are a number of wannabe closers (Julian Tavarez, Alan Embree, Eric Plunk) who are equally capable of functioning in his role should he falter. Remember, the dominant closer population has virtually turned over every two years or so during the past decade.

	W	SV	ERA	IP	H	BB	SO	B/I	$
1994 Cleveland AL	7	2	3.82	73	71	26	63	1.33	9
1995 Cleveland AL	3	46	1.13	64	49	17	58	1.03	54
1996 Projection >>>	6	38	3.76	95	84	26	77	1.16	48

MESEWICZ, MARC - TL - Age 26
A left-hander, Mesewicz has pitched decently since being the Pirates' 26th-round draft pick from Ohio State. He is not considered a prospect but the Pirates will hang on to him with knowledge that lefties sometimes develop late.

MICELI, DANNY - TR - Age 25
The Pirates haven't had anyone seize their closer's job since Kent Tekulve was in his heyday. Though inconsistent at times in 1995 during his first full major-league season, Miceli showed he has the chance of doing the job for a long time. He throws 95 MPH, has developed a good slider and has the right mentality for short relief. The only thing holding him back from being a premier closer is experience.

	W	SV	ERA	IP	H	BB	SO	B/I	$
1994 Buffalo AAA	1	2	1.88	24	15	6	31	0.88	
1994 Pittsburgh NL	2	2	5.93	27	28	11	27	1.43	1
1995 Pittsburgh NL	4	21	4.66	58	61	28	56	1.53	17
1996 Projection >>>	4	25	4.94	61	64	28	59	1.50	18

MILACKI, BOB - TR - Age 31
Soft-tosser Milacki continues to fool Triple-A hitters (3.33 ERA, 8-3 record) but hasn't been a good major league pitcher for years. He'll hang around the major league fringe waiting for a call. In the meantime, Milacki is just minor league roster filler.

	W	SV	ERA	IP	H	BB	SO	B/I	$
1994 Kansas City AL	0	0	6.14	55	68	20	17	1.58	-
1995 Tacoma AAA	6	0	5.27	71	94	23	31	1.64	

MILCHIN, MIKE - TL - Age 28
Milchin once was a highly touted prospect in the Cardinals organization. Last year, he pitched reasonably well at Albuquerque, but the Dodgers didn't protect him. Milchin simply does not have strikeout power.

	W	SV	ERA	IP	H	BB	SO	B/I	$
1995 Albuquerque AAA	8	0	4.32	83	94	30	50	1.48	

MILITELLO, SAM - TR - Age 26
The Sporting News once rated him the top prospect in the minors. Baseball America named him the number one prospect in the International League. In the minors, he just toyed with the opposition, compiling a 34-8 record and a 1.44 ERA without a dominating fastball. But then he developed arm problems and has gone nowhere in three years.

MILLER, ERIC - TR - Age 24
Despite his excellent strikeout record, Miller was stuck behind Kirk Bullinger in Springfield's bullpen in 1993. Last year he not only took the closer's job from Bullinger, but also was voted the best reliever in the Florida State League.

MILLER, KURT - TR - Age 23
Once upon a time, Miller was considered the best pitching prospect in three different organizations - Pirates, Rangers and Marlins. However, Miller's velocity began to betray him back in 1993, and he compensated by losing aggressiveness and nibbling around the edges of the plate. His woes intensified when he was exposed to the dreaded Pacific Coast League in 1994. He's still young, but Miller needs to display increased velocity before the Marlins will grant him another major league trial.

	W	SV	ERA	IP	H	BB	SO	B/I	$
1994 Florida NL	1	0	8.10	20	26	7	11	1.65	-
1995 Charlotte AAA	8	0	4.62	126	143	55	83	1.57	

MILLER, PAUL - TR - Age 30
Miller was once a promising pitcher but shoulder injuries and age now make him nothing more than a journeyman at Class AAA. He throws in the 90s, so he can't be entirely counted out. However, he isn't in the Pirates' plans anymore.

MILLER, TRAVIS - TL - Age 23
A lefthander who was the Twins' supplemental first round pick out of Kent State University in '94, Miller showed a good arm and control at Double-A Hardware City in his first full pro season. He rates alongside fellow Tigers southpaws Dan Serafini and '95 draftee Mark Redman as future number three starters.

MILLER, TREVER - TL - Age 23
A young lefthander with potential, Miller returned to Double-A in '95 and lowered his ERA while working from the bullpen for the first time in his career. If the Twins show patience he could eventually produce in a short relief role.

MILLION, DOUG - TL - Age 21
His name says it all. Coming right out of high school, the top draft choice mowed down 75 batters in 58 innings at Class A Bend. The lefty throws in the low 90's and could be the ace of the Rockies staff in three to four years.

MILLS, ALAN - TR - Age 29
Following some good years as a set-up man, Mills has struggled for two years in a row. He was demoted to Triple-A last year, and Manager Phil Regan said that he couldn't rely on just a fastball to be effective. He came down with an injury. It's possible that Mills can regain his touch in 1996.

	W	SV	ERA	IP	H	BB	SO	B/I	$
1994 Baltimore AL	3	2	5.16	45	43	24	44	1.48	3

	W	SV	ERA	IP	H	BB	SO	B/I	$
1995 Baltimore AL	3	0	7.43	23	30	18	16	2.09	-
1996 *Projection* >>>	1	0	5.52	22	23	13	18	1.65	-

MIMBS, MARK - TL - Age 27
The Mimbs brother that has not made the majors looks like he may get a chance soon. After missing most of 1994 with injuries, he posted an excellent 2.97 ERA in 16 starts at Albuquerque with a better than 4:1 strikeout to walk ratio. The Dodgers have plenty of lefthanded relievers, but they could use a lefthanded starter.

	W	SV	ERA	IP	H	BB	SO	B/I	$
1995 Albuquerque AAA	6	0	2.97	106	105	22	96	1.20	

MIMBS, MIKE - TL - Age 27
The Phils got major mileage out of Mimbs, an offseason Rule 5 acquisition, in 1995. He was a serviceable starter in the early going and functioned well out of the bullpen late. He is not overpowering, but his curve ball is very tough on lefties (.214 average in 1995). He needs to be more aggressive - many of his 75 walks were a result of his nibbling around the edges of the plate. He would likely be most effective in a setup relief role, but the Phils may require his presence in the 1996 rotation, where he would be a number four starter, at best.

	W	SV	ERA	IP	H	BB	SO	B/I	$
1995 Philadelphia NL	9	1	4.15	136	127	75	93	1.48	3
1996 *Projection* >>>	7	0	4.35	136	133	74	93	1.52	-

MINCHEY, NATE - TR - Age 26
Minchey has made two short appearances in the majors but has been traded three times as a minor leaguer, the last time to the Cardinals before the 1995 season. He had his usual solid Triple-A campaign as a reliable starter for Louisville. He's not an overpowering pitcher but succeeds by pitching intelligently. He'll get another shot at the big leagues in 1996.

	W	SV	ERA	IP	H	BB	SO	B/I	$
1994 Pawtucket AAA	11	0	3.03	151	128	51	93	1.18	
1994 Boston AL	2	0	8.61	23	44	14	15	2.52	-
1995 Louisville AAA	8	0	3.73	147	153	42	67	1.33	

MINOR, BLAS - TR - Age 30
A capable middle relief workhorse, Minor features a fastball, curve, and splitter. His skills are solid, but on a team with deep pitching talent, righty relievers can fall into obscurity rather easily.

	W	SV	ERA	IP	H	BB	SO	B/I	$
1994 Buffalo AAA	1	11	2.98	51	47	12	61	1.15	
1994 Pittsburgh NL	0	1	8.05	19	27	9	17	1.89	-
1995 New York NL	4	1	3.66	46	44	13	43	1.22	3
1996 *Projection* >>>	3	1	4.13	49	49	14	45	1.29	2

MINTZ, STEVE - TR - Age 27
Mintz is old for a prospect, but pitched decently at Triple-A and was rewarded with his first stint in the majors, where he posted a 7.45 ERA. He may not get a second stint.

	W	SV	ERA	IP	H	BB	SO	B/I	$
1995 Phoenix AAA	5	7	2.39	49	42	21	36	1.29	
1995 San Francisco NL	1	0	7.45	19	26	12	7	1.97	-

MINUTELLI, GINO - TL - Age 31
Eleven years in the minors have earned Minutelli just 40.2 innings in the majors. He was released after sixteen unimpressive innings for Triple-A Richmond in 1995. Minutelli might finally be finished, but you never can be sure about lefties.

MIRANDA, ANGEL - TL - Age 26
Brewers fans are still waiting for him to put it together. It's not too late. Has the potential to be the ace of the Brewers staff.

	W	SV	ERA	IP	H	BB	SO	B/I	$
1994 Milwaukee AL	2	0	5.28	46	39	27	24	1.43	0

	W	SV	ERA	IP	H	BB	SO	B/I	$
1995 Milwaukee AL	4	1	5.23	74	83	49	45	1.78	-
1996 *Projection* >>>	4	1	4.95	81	82	49	49	1.62	-

MISURACA, MIKE - TR - Age 27
During the 1994 season, Misuraca ranked ahead of Brad Radke among Minnesota pitching prospects. But while Radke advanced to the Twins rotation, Misuraca was in and out of the rotation with Triple-A Salt Lake City. The biggest difference was that he couldn't get strikeouts when he needed them.

	W	SV	ERA	IP	H	BB	SO	B/I	$
1995 Salt Lake AAA	9	0	5.34	143	174	36	67	1.47	

MITCHELL, LARRY - TR - Age 24
The Phils' 1992 fifth round pick struggled with his control at Double-A Reading for the second consecutive season. He has a diversified repertoire, and has tossed some low-hit games in his two Double-A seasons, but his overall progress has been minimal. Now, the Phils' best pitching prospects are running up his back, so he must produce or perish in 1996. He could well respond to the challenge and could be one of the first Phils' starters summoned from Triple-A for an audition in midseason.

MIX, GREG - TR - Age 24
Mix is a nondescript swingman drafted by the Marlins from Stanford in the 21st round in 1993. He does not throw hard, but has maintained his exemplary control while being shuttled between the rotation and the bullpen, most recently at Double-A Portland. However, he has never been entrusted with a prime responsibility, such as staff ace or closer. Mix has likely reached the apex of his minor league career, and should not expect to materially extend his tenure in the pros.

MLICKI, DAVE - TR - Age 27
A surprising success as a starter in 1995 (coming back from elbow surgery) Mlicki faces touch and talented challengers for his starter's role if he stays with the Mets. Spot starting and fill-in work, if not a trade, appeared to be in Mlicki's future when 1995 drew to a close. At least after the 1995 opportunity he has proven himself, finally.

	W	SV	ERA	IP	H	BB	SO	B/I	$
1995 New York NL	9	0	4.26	160	160	54	123	1.33	5
1996 *Projection* >>>	6	0	4.26	109	108	36	83	1.33	2

MLICKI, DOUG - TR - Age 24
Mlicki, the younger brother of Dave Mlicki of the Mets, has pitched consistently well in his four years in the Astro system until experiencing some difficulty when he was promoted to Triple-A Tucson during the 1995 season. He has an excellent curveball and an average fastball and change-up. He needs to keep his pitches down to be effective. With a strong year at Triple-A in 1996 he could be in a position to compete for a starting job in the majors in 1997.

	W	SV	ERA	IP	H	BB	SO	B/I	$
1995 Tucson AAA	1	0	5.56	34	44	6	22	1.47	

MOEHLER, BRIAN - TR - Age 24
Moehler has been near .500 in each of his three pro seasons. His value is that he takes the ball every five days and gets his team about six innings per start. That's not enough even in the Detroit organization.

MOELLER, DENNIS - TL - Age 28
Moeller returned to the Royals after a forgettable year with the Pirates. Lacking an outstanding pitch and throwing below average breaking balls and fastballs, Moeller is probably stuck at Triple-A. Being lefthanded may help Moeller get back to The Show, but he'll never be big box office.

MOHLER, MIKE - TL - Age 27
He's a one-out lefty who has walked more batters than he has struck out in his short major-league career. It's unlikely he'll get many saves.

	W	SV	ERA	IP	H	BB	SO	B/I	$
1995 Oakland AL	1	1	3.04	23	16	18	15	1.44	1

MONGIELLO, MIKE - TR - Age 28
Mongiello was used as both a starter and reliever for Triple-A Nashville in 1995. He's a strikeout pitcher with a good

fastball who could pitch in the majors, but needs to move quickly as he's beginning to look like a career minor leaguer.

	W	SV	ERA	IP	H	BB	SO	B/I	$
1995 Nashville AAA	3	1	5.14	91	104	37	72	1.55	

MONTALVO, RAFAEL - TR - Age 32
After four years out of organized ball, Montalvo returned last spring as a Dodgers replacement player. He hung around all season in Albuquerque's bullpen, but LA then let him go as a minor league free agent. His one major league appearance was 10 years ago with Houston.

	W	SV	ERA	IP	H	BB	SO	B/I	$
1995 Albuquerque AAA	3	4	2.65	98	105	34	65	1.41	

MONTELEONE, RICH - TR - Age 33
Monteleone has appeared in 189 major league games over eight years without recording a save. That observation notwithstanding, he has pitched effectively. His role is middle relief and mop-up.

	W	SV	ERA	IP	H	BB	SO	B/I	$
1994 San Francisco NL	4	0	3.18	45	43	13	16	1.24	4
1995 Vancouver AAA	1	1	3.24	16	19	3	7	1.32	
1995 California AL	1	0	2.00	9	8	3	5	1.22	0
1996 *Projection* >>>	3	0	4.40	34	32	11	15	1.27	1

MONTGOMERY, JEFF - TR - Age 34
Aging gracefully, Montgomery is one of the league's senior closers with 217 saves over the last seven years. 1995 was more of the same as he mixed in breaking stuff with his low-90s fastball. He didn't get much help in the bullpen and often was the Royals only reliable reliever. The Royals frugal approach and Montgomery's high salary make him trade bait for 1996.

	W	SV	ERA	IP	H	BB	SO	B/I	$
1994 Kansas City AL	2	27	4.03	44	48	15	50	1.41	35
1995 Kansas City AL	2	31	3.43	65	60	25	49	1.29	33
1996 *Projection* >>>	3	33	3.43	72	67	25	61	1.28	39

MONTGOMERY, STEVE - TR - Age 25
Montgomery tied a Texas League record with 36 saves for Double-A Arkansas in 1995. He's a crafty pitcher who lacks overpowering stuff and should get to Triple-A Louisville in 1996, or even to the majors. Beware of his saves total, though, as Cardinals' minor leaguers have a habit of piling up saves before fizzling in the majors.

MONTOYA, WILMER - TR - Age 22
Montoya was recognized for having the best breaking pitch in the low A-ball South Atlantic League by circuit managers. Another in a long line of Indians' short reliever prospects, Montoya is a converted starter whose slight build (5'10", 165 lbs.) made him a fine candidate for conversion to the pen. His excellent curve is a strikeout pitch at lower levels, but will likely not fool higher level hitters. With his strong two-inning arm, his best bet for future success is as a setup man. Look for him at high A-ball Kinston in 1996.

MOODY, RITCHIE - TL - Age 25
The Rangers' baffling decision to convert Moody into a starter was aborted when Moody came down with a sore left shoulder. After an initial misdiagnosis, a rotator cuff injury was discovered, and Moody underwent season ending surgery. Moody has been a power pitcher, and it may take some time for him to regain effectiveness.

MOORE, JOEL - TR - Age 23
Moore has won 25 games the last two seasons. He's 6-3, 200, but lacks a fastball that can dominate batters above the Double-A level where he pitched last season. With one complete game in 67 pro starts, he may make it to the Rockies as a reliever if at all.

MOORE, MARCUS - TR - Age 25
Moore is a prospect in the Steve Dalkowski mold, striking out (and walking) about a hitter per inning. He was shelled in two brief trials with the Rockies before being acquired by the Reds. Hard throwing, wild prospects like Moore are long shots to develop into major league pitchers, but if they come in the payoff is huge.

MOORE, MIKE - TR - Age 36
Moore's career continued its rapid decline in '95 as his ERA ascended to become an all-time major league record (!) and earned him a release from the Tigers. He could possibly mount a comeback as a reliever, but I wouldn't want to bet on it.

	W	SV	ERA	IP	H	BB	SO	B/I	$
1994 Dertoit AL	11	0	5.42	154	152	89	62	1.56	-
1995 Detroit AL	5	0	7.53	132	179	68	64	1.87	-

MOORE, TIM - TR - Age 25
The lanky (6-4, 190) Moore has been a strikeout pitcher in the low minors, but didn't show that ability at Double-A Birmingham in 1995. The White Sox haven't yet decided whether he's a starter or a reliever, but he'd have a better shot with them out of the bullpen.

MOREL, RAMON - TR - Age 21
One of the Pirates' top pitching prospects, Morel held his own in a few major-league relief appearances last season. He does not have one exceptional pitch but throws strikes and knows how to set up hitters. He'll likely spend this season at Triple-A Calgary with a good shot of cracking the major-league rotation in 1997.

MORGAN, MIKE - TR - Age 36
Traded from the Chicago Cubs to St. Louis early last season, Morgan had a solid 1995 after a horrendous 1994. The main key was health. He's not a great pitcher by any means. However, when he stays off the disabled list, he'll give a team innings and keep them in games. That's why he expected to be pursued by many clubs as a free agent over the winter.

	W	SV	ERA	IP	H	BB	SO	B/I	$
1994 Chicago NL	2	0	6.69	80	111	35	57	1.81	-
1995 St. Louis NL	7	0	3.56	131	133	34	61	1.27	7
1996 *Projection* >>>	8	0	4.00	160	175	49	85	1.40	3

MORMAN, ALVIN - TL - Age 27
After posting a 17-2 record in his first three seasons, Morman was considered one of the brightest prospects in the Astro organization. However, he has spent the last two years as a middle reliever at Triple-A Tucson with only modest success. As a lefthanded reliever, he should get a major league opportunity at some point.

	W	SV	ERA	IP	H	BB	SO	B/I	$
1995 Tucson AAA	5	3	3.91	48	50	20	36	1.45	

MORONES, GENO - TR - Age 25
When the Royals traded Brian McRae and his salary to the Cubs, Morones was part of the package they got in return. An arm injury hid his potential and limited him to 79 innings at Double-A Wichita in 1995. When healthy Morones is a dependable starter with a good strikeout ratio.

MORRIS, JACK - TR - Age 40
Morris was a truly great pitcher for many years, but has been a beneficiary of unusual run support. He is one of only a handful of 20-game winners with 4.00+ ERAs (1992). If you listen to him, he's personally responsible for all of his teams' successes, but not responsible for any of their shortcomings.

MORRISON, KEITH - TR - Age 26
Morrison has struggled in Triple-A for the past two years. Although he improved his record last year, it was still a poor record overall, indicating that he is a very hittable pitcher.

	W	SV	ERA	IP	H	BB	SO	B/I	$
1995 Vancouver AAA	14	0	4.93	160	178	40	84	1.36	

MORTON, KEVIN - TL - Age 27
Good enough to get 15 starts with the Red Sox in 1991, Morton regressed in 1992, when his Pawtucket ERA was 5.45. In 1995 the Cubs had him stored as a reliever and spot starter but never quite tapped his level in their depth chart.

	W	SV	ERA	IP	H	BB	SO	B/I	$
1995 Iowa AAA	1	0	4.79	92	97	42	49	1.51	

MORVAY, JOE - TR - Age 25
The jury is still out on this Rangers' prospect. He hasn't had much pro experience and his numbers at Double-A Tulsa were disappointing, but he did have a good second half in 1995 and is a better pitcher than his marginal numbers would indicate.

MOTEN, SCOTT - TR - Age 23
Moten had some success as a set-up man with the Twins' New Britain farm, but a Double-A set-up man is a long way from the majors.

MOUNCE, TONY - TL - Age 21
Mounce was Houston's seventh round draft choice out of high school in 1994 and has been the surprise of the draft. He has had two strong seasons and outperformed the more highly touted Scott Elarton at Class-A Quad Cities in 1995. He had the lowest ERA in the Astro minor league system in 1995 and was second in both wins and strikeouts. He is on track for a shot at a major league job in two or three years.

MOYER, JAMIE - TL - Age 33
Since he doesn't throw very hard, Moyer relies on pin-point pitch location and changing speeds to be effective. He can get hammered when things are not working perfectly for him. He is usually more effective against right handed batters than the lefties, an unusual differential for a southpaw. At best Moyer can be a fifth starter giving you some innings, perhaps winning 10 games.

	W	SV	ERA	IP	H	BB	SO	B/I	$
1994 Baltimore AL	5	0	4.77	149	158	38	87	1.32	7
1995 Baltimore AL	8	0	5.21	115	117	30	65	1.27	5
1996 *Projection* >>>	9	0	4.85	156	161	39	89	1.28	7

MULHOLLAND, TERRY - TL - Age 33
1995 was the second consecutive disastrous season for Mulholland, whose problems are partly physical and partly mental, but whose results are disturbingly awful. Never a huge strikeout pitcher and thus unlikely to have a long career in any event, Mulholland will likely show up again on someone's roster.

	W	SV	ERA	IP	H	BB	SO	B/I	$
1994 New York AL	6	0	6.49	120	150	37	72	1.55	-
1995 San Francisco NL	5	0	5.80	149	190	38	65	1.53	-
1996 *Projection* >>>	3	0	5.71	112	137	30	56	1.49	-

MUNOZ, BOBBY - TR - Age 28
Much was expected of Munoz after his fine first season with the Phils in 1994. Alas, he showed up at spring training in poor shape, and made only three midseason starts before requiring elbow surgery. Munoz is also subject to wild weight fluctuations (he is listed at 6'8", 252 lbs.), and his plans to play pro basketball in Puerto Rico during the strike call both his judgment and dedication into question. He must regain his "A" fastball to have a chance at being a major league starter again - the pitching-starved Phils will give him every opportunity.

	W	SV	ERA	IP	H	BB	SO	B/I	$
1994 Philadelphia NL	7	1	2.67	104	101	35	59	1.30	11
1995 Philadelphia NL	0	0	5.74	15	15	9	6	1.53	-
1996 *Projection* >>>	3	0	3.71	59	58	25	32	1.40	1

MUNOZ, J.J. - TL - Age 28
Munoz' minor league career has been plagued by injuries, but he's been pretty good as a middle reliever when healthy, like he was at Triple-A Omaha in 1995. A hard thrower, Munoz will get a chance as a long reliever with the Royals in 1996.

	W	SV	ERA	IP	H	BB	SO	B/I	$
1995 Omaha AAA	2	6	3.38	56	48	19	51	1.20	

MUNOZ, MIKE - TL - Age 30
Munoz was overused in the early part of the 1995 season, which contributed to his comparatively poor year statistically. He lacked the pinpoint control he exhibited in 1994, but was usually effective in limited roles against left-handed hitters. He will likely continue to be one of the workhorses of the Rockies' pen in 1996.

	W	SV	ERA	IP	H	BB	SO	B/I	$
1994 Colorado NL	4	1	3.74	45	37	31	32	1.49	2
1995 Colorado NL	2	2	7.42	43	54	27	37	1.85	-
1996 *Projection* >>>	3	1	5.91	51	54	32	40	1.71	-

MUNOZ, OSCAR - TR - Age 26
Munoz straightened out his control in '95, increasing his chances of earning a permanent bullpen job. Young Twins pitchers are unlikely to post good numbers in '96, but Munoz looks like a major league pitcher on the rise.

	W	SV	ERA	IP	H	BB	SO	B/I	$
1994 Salt Lake AAA	9	0	5.88	139	180	68	100	1.77	
1995 Salt Lake AAA	8	0	4.95	112	121	35	74	1.39	
1995 Minnesota AL	2	0	5.60	35	40	17	25	1.62	-
1996 *Projection* >>>	2	0	5.09	109	119	43	77	1.49	-

MURPHY, ROB - TL - Age 35
The simple fact that Murphy is a southpaw has enabled him to carve out an eleven year major league career (and a handsome standard of living). Alas, the gravy train may finally be reaching its end, as Murphy was rocked in his brief tenure with the Marlins before being released. The excellent velocity he displayed in the late 1980's with the Reds is long gone, but I still wouldn't be surprised to see this familiar name on a Triple-A roster in 1996, if not in the majors.

	W	SV	ERA	IP	H	BB	SO	B/I	$
1994 Two Teams	4	2	4.29	42	38	13	25	1.21	6
1995 Two Teams	1	0	10.95	12	14	8	7	1.78	-
1996 *Projection* >>>	1	0	5.48	31	31	12	18	1.40	-

MURRAY, HEATH - TL - Age 22
Murray is a talented young southpaw starter who had a very good record in Single-A in 1994, but he struggled in Double-A last year. He has an average fastball and an excellent breaking ball. Murray is a top Padre prospect, but he needs to improve on some things and become more consistent before he can move up higher.

MURRAY, MATT - TR - Age 25
Murray caused a stir by going unbeaten deep into last season with the Braves' Double-A and Triple-A farms. He was hammered mercilessly in the majors with Atlanta, and again after being traded to Boston. Despite his size (6-6, 235 lbs.), Murray doesn't throw hard and is a marginal prospect.

	W	SV	ERA	IP	H	BB	SO	B/I	$
1995 Two Teams	0	0	9.64	14	21	8	4	2.07	-

MUSSELWHITE, JAMES - TR - Age 24
After showing the best control in the Florida State League, Musselwhite had similar success after his promotion to Double-A. The Yankees drafted him in the seventh round in 1993.

MUSSETT, JOSE - TL - Age 27
Musset, acquired from the Angels before 1994, missed almost all of that season because of a sore shoulder. His work at Double-A in 1995 (4-1 with 4 saves and a 3.33 ERA working out of the pen) kept hopes alive.

MUSSINA, MIKE - TR - Age 27
Mussina would have won over 20 games, but he got off to a slow start because of the short spring training. He was 10-4 with a sparkling 2.02 ERA in the second half, the best ERA in the American League. Mussina is one of the best pitchers in baseball, and he could win the Cy Young award in 1996.

	W	SV	ERA	IP	H	BB	SO	B/I	$
1994 Baltimore AL	16	0	3.06	176	163	42	99	1.16	27
1995 Baltimore AL	19	0	3.29	221	187	50	158	1.07	30
1996 *Projection* >>>	20	0	3.30	221	188	68	147	1.16	30

MUTIS, JEFF - TL - Age 29
A former minor league standout, Mutis found out what happens to minor league finesse pitchers in the majors, as he was pillaged to the tune of a 6.48 career major league ERA from 1990-1994. How far did his star fall with the Marlins in 1995? Well, they trotted out the likes of Buddy Groom, Rob Murphy, Rich Scheid and Mike Myers as lefty relievers

in 1995, and never gave Mutis the call. Mutis will likely linger as Triple-A roster filler for an indefinite period, likely in a different organization.

MYERS, JASON - TL - Age 22
San Francisco's 10th-round draft choice in 1993 became a prospect with a good year in the Midwest League.

MYERS, JIMMY - TR - Age 26
Myers has bounced around several organizations, landing in the Oriole system last year. He has a history of walking as many as he strikes out, and he doesn't strike out very many batters. He looks like a soft tosser with poor control, a bad combination. He has very little chance of making the Orioles.

	W	SV	ERA	IP	H	BB	SO	B/I	$
1995 Rochester AAA	0	6	3.06	64	72	29	31	1.57	

MYERS, MIKE - TL - Age 26
How does one explain the fact that Myers was actually summoned to the Marlins for two relief appearances in 1995 after stinking up the joint at Triple-A for three seasons? Why, simply because he flings the ball with his left wing. Myers had good stuff once, shortly after being drafted in the fourth round by the Giants in 1990, but has experienced numerous arm miseries since. He does not appear to be a serious competitor for a big league role.

	W	SV	ERA	IP	H	BB	SO	B/I	$
1995 Toledo AAA	0	0	5.40	45	47	18	32	1.45	
1995 Two Teams	1	0	9.95	8	11	7	4	2.25	-

MYERS, RANDY - TL - Age 33
For all the saves Myers collects he sure gives up a lot of big time pressure homers. He's a fastball pitcher who likes to challenge hitters, but the trouble is - his fastball isn't what it used to be and he hasn't made the adjustment to using other pitches. Myers is in for some hard times until he makes the necessary transition. There is no truth to the rumor that he's considering a pro wrestling career after his late season bout with a Wrigley Field denizen.

	W	SV	ERA	IP	H	BB	SO	B/I	$
1994 Chicago NL	1	21	3.79	40	40	16	32	1.39	27
1995 Chicago NL	1	38	3.88	55	49	28	59	1.39	32
1996 *Projection* >>>	1	30	3.90	62	56	28	62	1.36	25

MYERS, ROD - TR - Age 26
A sore right shoulder through much of his minor league career prompted a move to the bullpen by Myers in 1994. He struggled in his first year at Triple-A Omaha, despite a good start to his 1995 season. 1996 will be a pivotal year for Myers to prove himself as a true prospect.

	W	SV	ERA	IP	H	BB	SO	B/I	$
1995 Omaha AAA	4	2	4.10	48	52	19	38	1.47	

MYSEL, DAVE - TR - Age 25
Mysel is a big hard thrower who the Tigers see as a closer. He is being used as a starter in the minors to get more innings and experience. Tiger coaches are trying to improve his mechanics.

NABHOLZ, CHRIS - TL - Age 29
Nabholz has now had two straight lost seasons after doing very little for the Cubs in 1995. He's a sinkerball pitcher with usually good control who always finds a way to make the wrong pitch at the wrong time. Even though he's just a marginal major league pitcher, being lefthanded will get Nabholz at least one more chance in the big leagues.

	W	SV	ERA	IP	H	BB	SO	B/I	$
1994 Two Teams	3	0	7.64	53	67	38	28	1.98	-
1995 Iowa AAA	0	0	6.41	19	27	12	16	1.99	
1995 Chicago NL	0	0	5.40	23	22	14	21	1.56	-
1996 *Projection* >>>	1	0	5.49	33	35	21	22	1.70	-

NAGY, CHARLES - TR - Age 28
Nagy's excellent 1995 won-lost record is quite deceiving. He received the best run support (6.83 runs per start) among AL ERA title qualifiers, and allowed lefties to carve him up at a .313 clip. None of this is much cause for alarm, as

Indians' starters have a much larger safety net, and Nagy, whose stuff and control remains sound, should rebound to previous form with modestly improved location within the strike zone. Expect him to pitch as well as he did in 1994 (3.45 ERA), with a record approximating his 1995 mark over the next two or three seasons.

	W	SV	ERA	IP	H	BB	SO	B/I	$
1994 Cleveland AL	10	0	3.45	169	175	48	108	1.32	17
1995 Cleveland AL	16	0	4.55	178	194	61	139	1.43	9
1996 *Projection* >>>	14	0	4.29	196	211	64	142	1.40	10

NARCISSE, TYRONE - TR - Age 24
Narcisse is well known by the Houston major league staff through his participation as a replacement player last spring. He has had trouble winning in the minor leagues, especially in 1995 when he was 5-14 despite a 3.24 ERA at Double-A Jackson. Similar in mannerisms and appearance to J.R. Richard, but without his fastball and slider, Narcisse remains an interesting project. A big year at Triple-A in 1996 could make him a candidate for one of the Astro starting jobs in 1997 when Drabek and Swindell will have completed their contracts.

NAULTY, DAN - TR - Age 26
Naulty has been promoted steadily through the Minnesota organization. He's only 2-13 above Class A. However, he's a 6-6, 202-pound fireballer whose further advancement is dependent on his control.

	W	SV	ERA	IP	H	BB	SO	B/I	$
1995 Salt Lake AAA	2	4	5.18	90	92	47	76	1.54	

NAVARRO, JAIME - TR - Age 28
Navarro's fine 1995 campaign is not a fluke. He was more aggressive with the Cubs than he had been with the Brewers. He has always had a good arm and had more of a take charge attitude last year. Expect continued success for Navarro in 1996.

	W	SV	ERA	IP	H	BB	SO	B/I	$
1994 Milwaukee AL	4	0	6.62	89	115	35	65	1.67	-
1995 Chicago NL	14	0	3.28	200	194	56	128	1.25	15
1996 *Projection* >>>	13	0	4.15	194	205	60	125	1.36	5

NEAGLE, DENNY - TL - Age 27
Neagle emerged as the ace of the Pirates' staff and one of the National League's top left-handed starters last season at age 26. His best pitch is a changeup, which makes his otherwise ordinary stuff look even better. Neagle is an extremely bright guy and knows how to spot the change to set hitters up. He should be a consistent 15-game winner for many years to come.

	W	SV	ERA	IP	H	BB	SO	B/I	$
1994 Pittsburgh NL	9	0	5.12	137	135	49	122	1.34	3
1995 Pittsburgh NL	13	0	3.43	209	221	45	150	1.27	14
1996 *Projection* >>>	13	0	3.80	207	214	53	160	1.29	11

NEESE, JOSHUA - TR - Age 24
Neese made an impressive debut in pro ball in 1993 going 12-3 with a nice 2.54 ERA for Niagara Falls. But he came down with an elbow problem and missed all of 1994.

NEIER, CHRIS - TR - Age 24
Neier has pitched most effectively as a swing man in his four pro seasons. He has neither the repertoire to be an effective starter nor the one dominating pitch he'd need to be a closer. His 1995 season with Colorado's Double-A farm at New Haven was his best to date.

NELSON, JEFF - TR - Age 29
Nelson and Bill Risley were animals in setting up Ayala and Charlton. Nelson's had good number before, but really pitched beautifully almost the entire year. He was one of the few non-closers relievers with any value in 1995, and his ALCS performance only increases his confidence.

	W	SV	ERA	IP	H	BB	SO	B/I	$
1994 Calgary AAA	1	8	2.84	25	21	7	30	1.11	

	W	SV	ERA	IP	H	BB	SO	B/I	$
1994 Seattle AL	0	0	2.76	42	35	20	44	1.30	2
1995 Seattle AL	7	2	2.17	78	58	27	96	1.08	14
1996 *Projection* >>>	4	3	2.79	77	60	30	89	1.16	12

NEN, ROBB - TR - Age 26
Nen proved his that his 1994 breakthrough season was not an illusion as he posted another solid season as Marlins' closer despite his deceptive 0-7 won-lost record. He recovered from early season struggles, and was nearly unhittable in the second half. He has a blistering fastball, which he has learned to control after spells of wildness throughout his minor league career. He is effective against righthanders (.218 opponent batting average in 1995), and with Bryan Harvey no longer being relied upon, Nen is the Marlins' closer for the foreseeable future. His only flaw is that opponent baserunners can steal at will, going 12 for 12 in 1995.

	W	SV	ERA	IP	H	BB	SO	B/I	$
1994 Florida NL	5	15	2.95	58	46	17	60	1.09	23
1995 Florida NL	0	23	3.29	65	62	23	68	1.29	21
1996 *Projection* >>>	2	31	3.43	74	67	27	75	1.27	29

NEWLIN, JIM - TR - Age 29
Newlin has been with several organizations, spending last year in the Baltimore system. He relies on a deceptive motion be effective and enjoyed some success in the lower minors. The Orioles have released Newlin.

NICHOLS, ROD - TR - Age 31
This veteran pitcher earned another shot in the big leagues by leading Triple-A Richmond with 25 saves. After years as a struggling starter, he may have finally found a role in the bullpen. Nichols doesn't throw very hard but had outstanding control in Richmond. The Braves bullpen is crowded but Nichols should find work in the majors in 1996, probably as a long man in the pen.

NICKELL, JACKIE - TR - Age 25
Nickell's control was voted the best in the California League in Baseball America's poll in 1994. He improved further in another year at Double-A in 1995 but still didn't get promoted. Look for him at Triple-A in early '96 and, if he does well, the majors later in the year.

NICHTING, CHRIS - TR - Age 29
The 29-year old rookie didn't show anything at the major league level, but he was very impressive at Triple-A Oklahoma City. He can probably pitch for several more years in the minors, but isn't likely to get another shot at the bigs.

	W	SV	ERA	IP	H	BB	SO	B/I	$
1995 Oklahoma City AAA	5	1	2.13	67	58	19	72	1.14	
1995 Texas AL	0	0	7.03	24	36	13	6	2.01	-

NIED, DAVE - TR - Age 27
A strained elbow ruined 1995 for the Rockies' first expansion draft pick (from Atlanta). His only two appearances in August were in relief, and he was hammered. Nied agreed to play winter ball in Puerto Rico to strengthen his arm and regain his control. He'll be in the thick of the competition for a starter's role in 1996, where he's demonstrated in past years that he can pitch brilliantly if he's healthy, which has been rare indeed.

	W	SV	ERA	IP	H	BB	SO	B/I	$
1994 Colorado NL	9	0	4.80	122	137	47	74	1.51	2
1995 Colorado Springs AAA	1	0	4.99	30	31	25	21	1.83	
1996 *Projection* >>>	4	0	5.59	63	75	26	38	1.60	-

NIELSEN, JERRY - TL - Age 29
The former Yankee and Angel now lacks ability to get Double-A hitters out.

NITKOWSKI, C.J. - TL - Age 23
The Tigers received this young curveballing lefty from Cincinnati for David Wells. Nitkowski was the Reds' first round pick in '94 out of St. John's University, and he has a bright future. He has been compared to Frank Viola; remember that even two-time Cy Young winner Viola needed a couple of years to gain experience before he won consistently.

	W	SV	ERA	IP	H	BB	SO	B/I	$
1995 Cincinnati NL	1	0	6.12	32	41	15	18	1.74	
1995 Detroit AL	1	0	7.09	39	53	20	13	1.87	-
1996 *Projection* >>>	8	0	5.11	165	178	68	93	1.49	-

NIX, JAMES - TR - Age 25
After working as starter in 1994, Nix was moved to the bullpen in 1995. His season at Double-A Chattanooga was promising enough that the Reds sent Nix to the Arizona Fall League. Nix was a 19th round draft pick in 1992 and has posted good strikeout totals throughout his minor league career.

NOMO, HIDEO - TR - Age 27
The Tornado turned in a brilliant first half (1.99 ERA, .158 opponents batting average) before fading to "above average" the second half (3.03 ERA, .204 OBA). Nomo features a good fastball but his best pitch is his forkball, which reminds me of Mike Scott's or Bruce Sutter's in their prime. His unconventional windup serves to hide the ball from the hitter until the last possible moment. His season was similar to Mike Scott's brilliant 1986, giving up very few hits, a few more walks than one would like, and a phenomenal strikeout rate. The only question about Nomo is his durability, as he was worked hard in Japan and Tommy LaSorda is a notorious abuser of fragile pitchers.

	W	SV	ERA	IP	H	BB	SO	B/I	$
1995 Los Angeles NL	13	0	2.54	191	124	78	236	1.06	23
1996 *Projection* >>>	15	0	3.14	202	146	88	210	1.16	22

NORRIS, JOE - TR - Age 25
Norris might well carve a spot in the Twins bullpen in '97. Drafted by Montreal, this big righthander has spent the last two seasons working at Double-A for Minnesota. He has shown improvement and will move to Triple-A in '96.

NOVOA, RAFAEL - TL - Age 28
A one-time top prospect and ex-major leaguer, Novoa was on the rehab trail in 1995, working seven games on the White Sox farm. Keep your eye on that "TL" asset.

NUNEZ, CLEMENTE - TR - Age 21
Despite a solid 1994 campaign as one of the high A-ball Florida State League's youngest starters, Nunez returned there in 1995. Nunez displayed only average velocity but pinpoint control, walking 1.5 batters per nine innings. Despite his relatively small (5'11", 181 lbs.) stature, he averaged nearly seven innings per start. A pitcher's toughest jump is from high A-ball to Double-A - that test in 1996 will determine Nunez' worth as a prospect. If all goes well, he could contend for a spot with the Marlins by mid-1997.

NYE, RYAN - TR - Age 22
Nye was the Phils' number two pick in 1994, and was conspicuously retained at high A-ball while opening day teammates Carlton Loewer and Matt Beech were promoted to Double-A. Nye possesses impeccable control and has a diversified repertoire featuring an average fastball, slider and changeup. As with most pitchers, Nye's key test will be the jump to Double-A - if he maintains his average power and excellent control at that level, he will be a viable big league prospect. He is two full seasons away if all goes well.

Do You Surf The NET?

Visit **John Benson's** Web Site:

hhtp://www.johnbenson.com

For the latest news on products and services.

Download Benson's Draft Software DEMO - FREE !!

See what Benson said last year about hundreds of players.

O'DONOGHUE, JOHN - TL - Age 26
The son of the ex-major league lefthander of the same name, O'Donoghue found himself with other organizations' castoffs on the Albuquerque staff last season. The 6-6, 210-pounder has been a .500 pitcher in Triple-A because he hasn't dominated lefthanded batters.

	W	SV	ERA	IP	H	BB	SO	B/I	$
1994 Rochester AAA	4	1	5.72	105	142	55	78	1.87	
1995 Albuquerque AAA	5	0	3.82	92	97	25	59	1.33	

OEHRLEIN, DAVE - TL - Age 26
Oehrlein's first year at Double-A Arkansas was a disappointment and he has fallen from prospect status in the eyes of Cardinals' brass. Being a lefty will help him advance but he'll have to do better in 1996 to have any real chance at the big leagues.

OGEA, CHAD - TR - Age 25
It was long overdue, but Ogea finally got an extended chance to prove his value to the Indians in 1995. After watching the club import such relics as Jack Morris and Bud Black, Ogea proved his worth with his exceptional breaking ball repertoire which he can seemingly place anywhere he wishes. Ogea needs to learn to hold baserunners better, and must maintain his superb precision because of a lack of velocity, but he appears to have clearly earned a full season berth in the fourth or fifth spot in the Indians' rotation, an attractive role on such a strong club.

	W	SV	ERA	IP	H	BB	SO	B/I	$
1994 Charlotte AAA	9	1	3.85	164	146	34	113	1.09	
1994 Cleveland AL	0	0	6.06	16	21	10	11	1.90	-
1995 Cleveland AL	8	0	3.05	106	95	29	57	1.17	12
1996 *Projection* >>>	10	0	3.31	162	150	49	89	1.23	17

OHME, KEVIN - TL - Age 24
The Twins are high on Ohme, who missed most of the 1994 season and was brought along slowly last year in Double-A. He has tended to nibble at corners and fall behind in the count. He was used as a reliever in the Arizona Fall League.

OJALA, KIRT - TL - Age 27
Ojala was once the Yankee organization's pitcher of the month, and he's 19-14 with ERA's under four in his last two Triple-A seasons, but he would have a better chance to advance in another organization.

	W	SV	ERA	IP	H	BB	SO	BPI	$
1995 Columbus AAA	8	1	3.95	145	138	54	107	1.32	

OJEDA, BOB - TL - Age 38
The Yankees brought Ojeda to spring training for a long look in '94, and eventually called him up and gave him two starts. But he got crushed in both outings and was released 5/6/94.

OLIVARES, OMAR - TR - Age 28
Starved for pitching, the Phils were happy to find a relatively young pitcher with a live fastball available. It took the Phils only a brief period to discover what the Cards and Rockies already knew - that Olivares has lost the edge on his fastball, and he generally whines too much for a marginal major league pitcher. All he showed as a Phillie was a good bat for a pitcher, not exactly a high priority.

	W	SV	ERA	IP	H	BB	SO	B/I	$
1994 St. Louis NL	3	1	5.74	73	84	37	26	1.64	-
1995 Scranton AAA	0	0	4.87	44	49	20	28	1.56	
1995 Philadelphia NL	1	0	6.91	41	55	23	22	1.87	-
1996 *Projection* >>>	2	1	5.88	71	84	32	32	1.63	-

OLIVER, DARREN - TL - Age 25
When healthy, Oliver's fastball and slurve are extremely tough on lefthanded hitters. Problem is, Oliver is seldom healthy. Oliver's season ended in late June with a partially torn left rotator cuff, the third injury to his left shoulder in five seasons. He has also undergone ligament transplant surgery in his left elbow. Oliver had been added to the starting rotation shortly before suffering the injury, although he had also been considered a closer candidate.

	W	SV	ERA	IP	H	BB	SO	B/I	$
1994 Texas AL	4	2	3.42	50	40	35	50	1.50	5
1995 Texas AL	4	0	4.22	49	47	32	39	1.61	1
1996 *Projection* >>>	4	1	3.90	54	49	30	48	1.46	2

OLSEN, STEVE - TR - Age 26
Olsen is a 6-4, 225-pound control pitcher. He pitched well for the White Sox Triple-A affiliate at Nashville in 1994, but last season the Sounds had to send him back to Double-A Birmingham.

OLSON, GREGG - TR - Age 29
This former Orioles closer has finally shown something of major league quality after his serious elbow injury in 1993. He still throws the great curveball, but with a little less snap and his control isn't quite as good as it needs to be. But, he's very close to being an effective short reliever again and might be the leading candidate to replace Jeff Montgomery as the Royals closer should Monty be dealt in a cost cutting move.

	W	SV	ERA	IP	H	BB	SO	B/I	$
1994 Atlanta NL	0	1	9.20	14	19	13	10	2.18	-
1995 Two AAA Teams	1	13	2.38	22	16	10	26	1.15	
1995 Cleveland - Kansas City AL	3	3	4.09	33	28	19	21	1.42	4
1996 *Projection* >>>	2	5	4.70	33	31	20	23	1.53	4

ONTIVEROS, STEVE - TR - Age 35
His 1994 ERA title made for a good human interest story, and Ontiveros is a decent pitcher, but injuries and other problems resulted in an increase of almost two runs in his ERA in 1995. He's returned from the dead before, but Ontiveros is now 35 years old and must be considered a risk at this point.

	W	SV	ERA	IP	H	BB	SO	B/I	$
1994 Oakland AL	6	0	2.65	115	93	26	56	1.03	18
1995 Oakland AL	9	0	4.37	129	144	38	77	1.40	6
1996 *Projection* >>>	8	0	4.49	138	150	54	77	1.48	2

OQUIST, MIKE - TR - Age 27
Oquist has below average stuff. He pitched in middle relief for Orioles for a time last year, but they decided he just couldn't get it done in the majors.

	W	SV	ERA	IP	H	BB	SO	B/I	$
1994 Baltimore AL	3	0	6.17	58	75	30	39	1.80	-
1995 Rochester AAA	0	2	5.25	12	17	5	11	1.83	
1995 Baltimore AL	2	0	4.17	54	51	41	27	1.70	-
1996 *Projection* >>>	1	0	4.95	37	39	21	21	1.62	-

ORELLANO, RAFAEL - TL - Age 22
The slightly built (6-2, 160) Orellano stayed healthy all last season for Trenton, the Red Sox Double-A affiliate. Think of him as a lefthanded Julian Tavarez. Orellano can be a strikeout-an-inning pitcher. He gets into trouble by walking batters or by falling behind in the count and serving up home run pitches.

OROSCO, JESSE - TL - Age 38
When Orosco posted a 5.08 ERA with Milwaukee in 1994, he was thought to be washed up. But the Orioles took a chance, and Manager Phil Regan quickly found that Orosco's pitch selection was very predictable. Regan got Orosco to mix up his pitches and to throw more breaking balls, and he quickly became the star of the O's bullpen. The O's like Jesse so much, they signed him for 1996, and he will again be in a set-up role with situational pitching as needed.

	W	SV	ERA	IP	H	BB	SO	B/I	$
1994 Milwaukee AL	3	0	5.08	39	32	26	36	1.49	0
1995 Baltimore AL	2	3	3.26	49	28	27	58	1.11	7
1996 *Projection* >>>	2	2	3.78	56	37	31	61	1.22	5

OSBORNE, DONOVAN - TL - Age 26
Osborne did OK last season after missing all of 1994 because of shoulder surgery. He's a good pitcher, capable of winning 15 games on a regular basis now that his arm woes are behind him. He will at least triple his 1995 win total in 1996.

	W	SV	ERA	IP	H	BB	SO	B/I	$
1994 St. Louis NL			Did Not Play						
1995 St. Louis NL	4	0	3.81	113	112	34	82	1.29	4
1996 *Projection* >>>	13	0	3.70	174	172	49	126	1.27	11

OSTEEN, GAVIN - TL - Age 26
For the third straight season, Osteen struggled at AAA Tacoma. He has pitched well during this time in the lower minors, and is only 25 years old. He could still have a good major league career, although you don't often hear him mentioned as a top Oakland prospect, and his AAA performances leave something to be desired.

OSUNA, AL - TL - Age 30
The Dodgers acquired Osuna from Houston to become one of those get-one-lefty-out relievers. When he didn't get those batters out, in a trial lasting only 8.2 innings, his four years of major league success were dismissed as irrelevant, and he went to Albuquerque, where he had some success as a setup and short reliever, and then on to the Mets farm, where he's had even more success.

	W	SV	ERA	IP	H	BB	SO	B/I	$
1994 Albuquerque AAA	1	3	2.82	44	39	14	41	1.19	
1995 Norfolk AAA	3	0	3.00	42	39	12	31	1.21	
1996 *Projection* >>>	1	0	4.87	31	32	14	25	1.50	-

OSUNA, ANTONIO - TR - Age 22
Despite an injury plagued and generally ineffective season in a setup role, Osuna is the Dodger's closer of the future. He features a great fastball and not much else, consistently striking out over a batter an inning throughout his minor league career. If (when?) Todd Worrell goes down, Osuna will get the first chance to replace him as closer.

	W	SV	ERA	IP	H	BB	SO	B/I	$
1995 Los Angeles NL	2	0	4.43	44	39	20	46	1.32	-
1996 *Projection* >>>	1	3	4.43	30	26	14	31	1.32	2

OTTO, DAVE - TL - Age 31
An intelligent guy, he couldn't break a pane of glass with his best fastball despite being built like Paul Bunyan. He has no value.

PAINTER, LANCE - TL - Age 28
Painter made only one start for the Rockies, and spent most of the latter part of the season in spot relief duty after being called up from Triple-A. The Rockies sorely need a lefty starter, but the most promising southpaws are still deep in the farm system. Painter could see limited action in the starting rotation in 1996 if he can keep his breaking ball down.

	W	SV	ERA	IP	H	BB	SO	B/I	$
1994 Colorado NL	4	0	6.11	73	91	26	41	1.59	-
1995 Colorado NL	3	1	4.37	45	55	10	36	1.44	1
1996 *Projection* >>>	5	1	4.55	89	95	34	59	1.45	-

PALACIOS, VICENTE - TR - Age 32
Palacios had a horrible 1995 season, marred by injuries. He's had his moments - though not enough - with both the Pirates and Cardinals but appears to be at the end of his career.

	W	SV	ERA	IP	H	BB	SO	B/I	$
1994 St. Louis NL	3	1	4.44	117	104	43	95	1.25	5
1995 St. Louis NL	2	0	5.80	40	48	19	34	1.67	-
1996 *Projection* >>>	1	0	5.72	31	36	14	22	1.60	-

PALL, DONN - TR - Age 34
This veteran reliever is an eleventh man on a major league staff at best. Pall has spent parts of seven years in the big leagues, but he can't work as frequently as he used to, and his lukewarm velocity has left him more hittable in recent years.

	W	SV	ERA	IP	H	BB	SO	B/I	$
1994 Two Teams	1	0	3.69	39	51	10	23	1.56	-
1995 Nashville AAA	4	3	3.98	86	89	20	79	1.27	

PARK, CHAN-HO - TR - Age 22
1994's Grapefruit League sensation struggled with his control at Triple-A Albuquerque, walking 6.2 batters per nine innings. He should not be compared to Nomo (or vice versa), who was a veteran major league pitcher when he arrived in the US, having to deal "only" with the cultural adjustment. Park was signed as a college sophomore, so he must adjust to both the rigors of a full season schedule and the cultural adjustment. Both can be major hurdles. He still is a good prospect - for 1997 or 1998 after he harnesses his tremendous stuff.

	W	SV	ERA	IP	H	BB	SO	B/I	$
1995 Albuquerque AAA	6	0	4.91	110	93	76	101	1.54	
1996 Projection >>>	2	0	4.90	76	73	41	70	1.50	-

PARRA, JOSE - TR - Age 23
This young Dominican came over from the Dodgers in the Tapani deal. The Twins used him as a starter, a role to which he is ill suited. Parra will develop into a reliable reliever when Minnesota obtains some starting help from their farm system. He does not throw hard enough to be a prospect for closer duty.

	W	SV	ERA	IP	H	BB	SO	B/I	$
1995 Los Angeles NL	0	0	4.35	10	10	6	7	1.55	
1995 Minnesota AL	1	0	7.59	61	83	22	29	1.70	-
1996 Projection >>>	4	0	5.82	144	186	54	72	1.67	-

PARRETT, JEFF - TR - Age 34
Parrett spent 1995 with the Cardinals. Though it might seem to be the case, he has NOT pitched with every club in the majors now. He had a pretty decent year in St. Louis and will be in someone's bullpen as a middle reliever in 1996.

	W	SV	ERA	IP	H	BB	SO	B/I	$
1994 Omaha AAA	0	0	3.96	38	34	14	35	1.24	
1995 St. Louis NL	4	0	3.64	76	71	28	71	1.29	3
1996 Projection >>>	3	0	3.78	52	48	19	48	1.29	1

PARRIS, STEVE - TR - Age 28
After a great start at Double-A Carolina, Parris was promoted to the Pirates' starting rotation last June and he acquitted himself pretty well in spite of less-than-stellar numbers. His fastball is average but he's tough when he's able to spot a good curveball for strikes. He's been through a lot, including reconstructive elbow surgery and being released by Philadelphia, Los Angeles and Seattle. However, Parris has perservered and should hang around a few years as a decent Number four or five starter.

	W	SV	ERA	IP	H	BB	SO	B/I	$
1995 Pittsburgh NL	6	0	5.38	82	89	33	61	1.49	-
1996 Projection >>>	7	0	4.97	163	170	65	121	1.44	-

PATRICK, BRONSWELL - TR - Age 25
Patrick has spent eight years in the minor leagues but only one in the Houston system. He appears to have found his niche as a Triple-A middle reliever.

	W	SV	ERA	IP	H	BB	SO	B/I	$
1995 Tucson AAA	5	1	4.19	81	91	21	62	1.37	

PATTERSON, BOB - TL - Age 36
Patterson had a very good season last year in his usual role of lefty set-up man and middle reliever. In the same genre as lefties Jesse Orosco and Paul Assenmacher, such pitchers quietly do their excellent jobs without much fanfare, but they are very valuable in keeping the lid on things usually pitching only an inning until the closer can get into the game.

	W	SV	ERA	IP	H	BB	SO	B/I	$
1994 California AL	2	1	4.07	42	35	15	30	1.19	4
1995 California AL	5	0	3.04	53	48	13	41	1.14	6
1996 Projection >>>	3	1	3.50	59	53	16	45	1.17	6

PATTERSON, DANNY - TR - Age 25
Patterson has moved steadily through the Rangers' farm system, pitching mostly in relief. He has received mid-season promotions in each of the last two years, and was slated to pitch in the Arizona Fall League.

	W	SV	ERA	IP	H	BB	SO	BPI	$
1995 Oklahoma City AAA	1	2	1.65	27	23	9	9	1.17	

PATTERSON, JEFF - TR - Age 27
After seven years on the farm, mostly in the Phillies system, Patterson finally reached the majors in '95. Unfortunately this career minor league reliever reached his peak back in 1992-1993 with 36 saves as he advanced to Triple-A and held his own with a 2.69 ERA at Scranton in '93, when the major leagues didn't need him.

	W	SV	ERA	IP	H	BB	SO	B/I	$
1995 Columbus AAA	5	0	3.61	62	56	30	36	1.38	

PATTERSON, KEN - TL - Age 31
For his bullpen work, Patterson has a good major league record. But he blew out his elbow in early 1994, missing almost two years. He came back last year, pitching in Triple-A. Patterson's role has always been the lefty set-up man out of the bullpen.

PAVELOFF, DAVE - TR - Age 27
Paveloff is a 26 year old middle reliever and mop up man who pitched in Class AA last year. He spent almost four years in Class A where he posted some good records. Overall had a 2.69 ERA on the Orioles farm.

PAVLAS, DAVE - TR - Age 33
A solid year at Triple-A got this ex-Cub another shot at the majors. He's not going to find a big role with any team, but Pavlas is a crafty veteran who can throw strikes in spot relief work.

	W	SV	ERA	IP	H	BB	SO	B/I	$
1995 Columbus AAA	3	18	2.61	58	43	20	51	1.07	
1995 New York AL	0	0	3.18	5	8	0	3	1.41	-
1996 Projection >>>	1	0	3.77	31	33	11	16	1.41	0

PAVLIK, ROGER - TR - Age 28
Pavlik came back nicely from a partially torn rotator cuff, finishing strongly after reverting to his unorthodox, cross-body style of pitching. There is concern that his delivery puts undue strain on his shoulder, and there is always the possibility of re-injury. Pavlik will never be a low ratio pitcher, but, health permitting, he is a good bet to be a consistent winner.

	W	SV	ERA	IP	H	BB	SO	B/I	$
1994 Texas AL	2	0	7.69	50	61	30	31	1.81	-
1995 Texas AL	10	0	4.37	191	174	90	149	1.38	9
1996 Projection >>>	11	0	4.69	167	153	81	127	1.40	5

PEDRAZA, ROB - TR - Age 23
A sterling 13-3 record with a 3.24 ERA is going to move Pedraza along to Triple A permanently next year. He had seven starts with a 9.37 ERA, but learned a lot. He averaged 1.7 walks per nine innings in first three years with Montreal farm teams.

PEEVER, LLOYD - TR - Age 24
The 4th round pick in the '92 draft looked good with a 3.43 ERA at Double-A New Haven in 1994, but struggled in a '95 season limited to eight starts.

	W	SV	ERA	IP	H	BB	SO	BPI	$
1995 Colorado Springs AAA	3	0	5.36	42	45	16	25	1.46	

PELTZER, KURT - TL - Age 27
This lefty reliever has posted good numbers in five minor league seasons, although he has never been used as a stopper. He could help a team as a lefty specialist. Had a 2.84 ERA with one save at AA Shreveport.

PENA, ALEJANDRO - TR - Age 36
Have arm, will travel. Pena pitched for three teams in 1995 and has changed teams six times in the last six years. He was mostly useless in Boston, but fared better for Florida before joining the Braves' playoff roster. Pena keeps blowing out his elbow, so his career is just one pitch away from ending at any time.

	W	SV	ERA	IP	H	BB	SO	B/I	$
1994 Pittsburgh NL	3	7	5.02	28	22	10	27	1.12	9
1995 Boston AL	1	0	7.40	24	33	12	25	1.85	-
1995 Florida - Atlanta NL	2	0	2.61	31	22	7	39	0.94	0
1996 Projection >>>	2	2	4.40	49	49	18	49	1.36	1

PENNINGTON, BRAD - TL - Age 26
The Reds acquired Pennington in June and sent him to Triple-A after seeing his alleged mechanics, which make Rob Dibble look as controlled and smooth as Greg Maddux. Pennington has a great fastball and is lefthanded, so he should get about a thousand more chances to make the majors.

	W	SV	ERA	IP	H	BB	SO	B/I	$
1996 Projection >>>	1	1	6.12	30	31	18	31	1.62	-

PERCIBAL, WILLIAM - TR - Age 22
Percibal is a smooth reliever with four above-average pitches, including a good slider. Orioles Farm Director Syd Thrift called him "a young Satchel Paige." Percibal could rise rapidly in the Orioles organization and could be in their bullpen in late 1996.

PERCIVAL, TROY - TR - Age 26
Percival throws a dominating fastball and is the Angels closer-in-waiting to replace Lee Smith. His fastball hits the radar guns in the high-90's MPH range. Last year was Percival's first taste of the major leagues, and he exceeded the Angels' expectations with an outstanding year.

	W	SV	ERA	IP	H	BB	SO	B/I	$
1994 Vancouver AAA	2	15	4.13	61	63	29	73	1.51	
1995 California AL	3	3	1.95	74	37	26	94	0.85	15
1996 Projection >>>	3	9	2.80	68	55	20	71	1.11	17

PEREZ, CARLOS - TL - Age 25
Perez's theatrics aside, this lefty had a good rookie season with the Expos in 1995 and was one of the top rookie starters in the majors. His herky-jerky delivery makes it tough for hitters to pick up his pitches and he also throws hard. He has the makings of a consistent winner but his career could be sidetracked after off-field problems last September.

	W	SV	ERA	IP	H	BB	SO	B/I	$
1995 Montreal NL	10	0	3.69	141	142	28	106	1.20	10
1996 Projection >>>	12	0	3.78	171	172	37	128	1.22	12

PEREZ, DAVID - TR - Age 27
Perez didn't do anything at Triple-A Oklahoma City to suggest that he is ready to pitch effectively in the majors. He'll get yet another season at Triple-A in 1996.

	W	SV	ERA	IP	H	BB	SO	BPI	$
1995 Oklahoma City AAA	5	0	5.57	103	120	34	74	1.49	

PEREZ, MELIDO - TR - Age 30
Perez slumped and then went out with a sore shoulder in 1995. His ailments have now put him on the DL two of the last three seasons, and he hasn't produced a really good year since 1992. If he's physically OK he can still dominate with his fastball/forkball 1-2 punch, but health is a big question.

	W	SV	ERA	IP	H	BB	SO	B/I	$
1994 New York AL	9	0	4.10	151	134	58	109	1.27	13
1995 New York AL	5	0	5.58	69	70	31	44	1.46	0
1996 Projection >>>	6	0	4.78	90	86	37	64	1.36	2

PEREZ, MIKE - TR - Age 31
Perez is a good middle reliever, but not much else. He has a publicly announced aversion to closing games and is much better as a setup man. A rubber arm allows Perez to be used in many different situations. He'll continue in the same role in 1996.

	W	SV	ERA	IP	H	BB	SO	B/I	$
1994 St. Louis NL	2	12	8.71	31	52	10	20	2.00	6

	W	SV	ERA	IP	H	BB	SO	B/I	$
1995 Chicago NL	2	2	3.66	71	72	27	49	1.39	3
1996 *Projection* >>>	3	2	4.49	68	77	24	47	1.48	0

PEREZ, YORKIS - TL - Age 28
There are situational relievers, and then there's Yorkis Perez. The designated lefty in the Marlins' bullpen has pitched a grand total of 92 innings in his 116 big league appearances. He shut down lefties, holding them to a .157 average in 1995, but was betrayed both by his control, and by relievers like Randy Veres and Terry Mathews, who consistently allowed Perez' baserunners to score. Unless prospect Vic Darensbourg, who missed all of 1995, is 100%, there is little immediate competition for Perez from within the organization. Expect improvement from Perez in 1996.

	W	SV	ERA	IP	H	BB	SO	B/I	$
1994 Florida NL	3	0	3.54	40	33	14	41	1.16	3
1995 Florida NL	2	1	5.21	46	35	28	47	1.35	0
1996 *Projection* >>>	4	2	4.61	49	37	24	49	1.27	2

PERIGNY, DON - TR - Age 27
Perigny went from starter to closer for the Marlins' Portland Double-A affiliate. Despite a mediocre ERA, he furnished a three to one strikeout/walk ratio, and struck out nearly a batter per inning. He'll likely be tested in the unfriendly (to pitchers) Triple-A Pacific Coast League in 1995.

PERSCHKE, GREG - TR - Age 28
Occupation: organizational pitcher. Has been brilliant at Double-A but keeps struggling at Triple-A, most recently for the Cubs' Iowa farm in 1994.

PERSON, ROBERT - TR - Age 26
Although he made one great start late in 1995, Person is being groomed as a short reliever for the long-term. He went to Arizona Fall League for the second consecutive season to polish his game-finishing skills.

	W	SV	ERA	IP	H	BB	SO	B/I	$
1995 Norfolk AAA	2	0	4.50	32	30	13	33	1.34	
1995 New York NL	1	0	0.75	12	5	2	10	0.58	2
1996 *Projection* >>>	1	1	4.24	34	33	16	28	1.45	-

PETERSEN, MATT - TR - Age 25
The Marlins 1992 29th-round pick from Iowa State ranked among organizational strikeout leaders in two of his first three seasons but keeps running into trouble above the Class A level. 1996 looms as a make-or-break year for him.

PETERSON, JAYSON - TR - Age 20
Peterson's reward for an undefeated season at Denver's East High School was being drafted in the first round by the Cubs. He had a lot of trouble throwing strikes as a pro.

PETERSON, MARK - TL - Age 25
Peterson had awesome numbers at Double-A last year. His future could be a lefty who rises above the one-out role. He's still a couple of years away.

PETKOVSEK, MARK - TR - Age 30
This journeyman right-hander added a little stability to a woeful Cardinals rotation last year. He doesn't have one great pitch but is a bright guy who gets the most out of his ability. The Cardinals inexplicably dropped him from the rotation last September. He's not going to be a Cy Young candidate but he deserves another chance, either in St. Louis or somewhere else.

	W	SV	ERA	IP	H	BB	SO	B/I	$
1994 Tucson AAA	10	0	4.62	138	176	40	69	1.56	
1995 St. Louis NL	6	0	4.00	137	136	35	71	1.25	6
1996 *Projection* >>>	5	0	4.26	93	97	26	48	1.33	1

PETT, JOSE - TR - Age 20
The Brazilian Pett got his most extensive pro experience last season with the Blue Jays' Double-A farm at Knoxville. Despite a fastball timed as high as 94 MPH, the 6-6, 190-pound Pett has not been a strikeout pitcher. Monitor his progress at Syracuse this year.

PETTIFORD, CECIL - Age 28
Pettiford spent five years in rookie and Class A leagues before making it to Class AA as a middle reliever last year.

PETTIT, DOUG - TR - Age 25
It's often said that a low draft pick must constantly prove himself, and that might not even be enough. All the 41st-round pick has done since being drafted out of Texas in 1992 is to lead his team in saves each year 1992 through 1994 and compile a cumulative four to one strikeout/walk ratio in his first three pro seasons. Finally promoted above Class A in 1995, Pettit was competent if somewhat less spectacular (3-1 with 2 saves and a 3.69 ERA in 31.2 innings for Double-A Portland). At least the promotion showed that somebody is watching him.

PETTITTE, ANDY - TL - Age 23
A big force in the Yankees late 1995 surge, Pettitte has a 93 MPH heater and credits his major league success to a cutter taught him by coach Billy Connors ("the same cut fastball Billy taught Greg Maddux when they were with the Cubs). Pettitte is well-suited to Yankee Stadium.

	W	SV	ERA	IP	H	BB	SO	B/I	$
1995 New York AL	12	0	4.17	175	183	63	114	1.41	9
1996 Projection >>>	11	0	4.05	180	182	61	117	1.35	11

PHILLIPS, TONY - TR - Age 26
Once a hot prospect in the Mariners' lower minors, Phillips has stalled at Triple-A due to lack of a strikeout pitch. He still has pretty good control, and a 4.12 ERA is not too bad for the Pacific Coast League. Still, for Phillips to get more than a cursory look in the majors he'll have to start fanning a few more batters.

	W	SV	ERA	IP	H	BB	SO	B/I	$
1995 Tacoma AAA	3	1	4.12	87	98	14	44	1.28	

PHOENIX, STEVE - TR - Age 28
This career minor-leaguer hints at something greater, but has not gotten the opportunities, for whatever reason.

	W	SV	ERA	IP	H	BB	SO	B/I	$
1994 Huntsville AA	6	20	1.29	48	42	16	40	1.19	
1994 Tacoma AAA	0	9	1.23	22	16	4	16	0.91	
1995 Edmonton AAA	4	5	4.50	64	66	28	28	1.47	

PICHARDO, HIPOLITO -TR - Age 26
Pichardo was one of the few bright spots in a dismal Royals bullpen in 1995. He throws a good sinker and managed to reign in his whirling delivery enough to control his pitches better. Pichardo has been an occasional starter in the past and could return to that role in a pinch. But, based upon his recent bullpen success, he'll probably remain a righthanded long relief/ situational specialist.

	W	SV	ERA	IP	H	BB	SO	B/I	$
1994 Kansas City AL	5	3	4.92	67	82	24	36	1.57	4
1995 Kansas City AL	8	1	4.36	64	66	30	43	1.50	4
1996 Projection >>>	5	1	4.48	88	97	35	51	1.50	2

PICKETT, RICKY - TL - Age 26
A wild fireballer who could never find the plate while in the Reds organization, Pickett walked only 9 in 21 innings for the Giants' Double-A club while still striking out more than one batter per inning. If he has truly found the plate, he could be a real sleeper. Watch his 1996 stats closely.

PIERCE, ED - TL - Age 27
Pierce's repertoire is too limited for effective starting duty, his breaking stuff isn't of major league quality and he walks too many for a pitcher who isn't overpowering. While Pierce was once on the verge of breaking through to the majors, it's now safe to assume that he won't be a serious big league contributor. Lefthanded relief help is always in demand, so Pierce may get a set-up job eventually. In the meantime he'll be stored at Triple-A as bench help for the Royals.

PIERCE, JEFF - TR - Age 26
An overachieving strikeout pitcher, Pierce fanned more than a batter per inning pitching long relief and made three

spot starts for Triple-A Pawtucket in 1995. He's no prospect, but could earn a middle relief role with in weaker major league bullpen.

	W	SV	ERA	IP	H	BB	SO	B / I	$
1995 Pawtucket AAA	4	0	4.14	41	34	16	43	1.21	
1995 Boston AL	0	0	6.60	15	16	14	12	2.00	-

PIERSON, JASON - TL - Age 25
Finally given a chance above Class A in 1995, Pierson was roughly greeted in his four starts for Double-A Birmingham. As a southpaw who can throw strikes, he can look forward to more chances with better results.

PINEDA, LEONEL - TR - Age 19
Remember this name. Signed by the Marlins as a 16 year old free agent from the Dominican Republic, Pineda made his minor league debut late in 1995. Though he was hit hard in his five low Class-A starts, Pineda showed exemplary control and an uncanny ability to extricate himself from trouble. His 6'2", 175 lbs., body is still growing, and if his fastball gets a slight boost, Pineda could develop into a dominating starter. He's got a long way to go, but he has the tools.

PISCIOTTA, MARK - TR - Age 25
Colorado thought enough of Pisciotta to select him from the Pirates in the Rule Five Draft at the 1993 winter meetings. Pisciotta didn't make the Rockies, returned to the Pirates' organization and has watched his progress stall during the past two seasons. No longer considered the closer of the future, he'll have to fight to make it to the majors as a middle reliever.

PITTSLEY, JIM - TR - Age 22
The Royals 1992 first-round draft pick was supposed to open the 1995 season at Double-A Wichita, instead pitching well enough in the spring to begin the year at Triple-A Omaha. An impressive start earned Pittsley a promotion to the majors where he blew out his elbow after just one start. Off-season surgery and rehabilitation will slow his development, but the big (6'7") righthander has great control of a live fastball and an impressive curve, so he'll be given a lot of time to recover.

	W	SV	ERA	IP	H	BB	SO	B / I	$
1995 Omaha AAA	4	0	3.21	47	38	16	39	1.13	
1996 Projection >>>	2	0	4.23	55	61	21	28	1.50	-

PIVARAL, HUGO - TR - Age 19
The Dodgers must be scouting junior high schools all over the world. Their latest international rising star is the Guatemalan Pivaral. He cooled off after a very hot start in the Florida State League in 1994 and then delivered a workmanlike season at Class A San Bernadino in 1995. Stay tuned on this youngster.

PLANTENBERG, ERIK - TL - Age 27
Plantenberg is a southpaw reliever who spent some time in the majors with Seattle in 1993 and '94, getting into 20 games in '93. He has been used as a situational reliever to get out a single lefthanded batter, and he may catch on with the Padres or another team in that role.

PLESAC, DAN - TL - Age 34
Not bothered by shoulder tendinitis for the first time since his closer days in Milwaukee, Plesac had a solid 1995 after signing with the Pirates as a free agent. Plesac still throws hard and can get an occasional save. However, he is better suited as a set-up man at this point in his career.

	W	SV	ERA	IP	H	BB	SO	B / I	$
1994 Chicago NL	2	1	4.61	54	61	13	53	1.35	1
1995 Pittsburgh NL	4	3	3.58	60	53	27	57	1.33	5
1996 Projection >>>	4	2	4.02	70	69	26	65	1.35	3

PLUNK, ERIC - TR - Age 32
Very silently, Eric Plunk has been one of the most consistently dominant relievers in baseball over the last three years, giving up well under a hit per inning and striking out better than a batter per inning each season. He absolutely devastates righthanders (despite Jay Buhner's postseason homer), holding them to .171 average in 1994 and .200 average in 1995. He's a manager's dream - though he has every right to whine for some closing opportunities, he's

perfectly content in a supporting role. Plunk will remain the second righthander in the Tribe bullpen for the foreseeable future.

	W	SV	ERA	IP	H	BB	SO	B/I	$
1994 Cleveland AL	7	3	2.54	71	61	37	73	1.38	12
1995 Cleveland AL	6	2	2.67	64	48	27	71	1.17	10
1996 Projection >>>	4	2	3.00	80	64	36	86	1.25	10

POLLEY, DALE - TL - Age 30
Polley grabbed the attention of Braves brass with his performance at Triple-A Richmond in 1995, posting a 1.56 ERA in a team-leading 47 appearances. He earned seven saves and struck out a batter per inning, showing that he can work in either a setup or closer role. Polley is too old to be a real prospect, but he could earn a major league job as a situational or setup bullpen lefty.

	W	SV	ERA	IP	H	BB	SO	BPI	$
1995 Richmond AAA	3	7	1.56	63	51	20	60	1.12	

POOLE, JIM - TL - Age 29
An unobtrusive journeyman whose sole major league mission is to retire key lefties, Poole was an excellent #3 lefty out of the Indians' pen in 1995. His role will never expand - a solid indicator of his one-dimensional nature is his ratio of games to innings pitched - in 186 career outings, he has pitched only 177 innings. It was only fitting that Poole pitched 1995 in the same pen as Paul Assenmacher, an older version of himself. Poole should age similarly.

	W	SV	ERA	IP	H	BB	SO	B/I	$
1994 Baltimore AL	1	0	6.64	20	32	11	18	2.11	-
1995 Cleveland AL	3	0	3.75	50	40	17	41	1.13	4
1996 Projection >>>	3	0	3.92	48	42	17	38	1.24	2

PORTUGAL, MARK - TR - Age 33
Portugal performed poorly when he was acquired by the Reds in July, but finished strong to post a typical Portugal year. He mixes his pitches well, usually posts a league average or better ERA, wins more than he loses, is vulnerable to the longball, and has good control. Portugal will remain in the Reds rotation in 1996.

	W	SV	ERA	IP	H	BB	SO	B/I	$
1994 San Francisco NL	10	0	3.93	137	135	45	87	1.31	9
1995 Two Teams	11	0	4.01	181	185	56	96	1.33	7
1996 Projection >>>	13	0	3.85	201	201	64	114	1.32	9

POTE, LOU - TR - Age 24
Still coming back from arm injuries, Pote had a 2.83 ERA in five Class AA starts for Shreveport in 1994 but frequently struggled during 1995 while working mainly out of the pen, first for Shreveport and then for the Expos at Double-A.

POTTS, MICHAEL - TL - Age 25
Potts has unimpressive stuff, but has been relatively successful as a middle reliever since converting from starting duty two years ago. In two years at Triple-A Richmond he has a 3.73 ERA. Potts lacks an outstanding pitch and walks too many batters for a soft-tosser. The Braves have several good lefthanders in their major league bullpen, so Potts has no chance of reaching Atlanta; he'd be better off with another organization.

	W	SV	ERA	IP	H	BB	SO	BPI	$
1995 Richmond AAA	5	1	3.79	73	79	37	52	1.57	

POWELL, DENNIS - TL - Age 32
Veteran lefty Powell spent a disappointing 1995 with the Kintetsu Buffaloes in Japan's Pacific League, going 2-7 with a 3.81 ERA. He had made 207 major league appearances over eight seasons in the US. Powell could earn a long relief role should he return to the States.

POWELL, JAY - TR - Age 24
The Marlins acquired the Orioles' 1993 top draft pick in a deal for Bret Barberie just prior to the 1995 season. He was moved into the closer role after starting throughout his first two pro seasons, and was quite successful. His 90+ MPH fastball maintained its velocity much better when he was used in short spurts, and he was not intimidated in a late season major league trial, though his control was wobbly. Powell will get a clear shot at becoming a Marlins' setup man in 1996 - if he falls short, he will close at Triple-A Charlotte.

	W	SV	ERA	IP	H	BB	SO	B/I	$
1996 *Projection* >>>	1	1	3.80	34	35	13	20	1.40	0

POWELL, ROSS - TL - Age 28
He has had chances with Cincinnati, Houston and the Pirates over the past three seasons and the only thing that has distinguished him is that he is left-handed. He'll keep getting chances, though probably no more in Pittsburgh. If he was right-handed, he'd be seeking a new line of work.

	W	SV	ERA	IP	H	BB	SO	B/I	$
1995 Pittsburgh NL	0	0	6.98	29	36	21	20	1.92	-

POWER, TED - TR - Age 41
Power retired in spring training 1994 right around the time Lou Piniella was discovering Bobby Ayala as the closer.

PRADO, JOSE - TR - Age 23
Exclusively a starter for much of his pro career, Prado moved to the bullpen in mid-season at Double-A San Antonio and experienced some success. He had a fine 1994 campaign in the California League but his future is muddier as a reliever.

PRESLEY, KIRK - TR - Age 21
Until last season, he was known only as Elvis Presley's third cousin and the Mets' 1993 first-round draft pick. Minor league fans finally got a chance to see his 90 MPH fastball and near-major league curve.

PRICHER, JOHN - TR - Age 25
The hard-throwing Pricher looked like a big-time closer prospect until 1994, when his control deserted him. He fell all the way to Sioux City (Independent) in 1995.

PRIETO, ARIEL - TR - Age 26
His was another good human interest story that covered up mediocre pitching. Prieto had control problems in his first major-league season, without posting big strikeout numbers, and also had injury troubles. He's more famous than good at this point. However, Indians Manager Mike Hargrove said of Prieto: "He's outstanding. His motion is so smooth...guys like that are real sneaky. This guy has a chance to be real good." Prieto's fastball measures in the 91-94 MPH range.

	W	SV	ERA	IP	H	BB	SO	B/I	$
1995 Oakland AL	2	0	4.97	58	57	32	37	1.53	-
1996 *Projection* >>>	6	0	4.74	149	144	77	95	1.48	1

PUGH, TIM - TR - Age 29
Pugh pitched fairly well for the Reds working as a spot starter/reliever before he was sent down to Indianapolis when the Reds acquired David Wells. At Indianapolis he did not pitch well. Pugh suffers from chronic back problems and is unlikely to crack the Reds rotation in 1996. He relies on a sinker and guile to be effective.

	W	SV	ERA	IP	H	BB	SO	B/I	$
1994 Cincinnati NL	3	0	6.04	47	60	26	24	1.80	-
1995 Indianapolis AAA	2	0	4.68	42	42	14	20	1.32	
1995 Cincinnati NL	6	0	3.84	98	100	32	38	1.34	3
1996 *Projection* >>>	4	0	4.50	93	99	31	41	1.40	-

PULIDO, CARLOS - TL - Age 24
This lefthanded reliever spent '95 in the Triple-A Salt Lake City bullpen after starting fourteen games for Minnesota in '94. He needs to make some strides forward to gain another chance at the majors.

	W	SV	ERA	IP	H	BB	SO	B/I	$
1994 Minnesota AL	3	0	5.98	84	87	40	32	1.51	
1995 Salt Lake AAA	8	3	4.67	71	87	20	38	1.50	
1996 *Projection* >>>	1	0	5.49	35	37	16	13	1.47	-

PULSIPHER, BILL - TL - Age 22
An elbow sprain ended Pulsipher's 1995 season in mid September. Before that, he was a big-talent, big-repertoire

rookie, often carrying the staff on the strength of his 90+ fastball, cutter and big curve. Adding a reliable straight change would elevate him to the staff ace level any time now.

	W	SV	ERA	IP	H	BB	SO	B/I	$
1995 New York NL	5	0	3.98	126	122	45	81	1.32	4
1996 *Projection* >>>	10	0	3.90	156	150	51	100	1.29	7

PURDY, SHAWN - TR - Age 27
Purdy picked up 21 saves for Double-A Shreveport. He's otherwise undistinguished.

PYC, DAVE - TL - Age 25
Power pitcher Pyc was consistent for most of the year at Double-A San Antonio but got very little run support. The Dodgers have questioned his attitude, but he's still considered a good prospect who should advance to Triple-A Albuquerque in 1996.

QUANTRILL, PAUL - TR - Age 27
Due to a rash of injuries, Quantrill was the only Phils' starter who pitched enough innings to qualify for the ERA title. Quantrill has mediocre velocity and relies on precise control of his sinker/slider repertoire for success.

	W	SV	ERA	IP	H	BB	SO	B/I	$
1994 Two Teams	3	1	4.92	53	64	15	28	1.49	0
1995 Philadelphia NL	11	0	4.67	179	212	44	103	1.43	1
1996 *Projection* >>>	4	1	3.86	86	90	23	55	1.32	3

QUIRICO, RAFAEL - TL - Age 26
Quirico became a full-time reliever in 1994. If you've read this far into the book, you know you never should give up on a lefthander. The Yankees haven't. Quirico has a career 3.51 ERA after seven minor league seasons.

RACZKA, MIKE - TL - Age 33
Veteran reliever Raczka had limited major league experience with Oakland in 1992 and is now trying to get back to the bigs as a situational lefty. Despite a successful year at Triple-A Louisville in 1995 Raczka is not in the Cardinals' immediate plans.

	W	SV	ERA	IP	H	BB	SO	BPI	$
1995 Louisville AAA	5	1	3.86	49	49	20	43	1.41	

RADINSKY, SCOTT - TL - Age 28
Chemotherapy and radiation treatments used to battle Hodgskin's disease have sapped Radinsky's strength; he was throwing hard for most of 1995, but pitched better at the end of the year. He needs his good velocity to succeed. Radinsky didn't get along well with Manager Terry Bevington, so it's hard to say what his role will be in 1996.

	W	SV	ERA	IP	H	BB	SO	B/I	$
1995 Chicago AL	2	1	5.45	38	46	17	14	1.66	-

RADKE, BRAD - TR - Age 23
Although he seemed better suited to relief or Triple-A, Radke gutted out a good year in the Twins rotation in '95. He has never been regarded as a top prospect and will have to prove his eleven wins were not a fluke. Look for him to succeed only if the other Twins starters (Robertson, Trombley, Rodriguez, and Hawkins) are able to contribute a lot of innings; he'll need a lot of help from the bullpen to repeat his '95 record.

	W	SV	ERA	IP	H	BB	SO	B/I	$
1995 Minnesota AL	11	0	5.32	181	195	47	75	1.34	6
1996 *Projection* >>>	9	0	4.93	147	154	36	61	1.29	6

RAIN, STEVE - TR - Age 20
A hard thrower who keeps the ball down, Rains got 23 saves for the Cubs Class-A Rockford team.

RALPH, CURTIS - TR - Age 27
The Pirates signed this journeyman away from the New York Yankees as a six-year free agent following the 1994 season. He doesn't have major-league ability.

RALSTON, KRIS - TR - Age 24
Three consistent seasons have established Ralston as a legitimate prospect. He works off a good fastball and has steadily advanced each season. Look for Ralston at Triple-A Omaha in 1996.

RAPP, PAT - TR - Age 28
Rapp took a major step forward in 1995, becoming the unquestioned ace of the Marlins' staff. He overcame career-long problems with righthanded hitters, limiting them to a .262 average. Rapp doesn't throw particularly hard, and his control is only marginal - he is adept at pitching out of trouble, avoids the home run ball, and is among baseball's best at holding baserunners (would-be basestealers were only five for 20 against Rapp). His stamina is questionable, as he has averaged fewer than six innings per start in the majors. 1995 will likely go down as his career peak, but he should remain a serviceable starter for the time being.

	W	SV	ERA	IP	H	BB	SO	B/I	$
1994 Florida NL	7	0	3.85	133	132	69	75	1.51	4
1995 Florida NL	14	0	3.44	167	158	76	102	1.40	9
1996 *Projection* >>>	13	0	3.44	178	169	77	106	1.38	9

RASMUSSEN, DENNIS - TL - Age 36
In a career that will not die, Rasmussen keeps winning in Triple-A (6-3, 2.89 ERA for Omaha in 1995), but flopping in the bigs. He uses his height to drive American Association hitters off of the plate, but major leaguers aren't intimidated. Rasmussen is always one month away from a complete fadeout.

RATEKIN, MARK - TR - Age 25
Ratekin advanced from Double-A to Triple-A during the 1994 season, usually a good sign. Unfortunately Ratekin has been hit hard ever since. Even a return to Double-A didn't help him regroup (5.94 ERA for Class AA Midland).

RATH, GARY - TL - Age 23
Rath pitched very well with Double-A San Antonio, then struggled after a promotion to Albuquerque. His fastball and curve are no more than average, but poor control hurt him more than anything else in the Pacific Coast League. Still, he's the pitching prospect closest to making the Dodgers roster.

	W	SV	ERA	IP	H	BB	SO	BPI	$
1995 Albuquerque AAA	3	0	5.08	39	46	20	23	1.69	

RATLIFF, JON - TR - Age 24
Ratliff, a first-round draft choice by the Cubs in 1993, had his healthiest and best season last year with Double-A Orlando. The 6-5, 200-pounder came out of LeMoyne College, the same as Tom Browning and Jim Deshaies, but throws a bit harder.

RAWITZER, KEVIN - TL - Age 25
Rawitzer was impressive in his first two seasons of Class-A ball, but struggled in 1995 at Double-A Wichita. He needs another, better year at Double-A to regain stature as a prospect.

RAY, KEN - TR - Age 21
Another impressive year at Class-A earned Ray a mid-season promotion to Double-A Wichita where he struggled in 1995. He improved down the stretch and looked especially good in the Texas League playoffs. Ray has a decent fastball, but needs to improve his curveball. He'll have time to develop both with a return to Double-A in 1996.

REARDON, JEFF - TR - Age 40
Reardon tried to hang on in 1994 with a knuckleball, even getting a couple more saves into the record books before calling it quits.

REDMAN, MARK - TL - Age 22
Redman was the Twins' first round pick in last June's draft. He pitched well at Class A, and college lefthanders have a way of finding their way to the majors quickly. Redman has the talent to be a #3 starter in the majors.

REED, RICK - TR - Age 31
Reed posted another solid Triple-A season and finally got a chance when half the Reds rotation was on the DL. This would not be a big deal except that Reed was a replacement player. After the usual whining and hand wringing by

the union, Reed took a no-hitter into the seventh in his first start, which made it easier for his teammates to accept him. Unfortunately for Reed that was his only good start and he was quickly returned to the minors. Reed has excellent control and can pitch in the majors, but he hasn't had a decent opportunity since 1992.

	W	SV	ERA	IP	H	BB	SO	B/I	$
1995 Indianapolis AAA	11	0	3.33	135	127	26	92	1.14	
1995 Cincinnati NL	0	0	5.82	17	18	3	10	1.24	-

REED, STEVE - TR - Age 30
Sidewinding Reed developed a change-up during the 1994 off-season which greatly enhanced his effectiveness against lefties in 1995. He kept his ERA below 2.00 most of the season - including an astounding 3.07 ERA at Coors Field - while appearing in more games than all but one staff member. Reed is a workhorse who will be a key to the Rockies success in 1996.

	W	SV	ERA	IP	H	BB	SO	B/I	$
1994 Colorado NL	3	3	3.94	64	79	26	51	1.64	2
1995 Colorado NL	5	3	2.14	84	61	21	79	0.98	14
1996 Projection >>>	3	3	3.40	92	82	28	80	1.20	8

REKAR, BRYAN - TR - Age 23
Rekar spent all of 1994 at Class-A Central Valley and started last season at Double-A New Haven before his promotion to the big leagues in mid-July. He pitched effectively in most of his 14 starts, and seemed unruffled by the credentials of even the best batters he faced. Rekar has a strong fastball and a bright future, but could benefit from some seasoning at the Triple-A level in 1996.

	W	SV	ERA	IP	H	BB	SO	B/I	$
1995 Colorado NL	4	0	4.98	85	95	24	60	1.40	-
1996 Projection >>>	7	0	4.89	146	161	39	103	1.37	2

REMLINGER, MIKE - TL - Age 30
The Reds acquired the former Giants prospect from the Mets in May and sent him to Indianapolis after a brief look in Cincinnati. Remlinger was moved to the bullpen and showed some signs of a comeback, with 58 strikeouts in 47 innings although control was still a problem. The Reds are becoming a halfway house for failed pitching prospects, hoping that one will hit big.

	W	SV	ERA	IP	H	BB	SO	B/I	$
1994 New York NL	1	0	4.61	54	55	35	33	1.65	-
1995 Indianapolis AAA	5	0	4.05	46	40	32	58	1.55	
1995 Two Teams	0	0	6.75	6	9	5	7	2.10	-
1996 Projection >>>	1	0	4.95	31	33	20	21	1.72	-

RENKO, STEVE - TR - Age 28
Renko has struggled both starting and relieving in Double-A for two years and is a very hittable pitcher; he pitched for Midland in the Texas League last year, a hitter's paradise. The Angels saw some potential and promoted him to Triple-A in mid-year.

REVENIG, TODD - TR - Age 26
Revenig is a former "next Eck" who has been on the comeback trail from injuries for a few years. He led Triple-A Edmonton in saves with 10, but was otherwise unimpressive.

	W	SV	ERA	IP	H	BB	SO	BPI	$
1995 Edmonton AAA	4	10	4.31	54	53	15	28	1.25	

REYES, ALBERTO - TR - Age 24
Reyes is a former top minor league closer who is worth a look. He could be fine if Fetters falters.

	W	SV	ERA	IP	H	BB	SO	B/I	$
1995 Milwaukee AL	1	1	2.43	33	19	18	29	1.11	4
1996 Projection >>>	1	1	3.26	43	31	24	37	1.29	3

REYES, CARLOS - TR - Age 26
Reyes pitched very well in the Braves' system, but hasn't done much for Oakland. He's improved his control; he's unlikely to ever become a stopper, but might surprise as a fourth or fifth starter if given a chance.

	W	SV	ERA	IP	H	BB	SO	B/I	$
1994 Oakland AL	0	1	4.15	78	71	44	57	1.47	2
1995 Oakland AL	4	0	5.09	69	71	28	48	1.43	1
1996 *Projection* >>>	3	0	4.70	79	78	36	56	1.44	0

REYNOLDS, SHANE - TR - Age 28
Reynolds was Houston's most consistent starter until he faltered in five of his last six starts. His primary assets are excellent control and an outstanding split fingered fastball. His repertoire also features a 90 MPH fastball and a curve. He has ranked among the league leaders in strikeout to walk ratio in his two years as a starter and should have what it takes to be a consistent winner in the major leagues.

	W	SV	ERA	IP	H	BB	SO	B/I	$
1994 Houston NL	8	0	3.05	124	128	21	110	1.20	13
1995 Houston NL	10	0	3.47	189	196	37	175	1.23	12
1996 *Projection* >>>	12	0	3.33	181	187	34	165	1.22	15

REYNOSO, ARMANDO - TR - Age 29
Reynoso spent most of the first half of last season on the DL as a result of reconstructive elbow surgery in mid-1994. Even after his return, his usual effectiveness was limited by his lack of arm strength. Reynoso should be fully healed and will return to the starting rotation for 1996, he'll continue to rely more upon guile than power.

	W	SV	ERA	IP	H	BB	SO	B/I	$
1994 Colorado NL	3	0	4.82	52	54	22	25	1.45	0
1995 Colorado NL	7	0	5.32	93	116	36	40	1.63	-
1996 *Projection* >>>	8	0	4.97	154	176	50	73	1.47	-

RHODES, ARTHUR - TL - Age 26
It's hard to believe that the talented Rhodes has started 59 major league games over five years, and that he is still the same inconsistent and erratic pitcher now that he was back in 1991. He was so erratic last year that he was moved to the bullpen, where he had a few good outings. But he developed a shoulder problem requiring surgery to repair a slight tear in the labrum, the tissue surrounding the shoulder. Orioles ownership wants a winner now and are running out of patience with Rhodes.

	W	SV	ERA	IP	H	BB	SO	B/I	$
1994 Baltimore AL	3	0	5.81	52	51	30	47	1.54	-
1995 Baltimore AL	2	0	6.21	75	68	48	77	1.54	-
1996 *Projection* >>>	3	0	5.90	82	76	50	77	1.55	-

RICCI, CHUCK - TR - Age 27
A nine year minor league veteran from the Philadelphia area, Ricci realized a lifelong dream when he first reached the majors as a Phil late in 1995. He is a hard thrower who overcame career-long control woes to become a dominant closer at Triple-A Scranton-Wilkes Barre in 1994-95. His stuff translated well to the majors, as he maintained his high strikeout rate in his limited shot. Ricci cannot be discounted as a longshot contender for one of the last two relief spots on the Phils' 1996 roster.

	W	SV	ERA	IP	H	BB	SO	B/I	$
1995 Scranton AAA	4	25	2.49	65	48	24	66	1.11	
1995 Philadelphia NL	1	0	1.80	10	9	3	9	1.20	0

RICHEY, JEFF - TR - Age 26
Richey was the ace of San Jose's bullpen, using the best breaking pitch in the California League to get 19 saves. He had better control, and a better year, in the Midwest League in '93 (1.03 ERA, 28 saves). Still far below Rod Beck.

RIDENOUR, DANA - TR - Age 30
A former closer prospect in the Yankees' organization, he became a starter for the first time in 1994 at Triple-A Edmonton in the Marlins' organization. He has routinely posted admirable strikeout/walk ratios in his nine year minor league career, but his window of opportunity to break through at the major league level is probably closed.

RIGHETTI, DAVE - TL - Age 37
Far from retiring in 1995, Righetti pitched very well for Triple-A Nashville then took his Lazarus act to Chicago where he continued to be quite effective. He'll pitch somewhere in 1996; how long can this 1981 AL Rookie of the Year keep going?

Benson's Baseball Player Guide: 1996

	W	SV	ERA	IP	H	BB	SO	B/I	$
1995 Chicago AL	3	0	4.20	49	65	18	29	1.68	0
1996 *Projection* >>>	3	0	4.33	90	117	31	53	1.64	-

RIGHTNOWAR, RON - TR - Age 31
Rightnowar is another replacement player who had his moment in the sun, but is unlikely to be in the long range plans of the Brewers.

	W	SV	ERA	IP	H	BB	SO	B/I	$
1995 New Orleans AAA	1	10	2.67	30	37	9	22	1.58	
1995 Milwaukee AL	2	1	5.40	36	35	18	22	1.45	0
1996 *Projection* >>>	1	0	5.55	30	29	15	18	1.46	-

RIJO, JOSE - TR - Age 30
Rijo's often tender elbow finally gave out in July and Tommy John surgery followed in August. The surgery requires a lengthy rehabilitation and it's not likely that Rijo will be ready in April. Completely healthy, Rijo is one of the best pitchers in the league but after the trades for Portugal, Wells, and Burba, the Reds can afford to be patient.

	W	SV	ERA	IP	H	BB	SO	B/I	$
1994 Cincinnati NL	9	0	3.08	172	177	52	171	1.33	14
1995 Cincinnati NL	5	0	4.17	69	76	22	62	1.42	1
1996 *Projection* >>>	10	0	3.18	155	158	45	146	1.31	11

RISLEY, BILL - TR - Age 28
Risley was OK until late August then got belted around when his fastball lost some velocity and movement. Over the last two seasons he has been a first half gem, then fades in the second half.

	W	SV	ERA	IP	H	BB	SO	B/I	$
1994 Seattle AL	9	0	3.44	52	31	19	61	0.96	
1995 Seattle AL	2	1	3.13	60	55	18	65	1.21	6
1996 *Projection* >>>	5	2	3.25	63	55	22	70	1.23	8

RITCHIE, TODD - TR - Age 24
Ritchie once was highly rated in the Minnesota organization, but his career has stalled with three seasons in Double-A. Last year he was healthy, at least, but wasn't effective.

RITCHIE, WALLY - TL - Age 30
Ritchie saw time in 1994 with Cincinnati's Triple-A team. He can be a safe lefty short reliever if his manager uses him wisely. Has a very good changeup.

RITZ, KEVIN - TR - Age 30
Crackerman started last season penciled in as a middle reliever, but snuck into the rotation when Nied ended up on the DL. He was by far the Rockies' most consistent starter throughout the season, showing flashes of brilliance when his sinker was at its best - a must for success at Coors Field. Ritz should be a mainstay in the starting rotation in 1996.

	W	SV	ERA	IP	H	BB	SO	B/I	$
1994 Colorado NL	5	0	5.62	73	88	35	53	1.67	-
1995 Colorado NL	11	2	4.21	173	171	65	120	1.36	7
1996 *Projection* >>>	10	0	4.50	170	175	66	119	1.42	0

RIVERA, BEN - TR - Age 28
Big Ben's star continued to fall in 1994. The Phils disabled him in May, ostensibly due to a "tired" arm. In reality, he was sent out to lose weight and regain the focus he exhibited as a rookie in 1992. After his first time around the league that season, all of Rivera's numbers have been awful except for won-lost record, which has been propped up by run support. Rivera faces an uphill battle for a starting spot in 1995.

RIVERA, MARIANO - TR - Age 26
After getting rocked in his first callup, Rivera settled down and threw his 95 MPH fastball with more confidence from July 4th to the end of the '95 season. His live arm offers all kinds of possibilities, from starting to long relief to setup to closing. Whatever role he fills, success is highly likely.

	W	SV	ERA	IP	H	BB	SO	B/I	$
1995 New York AL	5	0	5.51	67	71	30	51	1.51	0
1996 *Projection* >>>	5	0	4.82	101	100	43	77	1.42	1

RIVERA, ROBERTO - TL - Age 27
Formerly Cleveland property, Rivera sank to Class-A for part of 1994 on the Cubs farm. Little chance to see a major league park without a ticket, but has excellent control.

ROA, JOE - TR - Age 24
An afterthought in the post-1994 season deal with the Mets which featured Dave Mlicki, Jerry DiPoto and Jeromy Burnitz, among others, Roa used his pinpoint control to post an awesome 1995 Triple-A season. Roa doesn't throw particularly hard, but has walked only 171 batters in 930 career innings. He is particularly tough on righthanded hitters and might be needed more as a situational reliever in Cleveland. Don't be fooled by the 17-3 record, though - this is no phenomenal prospect.

	W	SV	ERA	IP	H	BB	SO	B/I	$
1995 Buffalo AAA	17	0	3.50	164	168	28	93	1.19	

ROBERSON, SID - TL - Age 24
Junkball pitcher Roberson advanced to the majors for the first time in 1995, not so much on merit but due to Brewers desperation for pitching. Used as a swingman, Roberson made 13 starts and walked nearly as many as he struck out. Most alarming, he allowed 16 homers in just 84.1 innings, far too many for a non-strikeout pitcher. Roberson will contend for a long-relief/spot starter role with the Brewers in 1996.

	W	SV	ERA	IP	H	BB	SO	B/I	$
1995 Milwaukee AL	6	0	5.76	84	102	37	40	1.65	-
1996 *Projection* >>>	5	0	5.40	98	115	38	47	1.56	-

ROBERTS, CHRIS - TL - Age 24
Bill Pulsipher, who is more outspoken and throws harder, received more attention, but Roberts pitched equally well in the Eastern League on the Mets farm in 1994. Since then their paths have diverged. Pulsipher went on to the majors while Roberts went through a tough learning experience at Triple-A. He still has time to develop.

	W	SV	ERA	IP	H	BB	SO	BPI	$
1995 Norfolk AAA	7	0	5.52	150	197	58	88	1.70	

ROBERTSON, RICH - TL - Age 27
This tall Texan finished the season strong, pitching in the Twins rotation only a year after Pittsburgh released him. Robertson needs good control to be successful, and now that he has found it he can make 20-25 starts in '96. It isn't impossible that he will win eight to ten of those games.

	W	SV	ERA	IP	H	BB	SO	B/I	$
1994 Pittsburgh NL	0	0	6.89	15	20	10	8	1.91	-
1995 Salt Lake AAA	5	0	2.44	44	31	12	40	0.97	
1995 Minnesota AL	2	0	3.83	51	48	31	38	1.53	1
1996 *Projection* >>>	7	0	4.35	141	136	76	98	1.50	2

ROBINSON, KEN - TR - Age 26
Robinson was one of the Blue Jays' most effective relievers in his rookie season. He's a little guy (listed at 5'9" but some say even shorter) with a surprisingly hard fastball which he doesn't seem to need much command of. He's almost certain to be back in the major leagues in 1996 and could be a setup man on a young pitching staff.

	W	SV	ERA	IP	H	BB	SO	B/I	$
1995 Toronto AL	1	0	3.69	39	25	22	31	1.21	2
1996 *Projection* >>>	2	0	3.74	53	35	32	43	1.26	2

RODRIGUEZ, FELIX - TR - Age 23
Originally a catcher, Rodriguez was converted to pitching by the Dodgers in 1993. He is an extremely raw prospect, but promising enough to be placed on the Dodger 40-man roster. As you would expect, he features a great fastball and struggles with his control.

	W	SV	ERA	IP	H	BB	SO	B/I	$
1995 Albuquerque AAA	3	0	4.24	51	52	26	46	1.53	
1995 Los Angeles NL	1	0	2.53	10	11	5	5	1.50	0

RODRIGUEZ, FRANK - TR - Age 23
Rodriguez wrestled with his control in '95 after the trade for Rick Aguilera placed him in Minnesota's rotation. No one questions Rodriguez' talent, as he has a good fastball, slider, and mechanics. He needs two to four seasons of experience before he starts to win consistently. Rodriguez is a major factor in the Twins' rebuilding plans and they will give him every chance to succeed.

	W	SV	ERA	IP	H	BB	SO	B/I	$
1995 Boston - Minnesota AL	5	0	6.13	105	114	57	59	1.62	-
1996 *Projection* >>>	6	0	5.45	149	153	76	83	1.54	-

RODRIGUEZ, RICH - TL - Age 33
Once one of the more unsung left-handed relievers in the National League, Rodriguez appeared in only one game with the Cardinals last season because of injuries. If he can ever lift his arm over his head again, he could wind up back in the majors. However, his best days seem to be behind him.

ROGERS, BRYAN - TR - Age 28
Mets farmhand Rogers while in Triple-A in 1995 posted a 2.21 ERA along with 10 saves and 8 wins in 77 innings. On a less well-stocked team he could have expected a late-season callup.

ROGERS, CHARLIE - TL - Age 27
A bullpen ace in the Texas League, traditionally a hitters' league, but then he had a 6.35 ERA after moving up to Triple-A on the Brewers farm.

ROGERS, JIMMY - TR - Age 29
Rogers finally made it to the major leagues as a reliever after seven professional seasons in the Toronto organization, most of them as a starter. He has good control despite the 18 walks he gave up with the Jays. At his age, if he isn't in the major leagues on opening day, he will have a tough time getting back.

	W	SV	ERA	IP	H	BB	SO	B/I	$
1995 Toronto AL	2	0	5.70	23	21	18	13	1.65	-

ROGERS, KENNY - TL - Age 31
Rogers has finally emerged as one of the premier lefthanders in the American League. He has a good enough fastball to challenge hitters and an outstanding curve. He'll also have a big contract, since he was a free agent at the season's end.

	W	SV	ERA	IP	H	BB	SO	B/I	$
1994 Texas AL	11	0	4.46	167	169	52	120	1.32	12
1995 Texas AL	17	0	3.38	208	192	76	140	1.29	20
1996 *Projection* >>>	15	0	3.77	232	222	79	159	1.30	19

ROGERS, KEVIN - TL - Age 27
Rogers was, at one point, perhaps the Giants' most appealing pitching prospect, but he missed the entire 1995 season due to injury and is a question mark until he proves he can pitch. Before the injury, Rogers was an excellent and relatively unknown pitcher.

ROJAS, MEL - TR - Age 29
Rojas took over as the Expos' closer after John Wetteland was traded to the Yankees in spring training. He posted 30 saves, however, he was also unreliable and became very hittable when used on consecutive days. He complained when he was the set-up man and didn't stop last season after moving into the closer's role. Former Expos GM Kevin Malone dubbed Rojas "The Excuse Man." Being Expos manager Felipe Alou's nephew doesn't insure that Rojas will remain the closer if he struggles at the outset of the 1996 season. He could even be traded before that.

	W	SV	ERA	IP	H	BB	SO	B/I	$
1994 Montreal NL	3	16	3.32	84	71	21	84	1.10	25
1995 Montreal NL	1	30	4.12	67	69	29	61	1.45	25
1996 *Projection* >>>	2	26	3.69	90	84	31	81	1.29	25

ROPER, JOHN - TR - Age 24
Roper came over from Cincy with Deion Sanders. He was injured most of the year, and so while he is considered a top prospect, he must be viewed with skepticism until he demonstrates he has recovered from his injuries and can pitch well at the major-league level.

ROSE, SCOTT - TR - Age 25
Rose led Double-A Huntsville in saves, but was otherwise unimpressive.

ROSENGREN, JOHN - TL - Age 23
Rosengren had a very good record in Class A, but stumbled after moving up to Double-A in 1994. In 1995 he did better in another year split between Class A and Double-A (3.99 and 4.52 ERA's respectively). There isn't much pitching talent ahead of him in the Tigers organization. There is also a shortage of lefthanded pitchers. And Rosengren just turned 23 in August.

ROSSELLI, JOE - TL - Age 23
Rosselli was the California League Pitcher of the Year in 1992, but it's been downhill ever since. Rosselli was injured in 1993 and has yet to recover. His K/IP ratio was poor at Triple-A in 1995 and with the Giants.

	W	SV	ERA	IP	H	BB	SO	B/I	$
1995 Phoenix AAA	4	0	4.99	79	94	12	34	1.34	
1995 San Francisco NL	2	0	8.70	30	39	20	7	1.97	

RUEBEL, MATT - TL - Age 26
This left-hander emerged as one of the Pirates' top pitching prospects in 1995 as he was Pitcher of the Year in the Double-A Southern League. He does not throw particularly hard and is the typical finesse lefty. However, he throws strikes, understands his craft and has a future.

RUETER, KIRK - TL - Age 25
Rueter won the first 10 decisions of his major-league career in 1993-94 but the Expos farmed him out after he got off to a horrible start in 1995. Rueter, though, returned from Triple-A Ottawa late last season and pitched some terrific games. He's strictly a finesse lefty and has to be just right with his all his pitches to win. You usually never know what to expect with those kind of pitchers from one year to the next.

	W	SV	ERA	IP	H	BB	SO	B/I	$
1994 Montreal NL	7	0	5.17	92	106	23	50	1.40	2
1995 Montreal NL	5	0	3.23	47	38	9	28	0.99	5
1996 *Projection* >>>	7	0	4.12	143	142	31	78	1.21	7

RUFFCORN, SCOTT - TR - Age 26
Ruffcorn suffered through some arm trouble in 1995 and really didn't pitch well when he wasn't hurt. He appears to have stalled at Triple-A and has had three terrible trips to the big leagues. Ruffcorn has a great arm, but will probably need a trade to reach his potential.

RUFFIN, BRUCE - TL - Age 32
Ruffin had the Rockies' best ERA in 1995, despite a nagging forearm injury which limited his innings and diminished his saves. He went on the DL for two-and-a half months during the middle part of the season, but returned in late August with his wicked slider intact. He should remain effective in 1996 as a late-inning stopper.

	W	SV	ERA	IP	H	BB	SO	B/I	$
1994 Colorado NL	4	16	4.04	55	55	30	65	1.53	18
1995 Colorado NL	0	11	2.12	34	26	19	23	1.32	11
1996 *Projection* >>>	2	10	3.27	60	55	32	55	1.45	9

RUFFIN, JOHNNY - TR - Age 24
Ruffin is a very promising reliever who features a moving fastball and slider; he was acquired in the Tim Belcher trade. He split the year between Indianapolis and Cincinnati before ending his season with one of the all time weird injuries - tearing a knee ligament while getting off the couch to change channels. He is expected to recover fully and will compete for a setup role in 1996.

	W	SV	ERA	IP	H	BB	SO	B / I	$
1994 Cincinnati NL	7	1	3.09	70	57	27	44	1.20	9
1995 Cincinnati NL	0	0	1.35	13	4	11	11	1.13	0
1996 *Projection* >>>	3	1	2.96	42	33	19	29	1.24	4

RUNION, TONY - TR - Age 24
Runion was drafted in the 58th round by the Indians in 1993 and he chalked up a spetacular season as a spot starter/middle reliever for Single-A Columbus. He struck out well over a batter per inning pitched and had a strikeout/walk ratio of three to one. However, he has yet to pitch at even a high Class-A level, a negative at his age. Don't brand him a prospect just yet.

RUSCH, GLENDON - TL - Age 21
Rusch was outstanding for Class-A Wilmington in 1995. He has great poise and even better control, but needs to improve his breaking stuff to have similar success at high levels. Rusch is a good young prospect but still must prove himself at Double-A Wichita in 1996.

RUSSELL, JEFF - TR - Age 34
For the first half of the season, Russell was one of the more effective closers in the A.L. Around the All-Star break, he went on the disabled list with a bad back, and he was used very sparingly for the rest of the season. Although Russell has hinted at retirement from time to time, he was expected to return in 1996, but health may be a limiting factor. Depending upon where he winds up, he may or may not get save opportunities.

	W	SV	ERA	IP	H	BB	SO	B / I	$
1994 Two Teams	1	17	5.09	40	43	16	28	1.45	20
1995 Texas AL	1	20	3.03	32	36	9	21	1.38	20
1996 *Projection* >>>	1	18	3.79	44	47	16	30	1.44	18

RYAN, KEN - TR - Age 27
Ryan completely lost it in 1995, first losing his closer role, then getting demoted to the minors. He seemed to lose confidence in his fastball, then couldn't get the slider or forkball over. Once he started falling, Ryan plummeted quickly, falling all the way to Double-A Trenton; he didn't pitch any better at either minor league stop, either. Ryan will have to fight for a setup spot in the Red Sox bullpen in 1996; he might have a better chance with a different organization.

	W	SV	ERA	IP	H	BB	SO	B / I	$
1994 Boston AL	2	13	2.44	48	46	17	32	1.31	20
1995 Boston AL	0	7	4.96	32	34	24	34	1.78	4
1996 *Projection* >>>	2	2	4.90	36	35	20	31	1.53	0

RYAN, KEVIN - TR - Age 25
Ryan pitched decently in Double-A last year, but struggled in a brief Triple-A trial. He will likely pitch in Triple-A in 1996, and if he's effective, he may get a shot at the Orioles bullpen.

RYAN, MATT - TR - Age 24
Ryan burst into prospect status in the Pirates' organization last season by posting phenomenal numbers with Double-A Carolina and Triple-A Calgary. The Pirates sent him to pitch winter ball in the Dominican Republic and he could very well contend for a major-league set-up job this spring.

RYCHEL, KEVIN - TR - Age 24
A hard-throwing right-handed reliever who has begun harnessing a very good fastball, Rychel could contend for a job in the Pirates' bullpen this year.

SABERHAGEN, BRET - TR - Age 31
Sabes joined the Rockies in late July of 1995. His sore shoulder resulted in less velocity and movement on his pitches, along with more walks than in past years, but his determination served as an inspiration for the Rockies' young pitchers. Off-season arthroscopic surgery may slow his early performance in 1996, but few question Saberhagen's resolve to return as the number one or two starter.

	W	SV	ERA	IP	H	BB	SO	B/I	$
1994 New York NL	14	0	2.74	177	169	13	143	1.03	27
1995 Two Teams	7	0	4.18	153	165	33	100	1.29	5
1996 *Projection* >>>	10	0	4.80	192	218	43	137	1.36	-

SACKINSKY, BRIAN - TR - Age 24
Sackinsky has below average stuff, but has good control and could blossom into a good finesse pitcher in the majors. It usually takes the finesse guys longer to develop into effective pitchers than the hard throwers, and Sackinsky may have to spend another year or two in the minors perfecting his craft.

SAGER, A.J. - TR - Age 31
Sager had advanced slowly through the Padres' farm system, first reaching the majors in 1994. Despite a 3.50 ERA and 8-5 record in 22 starts at Colorado Springs in 1995, he appears to have topped out at Triple-A. Sager will remain a fringe major leaguer while he becomes a Triple-A journeyman pitcher for the next few seasons.
Sager has been in the minors since 1988 and didn't pitch well at Triple-A Las Vegas. He has almost no chance of making it back to the Padres.

	W	SV	ERA	IP	H	BB	SO	B/I	$
1994 San Diego NL	1	0	5.98	46	62	16	26	1.67	-
1995 Colorado Springs AAA	8	0	3.50	133	153	23	80	1.32	
1995 Colorado NL	0	0	7.36	14	19	7	10	1.77	-

SALKELD, ROGER - TR - Age 25
The third pick overall in the 1989 draft, Salkeld was acquired by the Reds in May in exchange for Tim Belcher. At Triple-A Indianapolis, Salkeld posted his best season since 1991. His control improved and he limited the opposition to 7.3 hits per nine innings. Salkeld is still young and the Reds can afford to be patient.

	W	SV	ERA	IP	H	BB	SO	B/I	$
1994 Seattle AL	2	0	7.17	59	76	45	46	2.05	-
1995 Indianapolis AAA	12	0	4.22	119	96	57	86	1.30	

SANDERS, SCOTT - TR - Age 27
Sanders was expected to have a good season last year, but he came down with an elbow ligament problem requiring rest. It was the second year in a row that he came down with the same injury. The Padres expect him to be ready for spring training, and with his excellent stuff, he can have a very good year.

	W	SV	ERA	IP	H	BB	SO	B/I	$
1994 San Diego NL	4	1	4.78	111	103	48	109	1.36	3
1995 San Diego NL	5	0	4.30	90	79	31	88	1.22	4
1996 *Projection* >>>	10	0	4.20	125	113	47	121	1.28	5

SANDERSON, SCOTT - TR - Age 39
The Angels were counting on the righthanded veteran starter Sanderson to counterbalance their lefty starters. But he herniated a disc in his lower back in May, requiring surgery and putting him on the disabled list for the rest of the season. It's doubtful that will come back in 1996, but if he does, it should be noted that he was losing his effectiveness in 1994.

	W	SV	ERA	IP	H	BB	SO	B/I	$
1994 Chicago AL	8	0	5.09	92	110	12	36	1.33	6
1995 California AL	1	0	4.12	39	48	4	23	1.32	1

SANFORD, MO - TR - Age 29
Sanford is a big righthander who, despite disappointing at the big league level, could still develop into a good reliever. Considering the Twins' recent desperation for pitching, his failure to establish himself is disquieting.

	W	SV	ERA	IP	H	BB	SO	B/I	$
1995 Salt Lake AAA	0	0	6.35	5	6	4	8	1.77	
1995 Minnesota AL	0	0	5.30	18	16	16	17	1.71	-

SANTANA, JULIO - TR - Age 23
Santana has an excellent fastball and changes speeds well. He needs a more reliable breaking pitch if he is to advance further. Santana will likely spend 1996 at Triple-A Oklahoma City, and could be in the majors by 1997.

SATRE, JASON - TR - Age 25
Despite two near no-hitters for the Orioles Triple-A franchise at Rochester, Satre was released after the season and hooked on with the Red Sox. He had the worst season of his pro career in 1995, going 1-5 with a 6.16 ERA in five starts at Triple-A Pawtucket before earning yet another release. Satre is still young enough to get another shot, but he'll have to do a lot more with it to stay in baseball.

SAUNDERS, TONY - TL - Age 22
Saunders is a control artist who has battled injury woes in each of his last two seasons in the Marlins' chain, both at high Class-A Brevard County. After each extended absence, the resilient Saunders bounced back and exhibited uncanny precision. The jump to Double-A should be telling - if he can maintain his control against upper level hitters who will be more inclined to lay off of his average stuff, Saunders could be a prime breakout candidate for 1996. He's a lefty, so he'll get plenty of chances.

SAUVEUR, RICH - TL - Age 32
Sauveur split the closer/setup duties at Triple-A Indianapolis in a platoon tandem with righthander Scott Service. He had a marvelous year in 1995 furthering his chance to return to the majors. Sauveur can be a successful lefty situational reliever in the right situation.

	W	SV	ERA	IP	H	BB	SO	B/I	$
1995 Indianapolis AAA	5	15	2.05	57	43	18	47	1.07	

SCANLAN, BOB - TR - Age 29
He's had a long struggle as a reliever and as a starter.

	W	SV	ERA	IP	H	BB	SO	B/I	$
1994 Milwaukee AL	2	2	4.11	103	117	28	65	1.41	6
1995 Milwaukee AL	4	0	6.59	83	101	44	29	1.74	-
1996 Projection >>>	4	1	5.44	107	125	44	51	1.58	-

SCHEID, RICH - TL - Age 31
This ten-year minor league veteran relies heavily on his curveball, which he hung way too often at both the Triple-A and major league levels in 1995. Scheid needs to work the corners of the strike zone to be effective, because of his marginal velocity - he simply caught too much of the plate with his pitches in 1995. His major league window of opportunity has likely closed, but he will linger on someone's Triple-A roster since he throws a baseball with his left hand.

	W	SV	ERA	IP	H	BB	SO	B/I	$
1994 Florida NL	1	0	3.34	32	35	8	17	1.33	1
1995 Charlotte AAA	1	0	5.93	54	74	15	37	1.63	
1995 Florida NL	0	0	6.10	10	14	7	10	2.03	-

SCHILLING, CURT - TR - Age 29
Schilling has missed significant chunks of each of the last two seasons with elbow and shoulder problems. Prior to 1995 shoulder surgery, Schilling had regained his top velocity and was again one of the NL's premier starters. He dominated righties and lefties with a plus fastball and biting slider, striking out a batter per inning with one baseball's best strikeout/walk ratios. He is again expected to regain full strength, but will have to accept a pay cut to return to the Phils.

	W	SV	ERA	IP	H	BB	SO	B/I	$
1994 Philadelphia NL	2	0	4.48	82	87	28	58	1.40	1
1995 Philadelphia NL	7	0	3.57	116	96	26	114	1.05	10
1996 Projection >>>	6	0	4.40	80	73	20	70	1.17	4

SCHMIDT, CURT - TR - Age 26
This sidearmer was a surprise member of the Expos' opening-day roster last season but was quickly back in the minors. He has a chance to become a decent middle reliever but has little star potential.

	W	SV	ERA	IP	H	BB	SO	B/I	$
1995 Ottawa AAA	5	15	2.22	52	40	18	38	1.11	
1995 Montreal NL	0	0	6.97	10	15	9	7	2.32	-

SCHMIDT, JASON - TR - Age 23
Last year, Angels prospect Schmidt had the misfortune of having to pitch in Midland in the Double-A Texas League, a hitter's paradise and a pitcher's hell. He lost seven consecutive decisions at mid-season, but showed some potential.

	W	SV	ERA	IP	H	BB	SO	B/I	$
1995 Richmond AAA	8	0	2.25	116	97	48	95	1.25	
1995 Atlanta NL	2	0	5.76	25	27	18	19	1.80	-

SCHMITT, TODD - TR - Age 26
Schmitt's record fell off from his '93 season in the Midwest League. An undrafted free agent, he was voted the best reliever in the California League in 1994.

	W	SV	ERA	IP	H	BB	SO	B/I	$
1994 Rancho Cucamonga A	2	29	1.95	51	43	24	45	1.31	
1995 Las Vegas AAA	0	2	7.82	12	16	9	6	1.98	

SCHNEIDER, PHIL - TL - Age 25
The lefty came on strong at end of the '94 campaign with New Haven. The 49th round draft choice may surprise some people and end up in Colorado Springs soon. Doesn't throw hard, but has good control and a great change.

SCHOOLER, MIKE - TR - Age 33
Schooler was the Mariners' ace closer in 1989 and '90 posting 33 and 30 saves respectively. But he came down with arm problems and struggled for a number of years. Trying to make a comeback last year, he pitched very effectively in the Angels system with Midland in the Double-A Texas League, even making the Double-A All-Star team. It would not be a surprise to see Schooler back in a major league uniform in 1996.

SCHOUREK, PETE - TL - Age 26
Schourek was showing indications of his 1995 form in late 1994 when the strike hit. A small adjustment in his mechanics added four MPH to his fastball and gave him better control of his best pitch, a sharp breaking curveball. He had no weaknesses in 1995, holding runners well, displaying excellent control, a high strikeout rate, and making all of his starts. There is no reason to believe that 1995 is a fluke - given his age he should be one of the top lefthanders in the league for years.

	W	SV	ERA	IP	H	BB	SO	B/I	$
1994 Cincinnati NL	7	0	4.09	81	90	29	69	1.46	3
1995 Cincinnati NL	18	0	3.22	190	158	45	160	1.07	22
1996 *Projection* >>>	16	0	3.30	195	179	51	160	1.18	19

SCHRENK, STEVE - TR - Age 27
This finesse/groundball pitcher has persevered through arm and shoulder injuries and family problems and is now talked up as a possible fifth starter for Chicago. It's probably not going to happen; Schrenk has fine control and his best hope is for a deal to a pitching-thin team.

SCHUERMANN, LANCE - TL - Age 26
Schuermann was inconsistent in his first Triple-A season. Basically a control pitcher, Schuermann needs another year at Triple-A Oklahoma City and even then may not get much consideration for a major league spot.

	W	SV	ERA	IP	H	BB	SO	B/I	$
1995 Oklahoma City AAA	4	0	4.67	88	101	40	44	1.59	

SCHULLSTROM, ERIK - TR - Age 27
One of the Twins' many disappointments, Schullstrom posed no problem to AL hitters in '95. He will need to make some major adjustments to establish himself as a big league pitcher, and the jury is still out on whether he's capable of doing so.

Benson's Baseball Player Guide: 1996

	W	SV	ERA	IP	H	BB	SO	B/I	$
1995 Minnesota AL	0	0	6.89	47	66	22	21	1.87	-
1996 *Projection* >>>	2	0	5.94	37	44	16	20	1.61	-

SCHWARZ, JEFF - TR - Age 31
A late call up from Triple-A Vancouver, Schwarz pitched as well as any of the ineffective Angel relievers, which means his one walk an inning average will have him start in the minors again.

SCOTT, DARRYL - TR - Age 27
A very solid season as the Vancouver closer in 1993, then had a forgettable year for the Yokohama Baystars in 1994 and was released after 32 innings. Control has always been the problem. Scott has enough talent. He was welcomed back in the U.S. and can still have a major league impact if he can just show better control.

	W	SV	ERA	IP	H	BB	SO	B/I	$
1995 Colorado Springs AAA	4	4	4.70	95	113	41	77	1.61	

SCOTT, TIM - TR - Age 29
Scott has quietly emerged as an effective, though unheralded, setup reliever with the Expos over the last three years. His stuff is nasty and his fastball reaches 97 MPH. If the Expos grow tired of Mel Rojas' attitude, Scott could get a shot to close in Montreal.

	W	SV	ERA	IP	H	BB	SO	B/I	$
1994 Montreal NL	5	1	2.70	53	51	18	37	1.29	6
1995 Montreal NL	2	2	3.98	63	52	23	57	1.18	4
1996 *Projection* >>>	4	2	3.48	72	63	26	61	1.23	6

SCUDDER, SCOTT - TR - Age 28
Once considered among the Reds' best pitching prospects, Scudder never lived up to the hype. He has a wide repertoire which are all quality pitches, but he never seems to be able to do anything against major league hitters. And now, he's having problems with Triple-A hitters, too, going 1-4 with a 5.17 ERA for Indianapolis in 1995. His once-bright star is beginning to wink out.

SEANEZ, RUDY - TR - Age 27
Betting on this guy to be healthy is the equivalent of trying to draw two cards to an inside straight. His entire career has consisted of time on the DL (mostly back and arm problems) and brief flashes of a great fastball. Since he became a reliever in 1990, his career high in innings pitched is 56. The Dodger's have plenty of other hard throwing (and healthier) relief prospects competing for his job.

	W	SV	ERA	IP	H	BB	SO	B/I	$
1994 Los Angeles NL	1	0	2.66	23	24	9	18	1.39	1
1995 Los Angeles NL	1	3	6.75	34	39	18	29	1.64	-
1996 *Projection* >>>	1	2	4.47	34	33	18	27	1.52	-

SEELBACH, CHRIS - TR - Age 23
Seelbach was the player to be named later received by the Marlins from the Braves in the Alejandro Pena deal. Seelbach goes from being just one of the guys in the Braves' organization to being one of the most polished starting pitcher prospects in the Marlins' chain. The Braves' 1991 #4 pick has developed a maddening pattern of dominating Double-A hitters, but then pitching timidly after his promotions to Triple-A. He appeared to overcome that weakness with some strong late 1995 starts - look for Seelbach to start 1996 in Triple-A, and be one of the first in line for a midseason promotion.

	W	SV	ERA	IP	H	BB	SO	B/I	$
1995 Richmond AAA	4	0	4.66	73	64	39	65	1.41	

SELE, AARON - TR - Age 25
Serious shoulder problems wrecked Sele's season in 1995; he was just getting back to full strength as last season drew to a close. He's not overpowering but has good command of several pitches. Sele will be counted on by Boston as a number three starter in 1996. If completely healed Sele could be one of the year's better comeback stories.

	W	SV	ERA	IP	H	BB	SO	B/I	$
1994 Boston AL	8	0	3.83	143	140	60	105	1.40	10

	W	SV	ERA	IP	H	BB	SO	B/I	$
1995 Boston AL	3	0	3.06	32	32	14	21	1.42	2
1996 *Projection* >>>	9	0	3.52	163	158	68	118	1.39	11

SEMINARA, FRANK - TR - Age 28
Seminara had a passable year as a middle reliever at Triple-A Rochester before going back into the starting rotation in the Brewers system. A sinker/slider pitcher who has been slowed by injuries, Seminara had a 7.96 ERA in seven disastrous starts at Triple-A New Orleans. He's finished as a starting pitcher, but might revive his career as a long reliever.

	W	SV	ERA	IP	H	BB	SO	B/I	$
1994 Norfolk AAA	4	0	4.38	101	108	31	43	1.37	
1994 New York NL	0	0	5.82	17	20	8	7	1.65	-
1995 New Orleans AAA	2	0	7.96	37	54	14	19	1.83	

SENIOR, SHAWN - TR - Age 24
Senior, who is from Cherry Hill, N.J., felt right at home pitching for Double-A Trenton last season, his junior year as a pro. The stocky (6-1, 195) lefty is effective if he gets his curve over the plate.

SEPEDA, JAMIE - TR - Age 25
On one of the worst clubs in Double-A (Reading) Sepeda couldn't keep a spot in the rotation, posting a 4.99 ERA with nearly as many walks as whiffs in 1994. The Astros took a long look at Sepeda in 1995, but he fell all the way to Independent ball, and didn't do too well there, either.

SERAFINI, DAN - TL - Age 22
Serafini is a promising young lefthander whom the Twins have brought along slowly. He needs another two years to refine his control before he enters the Minnesota rotation for what should be a solid career. Most observers agree Serafini has the potential to be a consistent ten to twelve game winner.

SERVICE, SCOTT - TR - Age 29
Impressive strikeout totals make Service a perennial prospect. That he has already been let go from the Phillies, Expos, Chunichi Dragons, Reds, and Rockies suggest he will never make it past the prospect stage. He pitched OK for the Giants last year, and is likely to be given a chance to do the same in 1996.

	W	SV	ERA	IP	H	BB	SO	B/I	$
1994 Indianapolis AAA	5	13	2.31	58	35	27	67	1.06	
1994 Cincinnati NL	1	0	7.36	7	8	3	5	1.50	-
1995 San Francisco NL	3	0	3.19	31	18	20	30	1.23	2

SEXTON, JEFF - TR - Age 24
Sexton became a starter in 1995 after two years as a reliever in the Indians' low minors. Lacking a dazzling fastball, Sexton relied on location and exquisite control to dominate Class-A hitters in 1995. After high Class-A Kinston ace Bartolo Colon was shut down late in July, Sexton became the anchor the rotation that went on to win the Carolina League championship - he pitched eight innings of shutout baseball in Game One of the league finals. However, Sexton was among the older starting pitchers in his league in 1995, and he will be hard pressed to match his success at higher levels due to his relative lack of velocity.

SHAW, CURTIS - TL - Age 26
Shaw is a lefty strikeout pitcher and gets lots of chances, but he walked 88 batters in 98 innings for Triple-A Edmonton and is about to run out of those chances.

	W	SV	ERA	IP	H	BB	SO	B/I	$
1995 Edmonton AAA	6	2	4.67	98	91	88	52	1.82	

SHAW, JEFF - TR - Age 29
After two good seasons as a right-handed middle man in the Expos' bullpen, Shaw had a horrible 1995. He's decent but not good enough to avoid having to prove himself all over again this spring either in Montreal's camp - or somewhere else.

	W	SV	ERA	IP	H	BB	SO	B/I	$
1994 Montreal NL	5	1	3.88	67	67	15	47	1.22	6
1995 Montreal NL	1	3	4.62	62	58	26	45	1.35	3

	W	SV	ERA	IP	H	BB	SO	B/I	$
1995 Chicago AL	0	0	6.52	9	12	1	6	1.34	-
1996 *Projection* >>>	2	1	4.80	56	56	20	38	1.36	1

SHEA, JOHN - TL - Age 29
Shea has spent all or parts of five seasons pitching in Triple-A. He pitched decently last year, and it was his best Triple-A season. Shea could get a shot at the Orioles bullpen as lefty relievers are always in demand.

	W	SV	ERA	IP	H	BB	SO	B/I	$
1995 Rochester AAA	0	4	2.95	39	38	17	37	1.39	

SHEEHAN, CHRIS - TR - Age 27
Sheehan had great strikeout rates (about a batter per inning) in the lower minors, but didn't experience that kind of success at Double-A Wichita in 1995. He's really far too old to just be advancing above Class-A ball and is a distant prospect.

SHEPHERD, KEITH - TR - Age 28
Shepherd has had just one good month in the majors (June of 1993 for the Rockies) and made just two appearances for the Red Sox before being released. He'll have to fight for a major league bullpen role; look for Shepherd on a Triple-A roster in 1996.

SHIFFLETT, STEVE - TR - Age 30
Former Royals minor leaguer Shifflett has toiled at Triple-A for the last four years and had a poor 1995 campaign for Colorado Springs. He is imminently hittable and lacks the pinpoint control necessary for someone who doesn't throw especially hard. Shifflett will have to battle to stay at Triple-A in 1996.

	W	SV	ERA	IP	H	BB	SO	B/I	$
1994 Omaha AAA	3	2	3.70	92	99	24	39	1.33	
1995 Colorado Springs AAA	4	0	6.87	38	61	13	21	1.95	

SHOEMAKER, STEVE - TR - Age 26
He pitched well at Double-A in 1995, but is unlikely to do the same in the majors.

SHOUSE, BRIAN - TL - Age 27
The highlight of Shouse's career came following the 1992 season when former Pirates GM Ted Simmons inexplicably put him on the 15-man protected list for the expansion draft. Other than being one of the nicest guys you'd ever want to meet, the only thing he has going for him is that he's left-handed. He was sent to the Arizona Fall League at the end of last season, meaning he'll be given one last chance to show that he can really pitch in the majors.

SHUEY, PAUL - TR - Age 25
It seems like so long ago that Shuey was considered a leading candidate to be the Indians' 1995 closer. Shoulder problems gave him a late start in 1995 and once he recovered there was no room in the Indians' excellent major league pen. To his credit, Shuey continued to refine control of his low 90's heater, with a downright dominating Triple-A performance. He should secure a role in the 1996 Tribe pen, especially if Julian Tavarez graduates to the rotation. He remains the Indians' likely closer of the future.

	W	SV	ERA	IP	H	BB	SO	B/I	$
1994 Cleveland AL	0	5	8.49	11	14	12	16	2.23	
1995 Buffalo AAA	1	11	2.63	27	21	7	27	1.03	3
1996 *Projection* >>>	2	2	4.25	36	36	18	40	1.51	1

SHUMATE, JACOB - TR - Age 20
Shumate, the Braves' number one draft choice in 1994, averaged less than three innings and more than four walks per start in the Appalachian League. Control may continue to be a problem; he walked 55 in 65 innings for his high school team.

SILVA, JOSE - TR - Age 21
Silva's fastball was voted the best in the Southern League, but he had limited success with it after a big year in the South Atlantic League in '93. In 1994 he had a 4.14 ERA for Double-A Knoxville.

SIMAS, BILL - TR - Age 24
Simas was acquired by the White Sox from California in the Jim Abbott trade. He was highly regarded by the Angels and is destined for middle relief or even a set up role as early as 1996.

	W	SV	ERA	IP	H	BB	SO	B/I	$
1995 Chicago AL	1	0	2.57	14	15	10	16	1.79	-

SIMON, RICHIE - TR - Age 30
Now 30 years old, Simon has been pitching in the minors for nine years without impressing, although he did get 20+ saves on two separate occasions, most recently in 1993 on the Giants farm. He was to be the anchor for the Royals replacement team, so a major league future is all but over.

SIMMONS, SCOTT - TR - Age 26
Simmons is the definitive finesse pitcher and nearly led the Texas League in ERA for Double-A Arkansas in 1995 one year after an ERA championship for Arkansas in 1994. He throws nothing hard, but is very consistent with each pitch. Simmons doesn't immediately impress, but he gets results. He earned a late season promotion to Triple-A Louisville where he will begin the 1996 season.

SINNES, DAVID - TR - Age 24
Sinnes, drafted in the 19th round out of Notre Dame in 1993, was voted the best reliever in the South Atlantic League in 1994.

SIROTKA, MIKE - TL - Age 24
Sirotka is a lefty finesse pitcher who gets into trouble when he tries to get too fine with his breaking pitches, leaving them out over the plate. He advance a lot farther than expected in 1995, moving from Double-A Birmingham through Triple-A Nashville to the White Sox' rotation. He probably won't make the club's 1996 roster, but Sirotka is smart enough to eventually get back to the big leagues.

	W	SV	ERA	IP	H	BB	SO	B/I	$
1995 Nashville AAA	1	0	2.83	54	51	13	34	1.19	
1995 Chicago AL	1	0	4.19	34	39	17	19	1.63	-

SLOCUMB, HEATHCLIFF - TR - Age 29
After a phenomenal start, Slocumb cooled off considerably in the second half of 1995 and actually had quite ordinary numbers once you get past the illusory save total. He relies primarily on a fastball which is difficult to hit for distance (11 homers in 274 career innings) despite its relative lack of velocity. His control is very shaky, and he was quite a basket case on the mound by the end of 1995. He benefitted from the comfortable way Jim Fregosi utilizes his closers - like Mitch Williams before him, Slocumb was usually used for one inning or less, and he inherited eight runners all year. He won't hold the closer job through 1996.

	W	SV	ERA	IP	H	BB	SO	B/I	$
1994 Philadelphia NL	5	0	2.86	72	75	28	58	1.42	5
1995 Philadelphia NL	5	32	2.89	65	64	35	63	1.52	30
1996 Projection >>>	6	19	3.30	78	78	39	69	1.50	18

SLUSARSKI, JOE - TR - Age 29
Slusarski never developed. He has featured a big fastball but not much else. He really needs another pitch. Starting to bounce around from team to team.

	W	SV	ERA	IP	H	BB	SO	B/I	$
1994 Scranton AAA	2	0	7.82	38	50	10	29	1.57	
1995 Two AAA Teams	2	11	2.39	64	55	15	39	1.10	
1995 Milwaukee AL	1	0	5.40	15	21	6	6	1.80	-

SMALL, AARON - TR - Age 24
This curveballer spent six years in the Blue Jays' chain before moving to the Marlins' organization in 1995. He was the primary Triple-A closer, but will never fill that role in the majors - he just doesn't have the stuff. However, he has the ability to be a situational major league reliever if he can consistently keep the ball down against righties. He will be one of several pitchers jockeying for the last spot on the Marlins' staff.

	W	SV	ERA	IP	H	BB	SO	B/I	$
1994 Syracuse AAA	3	0	2.22	24	19	9	15	1.15	

	W	SV	ERA	IP	H	BB	SO	B/I	$
1995 Two AAA Teams	2	10	2.98	42	39	11	33	1.18	
1995 Florida NL	1	0	1.42	6	7	6	5	2.05	-

SMALL, MARK - TR - Age 28
Small was the primary closer at Triple-A Tucson in his seventh year in the Astro system. He is an organization player who was slated to be the closer on the replacement team. Small has never been on the 40-man major league roster and does not rate as a prospect.

	W	SV	ERA	IP	H	BB	SO	B/I	$
1995 Tucson AAA	3	19	4.09	66	74	19	51	1.41	

SMILEY, JOHN - TL - Age 31
The veteran lefthander got off to a 10-1 start but was slowed in the second half with groin problems. Smiley has excellent command of four pitches and cut down on his gopher balls (usually a problem for him) in 1995. His only bad years in the majors occurred when he tried to pitch hurt.

	W	SV	ERA	IP	H	BB	SO	B/I	$
1994 Cincinnati NL	11	0	3.86	158	169	37	112	1.30	12
1995 Cincinnati NL	12	0	3.46	176	173	39	124	1.20	14
1996 Projection >>>	14	0	3.60	197	199	44	137	1.24	14

SMITH, BRIAN - TR - Age 23
Blue Jays prospect Smith had an impressive year in Single-A in 1995 with a 0.87 ERA, a strike out/walk ratio over 4:1 and had 21 saves.

SMITH, DAN -TL - Age 26
The national poster boy for orthopedic surgery, Smith can't seem to make it through the year without unraveling. After missing almost all of the 1993 season, Smith did pitch in 1994, although he started and ended the season on the disabled list. Smith's latest malady, a partially torn rotator cuff, kept him from an Arizona Fall League stint. He's still a candidate for a big league roster spot when healthy.

SMITH, ERIC - TR - Age 26
The Phils' 30th round pick in 1992 out of Brigham Young was the closer at Single-A Clearwater. His main drawbacks are his age, lack of higher level experience, and sudden inability to strike out hitters (4.5 whiffs per nine innings, more walks than whiffs) in a pitchers' league.

SMITH, LEE - TR - Age 38
This future Hall-of-Famer had another solid year and is signed by the Angels through 1996. One possible problem that speedster Otis Nixon exploited last year was Smith's inability to field his position, particularly bunts. The usually stolid Smith got rattled on several occasions last year and gave up some key hits.

	W	SV	ERA	IP	H	BB	SO	B/I	$
1994 Baltimore AL	1	33	3.29	38	34	11	42	1.17	43
1995 California AL	0	37	3.47	49	42	25	43	1.36	37
1996 Projection >>>	1	30	3.46	55	48	27	53	1.35	33

SMITH, OTTIS - TR - Age 25
Acquired in the 1994 Anthony Young deal from the Mets, Smith displayed good control for Double-A Orlando, posting a 3.07 ERA. He earned a promotion to Triple-A Iowa where he was terrible, going 1-3 with a 10.45 ERA. He's a distant prospect, but could get some attention with a better year in Triple-A in 1996.

	W	SV	ERA	IP	H	BB	SO	B/I	$
1995 Iowa AAA	1	0	10.45	20	34	13	12	2.28	

SMITH, PETE - TR - Age 30
This former Brave and Met used to be a hard thrower who tantalized his employers with occasional dominance. After battling shoulder tendinitis in 1993, he has been forced to become a finesse pitcher, and he just doesn't have the precise control to excel with that style. Expect Smith to linger at the Triple-A level, with an extended major league opportunity only a remote possibility.

	W	SV	ERA	IP	H	BB	SO	B/I	$
1994 New York NL	4	0	5.55	131	145	42	62	1.42	-

	W	SV	ERA	IP	H	BB	SO	B/I	$
1995 Charlotte AAA	2	0	3.86	49	51	17	20	1.39	
1995 Cincinnati NL	1	0	6.66	24	30	7	14	1.52	-

SMITH, SCOTTY - TR - Age 25
A good first half at Double-A Tulsa was wrecked by Smith's horrible second half. While he's better than the 5-8, 6.11 record he posted in 1995, Smith is really not a good prospect.

SMITH, SHAD - TR - Age 28
Smith began last season pitching excellent baseball for Class AA Shreveport, was promoted to AAA Phoenix, had some trouble, and was demoted back to AA. Smith will be 28 years old in May and had a mediocre record prior to last season. He's no prospect, with only a marginal chance to make the majors.

SMITH, WILLIE - TR - Age 28
Looks like Lee Smith and pitches like Lee Smith; just hasn't been so successful. The Yankees' attempt to convert Smith into a starter was a failure and set back his career. He nailed down 29 saves with AAA Louisville in 1994, while averaging over a strikeout per inning. He came up to the bigs in 1994 and got shelled.

SMITH, ZANE - TL - Age 35
This crafty old lefty struggled through an injury-plagued year to post the worst ERA of 12 major league seasons; more than a run worse than his previous high. Smith's sinker didn't bite and he gave up too many hard hit fly balls. If he can overcome yet another round of rehab for his tender shoulder, Smith could again be an effective starter.

	W	SV	ERA	IP	H	BB	SO	B/I	$
1994 Pittsburgh NL	10	0	3.27	157	162	34	57	1.25	15
1995 Boston AL	8	0	5.61	110	144	23	47	1.51	0
1996 Projection >>>	8	0	5.14	136	160	29	54	1.39	2

SMOLTZ, JOHN - TR - Age 28
Smoltz bounced back very well from elbow problems in 1994 and again placed among league leaders in many pitching categories, including strikeouts. He has a good fastball, a hard slider and an effective change-up. Smoltz should remain one of the league's most effective righthanded starters in 1996.

	W	SV	ERA	IP	H	BB	SO	B/I	$
1994 Atlanta NL	6	0	4.14	134	120	48	113	1.25	8
1995 Atlanta NL	12	0	3.18	192	166	72	193	1.24	15
1996 Projection >>>	14	0	3.30	211	183	78	199	1.24	17

SODERSTROM, STEVE - TR - Age 23
Recovering from earlier injuries, Soderstrom pitched successfully at the Double-A level in 1995. He has great potential, but is still two years away from the majors.

SODOWSKY, CLINT - TR - Age 23
Sodowsky reached Double-A in his fifth pro season and pitched well, moving on to Triple-A Toledo and eventually joining the Tiger rotation in September. A control pitcher who needs the corners to be successful, Sodowsky will suffer some hard knocks with the Tigers over the next few seasons.

	W	SV	ERA	IP	H	BB	SO	B/I	$
1995 Detroit AL	2	0	5.01	23	24	18	14	1.80	-

SOLLECITO, GABE - TR - Age 24
Sollecito is a hard throwing closer who gets a lot of strikeouts, averaging more than one per inning, a good sign for the Tigers to be hopeful.

SOPER, MIKE - TR - Age 29
In 1991, Soper pitched for AA Kinston and led the minors with 41 saves. We are keeping him here as a future reference (the "Soper Rule") that minor league saves don't mean much, and Class A saves mean nothing.

SPARKS, STEVE - TR - Age 30
Sparks is a soft tossing junk/knuckleballer with some chance of long term success.

	W	SV	ERA	IP	H	BB	SO	B/I	$
1995 Milwaukee AL	9	0	4.63	202	210	86	96	1.47	5
1996 *Projection* >>>	8	0	4.80	136	143	60	65	1.49	1

SPENCER, STAN - TR - Age 27
The Expos' first round draftee had appeared to finally overcome a legacy of arm problems in 1994, excelling at Double-A Portland in the Marlins' chain. His always solid control betrayed him in 1995 - after walking 36 batters in 144 innings in 1994, he walked 43 in only 80 innings in 1995. Spencer's career may be ending just a year after he appeared to be in line for a major league opportunity.

SPOLJARIC, PAUL - TL - Age 25
Spoljaric continued his two and a half year slump despite posting some impressive strikeout numbers at Triple-A Syracuse. He has always shown that he can throw hard but his control disappeared when he was promoted to Double-A Knoxville back in 1993. Once a starter, he is making the transition to being a setup man. With Ricky Jordan competing for a spot in the Toronto bullpen, Spoljaric's future looks to be elsewhere or back in the rotation.

	W	SV	ERA	IP	H	BB	SO	B/I	$
1994 Syracuse AAA	1	0	5.70	47	47	28	38	1.59	
1995 Syracuse AAA	2	10	4.93	87	69	54	108	1.41	

SPRADLIN, JERRY - TR - Age 28
Spradlin quacks like a power pitcher, but he is not a power pitcher. Despite his imposing 6'7", 240 lbs., presence, he is a sinker/slider pitcher with impeccable control who can be particularly difficult on righthanded hitters. However, he was not among the 26 pitchers who got a look at the big league level for the Marlins in 1995. Do not be surprised if Spradlin earns another major league opportunity (albeit limited) and proves to be a serviceable middleman.

	W	SV	ERA	IP	H	BB	SO	B/I	$
1994 Indianapolis AAA	3	3	3.68	73	87	16	49	1.41	
1995 Charlotte AAA	3	1	3.03	59	59	15	38	1.25	

SPRINGER, DENNIS - TR - Age 31
The Phils' first knuckleballer in ages finally made it to the majors after a nine year tour of the minor leagues. He has solid control for a pitcher of his type, but his knuckler doesn't move as much as those of Tom Candiotti or Tim Wakefield. Sadly, Springer's best - and maybe last - shot at a big league win was ended by Heathcliffe Slocumb, who blew a three-run ninth inning lead in one of his four starts. Springer will likely return to Triple-A in 1996.

	W	SV	ERA	IP	H	BB	SO	B/I	$
1995 Scranton AAA	10	0	4.68	171	163	47	115	1.23	
1995 Philadelphia NL	0	0	4.84	22	21	9	15	1.34	-

SPRINGER, RUSS - TR - Age 27
The Phils acquired Springer in a mid-1995 deal for outfielder Dave Gallagher, and he was quite dominant out of the bullpen in the late going. His stuff has never been the problem - he has always been quite vulnerable to the big inning, as he labors with men on base and grooves pitches for multiple-run homers. He allowed an amazing 16 homers in 78 innings in both leagues in 1995. The Phils want him to spend lots of time with pitching coach Johnny Podres and will give him every opportunity to win a spot in their rotation in 1996. He could be a creditable fourth starter.

	W	SV	ERA	IP	H	BB	SO	B/I	$
1994 California AL	2	2	5.52	45	53	14	28	1.47	2
1995 California AL	1	1	6.10	51	60	25	38	1.65	-
1995 Philadelphia NL	0	0	3.71	26	22	10	32	1.20	-
1996 *Projection* >>>	6	0	4.88	115	119	48	92	1.45	-

ST. CLAIRE, RANDY - TR - Age 35
He spent last season, believed to be his 107th in professional baseball, serving as the closer for the Pirates' Triple-A Calgary farm club. Somehow, he keeps hanging on.

	W	SV	ERA	IP	H	BB	SO	B/I	$
1995 Calgary AAA	3	19	5.00	54	72	21	43	1.73	

STANTON, MIKE -TL - Age 28
A stretch-drive deal brought Stanton to Boston from Atlanta, where he had struggled through a dismal season. He

was just what the Red Sox needed to solidify their bullpen, giving them several quality outings in a lefty set-up role. Stanton will never again get a closer role (like he had for Atlanta in 1993), but he can be very successful if used as a situational lefthander.

	W	SV	ERA	IP	H	BB	SO	B/I	$
1994 Atlanta NL	3	3	3.55	45	41	26	35	1.47	5
1995 Atlanta NL	1	1	5.59	19	31	6	13	1.91	1
1995 Boston AL	1	0	3.00	21	17	8	10	1.19	1
1996 Projection >>>	3	2	4.02	52	55	23	35	1.51	2

STEED, RICK - TR - Age 25
It took Steed three years to get out of the Florida State League, but once he did he earned an in-season promotion to Syracuse, just one sore arm away from Toronto. A good start in Triple-A could get Steed a relief job with the Blue Jays.

	W	SV	ERA	IP	H	BB	SO	B/I	$
1995 Syracuse AAA	4	1	3.72	55	51	23	34	1.33	

STEENSTRA, KENNIE - TR - Age 25
A soft-tossing workhorse, Steenstra had his best season for Triple-A Iowa, going 9-12 with a 3.89 ERA while displaying excellent control. Because he lacks velocity on his pitches he'll have to have pinpoint control to succeed in the big leagues. Steenstra will have a shot at a fifth starter role in spring training for the Cubs in 1996, but he's not the front runner for that spot.

	W	SV	ERA	IP	H	BB	SO	B/I	$
1995 Iowa AAA	9	0	3.89	171	174	48	96	1.30	

STEPH, ROD - TR - Age 26
The Reds' 1991 12th round pick spent his first full season in the Indians' chain in 1995 and proved to be a reliable Double-A swingman. He relies on exceptional control, but just doesn't have the requisite velocity to get the ball past higher level hitters. Steph will have a difficult time making the step up to Triple-A - he has no major league future.

STEPHENSON, GARRET - TR - Age 24
Stephenson is a bright Oriole pitching prospect who had an excellent season last year. His high strikeout rate and the low number of hits allowed per inning are particularly impressive. He will probably begin 1996 in Triple-A, but he could be pitching for the Orioles sometime during the year.

STEVENS, DAVE - TR - Age 26
Stevens struggled at times in '95, as hitters managed 14 home runs off of him in 66 innings. Control of his breaking pitches often deserted him, leaving him with just his heater in pressure situations. In time Stevens will develop into a good closer, but '96 likely will be another season of rough seas.

	W	SV	ERA	IP	H	BB	SO	B/I	$
1994 Minnesota AL	5	0	6.80	45	55	23	24	1.73	-
1995 Minnesota AL	5	10	5.07	65	74	32	47	1.61	9
1996 Projection >>>	5	15	4.90	63	73	31	42	1.64	13

STEWART, DAVE - TR - Age 39
One of the game's classier guys and a real competitor, Stewart retired midway through 1995 when it became patently obvious he no longer had his stuff. He'll be long remembered as a guy who won 20 games four straight years and helped the Athletics to a World Series championship.

	W	SV	ERA	IP	H	BB	SO	B/I	$
1994 Toronto AL	7	0	5.87	133	151	62	111	1.60	-
1995 Oakland AL	3	0	6.89	81	101	39	58	1.73	-

STOTTLEMYRE, TODD - TR - Age 30
A lesson in the pitfalls of judging a pitcher by his W-L record. Todd Stottlemyre came to Oakland with a career ERA of 4.39 and a career Ratio of 1.401, leading some of us to believe the Athletics were stupid to give him a large contract. In 1995, pitching his home games in an excellent pitchers' park, Stottlemyre posted an ERA of 4.55 and a Ratio of 1.469; despite these mediocre numbers, many seem to believe Todd had a good season, simply because good run support helped him to a record of 14-7. Stottlemyre was not very good in 1995, nor has he had a very good career.

He could easily go 7-14 in 1996, with the same weak ERA/Ratio.

	W	SV	ERA	IP	H	BB	SO	B / I	$
1994 Toronto AL	7	1	4.22	140	149	48	105	1.40	9
1995 Oakland AL	14	0	4.55	209	228	80	205	1.47	-
1996 *Projection* >>>	14	0	4.48	208	226	78	183	1.46	6

STRANGE, DON - TR - Age 28
Former Braves minor leaguer Strange had a good season for Double-A Wichita in 1995. He throws several different pitches, but none are of major league quality. Strange has good control but hasn't had more than a nibble above Double-A in seven pro seasons. He's unlikely to reach the majors.

STULL, EVERETT - TR - Age 24
Stull blew away many Eastern League hitters last year. Others merely waited for him to walk them. The result was a lot of pitches thrown, and no complete games. He's a definite prospect if he can harness his fastball.

STUMPF, BRIAN - TR - Age 23
The Phils' 1994 45th round draft pick defied his low draft status to become a dominant closer at low Class-A Piedmont. He is not a flamethrower, but he has good movement on his pitches and has extremely good control. However, he was much older than most of his South Atlantic League peers and has the type of stuff that will be severely challenged as he advances. He is not major league closer material.

STURTZE, TANYON - TR - Age 25
Sturtze earned a brief (two innings) call-up to Chicago due to an emergency vacancy in the Cubs bullpen, then pitched quite a bit worse after being returned to Triple-A Iowa. It was his second straight fading year at Triple-A and he appears to have topped out at that level. Sturtze is not a strikeout pitcher and doesn't have the control necessary to succeed in the majors as a finesse pitcher.

	W	SV	ERA	IP	H	BB	SO	B / I	$
1995 Iowa AAA	4	0	6.80	86	108	42	48	1.74	

SULLIVAN, SCOTT - TR - Age 25
A 1993 second round pick out of Auburn, Sullivan reached the majors with the Reds briefly in 1995 during the spring roster expansion. He is being groomed as a reliever and relies on a fastball and slider.

	W	SV	ERA	IP	H	BB	SO	B / I	$
1995 Indianapolis AAA	4	1	3.53	58	51	24	54	1.28	

SUPPAN, JEFF - TR - Age 21
After an impressive half-season at Double-A Trenton, Suppan quickly jumped into the Red Sox rotation, filling an emergency starter's role. At age 19, he clearly wasn't ready for the majors, but his talent is obvious. A second round draft pick in 1993, Suppan struggled at Triple-A after his demotion from Boston. He'll have an outside chance to grab a fifth starter role in spring training, 1996. More likely he'll go to Pawtucket to gain some experience before a late-season return to the big leagues. He's a good looking prospect.

	W	SV	ERA	IP	H	BB	SO	B / I	$
1995 Pawtucket AAA	2	0	5.32	45	50	9	32	1.30	
1995 Boston AL	1	0	5.96	22	29	5	19	1.50	-
1996 *Projection* >>>	3	0	5.11	58	73	12	49	1.46	-

SUZUKI, MAKATO - TR - Age 21
Suzuki was a big part of the overselling of the Mariners before 1994. Then the Japanese fireballer went down with a sore shoulder that was still troubling the Seattle brass in the fall of '94. In the autumn of 1995 Suzuki went to the Arizona Fall League and delivered some adequate work as a pen man and spot starter.

SUTCLIFFE, RICK - TR - Age 39
Sutcliffe gave it one last valiant effort in spring training of 1995, but couldn't cut it and retired. A classy guy and former Cy Young winner, Sutcliffe could be a good pitching coach if he chooses.

SWAN, RUSS - TL - Age 32
Swan had a forgettable half-season for Triple-A Edmonton in 1995, going 3-3 with a 4.34 ERA. He hasn't been an

effective pitcher since 1991 and will probably find another venue in 1996.

SWARTZBAUGH, DAVE - TR - Age 28
Swartzbaugh got his fifteen minutes (and 7.1 innings) of fame due to an emergency bullpen vacancy with the Cubs in 1995; not that he didn't earn it. His 1.53 ERA in 30 appearances for Triple-A Iowa led the team as he continued to demonstrate good control. Swartzbaugh is a distant prospect, but could grab a middle relief role in the right major league situation.

	W	SV	ERA	IP	H	BB	SO	B/I	$
1995 Iowa AAA	3	0	1.53	47	33	18	38	1.09	

SWIFT, BILL - TR - Age 34
Swift battled nagging injuries all last season, but pushed himself to pitch on little more than guts at the end. The day after the Rockies were eliminated from the NL playoffs, he had arthroscopic shoulder surgery; he's expected to be fully recovered for the start of the 1996 season. Swift's sinker is the perfect pitch for Coors Field.

	W	SV	ERA	IP	H	BB	SO	B/I	$
1994 San Francisco NL	8	0	3.38	109	109	31	62	1.28	9
1995 Colorado NL	9	0	4.94	105	122	43	68	1.56	-
1996 *Projection* >>>	12	0	4.47	141	148	46	88	1.38	2

SWINDELL, GREG - TL - Age 31
Swindell recorded his third straight disappointing year with the Astros since signing a four year contract before the 1993 season. In all three years his ERA was over 4.00 and he gave up far more than one hit per inning. Without an outstanding pitch, his major asset is his control. He was used in relief late in the season and may find himself in the bullpen again in 1996.

	W	SV	ERA	IP	H	BB	SO	B/I	$
1994 Houston NL	8	0	4.37	148	175	26	74	1.36	6
1995 Houston NL	10	0	4.47	153	180	39	96	1.43	2
1996 *Projection* >>>	10	0	4.31	160	189	37	94	1.41	1

SWINGLE, PAUL - TR - Age 29
After a disastrous 1994 campaign in the Angels system when he went 2-9 with a 6.92 ERA, Swingle improved his control and had better results in 1995. He was used strictly out of the bullpen for the first time in years and had useful results for Triple-A New Orleans. A hard thrower, Swingle has a chance to earn a major league relief role in 1996 somewhere, if not with the Brewers.

	W	SV	ERA	IP	H	BB	SO	B/I	$
1995 New Orleans AAA	1	0	4.57	43	42	15	41	1.32	

TABAKA, JEFF - TL - Age 32
Tabaka came to the Astros from San Diego in the Phil Plantier trade in July. He occasionally has control problems but was reasonably effective as a lefthanded relief specialist. Tabaka should fill the same role in 1996.

	W	SV	ERA	IP	H	BB	SO	B/I	$
1994 Two Teams	3	1	5.27	41	32	27	32	1.44	1
1995 Two Teams	1	0	3.23	30	27	17	25	1.43	0

TAM, JEFF - TR - Age 25
Tam was unhittable in A ball, but very hittable in the Eastern League. See how he does in another try at Binghamton before getting excited about him. Still has a 2.21 career ERA on the Mets farm.

TAPANI, KEVIN - TR - Age 32
The new Rick Mahler. Tapani's last good year was 1993 and good control and durability are his only assets. With the Dodger defense, putting the ball in play is not a method that will produce good results. Given his age, stuff, and support cast, I would not expect a comeback in 1996.

	W	SV	ERA	IP	H	BB	SO	B/I	$
1994 Minnesota AL	11	0	4.62	156	181	39	91	1.41	9
1995 Minnesota AL	6	0	4.92	133	155	34	88	1.41	-
1995 Los Angeles NL	4	0	5.05	57	72	14	43	1.51	-
1996 *Projection* >>>	14	0	4.30	197	220	58	129	1.41	3

TAVAREZ, JULIAN - TR - Age 22
The kid who rocketed through the Indians chain, first arriving in the majors for a brief period at age 20, became a solid big league contributor in 1995 as baseball's premier setup man. Tavarez used his lively sinking fastball and killer curve to hold righties to a .205 average and fashion an excellent strikeout/walk ratio. Tavarez is capable of much more - it is only a matter of time before he becomes a top major league starter or premier closer. Don't be surprised if he excels while taking a regular starting turn for the Tribe in 1996.

	W	SV	ERA	IP	H	BB	SO	B/I	$
1994 Charlotte AAA	15	0	3.48	176	167	43	102	1.19	
1995 Cleveland AL	10	0	2.44	85	76	21	68	1.14	13
1996 *Projection* >>>	7	0	2.90	99	94	24	77	1.20	12

TAYLOR, BILL - TR - Age 33
Taylor, a 32 year old rookie in 1994, pitched well in a supporting role. Opportunity and age became the primary roadblocks in Taylor's way.

TAYLOR, BRIEN - TL - Age 24
Taylor missed all of 1994 after injuring his shoulder in an off-field brawl. While he was rehabbing, he complained that he was bored with baseball. In 1995 he made 11 starts in Rookie league, yielding a 6.07 ERA.

TAYLOR, KERRY - TR - Age 25
Taylor got into 36 games with the Padres in 1993 as a starter and reliever. He pitched poorly then, and he has pitched poorly in Triple-A for the past two years. His future doesn't look very promising.

	W	SV	ERA	IP	H	BB	SO	B/I	$
1995 Las Vegas AAA	2	0	4.38	37	44	21	21	1.76	

TAYLOR, ROB - TR - Age 30
An aging minor league closer remarkably similar to Bill Taylor's profile three years ago.

	W	SV	ERA	IP	H	BB	SO	B/I	$
1995 Iowa AAA	4	18	2.81	57	42	28	48	1.22	

TAYLOR, RODNEY SCOTT - TL - Age 28
Taylor pitched briefly for Boston in 1992 then disappeared, missing all of 1994 because of shoulder surgery. He knocked on the Pirates' door in spring training and was sent to Triple-A Calgary after throwing well in a tryout. He pitched pretty well in the Pacific Coast League and could resurface in the big leagues by virtue of being lefthanded.

	W	SV	ERA	IP	H	BB	SO	B/I	$
1995 Calgary AAA	5	0	4.11	140	144	35	83	1.28	

TAYLOR, SCOTT - TR - Age 29
Injuries at the big league level gave Taylor a golden opportunity to stick with the Rangers, but the results were disastrous. He pitched well at Triple-A Oklahoma City, though, so he merits another shot.

	W	SV	ERA	IP	H	BB	SO	B/I	$
1995 Two AAA Teams	8	0	3.55	129	132	41	74	1.34	
1995 Texas AL	1	0	9.39	15	25	5	10	1.96	-

TELEMACO, AMAURY - TR - Age 22
Thus far, Telemaco's talent has outdistanced his production. But the Cubs feel it's just a matter of time before he's ready to challenge hitters at Wrigley Field. Last season he was a strikeout-an-inning pitcher more because he could change speeds and hit spots than because he overpowered batters.

TELFORD, ANTHONY - TR - Age 30
Telford pitched as a long reliever/spot starter at two Triple-A sites in 1995, but did little to show he belonged back in the major leagues. A control specialist, Telford was 4-1 with a 1.46 ERA for Buffalo, but posted a 7.16 ERA at Edmonton. If he gets back to the bigs it'll be as a long reliever, and not a particularly effective one.

	W	SV	ERA	IP	H	BB	SO	B/I	$
1995 Buffalo AAA	4	0	3.46	39	35	10	24	1.16	

TELGHEDER, DAVE - TR - Age 29
Telgheder needs to throw his split-finger pitch for strikes consistently to be effective. So far he hasn't done that except for three promising starts in late 1993 and occasional streaks in the minors.

	W	SV	ERA	IP	H	BB	SO	B / I	$
1994 Norfolk AAA	8	0	3.40	158	156	26	83	1.15	
1994 New York NL	0	0	7.20	10	11	8	4	1.90	-
1995 New York NL	1	0	5.61	25	34	7	16	1.60	-
1996 Projection >>>									

TEWKSBURY, BOB - TR - Age 35
Tewksbury has always been the ultimate control pitcher - hittable, but very few walks. The walks are still few, but the hits are getting more frequent every year. Tewksbury is still an acceptable fourth starter on most teams, but he is clearly on the decline. Tewksbury was slowed toward the end of the season by a pulled muscle.

	W	SV	ERA	IP	H	BB	SO	B / I	$
1994 St. Louis NL	12	0	5.32	155	190	22	79	1.36	4
1995 Texas AL	8	0	4.58	129	169	20	53	1.46	4
1996 Projection >>>	12	0	4.76	174	231	27	79	1.48	3

THIGPEN, BOBBY - TR - Age 32
Thigpen saved eight games for the Fukuoka Daiei Hawks of the Japanese Pacific League in 1995, posting a 1.96 ERA. He managed to get hurt again, though, and it would appear his days as a useful major league reliever are near an end.

THOBE, J.J. - TR - Age 25
Thobe got his first taste of the majors last September when the Expos called him up; he didn't distinguish himself. He could fashion a decent big-league career if he stays healthy. But that's a big if. Boston claimed him off waivers in October as Red Sox GM Dan Duquette continues his quest to move everyone from his former organization to New England.

	W	SV	ERA	IP	H	BB	SO	B / I	$
1995 Ottawa AAA	5	5	3.27	88	79	16	36	1.08	

THOBE, TOM - TL - Age 26
J.J. Thobe's older brother, who originally signed with the Cubs in 1988, sat out the next four years when he was more interested in surfing than baseball. He has improved as he has advanced through the Braves organization the last three seasons, and even reached Atlanta in September. He's a candidate for a major league relief job.

	W	SV	ERA	IP	H	BB	SO	B / I	$
1995 Richmond AAA	7	5	1.84	88	65	26	57	1.04	

THOMAS, CARLOS - TR - Age 27
Thomas is an older minor league reliever who can't seem to get it together to move up past Double-A.

THOMAS, LARRY -TL - Age 26
Former top prospect Thomas really took off after switching to relief in 1995, posting a 1.34 ERA for Double-A Birmingham which earned him his first taste of the big leagues. He's a sinker/slider pitcher who should be the White Sox top bullpen lefty in 1996.

	W	SV	ERA	IP	H	BB	SO	B / I	$
1994 Birmingham AA	5	0	4.63	144	159	53	77	1.47	
1995 Chicago AL	0	0	1.32	13	8	6	12	1.02	1

THOMAS, MIKE - TL - Age 26
Had 20 saves in 1991, 15 in 1993 and 20 in 1994. Moving up slowly but steadily, with plenty of strikeouts along the way.

THOMAS, ROYAL - TR - Age 26
Thomas reached Triple-A for the first time in 1995, going 7-7 with a 3.48 ERA pitching long relief and making spot starts in Richmond. His too-straight fastball and lack of control with his breaking pitches will prevent Thomas from advancing to Atlanta.

	W	SV	ERA	IP	H	BB	SO	B/I	$
1995 Richmond AAA	7	0	3.48	88	103	24	39	1.45	

THOMPSON, JUSTIN - TL - Age 23
Thompson has tempted the Tigers with his left arm's potential since they drafted him in '91, and from his performance in '95 the hometown fans won't have to wait much longer. He pitched well at Double-A, just missing the league's top ten prospects list. Thompson and C.J. Nitkowski will eventually form a good pair of lefties in the Detroit rotation.

THOMPSON, MARK - TR - Age 24
Thompson divided his time between the Rockies and Triple-A Colorado Springs last season. He has a decent fastball and improved the effectiveness of his changeup in 1995. Thompson must improve his control and avoid going deep into counts so often to gain more playing time with the Rockies in 1996.

	W	SV	ERA	IP	H	BB	SO	B/I	$
1995 Colorado Springs AAA	5	0	6.10	62	73	25	38	1.58	
1995 Colorado NL	2	0	6.53	51	73	22	30	1.86	-
1996 *Projection* >>>	2	0	5.77	31	39	16	18	1.78	-

THOMSON, JOHN - TR - Age 22
Don't confuse Thomson with Mark Thompson, who already is with the Rockies. Thomson pitched better in hitters' parks for Colorado's Class A farms than he did in the pitchers' park at Double-A New Haven. He probably will need another year in the Eastern League.

TIMLIN, MIKE - TR - Age 30
Despite an injury-shortened year, Timlin enjoyed his best season in the major leagues, holding righthanded hitters to a .159 average. He still has the nice sinker and the good fastball but now showed both confidence and a willingness to pitch inside. Unnoticed by many, he has the velocity and the makeup to be a closer.

	W	SV	ERA	IP	H	BB	SO	B/I	$
1994 Toronto AL	0	2	5.18	40	41	20	38	1.53	1
1995 Toronto AL	4	5	2.14	42	38	17	36	1.31	9
1996 *Projection* >>>	3	8	3.42	51	48	20	45	1.35	11

TOMLIN, RANDY - TL - Age 29
Tomlin never fully recovered from the elbow surgery he had late in the 1993 season, was farmed out to Class AAA Buffalo by the Pirates early in 1994 then didn't pitch after mid-July because of shoulder tendinitis. If he is healthy, Tomlin is a functional major league starter, though that 14-win season of 1992 seems like it happened a decade ago.

TORRES, DILSON - TR - Age 25
Another Rule Five draftee by the Royals, Torres got by for a while with his slider and forkball, but lost command of both pitches and spent a lot of the year at Triple-A Omaha. He's not going to be a big winner, but Torres has a solid future in a major league bullpen.

	W	SV	ERA	IP	H	BB	SO	B/I	$
1995 Kansas City AL	1	0	6.09	44	56	17	28	1.65	-
1996 *Projection* >>>	2	0	5.26	60	73	21	38	1.57	-

TORRES, SALOMON - TR - Age 24
He's going to arrive one of these days. But don't bet on 1996. He has already shown flashes of brilliance at the major league level. He has also shown flashes of mental anguish, serious enough that it is almost impossible to guess what Torres' career will look like ten years from now. The range of possibilities would seem to range from Denny McLain when he won 31 games, to Denny McLain when he lost 22 games.

	W	SV	ERA	IP	H	BB	SO	B/I	$
1994 San Francisco NL	2	0	5.44	84	95	34	42	1.53	-
1995 Two AAA Teams	1	0	3.00	30	22	13	24	1.17	
1995 Two Teams	3	0	6.30	80	100	49	47	1.86	-
1996 *Projection* >>>	5	0	5.10	94	104	47	52	1.61	-

TOTH, ROBERT - TR - Age 23
A control pitcher with an incredible change-up, Toth lacks the other pitches needed to be a big winner. Still, his recent

success should mean another promotion in 1996, this time to Triple-A Omaha. Toth may get a long relief role in the majors by 1997.

	W	SV	ERA	IP	H	BB	SO	B/I	$
1995 Omaha AAA	1	0	3.61	47	53	8	31	1.29	

TOUCHET, SEAN - TR - Age 23
An extremely long-range, unpolished prospect, Touchet has struck out over 13 batters per nine innings in two years of short-season ball, but has walked more than seven per nine innings. He has been used as a closer by the Marlins' organization to this point, and could become an interesting prospect if he sharpens his control significantly.

TRACHSEL, STEVE - TR - Age 25
Trachsel's really a pretty good pitcher but he simply can't win in Wrigley. It's gotten so bad that it's really a mental thing now, so he'll need a to reach his potential. Trachsel can be a 15-game winner in the right circumstances.

	W	SV	ERA	IP	H	BB	SO	B/I	$
1994 Chicago NL	9	0	3.21	146	133	54	108	1.28	13
1995 Chicago NL	7	0	5.15	160	174	76	117	1.56	-
1996 Projection >>>	9	0	4.45	172	170	72	126	1.41	0

TRANBARGER, MARK - TL - Age 26
Not to be confused with Mark Tranberg, Tranbarger is a rising relief ace who had a dominant year at Double-A Chattanooga, going 3-1 with a 1.95 ERA. He's probably not going to be a big league closer, but he could eventually win a lefty setup role. His progress at Triple-A Indianapolis in 1996 will be an indication of his prospects for major league play.

TRANBERG, MARK - TR - Age 27
Not to be confused with Mark Tranbarger, Tranberg is a dismal righthanded prospect who has only recently begun to pitch well above Class A. Of course, he's far too old to be at Double-A, where he went 6-6 with a 3.73 ERA. Also, his control is not especially good for a non-strikeout pitcher.

	W	SV	ERA	IP	H	BB	SO	B/I	$
1995 Scranton AAA	1	0	7.23	23	32	6	15	1.61	

TRINIDAD, HECTOR - TR - Age 22
Trinidad was traded for a team president. He went to the Twins as compensation for the Cubs' hiring Andy MacPhail. Trinidad, a control pitcher, struggled in his first full Double-A season.

TRLICEK, RICK - TR - Age 26
A control pitcher, Trlicek's below average stuff is barely good enough to get Triple-A hitters out. In his best season, 1993, he had a 4.08 ERA for the Dodgers, but has regressed since; he went 5-4 with a 5.29 ERA for Triple-A Phoenix in 1995. Should Trlicek somehow get back to the majors he'd be a middle innings reliever.

TROMBLEY, MIKE - TR - Age 28
The Twins gave Trombley another chance at the starting rotation in '95, and he posted more mixed results. A control pitcher, he needs to walk fewer batters than he did in '95, and his mechanics looked less sound than in previous seasons.

	W	SV	ERA	IP	H	BB	SO	B/I	$
1994 Minnesota AL	2	0	6.33	48	56	18	32	1.53	-
1995 Minnesota AL	4	0	5.62	97	107	42	68	1.53	-
1996 Projection >>>	4	0	5.68	98	109	40	68	1.52	-

TROUTMAN, KEITH - TR - Age 22
Troutman pitched well in limited action for Double-A San Antonio in 1995. He has good control and decent stuff, but should return to Double-A in 1996. Troutman is not considered a top prospect.

TSAMIS, GEORGE - TL - Age 28
This lefty finesse artist has struggled above Double-A. He posted a combined 3.38 ERA at two Double-A stops in 1995. It's hard to see Tsamis getting a reprise of his 1993 Twins bullpen role.

TURNER, MATT -TR - Age 29
A better human interest story than a pitching prospect, Turner was done a huge favor by the Indians when they released him shortly before the 1994 players' strike so that he could still get paid for the rest of the year while he recovered from Hodgkins' Disease. Turner returned to the Indians Triple-A Buffalo club late in the year and put up forgettable numbers. He still has a chance to return to the majors when he regains his strength. The Indians are to be commended for an under-publicized act of human kindness.

URBANI, TOM - TL - Age 28
Though the numbers weren't great, Urbani had a pretty fair 1995 as a swingman with the Cardinals. He has never been given a clear role during his three years in St. Louis. A crafty lefty who knows how to move the ball around, he'd be a decent fourth or fifth starter if the Cardinals would quit jerking him around.

	W	SV	ERA	IP	H	BB	SO	B/I	$
1994 St. Louis NL	3	0	5.15	80	98	21	43	1.48	-
1995 St. Louis NL	3	0	3.70	82	99	21	52	1.45	1
1996 Projection >>>	4	0	4.04	96	115	25	56	1.47	-

URBINA, UGUETH URTAIN - TR - Age 22
Urbina got a chance with the Expos last season but clearly wasn't ready to pitch in the major leagues. However, he has a live fastball and good breaking stuff. The next time around, he'll be ready and eventually blossom into a top-shelf starter.

	W	SV	ERA	IP	H	BB	SO	B/I	$
1995 Ottawa AAA	6	0	3.04	68	46	26	55	1.06	
1995 Montreal NL	2	0	6.17	23	26	14	15	1.71	-
1996 Projection >>>	6	0	4.00	85	82	48	55	1.53	-

VALDES, ISMAEL - TR - Age 22
Overlooked in the attention Hideo Nomo received was the brilliant rookie season posted by Valdes. He was the Dodgers second most effective pitcher (behind you know who) but received only 4.0 runs per game to work with. He features a good fastball, slider, and excellent control for a power pitcher. Valdes should be an excellent starter until Lasorda works him into the ground.

	W	SV	ERA	IP	H	BB	SO	B/I	$
1994 San Antonio AA	2	0	3.38	53	54	9	55	1.18	
1994 Los Angeles NL	3	0	3.18	28	21	10	28	1.09	
1995 Los Angeles NL	13	1	3.05	197	168	51	150	1.11	21
1996 Projection >>>	15	1	3.16	190	166	52	148	1.15	22

VALDES, MARC - TR - Age 24
The Marlins' top pick in 1993, Valdez took a step backwards after becoming the Marlins' foremost starting pitcher prospect in 1994. He got off to a woeful start at Triple-A Charlotte, where he experienced difficulty getting the ball past hitters for the first time in his pro career. He has a diversified repertoire which features a high 80's fastball and solid breaking stuff, all of which he throws consistently for strikes. However, he was ravaged after being summoned to the majors - of most concern was his admission that he was awed and scared by the experience. It appears that he will need further minor league seasoning - he'll be ready when he gets his strikeout rate back up.

VALDEZ, CARLOS - TR - Age 24
Valdez pitched extremely well at both Double-A and Triple-A, then got bombed in a late-season callup with the Giants. He needs more time at Triple-A, but is worth watching.

	W	SV	ERA	IP	H	BB	SO	B/I	$
1995 San Francisco NL	0	0	6.14	14	19	8	7	1.84	-

VALDEZ, SERGIO - TR - Age 30
He's been around forever, mostly as a reliever when in the majors, but he became a member of the Giants' rotation after a decent half-season as a starter in Triple-A. He has good control and is not a bad pitcher.

	W	SV	ERA	IP	H	BB	SO	B/I	$
1994 Boston AL	0	0	8.16	14	25	8	4	2.30	
1995 San Francisco NL	4	0	4.75	66	78	17	29	1.43	0
1996 Projection >>>	5	0	4.68	71	82	18	30	1.41	-

VALENZUELA, FERNANDO - TL - Age 35
Fernando's age is published as 35, but there is speculation that he may be in his 40's. He had some good outings last year as a starter and reliever, but overall, it was a poor year. Fernando may have finally reached the end of his major league career.

	W	SV	ERA	IP	H	BB	SO	B/I	$
1994 Philadelphia NL	1	0	3.00	45	42	7	19	1.09	4
1995 San Diego NL	8	0	4.98	90	101	34	57	1.49	-
1996 *Projection* >>>	3	0	5.00	69	75	25	38	1.45	-

VALERA, JULIO - TR - Age 27
Valera was once a promising pitching prospect in the Mets system. Traded to the Angels, he had a good year as a starter in 1992 going 8-11 with a 3.73 ERA in 188 innings. His future looked bright, but he came down with arm injuries requiring Tommy John-surgery and lengthy periods on the disabled list and minor league rehabs. But he showed that he's back with a neat complete game two-hitter last August versus Tacoma.

	W	SV	ERA	IP	H	BB	SO	B/I	$
1994 Vancouver AAA	1	0	5.28	60	70	20	43	1.50	
1995 Vancouver AAA	2	0	5.70	71	85	21	43	1.50	

VANDERWEELE, DOUG - TR - Age 26
A decent but not outstanding righthanded prospect on the Giants farm, he has good control but is otherwise undistinguished.

VANEGMOND, TIM - TR - Age 26
VanEgmond's stuff is nothing to get excited about; he's no better or worse than an average Triple-A starter at this point. Still, he's young enough to improve his control, which is the only way he'll get back to the majors for more than a cup of coffee.

	W	SV	ERA	IP	H	BB	SO	B/I	$
1994 Boston AL	2	0	6.34	38	38	21	22	1.54	-
1995 Pawtucket AAA	5	0	3.92	66	66	21	47	1.31	

VANLANDINGHAM, WILLIAM - TR - Age 25
Mature beyond his years, VanLandingham improved on his rookie season, walking fewer batters in forty more innings and increasing his K/IP ratio. He looks to be a solid pitcher for many years, not a staff ace but a good second starter. He has never lost a game at Candlestick Park.

	W	SV	ERA	IP	H	BB	SO	B/I	$
1994 Phoenix AAA	1	0	2.48	29	21	14	29	1.21	
1994 San Francisco NL	8	0	3.54	84	70	43	56	1.35	7
1995 San Francisco NL	6	0	3.67	122	124	40	95	1.34	5
1996 *Projection* >>>	10	0	3.63	172	166	63	128	1.33	8

VAN POPPEL, TODD - TR - Age 24
A flop since his famous signing in 1990, VanPoppel finally turned a corner last year. Prior to 1995, he had walked more batters than he struck out in the majors; last year, he struck out 122 in 138 innings and walked only 56. He often looked good coming out of the bullpen in midseason, and could become a dark horse candidate to take over from Dennis Eckersley as the A's stopper.

	W	SV	ERA	IP	H	BB	SO	B/I	$
1994 Oakland AL	7	0	6.09	116	108	89	83	1.69	-
1995 Oakland AL	4	0	4.88	138	125	56	122	1.31	4
1996 *Projection* >>>	3	0	4.84	93	84	39	82	1.32	1

VANRYN, BEN - TL - Age 24
Formerly a starter in the Dodgers' organization, VanRyn was acquired by the Angels and converted to a reliever last year. He pitched very well in his new role, and could move up quickly. He strikes out a lot of hitters, always a desired skill in a reliever, or a starter for that matter.

VASQUEZ, MARCOS - TR - Age 26
Originally signed by the Braves, the Reds signed Vasquez as a six year free agent in 1994. He has been moderately effective as a starter and reached Triple-A for the first time (for two innings) in 1995.

VERAS, DARIO - TR - Age 23
Veras is a young reliever with a very good minor league record over the past two years. If he continues to pitch well, he could be pitching for the Padres soon, probably as a middle reliever.

VERES, DAVE - TR - Age 29
Veres was by far the Astros' most consistent reliever, if not their most valuable pitcher in 1995. He led the league in relief innings with 103 in 72 games. Veres is a tireless worker with a good fastball, a sinker, a slider and excellent control. He should fill the same role in 1996.

	W	SV	ERA	IP	H	BB	SO	B/I	$
1994 Houston NL	3	1	2.41	41	39	7	28	1.12	6
1995 Houston NL	5	1	2.26	103	89	30	94	1.15	11
1996 *Projection* >>>	4	1	3.00	95	85	28	82	1.19	9

VERES, RANDY - TR - Age 30
This journeyman slopballer had his fourth, and longest, major league trial in 1995 with the Marlins. He nibbles around the edges of the strike zone with his pedestrian stuff, a sure recipe for a mediocre strikeout/walk ratio. His 1995 ERA was deceptively low, as he allowed an unacceptable 15 of 42 inherited runners to score. He was the beneficiary of injuries to Bryan Harvey and Jeremy Hernandez - only another rash of injuries will allow him to spend another full season in the majors.

	W	SV	ERA	IP	H	BB	SO	B/I	$
1995 Florida NL	4	1	3.88	48	46	22	31	1.40	2
1996 *Projection* >>>	4	1	3.91	45	43	21	29	1.41	1

VIANO, JACOB - TR - Age 22
In his second go-around at Double-A New Haven, Viano was much more successful. The power pitcher nailed down the closer's job. In an organization desperate for a bullpen stopper, he could rise fast. The Rockies think enough of him that they've sent him to the Arizona Fall League each of the last two years.

VIERRA, JOEY - TL - Age 30
Selected to the 1995 Triple-A all-star team, Vierra has good location and great off-speed stuff. For Triple-A Nashville he was used mostly to baffle lefthanded hitters. He's working on a knuckle ball to add to his repertoire. The little (5'7") lefty is a marginal prospect at best, but has a lot of good things going for him; don't be surprised if he gets a short major league stint in 1996.

	W	SV	ERA	IP	H	BB	SO	B/I	$
1995 Nashville AAA	2	4	4.17	58	47	19	57	1.14	

VILLONE, RON - TL - Age 26
Villone came to the Padres in the Andy Benes trade. He throws very hard and has an excellent change-up. He could move into the closer role should Trevor Hoffman have problems coming back from surgery, and young phenom Dustin Hermanson prove to be not ready. Villone could become another Randy Myers.

	W	SV	ERA	IP	H	BB	SO	B/I	$
1995 Seattle AL	0	0	7.91	19	20	23	26	2.22	
1995 San Diego NL	2	1	4.21	25	24	11	37	1.36	-
1996 *Projection* >>>	3	4	4.44	60	45	39	84	1.40	2

VIOLA, FRANK - TL - Age 35
The Reds took a chance on Viola when it looked like their entire rotation was going to the DL. In his three major league starts, he would pitch well for three or four innings before tiring. Despite his mediocre performance, he probably would have made the post season roster as an extra lefty, had he not been sidelined for the year with a sprained neck. A comeback is possible, but not likely with the Reds due to their fully stocked rotation.

	W	SV	ERA	IP	H	BB	SO	B/I	$
1994 Boston AL	1	0	4.65	31	34	17	9	1.65	-

	W	SV	ERA	IP	H	BB	SO	B/I	$
1995 Cincinnati NL	0	0	6.28	14	20	3	4	1.60	-
1996 *Projection* >>>	2	0	5.22	31	35	13	12	1.55	-

VITKO, JOSEPH - TR - Age 26
Vitko had a September callup with the Mets in 1992, but since then has been injured. He missed virtually all of 1993, and spent time in 1994 on the DL.

VOISARD, MARK - TR - Age 26
Voisard was the closer for Double-A New Haven in 1994, but lost that job last year to Jake Viano. Time would appear to be running out for Voisard.

VOSBERG, ED - TL - Age 34
Vosberg was one of the nicer surprises for Texas in the designated lefty relief role. There isn't any reason that he shouldn't be able to continue to pitch in that role for the near future. In one of the year's more embarrassing stories, Vosberg was arrested trying to scalp complimentary All-Star Game tickets. Hey, it's tough living on $109,000 a year.

	W	SV	ERA	IP	H	BB	SO	B/I	$
1995 Texas AL	5	4	3.00	36	32	16	36	1.33	7
1996 *Projection* >>>	3	5	3.13	52	46	24	52	1.35	8

WADE, TERRELL - TL - Age 23
We've been hearing about Wade for so long we forget how young he is. At this point, though, the next opening that would arise in the Atlanta rotation would go to Jason Schmidt, who is four days younger. Wade will need more than his plus fastball to succeed in the majors.

	W	SV	ERA	IP	H	BB	SO	B/I	$
1995 Richmond AAA	10	0	4.56	142	137	63	124	1.41	

WAGNER, BILLY - TL - Age 24
Wagner was Houston's first round draft choice in 1993 and is their top pitching prospect. He made his major league debut in September after being named by Baseball America as one of the top 10 prospects in both the Double-A Texas League (2nd) and Triple-A Pacific Coast League (6th). Wagner has an overpowering fastball but may not yet have sufficient command of his off speed and breaking pitches to be a successful starter in the majors. He pitched in the Arizona Fall League and should be with Houston in 1996, possibly as a reliever, but he will eventually be in the rotation and could have an outstanding career.

	W	SV	ERA	IP	H	BB	SO	B/I	$
1995 Tucson AAA	5	0	3.18	76	70	32	80	1.34	
1996 *Projection* >>>	4	0	4.05	54	54	26	40	1.49	-

WAGNER, BRET - TL - Age 22
The Cardinals' 1994 first-round draft pick, Wagner used a 5-4, 2.12 season at Class-A St. Petersburg to earn an August promotion to Double-A Arkansas. He's a very good prospect who should begin the 1996 season in Arkansas but will advance quickly.

WAGNER, JOE - TR - Age 24
The fourth of Milwaukee's first-round draft picks in '92, Wagner is a fastball pitcher, and not afraid to throw inside. He finally made it Double-A in 1995 but got convincingly crushed in five starts for El Paso. He will get another try there in 1996.

WAGNER, PAUL - TR - Age 28
Wagner has all the ability in the world (96-MPH fastball, sharp-breaking slider) and no idea what to do with it. He's a bright guy with a degree from Illinois State but has no feel for the art of pitching. He needs to develop an off-speed pitch to succeed as a major-league starter and tried a palmball late last season. One school of thought says he could become a top-flight closer but the Pirates stubbornly keep trying to make him a starter.

	W	SV	ERA	IP	H	BB	SO	B/I	$
1994 Pittsburgh NL	7	0	4.59	119	136	50	86	1.55	0
1995 Pittsburgh NL	5	1	4.80	165	174	72	120	1.49	-
1996 *Projection* >>>	8	1	4.69	176	190	67	129	1.46	-

WAINHOUSE, DAVE - TR - Age 28
Wainhouse lost all of 1994 to injury, then made a nice recovery for Triple-A Syracuse. He throws hard enough to be an effective setup man in the bullpen, and might get the chance in the wide-open Blue Jays pen.

	W	SV	ERA	IP	H	BB	SO	B/I	$
1995 three teams AA-AAA	5	5	4.50	53	74	23	36	1.83	

WAKEFIELD, TIM - TR - Age 29
1995 provided a lesson on why you shouldn't write off a knuckleballer - and why you can't really count on him, either. Wakefield was unhittable for the first four months of the season, then stumbled down the stretch as his knuckler stopped dancing. Still, it was a season worthy of Cy Young consideration; he'll have to completely fall on his face to drop out of the Boston rotation in 1996.

	W	SV	ERA	IP	H	BB	SO	B/I	$
1994 Buffalo AAA	5	0	5.84	175	197	98	83	1.68	
1995 Boston AL	16	0	2.95	195	163	68	119	1.18	24
1996 Projection >>>	10	0	3.88	188	171	68	115	1.27	15

WALKER, JAMIE - TL - Age 24
Walker has made slow progress in his four years in the Astro system. He was on the replacement squad in the spring of 1995 and that will probably be the closest he gets to the major leagues.

WALKER, MIKE - TR - Age 29
In the midst of a good year in middle relief Walker was demoted to Triple-A Iowa where he continued to pitch well. He doesn't throw very hard and has to get batters to put the ball in play. Walker is a very replaceable reliever who has to battle for the last spot on a major league staff.

	W	SV	ERA	IP	H	BB	SO	B/I	$
1995 Iowa AAA	1	0	4.10	26	22	19	13	1.56	
1995 Chicago NL	1	1	3.22	44	45	24	20	1.54	1

WALKER, PETE - TR - Age 26
Walker's career took a step up when he became the Double-A Binghamton closer in 1993. But then he started 1994 on the DL with an elbow injury. He showed enough comeback progress to reach the majors in 1995, when his biggest problem became a Mets pen overcrowded with competent righties.

	W	SV	ERA	IP	H	BB	SO	B/I	$
1995 Norfolk AAA	5	8	3.91	48	51	16	39	1.39	
1995 New York NL	1	0	4.58	17	24	5	5	1.64	-

WALL, DONNIE - TR - Age 28
Wall has been a consistent overachiever in his seven years in the Astro organization and had a breakthrough season in 1995, leading the Pacific Coast League with 17 wins, 119 strikeouts and an ERA of 3.30 while being named the league's Most Valuable Player. Wall has excellent control, but he has marginal major league stuff. He must have pinpoint control to be successful; in two of his five starts with the Astros in September, he didn't have it and failed to survive the third inning. Wall has earned a chance to compete for a major league job but success is not assured.

	W	SV	ERA	IP	H	BB	SO	B/I	$
1995 Tucson AAA	17	0	3.30	177	190	32	119	1.25	
1995 Houston NL	3	0	5.55	24	33	5	16	1.56	-
1996 Projection >>>	3	0	4.98	60	70	21	40	1.51	-

WALLACE, B. J. - TL - Age 25
Wallace was the Expos' first-round draft choice in 1992. He started having shoulder difficulties in '93, and has been on and off the DL ever since.

WALLACE, DEREK - TR - Age 24
The Mets are perhaps a bit less stocked, but Lomon will have to be superb to hang on with them in '96.

WARD, BRYAN - TL - Age 24
Ward is a hard thrower who has worked both as a starter and reliever in his three years in the Marlins' organization.

He dominated as a starter for high Class-A Brevard County, showing excellent velocity and location with his fastball, then struggled slightly with his control after his promotion to Double-A Portland. Since he throws lefthanded and has a plus fastball, he's got a shot to make the majors by 1997, most likely as a situational reliever.

WARD, DUANE - TR - Age 31
It was painful to watch Duane Ward throw slow breaking ball after breaking ball in his four games with the Jays last year. After surgery that caused him to miss all of 1994 and the end of 1995, at least for now, the great fastball is gone. Ward believes in himself and shouldn't be underestimated given his persistance and history. He was a free agent entering the off-season and was looking to prove that he can work his way back. He could be a pleasant surprise.

	W	SV	ERA	IP	H	BB	SO	B/I	$
1994 Toronto AL			Did Not Play						
1995 Toronto AL	0	0	27.00	2	11	5	3	6.00	-

WARE, JEFF - TR - Age 25
He was great at Triple-A last year and showed promise in a September callup with the Blue Jays. He has all the elements to be a good pitcher except for control, which he can still learn. He'll see action in the spring.

	W	SV	ERA	IP	H	BB	SO	B/I	$
1995 Syracuse AAA	7	0	3.00	75	62	46	76	1.44	
1995 Toronto AL	2	0	5.47	26	28	21	18	1.86	-

WARING, JIM - TR - Age 26
Waring has put up some excellent numbers for Class A teams in his five years in the Astro system, but has not achieved much success in his trials above that level. A finesse pitcher without a major league fastball, Waring appears to be a career minor leaguer.

WARREN, BRIAN - TR - Age 28
Probably the most unheralded pitcher of the Triple-A Indianapolis staff in 1995, Warren is a great setup man. He isn't afraid to attack the hitters but walks very few batters. Although he's too old to be a prospect, Warren has earned a chance in a major league bullpen.

	W	SV	ERA	IP	H	BB	SO	B/I	$
1995 Indianapolis AAA	2	2	1.61	56	56	9	35	1.16	

WARREN, DESHAWN - TL - Age 21
Because of poor control, Warren threw so many pitches last season that he averaged less than five innings per start. The young, hard-throwing lefthander will get plenty of chances to improve.

WASDIN, JOHN - TR - Age 23
The outstanding prospect pitched better than his 5.52 ERA suggests in the offense-happy Pacific Coast League, then had mixed results in a handful of late performances for Oakland. The combination of the high Triple-A ERA and his relative unknown status makes Wasdin a potential out-of-nowhere surprise for 1996.

	W	SV	ERA	IP	H	BB	SO	B/I	$
1995 Edmonton AAA	12	0	5.52	174	193	38	111	1.33	
1995 Oakland AL	1	0	4.67	17	14	3	6	0.98	1

WATKINS, SCOTT - TL - Age 25
Watkins showed drastic improvement upon returning to Triple-A Salt Lake City, thriving as a closer. He pitched well enough to earn a promotion to the big leagues, where the results were mixed. Watkins has the ability to have some good years in relief.

	W	SV	ERA	IP	H	BB	SO	B/I	$
1995 Minnesota AL	0	0	5.40	21	22	11	11	1.52	-

WATSON, ALLEN - TL - Age 25
Watson is close to becoming a major disappointment, compared to earlier expectations. He joined the Cardinals during the 1993 season and started off 6-0. Since then, he's gone 13-21. His greatest asset right now is that he's only 25, giving him time to improve, and he did put together one long impressive streak in late summer 1995, which went largely unnoticed and remains hidden behind some bad full-year numbers.

	W	SV	ERA	IP	H	BB	SO	B/I	$
1994 St. Louis NL	6	0	5.52	115	130	53	74	1.58	-
1995 St. Louis NL	7	0	4.96	114	126	41	49	1.46	-
1996 *Projection* >>>	11	0	4.12	178	180	67	101	1.39	3

WATSON, RON - TR - Age 27
Watson is a big hard thrower with a wildness problem. His 17 saves for Double-A Midland in 1994 will probably stand as his career peak, as he showed no progress in 1995.

WEATHERS, DAVE - TR - Age 26
Marlins' brass are becoming tired of associating the term "potential" with Weathers - it is about time they saw some results. Weathers clearly possesses a major league repertoire, with an upper 80's fastball and decent breaking stuff. However, he alternates between nibbling around the edges of the strike zone and walking batters, and grooving the ball in an effort to get ahead of hitters. Both approaches tend to yield disastrous results. Weathers will no longer be handed a starting role and is likely to open 1996 either in the bullpen or the minors.

	W	SV	ERA	IP	H	BB	SO	B/I	$
1994 Florida NL	8	0	5.27	135	166	59	72	1.67	-
1995 Florida NL	4	0	5.98	90	104	52	60	1.73	-
1996 *Projection* >>>	5	0	5.33	92	110	44	56	1.67	-

WEAVER, ERIC - TR - Age 22
A big (6'5") guy who has bouts of control problems, Weaver was shaky at the start of 1995 with Double-A San Antonio. He fought his control all year but pitched much better as the season wore on. Weaver is still a raw prospect; he needs more time in Double-A.

WEBER, BEN - TR - Age 25
With a promotion to Triple-A Syracuse, Weber suffered his first bad season in professional ball. He has exceptional control but it doesn't seem to be enough to get him over the hump as he always allows more hits than his share. He appears to be as nothing more than a spot starter at Triple-A.

	W	SV	ERA	IP	H	BB	SO	B/I	$
1995 Syracuse AAA	4	1	5.38	92	111	27	38	1.50	

WEBER, WESTON - TR - Age 32
Weber is an older pitcher who has toiled in Double-A and Triple-A for the past six years, never making it to the majors, not even for a cup of coffee. His record is undistinguished, and Triple-A looks like the peak for him.

	W	SV	ERA	IP	H	BB	SO	B/I	$
1995 Two teams AAA	6	0	4.67	150	170	50	86	1.51	

WEGMAN, BILL - TR - Age 33
Wegman appears to have fulfilled all of his potential as he continues to fade from "reliable" status.

	W	SV	ERA	IP	H	BB	SO	B/I	$
1994 Milwaukee AL	8	0	4.51	115	140	26	59	1.44	6
1995 Milwaukee AL	5	2	5.35	70	89	21	50	1.56	2
1996 *Projection* >>>	3	1	4.87	54	66	15	32	1.50	0

WEGMANN, TOM - TR - Age 27
Wegmann has below average stuff, but is always around the plate. The Orioles tried him as a starter in Triple-A but he was ineffective and very hittable. They sent him to Double-A only because they needed a pitcher there, not because he couldn't be a reliever in Triple-A. At best, Wegmann is a Triple-A pitcher.

WELLS, BOB - TR - Age 29
Wells looked fairly promising coming off 1995. He's still worth an entry on your prospect page, but he's no kid.

	W	SV	ERA	IP	H	BB	SO	B/I	$
1995 Seattle AL	4	0	5.75	76	88	39	38	1.66	-
1996 *Projection* >>>	4	0	5.49	46	52	23	23	1.63	-

WELLS, DAVID - TL - Age 32
The underrated Detroit starter was acquired by the Reds in exchange for 1994 top draft pick CJ Nitkowski. Wells is similiar to the other Reds lefthanders, featuring a good fastball and curve with good to excellent control. With the Reds fine defense behind him in 1996, one should expect a 15 win season.

	W	SV	ERA	IP	H	BB	SO	B/I	$
1994 Detroit AL	5	0	3.96	111	113	24	71	1.23	9
1995 Detroit AL	10	0	3.04	130	120	37	83	1.20	17
1995 Cincinnati NL	6	0	3.59	72	74	16	50	1.24	17
1996 Projection >>>	15	0	3.40	203	197	50	134	1.22	17

WENDELL, TURK - TR - Age 28
Flaky Wendell has made a name for himself with his antics, not with his pitching. He has always pitched well enough in Triple-A but is really just a marginal major leaguer who, as a right-handed middle reliever is imminently replaceable.

	W	SV	ERA	IP	H	BB	SO	B/I	$
1994 Iowa AAA	11	0	2.95	168	141	28	118	1.00	
1995 Chicago NL	3	0	4.92	60	71	24	50	1.57	-
1996 Projection >>>	2	0	5.76	49	60	21	39	1.65	-

WENGERT, DON - TR - Age 26
Wengert pitched better for Oakland in 1995 than he did in Triple-A. Mainly a starter in the minors, he was used in the bullpen for Oakland. He went to the Arizona Fall League to get more seasoning in 1994.

	W	SV	ERA	IP	H	BB	SO	B/I	$
1995 Oakland AL	1	0	3.34	29	30	12	16	1.42	1
1996 Projection >>>	2	0	3.70	40	40	17	22	1.44	0

WERTZ, BILL - TR - Age 29
Veteran minor league reliever Wertz had his worst pro season in 1995, going 4-5 with a 5.80 ERA for Triple-A Pawtucket. A former Indians' farmhand, Wertz is not a good prospect, but could earn a middle relief role in a major league bullpen - he'll have to do better than his 1995 performance to have a chance, though.

WEST, DAVID - TL - Age 31
West is yet another member of the Phils' 1995 staff who had his season ruined by shoulder surgery. As a starter, West has been difficult to hit, but has struggled with his control, consistently running deep counts and forcing himself out of the game in the middle innings due to high pitch totals. First and foremost, West must prove that he is healthy and has retained his fastball - he will never cut it as a finesse pitcher. Given those factors, he must then improve his conditioning dramatically. A move back to the bullpen could be in his best interests.

	W	SV	ERA	IP	H	BB	SO	B/I	$
1994 Philadelphia NL	4	0	3.55	99	74	61	83	1.36	5
1995 Philadelphia NL	3	0	3.79	38	34	19	25	1.39	1
1996 Projection >>>	4	0	3.82	76	62	44	60	1.40	1

WESTON, MICKEY - TR - Age 35
Weston was Triple-A Toledo's most reliable starter in 1995, going 11-7 with a fine 2.90 ERA. He's hardly a prospect, though, having spent parts of five years in the majors with four different teams several years ago. He's a Triple-A pitcher at best, and has maybe two or three years left at that job.

	W	SV	ERA	IP	H	BB	SO	B/I	$
1995 Toledo AAA	11	0	2.90	180	170	41	69	1.18	

WETTELAND, JOHN - TR - Age 29
Wetteland had a few rough spots in his 1995 campaign but ended on a high note with a 0.84 ERA and eight saves in September. His blow-'em-away heat is as good as ever.

	W	SV	ERA	IP	H	BB	SO	B/I	$
1994 Montreal NL	4	25	2.83	63	46	21	68	1.05	34
1995 New York AL	1	31	2.93	61	40	14	66	0.88	37
1996 Projection >>>	3	35	2.72	77	55	22	84	1.01	47

WHISENANT, MATT - TL - Age 25
Whisenant was one of two minor leaguers acquired from the Phils for Danny Jackson in 1993 on the date of the expansion draft. Whisenant is a hard throwing lefty who made his first appearance above Single-A in 1995. His control is marginal, but he has allowed far less than a hit per inning at each minor league stop. A player of his age who has never appeared in Triple-A cannot be considered a top prospect, but he does have the ability to become an effective major league situational reliever, perhaps sometime in 1996.

WHITAKER, STEVE - TL - Age 25
Last year we advised you to watch his walk totals to see if he'd finally found some control. In 1995 he walked 48 men in 76 innings across three different minor-league levels. He's not a big strikeout pitcher; along with the control problems, he would seem an unlikely prospect.

	W	SV	ERA	IP	H	BB	SO	B/I	$
1995 Phoenix AAA	0	0	7.00	54	72	36	30	2.00	

WHITE, CHRIS - TR - Age 26
White has been in the Astro system for five years and appears to have topped out at the Double-A level.

WHITE, GABE - TL - Age 24
Like so many other pitchers in the Expos' farm system, White has been hyped for a long time now. Yet, he has shown absolutely no promise in his major-league stints. Could it be that he's not as good as his press clippings? It's starting to look that way.

	W	SV	ERA	IP	H	BB	SO	B/I	$
1994 Ottawa AAA	8	0	5.05	73	77	28	63	1.43	
1994 Montreal NL	1	1	6.08	23	24	11	17	1.48	-
1995 Ottawa AAA	2	0	3.90	62	58	17	37	1.21	
1995 Montreal NL	1	0	7.01	25	26	9	25	1.36	-
1996 Projection >>>	5	0	4.92	68	69	26	60	1.40	-

WHITE, RICK - TR - Age 27
After a good rookie year in 1994, White showed up overweight at spring training then strained an elbow ligament. He wound up being demoted to Triple-A Calgary for a good portion of the season. He looked better upon returning to the Pirates in September, but ended up facing surgery on that ligament after the '95 season.

	W	SV	ERA	IP	H	BB	SO	B/I	$
1994 Pittsburgh NL	4	6	3.82	75	79	17	38	1.27	11
1995 Calgary AAA	6	0	4.20	79	97	10	56	1.35	
1995 Pittsburgh NL	2	0	4.75	55	66	18	29	1.53	-

WHITEHURST, WALLY - TR - Age 31
Whitehurst didn't perform at Triple-A and therefore hurt his chance to make it back to the major leagues. He still challenges hitters but has already had too many mediocre major league innings.

	W	SV	ERA	IP	H	BB	SO	B/I	$
1994 San Diego NL	4	0	4.92	64	84	26	43	1.72	-
1995 Three teams AAA	4	0	5.17	72	88	20	41	1.50	

WHITEMAN, GREG - TL - Age 22
A college lefthander with potential, Whiteman was the Tigers' third round pick in the '94 draft. He spent the '95 season at low Class A and is three years away from the major leagues.

WHITESIDE, MATT - TR - Age 28
Whiteside had his most effective season since his rookie year as the Rangers were able to avoid overusing him for most of the season. Whiteside cut down on his walks and boosted his strikeout total in a middle relief role.

	W	SV	ERA	IP	H	BB	SO	B/I	$
1994 Texas AL	2	1	5.02	61	68	28	37	1.57	0
1995 Texas AL	5	3	4.08	53	48	19	46	1.26	7
1996 Projection >>>	4	4	4.35	72	67	25	53	1.28	7

WHITESIDE, SEAN - TL - Age 24
A lefthanded relief prospect, Whiteside had a generally disappointing year; his brief callup to the majors was based on his '94 season. He needs two more years in the minor leagues to straighten out his control.

WHITTEN, CASEY - TL - Age 23
The Indians' second round pick in 1993 established himself as a viable major league prospect by demonstrating excellent control, a high-80's fastball, and a solid offspeed repertoire at Double-A Canton-Akron in 1995. He's a tad undersized at 6'0", 175 lbs,, but he is a solid Triple-A campaign away from being a prime competitor for the rotation spots currently held by greybeards Dennis Martinez and Orel Hershiser. He will not be a major league ace, but should be a solid third or fourth starter.

WICKANDER, KEVIN - TL - Age 31
He even pitched well in Tiger Stadium. On the downside, he nibbles a lot and walks too many batters. That can be a very dangerous situation when hitters again start to lay off the marginal pitches and talk a base on balls. On the plus side, he appears to have improved his control, if the batters are swinging.

	W	SV	ERA	IP	H	BB	SO	B/I	$
1995 Two Teams	0	1	1.93	23	19	12	11	1.33	2
1996 *Projection* >>>	2	1	3.96	48	46	21	23	1.40	1

WICKMAN, BOB - TR - Age 27
Wickman features a cut fastball and slider which induce frequent groundouts. He's well-suited to setup work, especially when coming into a game with men on base. He can extend himself for an extra inning when needed, and even close a game on occasion.

	W	SV	ERA	IP	H	BB	SO	B/I	$
1994 New York AL	5	6	3.09	70	54	27	56	1.16	16
1995 New York AL	2	1	4.05	80	77	33	51	1.38	3
1996 *Projection* >>>	5	2	4.00	97	90	40	65	1.34	7

WILEY, CHAD - TR - Age 24
Wiley has made steady progress through his four-year pro career to reach Double-A Tulsa in 1995. He started off the season 5-1, but got very little run support the rest of the way and finished 6-9 with a 3.89 ERA. Wiley should begin 1996 at Double-A but could be knocking on the door of a major league opportunity before the year is out.

WILKINS, MARC - TR - Age 25
A swingman for the Pirates' Double-A Carolina farm club last year, he's a borderline prospect at best.

WILLIAMS, BRIAN - TR - Age 27
Williams is reliever and spot starter who has been in the majors for four-plus years with a career ERA near 5.00. He gives you innings, but that's about all.

	W	SV	ERA	IP	H	BB	SO	B/I	$
1994 Houston NL	6	0	5.74	78	112	41	49	1.95	-
1995 San Diego NL	3	0	6.00	72	79	38	75	1.63	-
1996 *Projection* >>>	4	0	5.89	82	93	41	71	1.64	-

WILLIAMS, JEFF - TR - Age 27
Williams, a converted closer, went to the 1994 Arizona Fall League to find a role. 1995 was a lost season for him as he worked in only eight games.

WILLIAMS, MIKE - TR - Age 27
With virtually all of the Phils' starting pitching candidates struck down by injury, Williams continued to get starting opportunities by default. Unlike most of the others, Williams made the most of his chances, using pinpoint location of his adequate fastball and offspeed pitches to consistently keep the Phils' in ballgames for six or seven innings. Most impressive was his deft handling of lefthanded hitters (.193 average). Williams will again go to Spring Training as the frontrunner for the fifth starter job - a role he has never held on Opening Day.

	W	SV	ERA	IP	H	BB	SO	B/I	$
1994 Philadelphia NL	2	0	5.01	50	61	20	29	1.61	-

	W	SV	ERA	IP	H	BB	SO	B/I	$
1995 Philadelphia NL	3	0	3.29	87	78	29	57	1.22	5
1996 *Projection* >>>	4	0	3.82	96	96	36	61	1.37	2

WILLIAMS, MITCH - TL - Age 31
The "Wild Thing" couldn't cut it with the Angels in a set-up role and retired in June, simply walking out and heading back to his Texas ranch. He didn't have the velocity or the fire in his belly for pitching. Some Phillies fans are probably very happy to see him retire. It's hard to believe Williams is only 31.

	W	SV	ERA	IP	H	BB	SO	B/I	$
1994 Houston NL	1	6	7.65	20	21	24	21	2.25	2
1995 California AL	1	0	6.75	10	13	21	9	3.19	-

WILLIAMS, SHAD - TR - Age 25
Starting pitching prospect Shad Williams has had two good years in Triple-A, in the tough Pacific Coast League. He improved last year, and the sharp 3.37 ERA, allowing fewer hits than innings pitched, and good strikeout-per-inning and strikeout-to-walk ratios all make him look like a guy who can win in the majors immediately. But as struggling hurlers like Pat Mahomes and Willie Banks can tell you, an outstanding Triple-A record doesn't always mean that a pitcher can win in the majors.

	W	SV	ERA	IP	H	BB	SO	B/I	$
1995 Vancouver AAA	9	0	3.37	149	142	48	114	1.27	

WILLIAMS, TODD - TR - Age 25
A submariner with good control but not much else, Williams got his first chance at the majors in 1995, and was not effective. At Albuquerque, he pitched well for the second straight year but did not record any saves, suggesting he is no longer the heir apparent for the Dodger closer job. Williams could be an effective set up man for a team that put a decent defense behind him.

	W	SV	ERA	IP	H	BB	SO	B/I	$
1995 Albuquerque AAA	4	0	3.38	45	59	15	23	1.64	
1995 Los Angeles NL	2	0	5.12	19	19	7	8	1.34	-

WILLIAMS, WOODY - TR - Age 29
Williams had just been converted to a starting pitcher when his season ended prematurely because of tendinitis in his right shoulder. His control has been off the last couple of years but he has made up for it with improved velocity and an ability to pound righthanded hitters inside. Assuming he's healthy, he'll have a very good shot to start the season in the rotation.

	W	SV	ERA	IP	H	BB	SO	B/I	$
1994 Toronto AL	1	0	3.64	59	44	33	56	1.30	3
1995 Syracuse AAA	0	1	3.52	7	5	5	13	1.31	
1995 Toronto AL	1	0	3.69	53	44	28	41	1.34	2
1996 *Projection* >>>	2	0	3.71	55	45	31	45	1.38	1

WILLIAMSON, MARK - TR - Age 36
It seems like middle and long reliever Mark Williamson has to fight for a job every year as the Orioles usually omit him from their plans. But his consistently solid pitching usually prevails over some erratic rookie. Williamson throws a fastball and a palmball and he will continue to be effective if he still has the fastball.

WILLIS, CARL - TR - Age 35
Willis surrendered seven earned runs in less than an inning of duty for Minnesota in '95. He had a couple of very good years with the Twins as a long and middle reliever, but he lost his effectiveness in 1994. He attempted a comeback in the Angels minor league system last year, but he struggled in Triple-A and it may be over for him.

	W	SV	ERA	IP	H	BB	SO	B/I	$
1994 Minnesota AL	2	3	5.92	59	89	12	37	1.70	0
1995 Vancouver AAA	2	1	4.11	35	40	11	17	1.46	

WILLIS, TRAVIS - TR - Age 27
The Pirates acquired Willis from the Chicago Cubs in the spring of 1994 after he saved 24 games for Double-A Orlando the previous season. But he hasn't been able to get anyone out in Triple-A the past two seasons, meaning his chances of pitching in the majors are nil.

	W	SV	ERA	IP	H	BB	SO	B/I	$
1995 Calgary AAA	2	0	7.15	39	57	15	13	1.85	

WILSON, GARY - TR - Age 26
The Pirates' minor-league pitcher of the year in 1994, Wilson began last season in the majors but wasn't ready, then was dogged by shoulder problems in the minors. His arm was sound by the end of the year. He's a finesse type pitcher and the best he'll probably be able to do at the major-league level is be a fifth starter or long reliever.

	W	SV	ERA	IP	H	BB	SO	B/I	$
1995 Pittsburgh NL	0	0	5.02	14	13	5	8	1.26	-

WILSON, PAUL - TR - Age 23
Wilson, the Mets' first draft pick in 1994, started his career slowly. He went 0-7 as a rookie, then struggled early on with Double-A Binghamton. After that, it was straight to the top for the ex-Florida State Seminole with a major league fastball and breaking pitch. He followed Bill Pulsipher and Jason Isringhausen through the farm system, and should follow them to New York sometime this season.

	W	SV	ERA	IP	H	BB	SO	B/I	$
1995 Norfolk AAA	5	0	2.85	66	59	20	67	1.19	
1996 *Projection* >>>	8	0	3.83	145	151	64	130	1.48	1

WILSON, STEVE - TL - Age 31
A seven-year major league veteran, Wilson has spent the last two years at Triple-A. He made a few spot starts and worked in long relief while having a generally poor season. His strikeout rates continue to deteriorate while opponent batting averages climb each year. Being lefthanded helps, but Wilson is barely hanging onto his pro career at this point.

	W	SV	ERA	IP	H	BB	SO	B/I	$
1995 Nashville AAA	2	1	4.56	51	60	17	26	1.50	

WILSON, TREVOR - TL - Age 29
It seems like we say the same thing about Wilson every season. He has lots of potential, is well-liked by management, teammates, and fans, but very injury-prone and thus completely unreliable. Also, despite all the positive hype that surrounds Wilson, he has never posted an ERA in the majors lower than 3.56, suggesting that even if he managed to stay healthy for a year, he would not be a superstar.

	W	SV	ERA	IP	H	BB	SO	B/I	$
1994 San Francisco NL				Did Not Play					
1995 San Francisco NL	3	0	3.92	82	82	38	38	1.45	1
1996 *Projection* >>>	8	0	3.86	99	98	43	46	1.43	2

WIMBERLY, LARRY - TL - Age 20
The Phils' 1994 third round pick had a sensational season. His main drawback is a lack of velocity - he struggles to reach 85 MPH, but that could change as his 6'2", 185 lbs., body matures. He also throws a curveball and changeup with pinpoint accuracy, regardless of the count or game situation. He should be promoted rapidly as one of the few lefthanded starting pitcher prospects in the Phils' chain. A surge in power could propel him from very good to great - watch him.

WINSTON, DARRIN - TL - Age 29
Winston was once a good-looking prospect in the Montreal farm system before being plagued with arm trouble. The Pirates signed him as a six-year free agent last year and he did OK at Triple-A Calgary. The Pirates like him, though, making him worthy of keeping an eye on.

	W	SV	ERA	IP	H	BB	SO	B/I	$
1995 Calgary AAA	4	2	4.80	50	59	17	40	1.50	

WISHNEVSKI, ROB - TR - Age 29
Wishnevski had another nice season in Triple-A. He can probably keep pitching at that level for several years, but making it to the majors is unlikely at this point.

	W	SV	ERA	IP	H	BB	SO	B/I	$
1995 Oklahoma AAA	6	3	3.47	109	101	53	78	1.42	

WITASICK, JAY - TR - Age 23
This big (6'4") strikeout pitcher is considered a top prospect in the St. Louis organization. A hard thrower who was a Class-A All-Star, Witasick fanned more than a batter per inning at St. Petersburg in 1995, earning a promotion to Double-A Arkansas. He'll begin 1996 where he left off - at Arkansas. Witasick was the Cardinals' second round draft pick in 1993.

WITHEM, SHANNON - TR - Age 23
Withem appeared to be on his way after a 10-2 season in the Florida State League in 1993. But he has been no more than ordinary in two Double-A seasons in the Detroit organization. He was hit hard last year.

WITT, BOBBY - TR - Age 31
Witt's struggles to control a good fastball has become legendary; he's now walked more than 1000 batters in his ten year major league career. Witt was marginally effective in short burst for the Marlins and Rangers in 1995. He's beginning to bounce around from team to team like a journeyman. Look for Witt at yet another venue in 1996.

	W	SV	ERA	IP	H	BB	SO	B/I	$
1994 Oakland AL	8	0	5.04	135	151	70	111	1.63	0
1995 Florida NL	2	0	3.90	110	104	47	95	1.36	5
1995 Texas AL	3	0	4.55	61	81	21	46	1.66	5
1996 Projection >>>	10	0	4.31	195	211	82	155	1.50	4

WOHLERS, MARK - TR - Age 26
Wohlers finally proved himself to the Braves brass and they gave him the closer's job for good in 1995. Now that he's learned the value of throwing strikes with that blazing fastball, Wohlers has become almost untouchable. He struck out a third of the batters he faced (12.5 per nine innings), fanning fifteen more hitters than he allowed to reach base. Wohlers has arrived for good and was the league's most dominant closer by the end of 1995.

	W	SV	ERA	IP	H	BB	SO	B/I	$
1994 Atlanta NL	7	1	4.59	51	51	33	58	1.65	2
1995 Atlanta NL	7	25	2.09	64	51	24	90	1.16	29
1996 Projection >>>	6	40	2.77	71	57	27	91	1.18	41

WOJCIECHOWSKI, STEVE - TL - Age 25
Wojo has shown gradual improvement in the minors, but was overmatched in his first major-league stint, walking more than twice as many batters as he struck out with an ERA of 5.18. He's still young enough to improve, but running out of time.

	W	SV	ERA	IP	H	BB	SO	B/I	$
1995 Oakland AL	2	0	5.18	48	51	28	13	1.62	-

WOLCOTT, BOB - TR - Age 22
Wolcott was thrust into the ALCS in a must win situation against the Indians, and did just fine. His confidence and chances for a permanent spot in the Mariners rotation are enhanced.

	W	SV	ERA	IP	H	BB	SO	B/I	$
1995 Seattle AL	3	0	4.42	36	43	14	19	1.55	
1996 Projection >>>	5	0	4.82	90	102	34	52	1.51	-

WOODALL, BRAD - TL - Age 26
Woodall was unable to build on his 1994 season when he was rated by Baseball America as the International League's best pitcher. He pitched briefly in Atlanta before stumbling through a dismal year at Triple-A Richmond and spending half the year on the disabled list. When he's healthy, Woodall has great control and throws a superior change-up. He'll eventually be a major league starting pitcher, but not in 1996, unless he's traded to another organization.

	W	SV	ERA	IP	H	BB	SO	B/I	$
1995 Richmond AAA	4	0	5.10	65	70	17	44	1.34	
1995 Atlanta NL	1	0	6.10	10	13	8	5	2.03	-

WOODFIN, CHRIS - TR - Age 27
Woodfin has been the closer for Double-A Birmingham the last season and a half. He needs a chance to show whether he can overpower Triple-A hitters before the White Sox can assess his major league chances.

WOODSON, KERRY - TR - Age 26
Anyone who makes it to the majors at his young age has to be good. In 1990, he was 8-6 with a 3.03 ERA at single-A. The next year he was only 4-6 but kept his ERA at 3.06 while moving up a level. Despite the two quality seasons as a starter, the Mariners moved him to relief.

WORRELL, TIM - TR - Age 28
Worrell had Tommy John-type ligament-transplant surgery in 1994. He came back to pitch near the end of 1995, and he should return in 1996 to compete for a slot in the Padres rotation.

	W	SV	ERA	IP	H	BB	SO	B/I	$
1994 San Diego NL	0	0	3.68	14	9	5	14	0.95	0
1995 San Diego NL	1	0	4.73	13	16	6	13	1.65	-
1996 Projection >>>	5	0	4.54	122	121	50	96	1.40	-

WORRELL, TODD - TR - Age 36
1995 was an unlikely comeback for the often injured Worrell, who posted his best year since 1988 and set the Dodger team record for saves. Given his injury history, a repeat isn't likely but none of the numerous young Dodger closer candidates will beat him out of the job if he is healthy in 1996.

	W	SV	ERA	IP	H	BB	SO	B/I	$
1994 Los Angeles NL	6	11	4.29	42	37	12	44	1.17	16
1995 Los Angeles NL	4	32	2.02	62	50	19	61	1.11	34
1996 Projection >>>	5	30	2.89	64	56	20	63	1.20	31

WRIGHT, JAMEY - TR - Age 21
For a change, the Rockies made a high school pitcher their first draft choice in 1993. Wright throws a change, and a slider, but his fastball reaches only the high 80s. He was hit hard in the Sally League, but he'll receive the multiple chances requisite for a number one pick.

WRIGHT, JARET - TR - Age 20
The Indians' top 1994 pick has some lofty expectations to challenge him, as he was ranked as the top prospect in the fine Indians' organization entering 1995. Wright's calling card is his 95 MPH fastball, which he still has trouble controlling properly. His breaking ball repertoire is also in the early developmental stages. He had the best fastball in the low Class-A South Atlantic League, according to league managers, but he still remains a rather raw gem. Pencil him in for high Class-A Kinston in 1996 - he could become an excellent closer someday.

WUNSCH, KELLY - TL - Age 23
Wunsch, a 1993 first-round draft pick by the Brewers, he's a pitcher has to be wild to do that, and Wunsch was so wild he found himself back in the Pioneer League.

YAUGHN, KIP - TR - Age 26
Yaughn came back from injury, and pitched both as a starter and as a closer last season. He'll have to show more progress in '95 to remain a prospect.

YORK, CHARLES - TL - Age 25
After overpowering hitters in his first two pro seasons, the big (6-4, 240) Indians' lefty was torched at Single-A Kinston, eventually being relegated to mop-up duty. At his age, he should be experiencing success at Double-A, at the very least. His ability to throw lefthanded is his only hope at this point.

YOUNG, ANTHONY - TR - Age 30
Young returned from "Tommy John" elbow surgery to pitch very well much sooner than expected. He hadn't pitched much in relief before 1995, but the surgery has diminished his arm strength so he's likely to remain in a relief role in the future.

	W	SV	ERA	IP	H	BB	SO	B/I	$
1994 Chicago NL	4	0	3.92	114	103	46	65	1.30	5
1995 Chicago NL	3	2	3.70	41	47	14	15	1.48	2
1996 Projection >>>	3	2	3.83	67	68	26	35	1.40	2

YOUNG, PETE - TR - Age 28
Young was a beneficiary of Red Sox general manager Dan Duquette's pipeline back to the Montreal organization. It's doubtful that Young, a finesse pitcher, ever can benefit the Boston bullpen.

ZIMMERMAN, MIKE - TR - Age 27
The Marlins picked up Zimmerman, who had a losing record in five minor league seasons, on waivers from the Pirates organization. He surprised his new team by pitching well as a spot starter in 1994, but in 1995 he made it look like the Pirates knew what they were doing when they let him go.

	W	SV	ERA	IP	H	BB	SO	B/I	$
1995 Charlotte AAA	2	0	5.30	69	84	41	30	1.80	

ZOLECKI, MIKE - TR - Age 24
The oft-injured Zolecki started making his way back last season through the Rockies' two Class A teams and their Double-A farm at New Haven, where he had a 3.25 ERA. He pitched well, but needs more time to prove he's healthy.

GOT A QUESTION?
CALL JOHN BENSON LIVE

Your Question - Your Roster - Your Situation

Let the top analyst in the business help you!!

1-900-773-7526

$2.49/minute

1 pm to 11 pm Eastern Time - 7 days a Week

The 1995 Amateur Draft: REPORT CARDS
by Jim Callis, Managing Editor, Baseball America

As Drayton McLane and George Steinbrenner know all too well, throwing cash at free agents isn't the best way to take your team to the World Series. Building through the amateur draft may require more patience, but it's much more reliable. Just ask the Braves or Indians. With that in mind, we take our annual look at the best players drafted in June 1995:

AMERICAN LEAGUE

Catcher--Craig Wilson, Blue Jays, second round. Wilson is more accomplished offensively than defensively. A high school player out of Huntington Beach, Calif., he had one of the sweetest swings in the prep ranks last spring. He went straight to the Pioneer League, which features several more experienced college pitchers, and batted .283 with seven homers in 184 at-bats. ETA: Early 1999.

First Baseman--Sean Casey, Indians, second round. An unheralded high school player in Pittsburgh, Casey blossomed into a NCAA Division I batting champ with a .461 average at Richmond last spring. Cleveland believed Casey was the best pure hitter available in the draft, and he did bat .329 with 18 doubles in 207 New York-Penn League at-bats. The Indians took another college first baseman, Clemson's David Miller in the first round, but he's moving to the outfield and won't block Casey. ETA: Early 1998.

Second Baseman--Ryan Freel, Blue Jays, 10th round. Freel was the leadoff man for the 1994 U.S. 16-18 national team that finished second at the World Junior Championships in Brandon, Manitoba. A 13th-round pick by the Cardinals in 1994, he chose to attend Tallahassee (Fla.) CC rather than sign. His best tool is his speed, and he also showed some hitting ability with a .280 batting average in the New York-Penn League, a lofty-assignment for a 19-year-old. ETA: Late 1998.

Third Baseman--Jeff Liefer, White Sox, first round. Liefer is an advanced lefthanded hitter who should be able to produce for both power and average, somewhat similar offensively to Robin Ventura. Liefer also played left field and first base at Long Beach State, but Chicago believes he can stick at third base. He signed late in the summer, so he won't make his pro debut until 1996. ETA: Early 1998.

Shortstop--Mark Bellhorn, Athletics, second round. Bellhorn is solid defensively, but it's his bat that made him a second-round pick. The former Auburn All-American has rare power for a middle infielder. Oakland sent him straight to the California League, a full-season high Class A circuit, and he hit .258 with 12 doubles and six homers in 229 at-bats. ETA: Late 1997. Also keep an eye on: Duan Johnson, Mariners, fourth round.

Left Field--Jose Cruz Jr., Mariners, first round. The son of the former Astros all-star may be able to solve Seattle's left-field vacancy in his first full pro season. One of the most dangerous power hitters in college baseball, Cruz helped Rice rise to national prominence. He also should hit for average, steal an occasional base and play acceptable defense. He spent most of last summer in the Cal League, hitting .257 with seven homers in 144 at-bats. ETA: Late 1996.

Center Field--Darin Erstad, Angels, first round. California may have a crowded outfield picture, but Erstad quickly will make a place for himself. He could contend for batting titles while hitting 15-20 homers per season, and he runs so well that he might be able to play a big league center field. In a further display of athleticism, he also was the punter and long-distance field-goal kicker on Nebraska's 1994 national champion football team. After batting a sizzling .363 with seven doubles and five homers in 113 Cal League at-bats, he proceeded to tear up the Arizona Fall League. ETA: Late 1996.

Right Field--Geoff Jenkins, Brewers, first round. Jenkins comes from the John Daly school of hitting: grip it and rip it. He takes a fierce uppercut swing that drives baseballs great distances, and he makes consistent contact despite swinging from his heels. The former Southern California All-American reached Double-A in his first pro summer, batting .278. ETA: Late 1996.

Designated Hitter--Shawn Gallagher, Rangers, fifth round. Gallagher may be the most accomplished high school hitter ever. Last spring, he tied national records with a five-homer game and a 51-game hitting streak playing for national power New Hanover of Wilmington, N.C.. He tore up the Gulf Coast League, batting .338 with 13 doubles, seven homers and 17 steals in 210 at-bats. Think Gregg Jefferies. ETA: Late 1998. Also keep an eye on: Doug Blosser, Royals, third round.

Starting Pitcher--Mike Drumright, Tigers, first round. The 1995 GTE Academic All-American of the Year also enjoys a lot of success on the mound. Drumright blossomed from raw thrower to power pitcher at Wichita State, and consistently throws 92-95 mph. He'll be rushed through the minors to help Detroit's beleaguered big league staff., and he already has hit Double-A, where he went 0-1, 3.69 with 34 strikeouts in 32 innings. ETA: Early 1997. Starting Pitcher--Jonathan Johnson, Rangers, first round. Following in the footsteps of Chris Roberts (Mets, 1992), John Wasdin (Athletics, 1993) and Paul Wilson (Mets, 1994), Johnson gave Florida State a first-round pitcher for the fourth consecutive season. He went 34-5 in three years for the Seminoles, and was the most polished pitcher available in the draft. Team USA's ace in 1994, he complements a dominant curveball with an average fastball. Johnson went 1-5, 2.70 in eight Florida State League starts. ETA: Early 1997.

Starting Pitcher--Andy Yount, Red Sox, first round. A former shortstop, Yount didn't become a full-time pitcher for Kingwood (Texas) High until the fall of 1994. Aided by a 95-mph fastball, he didn't need much time to adapt. He went 0-1, 2.76 with 17 strikeouts in 16 Gulf Coast League innings in his pro debut, and should get better with experience. ETA: Late 1998. Also keep an eye on: Roy Halladay, Blue Jays, first round; and Mark Redman, Twins, first round.

Closer--Alvie Shepherd, Orioles, first round. Shepherd has legitimate power as a first baseman-DH, but Baltimore doesn't plan on letting him pick up a bat. His 97-mph fastball was the hardest in college baseball last spring, though he had little success at Nebraska. Look for him to either make it big as a heat-throwing closer, or flame out quickly. He spent all summer negotiating, so he has yet to pitch professionally. ETA: Early 1998.

NATIONAL LEAGUE

Catcher--Ben Davis, Padres, first round. Baseball America's 1995 High School Player of the Year is the most exciting prep catcher since Dale Murphy two decades ago. Davis, a Malvern, Pa. product, is a switch-hitter with power from both sides of the plate, excellent defensive skills and uncommon athleticism for a catcher. He held his own in the Pioneer League, hitting .279 with five homers in 197 at-bats. ETA: Early 1998. Also keep an eye on: Ben Petrick, Rockies, second round.

First Baseman--Todd Helton, Rockies, first round. Helton was Mr. Everything at Tennessee: clutch-hitting first baseman, a winner as both a starting pitcher and closer, Baseball America's 1995 College Player of the Year, even a quarterback until his injury paved the way for Peyton Manning in the fall of 1994. He has the swing to take Andres Galarraga's job, and his line-drive power should be magnified by Coors Field. Helton hit .254 with 11 doubles in the full-season South Atlantic League last summer. ETA: Early 1997. Also keep an eye on: Billy Deck, Cardinals, third round; and Nate Rolison, Marlins, second round.

Second Baseman--Marlon Anderson, Phillies, second round. An All-America at South Alabama, Anderson is a rare legitimate prospect at second base who wasn't converted to the position after turning pro. He has top-of-the-lineup skills with above-average speed and a good batting eye. He produced across the board in the New York-Penn League, hitting .295 with 13 doubles and 22 steals in 312 at-bats. ETA: Early 1998. Also keep an eye on: Corey Erickson, Mets, fourth round.

Third Baseman--Chris Haas, Cardinals, first round. Haas, a high school player from Paducah, Ky., has huge power potential. Playing in the Appalachian League, he smacked 15 doubles and seven homers while hitting .269 in 242 at-bats, though he did strike out an alarming 93 times. His uncle Eddie, now an Expos major league scout, played in the big leagues and once managed the Braves. ETA: Early 1999.

Shortstop--Chad Hermansen, Pirates, first round. Hermansen broke into pro baseball in fine style, as managers named him the top prospect in both the Gulf Coast and New York-Penn leagues. He held his own in the advanced classification, and hit a combined .284 with 18 doubles and nine homers in 257 at-bats. He projected to hit for average, but his power surprised Pittsburgh a little bit. ETA: Early 1998. Also keep an eye on: Gabe Alvarez, Padres, second round.

Left Field--Reggie Taylor, Phillies, first round. Taylor, a high school star from Newberry, S.C., offered one of the most dynamic power-speed combinations in the draft. He showed more dash (18 steals) than bash (two homers) while hitting .222 in 239 Appalachian League at-bats, but Philadelphia isn't concerned. He's actually a pure center fielder, but someone has to play left on this team. ETA: Early 1999.

Center Field--Randy Winn, Marlins, third round. Winn was recruited by Santa Clara as a basketball player, but he found his niche on the diamond. His speed is the equal of any 1995 draftee, and he also wielded a potent bat in his first pro summer, hitting .315 with 19 steals in the New York-Penn League. Chuck Carr may be running out of time in Florida. ETA: Early 1998.

Right Field--Jaime Jones, Marlins, first round. Jones was the best pure hitter in the draft and did nothing to dispel that reputation with a .284 debut in the New York-Penn League at age 19. The San Diego product's bat should carry him through the minor leagues quickly. He also will hit for power and play a solid right field. ETA: Early 1998.

Starting Pitcher--Hansel Izquierdo, Marlins, seventh round. Izquierdo, who defected from the Cuban junior national team in 1994, makes this list based on what he showed before a series of injuries derailed him in 1995. He pitched just one Gulf Coast League inning last summer, but at age 16 he threw 92 mph and he regained his velocity, though not his command, in instructional league. If healthy, he'll be a frontline starter. ETA: Early 1999.

Starting Pitcher--Matt Morris, Cardinals, first round. The Seton Hall All-America at one point figured to be one of the first five selections draft, so St. Louis was elated to grab him with the 12th overall pick. A power pitcher, he maintained a plus fastball through instructional league. He went 3-2, 2.38 with 31 strikeouts in 34 Florida State League innings, and is poised to move quickly. ETA: Early 1997.

Starting Pitcher--Kerry Wood, Cubs, first round. Al Goldis, the Chicago scouting director who drafted Wood, swears the Grand Prairie, Texas high schooler is better than Dwight Gooden was at the same stage. Wood pitched just seven inconsequential innings in the Cubs system after being worked hard in high school. He eased any concerned by reaching 98 mph in instructional league. ETA: Late 1997. Also keep an eye on: Brett Tomko, Reds, second round; and David Yocum, Dodgers, first round.

Closer--Russ Ortiz, Giants, fourth round. Ortiz was something of a revelation after a quiet college career at Oklahoma. Using a 95-mph fastball, he dominated the Northwest League to the tune of 12 saves, a 0.52 ERA, 55 strikeouts and just 19 hits in 34 innings. Similar success in five California League outings has him on the fast track. ETA: Late 1997.

FIRST-DRAFT PICK GRADES

A--Potential major league star.
B--Potential major league regular.
C--Potential major leaguer.
D--Disappointment thus far.
F--Failure; no chance to play in majors.

1995 Note: many of these guys look really good now, because they are new and full of potential. Also, they reflect my praise above. Anyway:

The 1995 Draft

1. Darin Erstad, of, Angels — A
2. Ben Davis, c, Padres — A
3. Jose Cruz Jr., of, Mariners — A
4. Kerry Wood, rhp, Cubs — A
5. Ariel Prieto, rhp, Athletics — B
6. Jaime Jones, of, Marlins — A
7. Jonathan Johnson, rhp, Rangers — A
8. Todd Helton, 1b, Rockies — A
9. Geoff Jenkins, of, Brewers — A
10. Chad Hermansen, ss, Pirates — A
11. Mike Drumright, rhp, Tigers — B
12. Matt Morris, rhp, Cardinals — B
13. Mark Redman, lhp, Twins — B
14. Reggie Taylor, of, Phillies — B
15. Andy Yount, rhp, Red Sox — B
16. Joe Fontenot, rhp, Giants — B
17. Roy Halladay, rhp, Blue Jays — B
18. Ryan Jaroncyk, ss, Mets — B
19. Juan LeBron, of, Royals — B
20. David Yocum, lhp, Dodgers — B
21. Alvie Shepherd, rhp, Orioles — C
22. Tony McKnight, rhp, Astros — C
23. David Miller, 1b-of, Indians — B
24. Corey Jenkins, of, Red Sox — B
25. Jeff Liefer, 3b, White Sox — B
26. Chad Hutchinson, rhp, Braves — Did Not Sign
27. Shea Morenz, of, Yankees — B
28. Michael Barrett, ss, Expos — B

1994 Draft

1. Paul Wilson, rhp, Mets — A
2. Ben Grieve, of, Athletics — A
3. Dustin Hermanson, rhp, Padres — A
4. Antone Williamson, 3b, Brewers — B
5. Josh Booty, ss, Marlins — C
6. McKay Christensen, of, Angels/White Sox — C
7. Doug Million, lhp, Rockies — B
8. Todd Walker, 2b, Twins — A
9. C.J. Nitkowski, lhp, Reds/Tigers — C
10. Jaret Wright, rhp, Indians — B
11. Mark Farriss, ss, Pirates — C
12. Nomar Garciaparra, ss, Red Sox — B
13. Paul Konerko, c, Dodgers — A
14. Jason Varitek, c, Mariners — B
15. Jayson Peterson, rhp, Cubs — D
16. Matt Smith, 1b, Royals — C
17. Ramon Castro, c, Astros — B
18. Cade Gaspar, rhp, Tigers — B
19. Bret Wagner, lhp, Cardinals — B
20. Terrence Long, of-1b, Mets — B
21. Hiram Bocachica, ss, Expos — B
22. Dante Powell, of, Giants — C
23. Carlton Loewer, rhp, Phillies — B
24. Brian Buchanan, 1b-of, Yankees — C
25. Scott Elarton, rhp, Astros — B
26. Mark Johnson, c, White Sox — C
27. Jacob Shumate, rhp, Braves — D
28. Kevin Witt, ss, Blue Jays — B

1993 Draft

1. Alex Rodriguez, ss, Mariners — A
2. Darren Dreifort, rhp, Dodgers — C
3. Brian Anderson, lhp, Angels — C
4. Wayne Gomes, rhp, Phillies — B
5. Jeff Granger, lhp, Royals — C
6. Steve Soderstrom, rhp, Giants — B
7. Trot Nixon, of, Red Sox — A
8. Kirk Presley, rhp, Mets — C
9. Matt Brunson, ss, Tigers — D
10. Brooks Kieschnick, of, Cubs — A
11. Daron Kirkreit, rhp, Indians — C
12. Billy Wagner, lhp, Astros — A
13. Matt Drews, rhp, Yankees — A
14. Derrek Lee, 1b, Padres — B
15. Chris Carpenter, rhp, Blue Jays — B
16. Alan Benes, rhp, Cardinals — A
17. Scott Christman, lhp, White Sox — C
18. Chris Schwab, of, Expos — D
19. Jay Powell, rhp, Orioles/Marlins — B

20. Torii Hunter, of, Twins	C	
21. Jason Varitek, c, Twins	Did Not Sign	
22. Charles Peterson, of, Pirates	B	
23. Jeff D'Amico, rhp, Brewers	B	
24. Jon Ratliff, rhp, Cubs	C	
25. John Wasdin, rhp, Athletics	C	
26. Kelly Wunsch, lhp, Brewers	C	
27. Marc Valdes, rhp, Marlins	B	
28. Jamey Wright, rhp, Rockies	B	

1992 Draft

1. Phil Nevin, 3b, Astros/Tigers	C
2. Paul Shuey, rhp, Indians	C
3. B.J. Wallace, lhp, Expos	D
4. Jeffrey Hammonds, of, Orioles	B
5. Chad Mottola, of, Reds	B
6. Derek Jeter, ss, Yankees	A
7. Calvin Murray, of, Giants	D
8. Pete Janicki, rhp, Angels	C
9. Preston Wilson, of, Mets	B
10. Michael Tucker, of, Royals	B
11. Derek Wallace, rhp, Cubs/Mets	C
12. Kenny Felder, of, Brewers	C
13. Chad McConnell, of, Phillies	C
14. Ron Villone, lhp, Padres	B
15. Sean Lowe, rhp, Cardinals	C
16. Rick Greene, rhp, Det	C
17. Jim Pittsley, rhp, Royals	B
18. Chris Roberts, lhp, Mets	C
19. Shannon Stewart, of, Blue Jays	B
20. Benji Grigsby, rhp, A's	C
21. Jamie Arnold, rhp, Braves	C
22. Rick Helling, rhp, Rangers	C
23. Jason Kendall, c, Pirates	B
24. Eddie Pearson, 1b, White Sox	C
25. Todd Steverson, of, Jays/Tigers	C
26. Dan Serafini, lhp, Twins	B
27. John Burke, rhp, Rockies	C
28. Charles Johnson, c, Marlins	B

Baseball's Top 100
The Best Individual Seasons of All Time
by John Benson and Tony Blengino

Who's better? Mantle or Mays? Bonds or Thomas? Williams or DiMaggio? And Why??

By focusing on the individual season, this book achieves a clarity never before seen in any similar work. Essays by many of baseball's best writers, including Benson, Blengino, Peter Golenbock, Bill James, Dave Smith, Rob Wood, and many more.

Lavishly illustrated with dozens and dozens of full page photos, many previously-unpublished

A great gift for any baseball fan.
Perfect year-round reading for anyone interested in player performance measurement and ranking.

Mailing date: NOW
Just $19.95 plus postage
(see order form on back page).

STATS INC.
Meet the Winning Lineup...

Bill James Presents:
STATS 1996 Major League Handbook
- Bill James' exclusive 1996 player projections
- Career data for every 1995 Major League Baseball player
- Leader boards, fielding stats and stadium data
- **Price: $17.95, Item #HB96, Available NOW!**

Bill James Presents:
STATS 1996 Minor League Handbook
- Year-by-year career statistical data for AA and AAA players
- Bill James' exclusive Major League Equivalencies
- Complete 1995 Single-A player statistics
- **Price: $17.95, Item #MH96, Available NOW!**

STATS 1996 Player Profiles
- Exclusive 1995 breakdowns for pitchers and hitters, over 30 in all: lefty/righty, home/road, clutch situations, ahead/behind in the count, month-by-month, etc.
- Complete breakdowns by player for the last five seasons
- **Price: $17.95, Item #PP96, Available NOW!**

STATS Scouting Notebook: 1996
- Extensive scouting reports on over 700 major league players
- Evaluations of nearly 200 minor league prospects
- **Price: $16.95, Item #SN96, Available 1/1/96**

STATS 1996 Minor League Scouting Notebook
- Evaluation of each organization's top prospects
- Essays, stat lines and grades for more than 400 prospects
- **Price: $16.95, Item #MN96, Available 1/15/96**

Bill James Presents:
STATS 1996 Batter Versus Pitcher Match-Ups!
- Complete stats for pitchers vs. batters (5+ career AB against them)
- Leader boards and stats for all 1995 Major League players
- **Price: $12.95, Item #BP96, Available 1/15/96**

STATS 1996 Baseball Scoreboard
- Entertaining essays interpreting baseball stats
- Easy-to-understand statistical charts
- Specific coverage of every major team
- Appendices that invite further reader analysis
- **Price: $16.95, Item #SB96, Available 3/1/96**

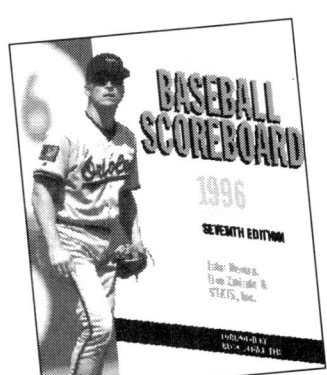

STATS 1995-96 Pro Basketball Handbook
- Career stats for every player who logged minutes during 1994-95
- Team game logs with points, rebounds, assists and much more
- Leader boards from points per game to triple doubles
- **Price: $17.95, Item #BH96, Available NOW!**

STATS 1996 Pro Football Handbook
- A complete season-by-season register for every active 1995 player
- Numerous statistical breakdowns for hundreds of NFL players
- Leader boards in a number of innovative and traditional categories
- **Price: $17.95, Item #FH96, Available 2/1/96**

Pro Football Revealed: The 100-Yard War (1996 Edition)
- Profiles each NFL team, complete with essays, charts and play diagrams
- Detailed statistical breakdowns on players, teams and coaches
- Essays about NFL trends and happenings by leading experts
- **Price: $16.95, Item #PF96, Available 7/1/96**
- **1995 EDITION AVAILABLE NOW for ONLY $15.95!**

Order from STATS INC. Today!
Use Order Form in This Book, or Call 1-800-63-STATS or 708-676-3383!

STATS INC Order Form

Name_____ Phone_____
Address_____ Fax_____
City_____ State_____ Zip_____

Method of Payment (U.S. Funds Only):
❏ Check/Money Order ❏ Visa ❏ MasterCard
Cardholder Name_____
Credit Card Number_____ Exp. _____
Signature_____

BOOKS

Qty	Product Name	Item #	Price	Total
	STATS 1996 Major League Handbook	HB96	$17.95	
	1996 Major League Hndbk. (Comb-bnd)	HC96	$19.95	
	STATS 1996 Projections Update	PJUP	$9.95	
	The Scouting Notebook: 1996	SN96	$16.95	
	STATS 1996 Player Profiles	PP96	$17.95	
	1996 Player Profiles (Comb-bound)	PC96	$19.95	
	STATS 1996 Minor Lg. Scouting Ntbk.	MN96	$16.95	
	STATS 1996 Minor League Handbook	MH96	$17.95	
	1996 Minor League Hndbk. (Comb-bnd)	MC96	$19.95	
	STATS 1996 BVSP Match-Ups!	BP96	$12.95	
	STATS 1996 Baseball Scoreboard	SB96	$16.95	
	STATS 1995-96 Pro Basketball Hndbk.	BH96	$17.95	
	Pro Football Revealed (1996 Edition)	PF96	$16.95	
	STATS 1996 Pro Football Handbook	FH96	$17.95	
	For previous editions, circle appropriate years:			
	Major League Handbook 91 92 93 94 95		$9.95	
	Scouting Report/Notebook 92 94 95		$9.95	
	Player Profiles 93 94 95		$9.95	
	Minor League Handbook 92 93 94 95		$9.95	
	Baseball Scoreboard 92 93 94 95		$9.95	
	Basketball Scoreboard 94 95		$9.95	
	Pro Football Handbook 95		$9.95	
	Pro Football Revealed 94 95		$9.95	

FANTASY GAMES & STATSfax

Qty	Product Name	Item #	Price	Total
	Bill James Classic Baseball	BJCG	$129.00	
	How to Win The Classic Game (book)	CGBK	$16.95	
	The Classic Game STATSfax	CGX5	$20.00	
	Bill James Fantasy Baseball	BJFB	$89.00	
	BJFB STATSfax/5-day	SFX5	$20.00	
	BJFB STATSfax/7-day	SFX7	$25.00	
	STATS Fantasy Hoops	SFH	$85.00	
	SFH STATSfax/5-day	SFH5	$20.00	
	SFH STATSfax/7-day	SFH7	$25.00	
	STATS Fantasy Football	SFF	$69.00	
	SFF STATSfax/3-day	SFF3	$15.00	

STATS ON-LINE

Qty	Product Name	Item #	Price	Total
	STATS On-Line	ONLE	$30.00	

For faster service, call 1-800-63-STATS or 708-676-3383, or fax this form to STATS at 708-676-0821

1st Fantasy Team Name (ex. Colt 45's):_____ _____
  What Fantasy Game is this team for?_____
2nd Fantasy Team Name (ex. Colt 45's):_____ _____
  What Fantasy Game is this team for?_____

NOTE: $1.00/player is charged for all roster moves and transactions.

For Bill James Fantasy Baseball
Would you like to play in a league drafted by Bill James?   ❏ Yes   ❏ No

TOTALS

	Price	Total
Product Total (excl. Fantasy Games and On-Line)		
For first class mailing in U.S. add:	+$2.50/book	
Canada—all orders—add:	+$3.50/book	
Order 2 or more books—subtract:	-$1.00/book	
IL residents add 8.5% sales tax		
Subtotal		
Fantasy Games & On-Line Total		
GRAND TOTAL		

FREE Information Kits:
❏ STATS Reporter Networks
❏ Bill James Classic Baseball
❏ Bill James Fantasy Baseball
❏ STATS On-Line
❏ STATS Fantasy Hoops
❏ STATS Fantasy Football
❏ STATS Year-end Reports
❏ STATSfax

BENS

Mail to: STATS, Inc., 8131 Monticello Ave., Skokie, IL 60076-3300

Do You Surf The NET?

Visit **John Benson's** Web Site:

hhtp://www.johnbenson.com

For the latest news on products and services.

Download Benson's Draft Software DEMO - FREE !!

See what Benson said last year about hundreds of players.

GET READY FOR 1996

John Benson's
Rotisserie Baseball Annual - 1996
Eighth Annual Edition - A Proven Winner
Reserve your copy now.

- The most complete, in-depth preview of the coming season
- The most accurate forecast stats and values of any publication
- The 1994 and 1995 editions both SOLD OUT, so order early!!

Now with a vastly expanded section on strategies, the Rotisserie Baseball Annual is the first, best, largest book for serious competitors, viewing every major league roster from the manager's and GM's viewpoint: who's going to play and how well they will do in the coming year, and why. In-depth analysis of every position on every team: which rookies are rising, and which veterans are fading. The best track record and most accurate forecasts of any publication -- and over a hundred tips on how to get the right players in drafts and auctions.

Get an early edge on your competitors!
The sooner you have it, the more
you will benefit from it.

NOW With More New Strategies!!!

Call Toll free, 24 hours a day **1-800-707-9090** for Mastercard and Visa orders.
For customer service, questions or Canadian orders, call **203-834-1231**
Or see the last page of this book for an order form.

The Benson Baseball Monthly

25 to 40+ PAGES EVERY MONTH, YEAR ROUND

- The ultimate publication for insider tips, news before it happens, and analysis of unfolding events.

- The first, best largest periodical for serious fans including scouts, management personnel, and Rotisserie league enthusiasts. Benson and his network of beat writers cover the major and minor leagues like no one else. Not just who's going to be traded, but who else gets affected and why and not just who's hurt or slumping or streaking, but who gets to play more, for how long, and why.

- The focus is always on the future. Benson's monthly features EXCLUSIVE QUOTES AND INTERVIEWS with players, coaches, managers, GM's and agents -- everyone with the most inside information and the power to make decisions. John Benson talks to GM's, front office executives, scouts, coaches, players and managers in their homes, offices, dugouts and clubhouses, for REAL, FIRST-HAND INFORMATION AND GENUINE SCOOPS!

- The Benson Monthly is featured in the book TOTAL BASEBALL, by John Thorn and Pete Palmer, as the pace-setter for the future in baseball analysis. Much too big to be called a "newsletter" the Benson Baseball Monthly packs every issue with 26 to 40+ pages of tips, commentary, letters, and insights from fifty writers and analysts nationwide.

- The Monthly offers both preseason forecast stats and values for all players, and in-season changes in forecasts and values -- always forward-looking.

Subscriptions are just $59 per year for FIRST CLASS MAIL. Or choose six months for $35, or the most popular option: two years for $99. A sample issue is $7.

Call Toll free, 24 hours a day **1-800-707-9090** for Mastercard and Visa orders.
For customer service, questions or Canadian orders, call **203-834-1231**
Or see the last page of this book for an order form.

NOW, The Best Permanent "How To" Books Available

ROTISSERIE BASEBALL
Volume I and Volume II

The most complete, most-advanced guide to winning Rotisserie baseball, in two volumes. Diamond Library is the exclusive distributor for the most popular, definitive, classic works, with advice that will last for years and years.

Volume I covers draft preparation, draft strategy, trading tactics, and tools for winning.

Volume II covers player valuation concepts with mathematical examples, optimal bidding, draft price inflation, competitive intelligence, and psychological warfare.

Call Toll free, 24 hours a day **1-800-707-9090** for Mastercard and Visa orders.
For customer service, questions or Canadian orders, call **203-834-1231**
Or see the last page of this book for an order form.

GOT A QUESTION?
ASK JOHN BENSON

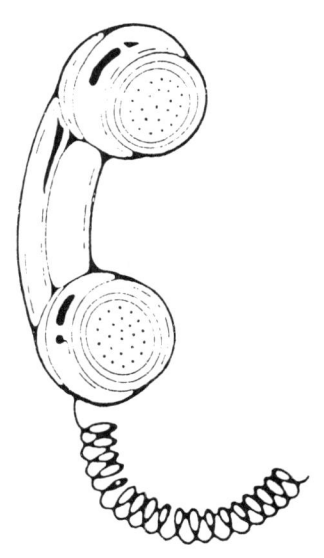

Your Question

Your Roster

Your Trades

Your Winter Strategies

Planning for This Year

LIVE -- NOT A TAPE

1-900-773-7526 (1-900-PRE-PLAN)
Just $2.49/minute

OPEN YEAR ROUND:
From 1 PM til Midnite-Eastern Time
Every Day

FUTURE STARS -
The Minor League Abstract

John Benson presents: FUTURE STARS - The Minor League Abstract. Knowing tomorrow's great players BEFORE they become famous -- that is the essence of FUTURE STARS. This book is packed full of vital information and insightful tips for minor league enthusiasts, Rotisserie leaguers, card collectors, and all baseball fans interested in the future of their favorite team.

FUTURE STARS combines two separate approaches to every player: statistical analysis and eyewitness scouting. John Benson expertly blends two approaches from two top analysts: Tony Blengino, pioneer on the frontiers of statistical analysis and forecasting player performance, and Lary Bump, baseball journalist who travels the country scouting minor league talent.

With these combined talents using different methods, FUTURE STARS gives you the most comprehensive look at the minor leagues today ... and for tomorrow.

Call Toll free, 24 hours a day **1-800-707-9090** for Mastercard and Visa orders.
For customer service, questions or Canadian orders, call **203-834-1231**
Or see the last page of this book for an order form.

JOHN BENSON'S DRAFT SOFTWARE

NOW AVAILABLE FOR DOS® or WINDOWS®
Fifth Year! A Proven Winner! The First - The Best!

BEFORE THE DRAFT

- View and Modify John Benson's 1996 Forecast Stats & Values for every player
- View & Compare 1996, 1995 & 3 year averages
- Change all options to fit <u>Your</u> League
  - Any roster size, Any dollar amounts
- Select AL/NL, mixed, or <u>ANY</u> group of teams
- Choose from over 20 stat categories
- Design your own stats (Windows® version)
- Use New Graphics to Spot Trends (Windows® version)

INSTANT PLAYER VALUATION to fit YOUR LEAGUE & your forecasts
Windows® version requires 386+ 4MB-HD+ V.3.1

DURING THE DRAFT

- One keystroke or click! Fast!!
- Keeps track of every player, every roster
- See Instantly at Every Moment:
  - Rosters for Every Team
  - Players taken, Money spent, Players Remaining, Money left
  - League Standings AT EVERY MOMENT
  - Potential Standings Impact of Every player on Every team
  - Draft inflation rates & adjusted values, updated continuously
  - John Benson's forecast stats & values & player notes

SPECIAL: IN-DRAFT TIPS!

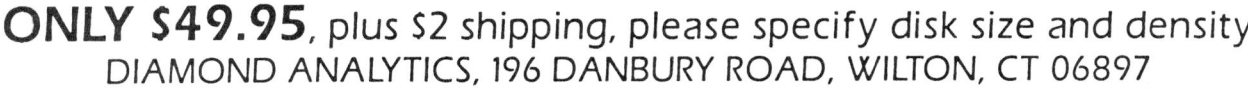

ONLY **$49.95**, plus $2 shipping, please specify disk size and density
DIAMOND ANALYTICS, 196 DANBURY ROAD, WILTON, CT 06897

FOR VISA/MASTERCARD ORDERS **1-800-707-9090**
FOR QUESTIONS OR CANADIAN ORDERS, CALL **203-834-1231**

DRAFT SOFTWARE DETAIL SPECIFICATIONS

John Benson's draft software is designed to help you study, prepare for, and execute, a successful draft or auction in a Rotisserie or fantasy league. The software has two basic program features:

(1) the EDIT module including the database editor and valuation program, and
(2) the DRAFT management program.

The Draft Software can be customized to suit almost any league. For example:
> Accommodates from 4 to 28 (36 in Windows Version) Fantasy/Rotisserie rosters
> DOS Version can handle active rosters with up to 12 pitchers and 24 hitters
> Windows Version can handle active rosters of any size (any number of hitters and any number of pitchers).
> Supports an unlimited number of players on Reserve and Ultra rosters.
  - Reserve Players count toward the team salary cap, but their stats do not affect the standings.
  - Ultra Players do not count toward the salary cap, nor do they affect the standings.
> Baseball players may be selected from any defined available pool. Each of the 28 major league teams may be included or excluded, as can Disabled List players, free agents, and/or minor league players
> Values and standings can accommodate any combination of hitting and pitching stat categories.
> The DOS version allows you to choose from 13 hitting categories (Avg, HR, RBI, SB, Runs, Runs + RBI, OBA, SLG, Runs + RBI - HR, SB-CS, 2SB-CS, Total Bases, and Walks) and 12 pitching categories (Wins, Saves, ERA, Ratio, K, Innings, W-L, 2W-L, K/BB, K/IP, Games, and Hits/9IP)
> The Windows version allows you to choose from 17 hitting categories (AB, PA, Avg, SLG, OBA, OPS, Hits, Singles, 2B, 3B, HR, RBI, Runs, SB, CS, BB, and K) and 11 pitching categories (Games, IP, Wins, Losses, Saves, Hits, Earned Runs, BB, K, ERA, and Ratio)
> The Windows version also allows you to combine the basic stat categories to create YOUR OWN custom categories, up to 2 custom hitting stats plus up to 2 custom pitching stats. Just add, subtract, multiply and divide the 28 give categories to create just about any stats you like.
> DOS version allow for up to 5 hitting and up to 5 pitching categories.
> Windows version allow for an unlimited number of categories.
> Hitting/Pitching categories can be unbalanced (e.g. with 5 hitting and 4 pitching categories).
> The Windows version allows for weighted stat categories. For example SBs can be weighted to be half the value of the other categories.
> Contains 1996 Forecast Stats by John Benson, plus 1995 full season and Three-Year average Stats for 1993-1995. The Windows version also contains 1993, 1994 and 1995 full season stats.
> Player values can be generated using any stats from any of the seasons including (1996 forecasts and three-year average) in the database.
> The Windows versions allows you to view a graph of EVERY PLAYER and see the Three-Year, 1995 full season and second half and 1996 forecast stats in an easy-to-view bar graph, either as absolute measures or on a per-at-bat basis for hitters or per-inning for pitchers.
> Dollar Values Support Draft or Auction mode. - in Draft mode, dollar values are for ranking players only - in Auction mode, dollar values work under a salary cap.
> Flexible Salary Scale for Auction mode - Salary Cap - Minimum Dollar Value - Minimum Salary Increment
> Custom Valuation of players using John Benson's formulas in accordance with your individual league rosters, salary structure, and stat categories.

> Support for a variety of Print Options. - Supports all Windows Printers - Print to File - Customize output by selecting fields to print - Sort on any category prior to printing

SEE NEXT PAGE FOR ORDERING INFORMATION

DRAFT SOFTWARE ORDER FORM - 1996

PROGRAM

Check One [ ]
NOTE: you MUST buy a program to run 1996 software!

DOS   - Runs 1996 Database.   [ ] $49.95 + $2 S&H   _____
or:
Windows   - Many New Features (See Detailed Spec. page)[ ]$49.95 + $2 S&H   _____

DATABASES:

	Dec. 15	[ ]	
Check at least one: [ ]	Jan. 2	[ ]	
	Jan. 15	[ ]	
First one FREE	Jan. 29	[ ]	
Second one $14.95	Feb. 12	[ ]	
Each Add. $9.95	Feb. 26	[ ]	
	Mar. 11	[ ]	
	Mar. 25	[ ]	
	April 1	[ ]	
	April 8	[ ]	total _____

S&H for data bases ----- Total Number of Databases_____ X $2.00 each   _____

Disk size and Density: 3.5 HI_____ 3.5 LOW_____ 5.25 HI_____ 5.25 LOW_____

Upgrade subtotal   _____

Database subtotal   _____

Total Draft Software Order   _____

NAME_____ADDRESS_____

CITY_____ST_____ZIP_____PHONE_____

Please send CHECK or MONEY ORDER to: Diamond Library
                                                    196 Danbury Road
                                                    Wilton, CT 06897

AVAILABLE FROM DIAMOND LIBRARY FOR 1996

Title: Quantity   Price   Total

The Rotisserie Baseball Annual 1996, by John Benson
  The biggest, most serious, most in-depth preview of the coming season
  NOW WITH MORE STRATEGIES.   _____ $ 22.95   _____
  Available February 25, 1996

Future Stars - The Minor League Abstract, by Tony Blengino & Lary Bump, John Benson editor
  Tomorrow's stars today - before they become famous
  Available February 25, 1996   _____ $19.95   _____

Baseball Player Guide A to Z, 1996, by John Benson
  Your complete player guide and who's who for 1996 -- over 2000 players
  with scouting reports and forecast stats.   _____ $19.95   _____
  Available NOW

Fantasy Football - Playing for Blood: -- Team-by-team coverage, strategies, and more
  from the best in the field. For the first time ever, **1996 projected
  stats** for over 500 players. Available July 1, 1996   _____ $19.95   _____

Rotisserie Baseball - Volume I and Volume II
The most complete, most-advanced guide to winning Rotisserie baseball, in two volumes. Definitive, classic works, with advice that will last for years and years. Volume I covers draft preparation, draft strategy, trading tactics, and tools for winning. Volume II covers player valuation concepts with mathematical examples, optimal bidding, draft price inflation, competitive intelligence, and psychological warfare.
  Volume I - Available NOW   _____ $12.95   _____
  Volume II - Available NOW   _____ $12.95   _____

Baseball's Top 100, by John Benson and Tony Blengino   _____ $19.95   _____
  The best individual seasons of all time, from Ruth and Cobb to Mantle and Maddux
  Available NOW

John Benson's ***Baseball Draft Software*** (Specify Windows or DOS and disk size)$49.95   _____
Windows _____   DOS _____   3.5 _____   5.25 _____

John Benson's ***Baseball Monthly*** -- exclusive news, quotes, interviews,
latest developments in player valuation and performance forecasting,
periodic review and update of entire player population. Letters, opinions.
Sample issue $7 -- Six months $35 -- One year $59 -- Two years $99 (Canada add 10%)   _____

Shipping: $3 per book, $2 per disk (Canada $5 per book, $4 per disk)   _____

                                                                                    Order Total   _____

Call Toll free, 24 hours a day **1-800-707-9090** for Mastercard and Visa orders.
For customer service, questions or Canadian orders, call **203-834-1231**
Or write: Diamond Library, 196 Danbury Road, Wilton, CT 06897

Please print your name _____   Address _____

City _____   State _____   Zip _____   Phone _____

Mastercard/Visa # _____ - _____ - _____ - _____   Exp _____   Signature _____
Please make check or M.O. payable to Diamond Library -- U.S. funds drawn on U.S. dollar accounts.
Rotisserie League Baseball is a registered trademark of R.L.B.A., Inc.